TENTH EDITION

SEMENOW'S QUESTIONS & ON ANSWERS REAL ESTATE

EDITED AND REVISED BY FRANK J. BLANKENSHIP

Pearson
Education

PRENTICE HALL
Englewood Cliffs, New Jersey 07632

Prentice-Hall International (UK) Limited, *London*
Prentice-Hall of Australia Pty. Limited, *Sydney*
Prentice-Hall Canada, Inc., *Toronto*
Prentice-Hall Hispanoamericana, S.A., *Mexico*
Prentice-Hall of India Private Limited, *New Delhi*
Prentice-Hall of Japan, Inc., *Tokyo*
Simon & Schuster Asia Pte. Ltd., *Singapore*
Editora Prentice-Hall do Brasil, Ltda., *Rio de Janeiro*

10 9 8 7 6 5 4 3 2 1

Library of Congress Cataloging-in-Publication Data

Semenow, Robert William
    Questions and answers on real estate / Robert W. Semenow: edited and revised by
Frank J. Blankenship.—10th ed.
        p.   cm.
    Includes index.
    ISBN 0-13-747593-4
    1. Real property—United States—Examinations, questions, etc. 2. Real estate
business—Law and legislation—United States—Examinations, questions, etc.
I. Blankenship, Frank J. II. Title.
KF570.Z9S4   1993
346.7304'3'076--dc20
[347.30646076]   92-37995
                                                                    CIP

ISBN 0-13-747593-4

PRENTICE HALL
Professional Publishing
Englewood Cliffs, NJ 07632
Pearson Education
Simon & Schuster. A Paramount Communications Company

Printed in the United States of America

About the Editor/Revisor

Dr. Frank J. Blankenship received his B.S. degree from the University of Maryland in 1954, his M.B.A. degree from the Harvard Graduate School of Business in 1956, and his Ph.D. degree (Business Administration-Real Estate) from the California Coast University in 1982.

During World War II and for several years later, he served as an officer in the U.S. Army Signal Corps. He is currently retired with the rank of Lieutenant Colonel. Immediately after his retirement from the Army he worked for several years with the General Electric Company and Univac Division of Sperry Rand, where he was National Sales Manager for the Original Equipment Department.

After moving to Utah in 1970, Dr. Blankenship became an active Real Estate Broker and practitioner of the real estate appraising profession. He held the designations of Senior Appraiser (IFAS) with the National Association of Independent Fee Appraisers and Certified Appraiser Consultant (CAC) with the American Association of Certified Appraisers.

Although officially retired from active real estate sales, since 1983, he continues to serve as a consultant to new REALTOR® organizations and as a director of his former company, All Points Realtors Inc. For eighteen years, Dr. Blankenship was an active Broker member of the Salt Lake City Board of REALTORS®, the Utah Association of REALTORS® and the National Association of REALTORS®.

Dr. Blankenship has served as Assistant Chairman, Education Committee, Utah Association of REALTORS®, and as contributing author to the "Salt Lake Realtor," a monthly publication of the Salt Lake Board. He has also served on the Utah State Committee for Real Estate Licensing Requirements.

He is the author of the *Prentice Hall Appraisal Deskbook,* 1986 and the *Prentice Hall Real Estate Investors Encyclopedia,* 1989.

From 1972 to 1985, Dr. Blankenship served as Adjunct Professor of Finance, Westminster College at Salt Lake, where he taught graduate and undergraduate courses in Marketing, Finance, Investments, and Real Estate. He is a former advisor, Real Estate Studies, at that institution.

Dr. Blankenship was listed in the *Marquis Who's Who in the West* 1986/87 and 1988/89 editions.

Preface

Since the First Edition of *Questions and Answers on Real Estate* was published in 1948, the book has been a significant study tool and reference for applicants taking licensing examinations. While it can still be useful in that regard, we see its current role more as a reference "at the elbow" of the modern broker, salesperson, and attorney. To date, more than 1,500,000 copies have been sold, which is an eloquent testimonial to its acceptance in the real estate and allied industries.

Attorneys will find the 10th Edition's numerous legal references and discussions an important adjunct to their own knowledge and experience. A special section (Appendix B) has been specifically designed to provide the real estate attorney with a quick reference, by subject, to key cases which have established legal precedence in the various subject areas.

While much of the basic content of the former editions has been maintained in this Tenth Edition, we have emphasized the elements that will improve it as an ongoing reference tool and source of continuing education for the real estate professional. The Questions and Answers, Problems, and Solutions have been somewhat reduced in number, without losing the comprehensive coverage of the various subjects.

The question/answer appendices have been designed for easy self study and review or as a broker's training tool. He can test the knowledge of his licensees by a periodic examination of the various aspects of real estate law and practices. These training sessions will be most beneficial in producing discussions among the daily practitioners who can share their experience and practical knowledge with the newer and less experienced agents.

Whereas in other editions the questions and answers were located in separate parts of the book, this new edition puts both questions and answers together. Where self study is desired, students may simply cover the answers as they review the questions, problems, and examples. If the answer is unknown or in doubt, they can easily check the adjacent answer column to clarify understanding.

Every state in the United States, the District of Columbia, the Virgin Islands, Guam, and the Canadian Provinces have enacted license laws that set forth prerequisites for licensure to guarantee the competency of its licensees. While a good reputation and professional competence are the cornerstones for a license, continuing education is a basic requirement to improved competency and professionalism. It is believed that this book will help achieve those goals.

I am grateful to the staff of Prentice Hall's Business and Professional

Publishing who provided me with the opportunity of furthering the work of Dr. Robert W. Semenow, deceased; and to his family, who, desirous of keeping his work alive and vital, have authorized this continuation of an illustrious contribution to the real estate profession.

Frank J. Blankenship

THIS TENTH EDITION is dedicated to Dr. Robert W. Semenow who provided the first comprehensive study guide for real estate trainees long before the advent of state required courses. Thanks to his help we passed our license examinations with flying colors.

CONTENTS

3 CONSIDERATIONS OF REAL PROPERTY OWNERSHIP

4 THE BROKERAGE BUSINESS

6   SALES AGREEMENTS

7   THE CLOSING AND PROPERTY TRANSFER

8   FINANCING THE PURCHASE

9   LANDLORD AND TENANT

10 VALUATION AND APPRAISAL OF REAL PROPERTY

APPENDICES

1

Your Guide to Professional Relationships: The Law, Ethics, and Practices

ETHICAL AND HONEST BEHAVIOR: A KEY TO SUCCESS

Successful real estate operations not only depends upon honest and ethical behavior of the broker and his agents but also upon the perception of the public in this regard. A true professional is a member of his professional trade association, THE NATIONAL ASSOCIATION OF REALTORS® (NAR), which has developed a strict Code of Ethics to which all members must strictly adhere. Many provisions of the code have been incorporated into the grounds for suspension or revocation of license in many state license laws. More importantly, the goals of NAR have been so successfully implemented that the public readily recognizes the competence, honesty, and integrity of its members.

The real estate licensee is often confused and intimidated by the many rules, regulations, and laws by which he is expected to live. He is cognizant of the perils of operating in an increasingly litigious society. He often wonders if it is possible to survive, let along make a living in his chosen profession. Staying out of trouble is really not that difficult. A good guide to this goal was provided by a broker who said, "In everything that you do, every statement you make, and every paper that you prepare, remember that there is a possibility that your action may be the subject of a court decision. Conduct yourself as if it is not only possible but likely." Perhaps the most important protection is your basic honesty, a liberal application of the *Golden Rule*—Treat others as you would want to be treated, if you were in their position—and a good working knowledge of the legal structure that regulates your industry.

1

Most problems are the result of financial difficulties that can sometimes force licensees to operate too close to the line that divides right and wrong. They are so anxious to make a deal that they forget to operate in a completely ethical manner. There is no excuse for "not knowing." An agent who is not sure of his actions should ask an experienced broker to guide him. The broker, on the other hand, can call upon his extensive experience or request the advice of his attorney.

There is ample help for the beginner who wants to learn. State and professional organizations have recognized the problems new agents face by providing excellent training and assistance. First, the states continue to increase their mandatory educational requirements for eligibility to prove your competence by comprehensive examination. Secondly, the NATIONAL ASSOCIATION OF REALTORS,® through its state and local boards, provides continuous training opportunities for its members. These instructional courses provide the licensee an opportunity to continuously upgrade his competence and the ability to earn advanced designations such as Certified Residential Broker. Someone once said that "knowledge is power." It certainly is true in the real estate profession.

UNDERSTANDING REAL ESTATE LAW

If you are to function successfully in the real estate industry, it is necessary that you have a basic understanding of the legal processes in which you will operate. You don't have to be a legal expert but you should have a basic understanding of the legal processes, how they were developed in the United States, and how they are applied to everyday problems and operations. While this book will not attempt to teach the law, per se, it will provide you with basic fundamentals and a little of the interesting history of how we got to where we are today.

THE LAW PROTECTS OUR RIGHTS

The rights that a person has in real estate are determined and protected by the law. The purpose of the law, it may be said, is to define and assert the legal rights and, as a collateral thereto, to prevent and punish legal wrongs. Blackstone defines law as, "A rule of civil conduct prescribed by the supreme power in the State, commanding what is right and prohibiting what is wrong." In the widest sense of the word, law may be said to be a "rule of action prescribed by a superior which an inferior is bound to obey." The social concept of law is that it consists of rules for the guidance of man in his relations to his fellow man and to organized society.

There are two types of law: (1) the written law, and (2) the unwritten law. Unwritten law refers to the custom of a community. In this regard *custom* should not be confused with *usage*. While custom has the force of law, usage is merely a fact. There may be usage without custom, but there can be no custom without usage. *Usage* consists merely of the repetition of acts, while *custom* is created out of that repetition.

Written law embraces constitutions, statutes, and court decisions. The federal Constitution is the fundamental law of the land and is representative of a system of laws and customs. A statute is a law enacted by the legislative body of a state, which defines its composition and jurisdiction. Courts, on the other hand, are not law-making bodies. They do have a very important function, which sometimes closely approaches legislation, in interpreting the Constitution of the United States, the laws passed by Congress, the state constitutions, and the state statutes.

This book considers all types of real estate law, but the emphasis is on *common law*. The common law is basically a set of cases that establishes the principles of law that are derived from court decisions, often tempered by the process of appeal to the higher courts. If a constitutional question is involved, for example, the deprivation of property without due process of law, recourse by appeal may be had to the federal court system up to and including the court of last resort, the United States Supreme Court. A system of courts of appeals, within the various states, provides for appeal recourse for questions of less than federal importance. Often these questions must be ultimately decided on their own merits and without the benefit of past experience, but where a similar case has been decided in another jurisdiction, that decision, even though it is not binding on the court, may be considered sufficiently persuasive to be adopted as a ruling. Thus, the precedence of common law is so important that it has been represented herein by approximately 850 cases, which are deemed key precedent-making decisions.

While federal laws apply throughout the country, each state has its own laws, based upon its own constitution, court decisions, customs, and the particular needs of its society. The fundamental concepts and principles of real estate law are applicable in almost all of the states, although the law relating to deeds, mortgages, landlord and tenant, and other aspects may vary materially from one state to another. The important concept to remember is that real property is subject to the laws of the state within which it is located and has nothing to do with the owner's domicile.

In most of the states in the Eastern part of the country, real property law, often referred to as real estate law, is based to a large extent upon English Common Law, which the colonists brought with them. This body of common law was established with the goal of providing a proper relationship between persons on a case by case basis. Thus, precedent continues to play an important role in the ongoing development of real estate law.

In the South and the West, codified law, resulting from the French and Spanish influences, is the rule. This is particularly noted in the community property laws in Texas, Arizona, and California.

Real estate law is further affected by a number of sources, including:

- The Constitution of the United States
- Treaties
- Acts of the Congress
- Federal Regulations

- State Constitutions and Legislative actions
- Rules and Regulations promulgated by State agencies
- Municipal Ordinances
- Precedence (Federal and State Court decisions)

THE BASIC FOUNDATIONS OF REAL ESTATE LAW

To understand the fundamentals of real estate law, one must accept the fact that there are no absolutes. The facts and circumstances of each situation are the determining factors of each case brought before the courts. Real estate conflicts and disputes are governed and resolved by two separate systems of law: (1) federal law and (2) state law. Whereas federal law is operational throughout the many states and possessions, state laws vary considerably from jurisdiction to jurisdiction. The only invariable part of these decisions lies in the application of *principles.* Wherever the judicial process is at work it is guided by basic principles, the most important of which are:

Principle of Jurisdiction—Any decree or order of a court must (a) be the result of a legally organized tribunal, (b) have jurisdiction over the person(s) and/or matter(s) in dispute, and (c) be empowered to grant an order or judgment.

Simply stated, the court must have the power to rule on the subject or dispute brought before it and it *must* be the court which rules on problems between those parties within its legal or geographic area.

Principle of Equity—Remedies must be based on rights and justice, where not otherwise addressable through strict rules of existing remedies and laws. That is, avoid going to court if there is an easier way to resolve the dispute.

The judicial process is constrained, to some extent, by one or more of the following:

Statutes of Limitations—These are based on the principle that an old and stale claim is difficult to prove. A statute of limitation prescribes a time within which an aggrieved person, who believes he has a just claim, can seek relief or redress. In other words, if you have a problem with another person you can't just wait and hope it will go away. If action is required, a prompt action is in order.

Doctrine of Laches—This doctrine logically follows the idea of the statute of limitations by eliminating undue delay in asserting a claim. Laches is an equitable defense in a court of equity, which will refuse relief to a party, who unreasonably delays the assertion of a claim against another. Under this doctrine, an equitable defense must be based on three factors: (1) knowledge of a party of his right to seek redress, (2) unjustified delay in asserting that right, and (3) some circumstance, such as a change in position by the other party, that would make a grant of relief inequitable.

Estoppel—An estoppel arises when, by a party's own declaration, act, or omission, that person has led another to believe a particular thing to be true and to act on that belief.

> *Example*—By intentional misrepresentation, misleading conduct, or wrongful concealment of facts, a person may be precluded from asserting legal title to land or from enforcing an encumbrance on, or maintaining an interest in, real estate.[1]

Doctrine of Clean Hands—This doctrine is usually explained as follows:

> Whenever a party seeks to set the judicial machinery in motion to obtain some remedy or redress for his aggrievance, he must not have violated conscience, good faith, or equitable principles in his prior conduct. If he has thus behaved, the doors of the court will be closed to him.

This doctrine is just good common sense. In effect it prevents the pot from calling the kettle black.

HOW DO COURTS AND JURIES RENDER DECISIONS?

Court decisions are not the mere results of successful presentations of the evidence to support the contentions of the litigant but also the careful weighing of this evidence by a judge or jury, guided by a number of rules that serve as aids in bringing about fair and just dispositions of the controversies brought before them. These rules are known as "Maxims of Jurisprudence." The most important of these maxims are:

- For every wrong there is a remedy—the law assumes that all problems have an equitable solution.
- The law helps the vigilant before those who sleep on their right.
- No one should suffer from the acts of another—if you are harmed, you are entitled to relief.
- Between rights, otherwise equal, the earliest is preferred—relief comes on a first come, first served basis.
- Interpretations of facts and laws must be reasonable—no "off-the-wall" decisions are allowed.
- When the reason for a rule ceases, so should the rule itself—laws are not kept after they are no longer useful.
- No one can take advantage of his own wrongdoing—there can be no profit in dishonesty.
- When one of two innocent persons must suffer, the one who caused the harm must suffer—if the only solution is to hurt one of the parties before the court, the one who caused the problem is the one to suffer.

---

[1] Mason v. Kierks Lumber and Coal Co., 94 Ark. 107; Hutter v. Weiss, 132 Ind. App. 244.

- The law neither *does* nor *requires* idle acts—actions are not taken just for the sake of doing something.

HOW THIS BOOK CAN HELP YOUR REAL ESTATE CAREER

A brief review of the table of contents will reveal those chapters which discuss the various aspects of real estate operations, the laws that have affected those operations and the detailed summaries of applicable legal cases which now encompass the body of "common law." Attorneys who are searching for specific references as precedence will find Appendix B most useful. Here, all of the cases discussed in the book have been sorted by subject matter along with the page number where specific cases are discussed in more detail. Each case or group of cases is briefly summarized to help identify the applicable legal problem.

Newly licensed real estate agents and those studying for their license examination will find Appendix A most helpful. Here, most of the terms to be encountered in your reading and study are clearly defined. You will also find Appendices C through J very helpful in your study efforts. Hundreds of questions and answers have been selected to illustrate the many problems to be encountered in the real estate profession. Just cover the answers provided to the right of the questions and review the questions one by one. If you are unsure of the correct answer, you can easily refer to the answer which you have hidden from view.

It is suggested that brokers may find this book useful in conducting review classes for their salespersons. The questions and answers in the appendices together with detailed discussions in the various chapters can provide many ready-made lessons with minimum required review.

2

Governmental Control
of Real Estate Operations

STATE LICENSING AND SUPERVISION

It has long been recognized that there is economic and social justification for the real estate broker and real estate salespersons in our society. However, not everyone is deemed qualified or worthy of the privilege of engaging in the business. The abuses that have been practiced in the past by some members of the real estate profession demonstrate that the justification of the broker and salesman exists only when the service that is rendered is efficient, intelligent, and honest. Because of the grave social consequences of incompetent or dishonest actions by brokers and salespersons, communities have learned that they must demand that the broker and his salespersons have certain qualifications of education and character. In the case of *Roman v. Lobe*,[1] the late eminent jurist, Justice Cardoza stated:

> The Legislature has a wide discretion in determining whether a business or occupation shall be barred to the dishonest or incompetent (citing cases). Callings, it is said, there are, so inveterate and basic, so elementary and innocent, that they must be left open to all alike, whether virtuous or vicious. If this be assumed, that of the broker is not one of them. The intrinsic nature of the business combines practice and tradition to attest the need of regulation. The real estate broker is brought by his calling into a relation of trust and confidence. Constant are the opportunities by concealment and collusion to extract illicit gains. We know from our judicial records that the opportunities have not been lost. With temptation so aggressive, the dishonest or untrustworthy may not reasonably complain if they are told to stand aside. Less obtrusive, but not negligible, are the perils of incompetence ..... The broker should know his duty. To that end, he should have a "general and fair understanding of the obligations between principal and agent".... Disloyalty may have its origin in ignorance as well as

---

[1] Roman v. Lobe, 243 N.Y. 51, 152 N.E. 461 (1926).

7

fraud. He should know, as the Legislature has said ... what is meant by a deed or a lease or a mortgage ...

We hold that the Legislature acts within its lawful powers when it establishes a system of license for real estate brokers with annual renewals.

Every state in this country, the District of Columbia, The Virgin Islands, Puerto Rico, and Guam as well as the Canadian provinces require a person engaging in the real estate business as a broker or salesperson, to be licensed. In order to obtain the required license, the applicant must be of good repute, have a minimum number of hours of formal, state approved instruction, and pass an examination to demonstrate competency.

Where regulatory laws are in effect, the technique used to accomplish the regulation is a system of licensing. Under these systems, persons must obtain a license in order to engage lawfully in the real estate brokerage business, and only those applicants who possess certain required qualifications are eligible for licensure. More importantly, *the continued privilege to engage in the business is conditioned upon the licensee abiding by certain prescribed standards of conduct in the operation of his business.*

The enactment of license laws has been the greatest single factor in elevating the real estate business to a recognized professional level. The courts have long held that the real estate business is of such public nature that it is a fit subject for regulation.[2]

THE CONSTITUTION SUPPORTS LICENSE LAWS

Licensure exists to deprive countless individuals of the privilege of engaging in the kind of vocation that they feel they have a natural and inalienable right to pursue. Because these laws restrict the free right to engage in the brokerage business, they have been challenged time and again in the courts of the various jurisdictions. The attacks have been on every conceivable front; hardly a legal weapon has been untried; yet, in the main, these laws have withstood every challenge, and their broad basic concepts have been established universally as valid and constitutional.

WHY STATES CAN SPECIFY WHO MAY BE LICENSED

The most important question touching the constitutionality of these license laws is, of course, whether the state has the right to demand at all that only persons with certain qualifications of knowledge, education, or character be permitted to engage in the real estate business. This kind of regulation, say the opponents of licensing laws, violates the *due process* clause of the Fourteenth Amendment of the Federal Constitution. The *due process* clause provides:

---

[2]
See Watson v. Muirlsead, 57 Pa. 161 (Pa. 1868).

...nor shall any State deprive any person of life, liberty, or property without due process of law; ...

It is argued that under this *due process* clause, or under similar provisions of state constitutions, every person is protected in his right to pursue a gainful occupation, and if one chooses to engage in the real estate brokerage business, the state cannot rightfully prohibit him from doing so, regardless of whether he be well- or ill-equipped and regardless of the social consequences of his engaging therein.

It is true that the due process clause does prohibit many forms of business regulation by the State. There can be no prohibition of the right to pursue a lawful and useful occupation under the guise of regulation. But where regulation of a business is needed for the protection of the citizenry and not the destruction of the business itself, the power of the state to enact required legislation cannot be denied. The due process clause has *never* been held to render the state powerless to protect citizen rights by enacting safeguards around any right an individual possesses.

There is a broad reservoir of power which inheres in every sovereign state, *to protect the health, safety, and property of her citizens.* This is known as "Police Power," under which the various states have sustained the state's right to restrict licensing of real estate personnel to those who possess certain educational and character qualifications. Thus, in an early case, *Riley v. Chambers*,[3] the argument was made before the Supreme Court of California, that it is an arbitrary invasion of private rights and liberties to prevent a person from engaging in a lawful and innocuous business occupation because of his moral character or reputation. The Court upheld the statute.

Licensing laws in all of the states are now firmly established as a result of countless court cases which attempted to overthrow one or more aspects of the legislative actions. The following is a representative list of cases in which the courts have sustained the right of states to regulate the real estate industry.

Arkansas	State v. Hurlock, 49 S.W. 2d 611 Cal.
California	Riley v. Chambers, 85 P. 855
	Breechen v. Riley 187 Cal. 121
Connecticut	Cyphers v. Allen 142 Conn. 699
Florida	State v. Rose 122 So. 225
	Shelton v. Florida Real Estate Commission 121 So. 2d 711
Kentucky	Sims v. Reeves 261 S.W. 2d 812
Louisiana	Zerlin v. Louisiana Real Estate Board 103 So. 528
New Mexico	State v. Spears 75 N.M. 400
New York	Groetzinger v. Forrest Hills Terrace Corp. 205 N.Y.S. 125

---

[3] Riley v. Chambers, 185 P. 855 (1919).

North Carolina	State v. Warren 114 S.E. 2d 660
Ohio	Hall v. Geiger-Jones Co. 242 U.S. 539
Pennsylvania	Young v. Dept.of Public Instruction 105 Pa. Super. Ct. 153
Tennessee	Davis v. Halley 227 S.W. 1021
West Virginia	State v. Jackson 120 W. Va. 521
Wisconsin	Payne v. Volkman 198 N.W. 438

CLOSE SUPERVISION OF LICENSEES IS ESSENTIAL

Every state now has passed legislation regulating the licensing and supervision of real estate brokers and salesmen. These acts are all very similar to Utah's Title 61, Chapter 2 as amended. The law reads:

> It shall be unlawful for any person, copartnership, or corporation to engage in the business, act in the capacity of, advertise or assume to act as a real estate broker or salesman within this state without first obtaining a license under the provisions of this . . .
>
> It shall be the duty of the state securities commission, herein referred to as the commission, to administer and provide for the enforcement of all provisions of this chapter....

The state laws typically authorize a Board or Commission to promulgate Rules and Regulations to implement the statutory authority. These rules must be reasonable and *not a usurpation* of legislative authority. In 1933 the Hawaii Real Estate Commission adopted a Rule and Regulation that an applicant for license was required to pass an examination. In the case of *Carlson v. Real Estate Commission of Hawaii*[4], the examination requirement was declared void. The next year the legislature amended the law to require an examination. Similarly, the Florida Commission adopted a Rule and Regulation that a real estate salesperson was required to devote *full* time to the real estate business. In *Lee v. Delman*,[5] the court held the Regulation invalid and expressed doubt that even a legislature could legally pass such a requirement.

In the case of *Real Estate Commission v. Roberts*,[6] the Supreme Court upheld the suspension order of the Pennsylvania Real Estate Commission because the broker had refused to permit the Commission's investigator to inspect the broker's escrow account without a warrant or subpoena. The appellant argued that the Commission violated his constitutional rights against self-incrimination and un-

---

4

Carlson v. Real Estate Commission of Hawaii, 38 Haw. 9 (1949).

5

Lee v. Delman, 66 So. 2d 252 (Fla. 1953).

6

Real Estate Commission v. Roberts, 271 A 2d 246 (Pa. 1970).

reasonable searches and seizures. The court held that the suspension order was proper, citing the "Required Record Doctrine" stated in the Shapiro case[7] that:

> The privilege which exists as to private papers cannot be maintained in relation to "records required by law to be kept in order that there may be suitable information of transactions which are appropriate subjects of governmental regulation and the enforcement of restrictions validly established.

The court cited the United States Supreme Court opinion in the *Morton Salt*[8], case which stated:

> Even if one were to regard the request for information in this case as caused by nothing more than official curiosity, nevertheless law-enforcing agencies have a legitimate right to satisfy themselves that (appellant's) behavior is consistent with the law and the public interest.

BROKERS MAY BE HELD ACCOUNTABLE FOR HIRING UNLICENSED AGENTS

It is important that a broker or salesperson renew his license promptly so as not to prejudice a claim for commission. The law charges the broker with knowledge whether or not his salespersons are properly licensed. A broker endangers his right to a commission where he employs an unlicensed salesperson who embarks upon a real estate deal before obtaining the necessary license. This is true even though application has been made and the examination taken. It is immaterial that the salesperson obtains a license prior to the consummation of the transaction.[9]

In short, an applicant for license is not legally qualified to engage in the real estate business until the license has actually been issued.

In an Arizona case, *Farragut Baggage and Transfer Co. v. Sharon Realty Inc.*,[10] the Court of Appeals reversed a $3,500 verdict in favor of a broker, where the salesperson was licensed by another broker on February 4, 1970. This connection was severed on March 16, 1970 and a salesperson's license was issued in the employ of the plaintiff broker on June 15, 1970. Lease negotiations were carried out by the salesperson in the latter part of March or early April 1970. Negotiations continued until June 29, 1970, when a formal lease was executed. The salesperson made application to the Real Estate Department for transfer of license on March 17, 1970, but the request was not accompanied by the transfer fee of $5.00. The fee was subsequently received on June 15, 1970 and the license issued. Accordingly, the salesperson was not licensed from March 16

---

[7] Shapiro v. U.S., 335 U.S. 1 (1948).

[8] United States v. Morton Salt Co., 338 U.S. 632.

[9] Certified Realty Co. v. Reddick, 456 P. 2d (Ore. 1969).

[10] Farragut Baggage and Transfer Co. v. Sharon Realty Inc., 501 P. 2d 88 (1972).

until June 15, while negotiations were being conducted. The court held that a plaintiff cannot recover where his cause for action cannot be established without showing that he had broken the law.

In the California case of *Firpo v. Murphy,*[11] a similar factual situation was presented and the court held that a broker who employs an unlicensed salesperson could not recover a commission for securing a lease of a building through such salesperson.

WHO IS EXEMPT FROM THE LICENSE LAWS?

The case of classes that most closely approaches the constitutional equality clause is that dealing with the validity of exemptions granted under the real estate licensing laws. All state licensing laws contain a provision for the exemption of certain classes of persons from the operations of the act. In other words, certain persons who do things contemplated by the licensing statutes are, nevertheless, not required to obtain a license in order to lawfully perform those acts. On the surface this does not appear to be obviously discriminatory, yet examined more closely, the typical exemptions found in the various statutes are found to have some reasonable basis for their existence. That is all the law requires to sustain them. In the case of *Southern Railway Co. v. Green*[12] it was stated:

> While reasonable classification is permitted, without doing violence to the equal protection of the laws, such classification must be based upon some real and substantial distinction, bearing reasonable and just relation to the things in respect to which such classification is imposed . . .

The following discussions provide some insight into the various exempted classes, the reasoning behind the exemptions and indication of the various challenges to their positions which have come before the courts.

ATTORNEYS-at-LAW

Almost all of the statutes exempt attorneys from the operation of the licensing law. This exemption was challenged in 1932 in the case of *Young v. Department of Instruction.*[13] The court upheld it as a constitutional discrimination. It should be pointed out, however, that the attorney is *only* exempt where he or she is acting in performance of his or her duties as an attorney, e.g., while acting as an attorney for the estate of a decedent. In *State v. Bodner*[14] it became clear that the attorney is also

---

[11] Firpo v. Murphy, 236 P. 968 (1925).

[12] Southern Railway Co. v. Green, 216 U.S. 400, 417, 54, L. Ed. 536.

[13] Young v. Department of Instruction, 105, Pa. Sup. 153 (1932)

[14] State v. Bodner, 99 So. 2d 785 (Fla. 1956).

exempt from any requirements pertaining to the required salesperson's examination.

Can an attorney, who assists a broker in disposing of a decedent's assets, share in the commission earned on the transaction? In the case of *Tobin v. Courshon, et al.*[15] a 3 to 2 majority opinion of the court held that the plaintiff attorney could not recover a commission even in an "isolated case" when there is a relationship to his duties as an attorney. Just because an attorney is familiar with the laws of conveyance, he or she cannot enter the real estate field on an independent venture.

TRUSTEES SELLING UNDER A DEED OF TRUST

This class of persons is exempt under almost all of the license laws. In the case of *Riley v. Chambers*,[16] the California Court upheld the trustee exemption, saying:

> . . . . trustees selling under a deed of trust are excepted, and no exception is being made of trustees doing anything else than selling, such as leasing, or renting or collecting rents. The reply is that a trustee, whether selling or doing something else, do not come within the purview of the Act. The express exception of trustees selling under a deed of trust adds nothing, and the Act would be the same if it made no mention of trustees. . . .

PERSONS HOLDING POWER OF ATTORNEY

This exemption is qualified and applicable only to those having specific power of attorney to *consummate* specific transactions. This exception is considered as valid, based on the California case, *Riley v. Chambers*[17] The exemption was further defined in Louisiana in the case of *Trentman Co. et al., v. Brown.*[18] The Louisiana Supreme Court said:

> It does not mean (the exemption) that one who is engaged in the business of real estate broker may exempt himself from the operation of the act by taking in each instance a power of attorney from the owner whose property he is seeking to sell. If the act meant this, it would soon be worthless as a piece of legislation.....

An unusual attack was made against the California real estate act[19] for bringing within its purview a class of persons who, in the earlier history of the license law legislation, were not considered properly to be within the purview of such acts—persons who engage in a single isolated act of brokerage without engaging in a course of business. In this important case, it was contended that

---

[15] Tobin v. Courshon, et al., 155 So. 2d 785 (Fla. 1963).

[16] Riley v. Chambers, 181 P. 589 (Cal.)

[17] Riley v. Chambers, 181 P. 589 (Cal.)

[18] Trentman Co. et al., v. Brown, 176 La. 854 (1933).

[19] Haas v. Greenwald, 196 Cal. 236, 237 P. 38 (1925).

insofar as the statute sought to prohibit one individual from employing another to handle a single transaction of the kind contemplated by the statute, it was unconstitutional as depriving persons of freedom of contract. The Supreme Court of California, in answering this contention said:

> No particular or convincing reason can be urged why the participants in a single negotiation of the sort defined by the Act should not be subjected to the same supervision as those engaged in a series of similar transactions, since at the last analysis every transaction of the kind coming within the purview of the statute is an isolated transaction, whether conducted singly or as a series of transactions carried on in the course of a business vocation, and since the lawmakers have seen fit to embrace the participants in each single transaction within the purview, requirements, and inhibitions of the act in question, we can see no adequate reason for holding that in so doing they have violated the constitutional right of freedom of contract any more than they would have done by confirming the scope of the statute to those carrying on such transactions in the course of a business or vocation.

This case eventually reached the U.S. Supreme Court which affirmed, without opinion, on the basis of *Bratton v. Chandler, supra.*[20]

RENTAL AGENCIES AND PUBLICATION SERVICES EXEMPT

Some rental firms have been the subject of litigation by real estate licensing commissions on the ground of operating as brokers without a license. Apparently, the agency does not enter into any agreement with the owner or with a prospective tenant; it simply makes available to the prospect a list of rental properties. The agency receives only an initial fee, say $20.

In the case of *Real Estate Commission v. Phares (Homefinders)*,[21] the Maryland Court of Appeals decided against the Real Estate Commission. The Maryland Legislature then amended the license law to include the definition of a real estate broker as "any person who aids, attempts, or offers to aid, for a fee, any person in locating or obtaining for purchase or lease any residential real estate."

In a 1974 suit (Civil 73-701-T), the United States District Court of Maryland dismissed the suit of Rhon Phares, DBA Homefinders, against the Real Estate Commission in Maryland, which sought an injunction against the Commission from enforcing the Act against them. The court held that the subject amendment bears a rational relationship to legitimate state objectives and that the law does not deny the plaintiff equal protection or due process. Contra is the case of *North Carolina Real Estate Licensing Board v. Rentex*[22], in which the Court of Appeals held that the licensing Act was in derogation of the Constitution, which guarantees

---

[20] Bratton v. Chandler, supra, in United States Supreme Court: 72 L. Ed. 415.

[21] Real Estate Commission v. Phares (Homefinders), 268 Md. 344 (1973).

[22] North Carolina Real Estate Licensing Board v. Rentex, 228 S.E. 2d 493 (N.C. App. 1976).

the right to pursue ordinary and simple occupations free from governmental regulation.

In the case of *Minnesota, etc. v. Beslanowitch*[23] the Supreme Court held that the licensing statute does not contemplate persons who merely compile and publish information about rental vacancies in a general manner. A dissenting opinion of three justices, quoting the New Jersey Real Estate Commission said, "The possibility of fraud, misinterpretation and sharp or unconscionable practices is great in the rental referral agency field."

Discriminations, other than exemptions, have been charged against provisions of the Acts. The California Act was challenged on the basis that a different penalty is prescribed for violations by an individual than that prescribed for violations by corporations. It was also attached because it prescribes penalties for individuals and corporate transgressors, whereas partnerships, as such, were left immune. Both of these objections were overruled by the District Court of Appeal and a hearing was denied by the Supreme Court.[24] This case also settled the idea that the charging of different license fees for salespersons and brokers was discrimination and that the requirement for certificates of character by two land owners for the broker and only the employer for salespersons was illegal. It should be noted that some states also require land owner certificates as a prerequisite for salesperson licensing. In Utah the requirement is three citizens who are land owners and have known the applicant for three or more years.

REGULAR EMPLOYEES ARE EXEMPT FROM LICENSURE

Many state license laws include regular employees of an owner as exempt from the license law requirement. In the case of *Brown v. Haverfield*,[25] the defendant was engaged in extensive livestock and ranching operations in Oregon and Idaho. One of the ranches, owned by the defendant, was the Big Muddy Ranch in Oregon. In December 1972, it was agreed that plaintiff would assist the defendant in locating cattle and other activities. Compensation was set at $50 per day, and it was anticipated that plaintiff would work 10 to 15 days each month. Defendant told the plaintiff that if plaintiff found a buyer for the Muddy Ranch, he would pay him a "darn good bonus." Compensation was to be $100,000 if the ranch sold for $42.50 per acre, and $50,000 if sold for $40.00 per acre. Plaintiff, in long hand, wrote the substance of the agreement, describing the compensation as a "finder's fee." Both parties signed and notarized the writing. The plaintiff, in late January 1973, contacted a friend, Doan, an employee of J.R. Simplot, to see if the latter might purchase the ranch. On March 19, 1973, defendant instructed plaintiff to "get after that Doan, and see if you can get something going on this thing." Upon plaintiff's

---

[23] Minnesota, etc. v. Beslanowitch, d/b/a Rental Directory

[24] People v. Schomig, 239 P. 413 (1925)

[25] Brown v. Haverfield, 557 P. 2d 233 (Ore. 1976).

urging, Doan spoke with Simplot, and a few weeks later one-half of the ranch was sold to a corporation controlled by Simplot. In 1974 the remainder acreage was sold in the same manner.

In support of his contention that he was a regular employee, the court found that considering the various duties which the plaintiff performed for the defendant and the compensation paid for them, the plaintiff was a regular employee within the contemplation of the Act and did not require a license in order to be paid compensation for the sale of Big Muddy Ranch.

WHY STATE LAWS ARE APPLICABLE TO RESIDENTS AND NON-RESIDENTS

The application of provisions of the license laws to out-of-state brokers brings into play another important provision of the United States Constitution—the comity clause. Article IV, section 2 of the constitution states:

> The citizens of each state shall be entitled to all of the privileges and immunities of citizens in the several states.

The object of this clause in the Constitution was that stated in its original form in the Articles of Confederation, which said:

> the better to secure and perpetuate mutual friendship and intercourse among the people of the different States in this Union.[26]

This constitutional provision secures to the citizen of every state all the rights and advantages in every other state that pertains to citizenship, in such state. Just what these rights and advantages are cannot be found enumerated in the Constitution, but it is left for the courts to decide what they are. One such very important privilege is the right to engage in business in the state. Thus, no state can say that the citizens of all other states, save her own, are ineligible for licensure to engage in the real estate business. The state of Florida attempted to do this very thing in 1927, but the Supreme Court of the state held the provision invalid insofar as it applied to natural persons. The Court, in *State v. Rose*,[27] said:

> That clause requiring every applicant to be a resident of the State of Florida is violative of Article IV, Section 2, and the Fourteenth Amendment, Constitution of the United States, and section 1, Declaration of Rights, Florida Constitution,

---

[26] Articles of Confederation, fourth article.

[27] State v. Rose, 122 So 225 (1929).

insofar as it applies to natural citizens. It denies to citizens of each State all of the privileges and immunities of citizenship of this State.

A NON-RESIDENT'S RIGHTS TO A REAL ESTATE LICENSE

In the 1926 case of *Land Co. v. Fetty,*[28] It was held that a Georgia lumberman employed for a single transaction of finding a purchaser for a tract of standing timber in Florida, but not licensed there, was not a broker within the statute defining a real estate broker.[29] The Court, stating that the Act was highly penal, construed the provision making a transaction the doing of business within the phrase "as a whole or partial vocation," as meaning that the Act was intended to apply to persons holding themselves out to the public as a real estate broker, and not to require every person specially employed for a specific transaction to take out a license.[30] In the New York case of *Aronson v. Carobine,*[31] it was held that where a real estate broker, licensed in New York is engaged in New York to sell property located in New Jersey and the broker finds a purchaser in New York, the broker is entitled to a commission, although he has not complied with the New Jersey law requiring a broker to be licensed. *Lex loci contractus* (law of the place of the contract) will govern. Later, in 1931 the Georgia court of appeals, in *Tillman v. Gibson,*[32] held to the same effect.

There is one well recognized exception to the law of the place of contract. In *Moore v. Burdine,*[33] a Mississippi broker conducted business in Louisiana in the sale of Mississippi Gulf Coast properties to prospects in Louisiana. Although the contract of employment was executed in Mississippi, it was held that the contract was to be performed in Louisiana; that the place of *performance* determined whether the contract could be legally executed. Since the plaintiff broker had not taken out a license in Louisiana, the contract was illegal and the court of Louisiana would not enforce it.

In the case of *Talbot v. Jones,*[34] the court held that an unlicensed broker cannot receive a fee for his services in arranging for financing through a vendor's lien and mortgage to enable the defendants to purchase certain real estate, even though it was a single or isolated transaction. The key to this decision was the Louisiana requirement that mortgage brokers to be licensed.

---

[28] Land Co. v. Fetty, 15 Fed. 2d 942 (1926).

[29] Florida Laws, 1923, Chap. 9177.

[30] 86 A.L.R. 640

[31] Aronson v. Carobine, 222 N.Y.S. 721 (1927).

[32] Tillman v. Gibson, 44 Ga. App. 440, 161 S.E. 630 (1931).

[33] Moore v. Burdine, 174 So. 279 (1937)

[34] Talbot v. Jones, 288 So. 2d (La. 1974).

In a similar case, *Webster v. Rushing,*[35] the Louisiana Court of Appeals denied a broker a $25,000 commission for negotiating a $2,500,000 loan. The Court also pointed out that he could not recover on a quantum merit basis, since he was acting in violation of the law requiring a license.

In a later case, *Frankel v. Allied Mills,*[36] an Illinois licensed broker went to New York and there negotiated a contract of sale of land in Illinois. The plaintiff broker sued for a commission in Illinois. The defendant contended that the brokerage contract was illegal because the plaintiff was not a licensed broker in New York. The New York statute forbids a person, partnership, or corporation from holding itself out or temporarily acting as a real estate broker or salesperson without being licensed. Further, the state forbids such person to sue for services rendered without alleging and proving he had a license. The law also makes a violation a misdemeanor and one act constitutes a violation. The court held that the contract was void under New York law where *it was made* and therefore it would not be enforced in the state of Illinois. The rule is well settled that validity, construction, and obligation of a contract must be determined by the law of the place where it is made or is to be performed, but the remedy is governed by the law of the forum—the rule is that when a statute declares that it shall be unlawful to perform an act, and impose a penalty for violation, contracts for such acts are void and incapable of enforcement. The objective of the statute is protection of the public, both vendor and purchaser.

Brokers who desire or contemplate doing business of listing or selling property in states other than their own should protect themselves by obtaining a license in the other state. Reciprocity between the states has made such cross licensing quite easy. Utah law, for instance provides:[37]

> A non-resident of this state may become a real estate broker by conforming to all of the provisions of this act, except that such non-resident broker regularly engaged in the real estate business as a vocation, and who maintains a definite place of business and is licensed in some other state, which offers the same privilege to the licensed brokers of this state, shall not be required to maintain a place of business within this state. The commission shall recognize the license issued to a real estate broker by another state as satisfactorily qualifying him for a license as broker...

STATES CONTROL LICENSEES THROUGH DISCIPLINARY ACTIONS

A broker's license is his livelihood. The laws under which it is obtained are enacted for the protection of the public and not to restrict competition in the

---

[35] Webster v. Rushing, 304 So. 2d. 66 (La. App. 1974).

[36] Frankel v. Allied Mills, 369 Ill. 578, 17 N.E. (2) 570 (1938).

[37] Par 61-2-6 (c), Title 61, Chapter 2 as amended.

industry. Every statute contains some statements to the effect that bad faith, untrustworthiness, incompetency or dishonest dealing shall be grounds for disciplinary action, and where warranted, revocation of the privilege.

The following 12 provisions for suspension, revocation or fine for illegal actions in the state of Utah are representative of other state statutes:

1. Making any substantial misrepresentation; or,

2. Making any false promises of a character likely to influence, persuade, or induce; or,

3. Pursuing a continued and flagrant course of misrepresentation, or of making false promise through agents or salesmen or advertising or otherwise; or,

4. Acting for more than one party in a transaction without the knowledge of the other parties thereto; or,

5. Representing or attempting to represent a real estate broker other than the employer without the knowledge and consent of the employer, or representing as salesman, employee, or having a contractual relationship similar to that of a salesman or employee with other than a licensed real estate broker; or,

6. Failing, within a reasonable time, to account for or to remit any moneys coming into his possession as a broker, which belongs to others; or commingling such funds with his own or with funds not held for others in the same capacity; or,

7. Paying a commission or valuable consideration to any person not licensed under the provisions of this chapter; provided, a commission may be shared with a licensed real estate broker of another jurisdiction; or,

8. Being unworthy or incompetent to act as a real estate broker or salesman in such manner as to safeguard the interests of the public; or,

9. Failing to furnish voluntarily copies of all listings and agreements of sale contracts to all parties executing the same; or,

10. Failing to keep a record of all transactions made which shall show the names of buyers and sellers, identification of the property, sales price, trust funds received, how trust funds are held and whether used by the broker, amount of commission and to whom paid and in what amount, and which records shall be retained for a period of three years and shall be open to inspection during business hours to the director or other duly designated representative of the board or commission; or,

11. Failing to disclose, in the purchase of property in the name of the broker or salesman, whether the purchase is made for himself or itself or for an undisclosed principal; or,

12. Any other conduct whether of a similar or a different character from that hereinbefore specified which constitutes dishonest dealing.

While New York provides only four grounds for disciplinary action, Ohio has 34 grounds. Most states, including New York provide a "catch-all" clause such as, "if found guilty of untrustworthiness, dishonesty, or incompetence in a real estate transaction."

Brokers who conduct their operations in an honorable manner and maintain their competence through continuing education have little to fear. On the other hand, those who assume they know it all and continuously operate close to the line of what is legal and right, often find themselves in court in defense of their actions. The following cases illustrate such problems.

In the case of *Haller v. Real Estate Commission,*[38] a real estate firm engaged in a questionable promotional practice whereby a buyer of a home would purport to sell an item of personal property, of insignificant value, and receive $1000 credit towards the purchase price of a home. A loan was then obtained through a federal savings and loan association, based on the sales price. The $1000 credit thus acted as a down payment in that amount. The Real Estate Commission suspended the broker's license for 90 days, finding that the federal statute that makes it unlawful to knowingly make any misrepresentation to a federally related mortgage institution, had been violated. The Court found that the Commission's action was not arbitrary or unreasonable, and that it acted within the scope of its authority.

Another case in which the commission's actions were upheld was the Oklahoma case of *Lee v. Real Estate Commission,*[39] where the Court said,

> The law required perfect good faith on the part of an agent towards his principal, not only in form, but in substance; and, the obligation of an agent to his principal demands the sincerest integrity, good faith and most faithful service.

The right of the Commission to suspend a broker's license was clearly established in the case of *Flagg v. Layman,*[40] which held that the Commission, upon its own initiative, or upon a complaint filed, may for cause, refuse, suspend, or revoke a license.

The most frequent complaints against licensees are misrepresentation, fraud or mishandling of money. Most license laws provide that if a licensee *is found guilty or pleads guilty* to certain specific crimes, his license may be revoked or suspended. The offenses most often resulting in revoking of the license are embezzlement, forgery, extortion, obtaining money under false pretenses, conspiracy to defraud (a felony).

Even in the case of a broker pleading *nolo contendere,* (no defense), revocation is usually upheld. In the case of *Handelsman v. Real Estate Commission,*[41] the New Jersey Supreme Court sustained the Commission's five-year revocation of a broker's license, where he pleaded *nolo contendere* to a charge of violation of F.H.A. regulations. Where the law provides for automatic revocation or suspension of license if the licensee is found guilty of certain offenses (violation of a state law),

---

[38] Haller v. Real Estate Commission, 253 N.W. 2d 280 (Neb. 1977).

[39] Lee v. Real Estate Commission, 516 P. 2d 1342 (Okla.1973).

[40] Flagg v. Layman, 517, P. 2d 329 (Or. App. 1973).

[41] Handelsman v. Real Estate Commission, 244 A. 2d 131 (N.J. 1968).

the Commission may not discipline a licensee by *its* finding such licensee guilty of the named state law crime. Absent a finding of guilt by *a court of competent jurisdiction,* the Court held, in the case of *Rifkin v. Florida Real Estate Commission,*[42] that the Commission had no right to discipline. The Commission can proceed against any licensee for fraudulent or dishonest dealing, under "proper safeguards."

A number of cases arises each year in each jurisdiction where a complaint is filed with the Real Estate Commission against a broker charging misrepresentation or fraud in the *sale of property owned by the broker.* The issue raised is whether such conduct by a licensee, acting as a principal, comes under the purview of the license law. Some cases have held in the negative and some in the affirmative. The weight of authority, and the most recent trend, is that a broker's license may be suspended or revoked on that account. In *McKnight v. Florida Real Estate Commission,*[43] the Commission's jurisdiction was upheld where the charge involved worthless checks, which were not issued as a result of a real estate transaction. The Court emphasized that the law requires a licensee to be honest, truthful, trustworthy, of good character, and that he bears a good reputation for fair dealing. The Court further stated:

> We think it would be ludicrous to construe the statutes to mean that a broker to be answerable to the real estate commission must commit the unlawful acts when engaged in real estate negotiations but should he commit the same unlawful acts when not engaged in real estate negotiations he would still be of good character and beyond the Commission's jurisdiction.

Perhaps the most clear statement, relative to broker honesty, was cited in the case of *State Real Estate Commission v. Tice,*[44] when the Court stated:

> We believe that a single standard of honesty and competency should guide a broker's real estate activities, whether he is performing as an owner or a broker.

In the instant case the broker has been charged with making certain misrepresentations, in connection with F.H.A. financing in the sale of his own property. This position was also taken by several other courts[45] at later dates.

The term "misrepresentation" is usually quite clearly understood by the public in general; however there are some cases where misrepresentation might be charged erroneously against the broker. Whereas a broker *can* be held liable for a seller's misrepresentations where, as a professional, he should have known better.

42
  Rifkin v. Florida Real Estate Commission, 345 So. 2d 349 (Fla. 1977).
43
  McKnight v. Florida Real Estate Commission, 202 So. 2d 199 (1967).
44
  State Real Estate Commission v. Tice, 190 A. 2d 188 (Pa. 1963).
45
  Fibus v. Real Estate Commission, 7 Pa. Com. Ct. 74 (1973); McKnight v. Florida Real Estate Commission, 202 So. 2d 420 and Boineau v. South Carolina Real Estate Commission, 230 S.E. 2d 440 (S.C. 1976).

He cannot be so charged for innocently and nonnegligently conveying a seller's misrepresentations; however, he is held to a standard of reasonable care and professionalism in this regard. These and similar situations are further discussed in Chapter 6.

The question often arises as to whether the jurisdiction of the Commission extends to acts committed outside the state by it's licensees. The case of *Williams v. Florida Real Estate Commission*,[46] is a case in point. The licensee in question was employed as a broker by a corporation engaged in selling real estate in the Bahamas Islands. The complaint alleged improper dealing in the sale of a lot located on Grand Bahamas Island. In ruling the Court said:

> We do not believe the Commission exceeded its jurisdiction simply because these checks were not issued as a result of a real estate transaction. The law specifically requires that a person in order to hold a real estate license must make it appear that he is honest, truthful, trustworthy, of good character, and that he bears a good reputation for fair dealing.
>
> Worthless checks are the antithesis of good reputation and fair dealings and this misconduct need not be done during the negotiation and/or sale of real estate in order to be punishable.

HOW REAL ESTATE LICENSE FEES ARE DETERMINED

Real estate license fees are usually set by the legislature and collected by the Real Estate Commission or Board. The Courts have ruled that fees must be *reasonable* as related to the actual cost of operation of the administration and enforcement of the licensing law. If set at an excessive rate, the fees will be held void and unenforceable. The subject of police power regulation fees was the subject of the Arkansas case of *Texarkansas v. Hudgins Products Co.*,[47] the Supreme Court said, inter alia:

> We think the reasonableness of an ordinance for the purpose of regulation may be said to be that, if it is such a sum as is so manifestly excessive and out of proportion, which would probably be required to make the ordinance effective, so that it is certain that the city will derive a profit from the ordinance, then in all such cases, that the purpose of the statute is to raise revenue, and such ordinances are void.

Two cases in which the subject of real estate licensing was considered, clearly established the limitations on fees charged. In a 1964 New Hampshire case, *William Coltin and Co. v. Manchester Savings Bank*,[48] the Supreme Court said:

---

[46] Williams v. Florida Real Estate Commission, 232 So. 2d 239 (1970).

[47] Texarkansas v. Hudgins Products Co., 164 S.W. 739.

[48] William Coltin and Co. v. Manchester Savings Bank, 197 A. 2d 208 (N.H. 1964).

The touchstone as to whether (the license law) is a revenue measure or a police power regulation is the intent of the legislature .... The purpose of the legislation was the protection of the public from unscrupulous brokers and salesmen.

The basis for fee establishment was further defined in 1977 in the case of *C. Dan Blackshear, et al. v. G.W. Hogan, et al.*[49] where the Georgia Association of Realtors challenged the license fees required under the 1973 Georgia Act as excessive, since the greater portion went into the state treasury. The Court found that the fees collected by the Real Estate Commission were *regulatory fees* assessed under the police powers of the state, and were not intended as a general revenue measure; however, the Court further declared that the license fees charged under the 1973 Act "to be unconstitutional and void." As a result, the 1977 legislature enacted a law which provides that "the Georgia Real Estate Commission shall be authorized to establish a reasonable amount for all fees provided for in the Act."

In the case of *Maury v. State,*[50] a statute was considered which imposed a license tax upon "each person, firm or corporation engaged in buying, selling, or renting real estate on commission," with a provision that if such person "also engages in the business of loaning money as an incident merely to the real estate business, they shall also pay an additional fee of fifty dollars." A majority of the court upheld the law.

Many of the states, such as Utah, have also included in their Acts provisions for assuring that the fees are adequate but not excessive. While the collected fees are paid into the general fund, and expenses of the commission paid from the resources of that general fund, the Commission is required to submit to the governor a budget of their requirements which is included in the overall budget submitted annually to the legislature for approval.

THE QUESTION OF "FINDER'S FEE" vs "COMMISSION" UNDER STATE LAWS

A finder's fee in most states refers to the payment of a commission to a broker for *obtaining a mortgage for the buyer.* It may also refer to a person who acts as a go-between to an owner and a purchaser, and receives a fee from the owner. In the latter capacity, a "finder" plays a very limited role, with minimal duties in a real estate transaction. He is, in a sense, an "originator" in the deal. A "finder" is one who finds, interests, introduces and brings together parties in a deal, even though he has no part in negotiating terms of the transaction.[51]

---

[49] C. Dan Blackshear, et al., v. G.W. Hogan, et al., File No. C-22561 - Civil Action, Fulton County Superior Court, Ga.

[50] Maury v. State, 93 So. 802, (1922).

[51] Consolidate Oil & Gas, Inc. v. Roberts, 425 P. 2d 282 (Colo 1967); Shoenfeld v. Silver Springs, U.S. Dist. Ct. Eastern Division (Wisc. 1971) and Brakage v. Georgetown Associates, Inc. 523 P. 2d 145 (Colo. App. 1974).

Court decisions are not in harmony in adopting a line of demarcation between what constitutes a person as a finder and when the activities fall within the definition of a real estate broker under the license law. Suppose Adams, a good fried of Costello, meets him at their country club and Adams learns that Costello wants to sell his home for $65,000. Adams tells him that he thinks he knows someone who would be interested at that price. Costello replies, "Send him over, and if he buys the property I will pay you $5,000." Adams sends Chase to Costello, and Chase buys the property at $65,000. Upon the facts stated, it would appear that Adams could recover the $5,000 as a finder's fee, even though he has no license.

A finder's fee was denied by the court to an unlicensed person in the sale of a hotel, since the real estate was a dominant feature of the transaction.[52]

In the California case of *Sullivan v. Collins*,[53] where the plaintiff did considerably more than introduce the prospect to the owner, the United States Court of Appeals affirmed a verdict of $55,000 as a finder's fee in favor of the plaintiff, an IBM operator and a musician. The court said,

> . . . what plaintiff did in addition to bringing the buyer and seller together was out of the spirit of helpfulness and not with expectation or purpose of award. These activities, if they affected the transaction at all, were purely incidental.

A person who sells stock in a corporation that owns and sells real estate cannot recover a finder's fee if he is not a licensed real estate broker.[54]

When a suit for commission on a real estate sale, filed by an unlicensed person, stated that the amount sought was an "incentive" or bonus payment, the court denied recovery, since plaintiff was not licensed in Louisiana.[55]

In *Evans v. Riverside International Raceway*,[56] the court states the distinction between finder and broker, to be:

> The services performed by finders may vary from case to case, but the distinction from the status of broker lies in their bringing the parties together, with no involvement on their part in negotiating the price or other terms of the transaction.

---

[52]
Sorice v. DuBois et al., 167 N.Y.S. 2d 227 (1966) and Cary v. Borden Co., 386 P. 2d 585 (Colo. 1963).

[53]
Sullivan v. Collins, 435 F. 2d 1128 (1970).

[54]
Brakage v. Georgetown Associates, 523 P. 2d 145 (Colo App 1974).

[55]
Parr v. Asaff, 322 So. 313 (La. App. 1975).

[56]
Evans v. Riverside International Raceway, 237 Cal. App. 2d 666 (1965).

OTHER STATE, COUNTY AND LOCAL LAWS AFFECTING REAL ESTATE OPERATIONS

TAXES

Real estate taxes consist of: (1) direct taxation, based on assessed value, and (2) special assessments, usually by local governments, for street, curb & gutter, sewer and other improvements based on lot size and/or street frontage. These assessments have generally followed the formula set by the 1966 Arizona case of *Weitz v. Davis.*[57] In a 1972 Washington case, the Court approved the assessment of property owners for the purpose of placing underground utilities.[58]

It is true, of course, that the entire community profits and benefits by the improvement of streets and other public service and indirectly, the entire tax-paying public participates in the maintenance of the original improvement. But where, for example, a street which serves only a limited number of properties is changed from a dirt street to one of brick, it is fair that only the immediate properties benefited should be assessed for the improvement.

In most jurisdictions, real estate is taxed at various levels of government. Real estate assets taxed by the legislature may provide a substantial portion of the state needs for administration, schools, highways, and other expenses. Counties typically raise the major portion of their operating funds from a further levy on the real estate asset base. Finally, incorporated cities and service districts may also obtain a substantial percentage of their needs from real estate taxation.

While school needs have, in the past, accounted for a major portion of the real estate taxes,[59] recent Court decisions have dictated the requirement to use other sources to provide for the educational needs of the state. Where the funds are based on real estate taxes only, the inevitable result is poor schools in poor counties and good schools in the rich counties. In 1989, the Kentucky legislature took the lead in assuring equal school quality based on student numbers rather than the ability to tax real estate assets.

OFFICIAL REAL ESTATE RECORDS

The county is the official keeper of all real estate records to include, property ownership records, mortgages, liens, judgments and other indebtedness. While the majority of these records are maintained in more or less the same manual methods of the past, many counties are modernizing their recordkeeping to provide real estate records on computer bases. In the not too distant future, it is expected that most record systems will not only be in computer bases but that citizens, having

---

[57] Weitz v. Davis, 4 Ariz. App. 209, 419 P. 2d 113, Aff'd Ariz. 40, 424 P. 2d 168 (1966).

[58] Citizens for Underground Equality v. Seattle, 6 Wash. App. 338, 492 P. 2d 1071 (1972).

[59] In Salt Lake County, Utah over 53% of the total residential tax is for school purposes.

need for access to these records, will be able to obtain them by on-line access. In Utah, private enterprises are addressing the need for rapid access to real estate by providing data such as tax records, plats and legal descriptions on compact discs. These data are made available to appraisers, attorneys, and other users at reasonable fees.

LOCAL AUTHORITIES CONTROL LAND USE

Master Planning and its operative "offspring," zoning ordinances, are implemented in local jurisdictions through authority of state enabling acts. In earlier times municipalities enacted zoning ordinances, to regulate the use of land, with no serious thought as to the eventual effect of their actions. As the boundaries of the municipalities grew to accommodate a rapidly increasing population, it became evident that zoning should be based on a plan which would permit the required growth in a logical and predetermined pattern rather than the result of "hodge-podge" zoning. Civic-minded real estate operators and brokers are in accord with the proposition that reasonable zoning regulations are essential to maintain and promote the attractive character of a city or town. To permit the unbridled development or careless use of land in accordance with the selfish interests of individual owners is bound to be reflected in the depreciated value of surrounding properties.

Today, almost all municipalities have established "Master Plans" which set aside designated areas for specific purposes. New area zoning and changes to older ones are closely supervised to assure conformance with the approved master plan. Zoning designations, which do not conform with the master plan are very few and approved only with well documented justifications and adequate public hearings. Legislation in the form of "spot zoning" may be allowed under special circumstances as indicated in the case of *Christopher v. Mathens, 362 Mo. 242 (1951),*[60]

The general purpose of zoning laws requires that such regulations shall be made in accordance with a comprehensive plan designed to:

- lessen congestion in the streets
- secure safety from fire, panic, and other dangers
- promote the health and the general welfare
- provide adequate light and air
- prevent the overcrowding of land, and
- avoid undue concentration of population or traffic flow.

Closely identified with zoning is the creation of planning commissions by the municipalities and/or districts. These bodies are charged with the responsibility of regulating the overall development of the community. Zoning and planning must be accomplished with due consideration to the character of the district and its

---

[60] Christopher v. Mathens, 362 Mo. 242 (1951) and Tennison v. Shomette, 379 A. 2d 187 (Md. App. 1977).

peculiar suitability for particular uses, and with a view to conserving the value of lands and buildings and encouraging the most appropriate use of land throughout the particular political subdivision.

It should be pointed out, however, that zoning laws have no application to the location of properties or their use *prior* to their enactment. This was pointed out by the court in the case of *Boise City v. Blaser*,[61] in which the court pointed out that the location of properties or their use prior to the enactment of zoning has no effect as long as the property continues as is and utilized in the same manner. The property is merely known as nonconforming use.

If any change in the property or its use occurs *after* the zoning change, it must be utilized in accordance with current zoning regulations. A case in point is *Goldfarb v. Dietz*,[62] where a building had been converted to multifamily use prior to the zoning change. When the building burned, permission to rebuild was denied as it no longer met current zoning regulations.

Zoning ordinances excluding the use of property by certain races are clearly illegal.

A recent court decision points out the problem of rezoning of undeveloped property that has been platted but not developed. In a Washington case, *Halverson v. City of Belleview*,[63] the court ruled that all parties having an interest in the property must approve of the change.

In a 1974 case, *Village of Belle Terre et al., v. Bruce Boraas et al.*,[64] involving housing zoned for single-family, the word family was defined as one or more persons *related by blood,* living and cooking together as a single-housekeeping unit. This early definition would appear to be obsolete as a result of the 1989 case of *Braschi v. Stahl Assoc. Co.*,[65] where the court gave a broad definition of *the family* which included lifetime partners whose relationship is long-time and characterized by emotional and financial commitment and interdependence and not limited to those people related by blood or law.

Where a zoning ordinance is in force, a property owner who desires to erect a structure must first obtain a building permit from the appropriate building inspector. If the purpose of the building meets the requirements of the building code and is not violative of any zoning restrictions, the desired permit will be issued. Where the contemplated use does not adhere to the zone set up for the particular location, the permit will be refused, although an appeal by an aggrieved party may be taken to the Board of Adjustment, or as it is sometimes known, the zoning board.

---

[61] Boise City v. Blaser, 352 P. 2d 892 (Idaho 1977). See also Norton Realty and Loan Co., Inc. v. Gainsville, 224 Ga. 166 (1968) and Walworth County v. Hartwell, 214 N.W. 2d 288 (Wis. 1974).

[62] Goldfarb v. Dietz, 506 P. 2d 1322 (Wash. 1973).

[63] Halverson v. City of Belleview, 41 Wash. App. 457, 704, P. 2d 1232 (1985).

[64] Village of Belle Terre et al., v. Bruce Boraas et al., (No. 73-191 April 1, 1974).

[65] Braschi v. Stahl Assocs. Co., 544 N.Y.S. 2d 784 (1989).

These boards have the power to hear and decide appeals, where it is alleged there is an error in the decision of an administrative official. The board can take cognizance of special conditions where a literal enforcement of the zoning ordinance will result in unnecessary hardship.

Further appeal to court is permitted, and ordinarily an appeal from the decision of the board operates to stay the proceedings upon the decision of the appealed, but the court may, upon application, grant a restraining order, upon cause shown and upon petitioner posting a bond as in any other case seeking injunctive relief.

In the case of *Nikola v. Township of Grand Blanc,*[66] the plaintiffs bought a property for the purpose of building and maintaining a mobile home park. The site was zoned for single residences other than mobile homes. The plaintiffs relied upon the representation by the township supervisor that rezoning for a trailer park would be no problem. A two-year delay ensued upon plaintiff's petition to build. One reason was it was anticipated that part of the land would be condemned for highway purposes, and thus the damages would be considerably increased. Another reason was the lack of sanitary sewers. Plaintiffs were led to believe that when these two factors no longer existed, rezoning would be granted. The court said:

> . . . . prospective purchasers and their counsel (should) be aware of the general enforceability of such claimed representations. It would be well for the purchasers to heed ancient adage of caveat emptor in this area of law, and get their rezoning problems adjudicated before purchase and not after. (emphasis supplied)

The court added, however, that in the instant case:

> . . . . we cannot possibly see how a mobile home park vis-a-vis single family residence can possibly affect Grand Blanc Township's morals, health or safety on the land in question.

Where a proposed zoning ordinance is controversial, the authorities may wish to take extraordinary care in determining the public's opinion prior to enactment. In one instance, in 1976, the city of East Lake, Ohio put the subject to a public referendum. Those who objected to this procedure alleged that the city had no right to delegate its power. The Supreme Court declared the referendum legal citing:

> (1) the referendum decision could not properly be characterized as a delegation of power, and (2) the referendum rezoning decision was properly reserved to the people under the Ohio Constitution.

As we will see in Chapter 12 in the discussion of land use, regulations, under the guise of zoning, which result in the destruction or confiscation of property, will fail. Courts, in the interest of justice and equity, may pertinently inquire into the valid or invalid exercise of this police power, keeping in mind whether the

---

66
Nikola v. Township of Grand Blanc, 209 N.W. 2d 803 (Mich. 1973).

challenged ordinances are necessary for the public health, safety, morals, or general welfare.

While the right of governments to regulate land use through the process of zoning is no longer questioned, the manner in which this is accomplished is subject to interpretations of the courts. Certain zoning actions may result in a claim of "Illegal Taking."

The following cases are considered *bellwether* tests for these claims.

LEGAL TESTS FOR ILLEGAL TAKING BY ZONING CHANGES

• Diminution of Value Test - Pennsylvania Coal Co.v. Mahore, 260 U.S. 393 (1922)

• Reasonable Use Test- Arvene Bay Constr. Co.v. Thatcher, 278 N.Y. 22, 15 N.E. 2d 587 (1938)

• Schere v. Freehold, 119 N.J. Super. 433, 292 A. 2d 35 *Cert. denied, 410 U.S. 93 (1972)*

• Balance of Public Benefit against Private Loss Test- LaSalle National Bank v. County of Cook, 60 Ill. App. 2d 39, 208 N.E. 2d 430 (1965)

• Harm-Benefit Test - Just v. Marienette Co., 56 Wisc. 2d 7, 201 N.W. 2d 761 (1972)

SOME ZONING MAY BE CONSIDERED A TAKING OF PRIVATE PROPERTY

San Diego Gas & Electric Co. v. City of San Diego (1981).[67] The gas company purchased a property as a possible site for a nuclear power plant. The city rezoned a part of the property, reducing the acreage available for industrial use. The company brought an action for *reverse condemnation*. The result was:

1. The Superior Court awarded damages.

2. The California Supreme Court reversed and transferred it to the Court of Appeals.

3. The Court of Appeals reversed the damage award and suggested that the case be retried on a basis of invalidating the ordinance.

4. The U.S. Supreme Court reviewed the case to determine the status of the California decisions. The final result was a mixed decision which indicated that *if* the case had become before the court for a decision, it was possible that the court would have awarded damages for the inverse condemnation, if the land owner could have proven that a taking had occurred.

---

[67]
28 U.S.C. 1259

It appears that the court has reasserted what it had previously held: an overly strict regulation of land can constitute a taking.

Chapter 12 discusses the problems of land use and defines the term "Reverse Condemnation" more thoroughly.

ARE LOCAL GOVERNMENTS SUBJECT TO ANTITRUST LAWS?

For a time local governments were reluctant to enforce zoning regulations which would appear to adversely affect one group while favoring another. The fear was that a municipality could be accused of restraint of trade under the Clayton Act. In 1984 Congress enacted a statute that appears to protect municipalities from damage liability under the Clayton Act. In 1985 the Supreme Court eliminated the requirement that a municipality show active supervision to qualify for antitrust immunity. Henceforth, it need only show that its anti-competitive actions were taken pursuant to a clearly articulated state policy.[68]

STATE'S AUTHORITY TO EXERCISE POWER OF EMINENT DOMAIN

Eminent domain may be defined as the power of the state to take private property for public use. The 5th Amendment to the Constitution of the United States states:

> No person shall be deprived of life, liberty, or property without due process of law, nor shall private property be taken for public use without just compensation.

Under the "due process" clause of the 14th Amendment,[69] this same prohibition is extended to the several states. Even though the state constitution contains no such provision, the right can, nevertheless, be exercised by the states as eminent domain is an inherent attribute of state sovereignty. The government is the supreme power in the state, and private rights are held under such supreme power and may be said to represent an indulgence by the sovereign power.

THE HISTORY OF THE EXERCISE OF SOVEREIGN POWER

The first recorded exercise of Sovereign Power was in 871 B.C.—Ahab, king of Samaria informed Nabob, the Jezreelite, that he had need of his vineyard for a garden for herbs.[70] In compensation the king said, "I will give thee for it a better vineyard than it; or, if it seems good to thee, I will give thee the worth of it in money." Nabob refused this condemnation saying the Lord forbade him to give away the inheritance of his father.

---

[68] Town of Hallie v. City of Eau Claire, 471 U.S. 34, 105,S.C.T. 1713, 85 L. Ed. 2d 24 (1985).

[69] Section 1 of the 14th Amendment reads: "Nor shall any state deprive any person of life, liberty or property without due process of law."

[70] I Kings XXI

Nabob apparently failed to avoid the condemnation as it is written that Ahab, having failed in his attempt at condemnation, was very unhappy. Jezebel, the king's wife in the name of the king, exercised the sovereign's power and directed that Nabob be killed in order that his land could be made available for the king's use.

The constitutional requirement of just compensation is a limitation on police power rather than a grant of power. The just compensation requirement in Anglo-American law may be traced back to the Magna Carta,[71] which provided that "no freeman shall be ..... deprived of his freehold....unless by the lawful judgment of his peers and by the law of the land."

It has been stated that eminent domain, as it presently exists, apparently grew out of the English common law proceeding known as "inquest of office" by which jurors inquired into any matter that entitled the King to possession of property and which became the proper proceeding at common law to acquire land for public use. Eminent domain was well recognized in England by the time of the American Revolution and was used in the colonies largely for roadway acquisitions.

CONDEMNATION RIGHTS RESERVED FOR THE STATE'S MUNICIPALITIES

The right of eminent domain exists not only in favor of the state but also for the benefit of any municipal subdivision of the state. In fact, any public corporation or any private corporation vested with a public use may exercise the extraordinary power when necessary for the public good. The emphasis here is "for the public good." In an early case, *Pittsburgh W. & K.R. Co,*[72] a railroad company sought to condemn a right of way across a steel mill, which would afford it access to a competing steel mill's land. Since it was primarily for the benefit of the second steel mill and for profit of the railroad company, eminent domain was refused. If the right to eminent domain did not exist for the public good, a single obstructionist property owner in a key position for a planned improvement could successfully stay the betterment and progress of a whole community with his refusal to sell or his unwillingness to sell at any but a prohibitive price.

The Supreme Court stated in *Armstrong v. U.S.,*[73] "the fifth amendment guarantees that private property shall not be taken for public use without just compensation was designed to bar Government from forcing some people alone to bear public burdens which in all fairness and justice, should be borne by the public as a whole." After all appropriation of private property does not mean confiscation of such land, for the owner is entitled to fair and just compensation for the taking.

---

[71] Art 39, Magna Carta (1215)

[72] Pittsburgh W.& K.R. Co., 8 S.E. 453 (W.Va.).

[73] Armstrong v. U.S., 364 U.S. 40,49 (1960).

Example—A public utility embarking upon a program of expansion, or a municipality in the development of a needed civic project, will endeavor to purchase the required properties for what is considered a fair and reasonable price. It is only when the negotiations fail that a resort is made to condemnation through eminent domain proceedings. The Court, upon failure of the interested parties to agree upon the sale price or to accept an award of court appointed viewers, will then determine a just price for the property in question.

It is not uncommon for a property owner to receive a higher price through court condemnation proceedings than is offered to him for a voluntary conveyance of the same land. Just compensation is held to be *the fair market value of the land and the improvements thereon.* Where only a part of the owner's tract is condemned, differences and difficulties arise as to the amount of compensation due. Certainly the claimant is entitled to the fair market value of the part taken, and it is equally well accepted that he or she is entitled, as an element of damage, to the depreciation in value, if any, to the land retained by him, caused by the taking. These two elements constitute his highest possible damage.

The term "Just Compensation" is not defined by any constitution, Federal or State. It is generally agreed, by the various courts that just compensation is determined by market value,[74] but even market value is not always the best measure of proper compensation, hence the courts have not established firm rules for evaluation.[75]

The Courts are constantly being besieged by land owners who feel that condemning authorities have failed to offer just compensation for their property. The following cases are illustrative of the complexity of this particular facet of the law and the decisions based on specific circumstances.

In *Defnet Land and Dev. Co. v. State*[76] the Court held that where only part of a property is taken, the measure of severance damage is the difference between market value of the remainder before and after the taking. This is considered a landmark case which set a precedence for future takings of this type.

In a 1973 case, *State Highway Commission v. Crooks,*[77] an award of $93,500 for taking 21 acres out of a tract of 196.32 acres, part of which was in a flood plain and part of which was hilly and in an industrial area, together with taking of right of access

---

[74]
Harwell v. United States, 316 F. 2d 791

[75]
United States v. Cors, 337 U.S. 325, 69 S. Ct. 1086

[76]
Defnet Land Dev. Co. v. State, ex re Herman 480 P. 2d 1013 (Ariz. App. 1971).

[77]
State Highway Commission v. Crooks, 282 So. 2d 451 (La. 1973).

to the proposed new highway, was fair and did not evidence bias, passion, or prejudice.

Factors to consider in a total taking of a dwelling under eminent domain are comparative sales data and reproduction cost.[78]

The Missouri Appellate Court held that the unsightliness of farm property caused by the construction of high-voltage transmission lines is a proper element of damage.[79]

In 1974 a South Carolina court ruled that undeveloped resources, such as valuable deposits of sand, gravel, and limestone, were a proper element in ascertaining land value.[80]

In the case of a partial taking and in the calculation of the value before and after the taking, the Florida Appellate court held that the owners were not entitled, as an element of compensation, to the increase in value of the property caused by the proposed improvement.[81] A limitation on this Florida ruling was established in the earlier case of *Levit v. State Department of Transportation.*[82] as follows:

> Such enhanced value is generally peculiar only to land lying adjacent to the improvement and within close proximity to the interchange exits and entrances leading to and from intersecting roads and highways.

Damage caused by a municipality in changing the level of a street from its natural level to an established grade is compensable.[83]

SOME CONDEMNATION LOSSES ARE NON-COMPENSABLE

While most losses due to a taking are compensable, certain restrictions apply. For instance, the loss of a liquor license was deemed not compensable, as such license is not "property" which is protected by the constitutional guarantees. A Delaware court, ruling on such a situation, considered a liquor license "a limited permit to engage in an enterprise, which would otherwise be unlawful."[84] Similarly, losses of intended *uses of property in the future* are not compensable.[85]

78
State of Louisiana v. Carmouche, 155 So. 2d 451 (La. 1963).

79
Missouri Public Service Co. v. Garrison, 454 S.W. 2d 628 (Mo. App. 1969).

80
Seaboard Coast Line R.R. v. Harrelson, 202 S.E. 2d 1 (S.C. 1974).

81
Pozin v. State Department of Transportation, 281 So. 2d 73 (Fla. App. 1973).

82
Levit v. State Department of Transportation, 248 So. 2d 542 (Fla. App. 1971).

83
Behlman v. City of Florissant, 548 S.W. 2d 619 (Mo. App. 1977).

84
Restaurants, Inc. v. City of Wilmington, 274 A. 2d 137 (Del. 1971).

85
Public Service Co. of Indiana v. Morgan County Rural Elec. Membership Corp., 360 N.E. 2d 1022 (Ind. App. 1977).

In general compensation for the loss of business due to the taking of *land* is not compensable. In the case of *Kayo Oil Co. v. State of Alabama*,[86] it was ruled that business profits are so remote from the land market value, on which the business is located, as to preclude the business as a proper indication of land value. However, an Alaskan court held the *loss of profits* compensable, and *"dammun absque injuria"* (injury without damages).[87]

Generally a condemnee is not entitled to compensation for personalty used in land taken (e.g., restaurant equipment). However, depreciation in value of personalty, in addition to physical damage, should be allowed.[88]

Compensation for trivial inconveniences caused by the taking are also not compensable. In *Dept. of Public Works, etc. v. Greenwell*,[89] condemnee claimed that the dead-ending of a road one-half mile East of her necessitated circuitry of travel for 800 feet. She could claim no damage as a result of the taking, thus the Court denied her claim.

Most important to any eminent domain proceedings is the requirement of the property owner to establish that public use is the direct and proximate cause of the *damage* complained of, and not merely such as is possible, as may be conceived by the imagination, or as merely affects the feelings of the property owner.[90]

CALCULATING JUST COMPENSATION IS NOT SIMPLE

If only a portion of the owner's land is taken for a public improvement and the project itself results in a significant benefit to the owner's remaining property, logic would seem to indicate that the owner should be charged for the benefits derived against the price paid to him or her. Lewis, on eminent domain, summarizes the law on benefits as follows (Sec.687):

> The law in regard to benefits is now pretty well settled in every State, either by decisions of its courts, or its statutes, or its constitution. While different and conflicting rules prevail in the different States under precisely the same constitutional provisions, it is evident that there can be but one absolute correct rule. In taking private property for public use, the State acts rightfully and not as a wrong doer. It guarantees just compensation and nothing more. In arriving at what is just compensation, the matter is to be viewed in the same light as though the State had bargained with the owner for a portion of his land and had agreed to make just compensation therefor. It is self-evident that, where a part of the tract is taken, the just compensation cannot be determined without considering the manner in which the part is taken, the purpose for which it is taken, and the

---

[86] Kayo Oil Co. v. State, 340 So. 2d 756 (Ala. 1976).

[87] State of Alaska v. Hammer, 550 P. 2d 820 (Alaska 1976).

[88] State of Alaska v. Ness, 516 P 2d 1212 (1973).

[89] Dept. of Public Works, etc. v. Greenwell, 359 N. E. 2d 780 (Ill. 1977).

[90] Frank v. Mercer County, 186 N.W. 2d 439 (N.D. 1971; Nichols on Eminent Domain Sec. 14.24.

effect of the taking upon that which remains. All the authorities concede this so far as damages to the remainder are concerned, and the justice of so doing may be taken for granted. But what justice is there in considering the effect insofar only as it produces damage? If a railroad is constructed through a farm and drains a valuable spring whereby the remainder is depreciated five hundred dollars, it is conceded that just compensation must include this five hundred dollars. But if, instead of draining a valuable spring, it drains a marshy tract so as to make it worth five hundred dollars more for actual use, the same sense of justice requires that this five hundred dollars of benefit should be considered.

A property owner is entitled to severable damages, if it is shown that the property taken is a part of a larger tract, which has been adversely affected by the taking: *Babinec v. State,*[91]

In the case of *United States v. 147.47 acres of land,*[92] the value of farm land on the outskirts of a growing town was deemed to be worth less than the value of such land, converted into a subdivision, on a lot basis. Of course the subdivider must have taken forward steps to make the change by the time of the taking. Incidents of such transformation would include such items as engineering, promotion of sales, advertising, plotting, and recording.

The above requirement for action to change the character of the land in order to consider a higher market value, appears to have been modified by later court decisions which base such considerations more on the possibility or probability of change rather than actual change taking place. In *United States v. 50.8 acres of land,*[93] the court said at 752:

> To what extent the possibility or probability of a change would affect the value as of the date of the taking, is dependent upon the degree of probability, the imminence of change, the effectiveness of the opposition, and other factors which are largely speculative and conjectural.
>
> To appraise the land as though the change had occurred, when in fact it had not, would be to totally disregard restrictions upon its use, which had been imposed by competent authority, for many years, and to permit the owner to receive compensation based on a prohibited use (citing cases). However, to deny the owner any increment in value attributable to the probability of a favorable change in zoning in the reasonably near future, would likewise, be unjust.

In the 1977 case of *State Department of Highways v. Miltenberger,*[94] the Court ruled that trees and shrubbery were not to be appraised independently of the land *unless* they have some unique value in addition to the fair market value of the condemned land. Thus natural trees along the border of farm land, taken for road widening would probably not be considered, whereas landscaping along the road

---

[91] Babinec v. State, 512 P. 2d 563 (Alaska 1973).

[92] United States v. 147.47 acres of land, 352 F. Supp. 1055 (Md/Pa. 1972).

[93] United States v. 50.8 acres of land, 149 F. Supp. 749.

[94] State Department of Highways v. Miltenberger, 344 So. 2d 705 (La. App. 1977).

of a private estate and having value as a noise screen, should be considered in the appraiser's evaluation.

LESSEES HAVE RIGHTS WHEN LEASED PROPERTY IS CONDEMNED

The examination of a commercial lease should determine what understanding exists under the lease, in regard to a taking of the leased property under eminent domain. If the lease does not specifically foreclose the lessee's right to damages, all elements affecting the value of the leasehold must be examined. In the case of *Barnini et al. v. Sun Oil Co.*,[95] the plaintiff's property was taken for highway purposes. The property was under lease to the defendant for a service station, with an option to renew. The Court said:

> The value of the lease is properly arrived at in the case of a complete taking by subtracting the rent provided for under the lease, from the fair market value of the lease. In a determination of what this amount should be, all elements legitimately affecting the value of the lease should be considered.

In *State Highway Commission v. Sambroski*,[96] it was declared that a lessee may be entitled to the reasonable market value of the unexpired period of the lease, unless fixtures upon the premises are obsolete at the time of the taking. Additional cases which dealt with this problem are: *County of Gennepin v. Holt* and *Wessels v. State of Alaska*.[97]

URBAN RENEWAL CONDEMNATION OF LARGE AREAS

In the mid-1970s, special authorities were created by Congress and the state legislative bodies for erecting public housing projects. These projects, intended to supply badly needed housing and to improve the standard of living for low income groups, have had an important effect upon the economic and social well-being of a large segment of our industrial population. In the fulfillment of the housing program, blighted areas have been condemned and destroyed for the erection of new structures. In this development, it is often necessary to resort to condemnation of an entire zone or district. This is known as *zone condemnation* and is the only practical and effective method of clearing slums. Zone condemnation is for a specific purpose. Even in public condemnation the cost is great, but the benefits of better health of the inhabitants and the elimination of crime are readily commensurate with the cost involved. Today state legislatures have created public

---

[95] Barnini et al. v. Sun Oil Co., 283 A. 2d 158 (Conn. 1971).

[96] State Highway Commission v. Sambroski, 463 S.W. 2d 896 (Mo. 1971).

[97] County of Gennepin v. Holt, 297 N.W. 2d 723 (Minn. 1973); Wessels v. State of Alaska, 562 P. 2d 1042 (Alaska 1977).

authorities with the right of condemnation for housing, sanitation, parking and public utility purposes.

Urban renewal is a *substantial state interest* that can justify taking property dedicated to religious use. In the case *Pillar of Fire v. Denver Urban Renewal Authority,*[98] the court ruled that church property is private property which can be taken for public use by eminent domain.

FEDERAL CONTROLS

FEDERAL CONSTRAINTS TO PROTECT THE ENVIRONMENT AND THE PUBLIC

While protection of the public is generally considered to be the province of the state and its local governments, certain aspects of this protection have been assumed by the federal government to assure conformance with the provisions of the federal constitution. These regulations apply primarily to: (1) protection of the environment, (2) property rights, and (3) the assurance that individuals will be free from discrimination because of race, age, or national origin.

FEDERAL ACTS TO PROTECT THE ENVIRONMENT

There are four federal acts that all REALTORS® should be aware of in the conduct of their business. These are the Comprehensive Environmental Response Compensation and Liability Act (CERCLA),[99] the Resource Conservation and Recovery Act (RCRA),[100] the Toxic Substance Control Act (TSCA)[101] and the National Environmental Policy Act (NEPA).[102]

CERCLA was designed to remediate sites contaminated by hazardous substances before further damage occurs. Typical CERCLA cases brought under this act are *United States v. Shell Oil* (1985), *FMC Corp. v. Northern Pump Co.,* and *United States v. Reilly Tar & Chemical Corp.* The Acts seek to accomplish its goals by imposing liability upon those who cause the contamination and by providing the federal government with enforcement tools and funding to address the contamination, if the responsible party(s) do not.

Under CERCLA provisions, the various classes of people who may be held liable are:

---

[98] Pillar of Fire v. Denver Urban Renewal Authority, 509 P. 2d 1250 (Colo 1973).

[99] 42 U.S.C. 9601-9675.

[100] 42 U.S.C. 6901-6991.

[101] 15 U.S.C. 2601-2654.

[102] 41 U.S.C. 4321.

Any person who by contract, agreement or otherwise arrange for disposal or treatment, or arrange with a transporter for transport for disposal or treatment, hazardous substances owned or possessed by such person, by any other party or entity, at any facility or incineration vessel owned or operated by another party, or entity and containing such hazardous substances.[103]

The following example illustrates how a rather casual connection can be a problem for a REALTOR®.

Example—If a buyer discovers hazardous waste during the inspection of property, the seller most often agrees to dispose of the waste, as a part of the selling agreement. The seller may then call his broker and ask the broker to arrange for disposal of the material. If the broker contacts companies, takes bids and arranges for one of the companies to clear the property at the seller's expense, the broker has exposed himself to possible liability if a spill occurs.[104]

In the case *New York v. Shore Realty*, the court found an officer and shareholder of a (Real Estate) Corporation personally liable for being in charge of a facility, noting that under New York law a corporation officer who actively participates in the conduct of the corporation is liable for torts of the corporation.[105]

HAZARDOUS SUBSTANCE DEFINED

The term Hazardous Substance is defined[106] as:

(A)any substance designated pursuant to section 311(b)(2)(A) of the Federal Water Pollution Control Act[33 USCS 1321 (b)(2)(A), (B) any element, compound, mixture solution, or substance designated pursuant to section 102 of this Act [42 USCS 9602], (C) any hazardous waste having the characteristics identified under or listed pursuant to section 3001 of the Solid Waste Disposal Act [42 USCS 6921] (but not including any waste the regulation of which under the Solid Waste Disposal Act has been suspended by Act of Congress), (D) any toxic pollutant listed under section 307(a) of the Water Pollution Control Act [33 USCS 1317(a)], (E) any hazardous air pollutant listed under section 112 of the Clean Air Act [42 USCS 7412], and (F) any imminently hazardous chemical substance or mixture with respect to which the Administrator has taken action pursuant to section 7 of the Toxic Substances Control Act [15 USCS 2605]. The term does not include petroleum, including crude oil or any fraction thereof which is not otherwise specifically listed or designated as a hazardous substance

---

103
   9607(a)(3).
104
   United States v. Bliss, 667 F. Supp. 1298 (E.D. Mo. 1987) United States v. Motalo, 629 F. Supp. 56 (D. N.H. 1984) City of Philadelphia v. Stepan Chemical Co., 544 F. Supp. 1135, 1140 (E.D. Pa. 1982)
105
   New York v. Shore Realty, 759 F. 2d 1032 (2d Cir. 1985)
106
   42 U.S.C. 9601(14)

under paragraphs (A) through (F) of this paragraph, and the term does not include natural gas, natural gas liquids, liquified natural gas, or synthetic gas usable for fuel (or mixtures of natural gas and such synthetic gas).

FORMER PROPERTY OWNERS MAY BE EXEMPT FROM LIABILITY

Prior landowners, who did not own the land at the time that hazardous substances were introduced are not liable under CERCLA for clean-up costs, even if the substances "migrated" underground during their ownership.[107]

Potential CERCLA liabilities are of legitimate concern to lenders because cleanup liabilities can extend to a lender that acquires property by foreclosure. Under CERCLA provisions, the lender would be classed as an *innocent landowner* exempt from liability *only* if, after due diligence, he or she had no reason to know of the presence of hazardous substances when he acquired the property.[108]

Accordingly, lenders in a real estate transaction should request the borrower's attorney to prepare a legal opinion. They may also wish to get an opinion from their own attorney. Cleanup liabilities may also limit the borrower's ability to use the property for its intended purposes.

It should also be noted that the U.S. may be granted a lien for CERCLA cleanup costs and damages, which may seriously dilute the lenders security. This provision has most recently come under fire in the case of *Reardon v. U.S. First U.S. Circuit Court of Appeals*.[109] The case involved a 16-acre site in Norwood, Massachusetts, contaminated with polychlorinated biphenyls. In 1989, the EPA filed a lien on the property with the Norfolk County Registry of Deeds. The lien was for an unspecified amount to cover all cleanup costs for which the owners were allegedly liable at that site. In its decision, the appeals court dismissed the EPA's arguments that the government's special interest in making sure it can recover cleanup costs justifies its practice of placing liens *without* conducting hearings.

Additional problems for lenders, regarding CERCLA violations, were recently imposed by the 11th Court of Appeals in the case *United States v. Fleet Factors Corp.*,[110] in which the court stated:

A lender, who has not acquired ownership at foreclosure, has not "operated" the facility, and has not been directly involved in decisions regarding disposal of toxic wastes may still be liable. The test is "Capacity to Influence".

RCRA concerns itself with the present day generation of waste and attempts to provide "cradle to grave" management of such waste. TSCA, on the other hand,

---

107
Ecodyne Corp. v. Shal, 718 F. Supp. 1454 (N.D. Cal 1989)
108
U.S.C. 9601(20 & 35), 9607 (1982).
109
Reardon v. U.S. First U.S. Circuit Court of Appeals, Boston, 90-1319.
110
United States v. Fleet Factors Corp., 901 F. 2d 1550 (11th Cir. 1990)

imposes testing, reporting and other use restrictions and recordkeeping requirements upon those who manufacture, process, or distribute chemicals that may adversely affect the health or the environment.

SOLID WASTE DEFINED

The term Solid Waste is defined as:[111]

> Any garbage, refuse, sludge from a waste treatment plant, or air pollution control facility or any other discarded material, including solid, liquid, semisolid, or containing gaseous material resulting from industrial, commercial, mining and agricultural operations, and from community activities, but does not include solid or dissolved material in domestic sewage, or solid or dissolved materials in irrigation return flows or industrial discharges which are point sources subject to permits under section 402 of the Federal Water Pollution Control Act, as amended (86 Stat. 923) [42 U.S.C. 2011 (et seq.).

NEPA requires federal agencies to prepare environmental impact statements on major federal actions that significantly affect the quality of the human environment. These reports must:

1. Show the impact of the proposed action.

2. Indicate adverse affects which cannot be avoided if the proposal is implemented.

3. Suggest alternatives to the proposal.

4. Indicate any relationship between local short-term uses and long-term productivity, and

5. List any irreversible and/or irretrievable commitments of resources that would be involved.[112]

THE REQUIREMENT FOR RECORDING HAZARDOUS WASTE SITES

The use of property as a hazardous waste site may forever poison the land which will make it unhabitable by man or livestock. Accordingly, the U.S. Environmental Protection Agency has promulgated regulations which require land owners to record a document, which will notify any potential purchaser, of the facts which may or may not indicate a future restriction in the use of the property. The recording of this information will serve as a record in perpetuity.

---

[111] 42 U.S.C. 6901-6992(k) 1989

[112] See Chapter 8; Appendix "B" ; Moskowitz, Joel S., *Environmental Liability and Real Property Transactions,* John Wiley and Sons, N. Y., 1989.

APPRAISER CONCERNS WITH ENVIRONMENTAL PROBLEMS

In the fall of 1990, the Society of Real Estate Appraisers Board of Governors suggested that all appraiser members of the Society include the following statements in their reports:

> In this appraisal assignment, the existence of potentially hazardous material used in the construction or maintenance of the building, such as the presence of urea formaldehyde form insulation, and/or existence of toxic waste, which may or may not be present on the property, has not been considered. The appraiser is not qualified to detect such substances. We urge the client to retain an expert in the field if desired.

As indicated in Chapter 10, the Society of Real Estate Appraisers merged with the Institute of Real Estate Appraisers, January 1, 1991, to form the Appraisal Institute. The above recommendation has been retained by the merged organization.

FEDERAL RIGHT TO EXERCISE THE POWER OF EMINENT DOMAIN

Any question regarding the right of the federal government to exercise the power of eminent domain was firmly established in 1875.[113] It should be pointed out, however, that most requirements for the exercise of this constitutional power is at the state or lower level of government; however, the United States Government in the exercise of its broad war powers has, in the interest of flood control, utilized large area (zone) condemnation to acquire extensive areas throughout the country.

FEDERAL OPEN HOUSING LEGISLATION: ANTI-DISCRIMINATION

Under the President's Executive Order of November 20, 1962, housing that related to or was aided by federal assistance came under an anti-discrimination mandate. The Order included new F.H.A. or V.A mortgage construction, public housing, housing assisted through urban renewal, and federally owned housing. Since then, statutes have been passed in a number of states, augmented by ordinances in some cities, making it illegal to discriminate against purchasers on the grounds of race, color, religion, national origin, or background. These regulatory measures vary as to their provisions and effectiveness.

On April 11, 1968, President Johnson signed an open housing law that is vitally important for all those in the housing and mortgage business. The law prohibits racial discrimination by most sellers and renters of dwellings, and also bans discrimination by all those who make loans to buy or improve residential property. For sellers and renters, the law took effect in three stages, but for lenders the effective date was Jan. 1, 1969. The agency charged with administering and enforcing the law is the Department of Housing and Urban Development (HUD);

---

[113]
Kohl v. United States, 91 U.S. 367, 23 L.Ed. 449

the Department of Justice also plays a role in those instances where violations reach the courts.

It is important to note that, by some state statutes, or by amendments to existing state laws, conviction of a real estate broker or salesperson as being a party to a discriminatory act constitutes grounds for disciplinary action by the Real Estate Commission.

The problem of housing is nationwide, and the states look to the federal government for leadership and guidance in alleviating the complex difficulties. The Congress acted and passed the Open Housing Law, which was signed by the President on April 11, 1968. A capsule analysis of the important provisions of the law follows (taken from Prentice Hall, Inc.—*Federal Aids to Financing Report, with permission:*)

The law prohibits discrimination on the ground of race, color, religion, or national origin in the sale, rental, or financing of dwellings. This includes setting harsher terms for publishing discriminatory advertising, telling persons that a dwelling is not available for sale or rental, when in fact it is, or "block-busting"(attempting to get a person to sell or rent by representations that people of a particular race, color, religion or national origin are entering or about to enter the neighborhood).

The law became effective in two stages:

(1) In 1968, it banned discrimination in the sale or rental of housing insured or guaranteed by the federal government or located in a federally assisted urban renewal or slum clearance project. The ban applies to all such housing backed by the government after November 20, 1962 (the date of the Executive Order banning discrimination in government-backed housing), unless payment was made before the date of enactment, namely April 11, 1968.

It also covers dwellings owned or operated by the federal government and dwellings built with the aid of loans, advances, grants, or contributions made by the federal government.

(2) Effective January 1, 1969, the ban applies to all dwelling units, no matter how financed, with these two exceptions:

(a) Single-family homes, provided the owner does not own more than three single-family homes at one time. If the owner is a nonoccupant of a single-family home he sells, he gets the exemption for only one sale within a 24-month period.

(b) One-to-four family dwellings, if the owner occupies one of the units.

Loans: Also effective January 1, 1969, banks, savings and loan agencies, mutual savings banks, insurance companies, and other lenders cannot discriminate in making loans on apartment buildings or homes—whether for purchase, repairs, or construction. Also forbidden is discrimination in setting the terms of the loans, such as the amount of the mortgage, the interest rate, and so on.

Enforcement of the Act is vested in the Secretary of Housing and Urban Development (HUD). The secretary, or his assistant, is limited in his powers in handling complaints to "education, conciliation, and persuasion." In this connection, he can investigate complaints, issue subpoenas, hold hearings, before issuing a final order. He cannot issue a "cease and desist order," nor fine an offender. For punitive damages for violation of the law, a complainant must file a suit in a Federal district court. If there is as "substantially equivalent" local or state fair housing law, the federal court generally will direct that complaint to be filed in the state or local forum.

The law gives the government the right to inspect the records of anyone charged with discrimination.

In addition to the enforcement provisions, the Attorney General can bring action in cases where there is a general pattern of discrimination or an issue of general public importance.

On June 17, 1968, the United States Supreme Court handed down its landmark decision on open housing, in the St. Louis case of *Jones v. Mayer Co.*,[114] involving the purchase of a homesite in a subdivision called Peddock Woods. The Supreme Court held that an Act of Congress passed in 1866 forbade racial discrimination in the sale or rental of housing in the United States. In a majority opinion (7-2), Mr. Potter Stewart said, inter alia,

> Negro citizens North and South, who won in the Thirteenth Amendment a promise of freedom—freedom to go and come at pleasure and to buy and sell when they please—would be left with a mere paper guarantee if Congress were powerless to assure that a dollar in the hands of a negro will purchase the same thing as a dollar in the hands of a white man.

The Act of 1968 contains many exemptions, including specifically single-family residential units sold without an agent. The Act of 1866 contains no such exemption and it lacks the federal enforcement machinery and other remedies available under the 1986 Act.

The law is still comparatively new and is not yet court tested as to any ambiguities or conflicts in its provisions, particularly in its relationship to the act of 1866 and the fairly recent Supreme Court decision. A number of legal experts are in good accord that the Supreme Court opinion in the Jones case has the effect of eliminating the several exceptions contained in the Act of 1968, without voiding the law itself. In support of this view, they call attention to the language of the 1866 Act, which states:

> All citizens of the United States shall have the same right, in every state and territory, as is enjoyed by white citizens thereof to inherit, purchase, lease, sell, hold, and convey real and personal property.

It would appear that a party plaintiff could petition for injunctive relief in a

---

[114] Jones v. Mayer Co., 392 U,S. 409 (decided June 17, 1968).

federal district court, on the basis that there is no irreconcilable conflict between the Act of 1968 and the Act of 1866. The total effect of the Supreme Court decision is to bring all property, personal as well as real, under anti-discriminatory regulation. In real estate, the decision creates an "open housing" law through out the country. However, it should be noted that buyers and renters can still reject for reasonable *cause,* but the grounds for rejection must apply equally to *all* persons.

An excellent reference for damages for racial discrimination in the Housing Market is found in *Clark v. Universal Builders, Inc.*[115] The latest authority for Discrimination on the basis of income is *Boyd v. Lefrak Organization.*[116]

The Fair Employment Practices Act is a segment of legislation designed to protect individuals from discrimination because of sex, age, religion, race, color, national origin, or ancestry. The legal reference for opinion on this law is *Evening Sentinel v. National Organization of Women.*[117]

Authority for a city to adopt a Fair Housing Ordinance is contained in the decision of *Chicago Real Estate Board v. City of Chicago.*[118]

BLOCKBUSTING

The federal provisions on fair housing are further buttressed by state acts, particularly in the area of anti-discrimination measures. The practice of "blockbusting," or panic peddling is by law an act of discrimination. This is an overt act on the part of a real estate broker to put pressure on owners of dwellings to sell their properties because of a threat that the neighborhood is being infiltrated by minority persons. It is an effort to create panic selling, prohibited by the Fair Housing Act.

In the case of *People, etc. v. Betts Realtors, Inc., et al.*[119] a prosecution was brought against a broker, charging unlawful solicitation for sale of residential property after receiving notice from the owner that he did not desire to sell or be solicited for sale. The Illinois Supreme Court, in this above cited case held that an act designated to prevent "blockbusting," or panic peddling, is constitutional and no longer open to question. The Illinois act also made it unlawful "to solicit any owner of residential property to sell or list such residential property after such person or corporation has notice that such owner does not desire to be solicited to seller list for sale such property." The Court rejected defendant's argument that the act was "an unconstitutional limitation of free speech, and that the right to engage in commerce and to earn a living is an unlawful investiture of legislative power, and is otherwise unconstitutional."

---

[115] Clark v. Universal Builders, Inc., 501 F. 2d 324 (7th Circuit), 88 Harvard Law Rev. 1610 (1975).

[116] Boyd v. Lefrak Organization, 509 F. 2d 1110 (N.Y. 1974).

[117] Evening Sentinel v. National Organization of Women, 357 A. 2d 498 (Conn. 1975).

[118] Chicago Real Estate Board v. City of Chicago, 224 N.E. 2d 793 (Ill. 1967).

[119] People, etc v. Betts Realtors, Inc. et al., 361 N.E. 2d 581 (Ill. 1977).

3

Considerations of Real Property Ownership

WHAT IS REAL PROPERTY?

It is important to remember that certain words and phrases in connection with real estate have a technical meaning and a different interpretation from that generally attributed to them by the average layman. The all-inclusive term "property" may be said to be the rights or interests which a person has in lands and chattels to the exclusion of all others. Blackstone defines land as comprehending all things of a permanent and substantial nature. Lands are "realty"; chattels are "personalty."

Realty includes a two-fold classification, *corporeal* realty and *incorporeal* realty. Corporeal realty, like land and buildings, can be seen and felt. In other words, real property includes land and almost anything built upon, growing or affixed to the soil. Incorporeal property includes rights issuing out of, annexed to, or exercisable within land. A good example of this would be a right of way.

It is frequently stated that realty consists of three parts: (1) the land, (2) tenements upon the land, and (3) hereditaments. The term *land* refers to the surface of the Earth, the subsurface, and the space above the land. A land parcel which is legally described as a flat plane upon the Earth, extends from a point at the center of the Earth, to the surface where it encompasses the parcel described, then the boundary lines continue above the land to some point in which public rights prevail (the right to fly airplanes for instance). The common law maxim regarding land is expressed in Latin as: "Cujus est solum, ejus est usque ad coelum," or "he who owns the soil, owns it to the heavens." [1] The idea of air rights was established as early as 1906 in the case of *Butler v. Frontier Telephone Co.*[2] when the Court of

---

[1] Am. Jur. 2d 618, Blackstone Commentaries 18 (1836)

[2] Butler v. Frontier Telephone Co., 186 N.Y. 486, 491 (1906).

Appeals declared that ". . . . space above the land is real estate the same as space itself." *Tenements* include lands plus certain other things which are realty but which cannot be described as land. The best example of these are buildings erected upon the land. *Hereditaments* include all of the other things, usually of an incorporeal nature, such as rights of way.

WHAT IS AN ESTATE?

Estate means quantity of ownership, and *title* is the evidence of ownership. The quality of the estate is evidenced by the title. Estates are generally categorized into two main subdivisions: "freehold estates" and "less than freehold estates." The freehold designation originated under the old English feudal system. Today we simply refer to freehold estates as *interests in land* whereas "less than freehold" covers easements, leases, and other interests which are generally considered as personal property. Many real estate interests are often a combination of freehold estates and some other aspect of less than freehold.

FREEHOLD ESTATES

Freehold estates are subdivided into two main categories: (1) estates of inheritance, and (2) estates not of inheritance. An estate of inheritance is by far the most important in that it gives the owner rights which continue during his lifetime and which eventually pass to his heirs. Estates not of inheritance are of lesser quality in that the rights attached thereto continue only for the life of the holder or some lesser period.

ESTATES OF INHERITANCE

Under the estate of inheritance category, the highest type of ownership is known as the "fee simple estate." Under the old English feudal system, a fief or fee granted by the king to his tenants was held for their lifetime or at the king's will and command, the fee was conveyed to the tenant with the additional statement, "to his heirs and assigns forever." Thus, an estate of inheritance was established.

FEE SIMPLE OWNERSHIP RIGHTS

The fee simple estate, sometimes referred to as fee simple absolute, involves three basic rights associated with the interest therein:

1. *The exclusive right of possession* which gives the owner complete and absolute control of his property. The owner may mortgage, lease or bar entry upon the property to others.

2. *The right of quiet enjoyment* which means that from a legal standpoint he

can utilize his land in any manner he chooses consistent with local laws. He may use the land himself or rent to others and receive rents.

3. *The right of disposition* which allows the owner use of the land during his lifetime or to sell it to others if he so chooses. He may also dispose of his property at death by will. Only by operation of the law may he be deprived of his ownership. This can occur if he fails to pay his taxes or just debts or if the state requires his lands for the use of the public, in which case he must be compensated for the loss under the rules of eminent domain.

If the owner decides to dispose of his property, he may grant or deed to the new owner an unrestricted right "fee simple absolute" or one of two lesser titles, "fee simple determinable" or "conditional fee." *Fee simple determinable* indicates a transfer in fee with a condition that the transfer is effective only as long as certain conditions prevail. Example, a transfer to a church for parking of cars. When the specified use or need no longer prevails, title reverts to the grantor or original owner. *Fee simple conditional* is a transfer in which certain conditions of use are stipulated in the deed of transfer and which permits the original owner to recover the property when these conditions are no longer met. Unlike the fee simple determinable, title reversion is not automatic but reverts only when the original owner repossesses the property after the conditional terms have been broken.

4. *Air, scenic, mineral, and water* rights are becoming more important than in previous periods. Although air, mineral, and water rights have long been recognized, scenic rights (a view beyond the owner's property) have only recently been deemed legitimate rights of property owners.

AIR RIGHTS

Air rights involve the right to the use and enjoyment of space above the ground level. In some locations, where land has become extremely valuable, owners of property have found a ready market for unused space above the ground. These rights are sold or leased for uses such as highways, railroads, or buildings, which constitute "vertical subdivisions." Several examples of these uses can be found in New York City, Boston, and Chicago.

In addition to the aerial rights, users must obtain easements on the lower levels for the construction and maintenance of supporting pillars.[3]

Some good examples of the use of air rights are New York's new Madison Square Garden constructed over the Pennsylvania railroad station, Boston's freeway system over the downtown rail yards, and the Pan American Building constructed over New York's Grand Central Station.

---

[3]
Blankenship, Frank J., *The Prentice Hall Real Estate Investment Encyclopedia,* Englewood Cliffs, N. J., 1989, p. 21.

SCENIC RIGHTS

The subject of scenic rights is just beginning to come before the courts. Building lots, sold primarily for their unobstructed views, have a need for covenants or other protection to assure the continuation of scenic enjoyment. Similarly, the increased use of solar energy can be expected to raise additional problems of exposure to the sun. Also, increased utilization of satellite receivers mandates protection of line-of-sight acquisition of available signals.

MINERAL RIGHTS

Valuable minerals, including oil and gas, have long been recognized as a part of the land. Legal problems, in regards to those rights, are more often concerned with the method of extraction, inconvenience caused to surface dwellers and the problems of how the land surface is left after the minerals have been extracted. A detailed discussion of mineral rights is not deemed appropriate for this work. It is sufficient to recognize their significance to land ownership.

WATER RIGHTS

Property rights in water and in the use and enjoyment of it are well established as rights in the soil over which it flows. But water, from its very nature, does not readily adapt itself to possession as does land, so that property right in water is usually only a usufructory right, except in the Far West where rights to specific amounts of flow are actually owned, sold or deeded with or without the property. Water rights are usually defined as a number of wells permitted on the property, the number of acre-feet or second-feet of flow from an irrigation canal or stream, or as watershares that define the amount of water available per unit of ownership.

Except in the West, where the natural channel of a watercourse lies along or through the lands of different owners, the water therein is common and indivisible property of all. They have equal privileges to it in all respects insofar as a right to its use for domestic or business purposes. An upper owner, whose land is traversed by a steam, cannot exercise his use to deprive the lower owners of a similar enjoyment. That is to say, he cannot divert the water, dam it up, or interfere with its natural flow. If, however, in the ordinary, normal and reasonable exercise of his rights to use, the result is to prevent a subjacent owner of similar use, the lower owner has no redress. This is the common law rule of the doctrine of riparian rights. On the other hand, a mining company would be liable if pollution of the stream results from an artificial diversion of the stream.

An upper property owner cannot interfere with the natural drainage of surface water so as to increase the area of flooding to the land of lower owners. Such a continuing nuisance was enjoined by the cases of *Glassman v. Weldin Farms*, and

Tyler v. Vanelst.[4] In the latter case, the defendants were working with a bulldozer to clear brush which caused the waters of Cozy Nook Creek to be muddied upstream from plaintiff's diversion system. The mud, silt, and debris dislodged thereby caused problems with the plaintiff's water system. The defendants were enjoined from such interference.

In the Western states, as mentioned above, the common law rule has been rejected by reason of the arid conditions of the land and the necessities of the inhabitants. The policy there permits a diversion of the stream of water from its natural course and protects *the first* appropriation as a recognized proprietary right.

Three elements must exist for a valid appropriation:

1. *Intent to appropriate the water* to some beneficial use existing at the time or contemplated in the future.

2. *An actual diversion from the natural channel* by means of a ditch, canal or other conduit, and

3. *The practical application of the water* within a reasonable time to some useful purpose.

These three considerations are the tests by which an appropriation is considered legal. One of the most famous of all Western appropriations was the flow of the Colorado river through the states of Idaho, Utah, Colorado, Arizona, and California. In an 1800s decision of the courts, the entire flow of this large stream was allocated to the affected states. Although many attempts have been made and continue to be made to reallocate the Colorado's flow, the ownership of available water remains basically as originally divided.

The question of liability is frequently raised relative to the overflow of water from one property to another. The law is clearly established that the first owner may not construct a natural channel for the flow of the water or channel that has acquired the character of an easement, nor may he gather surface water into a body and discharge it upon adjacent land. He may not act negligently in directing the flow so as to do unnecessary damage to others. But so far as he acts upon his rights to the enjoyment of his own property, any accidental damage to a neighbor is, in the eyes of the law, *damnum absque injuria* (injury without wrong). In other words the injured party has no legal remedy.

HOMESTEAD RIGHTS

The broad purpose of the homestead laws has been aptly stated to be "to promote security of home and to place homestead property beyond the reach of consequences of homeowner's economic misfortunes.[5]

---

[4] Glassman v. Weldin Farms, 359 A. 2d 669 (Del. Ch. 1976) and Tyler v. Vanelst, 512 P. 2d 760 (Wash. App. 1973).

[5] Swearingen v. Byrne, 136 Cal Reptr. 736 (1977).

Homestead property resembles an estate by the entireties. Homestead laws exist in Alabama, Alaska, Arizona, Arkansas, California, Florida, Georgia, Idaho, Iowa, Louisiana, Massachusetts, Michigan, Missouri, Mississippi, Oklahoma, South Dakota, Texas, Vermont, Virginia, West Virginia, Wisconsin, and Wyoming. Property owned and occupied as a home, in a certain amount, is known as a family homestead. Both husband and wife must join in any deed or mortgage for this property. In the interest of public policy for the preservation of the family, homestead property cannot be sold to satisfy a judgment against one spouse.

In the case of *Solomon v. Solomon,*[6] the Court held that the provisions of the Texas Uniform Reciprocal Enforcement of Support Act did not authorize a levy of execution upon the homestead property in a case involving a suit to collect arrearage for support of children under a divorce decree.

Certain elements must be present to establish a homestead. There must be a family of two or more persons living together under a family head and actually occupying the land in question. The proper declaration must be filed that the property is actually occupied as a homestead. The homestead laws provide maximum areas and values of the homestead. In Arkansas, for instance, the statute sets up two types of homesteads: (1) the rural homestead, outside of an urban area, owned and occupied as a residence consists of land not exceeding 160 acres, but no less than 80 acres, and not exceeding $10,000 in value; (2) the urban homestead in a city or town or village , occupied as a residence which cannot exceed one acre of land or less than one quarter acre, and not exceed in $2,500 in value. It is not necessary for a person to live on a homestead in order to claim homestead rights, but he must be in intention to return to the homestead.

In Texas, property upon which the head of the family conducts his business is known as his "business homestead." In California, the exemption from execution on homestead property is $7,500. In Florida, homestead exists as to 160 acres outside the incorporated city or town, and as to one-half acre, located within a city or town, which is exempt from execution for debt. There is a $5,000 tax exemption of the property assessment. In California, the value of a homestead that may be claimed by heads of family and persons 65 or older is over $30,000, and for other persons $15,000.

In Wisconsin, not exceeding one quarter acre residential or 40 acres of rural land can be held as a homestead.

In *Heard v. Mathis,*[7] the Court held that a test of a "family" for homestead purposes, which must be met singly or in combination, are: (1) a legal duty arising out of a relationship, and (2) a continuing communal living by at least two individuals, where one is regarded as the person in charge.

---

[6] Solomon v. Solomon, 546 S.W. 2d 129 (Tex. 1977).

[7] Heard v. Mathis, 344 So. 2d 651 (Fla. App. 1977).

ESTATES NOT OF INHERITANCE

There are various estates dictated by statutory law. They include life contracts and the various methods of taking title permitted by the state in which the property is located. These estates include the ordinary or standard life estate; an estate for years, which is granted for a definite time period (leasehold); and three others that are closely related—an estate at will, an estate at sufferance, and the legal life estate.

The ordinary life estate is one granted to another by deed or will for the natural life of the grantee. At his death the property reverts to the grantor, his heirs (reversion) or to the person named in the deed to succeed the life tenant (remainderman). The life tenant is entitled to the full benefits of the property, but he cannot suffer the property to go into disrepair or commit waste, as pointed out in *Gibbons v. Gibbons,.*[8] However, the mere nonuse of premises is insufficient to cause a surrender of the life estate as pointed out in *Fabianski, v. Boutin,*[9] Although the life tenant, in effect, has full use of the property he cannot lease it beyond his life time, due to the temporary nature of his estate possession.[10]

A conditional fee estate is analogous to ordinary life estate in that the property reverts to the grantor when a certain condition is not met: in the case of an ordinary life estate, the condition is the lifetime of the grantee, and in the case of a conditional fee estate, the condition is the purpose for which the property is being used. A conditional fee estate is a conveyance for property to be used for a specific purpose, such as a school or church, and when that use is abandoned, the property reverts to the grantor or his heirs.

An estate from year to year, also referred to as an estate for years, is one for a definite time period, which then continues indefinitely until one of the parties (to a lease for example) elects to terminate it by giving proper notice. This subject is more fully covered in Chapter 9, Landlord and Tenants.

An estate at will is a kind of nonformal permissive lease which may be terminated by the grantor at any time and without formal notice. For instance, a landlord might give permission for the use of a property without a formal lease or rental agreement.

An estate at sufferance is one where a person comes into possession of the premises lawfully, under a definite term lease, and then continues in possession at the expiration of the term without the owner's permission.

Another variation of the less than freehold estate is the "estate pur autre vie" in which the property is granted to another to be held for the lifetime of a third party. For instance A wills his home to B for the lifetime of his daughter C. When

---

[8] Gibbons v. Gibbons, 287 So. 2d (Miss. 1974).

[9] Fabianski v. Boutin, 371 A. 2d (N.H. 1977).

[10] Drees Farming Ass'n. v. Thompson, 246 N.W. 2d 883 (N.D. 1976).

C dies the life estate terminates and reverts to the remainder-man (D), another person named in the will or deed.

There are several versions of the legal life estate. Among those are the "curtesy", "dower", "tenancy by the entireties" and the "community property." Curtesy refers to the right of the husband to a lifetime ownership in property owned by his wife at the time of her death. State laws vary somewhat in regards to the curtesy provisions, but most require that the marriage be legal and require the birth of a child to the couple during the marriage. Dower right is very similar to that of the curtesy except it applies to the right of a widow to an interest in her husband's property. Again, state laws vary considerably as to what this means. Under common law the wife was entitled to a 1/3 interest in her husband's property. In states providing for a dower, an inchoate or consummate dower interest is provided. Inchoate dower means the interest the wife has in her husband's land which cannot be changed by the husband or his will. In other states the wife assumes all rights and obligations of a conventional life estate tenant upon the death of her husband.

SOME TYPES OF JOINT ESTATES

Although closely related, property ownership and types of estates are not the same: ownership is the act of owning and an estate is what is owned. Real estate ownership may be single ownership, or joint or multiple ownership. The term single ownership is self explanatory; however, joint ownership is more complicated. Joint ownership by two or more persons can be in the form of "tenancy in common" or "joint tenancy."

Tenancy in common means the owners hold an undivided interest equal to any portion of the whole, i.e., one quarter, one half or higher percentage. Tenancy in common is distinguished by the following characteristics:

- It permits ownership in unequal shares.
- There is no right of survivorship.
- The ownerships may be created at various points of time.
- By agreement the property can be partitioned according to each owner's share of the whole.

The principal characteristic of joint tenancy is the right of survivorship in which the survivor(s) becomes the sole owner(s) at the death of another owner. To create a joint tenancy four factors must exist:

1. A unity of interest, such as husband and wife.

2. Unity of time—both ownerships occur at the same time or as the result of one event such as a purchase.

3. Unity of title—there is only one title listing the parties in the ownership.

4. Unity of possession—all parties possess the property together.

Joint ownership can result in a multitude of problems when death, divorce, or other events require a decision in regards to who owns what or who has the right to do certain things. These problems are fully covered later in this chapter. Some very special types of joint ownership such as condominiums and cooperatives are discussed in Chapter 13, Special Property Ownership Types.

In states that provide for tenancy by the entireties, ownership of property is treated as if the husband and wife were one person. In other words, the surviving husband or wife assumes ownership of the entire property; however, neither the husband nor wife may convey or partition the property during the lifetime of the other. Upon the death of either party, the property is owned entirely by the survivor. In some states this type of estate is referred to as "joint tenancy."

Joint tenancy is not limited to married couples. But it is especially important for unmarried persons who own real estate together to remember that the language to create a joint tenancy must be clear and explicit; otherwise, the parties will be deemed to hold in common. In a joint ownership, a deceased party's interest in the property goes to the surviving owner(s) and not the decedent's heirs.

Example—A deed from Roger Harris to Carl Parsons and Edward F. Lundquist, "as joint tenants, with right of survivorship and not as tenants in common" would clearly create a joint estate. Upon the death of Carl Parsons, the property would vest absolutely in the surviving party, Edward F. Lundquist.

If, on the other hand, the conveyance from Harris simply stated, "Carl Parsons and Edward F. Lundquist" the grantees would hold as owners in common, and upon the death of Carl Parsons would not vest to Edward F. Lundquist, but would go to Carl's heirs.

Joint owners must acquire ownership by a single deed and there must be four *unities*: (1) time, (2) title, (3) interest, and (4) possession.

It is most important that joint tenancy title be taken in a manner that will preclude any misunderstanding as to the intentions of the parties. A typical problem in this regard is represented by the case of *Zomisky v. Zomisky,* [11] in which the grantor conveyed land to himself and his son as "joint tenants and as in common with the right of survivorship." Upon the father's death, the son claimed title to the land and the other children of the decedent brought suit, claiming that the deed created a tenancy in common. The Supreme Court, in affirming the lower court, held that the language in the deed was sufficiently clear to create joint tenancy, *with the right of survivorship.*

In another interesting case, *Yannopoulos v. Sophos,* [12] a property was owned

---

[11] Zomisky v. Zomisky, 449 Pa. 239 (1972).

[12] Yannopoulos v. Sophos, 365 A. 2d 1312 (Pa. 1976).

by a brother and sister as joint tenants with right of survivorship. An agreement of sale for the property was signed by the brother on November 12, 1973. The sister, residing in Mississippi, sent a telegram to the broker, approving the sale. The brother died on November 16, 1973. The question before the court was whether the sister was entitled to the entire proceeds of the sale or whether the deceased brother's estate was entitled to one-half. The court held that the execution of the agreement of sale by the deceased brother alone terminated the joint tenancy and created a tenancy in common. The executed agreement of sale by the brother vested title in the purchaser, and the vendor's then became trustees, holding the bare legal title for the purchaser, who became trustee for the seller for the balance of the selling price. One half of the proceeds of the sale was due to the brother's estate.

In regard to severance of joint tenancy, where two owners lease the property so held, the tenancy is not severed.[13]

Joint ownership presents many difficult situations which require the courts to render decisions. For instance, a conveyance of a farm to Francis Lucas, a single man, and to Joseph and Matilda Lucas, husband and wife, raised the question whether each of the three grantees own an undivided one-third interest, whether Francis owns a one-half interest and Joseph and Matilda own the other half by the entireties, or whether Joseph owns a one-third interest and the married couple own the other two-thirds by the entireties. With no more language than that shown above, the court, in the case of *Heatter v. Lucas*,[14] ruled that Francis owned a one-half interest and Joseph and Matilda owned the other half by the entireties.

In a similar situation a conveyance was made to James C. Miller, unmarried, and Dimitri Katsowney and Elfena Katsowney, his wife, as joint tenants and not as tenants in common. James C. Millona (Miller) died. There was no question raised as to the Katsowney's holding an estate in the entireties. The issue became whether Miller, the co-grantee, became a joint tenant or a tenant in common. It is clear that Miller was a tenant in common and at his death the sale of his interest, by the administrator, was valid.

A special form of joint tenancy called a "tenancy in partnership" is provided for in the Uniform Partnership Act. Such property must be purchased with partnership funds and used for partnership purposes. The deed must clearly indicate that the conveyance is to a partnership, as such, otherwise, the grantees will be considered as tenants in common. In case one partner dies, his surviving widow would have no dower right or claim in such estate. The value of the deceased partner's interest in the property would become a part of his estate. This situation is different from the case where two or more persons purchase real estate "as

---

[13] Tenhet v. Boswell, 133 Cal. Rptr. 10 (1976).

[14] Heatter v. Lucas, 397 Pa. 296 (1951).

partners" which would not constitute partnership property within this special law. Instead, they would own the property as tenants in common.

A special inheritance and estate tax situation arises when a deceased joint owner's property is the subject. Where four persons hold title in this manner and one dies, the tax liability will be based on a one-fourth value of the property as of the time of death.

A sale by one of three joint owners of his interest does not destroy the joint ownership of the remaining owners two-thirds interest. The purchaser of the one-third interest would just become a tenant in common with the other two tenants.

ESTATES BY THE ENTIRETIES

In earlier times it was commonly believed that the husband and wife were one and that the husband was *the* one. Currently when property is held in the name of husband and wife, it is known as joint tenancy and in some states as tenancy in the entireties. This latter form of title ownership is operative in the states of Alaska, Arkansas, Delaware, Florida, Indiana, Kentucky, Maryland, Massachusetts, Michigan, Missouri, New Jersey, New York, North Carolina, Oklahoma, Oregon, Pennsylvania, Rhode Island, Tennessee, Vermont, Wisconsin, and Wyoming.

In the Tennessee case of *Ballad v. Farley,*[15] the court held that a conveyance to a named person "and wife" without naming her was sufficient to create an estate by the entireties. This type of ownership exists only in favor of husband and wife and has certain advantages to recommend it. A deed from John Steel to Adam Taylor and Anna Mae Taylor, his wife, would automatically create an estate by the entireties. Both signatures are absolutely essential to transfer title. Where the parties are separated, neither spouse can convey or lease without the joinder of the other.[16] Upon the death of one, the property automatically vests in the surviving spouse; no court proceedings are necessary. Also, the property is usually free from state inheritance taxes, and in most states a judgment against one of the parties does not automatically become a lien on the property unless the survivor is the debtor spouse.

In the case of *Sawada v. Endo.,*[17] a judgment was entered against the husband alone, as a result of an automobile accident. After the start of the suit, the husband and wife conveyed real property to their sons. The judgment creditors challenged the transfer as fraudulent. The Supreme Court decided otherwise, holding that the subject property could not be severed into separate interests, and therefore, was not subject to the judgment against one spouse.

---

[15] Ballad v. Farley, 226 S.W. 544 (1920).

[16] Schweitzer v. Evans, 63 A. 2d 39 (Pa. 1949).

[17] Sawada v. Endo, 561 P. 2d 1291 (Hawaii 1977).

Both parties can join in a good conveyance of the property, free and clear of the judgment against the other party. A judgment entered against the husband, for example, would not be extinguished by such sale of property; however, if a judgment exists against one spouse, and the husband and wife wish to obtain a mortgage, there may be a problem, since the judgment antedates the mortgage, the real possibility exists that the wife may die before the husband and the judgment creditor would have precedence over the mortgage.

The distinction between sale of the property, free from judgment and lien, and mortgaging the property, subject in a qualified sense to a judgment, lies in the fact that a mortgage is only a temporary transfer of the property, and when paid off, the title to the property reverts to husband and wife as an estate in the entireties. Then the judgment creditor must await the fortuitous circumstance that the wife dies before her husband in order to proceed against the property.

Most couples, in states adhering to the estate by the entireties concept, prefer to hold property in this manner. So long as there is a harmonious relationship, it would be recommended in most cases. Where federal estate liability is a possibility, this type of ownership may not be advantageous.

It is generally accepted that both husband and wife must join in a deed (or lease) to convey property with good title. However, in New York and New Jersey it has been held to the contrary. In these two cases, it was pointed out that both parties share equally in the rents and profits and each spouse can compel an accounting in this connection, but not where one of the parties uses the residence as a home.[18]

In a related Pennsylvania case, *Garner v. Pierce*,[19] a property owned by the entireties was leased by the husband alone to a tenant, who paid rent to the husband for a while and then, for two months, it was paid to the wife. The husband then distrained upon the tenant's goods. The Supreme Court held that either spouse could lease the premises, but both were entitled to the income. The lessee was relieved from further obligation.

Divorce will terminate the ownership by the entireties and each spouse will then own a one-half interest in the property as tenants in common. Unless both parties can agree amicably to a joint deed in the property, it would be necessary for the spouse desiring to sell to enter a court action for sale of the property. The proceeds would then be divided equally between the former husband and wife.

Where a conveyance is made to two married persons and their spouses and it is intended that each couple shall hold by the entireties, the names and status of the respective parties should be carefully set forth as follows:

---

[18] Zanzonico v. Zanzonico, 124 N.J. Eq. 477 and Martose v. Martose, 134 N.Y.S. 2d (1954).

[19] Garner v. Pierce, 134 A. 494 (Pa. 1926).

THIS DEED, made the 10th day of June, 1992, between JOHN T. STEEL and FRANCES L. STEEL, his wife, of the city of Miami, County of Dade, and State of Florida,

a

n

d

WILLIAM C. GRAY, JR., and THELMA T. GRAY, his wife, and CARL T. FRYE and ALICE L. FRYE, his wife, of the same place, AS TENANTS BY THE ENTIRETIES AS TO THE RESPECTIVE SHARE OF EACH HUSBAND AND WIFE AND AS TENANTS IN COMMON OF THE WHOLE.

Today, it is not uncommon for a man and woman to take title to property as husband and wife, when they are not so in fact. Such a tenure is not void, but they will hold title as joint tenants or tenants in common, depending upon what the court could determine as their intention from all the facts. In the Maryland case of, *Michael v. Lucas*,[20] property was deeded to Joseph H. Kuntz and Emily H. Kuntz, as tenants by the entireties, the survivor of them, his or her heirs, personal representatives and assigns. The grantees were unmarried. Emily acquired title, as the survivor joint tenant, since that was clearly the intentions.

Owners in common have a mutual obligation to pay charges upon the property and the equity of one owner should not be enlarged by any expenditures made by the other party.[21]

COMMUNITY PROPERTY LAW

Community property laws exist in several of the Western states and is a type of old Spanish law which recognizes two types of property ownership: (1) Separate property, which was owned by one of the marital partners at the time of the marriage, received as a gift or was inherited, and (2) Community property, which is property acquired by either party during marriage with community funds. Each marital partner has an undivided one-half interest in community property. Unlike tenancy in the entireties, in community property the decedent's one-half ownership at death is disposed of in accordance with his will. Tenancy in common can terminate on death of either part, by divorce, or agreement of husband and wife.

The community property concept was introduced into the United States though the Spanish-influenced laws of Mexico. This institution exists in California,

[20] Michael v. Lucas, 152 Md. 512 (1927); Adams v. Foster, 466 S.W. 2d 706 (Mo. 1971).

[21] Singer v. Singer 341 So. 2d 861 (Fla, App. 1977)

Louisiana, New Mexico, Texas, and Arizona. It has also been incorporated into the statutes of Nevada (1865), Idaho (1867), Washington (1889), Oklahoma and Hawaii (1945), Michigan, Nebraska, Oregon, and Pennsylvania (1947).[22]

The enactments of community property laws were prompted by a desire to reduce federal income taxes payable by the income-producing husband. Court decisions are not uniform as to the allocation of income received by each spouse from different sources. Texas cases hold that *all* income received during marriage is community property, including income from a trust in which one of the parties has a life estate. In California, the Supreme Court held to the contrary, maintaining that a wife's income from her separate estate remained as her separate property. In Idaho and Texas, such separate property of the wife is considered community property. The community ownership is terminated by death of one of the spouses, or by divorce. When real estate, held as community property is conveyed, both husband and wife must join in the deed.

ESTATES LESS THAN A FREEHOLD

Estates less than a freehold generally refer to various types of leases, in which possession is granted to others for a limited time and under the specific conditions enumerated in the leasehold agreement. These tenancies are "estates for years," "periodic tenancies," "tenancy at will," and "tenancy at sufferance." A complete discussion of these can be found in Chapter 9, Landlord and Tenant.

THE OWNERSHIP STATUS OF UNMARRIED CO-HABITANTS

The law, concerning rights of co-habitants, whether married or unmarried, is in its early stages of development. The first significant case to come before the courts involved the distribution of assets in the probate of a homosexual in which the surviving partner claimed an oral agreement to share equally income and assets acquired during the term of their relationship. In this case,[23] the claim was denied based on the assumption that the oral contract provided for a payment for sexual services, an inseparable part of the agreement.

In an earlier case of co-habitation, *Marvin v. Marvin,*[24] the initial claim of the plaintiff was refused. This decision was later reversed by the California Supreme Court, stating:

> In summary, we base our opinion on the principal that adults who voluntarily live together and engage in sexual relations are nonetheless as competent as any

---

[22]
The Pennsylvania Act was declared unconstitutional in the case of Wilcox, v. Penn Mutual Life Ins. Co., 357 Pa. 581 (1947).

[23]
176 Cal. Rptr. 132 (1981).

[24]
Marvin v. Marvin, 557 P. 2d 106 (Cal. 1976).

other person to contract respecting their earnings and property rights ..... so long as the agreement does not rest upon illicit considerations, the parties may order their economic affairs as they choose, and no policy precludes the courts enforcing such agreements.

In a case a year later,[25] which involved a case of a married man living with a single woman, the court hinted that a person could, in such situations, incur obligations to a spouse and a lover at the same time.

In a somewhat related case in 1989[26] the court appeared to redefine the definition of *family* and provide eviction protection for a gay surviving partner. The court noted that the term *family* as used in the noneviction provisions of the New York rent control law, which protects surviving spouses of tenants or other members of deceased tenant's "family," are those who have been living with the tenant, including lifetime partners whose relationship is long-term and characterized by emotional and financial considerations and interdependence. The term is not limited to those people related by blood or law and includes gay partners.

PROPERTY USE RESTRICTIONS

The use of property may be restricted by "covenants," "easements" or by "zoning." A *covenant* is generally defined as an agreement between two or more parties, and entered into a deed, whereby one of the parties promises the performance or nonperformance of certain acts or that a given state of things does or does not exist. Covenants may also arise by implication of law, or from the conduct of the parties. An *easement* is defined as a liberty, privilege, or advantage which one proprietor may have in the lands of another, without profit in a material or physical sense (right of way). *Zoning* is the exercise of the police power of a municipality in regulating and controlling the character and use of property (single family, commercial, and industrial zoning, for example).

RESTRICTIVE COVENANTS

Restrictions in a deed, which limit the use of property conveyed, have been in existence for a very long time. For a restriction to be legal, it must be reasonable and not violate public policy. Restrictions have been employed to restrict types of buildings and/or limit their use. Such restrictions have been the cause of much litigation. Although restrictive covenants are not favored in law, they are strictly construed and every doubt is resolved against the existence of the restriction. In

---

[25] Re marriage of Baragry, 73 Cal. App. 3rd 444 (1977).

[26] Braschi v. Stahl Assocs. Co., 544 14 N.Y.S. 2d 784 (1989).

actuality the law favors the free and unrestricted use of property. For instance in the case of *Weber v. Les Petite Acadamies*,[27] it was ruled that any slight acquiescence in a breach will be construed as a waiver of the forfeiture.

Restrictions may arise by: (1) express covenants or by (2) implication from the language of the deed or from the conduct of the parties as ruled in *Witt v. Sternwehr Development Co.*[28]

Restrictive covenants are generally understood to be covenants running with the land. They are sometimes referred to as "negative covenants" since they take away some land uses. Such covenants may be created in a number of ways. First, the limitations of the use of the land may be explicitly set forth in the deed. Second, the restriction may be contained in a separate written instrument recorded or determined from a printed plan of the proposed development. Third, restrictive covenants may be brought into existence by estoppel through oral representations alone. Thus, where an owner sells part of a subdivision tract under representation that his entire plan is restricted to the same extent, he thereby restricts use of the remaining portion of his land to that extent. This was so held in *Burgess v. Putnam*[29] in 1971.

The owner of a subdivision sometimes imposes restrictions on some of the lots sold. These restrictions will not be defeated merely because similar restrictions are imposed upon the remainder of the lots. In the 1974 Delaware case *Hunt v. Collo*,[30] a developer conveyed one lot by deed containing building restrictions with a covenant that he would impose the same restrictions on the remainder of the lots to be sold. Subsequently he conveyed the remaining lots without restrictions in the deeds. The later grantees were bound by the restrictions to the former grantee. The ruling of the court was that these later grantees were bound to read the whole of the former deed and was bound by the recorded notice of the restriction.

It is a well-recognized principle of law that an owner has the right to restrain its use to his grantees and to limit its appropriation to purposes which will not in any way impair or lessen the value of that portion which he retains. These restrictions will be enforced by a court of equity unless they are against public policy. They are deemed enforceable, if reasonable and commensurate with the quality and character of the development. Where a tract of land is conveyed to a person with restrictions and he afterwards subdivides the land and conveys the several lots to third persons *without* restrictions, his several grantees or their purchasers would have no right to enforce, "inter se" (among themselves), the restrictions in the deed from the common grantor. Where the restrictions are

---

[27] Weber v. Les Petite Acadamies, 548 S.W. 2d. 847 (Mo. App. 1976)

[28] Witt v. Sternwehr Development Co., 400 Pa. 609 (1960).

[29] Burgess v. Putnam, 464 S.W. 2d 698 (Tex. Civ. App. 1971).

[30] Hunt v. Collo, 317 A. 2d. 545 (Del. 1974).

common to all the lot purchasers, each has a right to enforce the covenants and enjoin their violation. In *Beech Mountain Property Owners Ass'n v. Current*[31] a man sold lots in a plan with a 25-foot building line. The court ruled that the restriction was mutual to the extent that *any* lot owner could enjoin the violation of the building line restriction by any other lot owner.

A personal covenant, like a personal easement, is binding upon the original covenantor only and when he dies or disposes of the property, the restriction ends.

HOW RESTRICTIVE COVENANTS ARE ENFORCED

When considering relief by injunction against the breach of a restrictive covenant, the courts require due diligence upon the part of the plaintiff, and delay upon his part (laches) will ordinarily defeat his application. For instance, where an objector has permitted a violation to proceed without objection and the lot owner has incurred considerable expense in the building construction, relief would be denied. Equity aids the vigilant and not the sleeping, a well known maxim of jurisprudence. Another maxim that says, "he who comes into equity must do so with clean hands" would prevent a person who violates the restriction himself from enjoining a similar violation of another owner.

> *Example*—Where Jones converted a part of his residence into a store, in violation of a restrictive covenant, he would not succeed in enjoining Smith from using his building for a commercial purpose.

An injunction may be invoked or a building ordered to be torn down where a warning has not been heeded. Building restrictions are considered warranties rather than conditions. A breach generally gives rise to injunctions or money damages rather than forfeiture of the estate to the grantor as would be true if the restriction were construed to be a condition.

A release of restrictive covenants is not effective unless all persons who own property in the restricted subdivision join in the release. See *Amason et al. v. Woodman et al.*[32]

In the case of *Shea v. Sargent*,[33] it was pointed out that restrictive covenants are a derogation of the right of unrestricted use of property and are strictly construed. They will not be extended by implication to anything not clearly and expressly prohibited by their plain terms. Other states observe a more modern trend to the effect that a restrictive covenant is *not* strictly construed because they are said to protect land owners and the public rather than restrict the use of land. Such was the ruling in *Wallace v. St. Clair*.[34]

---

[31] Beech Mountain Property Ass'n v. Current, 240 S.E. 2d 503 (N.C. App. 1978).

[32] Amason et al. v. Woodman et al., 498 S.W. 2d 142 (Texas 1973).

[33] Shea v. Sargent, 499 S.W. 2d 871 (tenn. 1973).

[34] Wallace v. St Clair, 127 S.E. 2d 742 (W. Va. 1962).

LEGAL REQUIREMENTS FOR RESTRICTIONS

A property restriction requires five characteristics to assure its legality. These are:

1. *The language of the written instrument must be clear as to its meaning.* If ambiguous it will be struck down, as the courts are ever vigilant to protect the free alienation of property. Restrictions are strictly construed against persons seeking to enforce them and all doubts are resolved in favor of the natural rights. Any doubt must be resolved against the restriction and in favor of a free and unrestricted use of the property. Where the restriction limited the owner to a one dwelling house upon a lot, the erection of a duplex dwelling was held not to be in violation; however, a restriction for the erection of a private dwelling house would prohibit the erection of an apartment building housing a number of families. In the term "private dwelling" the word *dwelling* restricts the character of the building by eliminating all buildings for business or commercial purposes, such as stores, garages, warehouses, and so on. The word *private* further excludes buildings of a public nature, such as hotels, dormitories, and apartment houses.

2. *The intentions of the grantor must be clear* as regards whether the restriction is for the personal benefit or protection of the grantor or runs with the land. If Jones owns tracts 1 and 2, and sells 2 to Brown, reserving a right of way across the tract sold, the covenant would be personal to Jones alone and upon Jones's death or sale of tract 1, the restriction would cease. If, on the other hand, Jones reserved the right of way to himself, *his heirs and assigns*, the language use would clearly indicate an intention to create the right of way over tract 2 in favor of tract 1, regardless of the ownership of the latter. Any subsequent owner of tract 1 could enjoy the right of way.

3. *Restrictions should be limited as to time—20, 30, or 50 years.* If not limited the restriction would be perpetual and could become ineffectual due to evolution effecting a radical change in the character of the neighborhood. For example, a restriction could exist requiring all homes in an area to be constructed of brick, but later the area is rezoned for a parking lot. The restriction would be tempered to conform to the "change of the neighborhood," even before the time limit has expired.

4. *Care should be taken to ascertain how the restriction is to operate.* Prohibiting an erection of a commercial structure will not operate to prevent use of a residence for commercial purposes. In order to prevent such erection or use, the court in *Jones v. Park Lane Home for Convalescents,*[35] indicated the restriction clause should have read:

> That no building on said lot, or any hereafter erected, shall be erected for or used or occupied for business or trade, commerce, manufacturing, or for any offen-

---

[35]
Jones v. Park Lane Convalescents, 120 A. 2d 535)Pa. 1956).

sive or malodorous occupation, or be used for any purpose other than that of a private dwelling house with private garage.

5. *The restriction must not be contrary to public policy.* The courts have uniformly held that a prohibition by municipal ordinance effecting a racial restriction violates the constitution and is invalid.

Changes in local conditions may neutralize an otherwise valid restriction. In an Oregon case in 1971,[36] all deeds in a subdivision prohibited all buildings except a "private dwelling house." An owner of two vacant lots sought to build an eight-unit family type garden apartment. He established that other apartment buildings were in the vicinity and a ball park had been erected across the road. A tremendous amount of traffic resulted. As a result the city had changed the zoning from single family to garden apartments. The court held that the radical change of conditions in the area neutralized the deed restriction.

In another case,[37] a deed restriction in a development provided that no temporary nor unsightly structures were permitted; also anything offensive to a high class residential district was prohibited. An action was brought against the defendants, who moved their house trailer on a lot that had been purchased in the plan. The court held that "temporary structure" included a house trailer or mobile home.

A subdivision developer told purchasers of lots that only one-family homes could be erected. A number of lots were sold and single family residences were constructed. The deeds contained no such restriction. Later, the developer decided to permit buyers to use lots for trailer homes. Some of the original purchasers objected and brought an injunction action. The court held that oral testimony was admissible as the representations by the promoter constituted frauds. Relief was granted.[38]

A California court of appeals ruled that where all lots in a plan had been sold, the developer has no right to enjoin the violation of a restrictive covenant in the subdivision.[39] It should be noted, however, that any of the property owners in the subdivision could have enjoined the violation.

EASEMENTS

Easements may be classified as "appurtenant" or running with the land or "in gross" meaning personal to the owner in the nature of a license. In origin easements

---

[36] Albino v. Pacific First Federal Savings and Loan Association, 479 P. 2d (Ore. 1971).

[37] McBride v. Behrman, 272 N.E. 2d 181 (Ohio 1971).

[38] Burgess v. Putnam, 464 S.W. 2d 698 (Tex. Civ. App. 1971) and Faro v. Deutsch, 320 N.Y. 2d 778 (Sup. Ct. 1971).

[39] Kent v. Koch, 333 P. 2d 411 (Cal. App. 1958).

may be expressed or implied. Express easements are those which have been set forth in a deed or other writing, whereas an implied easement results as the result of legal implications. With the opening of the West to settlement, many situations arose in which roads and the boundaries between properties were improperly defined. As a consequence men trespassed over other's property in order to reach the main road. This resulted in the courts inventing the doctrine of "implied easements" which have been adopted throughout the country. As pointed out in the case of *Park County Rod & Gun Club v. Department of Highways*,[40] the grant of an easement is a grant for use and not a grant of title.

New types of easements are being created and recognized by the courts on a continuous basis. Examples of these newer types of easements are "scenic" and "solar." The recent additions to the easement types originate from the use and recognition of covenants in deeds, which are binding upon all landholders in the neighborhood. A very common easement, we are all familiar with, is the one granted to utility companies to run lines across our property.

Easement by Necessity

An easement by necessity is an exception to the general rule that an easement can only be created by deed, by prescription, or by adverse use for a statutory period. This was clearly pointed out in *Camp v. Milain*.[41] In *Soltis v. Miller*,[42] the law was clearly settled that where property is conveyed and so situated that access to it cannot be had except by passing over the remaining land of the grantor, the grantee is entitled to an easement by necessity over the grantor's land.

The prerequisites for an easement by necessity are that the properties in the controversy must come from a *common source;* and second, there must be a reasonable necessity for the creation of the easement, e.g., it must be the only practical means of ingress and egress as was the case of *Burrows v. Miller*.[43] In the case of *Oliver v. Ernel*,[44] an easement by necessity was granted against a grantor, where the land conveyed was land-locked and the grantee had no other access to a public road.

Implied Easements

The interest of public policy may dictate an implied easement where the circumstances surrounding the case make such an action desirable. The creation of

---

[40] Park County Rod and Gun Club v. Department of Highways, 517 P. 2d 353 (Mont. 1973).

[41] Camp v. Milain, 277 So. 2d 95 (ala. 1973).

[42] Soltis v. Miller, 444 Pa. 357 (1971).

[43] Burrows v. Miller, 340 So. 2d 779 (Ala 1976).

[44] Oliver v. Ernel, 178 S.E. 2d 393 (N.C. 1971).

such an easement must be based upon *necessity* and not *convenience*. There are no general rules for determining necessity but the courts normally judge that there is a necessity where the facts show that the original arrangement, which is clearly in the nature of an easement, has existed and where the disturbance of this arrangement could be inequitable to the party claiming the right.

An easement by implication was denied in the case of *Porter v. Griffith*[45] as it was shown that there had been no common grantor. This use was not limited by the manner in which it was used at the time it was created, but to vary with reasonable needs, present and future.

A good example of an implied easement is where the owner of two properties constructs a building upon one lot, and a cornice, roof or spouting encroaches over the other parcel. If he sells the unimproved property to another, the purchaser takes it subject to open, visible, permanent, and continuous servitude which has been placed upon it by the encroachment, and he cannot later demand the removal of the encroachment. To create an implied easement in favor of the improved property, it is necessary to show that the advantage which is claimed satisfies four requirements: (1) open, (2) visible, (3) permanent, and (4) continuous. In other words, it is a burden which can be readily seen by the intended purchaser before he pays for the property. Thus, he takes the property subject to the existing encroachment. If the encroaching building should burn down or be destroyed, the owner would not be permitted to rebuild so as to continue the encroachment. In rebuilding the new structure would have to be contained within the owner's own property. It should be noted that an implied easement cannot be extended to include land.

It should be noted that the doctrine of implied easement will not be enlarged to deprive an owner of the right of use or possession of his property, except in rare circumstances. Circumstances that might temper this principle might be where the *slight* encroachment of a building upon or near the dividing line or where the use of the encroachment upon land is claimed as a real necessity, the deprivation of which would cause a severe hardship.

In the case of *Westland Nursing Home Inc. vs. Benson*[46] the court held that where the deed uses the term "ingress and egress" without limitation, the easement was designed to serve a specific piece of property, rather than being personal to the grantor.

A "party wall" is a peculiar type of easement in that it is shared ownership with part standing one each of the owners' own property and with each owner having an easement on the other's property for support of his building. It is a structure for the common benefit and convenience of both tenements that it separates and both owners are equally liable for repairs and maintenance of the common wall.

---

[45] Porter v. Griffith, 543 P. 2d 138(Ariz. App. 1975).

[46] Westland Nursing Home, Inc. v. Benson, 517 P. 2d 862 (Colo. App. 1974).

Appurtenant Easements

Appurtenant easements are those connected with the ownership of nearby lands. Its principal characteristic is that there is a dominant tenant (owner of the land) on which the easement exists and a servient tenant, who is subject to the easement.

Example—Smith and Brown own adjacent parcels of land. Smith has the right of way across Brown's land. Smith is the dominant tenant and Brown is the servient tenant.

In the above example it should be noted that where both the dominant and servient tenants utilize a common right of way, both must share the expense of maintenance and repair. In *McDonald v. Bemboom*,[47] the dominant tenant sued the defendant owners of a servient tenement for a proportionate share of repair and maintenance costs for a private roadway, used by both parties as their principal means of ingress and egress. The defendant claimed that as an owner of the servient tenement they were not liable for any part of the repair and maintenance. The court found that since both utilized the roadway it was only fair that they share the expense of repair and maintenance, even though the agreement creating the easement was silent on the matter.

One of the most important things to remember about appurtenant easements is that they are not *personal grants* which die with the death of the person in whose favor they were made, nor are they extinguished when he parts with the property. The easements belong to the land and pass with it to all subsequent holders, unless excepted by the express provisions of the deed. It is also important to remember that the right of an easement belongs *to all and every part of the land*. The holder of any portion of the original tract, no matter how small a tract, is entitled to all the rights that he would possess if he owned the entire tract. The courts will permit the burden to be made greater where the additional servitude is due to the more complete development of the dominant tenement. The right of way which one farm possesses over another may be used very seldom so long as the tract is used for farming; but, when the ground is subdivided into lots, it is readily seen that the burden of the servient tenement is considerably increased. So long as the use is confined to those holders of any part of the original property, the courts will not intervene to release the servient tenement of any part of the extra burden. This is so because the easement belongs to the property, and to limit the full use and development would be contrary to public policy. The following cases are a reference to this point: *Garam v. Bender; Fristoe v. Drapeau; Ragonaud v. Dimaggio and Westland Nursing Home Inc. v. Benson.*[48]

---

[47] McDonald v. Bemboom, 694 S.W. 2d 782 (Mo. App. 1985).

[48] Garam v. Bender, 55 A. 2d 353 (Pa. 1947); Fristoe v. Drapeau, 215 P. 2d 729 (Cal. 1950); Ragonaud v. Dimaggio, 249 N.Y.S. 2d 705 (1964) and Westland Nursing Home Inc. v. Benson, 517 P. 2d 862 (Colo. App. 1974).

Easement in Gross

An easement in gross is one created for the benefit of the owner of a particular property (dominant tenant). There is no servient tenant because it is not connected with adjacent land. When the person for whom the easement was created dies, or sells the property, an easement in gross terminates. *An easement in gross is normally not transferable* as indicated in the case of *DeShon v. Parker.*[49]

Example—Stone permits his neighbor, Baker to use Stone's driveway, as it affords Baker a more convenient approach to his garage in the rear. If Baker sells the property to Chase, Stone could prevent Chase, the new owner, from continuing to use the driveway.

In the case of *Bunn v. Offutt,*[50] the court held that a right to the swimming pool on the property sold, which had existed in favor of the grantor, did not pass with the later transfer of the property, as it was an easement in gross.

The distinction between an easement in gross and an appurtenant easement is that in the gross clause creating the easement the essential words "his heirs and assigns" are not included.

Easements by Prescription

An easement, such as a walk or right of way, may not be voluntarily given but may be acquired by adverse use by individuals or the general public. Adverse use must be hostile in its inception in order to present a valid claim. This acquisition is known as "easement by prescription" and the general rules of adverse possession apply. The case of *Dickinson v. Pike,*[51] established the rule that prescriptive rights can only be acquired the use which is *open and notorious.* This rule was further refined by *George v. Dickinson,*[52] when the court stated that "long, continued, uninterrupted use of a roadway over farm land, creates an easement by prescription. In a 1977 Nebraska case, *Fisher v. Grinsberg,*[53] it was ruled that "permissive" use is not "adverse" and cannot ripen into an easement by prescription. This decision was further reinforced by two other decisions that same year.[54] It is now clear that the establishment of an easement by prescription requires use of an easement in such a way as to constitute "some actual invasion or infringement of the right to the owner of the subservient property for the legally prescribed time." This was made clear by the case of *Shultz v. Atkins.*[55]

49
DeShon v. Parker 361 N.E. 2d 457 (Ohio App. 1974).

50
Bunn v. Offutt, S.E. 2d 522 (Va. 1976).

51
Dickinson v. Pike, 201 S.E. 2d 897 (N.C. 1974).

52
George v. Dickinson, 504 S.W. 2d 658 (Mo. App. 1974).

53
Fisher v. Grinsberg, 252 N.W. 2d 619 (neb. 1977).

54
Pitts, v. Roberts, 562 P. 2d 231 (Utah 1977) and Union Hills Cemetery Ass'n v. Camp Zoe, Inc., 547 S.W. 2d 196 (Mo. App. 1977).

55
Shultz v. Atkins, 554 P. 2d 205 (Utah 1976).

Prescriptive easements were upheld, in a 1961 Massachusetts case, where the plaintiff acquired the right to use a driveway between two adjoining properties by his prescriptive use: *Flynn v. Korsac*.[56] In an Oklahoma case,[57] defendants were ordered to remove a chain-link fence and all other obstructions to a driveway. In a similar ruling in the case of *Stewart v. Bittle*,[58] a fence between two properties, which had existed for more than 30 years, was held to establish a boundary line.

In order for an owner to prevent a prescriptive easement from being established, he must take adequate measures to prohibit unlicensed use of his property. If a physical barrier is not effectual, application to a court for injunctive relief should be made. It should be noted that it is often difficult to determine whether the land itself has been acquired adversely, or merely a right of way over it. The subject of adverse acquisition of land is fully covered in Chapter 7.

WHEN IS AN EASEMENT AN ENCUMBRANCE?

In the case of *Rice v, Reich et al.*,[59] a purchaser sued a broker and owner to recover an earnest money deposit, because of an existing driveway (easement) which served the subject and the adjoining property. The executed agreement of sale required the seller to convey the property "free and clear of all liens and encumbrances." The court found that the buyer knew of the existence of the joint driveway at the time they executed the contract of sale, and could not recover. An easement which is fully known to a purchaser before he makes his contract to purchase, or which is so open, obvious and notorious that he must have known about it, is not an encumbrance within the meaning of the covenant. In the case of *Taxman v. McMahan*,[60] the court held that a party wall constitutes an encumbrance which rendered the title to the real estate defective, where there was a covenant to maintain and rebuild the wall.

SOME FINAL NOTES ON EASEMENTS

It should be remembered that an easement does not in any way give its beneficiary title to property which is subservient to it. It simply gives the right of use and not possession. The owner of the servient tract can sell the land over which his neighbor has certain rights, in the same way as though those rights did not exist. If, by mutual agreement, the easement is canceled, it is not necessary that the strip which has been subject to the servitude be deeded back to the owner of the servient

---

[56] Flynn v. Korsac, 175 N.E. 2d 397 (Mass. 1961).

[57] Whytock v. Green, 383 P. 2d 628 (Okla. 1963).

[58] Stewart v. Bittle, 370 S.W. 2d 132 (Ark. 1963).

[59] Rice v. Reich et al., 186 N.W. 2d 269 (Wis. 1971).

[60] Taxman v. McMahan, 124 N.W. 2d 68 (Wis. 1963).

tenement since he already possesses title to it. *An easement is an encumbrance* and a purchaser could refuse to accept a deed subject to a right of way or other privilege unless the agreement of sale provided that the conveyance was to be subject to the right.

In the case of *Toms v. Settipane,*[61] it was clearly ruled that nonuse, no matter for what period of time, will not per se, extinguish an easement.

ZONING THE SEVEREST TYPE OF PROPERTY RESTRICTION

We have already discussed the limitations upon a property owner's free use of property through the medium of restrictive covenants or easements provided to others. By far the most rigorous restriction on use is that which arise through zoning regulations. Zoning is the creation by law of districts in which regulations, which differ in the various districts, prohibit injurious or unsuitable structures and uses of structures and lands. Zoning, where reasonably exercised, represents a valid exercise of the police power of the state. Zoning is not a product of the state but of their municipalities in pursuance of enabling acts of the state permitting those municipalities to adopt zoning codes or ordinances. Zoning restrictions are closely allied to building restrictions, which result from a voluntary agreement of the parties.[62]

In the case of *City of Oakdale v. Benoit,*[63] the point was well made that zoning is a deprivation of rights of private ownership and it must be strictly construed in favor of the property owner; however, it must be enforced when its provisions are clear, unambiguous and no valid legal grounds exist to prevent its enforcement. In the case of *First National Bank of Des Plaines v. Cook County,*[64] it was again emphasized that the owner has the right to use his or her property in any way, subject to the restraints necessary to secure the public welfare.

The reasonableness of a zoning ordinance is for judicial determination. It is not the duty of the courts to fix district lines or to usurp the place of the zoning authorities. The work of zoning authorities is subject to review by the courts and, if an application is found to be unreasonable or confiscatory, it will be set aside. The United States Supreme Court has declared that "the inclusion of private land in a residential district under a zoning ordinance, with resulting inhibitions of the use for business and industrial buildings to the serious damage of the owner, violates the Fourteenth Amendment, if the health, welfare, safety, convenience, or general welfare of the part of the city affected will not be promoted thereby."

A good example of judicial determination of the legality of a zoning ordinance

---

61
  Toms v. Settipane, 317 A. 2d 467 (Conn. 1973).

62
  Village of Euclid, Ohio v. Ambler Realty Co., 272 U.S. 365.

63
  City of Oakdale v. Benoit, 342 So. 2d 691 (La. 1977).

64
  First National Bank of Des Plains v. Cook County, 360 N.E. 2d 1377 (Ill. App. 1977).

was the case of *Hackett v. Gale*,[65] in which the New Hampshire Supreme Court ruled that a real estate broker could not maintain an office in his home as an accessory use of its residence. The court said, "Real estate brokerage has been held to be a business rather than a profession." Many municipalities now allow real estate offices in residences but with many restrictions on their use such as:

- The office is used only for making and receiving telephone calls and other administrative tasks.
- The office cannot be used as a meeting place for customers and/or agents.
- The office use does not increase the traffic flow to or from the premises.
- A special exception must be issued as an adjunct to the business license and only after all of the above considerations have been resolved.

Court decisions are not permanent or perpetual, but subject to change with time. For instance, in the case of *Village of Belle Terre et al. v. Bruce Boraas et al.*,[66] the U.S. Supreme Court upheld the reasonableness of a village ordinance which restricted land use to one family dwellings and defined the word *family* to mean *"one or more persons related by blood, adoption or marriage, or not more than two unrelated persons, living and cooking together as a single-housekeeping unit."* Later, two 1983 cases appear to have changed the earlier definition.

The first case, in New York, involved an establishment of a residence for eight mentally disable adults, under the provisions of Sections 41.33 and 41.34 of the Mental Hygiene Law[67] was successfully contested. The second, the Ohio case of, *Beres v. Hope Homes, Inc.*,[68] redefined the term *family*. The court stated that if a structure is maintained as a private residence, even though occupied by persons unrelated by consanguinity, but who live together as a single household unit, the covenant for single family use was not violated.

A more detailed discussion of zoning which constitutes a taking and the various ramifications of legal zoning laws is found in Chapter 12 under Land Use.

---

[65] Hackett v. Gale, 179 A. 2d 451 (N.H. Sup. Ct. 1962).

[66] Village of Belle Terre et al. v. Bruce Boraas et al., (No. 73-191-April 1, 1974).

[67] Crane Neck Association v. N.Y.C./Long Island County Service Group, 92 App. Div. 2d 119, 460 N.Y.S. 2d 69 (1983).

[68] Beres v. Hope Homes, Inc., 6 Ohio App. 3d 71, 453 N.E. 2d 1119 (1983).

4

The Brokerage Business

THE REALTOR® MULTILISTING SERVICE

The local REALTORS® board's multilist service is the bread and butter of the REALTOR® as it lists all properties for sale by all REALTORS® of the membership and publishes a periodic list of all sales of properties that have closed. These sale items contain all of the original information originally shown on the listing card plus the sales data to include, sales price, date of sale, method of financing, and selling organization. Sales data is an essential requirement of the real estate appraiser.

Licensed brokers and salespeople, who are not members of the local board continue to challenge the legality of exclusion from the multilisting service, citing their reason for not being a member of the board variously as too expensive, too exclusive, and so on. An early case in 1971, *Oates v. Eastern Bergen Multilist*[1] held that such exclusion from the service was in restraint of trade since it deprived broker access to hundreds of properties, thereby lessening competition. Later, in 1973, an additional Pennsylvania challenge, *Collins v. Main Line Board of Realtors,*[2] again ruled that a Multilisting service cannot refuse a licensed broker admission to the multilisting service. Both of these decisions are apparently mute; however, as the result of the 1972 California case, *Marin County v. Palson,* previously cited, where it allowed *exclusion for cause.* In an even later case in 1976, the nonmember's position was eroded further in the decision of *Barrows v. Grand Rapids Real Estate Board,*[3] when it was ruled that exclusion from the multilist service is proper where it can be shown that a non-member is able to compete in the market place.

---

[1]
  Oates v. Eastern Bergen Multilist, 273 A. 2d 795 (N.J. 1971).

[2]
  Collins v. Main Line Board of Realtors, 304 A. 2d (1973).

[3]
  Barrows v. Grand Rapids Real Estate Board, 214 N.W. 2d 532 (Mich. 1974).

It should be noted that member access to the multilist publications is intended for the use of REALTORS® and their agents as an aid in selling listed properties. In the case of *Supermarket of Homes v. San Fernando Valley Board of Realtors,*[4] The court upheld the board's view that those who have legal access to the publications cannot use them for commercial purposes. The plaintiff in this case had been producing a publication for sale, which utilized data from the REALTOR® publication.

MULTILISTING MEMBER COOPERATION

All multilisting members have the advantage of access to *all* listing is the board's area. Thus, any REALTOR® may show any property listed to his client and share the commission with the listing broker, based upon a pre-published percentage arrangement. In *Oglesby and Barclif, Inc. vs. Metro MLS, Inc.,*[5] the legality of REALTOR® Board listing fee fixing was addressed. As a result of this decision, boards now allow individual members to establish their own fee (splits) with other members and to publish this in appropriate multilist publications.

In most states it is illegal for a broker to attempt to sell a property known to be listed by another broker and *without that broker's permission.* It is also a violation of the Code of Ethics of the NATIONAL ASSOCIATION OF REALTORS.[6] Failure of a broker to obtain permission may result in serious consequences. Several licensing laws provide it is ground for suspension or revocation of license if a licensee is found guilty of "having negotiated the sale, exchange or lease of any real property directly with an owner or lessor knowing that such owner or lessor had a written outstanding contract granting exclusive agency in connection with another real estate broker" *(O'Horo v. Ohio Real Estate Commission.)*[7] Membership in the multilist service precludes any such problem as all members are authorized to show any board-listed property. Brokers who sell other brokers' listings are subagents of the listing broker and are required to represent the seller in the same manner as if it was his own listing.

It is a generally accepted rule that a broker cannot effectively act as the agent for both parties in the same transaction. Each party is entitled to his broker's undivided efforts and to the unimpaired use of his skill, knowledge, and experience. It is not possible for a broker to fulfill these requirements if he is at the same time giving an equivalent service to the other party to the contract. The interest of the buyer and seller are diametrically opposed to each other.

4
Supermarket of Homes Inc., v. San Fernando Valley Board of Realtors, 304 A. 2d (1973).
5
Oglesby and Barclif v. Metro MLS, Inc. CCH TRR, Section 61, 064 (VA. 1976).
6
Article 21, Standard of Practice 21-3 and 21-4.
7
O'Horo v. Ohio Real Estate Commission, 4 Ohio App. 2d 75 (1964).

The seller is interested in getting the highest price for his property that he possibly can, while the purchaser is interested in obtaining the property at the lowest possible price. The agent must not, in other words, occupy the position of a judge, impartially weighing the merits of both sides. This general rule has been followed strictly in most states.

Serious consequences can befall the broker who does not assure that all parties are aware of his dual relationship. For instance, in the case of *Meerdink v. Krieger,*[8] two widowed sisters were awarded $19,000 damages. The broker advised them to purchase a $120,000 apartment building, upon which he received a fee. He was also to be compensated by the seller. The broker argued that under the purchase contract, he was to receive $10,000 for his services to the buyers. The broker was held liable for the forfeiture of his agent's commission, as well as damages.

In the case of *Hughes v. Robbins et al.,*[9] which involved a suit by a broker for commission, against seller and buyer in an exchange deal. The plaintiff claimed that both parties knew of the dual agency and there was no unfairness, double dealing, fraud or damage to the parties. Hood, a defendant, testified that he knew of the double employment. Robbins, the other defendant, emphatically denied knowledge. The Court denied recovery saying,

> We find that all of such evidence as was submitted is not sufficient to justify a finding that the defendants, Mr. & Mrs. Robbins, knew of, consented to, or acquiesced in the dual agency .... It should be further observed that even if the defendants Hood were aware of this dual agency, and the defendants Robbins were not so aware still the broker cannot recover from either of the defendants, his principals—the rule being that the broker cannot recover from either of his principals unless both with knowledge of, consented to and acquiesced in such double employment.

> It is understandable that "no servant can serve two masters, for either he will hate the one and love the other or else he will hold to the one and despise the other."

> The fact that no damage resulted from the conduct of the broker here cannot prevent the application of this general rule, which is intended not as a remedy for the actual wrong, but preventive of the possibility of it.

The case of *Ornamental and Structural Steel, Inc. v. BBT, Inc.*[10] was held to the same effect.

It is possible for a broker to legally perform in a dual capacity and recover from both parties in the transaction when: (1) he merely brings the parties together, (2) nothing is left to his discretion, (3) no special confidence reposes in him, (4) the fact the he is acting in a dual capacity is known to both parties, and (5) he is employed by both parties.

---

[8] Meerdink v. Kreiger, 15 Wash. App. 540 (1976).

[9] Hughes v. Robbins, et al., 164 N.E. 2d 469 (Ohio 1959).

[10] Ornamental and Structural Steel, Inc. v. BBT, Inc. 500 P. 2d 1053 (Ariz. 1973).

Where the subagent broker's decision is to represent the buyer, all parties must be informed of that decision and advised as to who is to pay the commission on the sale. Figure 4-1 is a typical Agency Disclosure form used by REALTORS® to advise interested parties as to agent representation. Many agents prefer to use this form regardless of whom he is representing. The seller's signature thereon signifies that he is fully cognizant of his agent's duties to him and the seller.

Sophisticated buyers often engage a REALTOR® to represent them in the search for a property. This employment often includes the payment of a commission for the service. If the buyer is paying the selling agent's commission, in a cross-board transaction, the seller may pay a lower commission equal to the agreed listing broker cut on such sales.

> *Example*—Broker A, a member of the multilist service, lists a home for sale with a 6 percent commission to be paid by the seller. Broker A's board-advertised percentage cut on other REALTOR® (cross-board) sales was 50 percent. Broker B obtained a seller who offered $100,000 for the property with the provision that the buyer would pay the selling broker's commission. In presenting the offer, Broker A recommended acceptance and agreed to accept a 3 percent commission (his agreed cut on cross-board sales), which would net the seller $97,000. Although the seller had wanted to sell at no less than $105,000, he realized that a full price sale with full commission would only net him $98,700 after paying a full 6 percent commission. The seller accepted the offer.

LISTING CONTRACTS

KNOWLEDGE OF REAL ESTATE LAW IS ESSENTIAL

If a real estate broker is to creditably discharge his duties that devolve upon him or her, it is essential that such person(s) have full knowledge of the laws applicable to real estate practice. Real estate agents represent a combination of the principles of the law of *principal and agent,* and the law of contracts. A real estate broker is an agent in the fullest sense of the word, in that he represents another (the owner) from whom he derives his authority.

The first contract in which the broker is involved is the listing contract, which is the contract between the owner and the broker. It spells out the agreed terms of sale, or lease, which is to be negotiated by the broker, the duration of the contract, and the compensation to be paid to the broker for his services, if he performs his contract. The compensation due the broker is called a commission. The subject of commissions will be covered in considerable detail later in this chapter.

The listing agreement should be clear and unambiguous as to its terms. Since the broker is the party who prepares the listing contract, ambiguity as to its meaning or doubt as to its interpretation will be construed most strongly against him.

In the case of *Roy Annett, Inc., v. Kellin*,[11] a farm was listed for sale with a broker under an exclusive listing. The extender clause provided "... if said property is sold by the owner within six months thereafter to any person with whom said broker negotiated with respect to a sale during the term," the owner was obligated to pay the broker a commission. The broker had a prospect during the original listing period. A second broker negotiated a sale to this prospect during the six months carry over period. The first broker sued for a commission. The Court decided against the broker, holding that the property was not sold "by the owner," but through another broker. The broker could have protected himself by stating in the extender clause "by whomsoever sold" or "if sold by the owner or anyone else."

However, in the Arkansas case of *Holbert v. Block-Meeks Realty Co.*,[12] where the broker had an exclusive listing contract "till 8/15/55" and the seller signed agreements of sale on that date, the court held that the broker was protected and could recover.

A listing contract that bore the heading "EXCLUSIVE LISTING AUTHORIZATION" but contained the words "gives the above named agent the exclusive right of sale or exchange" precluded the broker's recovery of a commission upon a sale made by the owner. In this case, *Bourgoin v. Fortier*,[13] the Court said,

> ... the contract is construed more strictly against the party who drew up the contract for he has created the troublesome ambiguity. No recovery of commission.

THE DURATION OF THE BROKER'S EMPLOYMENT IN "OPEN-TIME" LISTINGS

Where no time is fixed for the duration of a broker's employment, either party, acting in good faith, may terminate the contract at will. Ordinarily, the contract continues for a reasonable time. What is a reasonable time depends upon the circumstances in the particular case.[14] In the matter of a sale of the ordinary dwelling, a few months might be said to be a reasonable time within which the broker should procure a customer. Where a broker was put in charge of selling 250 lots under an agreement which specified no particular duration, and the broker had sold only two lots in four months, it was held that he demonstrated his inability to perform even though he was entitled to a reasonable time within which to do so. For this reason the owner was justified in terminating the contract by notice to the broker. A listing "for an unlimited period of time" is invalid.[15]

11
Roy Annett, Inc. v. Kellin, 112 N.W. 2d 497 (Mich. 1961).

12
Holbert v. Block-Meeks Realty Co., 297 S.W. 2d 924 (1957).

13
Bourgoin v. Fortier, 310 A. 2d 618 (Main 1973).

14
Richter v. First National Bank of Cincinnati, 82 Ohio App. 421 (1947); Roudebush Realty Co. v. Toby, 135 N.E. 2d 270 (1955); Beerland, Reiss, Murphy & Mosher, Inc. v. Schmidt, 261 N.W. 2d 540 (Mich. App. 1977)

15
Beerland, Reiss, Murphy & Mosher, Inc. v. Schmidt, 261 N.W. 2d 540 (Mich. App. 1977).

In the case of *Hunt v.Judd*,[16] the Court held that where several real estate brokers were employed to sell a property, sale of the property by one of the brokers terminates the authority of the others at once, although they have no actual notice of the sale. To the same effect is *Kennedy, et al. v. Vance*,[17] in which the Court said,

> Since the plaintiffs were not given an exclusive right to sell, they assume the risk of knowing that the land might be sold by the owner or another agent before they could find a purchaser, ready, able and willing to buy on the terms specified and that such a sale would ipso facto revoke their agency.

In the case of a listing contract with no stipulated duration of the appointment, the courts have held that the principal may terminate the agency at any time and discharge the broker, subject to the rule, however, that the purpose of revocation cannot be to deprive the broker of an earned commission. In other words, it must be in good faith. The notice may be in writing, oral, or implied from circumstances. An agency once terminated is not revived by subsequent acts.

If a purchaser is found within the time limit, it is immaterial that the actual sale was not consummated until afterwards. Where no time has been fixed, performance within a reasonable time will be sufficient, unless the offer to the broker has been withdrawn earlier. This is a question of *fact* to be determined in trial. A lapse of one year does not necessarily terminate the broker's authority, but the authority continues until revoked, and the lapse of time is merely one fact to be considered by the jury in determining whether the authority has been revoked.

A broker may recover any expenses incurred in connection with the agency previous to the revocation of his authority. For instance, Barns employed Adams to sell real estate. In an action in assumpsit by Adams against Barns to recover damages for a breach of contract, it appeared that Adams had agreed to sell a tract of land belonging to Barnes, which had been laid out in 449 building lots, for which Adams was to receive as compensation $100 for the sale of each lot. Adams erected a temporary office upon the land and incurred expenses amounting to $230. After Adams had sold two lots, it was found that Barnes' wife would not join in the deeds, and thereupon Barns notified Adams that he was unable to carry out the agreement. The court directed a verdict for Adams for the amount of his expenses.

Where there is an open listing and a broker has a sale imminent, the owner is liable for a commission even where he sells the property two days later to another party, but without the assistance of a broker. In the case of *Romine v. Green*,[18] the court held that the broker was entitled to a commission where the defendant accepted an offer to sell two days after the broker procured a purchaser at the same price. Since the broker had no notification of sale prior to his performance, the

---

16
Hunt v. Judd, 225 Ill App. 395.
17
Kennedy, et al. v. Vance, 201 Okla. 80 (1949).
18
Romine v. Green, 13 N.J. Super. 261 (1951).

owner was liable for a commission "unless he could prove a binding agreement for sale made so short a time before plaintiff's performance that reasonable opportunity to notify plaintiff was not afforded under the circumstances." Citing Mecham on Agency (Second Edition), page 625, *Kennedy and Kennedy v. Vance,*[19] the court stated as a general rule of law that the prior sale (of the owner) itself acts as a revocation of the power, if insufficient time has elapsed between the sale and the performance by the broker. However, a broker who obtains a buyer cannot be deprived of his commission merely because the owner is negotiating for the sale on his own account, even though the negotiations materialize into a sale at a later date. Mere preliminary discussions or negotiations are not enough. There must be a binding agreement for the sale.[20]

Some states, by Rule or Regulation, require that the original period for an exclusive listing shall not exceed one year. In the case of *Schechter v. Voltz,*[21] the appellate court held that a listing for a period "until sold" was not void, but was valid for a reasonable time. There is no *statutory* limitation on the duration of a listing contract. This is a matter of agreement between an owner and the broker.

LISTING CANCELLATIONS PRIOR TO STATED EXPIRATION TIME

Where a listing is in force and a broker has exerted efforts to negotiate a sale, the owner cannot arbitrarily cancel the listing and render himself immune to the broker's claim for a commission. In the case of *Blank v. Borden,*[22] the broker claimed a commission after a dispute arose between him and the owner, while the listing was in force. The owner then told the broker to take his sign off of the property and leave, because his service were no longer required. The subject listing was on a California Association of REALTOR® form which contained a clause,

> If said property is withdrawn from sale, transferred, conveyed, or leased without the consent of the agent, or made unmarketable by my voluntary act, the stated commission of 6 percent is due and payable.

The Court found that the broker had made a diligent effort to find a purchaser, had advertised the property, and that the owner's withdrawal of the listing was complete and unequivocal. The Court said,

> It is equally well settled in this state that a withdrawal from sale clause in an exclusive right to sell contract is lawful and enforceable; a claim for compen-

---

19
Kennedy and Kennedy v. Vance, 202 P. 2d 214 (Okla.1949).
20
Hartig v. Schrader, 190 Ky. 511 (1921) and Hawks v. Moore, 27 Ga. App. 555 (1921).
21
Schechter v. Voltz, 179 Pa. Superior Ct. 119 (1955).
22
Blank v. Borden, 524 P.2d 127 (Cal. 1974).

sation under such a clause being not a claim for damages for breach of contract but a claim of indebtedness under its specific terms (citing cases).

Judgment for plaintiff. [23]

TERMINATION OF LISTING WHERE THE AGENCY IS COUPLED WITH AN INTEREST

Where the employment is coupled with an interest of the broker in the subject matter of the employment, the owner cannot arbitrarily terminate the broker's employment. Such an employment is irrevocable even after death. The Arizona Supreme Court so held in the case of *Phoenix Title and Trust Co. v. Grimes.*[24] In this case a broker joined with others in the purchase, subdividing, development, and resale of desert land for the mutual benefit. The broker was given the exclusive right to sell the property. He performed all conditions of his contract for three years prior to his death. The defendants then served notice upon the broker's executor that they refuse to permit the executor to carry on, in performing the terms of the agreement. The court held that,

> If the agency or power of the agent is coupled with an interest in the subject matter of the agency, the power so coupled will survive to the personal representative of the agent upon the death. Although contracts to perform personal acts which can only be performed by the particular person contracted with are discharged by death of the person who is to perform such acts, this rule does not apply where the services were such that they could be performed by others acting on behalf of the personal representatives of the decedent: In re Burkes Estate 198 Cal. 163, 244 Pac. 340. We are convinced here that the executor could hire qualified licensed real estate agents to carry on the agency herein, which was coupled with an interest.

In the case of *Rucker & Co. v. Glenman,*[25] an owner entered into an agreement with a broker whereby the owner agreed to subdivide a plot of land and place it in the hands of the broker for sale. The owner was to receive a minimum of $4,000 from the sale of the lots and the net proceeds over this amount were to be divided equally between owner and broker. The court held that this was not an agency coupled with interest, but merely a method of providing for broker's commission by division of the proceeds. In *Banard v. Gardner Investment Co.,*[26] the court held that a listing "coupled with an interest" is revocable unless words used mean an interest in the land itself, as distinguished from an interest in the proceeds of the sale.

---

[23]
See also Buckaloo v. Johnson, 537 P. 2d 865 (Cal. 1975).

[24]
Phoenix Title and Trust Co.v. Grimes, 416 P. 2d 979 (1966).

[25]
Rucker and Co. v. Glenman, 130 Va. 511 (1921).

[26]
Barnard v. Gardner Investment Co., 129 Va. 346 (1921).

THE LISTING SHOULD SPECIFY THE RATE OF COMMISSION

If nothing is said in the contract of employment in regard to the rate of commission, then the broker is entitled to a reasonable rate of compensation, this rate being the one generally in the business in the particular locality in which the property is situated.[27] Since an owner entrusts his property for sale to a person whose ordinary business is to sell real estate on a commission basis, the law presumes, in the absence of any agreement to the contrary, that the commission compensation is to be paid for the services rendered. The rate is not fixed by any statute, but is a matter of custom or trade usage. The broker can recover on a "quantum meruit" basis in the event of dispute. To avoid controversy, it is highly recommended that the rate of compensation be negotiated in advance and at the time of employment.

The United States Department of Justice instituted suits against a number of metropolitan real estate boards alleging that the board rules fixing or recommending rates of commission were violative of the Sherman anti-trust law. Consent decrees have been entered in a number of these suits, whereby the boards agree to discontinue this practice. The consent decrees *require* that the broker *must* "negotiate" with the owner the amount of commission to be charged.

As a result of these cases, the NATIONAL ASSOCIATION OF REALTORS® have decreed that local boards will prepare their listing agreements in a manner to allow each broker to set his total commission and indicate what percentage of that commission will be paid to another cooperating broker selling his listing.

In states where a written listing is required in the statute, the listing must state the amount of commission agreed to be paid to the broker. It cannot be supplied later by an oral promise.[28] The rule followed in California is to the effect that the amount of commission may be shown by parole where there is sufficient memoranda to show the *fact* of employment.[29]

MOST BROKERS PREFER THE EXCLUSIVE LISTING

In an exclusive listing, the broker is assured that he or his agent will have the unrivaled right for a named period of time to negotiate the sale of the property in question. In return for this protection, the broker will advertise the property and make every effort to sell the property.

You should not be confused by the two types of listings containing the word "exclusive." These two types, *the exclusive agency contract* and *the exclusive right to sell contract* are quite different.

---

[27] It should be noted that most states now require the commission rate to be specified in the written listing.

[28] Gray v. Kohlhase and Lines, 502 P. 2d 169 (Ariz. 1973).

[29] Beazel v. Schrader, 381 P. 2d 390 (Cal. 1963).

FORM A   **SALES AGENCY CONTRACT**
                               (Exclusive Right to Sell)
              This is intended to be a legally binding agreement. Read it carefully.
                              If not understood, seek other advice.

.... A l l   P o i n t s   R e a l t y   I n c o r p o r a t e d ....
                  Member of Multiple Listing Service of Salt Lake Board of REALTORS®

1.   In consideration of your agreement to list the property described on Form B and to use reasonable efforts to find a purchaser or tenant therefor, I hereby grant you for the period stated herein, from the date hereof, the exclusive right to sell, lease or exchange said property or any part thereof, at the price and terms stated herein or at such other price and terms to which I may agree in writing.

2.   During the life of this contract, if you, your agent, your sub-agent or any other agent finds a party who is ready, able and willing to buy, lease or exchange said property or any part thereof, at said price and terms, or any other price or terms to which I may agree in writing, I agree to pay the Principal Broker listed below a commission of $_____ or ___6__% of such sale, lease or exchange price which commission, unless otherwise agreed in writing, shall be due and payable the date of closing the sale, lease or exchange.

3.   Should said property be sold, leased or exchanged within ___3___ months after expiration of this contract to any party to whom the property was offered or shown by me or you or any other party during the term of this listing, I agree to pay you the commission above stated if I am not obligated to pay a commission on such sale, lease or exchange to another Principal Broker pursuant to another valid sales agency contract entered into after the expiration date of this contract.

4.   You are hereby authorized to accept a deposit as earnest money from any potential buyer on the property as described on the property description and informational form (Form B). Said deposit to be held in a trust account.

5.   I hereby warrant the information contained on the property description and informational form (Form B) to be correct and that I have marketable title or an otherwise established right to sell, lease or exchange said property, except as stated. I agree to execute the necessary documents of conveyance and to prorate general taxes, insurance, rents, interest and other expenses affecting said property to agreed date of possession and to furnish a good and marketable title with abstract to date or at my option, a policy of title insurance in the amount of the purchase price and in the name of the purchaser. In the event of sale or lease of other than real property, I agree to provide proper conveyance and acceptable evidence of title or right to sell, lease or exchange.

6.   In case of the employment of an attorney to enforce any of the terms of this agreement, I agree to pay a reasonable attorney's fee and all costs of collection.

7.   You are hereby authorized to obtain financial information from any mortgagee or other party holding a lien or interest on this property.

8.   I hereby warrant and instructed to offer this property through the Multiple Listing Service of the Salt Lake Board of REALTORS®.

9.   You are hereby authorized to share the commission listed above (paragraph 2) with another (cooperating) Principal Broker, whether that Principal Broker represents the buyer(s) or the seller(s).

10.   You are hereby authorized to place an appropriate sign on said property.

11.   This Sales Agency Contract may not be changed, modified or altered, except by prior written consent executed by the Principal Broker and the owner(s) shown below, except that the listing price shall be changed by written request received from the owner(s).

> The parties hereto agree not to discriminate against any person or persons based on race, color, sex or national origin in connection with the sale, lease or exchange of properties under this agreement.

LISTED PROPERTY   3538 So. Appleblossom Lane, Salt Lake City, Ut.
                                              (Address)

_____
            (City)   (State)
LISTED PRICE $260,000

This contract is entered into this __4th__ day of __June__ , 19 __92__

This contract expires on the __4th__ day of __September__ , 19 __92__

All Points Realty Inc.   _Joseph T. Smith_
     Listing Company   Owner (Signature)
Frank J. Blankenship   _Elaine H. Smith_
  Principal Broker (insert name)   Owner (Signature)
BY   _Joe Grodman_
     Authorized Agent (Signature)

I hereby acknowledge receipt of completed copies of this document (Form A) and the property description and information form (Form B).

Complete both Form A and Form B.   _J. T. Smith_
1 copy to owner — 1 copy to listing office.   Owner

Figure 4-1

In an exclusive agency contract (Figure 4-1), which most brokers refer to as an exclusive listing, the broker is protected during the specified period against the sale of the property by another broker or any other person other than the owner. Under an exclusive right to sell listing, the broker is protected against a sale *by the owner* during the designated period. Should a sale by the owner occur, during the designated period, the listing broker is entitled to a commission on the sale as pointed out in the case of *Brown v. Miller.*[30] In the case of *Flynn v. LaSalle National Bank*,[31] the required operative words for an effective exclusive right to sell contract were defined. Such words as "I hereby give to Ajax Realty Co. the sole and exclusive right to sell; and to pay a commission upon the sale, exchange or lease with option to purchase by whomsoever the same may be made or effected" are necessary. See Fig 4-1 for an example of an Exclusive Right to Sell listing.

THE EXCLUSIVE RIGHT TO SELL LISTING HAS RESULTED IN MUCH LITIGATION

If an owner of real estate chooses to make a contract with a broker in which it is stipulated that the broker shall have the exclusive right to sell the property within a specified time and that he shall be entitled to receive a certain commission if the sale is made within the designated time, no matter who makes it, he is bound by its terms and cannot be relieved from a bad bargain because his agreement may have been foolish or improvident. The following cases illustrate this point.

Assume that an owner has been negotiating with several prospects in the recent past, before giving an exclusive right to sell listing. He may require that the broker agree that if the property is sold to any of these named prospects of the owner, he will not demand a commission. The names of the owner's prospects should, in this situation, be submitted in writing to the broker to prevent any misunderstanding in the future.

It is not unusual for an owner to give a listing one day and cancel it a few days later. If this occurs the broker has a cause for action, but what is the measure of his damages? It is not the commission that he *might* have earned on the deal, but rather the damages and expenses which he actually sustained *at the time of the breach of the contract.* If the time period from signing to cancellation is a few days, the amount is usually negligible as the Supreme Court of Arkansas so held in the case of *Nance v. McDougald,* and in the New Jersey case of *Barry Norman Agency, Inc. v. Elias.*[32] Where the time and effort are greater, it is possible for the court to award a full commission as in the case of *Jenkins v. Vaughn,*[33] involving a contract

---

[30] Brown v. Miller, 360 N.E. 2d 585 (Ill. App. 1977).

[31] Flynn v. LaSalle National Bank, 9 Ill. 2d 129 (1958).

[32] Nance v. McDougald, 211 Ark. 800 (1947); Barry Norman Agency, Inc. v. Elias, 245 A. 2d 80 (N.J. 1971).

[33] Jenkins v. Vaughn, 197 Tenn0. 578 (1955).

to sell a drugstore, in which the court said, "if broker had rendered a substantial performance by spending time and money in an effort to perform, the offer (listing contract) becomes binding and irrevocable."

Past court decisions have made it clear that where a principal revokes the broker's agency before the expiration of the listing period, he renders himself liable, unless such revocation is for cause. Damages which were the proximate result of the termination of the employment contract were awarded in the case of *Sinden v. Loabs,*[34] where it was shown that there were mutual promises, constituting consideration. The court ruled that even where obligations are imposed on one party (unilateral contract), the owner may not breach it if there has been substantial performance by the broker such as advertising expense and obtaining prospects. Clearly, in the cases just mentioned, considerations of practical justice warrant and require *substantial* performance on behalf of the broker. Where this has occurred the owner cannot arbitrarily cancel the employment before the expiration date.

In an allied 1946 Tennessee case involving a broker who had obtained a bona fide purchase before the cancellation was communicated to him, the court ruled that he was entitled to recover his commission on the sale.[35]

In the case of *Covino v. Pfeffer,*[36] the plaintiff broker sued the former owners to recover a commission, under the following facts: On April 11, 1968, the owners gave the broker an exclusive right to sell listing, which expired on July 11, 1968. During the last week of June 1968, the ultimate purchaser first saw the property. On or about July 7, 1968, the defendant property owner knew that the broker's prospect would buy the house. On July 9, 1968, the buyer made application for a mortgage loan. Even though the sales agreement was signed subsequent to expiration of the listing, the court held that the broker was entitled to a commission. The important aspect of this decision was that the court rejected the contention of the defendant that "the owners shall not be deemed to have sold the property, which is the subject of an exclusive sale contract, unless and until the negotiations with the prospective purchaser have been consummated, into a binding and enforceable contract of sale." In the case of *Ferris v. Meeker,*[37] the ruling of the court was that the expiration date of an exclusive listing may be waived, where after the time limit has expired the owner urges and encourages the broker to continue his efforts and the broker does so with the knowledge, approval and encouragement of the principal.

Since most states require a definite expiration date in an exclusive listing contract, a listing contract which provides for a definite time period (say 90 days)

---

[34] Sinden v. Loabs, 30 Wis. 2d 618 (1966).

[35] Hutchinson v. Dobson-Bainbridge Realty Co., 31 Tenn. App. 490 (1946).

[36] Covino v. Pfeffer, 160 Conn. 212 (1970).

[37] Ferris v. Meeker Fertilizer Co., 482 P. 2d 523 (Ore. 1971).

and states that the listing shall continue in force, unless the owner gives the broker 30 days *written notice of termination,* would be deemed an unethical practice.

CAN AN EXCLUSIVE RIGHT TO SELL CONTRACT BE TERMINATED EARLY?

Two questions arise in regard to exclusive listing expiration dates. These are:

1. Can a contract be terminated before the expiration date?

2. Is the broker entitled to a commission upon a sale to a prospect procured by him, who signs an agreement of sale subsequent to the expiration date in the listing?

The cases make a distinction in listing contracts as to whether they are unilateral or bilateral. In the unilateral contract, where the broker does not in any way *obligate* himself to advance the sale of the property in the interest of the owner, then what has been previously stated in regard to the owner writing a cancellation of employment applies. A unilateral listing contract imposes a duty upon the owner to pay a commission if the broker obtains a buyer; it imposes no duty on the broker to endeavor to get a buyer. However, in a bilateral contract where the broker expressly obligates himself to advance the cause of this principal's property, then the owner may not captiously or arbitrarily terminate the employment without being liable for damages to the broker. Such a clause creating a bilateral listing contract may read:

> I acknowledge that the listing of this property, and your endeavor and efforts to procure a purchaser, through advertising, co-brokers, to otherwise, shall constitute a good and sufficient consideration of this agreement.

In the Missouri case of *Chamberlain v. Grisham,*[38] the Court held that after a broker listed the property and endeavored to procure a purchaser, the contract became a bilateral one and was no longer revocable by the owner at will. In other words, if there is a substantial performance, the listing cannot be withdrawn. The listing contract must impose a duty or obligation upon the broker, as well as the owner, in order to give it a bilateral character. In some states, brokers use a form which recites, "In consideration of $1, receipt whereof is hereby acknowledged, etc."

In absence of a court decision in this area of subject matter, it would be presumptuous to speculate as to the bilateral quality of such a provision, where the broker does *nothing* to effectuate a sale; particularly in the light of court decisions oriented towards consumer and public protection.

A provision in the listing contract requiring the broker to relist the property promptly with the members of the multilisting organization, of which he is a

---

[38] Chamberlain v. Grisham, 230 S.W. 2d 721 (1950).

member, would indicate an irrevocable bilateral contract, when the property is so listed in the multilisting organization.

It is also well to provide a clause in the listing agreement that if the owner rescinds the contract before expiration, or is guilty of a breach, he agrees to pay the broker a designated sum, which may well be the amount of the commission as *liquidated damages,* and call it "liquidated damages." Incidentally, the contract of employment should be under seal.

THE EXTENDER OR CARRY-OVER CLAUSE IN AN EXCLUSIVE RIGHT TO SELL LISTING

The extender or "carry over" clause in an exclusive right to sell listing provides that the right of a broker to a commission will be protected by the owner, if the property is sold to a prospect, procured by the broker, within a specified time, *after* the expiration of the original listing period. The period of protection is usually three or six months, but may be any period designated. It is only fair and conscionable to include such a clause. Otherwise, an owner and buyer could conspire to postpone the closing until the listing period expired, and then close the deal— often at a price which squeezes out the amount of the broker's commission.

A typical extender clause reads:

> In the event that, after the expiration of the listing term, the undersigned owner shall sell, transfer, lease, or exchange the above property, directly or indirectly, within a period of 3 months from the expiration date of the listing contract, or any extension or renewal thereof, to any person or persons with whom XYZ Realty Inc. has been negotiating or dealing for the sale, lease, or exchange of said property, the undersigned owner agrees to pay XYZ Realty Inc. the above commission, which shall become immediately due and payable.

FAILURE OF THE OWNER TO CANCEL AN EXCLUSIVE AGENCY FOR AN INDEFINITE PERIOD

Many brokers mistakenly believe that they have an exclusive agency for an indefinite period, where the owner has given no notice to terminate. This is not the case, even where the contract contains language such as the following:

> The agent's authority hereunder may be revoked by the owner at any time after the expiration of the above term when no negotiations are pending for the sale or exchange of the property, but only upon and after 30 days notice in writing to that effect given to the agent. And if subsequently to such revocation, the property should be sold or exchanged to anyone with whom the agent had heretofore been negotiating the commission will be paid to said agent.

Suppose that a few days before the expiration of the listing, the broker showed the property to a prospective purchaser, who purchased the property through another broker 20 days after the listing expired, and the owner had not given notice to terminate the agency? This situation poses two questions: (1) Was the exclusive agency still in effect? (2) Was the sale made to one with whom the broker had "heretofore been negotiating"? The law is now well established that the contract above does *not* confer an exclusive agency after its original term and until it is revoked by 30 days written notice to the broker. *The exclusive character prevails only during the original term.* After that the agency continues only as an open or general listing, until revoked. During the original listing period the broker can recover a commission no matter who makes the sale. In order to recover after the expiration, the broker must prove that he was the procuring cause of the sale—more about this under the heading of "commissions."

Negotiating means more than introducing or pointing out a property to a prospect. To negotiate means to discuss and arrange the details—many REAL-TOR® boards require that the prospect be taken *to and through* the property. Merely to call attention to a property without further discussion or effort cannot be called a negotiation. On the other hand, suppose the owner Ashcraft, employed a broker Bonwit, to sell his property under the following agreement:

> The undersigned owner hereby employs Bonwit as the sole and exclusive agent for the term of three (3) months from the date hereof, and solely and exclusively thereafter until the expiration of thirty (30) days after written notice has been given to the broker by the owner.

Further, the contract calls for a 6 percent commission on the selling price, in event of a sale, whether made by another broker or by the owner himself. The contract of employment is dated January 3, 1992. No notice is given by Ashworth to Bonwit, but on May 3, 1992, Ashworth, himself, sells the property to Crane. Bonwith now claims a commission. In this case the broker could recover, because the *exclusive* character of the employment has been continued by *express agreement between the parties.*

It should be noted that an exclusive listing, for a definite period of time, may be extended *orally* for an additional period of time, by mutual agreement of the owner and broker.[39] It is difficult to prove that an oral listing is an exclusive right to sell rather than an exclusive agency:[40]

A very special type of exclusive listing is often used by brokers, where the property owner is reluctant to list his property and prefers to sell it on his own, thus saving a selling commission. Agents who have legitimate prospects for these "FSBO" (For Sale by Owner) properties often can procure commission protection and a right to show under a standard exclusive listing limited to *one named party.* These listings are referred to, in the trade, as one-party listings.

WHEN IS A BROKER EMPLOYED AS AN AGENT?

At the present time, 22 states do require a broker's employment to be in writing (Arizona, California, Hawaii, Idaho, Indiana, Kentucky, Louisiana,

---

[39] Samuels v. Firestone Tire and Rubber Co., 342 So. 2d 661 (La. 1977).

[40] Dorman Realty and Ins. Co., Inc. v. Stalvey, 212 S.E. 2d 591 (S.C. 1975).

Michigan, Minnesota, Mississippi, Montana, Nebraska, New Jersey, New Mexico, North Dakota, Ohio, Oklahoma, Oregon, Texas, Utah, Washington and Wisconsin—also the District of Columbia and the Province of Ontario). Georgia requires the exclusive listing to be in writing. All of these states require a definite expiration date in exclusive listing contracts. A number of states require a definite expiration date by rule and regulation of the Commission. A written listing eliminates misunderstandings and curtails litigation. In the long run, it inures to the benefit of the licensee, because it is strong evidence of employment. The written listing also protects the property owner from fraudulent and fictitious claims for commission. The written listing requirement does not apply to oral agreements between brokers, salespersons, or agents to share commissions.[41]

Where the law requires the listing to be in writing, it should contain:

1. A description of the property to be sold.

2. Terms of the agreed sale.

3. The negotiated amount or percentage of commission to be paid to the listing broker.

4. The expiration date of the listing contract.

5. Signature of the party granting the listing, and

6. Signature of the agent taking the listing on behalf of his broker.

In the Texas case of *Givens v. Dougherty*,[42] the court affirmed that a written listing (Texas requires all listings to be in writing) cannot be orally canceled. Broker Givens had a written listing on defendant's property. The defendant sold the property and refused to pay a commission, contending that the listing has been orally canceled. The Court stated that to allow the existence of a contract to be negated by parol evidence would render the statute of frauds a nullity.

In those states in which oral listings are valid, many problems can result from owner curiosity as to the value of their property in the current market or a half-hearted desire to sell. Later, if they change their minds a suit for commission results. For instance, in the case of *Windsor v. International Life Ins. Co.*,[43] there was a complete variance of facts presented to the Court. The broker paid an unsolicited visit to the defendant corporation and offered to exchange a business building for farm lands. An officer of the defendant company said he was not interested, but would be interested in exchanging farm lands for high class apartment properties. The broker said that he would see what he could do. *Nothing was*

41
Fowler v. Taylor, 554 P. 2d 205 (Utah 1976).

42
Givens v. Dougherty, 671 S.W. 2d 877 (Tex. 1984).

43
Windsor v. International Life Ins. Co., 29 S.W. 2d 1112 (1930).

said about commissions. Later the broker sued for commission and the Court held that there was no employment and so no recovery.

It is regrettable that all states do not require listing contracts to be in writing. The following examples of broker/owner misunderstandings illustrate that need.

In the case of *Yurgelin v. Emery,*[44] the Court held that a single inquiry by an owner as to the amount of commission the broker would charge was insufficient to warrant a finding that the owner expressly or impliedly contracted with the broker.

In a Tennessee and a Kansas dispute, the court held that where a broker asks an owner the price of his house, and introduces him to a customer who subsequently purchases it, he is not entitled to a commission, unless he was employed by the owner to make a sale, although he may have, to some extent, influenced the sale.[45]

No particular form of words is necessary to employ a broker although a mere statement to a broker of the price at which the owner will sell, is not, in itself, sufficient to imply a contract of employment. The broker *must act with the consent* of the principal, whether such consent be given by written instrument, orally or by implications from the conduct of the parties.[46]

In Corpus Juris Secundum, 32 Section 12, it is said:

> ... the mere leaving of a description of the property at the office of the broker, by the owner or his agent, wtih the request that the broker sell the property at a designated price and upon designated terms, amounts to employment of the broker; but the mere fact that a broker asks and obtains from the owner the price at which he is willing to sell does not of itself establish the relationship of principal and agent between them.

EMPLOYMENT BY IMPLICATION

A clear statement of the application of employment by implication rule is found in the annotation to *Reeves v. Shoemaker,*[47] reading:

> Where a broker approaches an owner of real estate and negotiates for the purchase of certain property, no promise to pay for the broker's services voluntarily rendered will be implied if the owner is justified by the circumstances in presuming that the broker is a prospective purchaser or is representing a prospective purchaser in the negotiations.

Similarly, in the case of *Morton v. Barney,*[48] the Court said:

> Nor can a broker by letters of his own and addressed to a possible purchaser or by writing an owner that he has offered the property to such proposed purchaser

---

[44] Yurgelin v. Emery, 282 Mass. 571 (1973).

[45] Sackett v. Ford, Tenn. 506 and Hunger v. Judy, 194 Kan. 159 (1965).

[46] Young v. Zimmer, 56 (Ill. App. 2d 298 1965).

[47] Reeves v. Shoemaker, (Iowa) 205 N.W. 742, 43 A.L.R. 839.

[48] Morton v. Barney, 140 Ill. App. 333 (1908).

make a contract of employment for himself, entitling him to a commission. *It takes two to make a contract of that kind* and an owner is under no obligation to respond to every letter he may receive from a real estate broker he has not employed. (emphasis supplied).

Misunderstandings between agents and principals in regards to employment are very common, this is particularly so if the contract is not in writing. In the Kentucky case of *O.L. Hamilton v. Booth*,[49] the question involved whether the contract of sale between owner and buyer constituted a *written* contract of employment between the broker and the owner, as required by Kentucky law. The Court said,

> This sales agreement between the defendant and the purchaser of his property has no resemblance of a contractual agreement between the defendant and plaintiff. It recites that the property was sold through Bud Hamilton's Realty Auction Co. (this is a printed form), but these words standing alone are meaningless. If the plaintiff was to recover on the basis of this writing, it would show an agreement with him and the terms of the agreement. It fails to show either. The plaintiff, therefore, has no claim based on this writing as a contract.

In another case where employment was disputed, the court held that the owner's liability to the broker for a commission on a sale the owner made directly with the prospective purchaser of the broker depended on whether the owner had knowledge, *before consummating the sale,* that the purchaser had been produced by the broker.[50]

BROKER ETHICS AND THE LISTING CONTRACT

Good ethics require that the broker voluntarily furnish the owner with a fully completed copy of the listing contract at the time it is signed. Some REALTOR® boards require that the listing submitted to the board contain the signature of the property owner, who certifies that he has been given a copy of the listing. The acknowledgement of receipt may be as follows:

> I hereby acknowledge receipt of a fully completed copy of the Listing Contract.

The above clause should be in prominent type. In those states, having the above rule, failure to furnish the owner with a copy of the listing may constitute grounds for suspension or revocation of license.

Some brokers are reluctant to give the owner a copy of the listing because

---

[49] O.L. Hamilton v. Booth, 332 S.W. 2d 252 (1960).

[50] Tucker v. Green, 96 Ariz. 371 (1964).

they do not want him to know, perhaps, that it may run on indefinitely, *unless written notice of cancellation is given to the broker.*

To obviate this practice, which is considered unethical in good real estate circles, many Commissions, by statute or Rule and Regulation, require a *definite* expiration date in listing contracts.

In the case of *Edwards v. Cobb,*[51] a broker, who entered into a buy/sell agreement with a purchaser was found liable for exceeding his authority and ordered to pay for damages suffered including the amount of appreciation in value between the date of the agreement and the date the action was brought.

In 1989 Levittown Norse Associates sued Joseph P. Day Realty Corp.[52] for published statements by Mr. Day that he was not interested in certain property because the owners were "difficult to deal with, and are currently being sued by other brokers and that the property owners lost an opportunity to open a second outlet in the area." The court ruled that these statements were "statements of opinion" and are not actionable.

Brokers are not only liable for their own actions but those of their subcontractors as well. In *Liftus v. American Realty Co.,*[53] a broker had an exclusive real estate listing requiring him to sell and assume the responsibility for performing tasks related to closing the transaction, one of which involved turning on the utilities. The broker hired an independent contractor to light the gas water heater. The contractor turned on the gas valve and the house exploded. The Court held that the *personal* service contract of the real estate broker was not delegatable and therefore the broker was liable for the loss.

A real estate broker is not personally responsible for an error or mistake which he honestly makes, unless he has been careless, grossly negligent, or has behaved contrary to his honest convictions and beliefs.

It sometime happens that a broker acts for an undisclosed principal, and the prospective purchaser deals exclusively with the agent as owner of the property. In such cases the agent is liable as if he were the principal. It is the duty of the agent, if he desires to avoid personal liability on the contract, not only to disclose the fact that he is acting in a representative capacity but also to disclose the identity of his principal. If he fails to do so, it must be taken that he assumes and intends to bind himself.

---

[51] Edwards v. Cobb, 451 So. 2d 1271 (La. App. 1984).

[52] Levittown Norse Associates v. Joseph P. Day Realty Corp., 541 N.Y.S. 2d 421 (App. Div. 1989).

[53] Liftus v. American Realty Co., 334 N.W. 2d 366 (Iowa Ct. App. 1983).

THE BROKER ALSO HAS A DUTY TO THE BUYER

Although the broker's *primary* duty is to safeguard and look after his principal's interests, nevertheless he also owes a high ethical duty to the purchaser. In the case of *Crogan v. Metz*,[54] the broker was held responsible to the purchaser when he represented that a certain property could *not* be purchased for less than $115,000, whereas it could be purchased for $100,000. In a similar case, the buyer recovered $15,000 realized by the broker in secret profits.[55]

In the case of *Wegg v. Broderick, Inc.*,[56] purchasers brought suit against a real estate broker and its agents for damages sustained in a land contract transaction. Under terms of the contract sale, the seller had the option, in event of default, of forfeiture or suit to collect delinquent payments. The seller refused to forfeit the equity of the buyers in the contract, but required performance. The buyers contended that the broker and its agents were negligent in not advising them that they could be relieved *of further obligation* upon forfeiting the payments made. The Court held that the broker had a duty to advise the purchasers that they would be relieved of further obligation upon forfeiting the payments made. The Court found that the purchasers "were relying on the superior knowledge they (defendants) possessed as real estate professionals." The broker and salesperson were held liable for damages.

WHO, BESIDES THE OWNER, HAS THE RIGHT TO LIST PROPERTY FOR SALE?

Where the property is listed with a broker by other than the owner, he should make careful inquiry as to such person's authority to sign the contract. Often a son or daughter of foreign or ill parents or those with little business experience, will do the negotiating with the broker. Should he obtain a buyer upon the terms requested, he may find that the old folks have changed their minds and want to continue in the neighborhood, where they have lived for many years. A suit for commission is futile unless the broker can prove that the child was the authorized agent of the parents. Agency is often difficult for a claimant to establish, as the affirmative burden of proof rests upon the plaintiff broker. The broker would have a cause of action against the child, but a judgment would probably be uncollectible.

In the case of *Sylvester v. Johnson*,[57] the defendant's daughter, who generally conducted the defendant's affairs, gave the broker the sole agency for the sale of a lot. He placed his "For Sale" signs on it. *This was done with the defendant's knowledge, and without objections.* The daughter referred the prospective buyer to the broker, with the statement that the matter was entirely out of her hands, and

---

[54] Crogan v. Metz, 303 P. 2d 1029 (Cal. 1956).

[55] Petersen v. Quvel, 552 P. 2d 538 (Or. 1976).

[56] Wegg v. Broderick, Inc., 557 P. 2d 861 (Wash. App. 1976).

[57] Sylvester v. Johnson, 110 Tenn. 392 (1903).

there was no denial of the existence of the agency. The broker was held to be the defendant's sole agent and he recovered.

Where a broker obtains a listing from a husband and knows that the wife, who is also an owner, will not sign a contract of sale, so that the buyer can obtain good title, the broker cannot collect a commission if he obtains a buyer. The marital relationship does not make one spouse the agent of the other, per se. The Court in the case of *Ginn v. MacAluso*,[58] held that it is important to obtain authority to sell from *both* parties.

In a more complicated case, *Virginia M. Pepper*,[59] it was revealed that the appellant had inherited certain property prior to her marriage, which she listed with the broker under her maiden name. The broker produced a buyer the next day and a contract was immediately executed by appellant under her maiden name. At settlement, however, appellant's husband refused to join in the conveyance and the sale was not consummated.

The appellant testified that at the time of signing she was unaware that her husband had to join in the conveyance, and that the broker failed to advise her, although he knew at the time she was married. The broker testified that he did not learn of her marriage until after the contract was executed. The Court said,

> In the case before us appellant testified that she was unaware of the necessity of having her husband join in the agreement. Nevertheless, we are of the opinion that the evidence supports the conclusion that the broker is entitled to a commission. It is clear from the finding that the broker did not learn appellant was married until after the contract was executed, and that he acted in good faith when he procured a purchaser acceptable to the appellant.

In the case of *Cohen v. Garlic*,[60] testimony revealed that an auctioneer firm was hired by the owner of real estate to sell it at auction. The auctioneer announced in effect that "broker participation" would be *allowed* to a broker representing the successful bidder at the time of his purchase if the broker registered his "client with us", and would be "paid by us after settlement." A broker for the successful bidder had duly registered him on a form stating that if "my client" is the successful bidder "I am to receive" such commission, "payable to me upon settlement." The Court held that the facts did not permit an inference that the owner of the property had authorized the auctioneering firm to bind him to pay such commission nor justify a ruling that the owner was liable to the successful bidder's broker therefor.

---

[58] Ginn v. MacAluso, 310 P. 2d 1034 (N.M. 1957).

[59] Virginia M. Pepper, appellant, v. J.C. Chatel, apellee, No. 30561, Municipal Court of Appeals for the District of Columbia (1962).

[60] Cohen v. Garlic, 344 Mass. 654 (1962).

THE REAL ESTATE COMMISSION

HAS A COMMISSION BEEN EARNED? THE PROBLEM MOST OFTEN BROUGHT BEFORE THE COURTS

It has been the general rule of law that a broker is entitled to his commission when an agreement of sale is signed by the seller and the buyer, produced by the broker. The main criteria are that *the broker has produced a purchaser, ready, able and willing to buy.* But alas, the signed agreement does not guarantee the broker's commission as we will see in much detail in the following case discussions.

THE OWNER OWES A DUTY TO THE BROKER

In the Oregon case of *Snyder v. Schram,*[61] a real estate broker was employed under an exclusive listing for a period of five months. The listing contained an extender period of 90-days. The broker worked diligently to obtain a buyer. One prospect was the U.S. Postal Service, with whom the broker's negotiations continued beyond the 90 day extender period. Seven months after the listing expired, the broker was notified that the seller considered the listing terminated. The Postal Service, shortly thereafter, signed an option to purchase the property, which it subsequently exercised. The broker sued for a commission. The lower court denied a recovery. Upon appeal, the appellate court reversed. It held that a seller has a corresponding duty of good faith to the broker. The court in review, found that the broker had been encouraged throughout the negotiations by the seller, that the seller had been advised as to the progress of negotiations, and that the sale was made on substantially the same terms as had been negotiated by the broker. Under the circumstances, there had been an implied extension of the listing beyond the termination date and the seller had not acted in the good faith required.

SPECIAL STATE RULES MAY OR MAY NOT BAR THE COLLECTION OF A COMMISSION

A Rule and Regulation of the Pennsylvania Real Estate Commission requires that in the use of exclusive right to sell contracts, the broker shall carry on the face of the listing statement, *in bold type,* "THE BROKER EARNS HIS COMMISSION ON THE SALE BY WHOMSOEVER MADE, INCLUDING THE OWNER." In the case of *Williams v. Brittingham,*[62] the broker sued the owner for a commission. The listing contract did not contain the required bold type language. The Court of Common Pleas stated,

> The act is a penal statute and must be strictly construed ... the same must follow in application of regulations promulgated under it by the commission...The

---

[61] Snyder v. Schram, 547 P. 2d 102 (Ore. 1976).

[62] Williams v. Brittingham, 38 D & C 342 (Pa. 1965).

purpose of the act is to police real estate brokerage operations, and not to change the substantive law of contracts or agency ... Had the legislature intended to make such violations a defense to an action to recover commissions, it would have done so ...

THE BROKER MUST BE EMPLOYED IF HE EXPECTS TO COLLECT A COMMISSION

One of the first criteria required for collecting a commission is that the broker can prove that he was employed by the seller. The cases are legion where brokers were unsuccessful in recovering a commission because they could not prove a contract of employment.

An excellent example of the employment problem is the case of *Sherman v. Bratton*,[63] involving a situation where the plaintiff, licensed as a broker, as an attorney, and as an engineer, sued for a commission in the leasing of property in Dallas. The broker's contract of employment with the owner was *verbal*. Since the broker was not employed in the capacity of attorney or engineer, but was employed as a broker, and the other professional services being only incidental to his employment, he could not recover in his suit for commission because Texas law required a broker's employment to be in writing.

In *Kelley v. J.R. Rice Realty Co.*,[64] a writing authorizing an agent to sell "property described on the reverse side of this card," was held sufficiently signed where the owner's signature appeared it the end of the face side of the card. In a similar case, *Svoboda v. De Wald*,[65] the court held that the broker's name on the agreement of sale constituted a written listing.

Some exceptions to the normal rule are found in the Nebraska case of *Mid-Continent Properties Inc. v. Pflug*,[66] in which the court held based on the above referenced Svboda v. De Wald case. In this case a licensed broker, *who did not have a written listing*, negotiated a sale of the defendant's property at $300,000. The contract of sale, executed by the owner and purchaser, included a clause that read, "Seller agrees to pay Mid-Continent Properties, Inc. a commission of 5 percent computed on the total purchase price ..." The agreement of sale was not signed by the broker. The plaintiff sued as a third-party beneficiary under the agreement of sale. The court said,

> In this case we deal with a contract that complies with all of the requirements of the statute save for the lack of the broker's signature. It is not a direct contract between broker and land owner, such as the statute contemplates, but a contract

[63] Sherman v. Bratton, 497 S.W. 2d (Tex. App. 1973).

[64] Kelley v. J.R. Rice Realty Co., 235 Ky. 643 (1930).

[65] Svoboda v. De Wald, 159 Neb. 594 (1955).

[66] Mid-Continent Properties Inc. v. Pflug, 249 N.W. 2d 476 (1977).

between the broker and the land owner for the commission sought to be recovered. No reliance on oral testimony is required; the agreement is definitely established and the object of the statute of frauds complied with . . . .

The Supreme Court reversed the District Court dismissal and remanded the case with directions.

A sign on the property reading, "SEE YOUR BROKER" does not create employment. The Pennsylvania Superior Court so held in the case of *Appeal of Lancaster Farmers National Bank,*[67] reversing an award in favor of a broker in a lower court. The testimony tended to show appellee (broker) had no specific contract to sell and that the was never contacted by the appellant (seller) and given authority to sell the property. The broker contacted the bank to ascertain whether the particular property was available *after* he learned that the Millers were interested in purchasing it. The bank had placed a sign on the property indicating that it was for sale and directing parties to *contact their broker.* The plaintiff broker had previously dealt with the bank, having sold a property for it and having received a commission on the sale. The Court said,

> The fact that the broker had previously made a sale and received a commission does not entitle him to a commission on a subsequent sale made by him for the same vendor, if he has not been employed to effect the sale. Thus, the previous transaction, not being probative in itself to create a subsequent agency, did not entitle appellee to a commission. Neither was the sign directing purchasers to contact their brokers an offer of employment. In *Lanard and Axilbund v. Thompson Printing Co.,* [68] defendant notified approximately 100 real estate brokers by postal card that it had property to rent. The Superior Court there held that: "The postal card amounted to no more than a notice that defendant had a property for rent. It did not authorize plaintiffs to secure a tenant." The sign in the instant case also was nothing more than a notice that the property was available. It created no agency.

A case in the same area of law, in which one broker sued another broker successfully, is the case of *Levit v. Bowers.*[69] In that case, the defendant REALTOR®, held an exclusive agency for the sale of a large plot of ground in Chicago. In June 1949, he mailed a letter to about one thousand real estate brokers in the Chicago Loop, offering to pay a full commission to a broker who "successfully negotiates a sale" of all or a portion of the property. The plaintiff broker recovered a verdict for $4,200 and the defendant appealed.

It was not the defendant's contention that the words "successfully negotiating sale" meant that no commission would be paid unless the sale was consummated. In regard to the meaning of the words in controversy, the Court said,

> The letter in question was prepared and signed by a REALTOR® and sent to

---

[67] Lancaster Farmers National Bank, 219 A. 2d 647 (1966).

[68] Lanard and Axilbund v. Thompson Printing Co., 84 Pa. Super. 199 (1924)

[69] Levit v. Bowers, 2 Ill. App. 2d 343 (1954).

1,000 real estate brokers—men who make their living as agents for buyers and sellers of real estate. The final transfer was beyond their control . . . If a sale had been consummated before the broker was entitled to his commission, then the solicitation by the defendant of the services of a thousand REALTORS® in the Chicago Loop was hardly more than a snare and a delusion . . . The property being vacant and the transaction being for cash (there) was left no matter of substance to be decided.

In dealing with an officer of a corporation owner, it is most important that the broker ascertain whether the officer has the necessary authority to list the property with the broker. The affirmative proof rests upon the broker and it may be difficult to discharge this burden as indicated in the case of *Barker v. Great Southern Dev. Co., Inc.*[70] In a related case in Florida, *McCabe v. Howard,*[71] a broker, seeking a commission, had shown a property to an officer of the corporation; the corporation president bought it in his own name. The broker had the affirmative burden to prove the president was acting as agent of the corporation, in order to recover.

In the case of *Lacalusa Inv. Co. v. Hess,*[72] a suit for commission was brought by a broker against a corporation for breach of a listing contract made with the corporate president. They held that the by-laws of the corporation were admissible to show that the president was only authorized to execute instruments in writing, which had first been approved by the directors, thus, no recovery.

In other situations, brokers were able to recover commissions for services, even though the corporations had not specifically authorized the solicitation of sales help. In a Pennsylvania case,[73] a broker produced a prospect as a result of an ad in the *Wall Street Journal* which named the vice-president as contact. The broker was informed by the vice-president to prepare a contract of sale, but the corporation claimed that he had no authority to act. The court decided in favor of the broker, since the paper named the vice-president as contact and the act was apparently within the scope of his authority.

In a later case, *Tierney v. American Urban Corporation,*[74] a commission was recovered based upon negotiations between broker and general manager where it was ruled that such a person has implied and ostensible power to do those things that are usual or necessary in ordinary corporate business.

In the case of *McGarry Realty Co., et al. v. McCrone, et al.,*[75] the plaintiff broker negotiated the sale of certain property and the plaintiff knew that the funds necessary to purchase the property were to be provided by the buyers' relatives.

---

[70] Barker v. Great Southern Dev. Co., Inc., 249 Miss. 662 (1964).

[71] McCabe v. Howard, 281 So.2d 362 (Fla. App. 1973).

[72] Lacalusa Inv. Co. v. Hess, 273 P. 766 (Cal. 1929).

[73] Simon v. Porter, 180 A. 2d 227 (Pa. 1962).

[74] Tierney v. American Urban Corporation, 365 A. 2d 1153 (Conn. 1976).

[75] McGarry Realty Co. et al. v. McCrone, et al., 97 Ohio App. 543 (1954).

The day following the execution of the agreement of sale, the purchasers called the plaintiff and told him that they could not get the money. The court said,

> We find no Ohio case where this question has been clearly presented, but no principle of law has been more clearly affirmed by the courts of this state than that an agent should not be permitted to benefit by his own failure to perform his full duty in representing his principal . . .

It would appear in this case that the broker should have had the agreement signed by the persons who would be furnishing the funds necessary for the purchase. After the deal was closed, such persons (the relatives) could transfer the property to the party for whom it was desired. It is the broker's duty to assure that the buyer is *able* to buy. Two cases have defined able buyer as *a purchaser of substance, financially—one who is able to command necessary money to close a transaction.*[76]

TO EARN A COMMISSION THE BROKER MUST BE THE EFFICIENT AND PROCURING CAUSE OF THE SALE

A general rule of law states that for a broker to succeed in asserting a claim for a commission, he must be the producing cause of the sale. In *Harkey v. Gahagan,*[77] the Court stated that "procuring cause" refers to efforts of the broker in introducing, producing, finding, or interesting a purchaser, and means that negotiations that eventually lead to a sale must be the result of some active effort of the broker. It may be said that a broker must initiate a series of events, which, without interruption, result in a sale. Where two or more brokers claim a commission, the decision of the court becomes more complicated.

Whether the broker is the efficient and procuring cause of the sale is a question of fact, which falls within the province of a jury to determine. It is not a question as to how much the broker does in the deal, but how *effective* were his actions. The case of *Mehlberg v. Redlin,*[78] is a point in this regard. The Court said,

> As background of the events of Friday, April 26, 1927, it should be noted that theretofore plaintiff had devoted time, effort and expense in establishing a market place to which both vendors and purchasers of real estate would be induced to resort. It was this preliminary activity of plaintiff which brought Redlin and Rev. Schumann to that office. These facts suggest that to conclude plaintiff's only contribution towards bringing Redlin and the synod together was the answering of a single phone call, is to ignore an important part of her activities.

The fact that a broker has established "a market place" for buyers and sellers

---

[76] Sharp v.Long, 283 So. 2d 567 (Fla. App. 1973) and Gopher State Bus. Opportunities, Inc. v. Stockman, 121 N.W. 2d 613 (Minn.1963).

[77] Harkey v. Gahagan, 338 So. 2d 133 (La. App. 1976).

[78] Mehlberg v. Redlin, 96 N.W. 2d 399 (S.D. 1959).

of real estate is significant. Some brokers have had the experience that, occasionally, an easy deal takes place—the property sells itself—and the broker receives a substantial commission. The seller is unhappy in that he feels he has paid the broker a substantial sum of money for "doing nothing." The owner has lost sight of the fact that the broker rendered quick service and that the broker's established place of business as "a real estate market" made this possible.

THE PROBLEM OF INTERSTATE OPERATIONS

Air travel has brought distant cities together in a matter of minutes or hours. It has multiplied the number of real estate transactions negotiated by two brokers whose offices are miles apart. In associating with a real estate broker from another state the licensee should make certain that the other broker is properly licensed in his home state and is eligible to cooperate. The NATIONAL ASSOCIATION OF REALTORS® publishes an annual directory of broker members in the United States which greatly assists members in their cooperative efforts.

The licensee should examine the law and the Rules and Regulations in his own state to ascertain whether he can share his commission legally with the nonresident broker. Apropos of this matter is the case of *Wheaton v. Ramsey*.[79] Ramsey was a licensed broker in Montana; Wheaton was licensed in South Dakota. At the time of the suit for a share of the commission, Ramsey was a resident of Idaho and for that reason, suit was brought in that state. In late 1963, Wheaton, appellant, contacted defendant, Ramsey, concerning her ranch listings in Montana and obtained from her certain information concerning Goat Mountain Ranch. The parties discussed the possible joint sale of the property and agreed that in such event, they would split the real estate commission. In October 1963, appellant traveled to Montana with the prospective purchasers, Mr. & Mrs. O. W. McPherson, and spent several days showing them the ranch. In December 1963, the McPhersons agreed with the defendant to purchase the ranch for $275,000. Upon completion of the sale in January 1964, the defendant received a 5 percent commission of $13,750. Ramsey refused to pay to appellant any share of the commission on the ground that her own Montana real estate license would be jeopardized, since Wheaton was not licensed in Montana. The Court said,

> The principal issue is whether by Montana law the understanding between appellant and respondent Ramsey constituted an illegal agreement, in as much as appellant was unlicensed in Montana, so that such agreement cannot now be enforced. Both parties concur that an agreement between real estate brokers to share a commission is not within the statute of frauds and may be made orally—two cases cited.[80]

The controlling statute is Montana's Real Estate Licensing Act of 1963. It

---

[79] Wheaton v. Ramsey, 436 P. 2d 248 (Idaho 1968).

[80] Reilly v. Maw, 146 Mont. 145 (1945) and Iusi v. Chase, 169 Cal. App. 2d 83 (1959).

provides that ". . . it is unlawful for any licensed broker to employ or compensate directly or indirectly any person for performing any of the acts regulated by this Act, who is not a licensed broker or licensed salesperson: provided, however, *that a licensed broker may pay a commission to a licensed broker of another state so long as such nonresident broker has not conducted and does not conduct in this state any service for which a fee, compensation, or commission is paid . . ."*

The statute is dispositive of appellant's complaint: it would be unlawful for respondent Ramsey to compensate appellant directly or indirectly pursuant to the fee-splitting agreement.[81] The agreement is therefore, unenforceable.

In the case of *Thorpe v. Ross J. Carte*,[82] a broker was to receive a commission of 6 percent. He orally agreed to share his commission with the unlicensed engineering and surveying firm that assisted in finding the buyer. There was an agreement that the seller, rather than the broker, would pay a part of the commission to the engineering firm. The court held that the contract was illegal and that the broker could not recover anything. The Court said,

> We see the effect of this contract to be the same as if Carte (the broker) had received the commission and then himself split it. What one does by another he does himself and the intents and purposes of (the law) could not be effectuated if a broker could do by manifestly obvious indirection what he is forbidden to do directly.

As we can see from the above referenced cases, all states have a real estate licensing law and one of the basic requirements for recovering a commission is broker proof of proper licensing to do business in the state. We should emphasize here that the operative words are "do business in the state." This is distinguished from the act of cooperating with a broker in another state, who performs the acts within that state. The following cases are representative of problems which have arisen due to improper broker actions.

A broker licensed in New York, but not licensed in New Jersey, obtained a listing in New York City for property in Newark, N. J. The broker sent a New York prospect to view the property. Shortly thereafter the prospect signed an agreement of sale in New York City for the subject property. The seller refused to pay a commission and the broker sued the owner in New York City. The Court held that the broker could recover so long as he did not conduct any negotiations in New Jersey.[83]

In the case of *Smirlock v. Potomac Development Corp.*,[84] a broker licensed in New York, but not licensed in Maryland, brought action for a commission. The Maryland licensing law includes in its definition of a real estate broker "any person

---

[81] Payment would have been legal had the out of state broker not performed services in the state.

[82] Thorpe v. Ross J. Carte, 250 A. 2d 618 (Md. 1969).

[83] Sutton v. Transcontinental, 222 N.Y.S. 2d 778 (1961).

[84] Smirlock v. Potomac Development Corp., 200 A. 2d 922 (Md. 1964).

who engages in any single real estate act or transaction." It further states that he must be licensed. The claim for commission, therefore, was refused. The Court pointed out that if the plaintiff had obtained a power of attorney, he would have been protected, since the act exempts a person holding a power of attorney, "where only one such transaction is involved."

A number of states require the broker to have been licensed at the time the cause of action arises. The phrase "time the cause of action arose" has been controversial. In the case of *Kemmemer v. Roscher,*[85] an exclusive listing was given "To Freeman F. Kemmemer and/or Fontana Realty Company, Inc., Broker, for a one-year period." At the time the listing was obtained, Kemmemer, the individual, was licensed, but Fontana Realty Company, the corporation, was not licensed. The property, in question, was sold during the one-year period through another broker. At the time the Agreements of Sale were signed, the corporation was licensed. In a suit for commission, the Court denied a recovery, citing an earlier case, *Payne v. Volkman,*[86] where an action was begun by two associated brokers, one of them being licensed, the other unlicensed. In that case, the court held that "the contract being invalid as to the unlicensed broker, the contract is invalid *in toto.*"

In the case of *Rosenthal et al., v. Art Metals, Inc. et al.,*[87] involved the provisions of a New Jersey law prohibiting a suit unless the broker was licensed "at the time the alleged cause of action arose." The plaintiff, licensed in New York, but not in New Jersey, at the time the listing was obtained. He did obtain a New Jersey license prior to the signing of the agreement of sale. The Appellate Court decided against the broker, since negotiations were carried on in New Jersey before he obtained a New Jersey license. Upon appeal, the Supreme Court affirmed. Later, in 1969, an Oregon court decided to the same effect.[88] An earlier New York Court reached a similar conclusion. That court[89] stated succinctly:

> Otherwise an unlicensed broker might negotiate sales with impunity up to the point of a complete agreement and then obtain his license for the purpose of recovering a commission on the execution of the formal contract. The law is not so toothless.

The United States Circuit Court of Appeals took an opposite view involving a similar issue to those discussed above. In the case of *Schreibman v. L.I. Combs and Sons, Inc. et al.,*[90] the plaintiff broker, licensed in New York, obtained a license

---

[85] Kemmemer v. Roscher, 100 N.W. 2d 314 (Wisc. 1960).

[86] Payne v. Volkman, 183 Wisc. 412, 198 N.W. 438 (1924).

[87] Rosenthal et al. v. Art Metals, Inc. et al., 101 N.J. Super. 156 (1968).

[88] Certified Realty Co. v. Reddick, 456 P. 2d 502 (ore. 1969).

[89] Bendell v. Dominicis, 167 N.E. 452 (1929).

[90] Schreibman v. L.I. Combs and Sons, Inc. et al., 377 F 2d 410 (1964).

in Indiana, "after" he secured a listing in Indiana. He was licensed at the time the agreement of sale was signed between the owner and buyer, procured by him. The Federal Court of Appeals held that since the plaintiff was licensed *at the time the action arose* (when the agreements were signed), the District Court was in error in dismissing the suit. The case was returned to the District Court for hearing on its merits. The California courts have also had occasion to examine their statute which is of similar import. In earlier cases of *Houston v. Williams; Davis v. Chapman and Wise v. Badis,*[91] citing the California cases as authoritative, the Iowa Supreme Court, in *Pound v. Brown,*[92] also decided in favor of the broker.

In this connection, the language of the Illinois license law requires the plaintiff broker to be licensed "prior to the time of offering to perform any such act or service or procuring any promise or contract for the payment of compensation for any such contemplated act or service."

In the case of *Quickshops of Mississippi, Inc. v. J. Bruce,*[93] the question was presented as to whether an unlicensed broker is entitled to recover a commission on a business opportunity property, where real estate, although significant, was not the dominant factor in the transaction. This presents a factual question for determination by a jury. The court sustained the verdict of the jury in favor of the broker.

The opinion of the Mississippi Supreme Court emphasizes the fact that the license law statute is penal in nature and must be strictly construed. The court referred to the New York rule,[94] which holds that a broker may recover a commission in the sale of a going business "despite the fact that real estate forms an incidental of the transaction and he does not hold a real estate broker's license."

Where the broker was employed to sell a business, and charged a commission of 10 percent for sale of the business and real estate, he could not collect for sale of the real estate since he was not licensed as a real estate broker.[95]

However, in the case of *Abrams v. Guston,*[96] where the sale of realty and the personal property located thereon constituted one complete and entire transaction, it being evident that the mill and machinery located on the leased property were of value to the purchaser only if he obtained the lease upon the property, the court held that the broker making the deal required a license.

This case differs from *Marks v. McCarty,*[97] where the real estate and the

---

[91]
Houston v. Williams, 200 P. 55; Davis v. Chapman, 282 P. 992 and Wise v. Badis, 242 P. 90.
[92]
Pound v. Brown, 140 N.W. 2d 183 (1966).
[93]
Quickshops of Mississippi, Inc.v. J. Bruce, 232 So. 2d 351 (1970).
[94]
Weingst v. Rialto Pastry Shop, 152 N.E. 693 (New York 1926).
[95]
Rockmatt Corp. v. Erlich, 294 So. 2d 412 (Fla. 1974).
[96]
Abrams v. Guston, 243 P. 2d 109 (1952).
[97]
Marks v. McCarty, 205 P. 2d 1025 (Cal. 1949).

personal property were each given separate sales prices in the escrow. In a similar case an unlicensed person was denied a commission in the sale of a restaurant, including stock and fixtures, lease and good will, on the grounds that the sale involved an interest in real estate, as a matter of law.[98]

Another landmark case in broker commission sharing is the case of *Hanks v. Hamilton*,[99] which was a suit by an unlicensed real estate salesman against a firm of brokers for a share of a $134,310 commission. The parties agreed in writing "that contingent upon the consummation of the sale of said property, resulting in the brokers receiving said commission, *it would be delivered to a closing agent, from which appellant would be paid $44,000 for 'services rendered'*. The Appellate Court said,

> Said agreement resulted in 'fee splitting' with unregistered people in the real estate profession. This is absolutely unlawful and the establishment of a 'fund' out of the commissions earned by a broker appears to be a device to split the fee and circumvent the law. This is the very thing that the law is trying to avoid.

WHO GETS THE COMMISSION WHERE BROKER EFFORT HAS APPARENTLY BEEN ABANDONED?

Clearly, if one broker abandons his efforts, he cannot later claim a commission if a sale is made by the owner, or through another broker, to his original prospect. For example, broker A had an open listing on a property for $30,000. She showed it to a prospect, Mrs. White, who was interested but did not make up her mind to buy it. Broker B showed Mrs. White various properties. He did not show the subject property, but mentioned it to her. She said that she had already seen it through broker A. About two weeks later, she called broker A and stated that she would like to go through the house again with her husband, but the broker told her it was too late—"the house is sold." A few days later she called broker B and when she mentioned that the house she was interested in was sold, he expressed surprise because he had received no notice of cancellation of the listing. He called the owner, who referred him to her attorney. The attorney told broker B that there was a signed agreement from a buyer, *but it was subject to the buyer's selling his present home and that he was going to advise his client, the owner, not to accept the deal*, whereupon the owner accepted the deal with Mrs. White. Now, broker A claimed a commission, as did broker B. Here A is not entitled to any commission as there was an abandonment of negotiations when A told Mrs. White, "the house is sold, you are too late," and did nothing more.

In the case of *Mammen v. Snodgrass*,[100] the Court said,

> The law is well settled in this state that the fact that a seller consummates a sale

---

[98] Cohen v. Scola, 80 A. 2d 643 (N.J. 1951).

[99] Hanks v. Hamilton, 339 So. 2d 1123 (Fla. 1976).

[100] Mammen v. Snodgrass, 13 Ill. App. 2d 538 (1957).

or that it is made upon different terms from those proposed by the broker, does not necessarily deprive the broker of compensation. If he is the efficient and procuring cause of the transaction, he is entitled to a commission.

But that a sale is finally brought about by the efforts of the principal with a person with whom the broker previously negotiated without success, does not furnish a basis for commission, if it appears that the broker has for a long time ceased negotiations with the purchaser and abandoned the property. A time must necessarily arrive after a prospective purchaser has declined to purchase when the owner may treat the negotiation at end and begin an entirely new and independent solicitation. . .

In the North Carolina case of *Jackson v. Northwestern Life Insurance Co.,*[101] the Court held that a broker was not entitled to a commission where he had failed to effect an agreement and abandoned his efforts, even though he may have introduced to each other parties who otherwise would never have met. The plaintiff broker did nothing for 14 months and the deal was closed through another broker. Whether there has been an abandonment of effort, so as to deprive the broker of a claimed commission, when a sale takes place to a prospect whom the broker contacted, is a question of fact, rather than law. Determination is within the purview of the jury.

If one of several brokers gives notice to his principal that he cannot effect a sale, he will not be entitled to a commission because another broker, who is informed by the first that the property is for sale, succeeds in finding a purchaser. So, if two brokers are employed, and one of them enters into a negotiation with a purchaser, which fails and is abandoned, he will not be entitled to a commission because another broker subsequently succeeds, wholly through his own efforts, in making a sale to the same person and upon substantially the same terms as those proposed by the first broker. The same results will follow where one broker has not been able within a reasonable time to effect a sale, and another broker afterwards succeeds in selling to a purchaser first approached by the former broker. The principal, acting in good faith and with no intentions of defeating the broker's claim, may revoke his authority, while his efforts are yet unsuccessful, even though the principal in person or through another broker subsequently sells to a purchaser to whom the first broker endeavored to sell.

THE CASE OF MULTIPLE BROKER EMPLOYMENT

Often the problem with commission payment is not *if* a commission is due, but which of several brokers involved in the transaction is the one who should be paid. The problem arises under several circumstances such as:

- Brokers licensed in different states are involved in the transaction.
- The sold property was listed with multiple brokers.

---

[101]
Jackson v. Northwestern Life Insurance Co., 133, F.2d 111 (1943).

- One broker abandons his effort with a prospect, who later buys through another broker.

- The owner sells the property assuming a prior listing was not in effect or he forgets about an agreement contained in a management contract.

Regardless of who is finally awarded the commission on a sale, it should be observed that even where a property has been listed with more than one broker, the owner is liable for *only one* commission. This fact was clearly pointed out in the case of *Watts v. Barker,* in 1938.[102]

The rule of law is that where two or more brokers possess concurrent authority to sell, and one makes a sale of the property, the agencies of the others are terminated by removal of the subject matter of the contract. While it is advisable for the owner to advise all brokers of that fact and that upon a sale by one or the other, the employment of the other brokers shall automatically cease. In Virginia, the law is that two or more brokers, knowing of the another employment(s) to sell the same land, the owner, if he shows no favoritism, may sell to the purchaser who is first produced and the broker producing the sale is the one entitled to the commission.[103]

The biggest problem of multiple broker agency is that often a single purchaser is the prospect of a number of brokers. When a sale results, which broker is entitled to the commission. The test for recovery is *which broker was the efficient and procuring cause of the sale.* Thus, it behooves each broker to keep his principal informed of the identity of every prospect shown the property. This is obviously not to imply that all a broker has to do is notify the owner of the name of his prospect and then sit idly by and await the fortuitous circumstance of a sale. He cannot be guilty of abandonment and then claim compensation because a sale is made to his original prospect. *He must activate the sale,* although in some instances the mere introduction of the principals may suffice, if that sets in motion a series of events that culminate in a sale. The West Virginia court stated the rule well in the case of *Averill v. Hart & O'Farrell,*[104] by stating "If a broker sets in motion machinery by which a sale is made, which without break in continuity, was the procuring cause of the sale, he is entitled to the commission, although he does not conduct *all* negotiations." In another multibroker dispute, *Dobson v. Wolf,*[105] the Court said,

> If a broker does not have the exclusive sale of property, he does not become entitled to a commission merely by showing property to the person who eventually buys it, but a personal introduction of the purchaser to the owner is not essential and it is sufficient if, through the efforts of the broker, the parties

---

[102] Watts v. Barker, 275 Ky. 411 (1938).

[103] Cannon v. Bates, 115 Va. 711.

[104] Averill v. Hart & O'Farrell, 101 W.V. 411 (1926)

[105] Dobson v. Wolf, 54 N.W. 2d 469 (South Dak., 1952).

are brought into communications with each other. It *is not enough that a broker's efforts may have contributed to the negotiations resulting in the sale.* If this were the rule, says the court in *Carney v. John Hancock Oil Co.,*[106] "no owner desiring to sell could safely employ more than one broker, for in the event of each of several being able to convince a jury that he had contributed anything to the sale, the principal might be held for as many commissions as there were brokers employed. The law contemplates no such absurdity.

In a very early New Jersey case, *Vreeland v. Vetterlein,*[107] the opinion was to the same effect as the above case. Here the court said,

> Where the property is openly put in the hands of more than one broker, each of such agents is aware that he is subject to the arts and chances of competition. If he finds a person who is likely to buy, and quits him without having effected a sale, he is aware that he runs the risk of such person falling under the influence of his competitor—and in such case, he may lose his labor. This is a part of the inevitable risk of the business he has undertaken.

Where claims for commissions have been advanced by several brokers, who claim to have produced the same purchaser for the owner's property, an owner should hesitate in voluntarily paying any commission. He may pay one broker and later have the courts decide that another was really the one who should have been paid, thus the owner would be stuck with two payments. *Where the owner is in doubt, he should pay the commission into court and there have the matter settled by a court of law,* thus avoiding further liability to himself in an interpleader suit. The law, in this regard, was succinctly stated in the case of *Julius Heller Realty Co. v. Jefferson Gravoco Bank,*[108] in which it said,

> In other words in these cases where an owner appoints more than one broker to procure a purchaser for his property, the rule is to the effect that *he who sows the seed and tills the crop is entitled to reap the harvest —rather than one who volunteers to assist in tilling the crop, the seed for which he has not sown.* The question of whether the plaintiff was procuring cause of the sale was for the jury to determine. Verdict in favor of the owner affirmed.

It is the broker who shakes the tree and not the one who runs up to gather the apples, who is entitled to the commission.[109] In this regard, it should be noticed that a number of courts have pronounced the rule that the sale of a property by one of the brokers *terminates the authority of the other brokers immediately, although they have no actual notice of the sale.*[110]

---

[106] Carney v. John Hancock Oil Co., 187 Minnesota 293.

[107] Vreeland v. Vetterlein, 33 N.J. 247 (1869).

[108] Julius Heller Realty Co. v. Jefferson Gravoco Bank, 144 S.W. 2d 174, 176 (Mo. 1940).

[109] Nichols v. Pendley, 331 S.W. 2d 673 (Mo. 1960) and Brennan v. Banner Realty, Inc., 436 P. 2d 894 (Ariz. 1968).

[110] Hunt v. Judd, 225 Ill. App. 395 (1922); Kennedy v. Vance, 201 Okla. 80 (1949) and Dino v. Cappelleri, 77 A. 2d 840 (Vt. 1951).

BROKERS SHOULD KEEP THEIR PRINCIPALS INFORMED OF THEIR ACTIONS

In multibroker situations, failure to keep the principal advised of the names of clients shown the property may result in a lost commission. Where a broker fails to acquaint the owner with the identity of his prospect, the owner may not know that the prospect is also the prospect of another broker at the same time. It is wise to keep the owner informed of negotiations as they proceed. Where this is done and a sale results, the owner, no doubt, will feel that the commission was well earned. It cannot be emphasized too strongly that a broker should acquaint the owner with the identity of *every* prospect to whom the property is submitted. One good commission saved, as a result of such notice, will adequately compensate a broker for the detailed work entailed.[111]

Failure of a broker to disclose the identity of a prospect who, later purchases the property, *during the term of the broker's listing,* is not fatal to the broker's claim for commission. In the case of *Lee C. Richards, Inc. v. Brewer,*[112] the court held that the nondisclosure to the owner appeared to be neither material or prejudicial.

PROBLEMS WHERE SEVERAL BROKERS CLAIM THEY FOUND THE BUYER

To determine which of several brokers is entitled to the commission, where each claims to have found the same purchaser, is often a problem of no little difficulty. Where all brokers are employed independently, at least it would seem that the ordinary rule applicable to the case of employment of a single broker would apply; that is, that the broker who was the efficient and procuring cause of the sale is entitled to the commission and that his right cannot be affected because of the principal in person, or by another agent, takes into his own hands and completes the transaction which the broker inaugurated.

Where two or more brokers are employed, there is no implied contract to pay more than one commission, and it therefore becomes necessary to lay down a rule for determining which one of the different possible claimants is entitled to be paid. Where several brokers have each endeavored to bring about a sale which is finally consummated, it may happen that each has contributed something without which the results would not have been reached. One may have found the customer, who otherwise would not have been found, and yet the customer may refuse to conclude the bargain through his agency. Another broker may succeed where the first has failed. In such cases, in the absence of express contract, the only one entitled to a commission is the one who can show that his services were the really effective means of bringing about the sale, or *the predominating efficient cause.*

---

[111] Tucker v. Green, 96 Ariz. 371 (1964).

[112] Lee C. Richards, Inc. v. Brewer, 548 S.W. 2d 196 (Mo. App. 1977).

Where several brokers are openly and avowedly employed so that each can be said to have undertaken the employment on that basis, it is held in many cases that the entire duty of the principal is performed by remaining neutral between them and that he has a right to sell to the buyer who is first produced by any of them without being called upon to decide which of several brokers was the primary cause of the sale.

Other cases state the rule somewhat less broadly, and it is everywhere agreed that in order to be entitled to the benefit of it, the principal must in fact have remained neutral, and he certainly must not knowingly permit, much less aid in or connive at, the appropriation by one man of the rewards of what was really the result of another person's effort. However, payment of the commission to one broker by an owner is not admissible as evidence in a suit by a second broker for a commission claimed in the sale to the same prospect.[113]

The general rule in law throughout the country is well stated in the case of *Trent Trust Co. v. McFarlane*,[114] where the court held that a broker is not entitled to a commission on a sale effected through another broker, even though a purchaser was introduced by the first broker or even though the sale may be aided by the first broker's previous efforts, provided the owner acts in good faith.

WHAT IF THE OWNER MAKES THE SALE?

In the case of *Essres Realty & Insurance Inc. v. Zeif*,[115] the Court held that where a broker opens negotiations but fails to bring buyer and seller together, and later, the owner sells to the same buyer without any further effort on the part of the broker, there can be no recovery of commission.

The case of *Realty Marts International, Inc. v. Barlow*,[116] raised the question of whether plaintiff-broker was precluded from obtaining a commission when the broker "failed to notify the owners that the subject property had been shown to the ultimate purchaser." The Court said,

> A REALTOR® is under no obligation to notify the owner every time the property is shown . . . the owners were notified that applicant's salesman had shown the property to the purchaser prior to the sale . . . The law is well settled that an owner is liable for a commission *where with the knowledge of pending negotiations between the broker and the purchaser, the owner completes the sale which the broker is the procuring cause.* (emphasis supplied)

A broker must produce a buyer while the premises are still on the market. In terminating employment an owner must act in good faith. Where an owner gives a second broker an exclusive listing agency, while an open listing is still in

---

[113] Walker v. Randall, 85 Pa. Super. 443 (1925).

[114] Trent Trust Co. v. McFarlane, 21 Hawaii 435 (1913).

[115] Essres Realty & Insurance Inc. v. Zeif, 512 P. 2d 650 (Colo. App. 1973).

[116] Realty Marts International, Inc. v. Barlow, So. 2d 63 (Fla. App. 1977).

existence, the open listing given to a broker earlier is not automatically terminated. The owner must give notice of cancellation of employment to the first broker. A broker is not entitled to compensation for merely procuring a customer to take an option that has never been exercised. To avoid any presumption that the employment of the broker is to continue until a sale is effected, the owner should take some action to notify the broker that his employment is terminated.

The mere introduction of the purchaser to the owner by the broker may be sufficient performance of the broker's contract of employment, depending, of course upon the facts in the particular case. If negotiations are taken up from the point of introduction by the buyer and seller without the aid or intervention of the broker and a sale results, the broker is entitled to a commission. The question is, "Did the broker set in motion a series of circumstances, which, without interruption, culminated in a sale?" If the introduction did that, the broker is considered the efficient and procuring cause of the sale, and he can recover.

It must be emphasized that it is not a question of how much work a broker did in a particular transaction, but rather, how effective was his work. If he did the spade work by obtaining a prospective purchaser, *the owner cannot then take the purchaser, deal with him directly, and turn the broker out of doors.* Nor can the owner take the matter into his own hands and complete the sale, either above or below the listing price, and then refuse to pay a commission. If a broker or salesperson brings to the owner, a purchaser who is willing and able to buy at a price below the listed price, the commission is earned if the owner actually sells the property to the prospect, or is willing to sell to that buyer.[117] That same rule applies if the property is sold, at a higher price than the listing given to the broker, by the owner to a prospect procured by the broker.

The general rule in these situations is that, where there has been no direct communication between the broker and the purchaser, it must *be shown affirmatively,* that the latter was induced to enter into the negotiations which resulted in the purchase through the means employed by the broker for that purpose.

If the broker employed other persons to aid him, whether under pay or not, or if he put up maps, signs, notices, or otherwise advertised the property, and if by means of these measures, a person was induced to open negotiations with the owner which resulted in his buying the property, the sale may be said to have been effected through the broker's instrumentality. *It must be made to appear that what the broker did was the immediate and efficient cause of such negotiations.* If the broker merely talked about the property with different persons and one of them, on his own accord and not on behalf of the broker, mentioned to another that the property was for sale, and such last-mentioned person thereupon looked into the matter and finally became the purchaser, the agency of the broker in inducing the sale was not sufficiently direct to entitle him to a commission.[118]

---

[117] Bass Investment Co. v. Banner Realty Inc., 436 P. 2d 894 (Ariz. 1968).

[118] Reap Realty Co. v. Hadock, 181 N.E. 2d 732 (Ohio 1961).

Where a broker posts a "For Sale" sign on a property listed with him and a prospect looks up the identity of the owner in the County records, and then deals with the owner directly, ignoring the broker, *it may be claimed that the broker was the instrumentality by which the sale was made.* Proof, however, may be difficult to establish in such a borderline situation.

A recent New York State case has added a new twist to the exclusive listing requirement that pays the broker, regardless to whom sold. In *Blake Realty Inc. v. Gilligan,*[119] the court ruled that a commission was payable to the broker even though the sale was to parties to whom the seller had already conducted negotiations. The court found that the broker and seller had never reached an agreement as to whether a commission was due in such instances.

In the case of *Adams and Leonard, Realtors, v. Wheeler,*[120] the plaintiffs had a Property Management Agreement for a definite period of time. The agreement contained the following provision:

> The agent shall have the sole exclusive right to sell and offer for sale the property covered herein, if the property is sold or offered for sale during the terms of this agreement.

The owner sold the property himself while the agreement was in force. The plaintiff did not have anything to do with the sale. The Court said:

> The broker performed no services concerning the sale of the property. Until he had performed some such services the contract was unilateral. The agreement could not be construed as constituting a completed and enforceable "right to sell" real estate listing contract. . . . We see no reason why a valid and enforceable "exclusive right to sell" contract could not be incorporated in a property management agreement, if the "exclusive right to sell" contractual provisions are complete concerning their rights and obligations if the property is offered for sale or sold. However, if the "exclusive right to sell" provisions are incomplete and unenforceable, and action for damages will not lie for breach of the unenforceable contract.

The Supreme Court affirmed the lower court's denial of a commission.

WHAT IF THE TERMS OF SALE ARE NOT THE SAME AS THE LISTING?

It is important that the broker have a definite understanding with the owner *that a commission will be paid,* if the broker obtains a buyer upon the seller's agreed terms. This is particularly true in the case of an oral listing.

A broker's right to recover a commission stands or falls upon the terms of offer made by the prospective purchaser. If the terms proposed vary in any material degree from those specified by the vendor, the broker cannot recover a commission.[121] A

---

[119] Blake Realty Inc. v. Gilligan, 547 N.Y.S. 2d 930 (N.Y. App. Div. 1989).

[120] Adams and Leonard, Realtors, v, Wheeler, 493 P. 2d 436 (Okla. 1972).

[121] Bell v. Warren Development Corporation, 319 A. 2d 299 (N.H. 1974).

broker is entitled, however, to his commission when he obtains a buyer upon the seller's terms, and the seller refuses to sign the agreement of sale.[122] If a broker negotiated an agreement of sale that was subject to obtaining a mortgage of $41,000 and the only mortgage obtainable contained a 1 1/2 percent prepayment penalty, which the buyer refused to accept, the broker could not recover a commission.

IS A COMMISSION DUE WHEN A SALE IS NOT COMPLETED?

Often a sales agreement is not finalized for one reason or the other, and the broker is deemed to have or have not earned a commission. The following situations illustrate some of these problems coming before the courts.

A broker may be due a commission if the buyer defaults. A case of great importance, which rejects the premise that an owner is liable to the broker for a commission after a buyer defaults on a signed sales agreement is *Ellsworth Dobbs, Inc. v. Johnson (owner) and Iarussi (buyer).*[123] In joining the buyer as defendant, the broker charged the buyer with breach of implied agreement to pay a commission if he failed to complete the purchase and thus deprive the broker of commission from the seller. The trial judge held, as a matter of law, that the broker's commission vested upon execution of the contract of sale, and the commission was not dependent upon the closing of title. The jury found for the broker in the amount of $15,000 against the owner. In reversing the lower court, the Supreme Court said,

> The present New Jersey rule as exemplified by the case cited is deficient as an instrument of justice. It permits the broker to satisfy an obligation to the owner simply by tendering a human being who is physically and mentally capable of agreeing to buy the property on mutually satisfactory terms, so long as the owner enters into a contract with such person. The implication of the rule is that the owner has the burden of satisfying himself as to the prospective purchaser's ability, financially or other wise, to complete the transaction; he cannot rely at all on the fact that the purchaser was produced in good faith by the broker as a person willing and able to buy the property . . . If it later appears that the purchaser is financially not able to close the title, or even that he never did have the means to do so, the owner must pay the broker a commission so long as he acted in good faith. Such a rule, considered in the context of the real relationship between broker and owner, empties the word "able" of substantially all of its significant content and imposes an unjust burden on vendors of property . . . Thus when the broker produces his customer, it is only reasonable to hold that the owner may accept him without being obliged to make an independent inquiry into his financial capacity. That right ought not to be taken away from him, nor should he be estopped to assert it, simply because he "accepted" the buyer . . . In a practical world, the tue test of a willing buyer is not met when he signs the agreement to purchase; it is demonstrated at the time of closing of title, and if he unjustifiably refuses or is unable financially to perform *then,* the broker has not produced a willing buyer.

---

[122] Wolfenberger v. Madison, 357 N.E. 2d 656 (Ill. App. 1976).

[123] Ellsworth Dobbs, Inc. v. Johnson (owner) and Iarussi (buyer), 50 N.J. 528 (1967).

It should be noted that when it became clear to the seller that there was no hope of the buyers completing the sale because they could not finance the purchase, the parties exchanged mutual releases, which the court held, under the facts present, did not and was not intended to amount to the equivalent performance of the contract. In holding the buyer responsible to the broker, the court said,

> This court has held that when a prospective buyer solicits a broker to find or to show him property which he might be interested in buying, and the broker finds property satisfactory to him which the owner agrees to sell at the price offered, and the buyer knows that the broker will earn a commission for the sale from the owner, the law will imply a promise on the part of the buyer to complete the transaction with the owner. If he fails or refuses to do so without valid reason, and thus prevents the broker from earning the commission from the owner, he becomes liable to the broker for the breach of the implied promise. The damages chargeable to him will be measured by the amount of commission the broker would have earned from the owner.

This New Jersey case has been cited with approval in *Staab v. Messier* in the east and on the west coast in the case of *Brown v. Grimm*.[124] This ruling has also been cited with approval in Connecticut, Iowa, Idaho, and Kansas.

In *Hersh v. Kelman*,[125] the plaintiff broker obtained a purchaser and a $200 deposit on an open listing. Before the owner would sign the agreement, he had the broker write into the agreement "commission to be paid when deal is consummated." The buyer moved to Detroit and defaulted. The seller sold the property through another broker and paid a commission. The first broker sued for a commission. The lower court decided in favor of the broker. The appellate court reversed saying,

> Failure of the prospective purchaser to consummate the deal, without any fault on the part of the seller, relieved the seller completely under the special terms of the contract from liability for the payment of commission.

In the case of *Jones v. Palace Realty, Co.*,[126] the North Carolina Supreme Court held that it was the event of closing the deal and not the date of its expected or contemplated happening that made the promise to pay a commission enforceable. In the case of *Bechtel Properties, Inc. v. Blanken*,[127] the agreement provided that "if the purchaser shall fail to make full settlement, the

---

[124] Staab v. Messier, 264 A. 2d 790 (Vt. 1970); Brown v. Grimm, 481 P. 2d 63 (Or. 1971) and Tristram's Landing, Inc.v. Wait, 327 N.E. 2d 727 (Mass. 1975. Both cases cited Ellsworth Dobbs, Inc. v. Johnson, op.cit.

[125] Hersh v. Kelman, 104, N.E. 2d 35 (1951).

[126] Jones v. Palace Realty Co., 226 N.C. 303 (1946).

[127] Bechtel Properties, Inc. v. Blanken, 299 F. 2d 928 (D.C. 1962).

deposit herein provided for may be forfeited at the option of the seller . . ." The agreement further provided that:

> The entire deposit shall be held by Sam Blanken & Co. until settlement hereunder is made or until the deposit is forfeited . . .

The broker had obtained a purchaser, who had shown himself ready, willing and able to perform. Certain matters arose which could not be resolved and the lower court said, "Apparently the transaction was just abandoned by the parties when the property was resold by the defendant." The appellate court said,

> In view of the fact that the contract was not settled, through no fault of the agent, and apparently by mutual agreement of the seller and the purchaser (or, if not by mutual agreement, at lease with the acquiescence of the seller), the commission agreement could not be performed in accordance with its terms. This is not to say however, that the agent is to be deprived by that reason, of his commission, which was in the total amount of $7,000.

In the New Mexico case of *Stewart Realty v. Brock*,[128] the broker had a listing of a ranch at $85,000; the broker's commission was to be 5 percent ($4,250). The broker obtained a buyer at that price, who paid $8,500 as a deposit. The buyer wanted to withdraw from the deal. The seller agreed, if the buyer would pay an additional $1,500. The buyer paid the $1,500. The broker claimed a commission of $4,250. The owner offered 5 percent of the $8,500 deposit, or $425. Upon suit, the court allowed the full amount of the commission claimed.

In the case of *Nelson v. Rosenblum Co.*,[129] a property was listed with a broker at $36,000 *net* and the broker obtained a purchaser who entered into a legally enforceable purchase agreement for the price of $37,500. Earnest money was paid by the purchaser to the defendant. Before the date of settlement, the purchaser advised the broker that they had taken employment in Florida and that they would default upon the contract and forfeit the earnest money. The owner demanded the entire deposit sum of $2,500. The court noted that the parties did not condition payment of the commission upon actual consummation of the purchase agreement. It held that if, without fraud, concealment, or other improper practice on the part of the broker, the principal accepts the person presented and enters into a binding and enforceable contract with the purchaser, the commission is fully earned.

Where the default or failure is on the part of the seller, the courts generally hold that the broker may recover the commission agreed upon. Where the failure or default is attributable to the purchaser, the rule is different.

---

[128] Stewart Realty v. Brock, 60 N.M. 216 (1955).

[129] Nelson et al. v. Rosenblum Co., 182 N.W. 2d 666 (Minn. 1970).

In every case the fundamental doctrine, under the varying forms of expression, is that the duty assumed by the broker to bring the minds of the seller and buyer to an agreement on a sale and on a price and terms upon which it is to be made and that, until this is done, his right to a commission does not accrue. A broker is not entitled to a commission when the customer through no fault of the seller refuses to complete the contract; but it is different when the customer has entered into a contract binding upon both parties or into an agreement to pay a stipulated sum as damages in case of refusal to complete the contract.

COMMISSION SHARING THROUGH MULTILISTS OR OTHER COOPERATIVE EFFORTS

Cooperative efforts between members of the multilisting organizations of the local realty boards is the backbone of the business. It is seldom that a dispute arises between members, regarding "commission splits" or "who is the selling agency." When these disputes do arise, the are generally settled by an arbitration committee of the local REALTOR® board.

However, in a Pennsylvania case, *Campbell v. Grange*,[130] the court denied a recovery to a cooperating broker of a real estate board. The court held that the selling broker was a sub-agent of the listing broker, and could not sue the owner, with whom the selling broker had no privity of contract.

Commissions to be paid by the seller are published for the information of all cooperating brokers, who may be interested in selling the property. The agreed listing broker–selling broker splits are a matter of record in the multilist publications. Each member of the multilisting organization is free to set his commission charge and his agreed split with cooperating brokers.

This latter arrangement came about as the result of United States Department of Justice suits against a number of metropolitan real estate boards alleging that the board rules that its members should follow, in practice, the recommended schedule of commission rates constitutes an illegal practice. A number of these boards entered into consent decrees agreeing to discontinue any schedule of commission rates and further agreeing that between brokers and owners, the commission rate should be negotiated. A related case, *Oglesby and Barclift, Inc. v. Metro MLS, Inc.*,[131] held MLS arrangements illegal; treble damages were awarded.

Where cooperation is outside of the multilisting organization, say non-realtor showing a REALTOR® listed property with consent of the REALTOR®, the problems can become more complicated, since the non-member broker is not bound by the rules of the multilisting organization.

---

[130] Campbell v. Grange, 23 D.& C. 2d 344 (1961).

[131] Oglesby and Barclift, Inc. v. Metro MLS, Inc., CCH TRR, Sec. 61,064 (Va. 1976).

When one real estate broker invites another broker to show property listed with him for sale and/or asks for help in selling it and the second broker sells it and collects the full commission, the first broker is entitled to a share of the commission. The second broker owes the first broker a duty of good faith and cannot place his interests ahead of the first broker.[132]

An agreement to divide a commission between two licensed brokers may be verbal.[133] Nor does the Statute of Frauds apply to the employment contract between broker and salespersons. It may be verbal,[134] although, for other reasons, such verbal employment might not be wise.

When one real estate broker sues another broker for a share of commissions after an agreement between them to that effect, the issue is not who was the "efficient and procuring cause" of the sale, but what were the terms of the agreement between the parties regarding a division of commissions earned. In the absence of an expressed contractual provision to the contrary, the commissions are to be shared equally, even though only one of the brokers did the major portion of the work.[135] In the DeBenedictis case the salesman's employment with the defendant was terminated on May 24, 1971. On April 27, 1971, he had arranged negotiations for the sale of certain restaurant property with a Mr. Zweben, a prospective purchaser. The quoted price was $850,000. The prospect offered $600,000. In the latter part of August 1971, the defendant negotiated further with Zweben, resulting in a sale for $625,000. The trial judge found that "if the plaintiff had not brought the parties together originally, the deal would never have been consummated," and awarded judgment to the plaintiff for 50 percent of the commission. The Appellate Court remanded the case to determine whether the salesperson-plaintiff action rested against the individual broker or the brokerage agency, of which corporation defendant was the president; and also *what* was the contract between them.

THE SALESPERSON'S RIGHT TO A COMMISSION

The situation frequently arises where a salesperson leaves a broker's employ after working on a deal with a prospect, and a sale is subsequently made, to that prospect. Is the salesperson entitled to a commission? The question depends upon the particular facts in the case. Pertinent facts would include the extent of the salesperson's activities in the transaction—was the deal "alive" and how long after the salesperson's departure were the agreements signed.[136] Clearly, if the agree-

---

[132]
Wheeler v. Waller, 197 N.E. 2d 585 (Iowa 1972).

[133]
J.A. Carter & Associates, Inc. v. Devore, 281 So. 2d 245 (Fla. App. 1973).

[134]
Fowler v. Taylor, 554 P. 2d 205 (Utah 1976).

[135]
DeBenedictis v. Gerechoff, 339 A. 2d 225 (N.J. App. 1975).

[136]
Clair v. Kall and Kall, Inc. N.Y. Misc. 2d (1960).

ments were signed before the salesperson left the broker's employ, but consummation occurred subsequent to his severance of employment, the salesperson is entitled to a commission.

Sometimes partners in a real estate firm agree to disagree and dissolve the firm. What happens in regard to commissions earned upon deals they were working on before the firm broke up? Here again, each case necessarily depends upon its particular facts. However, the case of *Pitt v. Kent*,[137] is illustrative of many similar situations. Pitt and Kent were partners in the real estate business. They were negotiating the sale of a large tract of land to Blitz and Price, but they could not obtain financing. Later, the real estate partnership was dissolved, but they agreed that if Blitz and Price bought the property, each would share equally in the commission.

An attorney obtained a group of investors to purchase the property, and later conveyed the property to Blitz and Price, at a profit. The court held that Pitt could recover one-half of the commission, as the transaction could be traced to the Blitz and Price original interest in the property while Pitt & Kent were partners.

Another situation develops where a salesperson's employer refuses to sue an owner, and the salesperson sues. In the case of *Turnblazer v. Smith*,[138] the Supreme Court refused recovery. It said,

> The real estate salesperson works merely for and under the control of the real estate broker and is engaged by and on behalf of a licensed real estate broker. Therefore, he works for the broker and does his bidding and is under his control. He does not perform services for others for which he may claim a commission.

WHO GETS THE MONEY WHEN A DEPOSIT IS FORFEITED BY THE BUYER?

Many listing contracts now in use provide "A deposit made, if forfeited by the buyer, shall first apply to the broker's commission, the balance, if any, shall belong to the owner."

While a broker is entitled to a return on his efforts, good conscience requires that it shall not be at the expense of an innocent principal. Suppose the clause in question is used and the broker obtains a purchase for the property at $100,000 and collects a deposit of $5,000. Later the buyer defaults and forfeits the deposit money. Should the broker be permitted to retain the entire amount on the grounds that the owner has a legal right to sue the defaulting buyer for specific performance, even though litigation may be futile? It is scarcely ethical that the broker keep all of the money and the owner be required to pursue litigation, entailing additional expense of cost and attorney's fees. In addition, the property may be tied up for a considerable period of time from the date from the date when the agreements were signed. Fair dealing requires that the down

---

137
   Pitt v. Kent, 179 A. 2d 626 (Conn. 1962).

138
   Turnblazer v. Smith, 379 S.W. 2d 772 (Tenn. 1964).

payment be divided equally between owner and broker, up to the amount where the broker receives full payment of his commission. A *common* provision used in the agreement of sale relative to the earnest money reads,

> Should the buyer fail to make settlement, as herein provided, the sum or sums paid on account of the purchase price, at the option of the seller, may be retained by the seller, either on account of the purchase price, the resale price, or as liquidated damages. In the latter case, the contract shall become null and void. In the latter event, all monies paid on account shall be divided equally between the seller and the broker, but in no event shall the sum paid to the broker be in excess of the amount of the commission due him.

Care must be exercised, however even with respect to the use of the above clause. In *Kulp Real Estate v. Rudolph Favoretto et ux.,*[139] the Court, following the landmark decision of the Dobbs case cited earlier, found such a clause in a listing agreement unenforceable and void against public policy. The Court found that there was ". . . a substantial inequality of bargaining position between the broker and vendors," because the broker was an experienced firm and the vendors, who had no prior real estate experience, signed the printed standardized form of brokerage agreement without benefit of counsel. While this holding may not be followed widely in other jurisdictions, it may be wise when employing such a clause to make sure that the client understands it before he signs the listing agreement.[140]

In the case of *Barry Norman Agency, Inc. of Morris County v. Elias,*[141] the broker sued the owner for the 7 1/2 percent commission, mentioned in the exclusive right to sell listing. The owner, in a telephone conversation, had revoked the listing 10 days after the listing was executed. The broker then decided "to let the listing run out." The broker did not advertise the property or show it to any prospective purchaser. It was sold through another broker. The Court stated that,

> the relationship between the broker and the seller has been characterized as one involving substantial inequality of bargaining power. Certainly it is a relationship that requires substantial scrutiny when brought before the Courts.[142]

The broker was entitled to such damages as he could prove, as well as the amount expected as a commission.

A BROKER MAY BE DENIED HIS COMMISSION IF HE FAILS IN HIS DUTY

A licensee must keep up with the applicable law that affects his employment. For example, the Texas license law *requires* a broker to advise a purchaser, in

---

[139] Kulp Real Estate v. Rudolph Favoretto et ux., 316 A. 2d 71 (N.J. 1974).

[140] House v. Erwin, 501 P. 2d 1221 (Wash. 1974).

[141] Barry Norman Agency, Inc. of Morris County v. Elias, 285 A. 2d 80 (N.J. 1971).

[142] Ellsworth Dobbs, Inc. v. Johnson, 236 A. 2d 843 (1967).

writing that the purchaser should have an abstract of the property examined by an attorney, or to be furnished with or obtain a policy of title insurance. Failure to comply precluded a broker from collecting a sales commission: *Jones v. Del Anderson and Associates.*[143]

The law is well settled that if a broker knows of any defect in the owner's title at the time he accepts a listing, or is aware of facts sufficient to put a reasonable prudent person on inquiry, he cannot collect a commission if he fails because of such defect.[144]

In the case of *Haymes v. Rogers,*[145] The plaintiff broker sued to collect a commission. The owner appealed a verdict in favor of the broker. After failing to sell the property at $9,500, the price originally listed with the broker, he stated to the purchaser his belief that the property could be bought for $8,500. After sale of the property for $8,500, the broker sued to recover his commission. The appellate court held, *as a matter of law,* plaintiff could not recover as there was a breach of fiduciary relationship. Mr. Justice Udall filed a vigorous dissenting opinion, in which he said,

> Will not the court's opinion be construed as holding that if a broker states to a purchaser or even indicates in any manner that property might be acquired for less than the listed price his right to a commission is thereby forfeited? If such be the declared law of this state, it will certainly give a wide avenue of escape for unscrupulous realty owners from paying what is justly owed to agents who have been the immediate and efficient cause of the sale of their property.
>
> It would be a most naive purchaser who would not know or assume that the owner of realty might sell for less than the original asking price.

A Louisiana case[146] is squarely opposed to the above decision. Other cases are in harmony with the Arizona decision, although other circumstances entered into the case, as where broker acted in his own interest, or withheld information from his principal.

In the case of *Heard, et al. v. Miles,*[147] two real estate brokers claimed a commission. The owner recognized the efforts of Joyner-Heard Realty Co., as procuring cause, but paid the money into the court, since there were two claims. The unsuccessful broker, Marx & Bensdorf, Inc., had negotiated three leases on the subject property. This broker also had negotiated several forbearance agreements on an existing mortgage. The last lease contained a *new* clause that a commission was to be paid "on any subsequent agreement to sell or exchange, made

---

[143] Jones v. Del Anderson and Associates, 539 S.W. 2d 348 (1976).

[144] Dail Realty v. Vodicka, 237 N.W. 2d 7 (S. Dak. 1975).

[145] Haymes v. Rogers, 319 P. 2d 339 (Ariz. 1950).

[146] Wolf v. Casamento, 185 So. 537 (1939).

[147] Heard, et al. v. Miles, 32 Tenn. 410 (1949).

with or through lessee." The property was sold to the tenant. No one ever called the owner's attention to the added clause. Although the court pointed out that the broker was not guilty of fraud, intentional bad faith or unfairness, it could not recover because it was the *duty* of the broker to disclose to its principal the provisions in the renewal lease for the benefit of the broker. The principle of disclosure, the court said, "is one of prevention, not remedial justice, which operates however fair the transaction may have been—however free from every taint of moral wrong."

If the suit had been between owner-lessor and the lessee, the *prime* parties to the lease, the owner would have been bound by the terms of the lease, whether she read it or understood it. But this was an action by an agent against his principal and the law is far more exacting.

In *Hughey v. Rainwater Partners,*[148] the court denied a broker his commission due to a breach of fiduciary duty to his client. The case revealed that a purchaser, through the defendant broker, made an offer to purchase plaintiff's home. The purchaser delivered a personal check as down payment in the amount of $5,000 and informed the broker that the check, at the time, would not clear. The plaintiff accepted the offer but was not informed that the check was known to not be good. The purchase agreement provided for retention of the down payment in the event of default. The deal failed and the plaintiff brought action against the broker for the $5,000 down payment. The broker was denied his agreed commission.

A broker with whom property is listed for sale must reveal to his owner the fact that he is to be a part purchaser of such property. In real estate parlance, this is where the broker "takes a piece of the action." His failure to do so will defeat his claim for a commission in the sale. In the case of *Thompson v. Hoagland,*[149] the court said,

> The broker was and is looked upon as a fiduciary and is required to exercise fidelity, good faith and a primary devotion to the interests of his principal . . .
> It is a corollary of the principal discussed above that the failure of the broker to inform the principal that the purchaser is an *alter ego* of the broker or a relative or partner renders the transaction voidable at the option of the principal.[150]

However, where the Court found that the broker had no interest in the corporation to which the property was conveyed, the broker could recover his commission on the sale.[151]

148
Hughey v. Rainwater Partners, 661 S.W. 2d 690 (Tenn. App. 1983).
149
Thompson v. Hoagland, 242 A. 2d 642 (N.J. 1968).
150
See also Brontonari v. Rollofo, 246 N.W. 2d 368 (Mich App. 1976).
151
Aeschlimann v. Rosbach, 558 P. 2d 1231 (Ore. 1977).

CAN AN AGENT APPOINT A SUBAGENT WITHOUT THE OWNER'S AUTHORITY?

Normally, an agent cannot appoint a subagent without the owner's authority, but in the case of property located out of state, it has been ruled by a South Dakota court,[152] that it is presumed the appointment of a subagent is necessary to facilitate the sale. In this case a broker sued for a commission. The defendant was a resident of Minnesota and owned a farm in Moody County, South Dakota. One Dwight Lloyd, an attorney in Flandreau, had authority to find a purchaser for the land and was acting as defendant's agent for that purpose. The plaintiff broker contacted the attorney and contends that Lloyd agreed that if the broker obtained a purchaser a commission would be paid to him. Later the broker obtained a prospect and negotiations were conducted with Lloyd but no sale resulted. Later the prospect saw Lloyd and rented the property for one year with an option to purchase. He later bought it. The court held that Lloyd was not authorized to hire a subagent at the expense of the defendant. There was nothing to show that the defendant had any knowledge that the plaintiff was the inducing cause of the sale, so there was no ratification by the seller. The case hung on the fact that where an owner knows that a broker, employed by him to sell land, has secured the services of a subagent by promising the subagent half of the commission from the owner and the owner assents thereto either expressly or by remaining silent, when it is his duty to object if he has an objection, the owner is directly liable to the subagent for his share of the commission. It should be noted that the case may have been decided differently if either of the states' (Minnesota and S. Dakota) license laws prevented the payment of out-of-state commissions.

COMMISSIONS ON LISTING WITH SPECIAL PERFORMANCE REQUIREMENTS

The amount of commission to be paid and/or conditions for payment are often made a part of the listing agreement. These provisions often result in disputes between brokers and sellers.

Where the owner has fixed a minimum net price, below which the agent may not sell the property, the question arises as to whether or not the broker is entitled to any excess realized over and above the net price. Let us assume that an owner has left property for sale with an broker, with the understanding that the property is not to be sold for less than $10,000, and the broker negotiates a sale at a price of $12,000. The question arises as to who is entitled to the excess $2,000. It must be remembered that the first duty an agent owes to his principal is that he must do everything legally possible to assert and protect the principal's interests; and so the courts have held that under the circumstances just outlined, the $2,000 belongs to

---

[152]
Croughaw v. Gerlach, 68 S.D. 93 (1941).

the owner. This is so unless it is *expressly* stipulated that the broker is to retain the excess as his commission. While net listings are used frequently, they are not looked upon with favor in good real estate circles. In fact, they are illegal in some jurisdictions.

Since it is agreed that the owner should receive the highest possible price for his property, a broker should look for his commission commensurate with his services. There is a creed that "labor is worthy of its hire." A broker who receives $1,200 commission (6 percent upon a $20,000 sale) has usually earned a fair return for his services. In a number of areas, consonant with inflation, the going rate of commission may be higher.

Where a property is listed with a broker upon a net listing basis of $30,000 and the broker obtains an offer of $37,500, it seems unconscionable that the broker will earn a 25 percent commission on the deal. Net listings, further, are conducive to fraud in that a broker is often sorely tempted to employ a straw purchaser and then resell the property at a handsome profit. Alabama, British Colombia, California, Georgia, Maryland, Michigan, Ontario, Tennessee, and Utah prohibit or regulate net listings.

In order for a broker to recover a commission under express contract requiring a net price to the owner, he must produce a purchaser at a price sufficiently in excess of the net price to cover his commission. An owner listed for sale with a broker certain real estate consisting of 13 houses. The owner wrote the broker, "I will think you may proceed and sell the entire 13 houses separately for $50,000 net cash to me. Your commission is 3 percent to come out of the last sale made." The houses were sold for an aggregate of $50,000. The owner refused to pay a commission and the broker sued for $1,500. The broker could not collect, because as the court stated,[153]

> Where one states to a broker that he will sell land for a certain sum "net" to him, the broker, on procuring a purchaser, is entitled to no commission unless the sum received exceeds the "net" price, the word "net" meaning that which remains after deducting all charges and outlay. We see no weakening of the effect of the word "net" by the words used in the communication which the prospective vendor sent to the broker, quoted above, that the commission was to come from the last sale made. The agreement was in writing and there was nothing in the case which would justify the departure from the evident purpose of the agreement that the vendor was to get $50,000 net cash, clear and above any commissions.

In another "net commission case," *Kerdyk v. Hammock Oaks Estates, Inc.,*[154] the broker who procured a buyer for a vacant tract of land at $50,000, was told the figure was to be a net price, after commissions. The broker disclaimed any net price

---

[153] Fink v. Dougherty, 90 Pa. Super. 443 (1927).

[154] Kerdyk v. Hammock Oak Estates, Inc., 342 So. 2d 833 (Fla. App. 1977).

agreement. The offer was refused. Three days later, the defendant conveyed the property to the sister-in-law of the president of the defendant's corporation. The same day, she conveyed the property to the broker's purchaser for $50,000. The Court held that the broker was entitled to a 10 percent commission on the sale.

In another case, *Quality Home Builders v. Harrick*,[155] an owner listed property for sale with a broker for $455,000 "net." The sale was ultimately consummated at $455,000, but the defendant refused to pay any commission to the plaintiff broker. The Court held that there was a special contract between the broker and owner predicated upon the consummation by the broker of a sale at the net price named. Since no sum was received over and above the net price designated, the broker could not recover a commission.

A broker may, by special agreement with his principal, contract to make his compensation depend upon the actual signing of the contract, or upon the actual passing of title, or other contingency.[156] Even under these conditions, a broker may recover his commission at the time fixed in the contract of sale if it develops that the negotiations fall through by reason of some defect in the title of the seller, or upon some arbitrary refusal of the seller to go through with the deal. The owner is not permitted to plead that his failure to consummate the transaction will operate to deprive the broker of his commission.

A broker who has earned his commission is generally not bound by any subsequent agreement that no commission is to be paid until the deed passes, for such an agreement is without consideration and cannot affect the obligation of the owner to the broker (in the listing contract); and the agreement is not more binding when it recites a nominal consideration or good and valuable considerations when in fact, none passed. The fact that the seller refused to make the contract unless the broker agreed to wait for his commission until the deal was closed has been said not to furnish sufficient consideration. If the agreement of sale provides that the broker's commission is to be paid *at settlement,* the contract means exactly what it states, and if the settlement does not materialize, the broker is not entitled to a commission, nor is this clause to be interpreted to mean that the commission to be paid when settlement *should have* taken place.

In the case of *Jones v. Palace Realty Co.*,[157] the Court held under contract for payment of commission to broker out of sales price of property,

> When the deal is closed up, he could not recover when the deal was never closed due to inability of the purchaser to comply. It was the actual event of closing the deal and not the date of its expected closing or contemplated happening that made the promise to pay enforceable.

155
Quality Home Builders v. Harrick, 173 S.E. 2d 846 (Va. 1970).
156
Gaynor v. Laverdure, 291 N.E. 2d 617 (Mass. 1973).
157
Jones v. Palace Realty Co., 226 N.C. 303 (1946).

To the same effect is the case of *Kostan v. Glasier*,[158] where the commission was "payable only when and if deal is finally closed." It is a well-settled law that language in an agreement of sale that a commission to the broker "payable when title closes, or upon delivery of deed" does not constitute a condition precedent for payment of commission, but rather the *time* when the commission is to be paid to the broker. However, the broker and owner may, by expressed language, make the broker's right to a commission depend upon a future happening, such as actual passage of title from seller to buyer. If the contingency does not materialize, it is fatal to the broker's claim for a commission.[159]

A clause that states "commission to be paid on the sale" is strictly construed. No actual sale-no commission. The Çourt so held in the case of *Tristam's Landing, Inc. v. Wait*.[160] In this case the agreement of sale provided that the commission was to be paid to the broker "on said sale." The buyer defaulted and the broker sued the seller. The Court construed this language as requiring that the said sale be consummated before the commission was earned. The same result follows where the agreement provides "no commission becomes due until the customer actually takes a conveyance and pays therefor." [161]

Also where an agreement of sale provides that the broker is not entitled to his commission until conditions are performed, the broker has no claim for commission until such condition is satisfied. This principle applies with equal force to oral and written brokerage contracts.[162]

In the case of *Richard v. Falletti*,[163] suit was brought by the broker to recover the unpaid half of a broker's commission earned on the sale of defendant's land. The lower court rendered judgment for defendant on ground that plaintiff's right was contingent on delivery of deed, which had not taken place. The Superior Court, Appellate Division, reversed, holding that obligation to pay full commission was not contingent on delivery of deed, and that broker completed performance, and earned commission, when he induced purchaser to sign a sales agreement.

A recent test of commission due, when the listing agreement modified the normal pay-out procedure with a clause saying the commission was to be paid from the "proceeds at closing" was the 1989 case of *Chamberlain v. Porter*.[164] The deal

---

[158] Kostan v. Glasier, 60 N.W. 2d 283 (1953).

[159] Amies v. Wesnofske, 174 N.E. 436 (N.Y. 1931).

[160] Tristam's Landing, Inc. v. Wait, 327 N.E. 2d 727 (Mass. 1975).

[161] Gaynor v. Laverdure, 291 N.E. 2d 617 (Mass 1973).

[162] Dixon v. Andres Tile & Mfg. Corp., 357 A. 2d 667 (Pa. 1976) and Stovall Realty & Insurance Co., v. Goff, 159 S.E. 467 (Ga. 1968).

[163] Richard v. Falletti, 13 N.J. Sup. 534 (1951).

[164] Chamberlain v. Porter, 562 A. 2d 675 (Me. 1989).

failed to close and the seller refused to pay. The Court ruled that since there was no closing and no proceeds, no commission was payable.

In a 1983 Arizona case, the subject of clearly defined commission rate in the listing agreement arose. In *Broadway Realty Trust, Inc. v. Gould,*[165] the Court clearly stated the requirement for a listing agreement to define the commission to be paid. Words such as "usual fee" and "standard fee" do not satisfy the requirements of the statute of frauds. The listing agreement provided, "In event the property is sold by the owner, owner agrees to pay a commission to the management pursuant in accordance with local real estate board commission schedule (or if none, the going rate in the area). The owner sold the property and refused to pay a commission. The court found that there was no real estate board commission schedule and the provisions of "usual" or "legal rate of commission" was insufficient to satisfy the requirement of the statute of frauds.

COMMISSION PAYMENTS PROBLEMS ON "EXTENDER CLAUSE" SALES

The extender clause in an exclusive right to sell listing provides protection to the broker if the property is sold by the owner to a prospect procured by the broker; within a specified period of time *after* the expiration of the original listing period. Many words are used in an endeavor to make the broker's entitlement to a commission effective, such as if the property is sold to anyone, to whom said property was "submitted" by said broker; to whom said property was "shown"; to whom the property had "been introduced"; to any person with whom the broker had "negotiated"; placed the owner "in touch with"; had "contact with", or the like. Should a sale result during the extender period, under any of the above terms, the broker would have his "foot in the door" so to speak, for a commission claim.

The word "negotiated" is used extensively, and in some areas, the following words are added: "and whose names have been filed with me on or before the expiration of the original listing." In the case of *Advance Realty Co. v. Spanos,*[166] the Court held that the words "to produce" a purchaser meant "to bring forth" or to be the cause of the sale.

Where the term (extender) of the listing has expired, the owner in the absence of fraud or bad faith, may contract with a prospect "introduced by the broker" within the period of performance, either upon the same terms or upon others, more or less favorable than those the broker was authorized, *without suffering any liability to compensate the latter for his services.*[167] In the case of *Bonn v. Summers,*[168] the

165
Broadway Realty Trust, Inc. v. Gould, 136 Ariz. 236, 555 P. 2d 580 (1983).
166
Advance Realty Co. v. Spanos, 348 Mich. 464 (1957).
167
Everson v. Phelps, 115 Oregon 523; Schmidt, Inc. v. Brock, 97 Ohip App. 469 (1953).
168
Bonn v. Summers, 249 N.C. 357 (1950).

listing contract involved required names of prospects shown the property to be filed within three days after the listing expired.

In the case of *E.M. Boerke, Inc. v. Williams,*[169] a property was listed exclusively with a broker, to remain in effect until January 15, 1957. It contained a 6-months' extender clause. The listing provided that the broker was to receive a commission if the property was sold during the extender period "to anyone with whom you negotiated during the life of this contract, and whose name you have filed with me in writing prior to the termination of this contract." On January 15, 1957, the plaintiff mailed a list of names (including name of the ultimate purchaser) to the defendants in Florida. The letter from the broker did not reach the defendants until after January 15, 1957. The plaintiff contended that the contract expired at midnight on January 15, 1957, so that the mailing was timely. The defendants argued that the contract expired 24 hours earlier. The court held that any ambiguity should be resolved against the broker, who prepared the listing contract. Also, that the mailing on January 15 did not satisfy the (time) requirement that the notice be "filed with me." The court said,

> To construe or define *mailing* as *filing* is to ignore the proper meaning of the word. Mailing merely initiates the process by which an article in the due course of the post will be delivered. The requirement of the contract in question is that the notice be filed or delivered to the party offering the property for sale.

In the case of *McGuire v. Sinnett,*[170] a broker had a listing contract that expired on August 23, 1936. A salesperson for the broker showed the property to a prospect before the listing expired. A second broker advertised the property after the listing expired and on September 1, 1936, the same prospect made an offer to purchase the property through the second broker and the deal closed. The first broker sued the owner for a commission, contending that he was protected for 90 days under a clause in his listing contract which provided that the owner would pay a commission if the broker placed the owner "in touch with a buyer to or whom, within 90 days after the expiration hereof, I (seller), may sell, exchange or convey said property." The Supreme Court permitted the broker to recover, stating:

> In the case before us, the broker is entitled to a commission in one of the three following instances: (1) If he found a buyer ready and willing to enter into a contract with the defendant on terms and price agreed to by the defendant; (2) if he placed the defendant in touch with a buyer to whom the defendant sold the property during the life of the contract or within 90 days after the expiration thereof; or (3) if he was the procuring cause of the sale.

The broker was entitled to the commission upon proving that he placed a

---

[169] E.M. Boerk, Inc. v. Williams, 137, N.W. 2d 489 (Wisc. 1965).

[170] McGuire v. Sinnett, 158 Ore. 390 (1938).

purchaser in touch with the seller during the term of the listing and the buyer consummated the deal within 90 days from the expiration date of the listing.

In all of these cases, it must be realized that the language of the listing contract is important. "In touch with" or "in contact with" is far different from "whom the broker had been negotiating." To negotiate means more than merely submitting or showing the property to a prospective purchaser. In the case of *Kalna v. Fialko*,[171] the court held that "to negotiate" means to transact business, to procure, to induce, to treat with another respecting a purchase or sale. In the 1968 case, *King v. Dean*,[172] the court stated that "negotiation is not a single act, but a process. It involves a dialogue or back-and-forth communication with a purpose; in this case, to sell real estate." The plaintiff also admitted that the owners were not informed that he had engaged in discussions with the buyers. In the case of *United Farms of Wisconsin, Inc. v. Klasen*,[173] the court ruled that the term "with whom the broker negotiated" in a listing agreement is to be accepted in its *broadest interpretation*.

Negotiations require that efforts of the broker to interest a prospect must have proceeded to a point where the prospect is considered a likely purchaser.[174]

The case of *Nichols v. Pendley*[175] involved a suit for a real estate commission. On March 2, 1958, the parties entered into a written contract whereby the owners appointed the broker as an exclusive agent for a period of two weeks to sell their residence at a price of $8,750. The contract further provided that "if this property is sold during the time of this agreement is in force, or if sold to anyone to whom said property was submitted by Nichols Agency within three months from the termination date hereof, then in that event the undersigned shall pay to said Nichols Agency, broker, 5 percent of the sales price as his commission due." It was admitted that within the two weeks exclusive period, a salesperson of the broker offered the property to the Woolevers for sale and took them through the house. They made an offer. The owners were present at the time. A sale was made to the Woolevers during the 90-day period following the expiration of the original term. The case turned on the interpretation of the word "submitted." The Court stated,

> The defendants contend that the word "submitted" means that the efforts of the broker must have proceeded to the point where the Woolevers were *likely purchasers*. Other cases cited referred to "negotiating." It has been held generally that "negotiating" implies a situation where the interest of the buyers has been aroused to the point that the purchaser may be considered a likely purchaser. Negotiations implies a discussion of terms, a bargaining. It is generally used in connection with the *consummation* of business matters. The word "submitted" means to leave or commit to the discretion of another.

---

[171] Kalna v. Fialko, 125 N.E. 2d 565 (1955).

[172] King v. Dean, 238 N.E. 2d 828 (Ohio 1968).

[173] United Farms of Wisconsin, Inc. v. Klasen, 112 Wisc. 2d 634, 334 N.W. 2d 110 (1983).

[174] Jessup v. LaPin, 150 N.W. 2d 342 (Wisc. 1967).

[175] Nichols v. Pendley, 331 S.W. 2d 673 (Mo. 1960).

The Court stated,

> It is a closed question. The acts of the plaintiff went far enough to fulfill the terms of the contract. But we are of the opinion that under the facts of this case plaintiff "submitted" the property to the purchasers within the exclusive period when it offered defendant's property to the Woolevers for sale and took them through the house in the presence of the defendants.

The broker recovered.

In a later case in Wisconsin, the term "anyone with whom the broker negotiated" was defined.[176] The case involved the provisions of the listing which provided for a commission if the seller sold "to anyone with whom the broker negotiated, during the term of the listing and whose name was submitted in writing before expiration of the listing." When the property was sold, a one-half interest to the seller's daughter and son in-law and the other half interest to one of the listed parties, the Court held that the language "anyone with whom the broker negotiated" was sufficiently broad to include the daughter and husband.

Failure to furnish the owner with a copy of the list of clients introduced to or taken through the property may not be fatal to the broker's recovery of a commission as in the case of *Fleetham v. Schneekloth*.[177]

In the case of *Dean v. King Service*,[178] a broker had an exclusive listing. He showed the property to a prospect on June 4, 1966. After the extender period expired, another broker showed the property to the same prospect on July 20, 1966. The property was deeded to that prospect on August 12, 1966. The first broker sued for a commission and won the case in the lower court. The Court of Appeals affirmed. However, the supreme court reversed. It held that,

> The law imposes upon an agent a duty to report his negotiations with prospective purchasers to his principal, especially where he expects to rely upon those negotiations as a basis for collecting a commission on the sale of their property after the expiration of the exclusive listing.

SPECIAL COMMISSION PROBLEMS INVOLVING LEASES

Most exclusive listings relate to a sale or exchange of an owner's property, but are silent as to the broker's right to a commission, if the owner and the broker's prospect sign a lease during the exclusive period of the listing, with an option to purchase. The parties may wait until the broker's listing has expired and then enter into a contract of sale during the term of the lease, circumventing the broker's commission.

In the case of *Cunningham v. Aeschliman*,[179] a seller and a prospect obtained

---

[176] United Farm of Wisconsin, Inc. v. Klasen, 112 Wis. 2d 634, 334 N.W. 2d 110 (1983).

[177] Fleetham v. Schneekloth, 52 Wash. 2d 176 (1958).

[178] Dean v. King Service, 249 N.E. 2d 45 (Ohio 1969).

[179] Cunningham v. Aeschliman, 296 N.E. 2d 326 (Ill. 1973).

by a broker entered into an option to purchase. This option was executed during the period of the broker's listing. The property was leased to the optionee. During the lease term, the property was sold by the owner to the broker's prospect. The Court permitted a commission recovery on the sale.

Dealing in options is a recognized real estate activity, and while many options are negotiated, a much smaller number of options are exercised. Unless the agreement between owner and broker provides for payment of a commission based upon money paid for the option, the broker is not entitled to a commission. It is the date when the option is exercised, rather than the date the formal agreements are executed, that determines the broker's right to a commission. Of course, the date the option is exercised must be before the option has expired.[180]

COMMISSION PAYMENTS ON CANCELLATION OF A LEASE

The question frequently arises as to the broker's right to collect commissions upon the unexpired term of a lease negotiated by the broker. The problem usually arises when the lease is terminated by a sale or where the management of the property is taken out of the broker's hands before the expiration of the lease term. Thus, two different situations are presented. In the first case, assume that the lease has been negotiated by the broker for a three-year period and the lease contains the provision that it can be terminated in the event of a sale of the property upon the owner giving the tenant 60 days' notice in writing. Suppose at the end of one year, the owner makes a bona fide sale and gives the tenant the required notice. The broker is obviously not entitled to a commission on the rent for the remaining 22 months since he negotiated the lease and is cognizant of the lease provisions. His remaining commission is contingent upon the tenant remaining in possession during the *entire* three-year period.

In the second case, where no sales clause is contained in the lease and the owner sells the property subject to the existing lease, the situation is different. Upon negotiation of the lease by the broker, he becomes entitled to a commission for the full period of the lease. Where the new owner takes the property out of the broker's hands, his rights against the original owner continue unabridged. However, custom, as evidenced by the practice among brokers or under the rules of the real estate board, may permit a reduction of the full amount of commission under these circumstances.

In the case of *Percy Galbreath & Son, Inc. v. Dehyco Co., Inc. et al.,*[181] the broker negotiated the lease for a five-year term. The lease included a provision wherein the lessor agreed to pay the broker "the usual commission for any subsequent lease that may be entered into by the Lessor and Lessee." A new lease was negotiated between the parties in 1974, after the expiration of the first five-year

---

180
Anthony v. Enzler, 132 Cal Rptr. 553 (1976).

181
Percy Galbreath & Sons, Inc. v Dehyco Co., Inc. et al., 548 S.W. 2d 664 (Tenn. App. 1976).

lease. In a suit for commission under the new lease, the broker was denied a commission. The Court said,

> There is no proof of what a *usual commission* was at the date of the original lease; nor, on the date of the new lease. . . . The plaintiff cannot prevail, having failed to prove the amount of commission to which he is entitled.

In the case of *Rosenfield v. Cadence Industries Corp.*,[182] the landlord *negotiated* the termination of a lease with the tenant, which still had 5 years and 6 months to run. The lease provided that the landlord would pay the broker a 5 percent commission on all rents collected. The lease also provided that no commission would be paid, if the lease was terminated by bankruptcy of the tenant, assignment for benefit of creditors, or destruction of premises by fire or other casualty. The court held that the broker was entitled to a commission for the unexpired term of the lease.

A broker's right to a commission is strengthened where the lease agreement states that the broker negotiated the sale or lease. It is fairly customary for an agreement of sale to state that "the Brookline Realty Co. negotiated the sale and the seller agrees to pay it a commission of 7 percent on the sale price," but is the same situation meaningful in the case of a lease agreement? In either case, the broker is a third party to the agreements. There are supreme court cases in Pennsylvania and Virginia which hold that the clause is meaningful and support a claim for commission. Both cases *arose in connection with such a clause in a lease.* In the case of *Richard B. Herman and Co. v. Stern*,[183] the plaintiff broker sued for a commission on the sale of certain business property, upon a clause in the lease negotiated by the broker that in the event the property were sold to the tenant, the broker would be entitled to a commission. The Court said,

> Appellant (Stern) obliges himself in clear and unambiguous language, for a recited consideration to the broker, under seal, to pay specific commissions. That this particular agreement is contained in the lease agreement between lessor, appellant and lessee, Sailor, is neither unusual nor legally objectionable. Its presence in the document can be only to create a binding agreement between principal, appellant and the agent, appellee, who signed as agent, for those commissions. Otherwise, its existence cannot be rationally explained. There is no legal or logical reason for prohibiting its inclusion of such promise. It is a practical manner of handling an everyday business matter in an efficient and legally effective manner, avoiding the necessity of other separate contracts.

To the same effect is the decision in the case of *W.D. Nelson & Co. Inc. v. Taylor Heights Development Corp.*[184]

182
Rosenfield v. Cadence Industries Corp., 348 N.Y.S. 2d 523 (1973).

183
Richard B. Herman and Co.v. Stern, 419 Pa. 272 (1965).

184
W.D. Nelson & Co. Inc. v. Taylor Heights Development Corp., 207 Va. 386 (1966).

COMMISSION PAYMENTS ON AN INSTALLMENT PURCHASE CONTRACT SALE

Sometimes, in an installment contract, the broker receives his commission as the installments are paid. In the case of *Hussey v. Stephens,*[185] the broker negotiated a sale of a motel for the sellers, who obtained a purchase money mortgage for $335,000, payable in annual installments of $25,000, in three payments of $8,333.33 each. The broker's commission was $10,000, with $2,000 paid at the time of sale and the balance at the rate of $727.27, beginning September 1, 1969, each time a $25,000 payment was made. The buyer made two annual payments, but on April 30, 1971, reconveyed the motel to the sellers for $30,000 and cancellation of the mortgage. The broker then sued for the balance of his commission. The Supreme Court held that the reconveyance of the property to the sellers did not constitute acceleration of the commission upon satisfaction of the mortgage, and reversed the lower court's award of commission.

A situation could arise where, under such installment contracts, the contract is rescinded before maturity, and in consideration of the return of the property the seller forgoes the remaining payments. As a cautionary measure, the listing agreement should anticipate this possibility and the broker should protect himself accordingly.[186]

COMMISSIONS ON NON-CASH SALES

Sometimes a broker, employed to sell real estate for a corporation, will procure a purchaser who agrees to accept the transfer of stock of the corporation, representing the purchase price for the property, instead of a deed. The broker is, nevertheless, entitled to a commission, despite the fact that there is a transfer of personal property rather than the conveyance of real estate. Where a corporation sells corporate stock, representing the value of real estate sold through the broker, and said stock is transferred to the buyer, the broker is entitled to his commission on the sale of the shares of stock.[187]

In the case of *Lyons v. Stevenson,*[188] the Court held that a licensed real estate broker who is not licensed as a securities broker may recover a commission, although he knows that the transaction will result in transfer of securities, if such transfer is *incidental* to the sale of the realty. See also *Baird & Wagner, Inc. v. Rudd.*[189]

---

[185] Hussey v. Stephens, 194 S.E. 2d 243 (S.C. 1973).

[186] Larkins v. Richardson, 502 P. 2d 1156 (Ore. 1972).

[187] Heymann v. Electric Service Mfg. Co. Inc., 194 A. 2d 429 (Pa. 1963).

[188] Lyons v. Stevenson, 135 Cal. Rptr. 457 (1977).

[189] Baird & Wagner, Inc. v. Rudd, 359 N.E. 2d 745 (Ill. App. 1976).

TRADE-INS, A NEW WAY TO EARN A COMMISSION

A new role for the broker is as a dealer in trade-in property. This has become even more important during a recessionary period when it is difficult to move listed property. Owners, during these periods, who desire to change properties or trade-up to a higher quality home, can often be persuaded to take the plunge where the broker will guarantee the sale of their current residence prior to closing on the new one.

This procedure can best be explained by an example. Mr. & Mrs. Adams contact a broker about a new home they have recently seen at the local "Parade of Homes." Their question is, "How good a chance do we have to sell our present home before we would have to close on the new on." The broker smelling a big sale and a good listing agrees to list the Adams' residence for the agreed price of $100,000 with the stipulation that if he is unable to find a buyer in 90 days, he will purchase the home himself at a price of 15 percent below the listed price. The broker is also to collect his normal 6 percent commission on the sale to himself.

The Adams then make an offer on the new home through their listing broker with a closing date set at 90 days from acceptance. If the broker is able to move the old home in the 90 days, he makes his usual 6 percent commission and is off the hook. If he is forced to buy the Adams' home at the end of 90 days, he has the 15 percent discount plus his 6 percent commission to work with. His only problem is to assure a sale before the 6 percent commission for the sale to himself plus the 15 percent discount plus the new commission of 6 percent on the resale of the Adams' old home, exceeds the use of his money in buying the property. This is not too great a risk for the total commission and discount amount of approximately $25,000 ($15,000 discount + 6 percent of $85,000 + 6 percent of $100,000 resale price) will support a $85,000 loan @ 12 percent rate for about 28 months. If he has properly appraised the value of the old Adams' home, there is little risk in losing and a good chance for a handsome profit.

The collection of two commissions (on sale to himself and on resale) was ruled legal in the 1908 case of *Jones v. Howard.*[190]

CONDEMNED PROPERTY IS NOT A SALE

Where property listed for sale is condemned before being sold, the owner's transfer of title does not constitute a sale for commission purposes.[191]

---

[190] Jones v. Howard, 234 Ill. (1908).

[191] Lundstrom, Inc. v. Nikkei Concerns, Inc. 788 P.2d 561 (Wash Ct. App. 1988).

5

Broker Relationships

The broker walks a tightrope in his relationships with three groups of people. First, he deals with the property owners to obtain listing agreements. In this capacity the broker acts as a principal party in contracting with property owners to obtain a buyer who is ready willing and able. The law is rather limited and very specific in regards to those duties.

Second, he must deal with buyers. In most situations he represents the seller as he shows the listed property to his prospects. At times, he may also represent the buyer when showing listings of other brokers. In this respect he is forbidden to serve two masters and must advise the property owner if he wishes to represent the buyer instead of the owner.

Third, he must recruit, train, and supervise the agents licensed to him. Their every action or lack of action is his responsibility. Licensed agents may serve as employees of the broker or as, in the majority of cases, independent contractors.

While there are many segments to the real estate business, most brokers concentrate their activities on real estate brokerage. It may be said that brokerage is the heart of the real estate business. Although those working in the real estate business consider themselves as professionals, real estate has been legally defined as a business and not a profession.[1]

WHEN IS AN AGENT AN EMPLOYEE

Agent employees are paid for their services on the basis of salary, salary plus commission, or commission only. As an employee he is responsible to the broker as to his hours of work, when he is expected to be in the office, and in the specific manner of his work performance. As an employee, he receives some advantages not available to the independent contractor. First of all, the broker is responsible

---

[1] Hackett v. Gale, 179 A. 2d 451, New Hampshire Supreme Court (1962).

for paying the employer's portion of social security taxes and for deducting the proper amount for the employees portion and for an additional amount representing income withholding taxes. The broker also provides unemployment insurance through the state employment agency and pays workmans' compensation insurance on behalf of this employee. In addition the broker may also elect to provide all or some portion of the employee's medical coverage and in some instances a retirement plan in the form of a pension or profit sharing plan. For all practical purposes the agent is treated the same as a clerk or bookkeeper in the office.

Most brokers prefer to have their agents work as independent contractors as it relieves them of social security and workmans' compensation payment and the administrative details of payroll withholding. In determining whether a salesperson is in fact an employee or independent contractor, the IRS has set some very firm requirements. First, it is absolutely essential that the independent contractor performs under a *written* contract. In this respect it is not the form of this agreement but the substance of it that controls. Naturally, the IRS would prefer that all salespersons work as employees.

Although the independent contractor performs the same kinds of services as the employee agent, his work habits are his own and may not be dictated by the broker. He may be requested to cover the phone or office but he may not be *required* to do so. The independent contractor may be furnished a desk in the brokerage office, provided training classes which he may or may not elect to attend, and is expected to abide by rules and regulations of the brokerage office. He pays his own social security taxes as an independent contractor and has no company paid insurance or retirement plans. The independent contractor is paid for his services by sharing in commission fees he earns for the brokerage. His cut of the pie is normally from 40 to 90 percent of his total commission contributions to the brokerage. The less supervision required and the greater his sales are the determining factors as to the percentage of commissions he takes home. A well trained agent with a history of substantial sales over the years may be able to command as much as a 80-90 percent commission share. In this case the agent is usually expected to pay for the advertising of his listed properties and any long-distance phone calls he makes on the office lines.

Some employment contracts provide that if a salesperson is discharged or resigns, he will not engage in real estate activity as a broker, or salesperson for another broker, within a certain area of the first broker's office or branch office, for a certain period of time. If such restraint of trade is reasonable, *as to area and time,* it will be upheld.

THE INDEPENDENT CONTRACTOR STATUS IS CONSTANTLY UNDER ATTACK

An early case in support of the independent contractor status was *Dimmitt-Rickhoff-Bayer Real Estate Co., v. Finnegan.*[2] In that case, the court held that

---

[2]

Dimmitt-Rickhoff-Bayer Real Estate Co., v. Finnegan, 179 F. 2d 882 (Mo. 1950).

salespeople for the plaintiff broker were not required to report to the broker's office daily, or at weekly sales meetings and were not required to keep fixed hours. The plaintiff made available office facilities and listings, assisted salesmen, divided commissions and furnished a booklet of general instructions. These facts did not constitute salespeople as "employees" of the plaintiff, so as to make remuneration of the salesmen subject to federal employment taxes.

In the case of *Bidwell v. Iowa Employment Security Commission*,[3] which involved an alleged nonpayment under the Iowa Employment Security law, the commission ruled that the salesman was an independent contractor in which the broker was obligated to pay the agreed-upon commission, when received by the broker.

A more recent court opinion also favors the independent contractor concept in the case of *Dept. of Employment v. Bake Young Realty*.[4] In reversing the Industrial Commission, the Supreme Court held that "real estate" salespeople are engaged in an independent occupation and thus are not "covered" employees for the purpose of the state's Employment Security Act. The court also relied upon the rationale in the case of *California Employment Stabilization Commission v. Morris*[5] which also involved a real estate salesperson; *Moore v. Idaho Employment Security Agency*,[6] involving a salesperson selling shares in mutual funds. The Idaho court subscribed to the view, espoused in the case of *Realty Mortgage and Sales Co. v. Oklahoma Employment Security Commission*,[7] that the association of broker and salesperson "is in the nature of a joint venture, in which each party to the arrangement makes certain contributions and performs certain services in order to produce a result mutually profitable to them . . . Each performs his function and receives his remuneration, not from the other, but from a third party. . . ."

Contrary to the above views, it has been contended that certain criteria establish that, in fact, the salesperson is an employee; to wit, the real estate license is in the custody of the broker, displayed in the broker's office; renewal of the license is handled by the broker; very often the salesperson has a drawing account; transfer of license from one broker to another broker by approval of the Real Estate Commission stymies the salesperson's freedom of doing business with brokers at large and initially, the salesperson must obtain recommendations of the particular broker with whom he will be associated exclusively.

A case that adopts the employer-employee rule is the case of *Hughes v.*

---

[3] Bidwell v. Iowa Employment Security Commission, (1973).

[4] Dept. of Employment v. Bake Young Realty, 560 P. 504 (Idaho 1977).

[5] California Employment Stabilization Commission v. Morris, 172 P. 2d 497 (1946).

[6] Moore v. Idaho Employment Security Agency, 367 P. 2d 291 (1961).

[7] Realty Mortgage and Sales Co. v. Oklahoma Employment Security Commission, 169 P. 2d 761 (Okla. 1946).

Industrial Commission,[8] holding that real estate sales persons are employees for the purposes of the Workmans' Compensation Act. In its decision the court emphasized that it is in the "right" to control and not the "exercise" of control that determines the status.

It appears that the employee/employer v. independent contractor controversy is likely to continue as states and the federal government become more anxious to raise their revenues. It is recommended that brokers now in the business and those just entering the business seek competent legal advice prior to employing agents. As pointed out above, a *written contract with the salesperson is a must.* In addition the specific wording in regards to duties must be carefully reviewed.

In preparing personnel contracts care should be exercised to assure that the broker is not liable for automobile accidents in which their salespersons may be involved and to assure that each agent is adequately insured for personal and property liability damage.

REALTORS® AND REALTOR-ASSOCIATES®

A REALTOR® is a licensed principal broker who is a member of his local real estate board, the state, and NATIONAL ASSOCIATION OF REALTORS.® A REALTOR-ASSOCIATE® is a licensed real estate agent, licensed to a principal broker and who is a member of his local real estate board, the state, and NATIONAL ASSOCIATION OF REALTORS.® The term other REALTOR® is a term sometimes used to define a licensed broker member who is not the principal broker of an organization but one who performs the same duties as an associate.

Applicants for membership in REALTOR® Boards must possess the required state licenses and pass an indoctrination course, which covers the policies, rules, and regulations of the local board, State Association and the National Association including the Code of Ethics of the National Association. A board of REALTORS® may require an applicant to meet the 8-point Membership Qualification Criteria of the National Association, if the applicant is applying for REALTOR® (principal) Membership. A Board of REALTORS® may require an applicant for membership to meet the 6-point Membership Qualification Criteria if an applicant is applying for REALTOR® (non-principal) Membership or REALTOR-ASSOCIATE® Membership.

In some localities attempts have been made to exclude certain licensed brokers and salesmen from membership in the local boards. In the case of *Marin County Board of Realtors v. Palson,*[9] the court ruled that California's Cartwright Anti-trust law forbids exclusion of part time brokers from REALTOR® Boards and multilist services; however, they may be excluded for cause. In a related case, *Guadango v. Mount Pleasant Listing Exchange, Inc.,*[10] the court held that residency

---

[8] Hughes v. Industrial Commission, 551 P. 2d 962 (Ariz. App. 1976).

[9] Marin County Board of Realtors v. Palson, 549 P. 2d 833 (1976).

[10] Guadango v. Mount Pleasant Listing Exchange Inc., CCH TRR Section 61, 065 (N.Y. 1976).

time limits are not in violation of N.Y. General Business Law. The board, in this case, had required the broker to maintain an office in the community for at least one year in order to be eligible for membership in the multilist service.

THE PRINCIPAL-AGENT RELATIONSHIP

If a real estate broker is to discharge his responsibilities which devolve from his office, it is necessary that he have a knowledge of certain cardinal and fundamental principles of law that affect the everyday practice of his business. Real estate brokerage *represents a combination of the principles of law of principal and agent and the law of contracts.* A real estate broker is an agent in the fullest sense of the word, in that he represents another from whom he derives his authority. A broker occupies a position of trust and confidence towards his principal and there are certain basic duties that every agent owes his principal. These are:

- Duty of loyalty.
- He must obey the instructions of his principal.
- He must not be negligent.
- He must act in person and cannot delegate his authority.
- He must account for money and property.

Good faith, loyalty, and fidelity are not a one-way street. The same virtues expected of the broker also apply to his principal, the property owner. This "other side of the coin" will be fully explored later in this chapter.

THE DUTY OF BROKER LOYALTY

The broker must be loyal to the trust of his principal. An agent cannot so exercise his duties as to garner a profit for himself at the expense of his principal. The courts have decided that in order for a broker to be loyal to his trust he must not sell himself, purchase for himself, or purchase from himself, unless the owner agrees. Where a property is listed with a broker for sale, it is the duty of the broker to determine a fair market value for that property and list it at that price. A broker will not be permitted to purchase a property, which has been listed with him, where he feels that the list price is below the normal market price and purchases it either in his own name or in the name of another person in trust for himself, and then resells the property at a profit. The reason for this rule is interestingly given in a New Jersey case in which the Court said as follows:

> Owing to the greed and selfishness of human nature there must, in the great mass of transactions, be a strong antagonism between the interest of the seller and the buyer, and universal experience shows that the average man, when his interests conflict with his employer's, will not look upon his employer's interests as more important and entitled to more consideration than his own.

In the Missouri case of *Blakeley v. Bradley et al.*,[11] The Supreme Court extended the principal that a broker should not purchase a property listed with himself unless this fact is made known to his principal in advance, to include also the broker's employees and their near relatives.

In a 1956 test of this principal a case involving a vacant lot in Kansas City, Mo. was listed with a broker and was sold a few days later to a "straw" party, for the real party in interest, a medical clinic. Three days later the "straw" party deeded the property to the clinic. In a suit for commission, these facts being established, a recovery was denied: *King v. Pruitt.*[12]

In the Maryland case of *Yerkie v. Salsbury,*[13] the Court pointed out that when a seller employs a broker to sell his property, he bargains for the disinterested skill, diligence and zeal of the broker for his (seller's) own exclusive benefit.

In construing loyalty, the courts have held that a real estate broker may not have a secret personal interest in the subject matter of his employment or make a secret profit or become the purchaser of his principal's property, indirectly, unless he discloses to his principal everything within his knowledge which might affect the principal's interests or influence his actions in relation to the subject matter of employment.[14]

In *Batson v. Strehlow,*[15] the court once again held that a broker cannot buy from himself or sell to himself, unless he makes full disclosure to the other party.

In the case of *Cox v. Bryant,*[16] a farm was listed with a broker at $40,000. Cox, a salesman, agreed to buy the farm at the listed price and agreements of sale were signed to that effect. The agreements recognized the Jim Morris Sales Co. as the broker in the deal and the Bryants agreed to pay the broker a 5 percent commission. The owners refused to go through with the deal and the salesman, Cox, brought suit for specific performance on the contract of sale. At the trial of the case, it developed that Cox was to receive 60% of the commission paid to his broker in the transaction. This fact was fatal to Cox's cause for action. The court said:

> In this case, before Cox could become the purchaser, it was his duty to terminate all agency relationships with the Bryants and thus place himself in the character and position of a purchaser.

---

[11] Blakeley v. Bradley et al., 281 S.W. 2d 835 (1955); Curroto v. Hammack, 241 S.W. 2d 897 (Mo. 1951).

[12] King v. Pruitt, 288 S.W. 2d 923 (1956).

[13] Yerkie v. Salsbury, 287 A. 2d 498 (Md. 1972).

[14] 8 Am. Jur. Secs. 89, 152.

[15] Batson v. Strehlow, 305 P. 2d 686 (Cal. App. 1957).

[16] Cox v. Bryant, 347 S.W. 2d 861 (Mo. 1961).

Among the facts that Cox should have disclosed to the Bryants was the fact that he was to receive a $1,200 commission for the sale to himself.

Note—This problem could have been easily avoided if the sales agreement had contained a statement such as:

The buyer hereby notifies all concerned that he is a licensed agent with the Jim Morris Sales Co. and will receive a portion of the agencies commission on this sale. It should also be known that this purchase is intended for the salesperson's own portfolio.

The Arizona case of *Nutter, appellant v. Becktel*,[17] was decided similarly to the above discussed case.

In the case of *Gallagher-Smith-Feutz Realty, Inc. v. Circle Z Farm Inc., et al.*,[18] the Court held that if a broker knows of the existence of a *better offer* at the time he tried to influence the seller to accept his purchaser, but fails to tell the seller of such an offer, he is deemed guilty of a breach of duty, and forfeits any claim for a commission.

The courts throughout the country have likewise adhered strictly to the principle of law that a broker is a fiduciary in the strictest sense of the word and owes a high degree of loyalty to his principal. In the case of *Cochrane v. Wittbold*,[19] a saleswoman employed by a broker caused her parents to purchase for her land listed for sale with her employer. She collected a commission on the sale, *without disclosing identity of the true purchasers to the seller,* and almost immediately resold the property to another for a profit. Such conduct, the Court held, was violative of the State Corporation and Securities Commission rules, prohibiting a broker from purchasing property listed with him, without making full disclosure to the listing owner. Such action was also contrary to the public policy of the state.

A broker is under a fiduciary duty to disclose to his owner *any knowledge he possesses concerning the planned resale of property* sold by the owner, unless the owner has knowledge of the agreement, prior to the sale.[20]

A BROKER MUST BE CAREFUL OF HIS REPRESENTATIONS

Where a broker is authorized to sell the property of his principal as well as to initiate negotiations, it is very important that the broker be circumspect in the representations which he makes to the prospective purchasers concerning the property for sale. Representations include not only actual statements made by the

---

[17] Nutter, appellant, v. Becktel, 433 P. 2d 993 (Ariz. 1967).

[18] Gallagher-Smith-Feutz Realty Inc. v. Circle Z. Farm, Inc. et al., 545 S.W. 2d 395 (Mo. App. 1976).

[19] Cocrane v. Wittbold, 102 N.W. 2d 459 (Mich. 1960).

[20] Case v. Business Centers, Inc. 357 N.E. 2d 47 (Ohio App. 1976).

broker, but also any impressions or beliefs that his conduct is calculated to produce in the mind of the other party as to facts. The law holds the broker responsible for his representations in almost the same manner as if he were acting for himself. Not only will the broker lose his right to a commission when he is guilty of misrepresentation, but in addition, he may find himself the defendant in an action brought by the disappointed purchaser, such as a fruitless action against the principal in the contract, for any damages or expenses incurred by the disappointed purchaser.

Even more important, the broker may find himself the defendant in an action before the Real Estate Commission for violation of the license law.

The general rule of law is well stated by the Nebraska Supreme Court,[21] as follows:

> A person is justified in relying on a representation made to him in all cases where the representation is a positive statement of fact and where an investigation would be required to discover the truth.

To answer an inquiry regarding termites by saying, "There are no termites in this house," is a statement of fact. But to say, "I have seen no termites," is not a misrepresentation, although there are termites, but the broker was unaware of that fact. The better practice would be for the broker to advise the prospect to inquire of the owner, or to have a professional termite inspection made.

In order to protect himself from a possible complaint, the broker, in filling out the data and information to be included in the listing contract, should receive all possible information from the owner. This information should be above the signature of the owner, with the statement:

"I/We represent the information contained in this listing, as a part thereof, is true and correct."

Unless the broker, as a licensee, held out to the public, qualified in the field of real estate, knows or should know, that a certain item of information could be false, he is held blameless, if it later turns out that the item is false. The owner would be responsible. On the other hand, if a broker makes an unauthorized or unwarranted representation, on his own initiative, the broker will be held personally responsible.

There is also a doctrine of law to be noted here called "puffing of goods." Where the broker makes extraordinary and extravagant statements regarding the property for sale, as, "It is the most beautiful spot in the world" and "The sun shines daily" and where there is no serious intent to include in the contract of sale that the property possesses all the magical power and charms claimed for it, the deluded victim has only his pains for his trouble and no remedy at law. A principal selling property is presumed to know whether the representations he makes concerning it are true or false, and if he knows them to be false, then he commits a positive fraud. If he does not know whether his representations are true or false, then actions

---

[21]
Martin v. Hutton, 90 Neb. 34 (1912).

constitute gross negligence, and in contemplation of law, representation founded on a mistake resulting from such negligence is fraud. The purchaser confides in the information furnished him by the owner on the assumption that an owner knows his own property. It is consequently immaterial to the purchaser whether the representations proceeded from mistake or fraud. The injury to him in both cases is the same, whatever may have been the motive of the seller.

The law imposes the same obligations upon an agent acting for an owner of the property. He must be just as scrupulous in the statements which he makes concerning it as the principal would be were he conducting the negotiations personally. If the misrepresentations made by the broker were made upon the information supplied by the owner, the broker is entitled to his commission from the owner if he procures a purchaser, and he is not liable to the buyer for damages.

BROKER-OWNERS ARE HELD TO A HIGH DEGREE OF FIDELITY

In selling his own property, a real estate broker must be especially careful that he is not guilty of material misrepresentation to a buyer. The penalty is severe, as he may be held responsible, even though acting as principal and not as a broker. It could mean the loss of the broker's license. To jeopardize his/her license is to jeopardize one's livelihood. In numerous cases, which have been brought before the courts it has been stated that "a single standard of honesty and competency should guide a broker's real estate activities, whether performing as a broker or owner."[22]

BROKERS MUST INFORM THE OWNER OF ALL OFFERS

It was held in *Simone v. McKee*,[23] that a broker retained by the owner owed that owner an affirmative duty to disclose second offers to the owner, and failure to disclose this information was equivalent to affirmative representation that *no* other offer existed.

A broker is bound to disclose *all offers*, even though he may believe the offer too low and informs the prospect that it would be an insult to submit such an offer to the owner: *E.A. Stout Agency v. Wooster.*[24] In a similar Colorado case in 1975, the court held that the broker is obligated to his principal to promptly communicate all definite offers to purchase, even if the broker feels that any particular offer is

---

22

Isaacs, 181 N.Y.S. 403; Maple Hill Farm v. New Jersey Real Estate Commission, 170 A. 2d 789 (1961); McKnight v. Real Estate Commission, 122 So. 2d 420 (Fla. 1976); Real Estate Commission v. Tice, 190 A. 2d 188 (Pa. 1963); Boineau v. S.C. Commission, 230 S.E. 440 (1976) and Blank v. Black, 512 P. 2d 1016 (Ore. App. 1973).

23

Simone v. McKee, 298 P. 2d 667 (Cal 1956).

24

E. A. Stout Agency v. Wooster, 99 A. 2d 689 (Vt. 1955).

inadequate; *this offer is imposed for the benefit of the purchaser as well as the vendor.*

To disclose a second offer is an affirmative duty of the broker and failure to do so is equivalent to a representation that no other offer exists. In the case of *Simone v. McKee,*[25] it was revealed that a broker received a $17,000 offer upon a property listed by him, which he failed to disclose to his principal owner, and only disclosed a $13,000 offer, which the seller was induced to accept. The broker was held liable for the difference in price.

BROKERS MUST INFORM OWNERS OF THE BROKER'S OWN INTERESTS IN LISTED PROPERTY

There is nothing illegal about a broker or salesperson purchasing a property listed with the broker's office, so long as the broker hides nothing from his owners and there is full disclosure of all facts which might influence his principal.

Sometimes, the listing contract will specifically provide that the listing broker has the option to purchase the property at the listed price. While not illegal, it raises a question of professional ethics. Should the broker exercise the option and shortly thereafter sell the property at a higher price to a third party, the owner will probably entertain serious reservations as to the broker's integrity and good faith.

It is highly recommended that when a broker or agent makes an offer for a brokerage listing that they include the following in the sales offer:

> By signatures hereon; (1) the seller hereby acknowledges that he has been informed of the buyer's status as a licensed real estate agent/broker and has no objection to the sale to said agent/broker and (2) the agent/broker buyer certifies that he is purchasing the property for his own use and/or investment portfolio and that as of the date of this agreement he has no plans for resale, trade or other disposition of the property.

In the case of *M.S.R. Inc. v. Lish,*[26] a corporate buyer was unable to maintain an action for specific performance on a contract negotiated by a broker who owned two-thirds of the stock of the corporation, a fact that was not disclosed to the seller.

Where the broker *does* make full disclosure of his interest, the law does not prevent him from purchasing property listed with him for sale and even making a profit. In the case of *Sylvester v. Beck,*[27] the plaintiff sued a real estate broker for damages alleging a breach of trust in the purchase of real estate. The plaintiff won a jury verdict in the amount of $9,000. The lower court entered judgment in favor

---

[25] Simone v. McKee, 298 P. 2d 667 (Cal. App. 1956).

[26] M.S.R. Inc. v. Lish, 527 P. 2d 912 (Colo. App. 1974).

[27] Sylvester v. Beck, 406 Pa. 607 (1962).

of the broker, notwithstanding the verdict. (Judgment N.O.V.). The plaintiffs appealed. The defendant was authorized to sell the property for $15,000 and he displayed the broker's for sale sign on the property. Later the plaintiffs agreed to sell the property to the broker for $14,000. Within one month, the broker sold the property for $25,000. A few weeks later, both deals were closed on the same day. Subsequently, when the plaintiffs learned that the defendant had realized a huge profit in a quick resale of the property, the entered the suit. The Court said:

> The fact that the defendant entered into a contract to resell the property twenty-seven days after he had contracted to purchase it and did not disclose this particular fact to the plaintiffs until the final settlement does not, in itself, entitle the plaintiffs to damages. The agency having ended when the plaintiffs agreed to sell, the agent was under no obligation to furnish his former principal with the details of events that took place subsequent to the termination of their relationship of principal and agent.

A BROKER-AGENT MUST OBEY INSTRUCTIONS OF HIS PRINCIPAL

A second fundamental duty that an agent owes to his principal is that *he must obey the instructions given him by his principal.* If a broker undertakes to judge that he may depart from the instructions of the owner, and that such variation would not be material, he does so at his own peril, and should any loss result by reason of the agent's deviation from given instructions, he will be personally liable. For example, where a broker is engaged to sell property on a cash basis but instead accepts notes which are later declared invalid, the agent will be held personally responsible for the resulting loss. The owner, however, should be specific in his instructions.

In *Jackson v. Williams,*[28] the broker was held liable for deposit money returned to the buyer, when the vendor had informed the broker *not to return the money.* In an allied case, *Earle v. Lambert et al.,*[29] a broker was held liable for damages where he reduced the price of the property in an exchange deal without authorization from his owner.

It must be recognized that a broker is a *special agent with limited authority.* A broker is employed for the specific purpose of negotiating a sale. When he accomplishes that purpose, his authority ends. *He has no authority once the agreement of sale is signed.* He cannot permit the purchaser to take possession of the premises prior to the closing of the deal, or to enter to make repairs or to decorate the premises.

---

[28] Jackson v. Williams, 510 S.W. 2d 645 (Texas App. 1974).

[29] Earle v. Lambert et al., 205 Cal. App. 2d 452 (1962).

If the deal fails to be consummated due to no fault of the buyer, the broker could be held personal responsible for the buyer's expense. The Iowa Supreme Court held that an agent, who contracted for a new well, and who was not authorized to represent the owners in doing so, was liable for the cost of drilling the new well.[30] If a buyer requests some special privilege or consideration, the request should be referred to the owner.

In the absence of any special agreement, it is the *principal's judgment and not the agent's* that is to control, so held the Court in *Gallagher v. Jones* and *Quinn v. Phipps.*[31]

In contrast to the above, where the agent *does not exceed his authority,* or where his representation to the buyer was only a repetition, in good faith, of a statement authorized by his principal, the agent is not personally liable to the buyer.[32]

A BROKER MUST NOT BE NEGLIGENT

A broker who is negligent in carrying out his duties may have his license suspended or revoked as in the case of a California broker who held an uncashed check for a period of time. A regulation of the California Real Estate Commission provides that "a check being held in an uncashed form must be specifically disclosed to the seller or offeree before he accepts the offer." In the referenced problem a salesperson accepted a deposit check for $5,000 on a five-acre tract of land. The check remained in the office for four months while negotiations continued. Finally the salesperson began to loose faith in the buyer and discussed his fears with his broker. The buyer was asked to issue a new check or authorize presentation of the original to the bank. He refused and it was learned that he had closed his account and that at no time did the buyer have funds on deposit to cover the check.

Most states have now enacted regulations regarding earnest money deposits and checks in particular. In Utah, for instance, the broker is subject to fine if he fails to deposit earnest moneys on the day following receipt or sooner.

Where a broker accepts a note from the purchaser as an earnest money deposit, in lieu of cash, the broker would be liable to his principal if the transaction was not consummated and the buyer failed to pay the note. Other situations which would be tantamount to negligence could be where the broker held a check or earnest money for an unduly long period of time, at the request of the buyer, or where he

---

[30] Cryder Well Co. v. Brown, et al., 136 N.W. 2d 519 (1965).

[31] Gallagher v. Jones 129 U.S. 195, 9 Ct. 335, 32 L Ed 658, 660 and Quinn v. Phipps, 113 So. 419.

[32] Peek v. Meadors, 500 S.W. 2d 333 (Ark. 1973)

accepted a post-dated check, unless he has advised his principal of the facts and the principal has approved.

It is common practice for brokers to accept checks for earnest money deposits. Where the broker deposits the check promptly and should the bank refuse payment because of insufficient funds, no liability can be visited upon the broker. Likewise, if the buyer dies, before the bank honors the check, the broker is not liable. It is the broker's duty to promptly inform his principal when any of the above situations occur.

Negligence was held in the case of *Wilson v. Hisey*,[33] when a real estate agent failed to recommend a title search to the buyer, and in representing, without knowing the real facts, that there was only one trust deed (mortgage) against the property, when there were two.

A broker cannot be found negligent for a mere mistake in judgment that does not result from failure to know or to do that which a person of ordinary prudence, under similar circumstances would do. So held the Court in the case of *Zwick v. United Farms Agency, Inc.*[34]

A BROKER CANNOT DELEGATE HIS AUTHORITY - HE MUST ACT IN PERSON

A broker cannot delegate to others the authority that he received from his principal, but must act in person. It must be realized that an owner hires a broker because of the confidence that he has in the ability and integrity of that broker. Thus a broker has no right to delegate his authority without the consent of his principal, *except as to those duties that are purely ministerial or mechanical in character, and where such delegation does not involve discretion, confidence or skill.*

An interesting situation occurs where the broker is a member of a multi-listing organization. In the California case of *Goodwin v. Glick*,[35] the defendant has given a listing to Petrol Realty Co. of San Pedro, on a San Pedro Realty Board form, which provided that a listing broker might refer the listing to members of the Board. The property was sold by another member of the Board. The Court said, inter alia,

> that the provision therein contained authorizing the agent named to refer the listing to the Realty Board, which in turn, is authorized to refer it to its members, must be construed as an authorization to Petrol Realty Co. to appoint members of the Realty Board to whom it is referred as its agent (Petrol's) and not as agents of the defendant (owner).

Circumstances may modify the generally accepted rule that a multilist selling

33
Wilson v. Hisey, 305 P. 2d 686 (Cal. App. 1957).
34
Zwick v. United Farms Agency, Inc. 556 P. 2d 508 (Wyo. 1976).
35
Goodwin v, Glick, 139 A C A Supp. 958 (1956).

broker is a subagent of the listing broker. In the case of *Wise v. Dawson*,[36] The Court held that the multilisting arrangements between listing and selling broker do not create an agent and subagent relationship so far as to visit liability upon the listing broker for misrepresentations allegedly made by the selling broker to buyers. This case was a suit for damages by the buyer and a tort action based upon fraud by the selling broker and could not be contracted away.

AN AGENT BROKER MUST ACCOUNT FOR ALL MONEY AND PROPERTY ENTRUSTED TO HIM

An agent must account for all money and property of his principal which has been entrusted to him and it must be kept separate and apart from his own funds. Most state license laws provide that the *commingling* of trust funds in the broker's personal or business account shall constitute grounds for suspension or revocation of license. Trust funds must be kept in a trustee account, which is subject to review and reconciliation at any time by members of the State Commission. So long as the agent exercises due care and caution in selecting a safe depository for such funds, he cannot be held liable for any later loss. One trust fund is adequate to hold all trust funds coming into the broker's hands.

Where there is a written listing, signed by the owner, it is important that it should contain a clause to the effect that the broker should hold all deposits of earnest money in escrow until the transaction is consummated or terminated. Under such authority, the broker should encounter no difficulty in convincing his owner that the broker should hold the earnest money deposit. Of course, money paid the broker by a purchaser can be recovered by the purchaser where the owner refuses to execute the agreement or is guilty of a breach of the agreement. This is so even though the agreement provides that, "It is understood that the broker is acting as agent only and will in no case whatever be held liable to either party for the performance of any terms of the covenant of this agreement or for damages for nonperformance thereof." This clause is not really necessary where the broker's principal is disclosed, since the action generally will be directed against the owner. But the buyer can sue the broker if the broker retains the deposit money, provided the buyer has a right of action against the owner.

In the event the agreement is not consummated and there is a disagreement as to who is to receive the earnest money deposit, the broker should pay the funds into the court for distribution as it directs. If there is no dispute, it is good broker practice for the broker to obtain a receipt, signed by the buyer and seller, acknowledging the receipt of funds and agreeing thereto.

In normal practice the amount of the earnest money deposit will be less than the amount of the broker's commission; however, the broker may not withdraw

---

[36] Wise v. Dawson, 353 A. 2d 207 (Del. 1975).

these funds until the deal has been closed. After closing, the amount received at the closing table plus the earnest money held will constitute the broker's commission and will be shown as a debit to the seller's statement.

If the amount of the earnest money, exceeds the broker's commission, he will be requested, by the closing agency, to provide a trust check for the difference. This check, together with the buyer's funds will be credited to the seller's account.

Regardless of where the earnest money deposit eventually ends up, the broker is accountable for these funds and must produce appropriate closing statements to show the reason for withdrawal from the trust account. Similarly, all trust funds being held must be accounted for by a log showing from whom received, date, and amount. The trust fund may not, at any time, contain less than the total of deposits taken in nor any excesses, which have not been withdrawn in accordance with closing statements.

CLIENTS HAVE A RESPONSIBILITY TO THE BROKER

Client-broker relationships are not a one-way street. A purchaser cannot accept the services of a broker and, when the deal is imminent, arbitrarily or capriciously dismiss the broker and refuse to do business with him. Nor can he circumvent the broker by using a third party as the purchaser for him. In *Orr v. Woolfolk,*[37] the Court said,

> Where a broker's prospect interests another who becomes the eventual purchaser of property which the owner listed with the broker for sale, the broker is entitled to a commission.

This does not mean, where a broker negotiated a sale of a property in a subdivision to a purchaser and the buyer interests a friend in an adjoining house, and a friend buys directly from the owner, that the broker is entitled to a commission on the second sale.

In *Beougher v. Clark,*[38] the Court has stated the principle as follows:

> The law will not permit one broker who has been entrusted with the sale of land and is working with a customer whom he has found, to be deprived of his commission by another agent stepping in and selling the land to the customer so found by the first broker. The utmost good faith must be exercised between principal and broker.

The same ruling applied in the case of *Greshman v. Lee.*[39] It sometimes happens that a broker brings a property to the buyer's attention and then the latter deals with the owner directly. Many brokers have instances where they show the outside of a listed dwelling and the prospect disclaims any interest and will not

---

[37] Orr v. Wolfolk, 250 Ky. 279 (1933).

[38] Beougher v. Clark, 81 Kan. 250 (1909).

[39] Greshman v. Lee, 152 Ga. 829 (1921).

even make the inspection of the interior. If the broker had previously notified the owner as to the identity of the prospect, he would have a good cause for action for a commission. Clearly, if the owner is unaware of the interest of the broker's prospect, it would be very difficult for the broker to recover a commission.

In the case of a multilisting cooperative brokers dispute as to who was the selling broker, the rule is usually "the one who showed the client *to and through* the property." A drive-by look or introduction is insufficient to establish a broker's position as selling agent.

A purchaser may lay himself open to a law suit for commission to a broker, by stating to the owner that there is no broker involved in the deal, after the broker has submitted the property to him.

A cautious or prudent seller, who has listed his property with one or more brokers for sale, will include a clause in the agreement of sale to the effect that the purchaser warrants that there are no brokers involved in the sale. In the case of *McCue v. Deppert*,[40] a broker, McCue of Rumson, New Jersey, sued the purchaser, Peter C. Deppert, under these very facts. The property was listed at $30,000, and a McCue salesman had shown Deppert the property. He said that he would return with his wife. Instead, he went directly to the owner, Kramer, who lived in nearby Lakewood, and bought the property for $25,000, "because there was no broker charge." The broker sued the buyer. The lower court decided against the broker, but upon appeal, the Superior Court held that the buyer could not "rely on his wrongful acts, in preventing the plaintiff from meeting the condition of procuring a ready, able, and willing purchaser."

Another similar case was decided by a lower court in Ohio in 1952, in the case of *Schlesinger v. Zeilengold*,[41] where the broker sued the buyer in an action of deceit and recovered a verdict of $2,800. The case involved a commercial property in Lynhurst, Ohio. There the buyer secured certain pertinent information about the property from the broker and then used it on his own. He then professed to be totally uninterested in the property and refused to enter into any discussion with the broker about its purchase. The buyer at the time was in direct negotiation with the owner. The Court's decision holds, in effect, that a prospective purchaser who perpetrates a fraud upon a broker, thereby preventing the broker from pursuing his lawful and legitimate rights under his employment contract, commits an actionable wrong in tort.

---

[40] McCue v. Deppert, 21 N.J. Sup. 591 (1952).

[41] Schlesinger v. Zeilengold, Ohio (1952).

6

Sales Agreements

LEGAL REQUIREMENTS FOR AGREEMENTS OF SALE

An agreement of sale is a contract in writing whereby one party agrees to sell and another agrees to buy certain real estate under such terms and conditions as are therein set forth. It must be remembered that a sales agreement is a contract. Hence, all essential elements of a valid contract must be present; these are:

- Offer and acceptance
- Seal or consideration
- Capacity of the parties
- Reality of consent
- Legality of object

Since the contracts discussed in this chapter relate to real estate, there is an additional formality to be observed. Under the statute of frauds, which exists in every state, a contract for the sale of real estate *must be in writing,* in order to be enforceable.[1] In the following section, each of the above requirements will be discussed in considerable detail.

In reviewing these discussions, you should be cautioned that the language of the real estate contract varies somewhat from a normal contract in which terms such as "contractor" and "contractee" are often replaced with the terms "vendor" and "vendee" or "buyer" and "seller."

---

[1] Hayman v. Ross, 22 N.C. App.624 (1974) and Fleming v. Romero, 342 So.2d 881 (La. App. 1977).

OFFER AND ACCEPTANCE

This term means that there must be a "meeting of the minds" on the subject matter and terms of the contract. The terms of the contract must be precise and definite.[2] It is the responsibility of the broker, who undertakes to prepare the agreement to see to it that the form and substance of the contract will meet any legal challenge. Most brokers agree that the agreement should be written as if one is going to court—very often that is the result. It should be understood that there can be many offers that arise from correspondence between parties, and a formal contract may never be signed or come into existence. That is, there was never a meeting of the minds on that particular offer. Subsequent negotiations may result in an acceptable offer, acceptance, and a contract.

SEAL OR CONSIDERATION

Although most offers for the purchase of real estate include a money deposit with the offer, it is not necessary that a money deposit be paid at the time the agreement of sale is signed, in order for the agreement to be valid and enforceable, as a mutual promise by the vendee to pay for the same at the same time constitutes good and legal consideration.[3] The deposit, normally accompanying the offer, is more often proffered in an amount to convince the seller that the buyer is earnest, capable of consummating the sale and unlikely to renege on his promise to buy, rather than in satisfaction of the contractual requirement.

CAPACITY OF THE PARTIES

Not every person has *full* contractual capacity. Included in this category are minors, mentally incompetent or insane persons, corporations and, to a limited extent in some states, married women. Currently, an increasing number of states have lowered the age of majority from the traditional 21 years to 18 years. During minority, most contracts entered into by minors are legal but voidable at the minor's option. Only contracts of necessaries are binding on a minor, but there is no hard and fast rule defining "necessaries." Certainly, maintenance, food, clothing, lodging, medical attention, and education in reasonable amounts should be legally included in this term. A voidable contract may be disaffirmed by a minor at any time during his minority or within a reasonable time after he attains his majority. Infancy is a defense personal to the infant alone. It cannot be pleaded by the other party to the contract as grounds for avoidance of contractual liability. In this connection, the appointment of a agent by an infant is generally void. In dealing with an infant owner of real estate, the other party should require the appointment of a guardian for the infant and all dealing should be conducted with that person.

---

[2] City of Roslyn v. Hughes Construction Co., 573 P.2d 385 (Wash. App. 1987).

[3] Cowman v. Allen Monuments, Inc. 500 S.W.2d 223 (Texas 1973).

A broker employed by an infant to sell property cannot collect his earned commission if the infant changes his mind and repudiates the contract of employment. It makes no difference that the sale arranged by the broker is advantageous to the infant. It should be recognized that an infant may appear to be of full age, but this has no bearing on his liability or freedom from liability in a contract. Even if there is no wrongful misrepresentation of age, the rule of law is the same: since he cannot make himself *sui juris* (of legal age) by falsifying his age, the infant can still disaffirm his contract. However, the injured party could sue the infant in a *tort* action for deceit.

An infant who elects to disaffirm his voidable contract must do so *in toto*. He cannot elect to ratify as much of the contract as will benefit him and reject that portion which will operate to his disadvantage. For example, an infant who agreed to purchase a commercial property for $10,000 by paying $2,500 cash and giving the owner a purchase money mortgage for $7,500 could not compel the seller to deed the property to him upon payment of the $2,500 cash and then disaffirm his obligation to execute the $7,500 mortgage.

In 1970, the U.S. Congress enacted a law permitting 18-year-old persons to vote in federal elections. This does not permit 18-year-old persons to enjoy full contractual capacity, unless the state law emancipates them from a minor incapacity to contract.[4] In the Arizona case of *Riley v. Stoves,* the court upheld the restriction of occupancy in a mobile home subdivision, to persons 21 years or older.

The law also protects persons mentally incompetent from their imprudent contracts. Mentally incompetent persons include the insane, those rendered incompetent due to age, and drunkards. To affect the contractual ability, the degree of mental derangement must be such as to render the person incapable of reasoning from cause to effect and thus understanding the effects of his/her acts. A person mentally incompetent is nevertheless liable for the necessaries furnished himself, his spouse, and children. Other contracts, if yet to be performed (executory), are voidable by him. The weight of authority is to the effect that where the contract has been executed so that the insane person has had the benefit and the parties cannot be restored to their former position, unaccompanied by any proof that the other knew, or ought to have known of the insanity, the contract will not be voided. If, however, the insane person has received no benefit, he may void the contract and recover what he has paid notwithstanding the other party's good faith.

To be on the safe side, a guardian or committee for the estate of the incompetent should be appointed by the court and the sale of real estate made under the direction of said court. The test of whether a guardian should be appointed for the estate of a person is the degree of mental unsoundness. If he is incapable of conducting the ordinary affairs of life so that to leave property in his possession

---

4

Riley v. Stoves, 526 P.2d 747 (Ariz. 1974).

and control would render him liable to become the victim of his own folly or of a designing person, a guardian should be appointed.

Any habitual drunkard may be regarded as an insane person and his capacity to contract is likewise limited. When a man or woman loses his/her mind, he/she is entitled to legal protection whether such loss is occasioned by his/her own imprudence or otherwise. This is true even though intoxication is voluntary and not procured by the intervention of another party.

The contractual powers of married women are based on statute. Today a married woman is almost completely emancipated in her capacity to contract. She may generally transact business in the same manner as a single woman (feme sole trader). In those states where she cannot sell her own real estate without the joinder of her husband, he should join in the execution of an agreement of sale. Even in those states, if a woman, before marriage, enters into an agreement to sell her real estate and marries before consummating the deal, and before the deed is delivered, the courts will honor her agreement of sale and *compel* her husband to join in the deed.[5]

The contractual powers of a corporation are defined and limited by their charters, the constitution and the states where they are formed. They have those powers expressly stated in their charters and such implied powers as may be necessary and incidental to carry out those expressed powers. Where a corporation exceeds those powers, the act is *ultra vires* and unenforceable. An agreement for the sale of real estate by a corporation should be executed in pursuance of a resolution by the board of directors authorizing and directing the particular conveyance. When the agreement is made under a general resolution authorizing the officer to execute deeds for any property which they may sell, it is doubtful whether such a sale is valid since the price and terms are left to the discretion of the officer. The reference here is those corporations formed for the express purpose of dealing in real estate. Here, requisite authority may be conferred upon its officers by general resolution to execute proper agreements and deeds as the occasion arises.

In general, foreigners, whether citizens of another state or nation, have full contractual authority. However, under the federal law prohibiting trading with an enemy, an affidavit by the parties to a real estate deal, stating that they are not enemy aliens, may be necessary.

In *Star Realty, Inc. v. Bower,*[6] involving action for specific performance brought by a buyer, the court denied specific performance. The court stated the well-settled case of *mental capacity to contract* is,

> whether the person in question possesses sufficient mind to understand in a reasonable manner, the nature and effect of the act in which he is engaged.

5
  Pepper v. Chatel (D.C. No. 3056 1962).

6
  Star Realty, Inc. v. Bower, 169 N.W.2d 194 (Mich. 1969).

However, to avoid a contract it must appear not only that the person was of unsound mind or insane at the time it was made, but that the unsoundness of mind was of such a character that he had no reasonable perception of the nature or terms of the contract.

In the case of *Watson v. Alford*,[7] a vendor, 100 years of age and in feeble health, sold for $200 a property which was valued at $6,750. The court held that the vendor's physical condition and the gross inadequacy of price were sufficient to require cancellation of conveyance.

REALITY OF CONSENT

A contract must be free of mistakes, misrepresentation, fraud, duress, and undue influence. That is, the consent to the contract must be *real*. The failure to achieve reality of consent may occur because of:

• Mistake
• Misrepresentation or fraud.

To avoid a contract on the grounds of mistake, the mistake must be mutual and substantial; that is, it must go to the heart of the agreement. Thus, where parties use ambiguous language and each has in mind an entirely different subject matter as the basis of the agreement, there is no contract.

Example—Where Ash owned considerable real estate, some of which was located on Jackson Street in Pittsburgh while another parcel was located on Jacksonia Street in the same city, an agreement was prepared for a parcel of real estate on Jackson Street. Due to the similarity in name, the buyer thought he was purchasing and intended to buy the tract on Jacksonia Street. The contract could be set aside on the grounds of a mistake.

Where the purchaser's attorney prepared the agreement of sale, and the purchaser had either actual or imputed knowledge of agreement of sale, a misdescription of land is not grounds for a recision of agreement. Once the buyer assumes the burden of examination, he cannot claim he was deceived to his injury, where such examination discloses correct information.[8]

In the case of *Roy S. Ludlow Inv. Co. v. Taggart*,[9] a purchaser was not permitted to take advantage of a typographical mistake in an agreement of sale. Lot 22 was not included in a group of 30 lots, which Taggart agreed to sell. However, Lot 22 was included, inadvertently, in the agreement. Ludlow knew that Taggart

[7] Watson v. Alford, 503 S.W.2d 897 (Ark. 1974).

[8] Ryan v. Brady, 366 A.2d 745 (Md. App. 1976).

[9] Roy S. Ludlow Inv. Co. v. Taggart, 509 P.2d 818 (Utah 1973).

wasn't the owner of Lot 22 because he had attempted to buy it from the *real* owner. Accordingly, no damages were allowed.

Misrepresentation and fraud are often confused. Misrepresentation is an *innocent* misstatement of a material fact, without intent to deceive, but which induces the contract.

> *Example*—If Jones should sell Smith certain building lots and represent that the lots were high ground and it later developed that they were not above tide level, Jones could not hold Smith to the contract even though he was honest in his representation. However, if the party to whom the representation was made did not rely upon it and made his own independent examination, he could not claim that the representation induced the contract.

Misrepresentation must be as to fact and not a mere expression of opinion. If a broker represents to a customer that certain real estate *cost* $10,000 to build and it only *cost* $7,000, there is fraudulent misrepresentation present. Where the broker states, instead, that the property is *worth* $10,000, that is a mere expression of an opinion and does not constitute misrepresentation.

LEGALITY OF OBJECT

The object of the contract must be legal. If the purpose contravenes the constitution, a statute, or federal treaty, the contract is void. Likewise a contract which tends to interfere with the public government or is injurious to the public at large, such as the perpetration of a nuisance, is unenforceable. In the day-to-day operation of the typical broker, the question of legality of object is seldom encountered.

BROKERS ARE NOT LIABLE FOR INNOCENT MISREPRESENTATIONS

A broker cannot be held liable for "innocently and nonnegligently conveying a seller's missrepresentations." In a 1987 case the court stated that brokers should be held to a standard of reasonable care and professionalism, but cannot be turned into guarantors.[10] On the other hand, he can be held accountable if reasonable care is not exercised. In a Kansas case,[11] the broker took the seller's word that a listed home was connected to a sewer. The sellers had shown the broker the old listing agreement in force when they purchased. It indicated "sewer connected per seller." A buyer of the property later had sewer problems and found that there was no sewer connection. The listing broker was held liable. It was shown that the broker should have suspicioned that the facts were incorrect since:

---

[10] Hoffman v. Connall, 746 P.2d 242 (1987).

[11] Johnson v. Geer Real Estate Co., 720 P.2d 660 (1986).

a. The home in question was 10-12 feet in elevation below the surrounding properties.

b. There was no sewer pump in the basement which would have been required to raise the effluent to the sewer level, and

c. The basement sewer drain was pointed away from the public sewer line.

The court further cited Kansas Stat. Ann. 58-3062 (a)(31), enacted in 1980 which requires brokers to "disclose material information, relating to the property, which the broker *knows or should know*."

DOES THE AGREEMENT SATISFY THE STATUTE OF FRAUDS?

The object of the Statute of Frauds, first passed in England in 1676, was to close the door to numerous frauds and perjuries in contracts which could be enforced only upon no other evidence than the mere recollection of witnesses.[12] However, partial performance of an oral contract to convey real estate may remove that contract from the operation of the Statute of Frauds where (1) there has been earnest money deposited, (2) the purchaser has gone in to possession, and (3) the purchaser has made improvements to the property. Under such circumstances, equity would intervene and entitle the buyer to a decree of specific performance.[13] In the case of *Harris v. Potts*,[14] the Court held that all three of the above conditions are indispensable and they must all exist.

It is often difficult to determine whether a writing is a mere receipt or a sufficient agreement under the Statute of Frauds. If the memorandum contains the names of the parties, a definite enough description to identify the property and the terms of sale, it will suffice.

Sometimes a broker will have the parties sign a preliminary agreement, such as an offer to purchase, although the advisability of using two separate instruments to do a single job is questionable when one is sufficient. Where there are conflicting clauses in the two papers, trouble may ensue. It does not always follow that the terms of the preliminary agreement are carried over to the later one. Even though the memorandum agreement is signed by both parties, it is not binding *where the parties agree that the terms should be spelled out in a subsequent agreement*. An agreement to make an agreement is not enforceable, where material terms are left to the future negotiations.[15] It is a contradiction in terms and imposes no obligation on the parties.[16]

[12] Haddock Construction Co. v. Snedigar Dairy, 510 P.2d 752 (Ariz. App. 1973).

[13] Zaborski v. Kutyla, 185 N.W.2d 586 (Mich. App. 1971); Walker v. Walker, 448 S.W.2d 171 (Tex. 1969) and Brotman v. Brotman, 353 Pa. 570 (1946).

[14] Harris v. Potts, 545 S.W.2d 126 (Tex. 1976).

[15] Ripps v. Mueller et al., 517 P.2d 512 (Ariz. 1973).

[16] Kenimer v. Thompson, 196 S.E.2d 363 (Ga. 1973).

The case of *Tompkins v. France,*[17] is pertinent. In that case, the preliminary agreement provided that the parties would execute the usual Chicago Real Estate Board sales contract form, embodying the terms, within five days. The contract submitted was not on the Chicago Board form, and it called for an earnest money deposit of $4,950, instead of $2,000, stated in the preliminary agreement to purchase. The court held that the buyer did not need to perform and he was entitled to a refund of his $2,000 deposit.

In another case involving a preliminary agreements, a writing that the conveyance of a particular piece of land (approximately 150 acres) would be mutually agreed upon in a future agreement, was not enforceable.[18]

The case of *Boekelheide v. Snyder,*[19] was an action for specific performance by the buyer. The writing upon which the action was based read,

> Received of H. H. Boekelheide $50 to apply on purchase of house and property of the old Young house. Balance $650.
>
> Margaret Snyder

Does the memorandum satisfy the Statute of Frauds, as a written contract of sale? The Court held the writing insufficient. It must be complete in itself, containing all the terms of the contract. Oral evidence is not admissible to supply defects in a written contract, which must be in writing under the Statute of Frauds. Payment of $50 did not constitute part performance.

To constitute an enforceable agreement, a written memorandum must disclose all essential elements of the sale of land, and cannot rest partially in writing and partially in parole. The court so stated in *Colrodas v. Russell*[20] where the time payment, manner of payment, and whether cash or credit was omitted from the writing.

A check for $1,000 from a purchaser to a seller, bearing only the notation "For lot 100 Earnest Money" did not constitute a contract for sale of the land, since lot 100 did not define the subject matter of the transaction.[21]

A dated memorandum signed by the owners, reciting merely that they had received from the purchaser the sum of $500 as deposit to purchase "Apt. at 20001 Conant, for $94,000" was sufficient to satisfy the Statute of Frauds. The Court decreed specific performance.[22]

---

[17] Tompkins v. France, 21 Ill. App.2d 227 (1959).

[18] Davison v. Robbins, 517 P.2d 1026 (Utah 1973).

[19] Boekelheide v. Snyder, 71 S.D. 470 (1947).

[20] Colrodas v. Russell, 289 So.2d 55 (Fla. App. 1974).

[21] Kenimer v. Thompson, 196 S.E.2d 363 (Ga. 1973).

[22] Klymshyn v. Szarek, 185 N.W.2d 820 (Mic. App. 1971).

A contract for sale of realty was held too vague and indefinite with respect to time within which the balance of the purchase price was to be paid. The contract stated that $11,000 of purchase price was to be paid in three equal installments.[23]

The Statute of Frauds does not require that a writing be one instrument. It may be created out of separate writings, connected with one another by the internal nature of the subject matter.[24]

ACCEPTANCE OF AN OFFER MAY CONSTITUTE A DEAL

A signed memorandum containing all of the essential elements of a formal agreement may be sufficient if the parties consider the execution of the latter agreement to be only a formality. In two Massachusetts cases, *Goren v. Royal Investments Inc.* and *Bloomendale v. Imbrescia*, the Massachusetts Appeals Court considered whether an executed agreement captioned "Offer to Purchase" constituted a final agreement, where one party to the contract refused to execute a more formal purchase and sale agreement provided for in the agreement.

In Goren,[25] both parties to a real estate transaction signed a document captioned "Offer to Purchase." The buyer's offer contained a description of the property, the selling price, method of payment, the closing date, provisions for leases currently encumbering the title, and required the seller to pay the broker's commission. Subsequent to the signing of the agreement, the seller received a higher offer and refused to close the first offer. The seller asserted that the parties had never agreed on the "boilerplate" provisions and the parties had not agreed to all significant terms. The judge found these arguments unpersuasive as the seller had agreed to the same terms with the third party. The court required the seller to perform specifically on the contract.

In *Bloomendale v. Imbrescia*,[26] the buyer/plaintiff relied upon a preliminary document, described by the court as "crude." The document declared that, upon the seller's acceptance of the deposit, the buyer would agree to sign "your usual real estate agreement." The standard form Purchase and Sale Agreement later submitted contained several new and unagreed upon provisions. Based upon the existence of these new elements, the trial judge dismissed the action, granting the seller's motion for summary judgment. On appeal, the Massachusetts Appeals Court affirmed the lower court's decision.

---

[23] Cook v. Barfield, 162 S.E.2d 417 (Ga. 1968).

[24] Lalone v. Modern Album and Finishing Co., Inc. 331 N.Y.S.2d 889 (1972).

[25] Goren v. Royal Investments, Inc, 25 Mass. App. Ct. 137, 516 N.E.2d 173 (1987).

[26] Bloomendale v. Imbrescia, Mass. App. Ct. 144, 516, N. E.2d 177 (1987)

WHAT IS A "BINDER"?

A binder, as the name implies, is an agreement to make a down payment for the purchase of real estate and is evidence of the purchaser's good faith. It is preliminary to the formal agreement of sale.

> *For Example*—A prospect inspects a "sample house" on a Sunday, likes it, and wants to be sure that he will get it, so he gives the broker or salesperson a check for $100 as a deposit. An agreement of sale can be prepared the following day and the buyer can pay an additional amount to constitute the earnest money deposit.

The case of *Picard v. Burroughs,*[27] involved a suit for specific performance of a land sale contract where the purchaser made a binder payment of $4,000. The Court denied relief because the binder agreement was too indefinite and ambiguous. Under the circumstances, the purchaser was entitled to a refund of his $4,000 binder payment. Thus, one difficulty of a binder is that too frequently, it is too brief to incorporate the essentials of an enforceable contract.

BROKER RESPONSIBILITY FOR PROPER PREPARATION OF THE SALES AGREEMENT

The responsibilities of a broker are much greater in preparing an agreement of sale than in preparing a listing agreement. In a listing agreement, the broker acts as a principal party and the law is rather limited in its scope to the two contracting parties—broker and owner. In an agreement of sale, the broker acts in the capacity of an agent for the owner. It is the owner and the purchaser, who are the principal parties. The broker's duties and responsibilities, as an agent, are considerably enlarged. The broker, in preparing the agreement of sale, must tailor it to the needs of the two principal parties. These needs vary from transaction to transaction.

Since the agreement of sale is between two principals, one of whom is the buyer and the other the owner, the broker preparing the contract is normally an agent of the party of the first part (owner). Although the broker is not a party to the contract, he may acquire important rights under it, if the agreement contains a clause which recognizes the broker as the one who negotiated the deal, and the owner agreed to pay him a commission for his services.[28] If the broker has conducted his operations properly, he does not have to rely on the sales agreement to guarantee his commission on the sale. He will have a valid contract (listing) with the owner, which guarantees a commission if he produces a buyer, ready, willing and able to buy.

---

[27] Picard v. Burroughs, 304 So.2d 455 (Fla. App. 1974).

[28] Herman v. Stern, 419 Pa. 272 (1965); W.D. Nelson & Co. Inc. v. Taylor Heights Development Corp., 207 Va. 386 (1966); Mid-Continent Properties, Inc. v. Pflug, 249 N.W.2d 476 (Neb. 1977) and Huber v. Gerahman, 300 S.W.2d 501 (Mo. 1957)

After finding a buyer who is ready, willing and able to buy, the broker's next important function is to negotiate a *valid* contract of sale between this principal, the owner, and the buyer. In this connection the broker prepares the agreement of sale, which, to a large extent, makes the law by which seller and buyer are governed.

While preparation by the seller's agent is more often the case, it should be recognized that under current legal authority, the contract of sale may be prepared by the buyer's broker, who represents the buyer only. In this case, the owner, being advised of this fact, should be assured that he is represented in the negotiations by his broker, who will advise him as to his possible acceptance, rejection, or possible counteroffer.

In a 1987 case, it was ruled that a seller's broker has no responsibility to the buyer and no obligation to explain the terms of the contract to a purchaser, even though that purchaser is not otherwise represented.[29] On the other hand, it has been recently ruled[30] that a purchaser's broker has no fiduciary responsibility to the seller, even though the purchaser's broker will derive his commission as a result of co-op brokerage effort. In the cited Colorado case, the purchaser's broker arranged for a sale for $100,000 knowing the subject property was far more valuable. In fact, he arranged for a resale prior to the closing of the transaction.

Regardless of which broker prepares the agreement, the need for care and accuracy is essential.

The broker or salesperson, preparing the sales agreement should be fully cognizant of the responsibilities which he assumes in undertaking to draw an agreement of sale. The instrument fixes legal right and obligations of the seller and buyer. It must adequately protect the seller, and at the same time, protect the buyer, who may be engaging in his *very first* real estate venture. A poorly drawn agreement of sale may not only lead to dissatisfaction and controversy, but to expensive litigation and waste of time as well. In addition, the person who prepared the agreement of sale, may find himself the defendant, not only in an action of law, but also in proceedings for revocation or suspension of license on the grounds of incompetency. *In many respects, the agreement of sale is more important than the deed, because it dictates and determines what goes into the deed.*

Where the agreement, prepared by a broker, is within the actual or apparent scope of the agent's authority, any ambiguity will be resolved against the principal, by whom he is employed. The broker's fundamental duty of loyalty to his principal is based on the principal-agent relationship. The broker's state license attests to his good repute and competency as a *professional*. In the case of *Yerkie, Jr. v. Salisbury*,[31] the Court said,

---

[29] Haldeman v. Gosnell Development Corp., 748 P.2d 1209 (Ariz Ct. App. 1987).

[30] Real Equity Diversification, Inc. v. Coville, 744 P.2d 756 (Colo. Ct App. 1987).

[31] Yerkie, Jr. v. Salisbury, 287 A.2d 498 (Md. 1972).

> Brokers and their salesmen ought to have sense enough to realize that many contracts of sale are important legal documents, the preparation of which ought to be left to lawyers. Quite often there is a great deal more to the drafting of a contract for the sale of land than filling in the blank spaces on a printed form.

Although we say that the broker drafts the agreement of sale, in actual practice, his drafting consists of filling in the blanks of a "state approved" form. To go beyond this more or less simple procedure, is to incur possible legal difficulties. If the intent of the parties cannot be adequately expressed on the approved form, or additional agreements are requireed to supplement the data on the form, buyers and sellers should be advised to seek the assistance of their respective attorneys.

BROKERS MAY BE PERSONALLY LIABLE

It is well established by law in every state that a broker is a fiduciary and the law exacts a high degree of loyalty and fidelity on the part of the broker towards his principal. This rule also applies to a salesperson and holds a broker responsible for the salesperson's acts, where the broker connives with his salesperson, is cognizant of what is going on, or benefits from an illegal transaction. The case of *Security Aluminum Window Mfg. Co. v. Lehman Associates, Inc. et al.,*[32] involved an action by seller against a broker and his agent for compensatory and punitive damages in relation to the sale of real property. The Appellate Court held, inter alia, that punitive damages should be assessed against both the real estate broker and his salesperson in relation to a fraudulent scheme involving the sale of property in which the seller was led to believe that an offer of $25,000 had been made for his property, when in fact an offer of $50,000 had been tendered by another party.

Where the broker knows that the buyer must sell his present home in order to provide funds for the purchase of his dream home, the broker or salesperson should be aware of the responsibilities he assumes if he guarantees to sell the buyer's present home within the time for closing on the new home, and he fails to do so.

The broker or salesperson may be well intentioned, but if he is unable to fulfill his promise, he is personally liable to the buyer for any loss which he may sustain. The same result is true if the broker promises to obtain necessary financing to make a real estate deal, and he fails to do so.

If the deal is subject to the sale of the buyer's present home, or to obtain necessary financing, a clause should be written into the agreement of sale to that effect. The owner may refuse to sign an agreement that contains a conditional clause, but the broker knows that he is taking a calculated risk, if the conditional clause is omitted and the broker has committed himself to selling the buyer's present home or obtaining financing.

---

[32] Security Aluminum Window Mfg. Co. v. Lehman Associates, Inc. et al., 108 N.J. Super.137 (1970).

This problem of disposition of the buyer's current home is often solved by the addition of a "24-hour contingency clause" which reads as follows:

This sale is contingent upon the buyer's selling and closing on his current residence at _____. Seller reserves the right to continue to offer this property for sale and if another acceptable offer is received, agrees to notify the buyer of said receipt and to wait 24-hours before accepting the second offer. The 24-hour period will provide time for the undersigned buyer to cancel this agreement or remove the contingency condition for selling his present home.

Thus, the seller is not required to take his home off of the market and may continue to seek a buyer. In the mean time, if the buyer is fortunate enough to obtain a buyer prior to receipt of the owner's second offer, he will be able to buy the property. If a buyer is not found by the time the second offer is received, he can either cancel the offer or cancel the contingency clause and suffer the possible consequences of double mortgage payments and the need for obtaining temporary financing for the down payment on the new home.

THE AGENT'S AUTHORITY IS LIMITED

The broker is a *special* agent with *limited* authority: he is employed to obtain a purchaser for the owner. This employment, generally, cannot be enlarged to empower the broker to sign, as agent of the owner, a binding agreement of sale.[33] A listing contract, per se, containing the words employment "to sell" does not confer such authority.[34] A broker without any express or special grant of power does not have the authority to bind his principal to a contract of sale.[35]

An architect is the agent of the owner in supervising the construction work as it progresses and has rather broad authority in this capacity.[36] However, he cannot enlarge upon the terms of an agreement of sale already signed by the builder and the purchaser.

Some printed listing contracts do authorize execution of a sales agreement by the broker, using such words as "and to contract in my name," or the like. This is not considered good ethical practice. Extenuating circumstances may dictate the use of such authority in the listing agreement authorizing the broker to sign as agent for the owner where, for example, the owner is going abroad for an extended time period, his itinerary is uncertain, and the owner is anxious to have the property sold.

With today's excellent communications throughout the world, the availability

---

[33] Peters v. Windmiller, 314 Ill. 496 (1925).

[34] Gallant v. Todd et al., 111 S.E.2d 779 (S.C. 1960).

[35] Fleming v. Romero, 342 So.2d 881 (La. App. 1977).

[36] Huber, Hunt & Nichols, Inc. V. Moore, 136 Cal. Rptr. 603 (1977).

of fax machines and direct-dial telephone services, it would be far better that the broker refuse this additional authority and depend, instead, on getting phone or fax approval of any agreement he may obtain.

An agent exceeds his authority when he permits a purchaser to take possession of the premises before the deal is closed, no matter how sympathetic he may be to the buyer's needs—for example, where the buyer is moving from another state, and his furniture and household effects are already in transit. Often, the buyer will ask the broker's permission to do some decorating, painting, or to make minor repairs before the deal is closed. Should the deal fail to close, the broker may find himself the defendant in an action for expenses and damages by the disappointed purchaser.[37] If the buyer wants some special privilege, the broker should refer him to the owner for permission.

The problem of early occupancy can be handled in a number of ways. In the case where furniture is on its way, it might be suggested to the owner that he permit unloading into the garage or home but not allow personal possession or provide a key to the building. Where personal occupancy is needed, a rental agreement can be drawn up providing for the purchaser to pay a normal rental until closing and then *requiring an excessive rental for each day beyond the scheduled closing that the buyer occupies the home.* This will assure that he will get out in a hurry if the deal doesn't close. The excessive charge should be 5-10 times the going rate for type of building rented.

A broker may bind his principal, if the act he committed is within the apparent or ostensible scope of his authority. The act committed must be such that it is related to the subject matter of the principal's contract and would appear to be within the *actual* authority. However, the *affirmative* burden of proof rests upon the agent who asserts it against the owner.

Employment of a broker "to sell" property would not be enlarged to permit a broker to enter into a binding agreement of sale for the owner.[38]

In the case of *McDonald v. Cullen,*[39] a buyer brought an action for specific performance. The sales agreement involved a loan commitment to be approved by May 2, 1975. However, no loan was approved or commitment made. On May 2, 1975, the broker submitted to the buyer a document, entitled "Contingency Release," stating that the loan approval clause had been met to the satisfaction of the purchaser. The defendant owners never authorized this Release, nor did they receive a copy. The Court held that the purchasers were not entitled to specific performance as the agent exceeded his authority.

Authority to perform one function cannot be expanded to authority to do other

---

37
Cryder Well Co. v. Brown et al., N.W.2d 519 (Iowa 1965).
38
O.L. Hamilton v. Booth, 332. S.W.2d 252 (Ky. 1960).
39
McDonald v. Cullen, 559 P.2d 506 (Ore. 1977).

allied functions. For instance, the broker authority to collect interest on a mortgage would not authorize the broker to collect payments on the principal.[40]

DRAFTING REQUIREMENTS FOR AN ACCEPTABLE SALES AGREEMENT

No particular form is necessary for an agreement of sale. However, most states have an approved form for the use of licensed brokers that, by its design, eliminates many of the problems encountered in the drafting process. It must be recognized that a broker is not allowed to practice law by drafting his own agreement, but is restricted to the use and minor modification of approved forms.

The legally binding agreement need only be signed by the vendor and need not be under seal. In actual practice the offer is signed by the purchaser, since the offer usually contains certain binding promises and other agreements. The writing should contain the following information:

1. The names of the parties to the contract (buyers and sellers).

2. A description sufficient to clearly identify the property.

3. Terms of the sale.

4. The purchase price to be paid.

The agreement, consisting of an offer and the acceptance, must be definite in all respects.

5. In addition to the above legal requirements, most state-approved forms also contain a section which serves as a receipt for earnest money deposits, which are acknowledged by the broker or salesperson.

Figure 6-1 shows a standard Earnest Money Sales Agreement, approved for use in the state of Utah. This form is adequate for most sale situations except for new construction. The following discussions explain the various parts of the form, the proper drafting of the various sections and the reasons for the wording suggested.

THE RECEIPT

Contains the date of preparation, the name of the buyer, as he wishes to sign in Line #12, the amount of the deposit and the form of that deposit. This is immediately followed by the name of the brokerage firm and phone number followed by the signature of the agent receiving the money.

---

[40] Shay v. Schrink, 335 Pa. 94 (1939).

EARNEST MONEY SALES AGREEMENT

Legend   Yes (X)   No (O)

This is a legally binding contract. Read the entire document carefully before signing.

REALTOR®

GENERAL PROVISIONS
(Sections)

A. **INCLUDED ITEMS.** Unless excluded herein, this sale shall *include* all fixtures and any of the following items if presently attached to the property, plumbing, heating, air-conditioning and ventilating fixtures and equipment, water heater, built-in appliances, light fixtures and bulbs, bathroom fixtures, curtains and draperies and rods, window and door screens, storm doors, window blinds, awnings, installed television antenna, wall-to-wall carpets, water softener, automatic garage door opener and transmitter(s), fencing, trees and shrubs.

B. **INSPECTION.** Unless otherwise indicated, Buyer agrees that Buyer is purchasing said property upon Buyer's own examination and judgment and not by reason of any representation made to Buyer by Seller or the Listing or Selling Brokerage as to its condition, size, location, present value, future value, income herefrom or as to its production. Buyer accepts the property in "as is" condition subject to Seller's warranties as outlined in Section 6. In the event Buyer desires any additional inspection, said inspection shall be allowed by Seller but arranged for and paid by Buyer.

C. **SELLER WARRANTIES.** Seller warrants that: (a) Seller has received no claim nor notice of any building or zoning violation concerning the property which has not or will not be remedied prior to closing; (b) all obligations against the property including taxes, assessments, mortgages, liens or other encumbrances of any nature shall be brought current on or before closing; and (c) the plumbing, heating, air conditioning and ventilating systems, electrical system, and appliances shall be sound or in satisfactory working condition at closing.

D. **CONDITION OF WELL.** Seller warrants that any private well serving the property has, to the best of Seller's knowledge, provided an adquate supply of water and continued use of the well or wells is authorized by a state permit or other legal water right.

E. **CONDITION OF SEPTIC TANK.** Seller warrants that any septic tank serving the property is, to the best of Seller's knowledge, in good working order and Seller has no knowledge of any needed repairs and it meets all applicable government health and construction standards.

F. **ACCELERATION CLAUSE.** Not less than five (5) days prior to closing, Seller shall provide to Buyer written verification as to whether or not any notes, mortgages, deeds of trust or real estate contracts against the property require the consent of the holder of such instrument(s) to the sale of the property or permit the holder to raise the interest rate and/or declare the entire balance due in the event of sale. If any such document so provides and holder does not waive the same or unconditionally approve the sale, Buyer shall have the option to declare this Agreement null and void by giving written notice to Seller or Seller's agent prior to closing. In such case, all earnest money received under this Agreement shall be returned to Buyer. It is understood and agreed that if provisions for said "Due on Sale" clause are set forth in Section 7 herein, alternatives allowed herein shall become null and void.

G. **TITLE INSPECTION.** Not less than five (5) days prior to closing, Seller shall provide to Buyer either an abstract of title brought current with an attorney's opinion or a preliminary title report on the subject property. Prior to closing, Buyer shall give written notice to Seller or Seller's agent, specifying reasonable objections to title. Thereafter, Seller shall be required, through escrow at closing, to cure the defect(s) to which Buyer has objected. If said defect(s) is not curable through an escrow agreement at closing, this Agreement shall be null and void at the option of the Buyer, and all monies received herewith shall be returned to the respective parties.

H. **TITLE INSURANCE.** If title insurance is elected, Seller authorizes the Listing Brokerage to order a preliminary commitment for a policy of title insurance to be issued by such title insurance company as Seller shall designate. Title policy to be issued shall contain no exceptions other than those provided for in said standard form, and the encumbrances or defects excepted under the final contract of sale. If title cannot be made so insurable through an escrow agreement at closing, the earnest money shall, unless Buyer elects to waive such defects or encumbrances, be refunded to Buyer, and this Agreement shall thereupon be terminated. Seller agrees to pay any cancellation charge.

I. **EXISTING TENANT LEASES.** If Buyer is to take title subject to an existing lease or leases, Seller agrees to provide to Buyer not less than five (5) days prior to closing a copy of all existing leases (and any amendments thereto) affecting the property. Unless reasonable written objection is given by Buyer to Seller or Seller's agent prior to closing, Buyer shall take title subject to such leases. If the objection(s) is not remedied at or prior to closing, this Agreement shall be null and void.

J. **CHANGES DURING TRANSACTION.** During the pendency of this Agreement, Seller agrees that no changes in any existing leases shall be made, nor new leases entered into, nor shall any substantial alterations or improvements be made or undertaken without the written consent of the Buyer.

Figure 6-1-1

K. **AUTHORITY OF SIGNATORS.** If Buyer or Seller is a corporation, partnership, trust, estate, or other entity, the person executing this Agreement on its behalf warrants his or her authority to do so and to bind Buyer or Seller.

L. **COMPLETE AGREEMENT — NO ORAL AGREEMENTS.** This instrument constitutes the entire agreement between the parties and supersedes and cancels any and all prior negotiations, representations, warranties, understandings or agreements between the parties. There are no oral agreements which modify or affect this agreement. This Agreement cannot be changed except by mutual written agreement of the parties.

M. **COUNTER OFFERS.** Any counter offer made by Seller or Buyer shall be in writing and, if attached hereto, shall incorporate all the provisions of this Agreement not expressly modified or excluded therein.

N. **DEFAULT/INTERPLEADER AND ATTORNEY'S FEES.** In the event of default by Buyer, Seller may elect to either retain the earnest money as liquidated damages or to institute suit to enforce any rights of Seller. In the event of default by Seller, or if this sale fails to close because of the nonsatisfaction of any express condition or contingency to which the sale is subject pursuant to this Agreement (other than by virtue of any default by Buyer), the earnest money deposit shall be returned to Buyer. Both parties agree that should either party default in any of the covenants or agreements herein contained, the defaulting party shall pay all costs and expenses, including a reasonable attorney's fee, which may arise or accrue from enforcing or terminating this Agreement or in pursuing any remedy provided hereunder or by applicable law, whether such remedy is pursued by filing suit or otherwise. In the event the principal broker holding the earnest money deposit is required to file an interpleader action in court to resolve a dispute over the earnest money deposit referred to herein, the Buyer and Seller authorize the principal broker to draw from the earnest money deposit an amount necessary to advance the costs of bringing the interpleader action. The amount of deposit remaining after advancing those costs shall be interpleaded into court in accordance with state law. The Buyer and Seller further agree that the defaulting party shall pay the court costs and reasonable attorney's fees incurred by the principal broker in bringing such action.

O. **ABROGATION.** Except for express warranties made in this Agreement, execution and delivery of final closing documents shall abrogate this Agreement.

P. **RISK OF LOSS.** All risk of loss or damage to the property shall be borne by the Seller until closing. In the event there is loss or damage to the property between the date hereof and the date of closing, by reason of fire, vandalism, flood, earthquake, or acts of God, and the cost to repair such damage shall exceed ten percent (10%) of the purchase price of the property, Buyer may at his option either proceed with this transaction if Seller agrees in writing to repair or replace damaged property prior to closing or declare this Agreement null and void. If damage to property is less than ten percent (10%) of the purchase price and Seller agrees in writing to repair or replace and does actually repair and replace damaged property prior to closing, this transaction shall proceed as agreed.

Q. **TIME IS OF ESSENCE—UNAVOIDABLE DELAY.** In the event that this sale cannot be closed by the date provided herein due to interruption of transport, strikes, fire, flood, extreme weather, governmental regulations, delays caused by lender, acts of God, or similar occurrences beyond the control of Buyer or Seller, then the closing date shall be extended seven (7) days beyond cessation of such condition, but in no event more than fifteen (15) days beyond the closing date provided herein. Thereafter, time is of the essence. This provision relates only to the extension of closing dates. "Closing" shall mean the date on which all necessary instruments are signed and delivered by all parties to the transaction.

R. **CLOSING COSTS.** Seller and Buyer shall each pay one-half (½) of the escrow closing fee, unless otherwise required by the lending institution. Costs of providing title insurance or an abstract brought current shall be paid by Seller. Taxes and assessments for the current year, insurance, if acceptable to the Buyer, rents, and interest on assumed obligations shall be prorated as set forth in Section 8. Unearned deposits on tenancies and remaining mortgage or other reserves shall be assigned to Buyer at closing.

S. **REAL PROPERTY CONVEYANCING.** If this agreement is for conveyance of fee title, title shall be conveyed by warranty deed free of defects other than those excepted herein. If this Agreement is for sale or transfer of a Seller's interest under an existing real estate contract, Seller may transfer by either (a) special warranty deed, containing Seller's assignment of said contract in form sufficient to convey after acquired title or (b) by a new real estate contract incorporating the said existing real estate contract therein.

T. **NOTICE.** Unless otherwise provided in this Agreement, any notice expressly required by it must be given no later than two days after the occurrence or non-occurrence of the event with respect to which notice is required. If any such timely required notice is not given, the contingency with respect to which the notice was to be given is automatically terminated and this Agreement is in full force and effect. If a person other than the Buyer or the Seller is designated to receive notice on behalf of the Buyer or the Seller, notice to the person so designated shall be considered notice to the party designating that person for receipt of notice.

U. **BROKERAGE.** For purposes of this Agreement, any references to the term, "Brokerage" shall mean the respective listing or selling real estate office.

V. **DAYS.** For the purposes of this Agreement, any references to the term, "days" shall mean business or working days exclusive of legal holidays.

THIS FORM HAS BEEN APPROVED BY THE UTAH REAL ESTATE COMMISSION AND THE OFFICE OF THE UTAH ATTORNEY GENERAL — JULY 1, 1987

Figure 6-1-2

EARNEST MONEY SALES AGREEMENT
EARNEST MONEY RECEIPT

Legend   Yes(X)   No(O)

DATE: __4-27-92__

The undersigned Buyer (s) __James A. & Jane P. Mills__ _____ hereby deposits with Brokerage
as EARNEST MONEY, the amount of __Five Thousand and 00/100 ----------------__ Dollars ($ __5,000.00__),
in the form of __Personal Check on Big Bank Inc., Jonesboro, Ark.__
which shall be deposited in accordance with applicable State Law.

__All Points Realty Inc.__ _____ Received by __Albert J. Slone, Agent__
Brokerage   Phone Number

OFFER TO PURCHASE

1. PROPERTY DESCRIPTION The above stated EARNEST MONEY is given to secure and apply on the purchase of the property situated at __121 North Main St.__ _____ in the City of __Jasper City,__ _____ County of __Holmes__ _____ , Utah, subject to any restrictive covenants, zoning regulations, utility or other easements or rights of way, government patents or state deeds of record approved by Buyer in accordance with Section G. Said property is owned by __Sam & Gloria Jones__ _____ as sellers, and is more particularly described as: __All of Lot 226, Peach Blossom Estates__

CHECK APPLICABLE BOXES:

☐ **UNIMPROVED REAL PROPERTY**   ☐ Vacant Lot   ☐ Vacant Acreage   ☐ Other _____
☒ **IMPROVED REAL PROPERTY**   ☐ Commercial   ☒ Residential   ☐ Condo   ☐ Other _____

(a) **Included items.** Unless excluded below, this sale shall *include* all fixtures and any of the items shown in Section A if presently attached to the property. The following personal property shall also be included in this sale and conveyed under separate Bill of Sale with warranties as to title: _____
__All Kitchen Appliances as installed, carpets and drapes as installed__

(b) **Excluded items.** The following items are specifically *excluded* from this sale: __Light Fixture in Dining Room to be__
__Replaced by Buyer's Selection up to cost of $300.00__

(c) **CONNECTIONS, UTILITIES AND OTHER RIGHTS.** Seller represents that the property includes the following improvements in the purchase price:

☒ public sewer   ☒ connected   ☐ well   ☐ connected   ☐ other   ☒ electricity   ☒ connected
☐ septic tank   ☐ connected   ☐ irrigation water / secondary system   ☐ ingress & egress by private easement
☐ other sanitary system _____   # of shares _____ Company _____   ☒ dedicated road   ☒ paved
☒ public water   ☒ connected   ☒ TV antenna   ☐ master antenna   ☐ prewired   ☒ curb and gutter
☐ private water   ☐ connected   ☒ natural gas   ☒ connected   ☐ other rights _____

(d) **Survey.** A certified survey ☐ shall be furnished at the expense of __Not Required__ _____ prior to closing, ☒ shall not be furnished.

(e) **Buyer Inspection.** Buyer has made a visual inspection of the property and subject to Section 1 (c) above and 6 below, accepts it in its present physical condition, except: __As Is Condition__

2. PURCHASE PRICE AND FINANCING. The total purchase price for the property is __$125,000.00__
__One Hundred Twenty-five Thousand__ _____ Dollars ($ __125,000.00__ _____) which shall be paid as follows:

$ __5,000.00__ which represents the aforedescribed EARNEST MONEY DEPOSIT:

$__40,000.00__ representing the approximate balance of CASH DOWN PAYMENT at closing.

$ _____ representing the approximate balance of an existing mortgage, trust deed note, real estate contract or other encumbrance to be assumed by buyer, which obligation bears interest at _____ % per annum with monthly payments of $ _____
which include: ☐ principal; ☐ interest; ☐ taxes; ☐ insurance; ☐ condo fees; ☐ other _____ .

$ _____ representing the approximate balance of an additional existing mortgage, trust deed note, real estate contract or other encumbrances to be assumed by Buyer, which obligation bears interest at _____ % per annum with monthly payments of $ _____
which include: ☐ principal; ☐ interest; ☐ taxes; ☐ insurance; ☐ condo fees; ☐ other _____ .

$__80,000.00__ representing balance, if any, including proceeds from a new mortgage loan, or seller financing, to be paid as follows: _____
at closing __from proceeds of a new mortgage to be applied for on acceptance of__
__this offer. Sales is subject to loan approval and granting.__

$ _____ Other _____

$125,000.00 TOTAL PURCHASE PRICE

If Buyer is required to assume an underlying obligation (in which case Section F shall also apply) and/or obtain outside financing, Buyer agrees to use best efforts to assume and/or procure same and this offer is made subject to Buyer qualifying for and lending institution granting said assumption and/or financing. Buyer agrees to make application within _____ days after Seller's acceptance of this Agreement to assume the underlying obligation and/or obtain the new financing at an interest rate not to exceed _____ %. If Buyer does not qualify for the assumption and/or financing within _____ days after Seller's acceptance of this Agreement, this Agreement shall be voidable at the option of the Seller upon written notice. Seller agrees to pay up to _____ mortgage loan discount points, not to exceed $ _____ . In addition, seller agrees to pay $ _____ to be used for Buyer's other loan costs.

Seller's Initials ( ) ( )   Date _____   Buyer's Initials ( ) ( )   Date _____

Figure 6-1-3

3. **CONDITION AND CONVEYANCE OF TITLE.** Seller represents that Seller ☐ holds title to the property in fee simple ☐ is purchasing the property under a real estate contract. Transfer of Seller's ownership interest shall be made as set forth in Section S. Seller agrees to furnish good and marketable title to the property, subject to encumbrances and exceptions noted herein, evidenced by ☐ a current policy of title insurance in the amount of purchase price ☐ an abstract of title brought current, with an attorney's opinion (See Section H).

4. **INSPECTION OF TITLE.** In accordance with Section G, Buyer shall have the opportunity to inspect the title to the subject property prior to closing. Buyer shall take title subject to any existing restrictive covenants, including condominium restrictions (CC & R's). Buyer ☐ has ☐ has not reviewed any condominium CC & R's prior to signing this Agreement.

5. **VESTING OF TITLE.** Title shall vest in Buyer as follows: James A. & Jane P. Mills as Joint Tenants with right of survival.

6. **SELLERS WARRANTIES.** In addition to warranties contained in Section C, the following items are also warranted: All kitchen appliances furnace, hot water heater and other mechanical items to be in good working order.
Exceptions to the above and Section C shall be limited to the following: _____

7. **SPECIAL CONSIDERATIONS AND CONTINGENCIES.** This offer is made subject to the following special conditions and/or contingencies which must be satisfied prior to closing: None

8. **CLOSING OF SALE.** This Agreement shall be closed on or before 5-30-1992 , 19 ____ at a reasonable location to be designated by Seller, subject to Section Q. Upon demand, Buyer shall deposit with the escrow closing office all documents necessary to complete the purchase in accordance with this Agreement. Prorations set forth in Section R shall be made as of ☒ date of possession ☐ date of closing ☐ other _____

9. **POSSESSION.** Seller shall deliver possession to Buyer on Closing unless extended by written agreement of parties.

10. **AGENCY DISCLOSURE.** At the signing of this Agreement the listing agent Brown Realtors Inc. represents (X) Seller ( ) Buyer, and the selling agent Albert J. Slone represents ( ) Seller (X) Buyer. Buyer and Seller confirm that prior to signing this Agreement written disclosure of the agency relationship(s) was provided to him/her. (X) ( ) Buyer's initials _____ Seller's initials.

11. **GENERAL PROVISIONS.** UNLESS OTHERWISE INDICATED ABOVE, THE GENERAL PROVISION SECTIONS ON THE REVERSE SIDE HEREOF HAVE BEEN ACCEPTED BY THE BUYER AND SELLER AND ARE INCORPORATED INTO THIS AGREEMENT BY REFERENCE.

12. **AGREEMENT TO PURCHASE AND TIME LIMIT FOR ACCEPTANCE.** Buyer offers to purchase the property on the above terms and conditions. Seller shall have until 11:00 (AM/PM) 4-28-92 , 19 ____, to accept this offer. Unless accepted, this offer shall lapse and the Agent shall return the EARNEST MONEY to the Buyer.

James A Mills	4-27-92	101 Smith St, Jonesboro, Ark	485-2101	402-16-1276
(Buyer's Signature)	(Date)	(Address)	(Phone)	(SSN/TAX ID)
Jane P. Mills	4-27-92	"	"	285-60-142c
(Buyer's Signature)	(Date)	(Address)	(Phone)	(SSN/TAX ID)

CHECK ONE:
☒ ACCEPTANCE OF OFFER TO PURCHASE: Seller hereby ACCEPTS the foregoing offer on the terms and conditions specified above.
☐ REJECTION. Seller hereby REJECTS the foregoing offer. _____ (Seller's initials)
☐ COUNTER OFFER. Seller hereby ACCEPTS the foregoing offer SUBJECT TO the exceptions or modifications as specified below or in the attached Addendum, and presents said COUNTER OFFER for Buyer's acceptance. Buyer shall have until _____ (AM/PM) _____, 19 ____ to accept the terms specified below.

Sam Jones	4-28-92	8:00 Am	121 N. Main	277-1819	515-50-61:
(Seller's Signature)	(Date)	(Time)	(Address)	(Phone)	(SSN/TAX ID)
Gloria Jones	4-28-92	8:00 Am	"	"	230-35-40.
(Seller's Signature)	(Date)	(Time)	(Address)	(Phone)	(SSN/TAX ID)

CHECK ONE:
☐ ACCEPTANCE OF COUNTER OFFER. Buyer hereby ACCEPTS the COUNTER OFFER
☐ REJECTION. Buyer hereby REJECTS the COUNTER OFFER. ——————— (Buyer's Initials)
☐ COUNTER OFFER. Buyer hereby ACCEPTS the COUNTER OFFER with modifications on attached Addendum.

James A. Mills	4-27-92	4:00 Pm	Jane P. Mills	4-27-92	4:00 Pm
(Buyer's Signature)	(Date)	(Time)	(Buyer's Signature)	(Date)	(Time)

DOCUMENT RECEIPT

State Law requires Broker to furnish Buyer and Seller with copies of this Agreement bearing all signatures. (One of the following alternatives must therefore be completed).

A. ☒ I acknowledge receipt of a final copy of the foregoing Agreement bearing all signatures:
SIGNATURE OF SELLER   SIGNATURE OF BUYER

Sam Jones	4-26-92	James P. Mills	4-28-92
	Date		Date
	Date		Date

B. ☐ I personally caused a final copy of the foregoing Agreement bearing all signatures to be mailed on _____, 19 ____ by Certified Mail and return receipt attached hereto to the ☐ Seller ☐ Buyer. Sent by _____

Figure 6-1-4

PROPERTY DESCRIPTION

In Line #1 the real property is identified as to address, city, county, and state. It is further identified by ownership and followed by additional language to completely identify the property to be purchased. Such words as "knows as the J.P. Smith Residence" or "Lot 126, Garden Subdivision" is appropriate.

The real property is further identified as unimproved or improved property and type. Under included items (item 1a), the drafter should include all personal property and even any real property which may be considered by the buyer or seller as *personal*. If any fixtures or personal property, now evident, are to be excluded it is essential that these exceptions be noted in item 1b. For instance, the owner might except an inherited antique chandelier in the dining room with the following statement: "Crystal chandelier in the dining room not included. Seller will replace this item with a buyer-acceptable item of value not to exceed $200.00." Section 1c further identifies the property amenities and the seller's signature will legally assure the accuracy of this listing. Item 1d provides for the subject of possible surveys, particularly where unimproved land is the subject. Completion of this section leaves no doubt as to whether a survey is to be made and who is to pay for it. Item 1e should be carefully considered. Does the buyer wish to inspect the property prior to closing? Is the closing subject to a satisfactory inspection? Will the property be inspected by a professional inspection firm and if so, who pays for the inspection. Is the owner planning to complete any repairs prior to closing? If so, will the buyer want to inspect the property prior to closing to assure proper completion. Where the form does not include sufficient space for these considerations, reference can be made to an addendum "attached to and made a part of this agreement."

PURCHASE PRICE AND FINANCING

Proper completion of this section should leave no doubt as to the total price to be paid, and the source of each and every dollar of that total. Where new financing or assumption of old financing is involved, the form clearly describes all requirements and actions required to consummate the transaction. It should also be noted that each of the parties are required to initial each completed page of the agreement signifying their agreement and full understanding of the words included.

CONDITION AND CONVEYANCE OF TITLE

Here the buyer certifies as to his type of ownership, agrees to furnish "good and marketable title" and either a policy of title insurance or an abstract of title. Abstracts of title are not currently recommended as they are opinions of the abstracter with no guarantee of accuracy. Title insurance policies, on the other hand, guarantee the buyer that the title is as represented in the policy.

INSPECTION OF TITLE

Item 4 guarantees the buyer the right to inspect the title, prior to closing, to assure that the property rights are as represented by the seller. This procedure is a standard part of the closing procedure, where the closing officer reviews the title documents and explains the various statement contained therein.

VESTING OF TITLE

The information contained in this section is used by the closing officer in the preparation of the deed. He may not change or modify this direction without agreement of the buyer(s). The subject of title is very complicated and has very large potential tax implications. Where the buyer is unsure as to how title should be taken, the broker or agent should not offer his opinion but rather refer this question to the buyer's attorney who can best advise the client as to the best manner of holding title.

SELLER WARRANTIES

Item 6 contains those seller warranties as to the condition of installed equipment and the condition in which he guarantees to deliver the real and personal property. Does the seller agree to leave the premises in a clean and sanitary condition and does he warrant that all electrical and mechanical equipment to be in working order at the time of closing? These guarantees should be enumerated here if they apply.

SPECIAL CONSIDERATIONS AND CONTINGENCIES

This is an area of considerable litigation. It is essential that any contingencies or considerations be carefully and clearly made a part of this agreement. This subject will be further examined in later paragraphs of this chapter.

CLOSING OF THE SALE

The date included here is a date both parties hope to meet. Any reasonable variation in this stated date will not be considered a failure to perform, *unless the date is made the essence of the agreement.* This item also provides for direction to the closing officer in regard to the proration of such items as taxes, existing insurance policies, rents, and so on, and the agreement between the parties as to the date of proration (closing or possession).

AGENCY DISCLOSURE

This item is a rather new legality and stems from the increasing change in the representation pattern of the realty profession. In former times, the selling agent was assumed to represent the seller and to some degree his buyer as well. Now, representation is an elective item of the buyer. More and more buyers desire that their agents represent their interests only and leave the owner representation to the listing broker. This does not necessarily mean that the buyer will pay his selling agent's commission, unless he so elects. In most cases, the commission still comes from the seller. The agency form, referred to here, is included as Figure 4-1, in Chapter 4.

GENERAL PROVISIONS

This item is self explanatory. A detailed discussion of pertinent legal aspects of the agreement are contained on pages 1 and 4 of the form.

AGREEMENT TO PURCHASE AND TIME LIMIT FOR ACCEPTANCE

This item provides for appropriate buyer and seller signatures, and identification of those persons. A full discussion of offer and acceptance, counter offers, delivery of contract etc. are discussed in more detail later in this chapter.

The agent should assure that the signature(s) of the buyers are exactly the same as in line #1 of the receipt. He should also determine that the seller(s) signature(s) are their legal and normal signatures. They need not be exactly as contained on the existing recorded deeds.

DOCUMENT RECEIPTS

Here, the buyers and sellers acknowledge the receipt of copies of the agreement bearing the signatures of all parties to the transaction. The three-part form provides for one copy of the offer to be provided to the purchaser as a receipt of his earnest money deposit. This is held by the purchaser until such time as he receives a copy of the "contract" containing all parties signature. A space is also provided for the drafter's (agent's) signature which certifies that copies have been provided to both buyers and sellers. In the event the seller is out of town, his copy must be mailed by Certified Mail and the receipt, when received, attached to the broker's record copy of the contract.

MOST BUY-SELL AGREEMENTS RESULT IN ROUTINE FULFILLMENTS

Most offers and acceptances result in satisfactory agreements between the parties and where the drafter has completed the offer in a competent manner, few problems are encountered. Nevertheless, there are many problems arising from misunderstandings between the parties, incomplete or incompetent drafting of agreements, changes in one or more of the parties status, or attempts to avoid the agreed consummation of the agreement. The following discussions describe problems which have arisen in the past and the decisions of the courts in resolving these disputes.

AGREEMENTS MUST BE DEFINITE AND COMPLETE

When the offer and acceptance are not definite, problems are sure to arise. For instance, a broker prepared an agreement of sale, and the buyer paid $1,000 deposit money, which was turned over to the seller. The buyer then sued the seller for the return of his money, claiming that the agreement of sale was inadequate, incomplete, and ineffective. The provision in controversy related to the mortgage. The agreement simply said, "Subject to purchaser obtaining a mortgage." It was silent as to the amount of the mortgage and all related aspects, such as interest rate, duration, monthly payment size, and whether the mortgagor had the right of anticipation. Clearly, the agreement lacked *detail,* the first essential in a meeting of minds. It would have been preferable to have stated, "Vendee will pay cash to highest loan obtainable at 9 percent or less." In this connection, a broker must be alert as to his responsibilities when he independently represents or warrants to the buyer that he will obtain the necessary financing. If the broker is unable to produce the required mortgage with the results of a failed deal, the buyer's deposit money is lost, and he has the right to sue the broker upon the latter's broken promise to produce the mortgage. It is considered an unethical practice to require the buyer to finance the property through the broker *alone, so that the broker cannot look for funds where he pleases.*

The same situation is true where the broker knows that the buyer must sell his present home in order to obtain funds necessary in the purchase of the new home. The broker, in good faith, may promise to sell the buyer's present home before the sale is consummated for the new home. If he fails to perform, the buyer can sue the broker for any loss he sustains. If the sale is contingent upon any condition, the broker should write that contingency into the contract of sale. Thus the owner, in considering the offer, knows that he has a contingent sale that may not materialize.

In another situation, a broker negotiated a $300,000 transaction and received a $10,000 deposit, which was to be the broker's commission. There was a $240,000 mortgage of record against the property. In referring to the mortgage in the agreement of sale, the broker stated that the buyer was accepting the property "under and subject to the mortgage," in the amount then due of $240,000. Note here, the amount of the mortgage should have been stated as "approximately" $240,000 as it varies from date to date, depending upon payments or lack thereof.

The seller's attorney tendered a general warranty deed to the buyer, at the closing. In referring to the unpaid mortgage, the deed stated it was "Under and subject to the mortgage balance of $240,000," which mortgage, the grantee *assumed and agreed to pay,* as part of the purchase price. The buyer refused to accept the deed because it did not conform to the agreement of sale. The buyer was correct. The broker had rendered a disservice to his principal, the seller, from whom he expected a $10,000 commission. Under the broker's mortgage clause, as drafted, the buyer would have suffered no personal liability in the event of a mortgage foreclosure sale, and a deficiency judgment was entered in favor of the mortgagee.

Under the mortgage clause in the deed, which was tendered, the buyer *assumed* the mortgage, and if foreclosure ensued, the buyer would have been obliged for any deficiency judgment. After a lengthy and costly controversy, the deal fell through and the broker lost a $10,000 commission.

Once a deed is accepted, rights which the parties had under the agreement of sale are merged into the deed. The sales agreement has been abrogated. No further action arises under the agreement of sale.[41] However, a closing statement, accepted by buyer and seller, may modify the agreement of sale if the figures are at variance with the sales agreement.[42]

Most sales require mortgage financing. The process is by purchaser-application to a lending institution, a commitment by the institution, examination of title and closing. It should be noted that "commitment" is not enough.

Suppose a man and wife applied for a loan based principally on the man's income and he dies after the commitment has been made. It is obvious that the death has seriously affected the security of the loan and it is most probably that the lender would not provide the funds previously committed and based on a certain income of the buyers.

The broker or salesperson plays an important role in obtaining a mortgage so that the sale can take place. The language in the agreement of sale, prepared by the broker in relation to the procurement of the mortgage, is all important. A clause such as "subject to obtaining a satisfactory mortgage in the sum of $50,000" is dangerous. A purchaser who desires to renege on the agreement can usually find that the mortgage proposed is *not satisfactory,* due to interest rate, terms or monthly payment. In the case of *Gaynes v. Allen,*[43] the Court held in an agreement of sale, "subject to the buyer obtaining satisfactory financing," that a mortgage obtainable from a Savings and Loan Association for a term of 25 years at 9 3/4% interest, and containing a provision that "the stipulated rate of interest may be increased, but only after a three-month written notice to the borrower," met the clause in the agreement for "available financing." From this, it is clear that the broker should have spelled out the mortgage contingency clause with far more clarity. A better clause in the agreement would have read:

> This sale is contingent upon the Buyer obtaining a commitment for a mortgage loan in the amount of $_____ for a term of not less than _____ years, at an effective interest rate of not more than ____% per annum and the loan being granted. Buyer shall obtain said commitment by _____, 19__(Contingency Date). Buyer shall make application in writing to a responsible mortgage lending institution within ten days from the date of the seller's acceptance of this agreement.
> If buyer applies for and cannot secure the commitment, Buyer shall, on or

---

[41] Dillahunty v. Keystone Savings Association, 303 N.E.2d 750 (Ohio 1973).

[42] S.G. Payne & Co. v. Nowak, 465 S.W.2d 17 (Mo. 1971).

[43] Gaynes v. Allen, 362 N.E.2d 197 (N.H.).

before the "Contingency Date," notify the Seller in writing either that (1) this Agreement is terminated, in which all of Buyer's earnest money Deposit will be returned to him and all rights and liabilities of the parties hereto shall thereupon cease and determine, or (2) Buyer waives the Mortgage Contingency Clause, in which event this Agreement shall continue in full force and effect as if no contingency had existed.

AMBIGUITIES IN THE AGREEMENT ARE CONSTRUED AGAINST THE PRINCIPAL WHOSE AGENT PREPARES THE AGREEMENT

Any ambiguity in the sales agreement was normally construed against the owner, since it was his agent who drafted the agreement. Where the mode of operation involving selling and buyer brokers is becoming more prevalent, it is assumed that future courts will hold the principal of the *drafting broker* responsible for ambiguities in the agreement. Few if any cases have been heard involving this new modus operandi to establish what future decisions are likely to be. Nevertheless, former decisions holding the owner responsible still apply and will have bearing on any future decisions.

In the case of *Baker v. Leight*,[44] the defendant broker prepared a deposit agreement and receipt, which stated that the buyers were "to assume an existing mortgage of approximately $52,000, payable at approximately $518.39 per month including 7 percent interest..." The seller wrote in a modification, among other, viz "5. The purchaser is to assume the legal obligation for the first mortgage." These modifications were accepted by the buyers. Later the parties became aware of the fact that the first mortgage contained the following clause:

16. It is expressly understood and agreed that this mortgage shall become due and payable forthwith at the option of the Mortgagee if the Mortgagors shall convey away the said premises or if title shall become vested in any other person or persons in any manner whatsoever.

The mortgage was a matter of record prior to the execution of the agreement of sale. When the buyers learned of the clause in question, they refused to go through with the deal. While other issues were also involved, the court said,

It was the seller's obligation to procure the waiver of clause 16 from the mortgagee and to come forward immediately upon being informed that the buyer elected to rescind because of the fact that clause 16 constituted a material breach of the contract. This the seller did not do.

The buyers made out a prima facie case. It was reversible error to direct a verdict for the defendants.

The Supreme Court remanded the case for further hearing.

It should be noted in Figure 6-1, that a situation such as the one outlined above

---

[44] Baker v. Leight, 370 P.2d 268 (Ariz. 1962).

could not occur in Utah as Section "F" of the approved form forces the seller to examine his mortgage agreement not less than five days prior to closing and divulge his findings to the seller.

In the case of *Beattie-Firth, Inc. v. Colebank*,[45] the broker lost his suit for a commission since his listing contract provided that he was to receive a commission: (1) if a buyer was obtained and a sale was consummated, or (2) if the sale was not consummated by reason of any default of the seller. The broker obtained a buyer. The sales agreement, prepared by the broker, recognized the plaintiff as the broker in the deal and the seller agreed to pay him a commission, subject to the two conditions listed above. The buyer defaulted and the seller refused to sue the buyer for damages or specific performance. Since the deal was not consummated and the seller was not at fault, neither of the two conditions was satisfied and the broker could not recover. The court held,

> . . . we would hesitate to enunciate a rule which would require a vendor whose promise is so conditioned to engage in expensive and perhaps fruitless litigation in order that the broker might be entitled to a commission. A burden so onerous cannot be imposed by implication.

ANY OFFER MAY BE REVOKED PRIOR TO ITS ACCEPTANCE

An element in a preliminary offer to purchase contract is that it usually provides that the seller has a certain period of time within which to accept the offer. The prospective buyer, however, is not *bound* to keep the offer open for the time specified in the written agreement. He can withdraw his offer at any time, if the seller has not accepted. Also, where a formal agreement of sale is prepared, which the buyer signs, it is still a naked offer, which can be withdrawn prior to acceptance. Thus, a broker should act promptly in seeing that his owner signs the agreement as soon as possible. *It takes two signatures to make a contract—buyer's and seller's.*

It is equally important that the broker deliver the seller's signed agreement to the buyer as soon as possible. In other words, it is not only necessary that the seller accept the buyer's offer by signing the agreement, but the acceptance must be *communicated* to the buyer. Until the acceptance has been communicated, the buyer can withdraw his offer to purchase, even though he has signed the agreement of sale.

In the case of *Reynolds v. Hancock*,[46] a broker sued the buyer for a commission upon the strength of a clause in an acceptance offer to purchase, which read,

> This offer is made subject to the approval of the seller by midnight March 27, 1857. In consideration of agent submitting this offer to the seller, purchaser agrees with the agent not to withdraw this offer during said period or until earlier rejection thereof by seller.

---

[45] Beattie-Firth, Inc. v. Colebank et al., 143 W.Va. 740 (1958).

[46] Reynolds v. Hancock, 53 Wash.2d 682 (1959).

After signing the offer to purchase, the buyer, prior to midnight March 27, 1957, notified the seller in California, that the offer was withdrawn. The Court held that there was no consideration to the buyers from the broker not to withdraw the offer prior to its expiration date. The broker could not recover. Using language that the offer is made *irrevocably* for a certain number of days may have some psychological effect, but it would not prevail in a suit at law.

Once the offer is signed by the owner and that fact communicated to the offeree, a binding contract is in effect. Thus, an offer may be accepted, or the offer may lapse through passage of a period of time (nonacceptance by seller), or it may be withdrawn before acceptance.

Acceptance by an authorized agent constitutes delivery. In *Little v. Rohauer*[47] the court was asked to force the defendants to perform on a contract to purchase. The defendants, with the aid of a Caldwell Banker agent, had found a suitable home to purchase from the plaintiff sellers. The listing was also with the Caldwell Banker agency. The sales contract, signed by both parties, provided that the purchasers were to receive a title commitment before July 10, 1981. The title commitment was received by the listing agent before July 10th, but he failed to inform the buyers. The purchasers, on July 14th, informed Caldwell Banker they would not perform on the contract because they had not received the title commitment as required.

The fact that the listing agent did not communicate the timely receipt of the commitment did not defeat the contract as he was an authorized agent of the buyers. Prior Colorado rules indicated that the selling broker, if different from the listing broker, was the listing agent's subagent and delivery to such broker would not constitute delivery.

A COUNTER OFFER CONSTITUTES A REJECTION

An acceptance must meet the exact terms of the offer in order to establish an enforceable contract. If a potential buyer, for example, receives an offer from the seller for the sale of the seller's home at $40,000, and in reply, injects certain conditions that the carpeting and drapes throughout the house are to be included in the sale, this is a counter-proposition and constitutes a rejection of the offer. An offer once rejected is gone forever, and cannot be accepted later, unless the offeror is receptive. A counter offer is, in effect, a new offer.[48]

In the case of *Stearns v. Western*,[49] purchasers of a certain property brought suit against the prospective seller to recover $1,000 earnest money deposit. The offer to purchase was subject to the conditions that the vendees were able to obtain,

---

[47]
Little v. Rohauer, 707 P.2d 1015 Colo. (Colo. App. 1985)

[48]
Ardent v. Horan, 366 A.2d 162 (R.I. 1976).

[49]
Stearns v. Western, 252 N.E.2d 126 (Ill. 1967).

within ten days, a $17,000 mortgage at interest not to exceed 5 3/4 percent for not less than 20 years. The buyer was unable to obtain financing on those terms within the ten days. The vendor then offered a mortgage loan, specifying five additional conditions over those enumerated above. These conditions were not shown to be matters of custom or usage. The court held this constituted a counter proposition and the buyers were entitled to a refund of their deposit.[50]

THE EARNEST MONEY DEPOSIT

Almost all offers to purchase are accompanied by an earnest money deposit, although such deposits are not necessary to validate the contract. The agreement should provide *more* than merely that the earnest money deposit shall be retained by the vendor as liquidated damages in case the buyer should fail or refuse to consummate the deal. The vendor should be afforded three alternative remedies:

1. Right to sue the buyer for specific performance of the contract.

2. The right to resell the property and sue the buyer for any loss on the resale, and

3. The right to retain the deposit money as liquidated damages.

A suggested clause to meet the above requirements might read:

> Should the buyer fail to make settlement, as herein provided, the sum or sums paid on account of the purchase price, at the option of the seller, may be retained by the seller, either on account of the purchase price, the resale price, or as liquidated damages. In the latter case, the contract shall become null and void. In the latter event, all monies paid on account shall be divided equally between the seller and broker, but in no event shall the sum paid to the broker be in excess of the usual rate of commission due him.

It is not necessary that a deposit of earnest money be paid at the time the agreement of sale is signed by the buyer and seller. The mutual concurrent promises that the buyer will pay a certain sum of money to the seller on a specific date and that the latter will execute and deliver a proper deed to the buyer on the same specified date, constitute good and sufficient legal consideration. A broker or salesperson would be rendering a disservice to the owner if he did not require a down payment from the buyer as evidence of good faith. The deposit should be in a sufficient amount to afford the seller financial protection, in case the buyer defaults. And yet, too many licensees accept a $500 deposit on a $25,000, or more property. Such a deposit falls far short of commission involved in the transaction. While it is true that the seller can sue the buyer for performance, the average seller is reluctant to engage in litigation. The size of the down payment should be commensurate with the amount of the consideration price for the property and also

---

[50] Pravorne v. McLeod, 383 P.2d 855 (Nev. 1963).

consider the waiting period before the deal will close. If the deal is to be closed more than 30 days from the date of the agreement, a large down payment should be obtained as a protection to the seller, since the real estate market might change during this longer period.

A 10 percent earnest money requirement upon the signing of an agreement of sale is reasonable. However, it often happens in real estate practice that a buyer does not have cash funds available for that large a deposit. It would be satisfactory for the broker to prepare a contract of sale for $17,500, with a cash deposit of $200, upon the signing of the contract. However, he should further provide that the buyer agrees to pay an additional sum of $1,300 or $1,800 within 30 days thereafter, *which date is of the essence of the agreement.*[51]

DISTRIBUTION OF EARNEST MONEY WHERE THE DEAL FAILS

BUYER WITHDRAWS OFFER PRIOR TO ACCEPTANCE

If the offer to purchase is withdrawn before it is accepted by the owner, the buyer is entitled to a refund of his deposit *immediately.* In one case, the broker sought to have the buyer sign a memorandum that if he ever bought a property in the future, it would be through the broker, before returning the deposit. This is unethical and clearly unenforceable. In 8 Amer. Juris. 1060, Sec. 130, it is said,

> If earnest money is paid to a broker, and the contract is broker by the principal, the broker, notwithstanding that he has disclosed his principal, is liable to the buyer for a refund of the deposit money, unless he has in good faith paid it over to his principal. The fact that the broker has a claim against his principal is no justification for refusal to return the deposit money.[52]

DEAL FAILS TO CLOSE

In spite of the above legality, the broker should avoid any charge against himself by not ignoring the express instructions of his principal. In *Polette v. Wall,*[53] the broker returned the earnest money to the buyer without the knowledge or consent of the sellers. The Missouri Court held that, by so doing, the broker exceeded his authority. Similarly, in the Washington case of *Somers v. Pix,*[54] the broker waived his commission by allowing the purchaser to withdraw the earnest money, because of objection to the title, which did not render it unmarketable.

The case of *Hicks v. Howell,*[55] involved an action by a buyer against an owner

---

[51] Cowan v. Allen Monuments, 500 S.W.2d 223 (Tex. 1973).

[52] Gosslin v. Martin, 56 Ore. 281, 107 P. 957 and Perry v. Thorpe Bros., Inc. 267 Minn. 29 (1963).

[53] Polette v. Wall, 256 S.W.2d 283 (Mo. 1953).

[54] Sommers v. Pix, 134 P. 932 (1913).

[55] Hicks v. Howell, 203 Va. 32 (1961).

and the broker to recover an earnest money deposit. The court held against the broker who received the earnest money deposit as agent for the sellers could not apply such funds to the payment of a commission where the vendors were unable to deliver a marketable title, as required. The broker was held liable to the buyers for the amount of the deposit.

In the case of *Eggerling v. Cuhel*,[56] the buyer signed an agreement to purchase a Knox County farm, on May 8, 1969, and gave a salesperson for the Thor Agency a deposit of $4,000. This check was turned over immediately to the broker and deposited in the broker's trust account. The sellers signed on May 9, 1969, and received a trust account check for $2,300, balance after deducting $1,700 commission. The broker and the salesperson split the commission evenly. The property was sold under an existing FHA mortgage. Possession was to be given on January 1, 1970. The buyer found that they could not proceed under FHA regulations. Negotiations continued without success until 1972. In May 1972, the sellers sold 57 acres of the property to another buyer. The Eggerlings then brought suit against the seller, broker, and salesperson. The court dismissed the suit against the salesperson and found in favor of the broker as well. The court stated that the license law statute was regulatory, and in the nature of a penal statute. Penalties for its violation involved suspension or revocation of license. Since there was no allegation of fraud or bad faith on the part of the salesperson or broker, the statute did not grant any new *civil* remedies against real estate brokers or salespersons. However, where the seller refuses to consummate a sale, without cause, the broker should return the deposit money to the purchaser.[57]

AGREEMENT MADE SUBJECT TO FINANCING

If the agreement is made subject to mortgage financing, it is important that the proposed terms be spelled out—amount, type, interest rate, commitment approval date, amount of appraisal required if VA or FHA financing, and so on.

Should the proposed mortgage be FHA, the agreement should expressly provide that, notwithstanding any other provisions of the contract, the buyer shall not be required to purchase the property if the appraisal is less than the selling price of the agreement. However, the buyer usually reserves the right to purchase the property even though it does not appraise for the full amount.

It is seldom that the mortgage company is willing to grant an FHA or VA loan without the payment of points. A point is 1 percent of the mortgage amount paid in advance to compensate the lender for lending money at less that the going rate

---

[56] Eggerling v. Cuhel, 246 N.W.2d 199 (Neb. 1976).

[57] Mathis v. Yarig, 176, 176 A.2d 794 (N.J. App. 1961).

(that specified by the FHA). By Government regulations these points *must be paid by the seller.* Consequently, agreements involving VA or FHA loans usually spell out the *maximum* points which the seller agrees to pay.

A Pennsylvania court has held that where an agreement for sale of a $24,000 dwelling was made subject to the purchaser obtaining a mortgage in the sum of $16,000, the purchaser had a right to expect a loan with at least a 20-year maturity and, upon his failure to obtain such a loan, he was entitled to a refund of his $2,000 deposit.[58]

PROBLEMS WHICH PREVENT THE CLOSING OF AN AGREEMENT

CLOSING DATES

A definite date for the closing of the transaction must be included in the agreement. If no date is specified for closing, the courts may well consider that the parties *intended* a reasonable time and would be governed accordingly. There is no hard and fast rule to determine what constitutes reasonable time. It depends upon a variety of circumstances—the activity of the real estate market, type of property involved, time of year, and so on. Thirty or 60 days in most cases would constitute a reasonable time.

The case of *Simmons and Associates v. Urban Renewal Agency,*[59] involved a suit to recover a deposit of $23,425 on the contract to purchase land for $475,000. The contract was dated April 25, 1965. The agency extended the time for submitting financing plans on eight separate occasions, over a period of 641 days. The court held that the retention of the deposit money as liquidated damages, under the contract, would be enforced.

Many purchasers are concerned that they will not be able to close a transaction upon the date specified in the agreement. Example, the mortgage money may not be available by the closing date, the buyers of the purchasers' home may not be ready to close on the purchasers' home, the moving company may not be available until a week after the closing date. Similarly, the sellers may not be ready to close on the date specified, because the house they are having built may not be ready.

If one of the parties wants to insist that the closing be held absolutely upon the date specified, the date must be made a vital and material part of the

---

[58] Tieri v. Orbell, 192 Pa. Super. Ct. 612 (1960).

[59] Simmons and Associates v. Urban Renewal Agency, 497 S.W.2d 705 (Ky. 1973).

agreement; such as, ". . . on Feb. 1, 1992, which date and time is of the essence of this agreement."

The time of essence clause may be waived by an extension agreement, as well as by conduct of the parties.[60]

Should the vendor be indulgent and waive the strict time obligation in one respect, he may well be held to a waiver of the other time obligations by the buyer. An oral extension of time negotiated by a vendor of "time is of the essence" clause agreement of sale is binding and need not be in writing under the statute of frauds.[61] Waiver may be shown by parol evidence, by way of circumstances or course of dealing.[62]

A seller of real estate may convert a sales agreement in which *time is not of the essence* to one which provides for time is of the essence by delivery of a notice to the purchaser *who has failed to close at the agreed time.* The time specified for the time is of the essence closing must be reasonable.[63]

In the case of *Robinson v. Abren,*[64] which was an action for specific performance brought by the purchaser. The closing date, per agreement of sale, was December 15, 1971, and *time was of the essence.* The cash payment on the contract was not received by the seller by December 15, 1971. It was mailed by the purchasers on December 16, 1971 and it was mailed *to the broker,* and not to the seller. The Court held that the buyer failed to show that the broker had express, implied, or apparent authority to accept payment after the closing date. Specific performance of the agreement was denied. See also Harris v. Potts, et al.[65]

PROBLEMS WITH MARKETABLE TITLE

Marketable title, which the seller agrees to furnish the buyer, is one free from liens, encumbrances or clouds; it is such a title that a court could compel a buyer to accept. If the sale is subject to a mortgage, easement, or restriction, it must be noted in the agreement, and made subject thereto. If the owner is permitted by the agreement and submits an abstract of title, the buyer shall have a certain number of days (10-20) within which to submit any objections, in writing. Most modern-day agreements insist upon title insurance; however, some sellers insist on furnishing an abstract of title. Where the owner insists, and the buyer is willing, the

---

[60]
Ricchio v. Oberst, 251 N.W.2d 781 (Wisc. 1977).

[61]
Kimm v. Anderson, 313 A.2d 46 (Me. 1974).

[62]
Smith v. Hues, 540 S.W.2d 485 (Texas App. 1976).

[63]
Tom Jones Realty Corp. v. Frick, 533 N.Y.S.2d 995 (N.Y. App. Div. 988).

[64]
Robinson v. Abren, 345 So.2d 404 (Fla. App. 1977).

[65]
Harris v. Potts et al., 545 S.W.2d 126 (Tex. 1976).

agreement should provide for the title to be brought up to date at the expense of the seller.

For a title to be marketable it need not necessarily be perfect, but a purchaser has a right to require that the title be of such a character that he will not be exposed to dangers of litigation on its validity. If the facts throw a cloud on the title, rendering it dubious in the minds of reasonable men, it is not merchantable.[66]

A broker is not liable to loss of commission, where he did not have knowledge of the seller's inability to deliver a good title because of the wife's refusal to join in the listing contract. The broker's prospect was able to purchase the property.[67]

CLOUDS UPON THE TITLE

Where the closing calls for the vendor to provide good and marketable title with title insurance, a preliminary search of the title may reveal one or more clouds on the title. These clouds generally are of one or two types: (1) judgments on the seller, or (2) liens on the property.

Liens are generally for small amounts that may be easily resolved in the closing process by payment of the amount owed. These liens are usually the result of filings by contractors or material suppliers for work on the property. Judgments, on the other hand are usually for much larger amounts and fall into two categories:

• Judgments in personam—which are judgments against the person (seller in this case), and as such bind all of his real estate, and

• Judgments in rem—which is a specific lien and against only one property.

JUDGMENTS, EARLY HISTORY

From early times (1688) lands of debtors have been subject to liens as security for debts. Although most people have a passing interest in the subject of judgments, few really understand the legal principles that apply.

What is a judgment? In legal parlance it may be defined as a decree of a court or competent jurisdiction declaring that one individual (debtor) is indebted to another (creditor), and fixing the amount of the debt. A verdict obtained in every court is not necessarily a judgment. Some other step may be required to reduce the verdict to a judgment.

The effect of a judgment is that a lien immediately attaches against the debtor's real estate upon the entry of the judgment. It automatically binds all the real estate located in the county where the judgment is entered. That is what is meant by the *lien* of the judgment. A lien may be defined, in technical language, as a hold or claim which one person has upon the property of another as a security for

---

[66] Ewing v. Plummer, 308 Ill. 585 (1923).

[67] Bryan, Appellant v. Jack Justice, 287 So.2d 331 (Fla. 1973).

some debt or charge. It is the right which the creditor has under the law to have the debt satisfied out of the debtor's property.

If the creditor has a claim not reduced to a judgment, the debtor can sell or mortgage his property, free and clear of such unsecured claim. If the creditor has reduced his claim to a judgment, a lien is thereby created against the real estate. A purchaser would then take the property subject to the lien and stand in the place of the debtor.

A judgment, other than a judgment *in rem,* binds every freehold interest in the land. A judgment entered against a life tenant will bind his interest in the property, which may be sold to satisfy a judgment. The purchaser would take the property for or during the lifetime of the debtor, as a tenant *pur autre vie* (for the life of another).

LIEN ON PERSONAL PROPERTY

Judgments are not liens on the personal property of the debtor as they are on his real estate. A debtor may convey good title to a bona fide purchaser of his automobile or other personal property even though there is a judgment of record against him. Personal property may, however, be seized in satisfaction of a judgment of debt. This is done by levy and attachment upon the direction of the sheriff, the executive officer of the court, to seize and sell the described property. A mortgage, while it deals with real estate, is personalty, but the court can direct the sheriff to levy on a mortgage belonging to the debtor and sell it. The same is true of a leasehold. In other words, a creditor is entitled to proceed against any property of his debtor to recover his debt. In a sense, a debtor is a trustee for his creditors.

RELEASE OF JUDGMENT

It is always important to remember that a judgment attaches and adversely affects real estate of a debtor, as a lien, just as soon as it is entered into the record. The judgment is a lien against all real estate owned by the debtor at the time the judgment is entered. The owner cannot give a purchaser good title to any part of the real estate owned by him. No prudent buyer would accept title thus encumbered, nor could the creditor be compelled to release any part of the debtor's real estate upon payment of any sum short of the full debt. A release is a matter of indulgence by the creditor. The real estate released should be noted on the margin of the recorded judgment.

When the debtor pays the judgment, he is entitled to have the judgment record marked "satisfied in full."

LIEN PERIOD

The lien of a judgment does not last forever. As between the original debtor-owner and judgment creditor, execution may be had against the debtor's property at any time, so long as the debtor continues to own it and rights of mortgagees or other judgment creditors have not intervened. The lien of a judgment lasts for a limited period of time, and, if the judgment is not revived within the prescribed period of time, the lien against a subsequent purchaser, mortgagee, or judgment creditor is lost. In Pennsylvania, the lien of judgment lasts for five years. If the judgment is for longer than the statutory period and no action taken to revive it, a purchaser from the debtor takes the property free from the judgment. In other jurisdictions, the judgment is a lien for ten years.

Even though the lien period is expired, it is not extinguished, but can be revived. If the debtor still owns the property, it can be sold on the judgment.

Where plaintiff's attorney quietly took default judgment on beginning of first day on which defendant's answer was delinquent, the trial court acted properly in setting aside judgment.[68]

A lien, as revived by a *scire facias* (to show cause) proceeding, attaches only as of the date of the revival.[69]

Judgments arise in several ways, among which are court decisions, default, and confession. Since litigation is always prevalent, a great many judgments arise through court action. Where the litigation takes place in a minor judiciary court, such as a Justice of the Peace, a transcript of the verdict or judgment can be filed in the proper county court so as to be a lien. A judgment by default arises where the law requires a person to take some sufficient legal step and he fails to do so. For example, Thompson sues Bryan and serves him with a copy of his statement of claim. Bryan is then required to file an answer within a certain period of time, say 20 days, and he fails to do so. Thompson can enter judgment against Bryan because of Bryans default. The great majority of judgments probably arise through confession, authorized in a note, bond, or lease. They are known as judgments DSB, which stands for *debitum sine brevi* and means "debt without a writ or declaration."

DEBT BY CONFESSION

A judgment by confession is as conclusive as a judgment on the verdict of a jury. The main distinction between a promissory note and a judgment note is that upon a default in payment of a promissory note, the holder must sue the maker before he can obtain a judgment. In the judgment note, the holder may enter upon a judgment upon a default, without any suit. This is so by reason of the language of the instrument which authorizes and empowers:

> ... any Attorney of any court of Record within the United States or elsewhere to appear for (me), and without declarations filed, confess judgment against (me) and in favor of said payee, his executors, administrators or assigns, as any term for the above sum with costs of suit. ...

In fact, the holder of the note may confess judgment at any time, even before default or maturity, but no execution can issue until default. If the obligor is deceased, judgment may not be confessed against him as death revokes the agent's power to

---

[68] Robinson v. Varela, 136 Cal. Rptr. 783 (1977).

[69] Mitchell v. Chastain, 233 S.E.2d 829 (Ga. App. 1977).

confess. Where one joint obligor dies, the note can be entered as a judgment against the survivor; it is irregular to enter the note against all of the obligor including the decedent. Judgment by confession operates in a very summary manner, and very often the debtor is unaware that a judgment has been entered against him until he tries to sell his property or place a mortgage upon it. If the debtor claims that the entry of judgment is unjust, he may petition the court to open up the judgment; and if the court, in the exercise of sound judicial discretion, believes that the debtor should be permitted to make a defense, it will open up the judgment and then the case is heard *de novo* (anew) to determine whether the plaintiff is entitled to a judgment.

A motion to enter summary judgment is to be granted only where there is no triable issue of material fact.[70]

A default judgment rendered without proof of the demand sufficient to establish a prima facie case must be set aside.[71]

In *Robinson v. Varela,*[72] the court of appeals stated:

> The law looks with disfavor upon a party who, regardless of the merits of the case, attempts to take advantage of a mistake, surprise, inadvertence, or neglect of the adversary. Thus, the "quiet speed" of a plaintiff's counsel in seeking default has been deemed a sufficient ground for setting aside a default . . .

A summary judgment should be granted, as a matter of law, where there is no genuine issue as to any material fact.[73]

To vacate such default judgment, it is essential for the defendant to show the existence of a meritorious defense and to present it with due diligence.[74]

A default judgment should be set aside in any case in which the failure of the defendant to answer before judgment was not intentional or the result of indifference on his part.[75]

Since a judgment can be entered summarily on a judgment (cognovit) instrument, because the debtor has authorized the confession of judgment against whom, the courts have said that it should be cautiously invoked.[76] The purpose of a

---

70

Kenne v. Wiggins, 138 Cal. Rptr (Cal. App. 1977).

71

Courville v. Southern Casualty Ins. Co., 304 So.2d 93 (La. 1974).

72

Robinson v. Varela, 136 Cal Rptr. 783 (Cal. 1977).

73

Kincaid v. Kingluen, 559 P.2d 1044 (Alaska 1977) and Keene v. Wiggins, 138 Cal. Reptr. 3 (Cal. App. 1977).

74

Lammert V. Lammert Industries, Inc., 360 N.E.2d 1355 (Ill. 1977).

75

Davis v. Thomas, 548 S.W.2d 755 (Tex. Civ. App. 1977).

76

Cardinali v. Planning Board of Lebanon, 373 A.2d 251 (Me. 1977).

summary judgment is not to try an issue in fact, but to ascertain whether there is a fact issue to be tried.[77]

A petition to set aside a default judgment is addressed to the sound discretion of the court, and must be supported by clear, strong and satisfactory evidence of mistake, inadvertence, surprise or neglect.[78] If the judgment appears erroneous upon its face, the proper proceeding is to strike off by motion. The court will examine the record to ascertain the form of the judgment but will not go into the merits of the debtor's claim as in a petition to open up the judgment. A great volume of judgments on notes or bonds accompanying mortgages are confessed. If there is a genuine issue of fact, a summary judgment is inappropriate.[79] A judgment, of course, can only be collected for the real debt due. Deficiency judgments are discussed, in relation with mortgage foreclosures in Chapter 8.

Although the majority of an infant's contracts are voidable at the infant's election, nevertheless a warrant of attorney by a minor to confess judgment against him is absolutely void. A judgment so confessed will be vacated upon a motion to strike it off. Since the confession is void, a minor is deemed incapable of ratifying it. A summary judgment may not be entered where there is disputed question of fact, which is materila to the disposition of the case.[80] Default judgments are looked upon with disfavor.[81]

In an action by a house purchaser against brokers and vendors, the question whether the realty firm knew about water problems was a factual issue *precluding* summary judgment.[82]

To vacate an ex parte judgment, a defendant must have a meritorious defense and must show that he exercised due diligence. It invokes the equitable powers of the Court, as justice and fairness require.[83]

In the Federal Court case of *Swarb v. Lennox*,[84] the Court held that the confession clause was a violation of the due process clause of the Constitution for persons having incomes less than $10,000. The United States Supreme Court, in the same case,[85] affirmed part of the lower court decision, holding that it was not

---

[77] Fishel v. Givens, 363 N.E.2d 97 (Ill. App. 1977).

[78] Edwards v. Edwards, 481 P.2d 432 (Colo. App. 1970) and Ute, Inc. v. Opfel, 518 P.2d 156 (Nev. 1974).

[79] Williams v. N. C. State Board of Education, 201 S.E.2d 889 (1974).

[80] Burough of Monroeville v. Effie's Ups and Downs, 315 A.2d 342 (Pa. Cmwlth. 1974) and Cardente v. Travelers Ins. Co., 315 A.2d 63 (R.I. 1974).

[81] Girkin v. Cook, 518 P.2d 45 (Okla. 1973).

[82] Cashion v. Ammadi, 345 So.2d 268 (Ala. 1977).

[83] Coronet Ins. v. Jones, 359 N.E.2d 768 (Ill. 1977).

[84] Swarb v. Lennox, 314 F. Supp. 1091 (1970).

[85] U.S. Supreme Court, 405 U.S. 191 (1972).

unconstitutional to enforce the confession of judgment against those earning over $10,000.

It has been previously stated that a judgment is a lien against all of the real estate which the debtor owns at the time the judgment is entered against him. It does not bind property he acquires by purchase or will after the date of entry of the judgment. Such after-acquired property can be brought under the lien of the creditor's judgment by reviving the lien of the judgment. This can be done at any time. After-acquired property, sold by the debtor before revival of the judgment, would pass clear title to a purchaser without notice.

A judgment creditor may take the necessary legal action to foreclose the property in order to obtain satisfaction of the debt and costs of sale. Frequently, however, the creditor may do nothing since foreclosure proceedings necessitate an advance of costs and payment of any delinquent taxes against the property. The creditor may feel, rather, that in time the debtor will desire to sell or mortgage the property and will then have to make peace with the creditor and pay him off. This often happens. The creditor should be alert that the lien of his judgment is not lost through the passage of time. The creditor instituting foreclosure proceedings must be circumspect in complying with all legal requirements as to notice and advertisement of the property for sale. The property is put up at a competitive public sale and sold to the highest bidder. Any excess funds realized at the sale, over and above the debts of record and costs, belong to the debtor-owner.

Where there is more than one creditor, the funds are distributed in the order of priority of liens. The creditor who initiates the sheriff's sale obtains no preference on that account, but takes his place in the distribution of funds according to the date when his judgment was entered. Where there is a first mortgage against the property, which is a first lien, and the property is sold on a later judgment lien, the first mortgage is not divested. The purchaser at the sheriff's sale takes the property subject to the first mortgage. If the property is sold on the first mortgage, all liens would be divested, and the purchaser would obtain clear title. Where there are two or more mortgages of record, without any prior or intervening judgments, sale on a subsequent judgment of record, would not divest any of the mortgages. The sheriff makes no warranty or guarantee of title. The risk and responsibility are entirely upon the purchaser.

FRAUD ON CREDITORS

A property sold, mortgaged, or liened in an effort to hinder, delay, or defraud a creditor may be set aside by the creditor's petition to the court for relief. A judgment entered the same day as a conveyance or mortgage of the property would constitute a prior lien against the property. In practice, a mortgagee may record his mortgage one day and disburse the funds the next day so as to have sufficient time to examine the records and ascertain that no judgment, mortgage, or adverse conveyance has been entered.

MECHANICS LIENS

A mechanics lien is given to contractors, laborers, and material men, by statute, for work performed or materials furnished. It is really special class legislation, but has nevertheless been sustained in the courts. There must be strict compliance with the legal requirements as to serving notice of intentions to file a lien. A distinction as to time of filing a mechanics lien is made between new construction and repairs, and as between a contractor and a subcontractor.

The contractor may enter into a "No Lien Contract" with the owner, and as the name implies, no mechanics liens can be filed for work or materials furnished on the job for the owner. If the "No Lien Contract" is recorded, subcontractors are bound by its terms, even though they had failed to take the precaution of examining the records. This does not give the owner "letter perfect" protection. If after the "No Lien Contract" is filed, the terms of the contract are materially changed between the owner and the contractor, the "No Lien Contract" filed would be inoperative.

Delivery of materials to the owner or his agent, either upon the premises or otherwise, for use upon or in a particular project, is sufficient to sustain a mechanic's lien.[86]

Even if there is a "No Lien Contract" filed, a subcontractor in some states, such as Pennsylvania, would have the right to file a mechanics lien for his labor, even though the owner has made his required payments to the contractor. An irresponsible contractor often visits unjust hardship upon the owner in this connection. In some states, a subcontractor can recover only the balance due and owing by the owner to the general contractor under the building contract. The owner, after receiving notice from a subcontractor as to the value of his services is privileged to hold out such amounts from the contract price and pay it directly to the subcontractor. Notice from the subcontractor is imperative. This is known as the "New York system."

In most states a mechanics lien dates back to the beginning of the construction job. Thus, mortgagees are apprehensive lest the mortgage be consummated and recorded before ground is broken. A prudent mortgagee will take the precaution to have photographs made of the site before any building or excavation has been performed at the time the mortgage was executed. This would be convincing evidence that no work had been done or any materials used.

A mechanics lien is subordinate to encumbrances recorded before commencement of work, but takes priority over all subsequent encumbrances.[87]

A prospective mortgagee of improved real estate is required to make a physical examination of the property to ascertain whether there has been recent work that might constitute a prior lien, even though the lien statement is not on file.[88]

---

[86] Kilgust v. Kemp, 235 N.W.2d 292 (Wis. 1975).

[87] Connolly Development, Inc. v. Superior Court of Merced County, 553 P.2d 637 (Cal. 1976).

[88] Lenexa State Bank and Trust Co. v. Dixon, 559 P. 776 (Kan. 1977).

A purchaser of property under construction is charged with any lien that is attached to the premises.[89]

The subcontractor has priority over a mortgage if the mortgage was recorded after the work was started, even though the subcontractor, a plumber for example, did not render any service until after the building was well advanced. The time for serving notice of intention to file a mechanics lien dates from the time when all of the work was completed. An owner can protect himself by requiring the general contractor to post a performance bond or by reserving to the owner the privilege of paying subcontractors claims upon certification of the architect that the work has been satisfactorily completed.

A purchaser from a contractor relies upon a release of liens, which must be executed by every subcontractor and material man who did work or furnished materials on the job. Unfortunately, in too many cases all of the material men or subcontractors have not executed the release. They may file a claim at a later date, which the purchaser must pay even though full payment of the purchase price has already been made to the builder. Also, the purchaser may be deceived by an unscrupulous builder who furnished a release, for example, signed by a lumber company that furnished only a small portion of the lumber used. The buyer may mistakenly believe that all claims for lumber have been paid, whereas the lumber company that furnished the bulk of the lumber has not signed a release nor has it been requested to do so. In purchasing a new building, it is recommended that title insurance be purchased insuring against mechanic's liens as well as defects in title. Unfortunately, in some states title insurance covering contractor and subcontractor liens is not available.

In the case of *United Benefit Life Ins. Co. v. Norman Lumber Co.*[90] a carpet and pad had been installed over unfinished plywood on the second floor, and long-lasting glue with tacks at great frequency used to hold down the carpet. The court held that the carpeting and pad were lienable items. In an insurance claim in the case of *Hartford Fire Ins. Co. v. Balch*,[91] the court found that the carpet in question was loosely tacked and glued in place; that the glue was merely intended to keep the carpet from slipping and therefore the property was personalty. Thus, the two cases are distinguishable.

A Minnesota case, *Reuben E. Johnson Co. v. Phelps*,[92] held that an architect, in the preparation of plans for improvement and the work of a surveyor in doing preliminary

---

[89]
    Hostetter v. Inland Development Corp. of Montana, 561 P.2d 1323 (Mont. 1977).

[90]
    United Benefit Life Ins. Co. v. Norman Lumber Co., 484 P.2d (Okla. 1971).

[91]
    Hartford Fire Ins. Co. v. Balch, 350 P.2d 514 (Okla. 1960).

[92]
    Reuben E. Johnson Co. v. Phelps, 156 N.W.2d 247 (1968).

survey of the property on which a mortgage is to be placed, did not permit liens filed after the mortgage, to attach and take effect as of the date of the plans and preliminary survey.

A bulldozer operator could not file a mechanics lien for work performed in removing brush and trees from a subdivision since the court held the work was done "to" the land and not "upon it."[93]

A subcontractor or material person cannot obtain a *personal* judgment against an owner on the basis of a quasi contract or unjust enrichment, in the absence of a contract or direct promise to pay.[94]

In the case of *Sears Roebuck & Co. v. Seven Palms Motor Inn*,[95] suit was entered to establish a mechanics lien for draperies and bedspreads, specially ordered and custom made for the motel. The draperies were attached to rods, which were attached to the building; the bedspreads were made to fit over the beds, and could be removed and used elsewhere. The draperies were held to be fixtures and lienable, but not the bedspreads.[96]

MARSHALLING

Where a creditor has two or more funds out of which to satisfy his debt, he cannot so elect as to deprive another creditor of his security who has but one fund. This is known as marshalling. For example, Benson entered judgment against Archer for $1,700 on June 16, 1991. Archer owns three parcels of improved real estate. On January 3, 1992, Chance places a mortgage on one tract for $1,500. Then on March 20, 1992, Benson issues execution against the mortgaged tract. Chance can compel Benson to first proceed against the other two properties owned by Archer. Of course, upon the sale of the other two tracts, Benson does not receive the amount of his judgment in full, he may then proceed against the other parcel upon which Chance holds a mortgage.

INDEXING JUDGMENTS

In concluding this discussion of judgments, your attention is directed to the necessity of identifying the debtor accurately in the judgment index. Omission of the middle initial or the debtor's name may prove fatal. The question is whether the debtor's name in the index is such as to put the searcher upon inquiry. Where property is held in the name of Daniel J. Murphy and judgment entered against Daniel Murphy, a court held the judgment was not a lien. Where land was owned by W.A. Black and judgment was entered against W. G. Black, the court held no

---

[93] Lambert v. Newman, 431 S.W.2d 480(Ark. 1968).

[94] Holiday Development Co. v. Tobin Construction Co., 549 P.2d 1376 (Kan. 1976).

[95] Sears Roebuck & Co. v. Seven Palms Motor Inn, 530 S.W.2d 695 (Mo. 1975).

[96] L.E.C., Inc. v. Collins, 332 So.2d 565 (La. App. 1976).

lien. However a judgment entered against Rosie Reustle was held a good lien against property held by Rosie C. Reustle. Rosie Reustle and Rosie C. Reustle were one and the same person, and the only person by that name in the county. A judgment against Caroline Kerl was a binding lien against the real estate owned by Caroline C. Kerl. Each case necessarily depends upon its concomitant circumstances. The Pennsylvania Court,[97] in determining what constituted sufficient constructive notice said:

> It is not necessary that the name of the judgment debtor, as docketed and indexed should be letter perfect, nor do the cases hold that omission of the middle initial in the entry of a judgment automatically and inevitably vitiates the entry and subordinates it to subsequent judgments more accurately docketed. Each case must depend upon concomitant circumstances.

Omission of a middle name may be misleading or harmful in cases where the surname is a relatively common one. The first or Christian name must be correct in the judgment. Title in name of Kathryn Steele, judgment entered against Catherine Steele was held invalid.

In the case of *McCausland v. Davis,*[98]

> . . . actual notice, implied notice (or implied actual notice) and constructive notice: *actual notice* stems from actual notice of the facts in question; *Implied notice* is factual inference of such knowledge, inferred from the availability of a means of acquiring such knowledge, when the party charged therewith had the duty of inquiry; *constructive notice* is the inference of such knowledge by operation of law, as under a recording statute . . .

In the case of *Maddox v. Astro Investments,*[99] a certificate of judgment was filed with the clerk of courts on May 2, 1973, but it was not indexed until June 4, 1973. In the interim, title was transferred by the debtor-owner. The judgment lien was not discovered in the title search. The court held that the judgment became a lien when it was delivered for filing with the clerk. Failure to index constituted negligence, as a matter of law.

ASSIGNMENT

A judgment is personal property. It is readily assignable in the same manner as a note or mortgage. The judgment creditor who transfers the judgment is the assignor. The party to whom the judgment is assigned is the assignee. The assignee takes subject to all equities existing between the original parties.[100]

---

[97] Coral Gables Inc. v. Kerl, 334 Pa. 441, 6 A.2d 275 (1939).

[98] McCausland v. Davis, 204 So.2d 335 (Fla 1967).

[99] Maddox v. Astro Investments, 343 N.E.2d 133 (Ohio App. 1975).

[100] L.C. Russell Co. v. Pipeguard Corp., 504 S.W.2d 596 (Tex. 1973).

EQUITABLE CONVERSION

With the signing of the agreement of sale, equitable (beneficial) title to the property vests in the buyer (vendee), and legal title continues in the vendor, until transferred by deed through the doctrine of equitable conversion. This means that any increase in the value of the property from the date of agreement signing until delivery of deed inures to the buyer.

Where, after an agreement of sale is executed, and before the deal is closed, a building on the land is destroyed in whole, or in part, by fire, or other casualty, the courts are not in full accord as to which party to the agreement must bear the loss. The weight of authority holds that an accidental loss falls to the purchaser, and he must complete the deal according to the terms of the agreement.[101]

In the case of *Insurance Co. of N.A. v. Erickson, 50 Fla. 419 (1905)*,[102] the Court stated,

> It has long been the law in Florida that under a binding executory contract for the sale of land, where the purchaser is regarded as equitable owner, the purchaser must ordinarily bear any loss that occurs . . .

See also *Sanford v. Breidenbach* and *Skendzell v. Marshall*.[103]

The minority view, followed in several New England states, holds that when the building is destroyed by fire, there is a failure of consideration under the law of contracts, and the loss falls upon the vendor.[104]

Where the property is insured by the vendor, the vendee is entitled to the benefit of the insurance as a set-off against the purchase price. In the case of *Dubin Paper Co., v. Insurance Co. of North America*,[105] the court held that where the insured (owner) enters into an agreement of sale of the property covered by the insurance policy, and a fire loss occurs before the deal is consummated, and the insured receives the proceeds of the policy, he holds these as trustee for the buyer. "Conscience of equity" so requires, and is given expression by creating a constructive trust for the benefit of the buyer.[106]

A number of states, as in California and New York, have adopted the Uniform Vendor and Purchase Risk Act. The Act in essence, places the assumption of risk loss upon the vendor, unless the buyer is in possession. Many agreements of sale

---

[101] Good v. Jamard, 76 S.E. 698 (S.C.) and Oaks v. Wingfield, 95 Ga. App. 871 (1957).

[102] Insurance Co. of N.A. v. Erickson, 50 Fla. 419 (1905).

[103] Sanford v. Breidenbach, 173 N.E.2d 702 (Ohio App. 1960) and Skendzell v. Marshall, 301 N.E.2d 641 (Ind. 1973).

[104] Thompson v. Gould, 20 Pick. 134 (Mass. 1838(; Libman v. Levenson, 128 N.E. 13 (Mass. 1920) and Durham v. McCready, 151 A. 544 (Me. 1930).

[105] Dubin Paper Co. v. Insurance Co. of North America, 361 Pa. 68 (1948).

[106] Beatty v. Guggenheim Explorations Co., 225 N.Y. 380.

in use include a clause placing the risk of loss upon the seller, unless the buyer is in possession of the premises. It is a wise precaution for the purchaser to obtain insurance upon the property, immediately upon signing of the agreement, protecting him against loss by fire, casualty or accident. The State of Utah standard sales agreement, General Provision "P" (Fig 6-1-4) places the risk of loss upon the seller.

EQUITABLE TITLE - ZONING CHANGE

Under the equitable title doctrine, any change in zoning ordinances of the municipality, affecting the property, are at the risk of the buyer. In the case of *Diodonate v. Reliance Standard Life Ins. Co.,*[107] the crucial decision was "which of the litigants (buyer or seller) bore the risk of loss attending the zoning change between the time of the Agreement of Sale and the settlement. The Court said,

> There appears to be no cogent argument for treating losses resulting from zoning changes occurring between the execution of the Agreement of Sale and settlement differently from casualty or other kinds of loss between those periods. The parties are always free to mold rights and responsibilities inter se (among themselves) in what ever fashion they desire. But when they are quiet, the law speaks in a voice of finality to set their dispute at rest.

Even if there is an agreement, subject to zoning contingencies, the buyer can elect to waive the contingency and accept the property "as is," without the desired change in zoning. An agreement of sale was made subject to the buyer's obtaining a variance of a prohibited use under the zoning ordnance by a certain date. He was unable to obtain the variance. The seller sued him. The buyer was unsuccessful in the lower court, but took an appeal. Since this would have taken time beyond the specific date, the buyer decided to take the risk involved, waved the contingency, and elected to take the property without variance. The seller refused and returned the deposit. The Alabama Supreme Court compelled specific performance without the subject contingency.[108]

In the case of *White Realty & Ins. Co. v. Moreland,*[109] which involved a suit for commission, the sales agreement contained the following controversial clause:

> Sellers warrant that the said location is zoned commercial at the time of the settlement.

The contract also provided that the seller was obligated to the broker for a commission "at or prior to the time of settlement, hereunder." The court held that the word "warrant" was not a promise by the sellers to secure a change in zoning, but that it was an agreement "that the vendee's duties would be conditional on the

---

107
   Diodonate v. Reliance Standard Life Ins. Co., 433 Pa. 219 (1969).
108
   La Grave v. Jones, 336 So.2d 1330 (1976).
109
   White Realty & Ins. Co. v. Moreland, 259 A.2d 461 (Pa. 1969).

future existence of the fact that the property was zoned as commercial property."
The Court said further,

> This interpretation is supported by the further principle that a contract which
> tends to interfere with the administration of Government are unenforce-
> able.(citing cases). To contract for the accomplishment of something that is
> within the legislative discretion of a municipal body, is to be discouraged as
> against public policy.

No recovery was made by the broker. See also *Wright v. City of Littleton;
Craig v. Presbyterian Church; and Gignilliat v. Borg.*[110]

In short, the agreement of sale should be made subject to zoning, permitting
the use intended, upon delivery of the deed. If a zoning change is required, the
agreement should spell out whether the deal is contingent upon such change, and
which party is to seek the change.

NEGLIGENT MISREPRESENTATION OR FRAUD

Negligent misrepresentation by a seller, which causes financial loss to a
buyer, can be the basis for an action for damages. [111]

If the following representations were untrue, they would constitute grounds
for recision of the agreement of sale: The heating plant, plumbing and electrical
wiring were in good condition; that an adjoining dilapidated house had been
condemned by the city and would shortly be torn down; that there was sufficient
land to sell a 60-ft lot off of the property, for which lot an offer of $2,000 had already
been made; that the cellar was dry and in good condition and that the roof was in
good repair.

These representations are such that the truth cannot be readily determined
from an inspection of the premises by one not skilled in the knowledge of home
construction and plumbing. It has been held that plumbing, electrical wiring, and
heating are not generally ascertainable on viewing. The same is true of the roof. A
sale is not dependent upon the fortuitous circumstances that a purchaser be
available when rain or snow is falling so that he can inspect the roof and determine
whether it is watertight and that the cellar is dry. An owner must be circumspect in
regard to the statements he makes.[112]

In the case of *Colby v. Granite State Realty,*[113] the prospects noted, during
negotiations, that the septic tank was overflowing. The owner's agent represented
that the defective tank would be repaired prior to the sale and that the well was in
good condition. The prospect then executed an agreement of sale which contained

---

[110] Wright v. City of Littleton, 483 P.2d 953 (Colo. 1971); Craig v. Presbyterian Church, 62 Mich. App. 617 (1975); and Gignilliat v. Borg, 205 S.E.2d (Ga. 1974).

[111] Wilson v. Caine, 366 A.2d 474 (N.H. 1976).

[112] Lake v. Thompson, 366 Pa. 352 (1950) and Karan v. Bob Post, 521 P.2d 1276 (Colo. 1974).

[113] Colby v. Granite State Realty, Inc. 366 A.2d 482 (N.H. 1976).

a standard provision merging all prior representations and oral statements. The seller stated, at closing, that the septic tank had been repaired and that the well was in operating condition, which was untrue. The court held that the purchaser, generally, is justified in relying on material statements of fact concerning matters peculiarly within the seller's knowledge. The purchaser was granted relief.

Where misrepresentation may be set up as grounds for avoidance of a contract, it does not lay any basis for an action of damages, but only for actual incurred expenses.

In the case of *Peoples Furniture and Appliance Co. v. Healy,*[114] a buyer sued for return of a $5,000 deposit, when the buyer elected not to complete the deal, upon discovering there was a possibility of flooding. Plaintiff was unable to obtain flood insurance. The Supreme Court held that flooding was material. The court said that, "the fact that plaintiff might have ascertained the situation from others is no defense if plaintiff had a right to rely on defendant's representation."

In the case of *Goggans v. Winkley, et al.,*[115] the purchasers sued the sellers for damages from alleged false representation by vendors in inducing the purchase of land. The Supreme Court held that a provision of the contract for deed that expense of surveying the premises should be borne by the purchaser did not preclude the purchasers from attempting to prove that certain representations were made by a real estate agent relative to a previous survey, and that these representations were properly relied upon and were incorrect.

Where a broker made certain misrepresentations concerning the gross income of a motel and the vendors made a correct disclosure prior to the time the transaction was closed, the buyers were not justified in relying on the previous misinformation furnished by the broker. Under such circumstances the broker cannot be held liable. If there had not been accurate disclosures before signing, the broker and vendors would have been jointly and severally liable.[116]

In the case of *Isaacs v. Cox,*[117] involved a action by purchasers for recision and damages for alleged fraud and misrepresentation in obtaining a real estate contract. The complaint alleged that there was misrepresentation as to the water system, construction of the house and that the defendants represented that certain additional work and materials would be provided after the date of the deed and possession by the plaintiffs. It was also charged that this had not been done. The general rule of the law is well settled that a principal is responsible for his agent's fraud in effecting a sale if made within the actual and apparent scope of his authority. The court held that misrepresentations, if any, made by the agent, as to water quality and supply, were material. The sellers contended that any statements

---

[114] Peoples Furniture and Appliance Co. v. Healy, 113 N.W.2d 802 (Mich. 1962).

[115] Goggans v. Winkley et al., 465 P.2d 326 (Mont. 1970).

[116] Viebahn v. Cudim et al., 273 Minn. 504 (1966).

[117] Isaacs v. Cox, 431 S.W.2d 494 (Ky. 1968).

made by them or their agent were not admissible in evidence, since the contract provided:

> We have read the entire contents of this contract and acknowledge receipt of same. We are not relying on verbal statements not contained herein. We further certify that we have examined the property described herein-above; that we are thoroughly acquainted with its condition and accept it as such.

The Court said,

> Those cases (cited by the defendants) held that the written contract of sale were controlling and that oral representations of a contradictory nature could not be introduced for the purpose of varying the contract. The buyers offer the testimony, not for the purpose of varying the contract, but in order to prove misrepresentations which induced them to enter into it. Such testimony is admissible even though the contract contained the above quoted provisions.

The court remanded the case to the lower court for further hearing.

The parole evidence rule, upon which the defendants relied, provides that no oral testimony can be introduced to vary, contradict, add to or subtract from, the terms of a written contract, or change its legal import, except for fraud, accident, or mistake. In spite of the "exonerations" clause in most agreements of sale that the buyer is not relying upon any verbal statements and it is being purchased as a result of personal inspections and examination, fraud can be introduced as grounds for overcoming the setting aside the clause in question.[118]

In another case, a clause, similar to the above was contained in a disputed contract. The court ruled that such clauses cannot exonerate the broker or his principal for any fraud or misrepresentation made by the broker, which *induced* the purchaser to enter into the agreement.[119] Similarly, clauses to the effect that the property is being purchased "as is" after inspection is not a defense for fraud or misrepresentation.[120]

Fraud may also consist of concealing material defect where there is duty to disclose. Silence as to a condition which the purchaser is not likely to discover (house built upon a gully, upon filled ground), may constitute fraud.[121]

While it is the general rule that the agreement of sale is merged in the deed, this principle, however, will not prevent reformation upon showing of mutual mistake of fact, misrepresentation, or fraud.[122]

Fraud is a tort as well as grounds for avoiding a contract and will sustain an action for damages. Unless a seller does something to conceal a defect or to throw

---

[118] Becker v. Lagerquist Bros. Inc., 348 P.2d 423 (Wash. 1960).

[119] Ritz v. Mymor Houses, Inc., 213 N.W.2d 470 (Iowa 1973).

[120] Colby v. Granite State Realty Inc., et al. 386 A.2d 482 (N.H. 1976).

[121] Lawson v. Citizens and So. National Bank, 193 S.E.2d 124 (S.C. 1972) and Webb v. Culver, 509 P.2d 1173 (Ore. 1973.)

[122] Bicknell v. Barnes, 501 S.W.2d 761 (Ariz. 1973).

him off the inquiry, the buyer has only himself to blame if the purchase turns out less valuable than he anticipated. An owner in selling a vacant lot to a person who desires to purchase it for the erection of a home, is not bound to disclose that the lot is "filled-in" land unless the buyer makes inquiry and the owner by word or deed, does something to disarm his suspicions and steer him away from the question. By the same token, a buyer in negotiating the purchase of farm land, is not bound to disclose the presence of underlying coal land which is the motivating the purchase in question. The parties deal at "arms length." It is wise to permit a prospective purchaser to make a thorough examination of the premises under consideration and then insert a clause in the agreement of sale to the effect that the purchase is being made as a result of buyer's inspection; or that he is buying the property "as is." As a general rule, the buyer takes the property subject to *patent* defects, i.e., those that are ascertainable upon view, or a reasonable inspection of the property. The buyer can rescind the contract, where he later discovered *latent* (hidden or concealed) defects which were not readily ascertainable upon view, such as a defective septic tank, plumbing or electrical lines.

In the case of *Dillahunty v. Keystone Savings Ass'n.,*[123] the court held that the principle of *caveat emptor* applies to a sale of real estate relative to conditions open to observation.

PROBLEMS WHEN EARNEST MONEY IS OTHER THAN CASH

Sometimes a broker will accept a "postdated check" which is not honored upon presentation to the bank. Unless the owner has consented to the acceptance of the check, the broker has violated his fiduciary responsibility to his principal and again jeopardizes not only his commission, but his license as well. A broker is within his rights in accepting an ordinary check for earnest money, even though the buyer immediately stops payment on the check, because it is an everyday business custom to do so. The broker, who accepts a check, is duty bound to deposit it immediately for payment. A postdated check, which is dishonored, or a check upon which payment has been stopped, had no effect upon the agreement of sale, if the seller takes action against the purchaser to enforce it. Sometimes, instead of cash, the buyer will give the broker a short-term promissory note. A broker is guilty of bad faith and jeopardizes his license, when he accepts a note in lieu of cash and fails to so inform his principal. As in the case of a bad check, default upon a note does not void a sales agreement.

The case of *Witherspoon v. Pusch,*[124] was a suit by an owner for breach of a written contract to purchase realty and to recover on a check for the down payment on which the payment had been stopped. The Supreme Court held that parole testimony of the buyer was permissible to show the understanding with the owner's

---

[123] Dillahunty v. Keystone Savings Ass'n., 303 N.E.2d 750 (Ohio 1973).

[124] Witherspoon v. Pusch, 136 P.2d 137 (Colo. 1960).

broker that the offer to purchase was not a firm offer. The check for the down payment was to be held until the buyer had an opportunity to investigate zoning restrictions and adaptability of the property as to intended use. There was no contract, and the buyer's actions were not an attempt to vary terms of the written contract. The plaintiff relied upon the signed contract, and a check for $1,500 marked "Payment Stopped." The court said,

> The check itself stands or falls upon the existence of good and sufficient contract between the parties. In this case, Mrs. Pusch testified that the signing of the offer and the giving of the check was a convenience which would make it unnecessary for the parties to meet again, if she found upon investigation that everything was satisfactory as to zoning classification and adaptability of plumbing for conversion of the building into apartments as required by the City and County of Denver.

The plaintiff contended that these conditions were made between Mrs. Pusch and the broker, they were not binding upon her because the broker was not a party to the contract. The court held that the broker was the agent of the owner and, therefore, there could be no recovery.

Where an agreement of sale has been signed and a check made payable to the broker, is given to that broker, as a deposit, and the buyer stops payment on the check, the owner cannot sue on the check, but the broker can. Under these circumstances, the court held, in the case of *Duncan v. Baskin*,[125] that upon dishonor by the maker, and subject to any notice of dishonor or protest, the holder of the check has an immediate right of recourse against the drawer. Production of the check entitled the broker to recover, without submitting further proof of damages, subject to whatever defenses the defendant raises.

In the case of *Staab v. Messier*,[126] a contract of sale was executed, which recited "Deposit $500." This deposit was in the form of a $500 check given by the prospective buyer to the broker "to be held, uncashed, by the plaintiff (broker) until Pepin (buyer) was able to ascertain whether or not he could raise the $15,000 purchase price by the closing date set forth in the contract." It was conceded that when the buyer gave the $500 check, he had insufficient funds in the bank to cover it. Broker lost his suit for commission. The court quoted with approval the case of *Ellsworth Dobbs, Inc. v. Johnson.*[127]

> The principle that binds the seller to pay commission if he signs a contract of sale with the broker's customer, regardless of the customer's financial ability, puts the burden on the wrong shoulders ... It follows that the obligation to fulfill

125
Duncan v. Baskin, 154 N.W.2d 617 (Mich. 1969).

126
Staab v. Messier, 264 A.2d 790 (Vt. 1970).

127
Ellsworth Dobbs, Inc. v. Johnson, 236 A.2d 843 (N.J. 1967).

monetary conditions of the purchase must be regarded as logically and sensibly resting with the broker.

Where the broker accepted a note instead of cash, as recited in the agreement of sale, the broker was unsuccessful in recovering a commission from the owner.[128] The failure of the broker to acquaint his principal with the fact that he was holding a note, instead of cash, was fatal to his recovery. In *Mecklenborg v. Niehaus*,[129] the court said,

> An agent owes a duty to his principal to inform him of all facts relating to the subject matter of the agency that would affect the principal's interest.

The facts should have been submitted to a jury to decide.

Where a broker signs a receipt of earnest money, which contains a notation that "check is to be returned if purchaser cannot get a mortgage to cover the balance (price of farm $4,200; balance $3,780)," and no mention is made of the mortgage condition in the formal agreement of sale signed by the buyer and seller, the broker is held personally responsible for the return of the down payment, if the mortgage is unobtainable.[130]

A broker who is authorized to negotiate a sale of property has implied authority to accept the initial down payment but no implied authority to accept subsequent payments made on account of the purchase price. In the case of *Gerig v. Russ*,[131] a broker in Salem negotiated a sale of 103 acres of land at $21,500 for Russ to Gerig. The earnest money receipt read,

> Received of David Gerig and Ellen I. Gerig the sum of $500 as earnest money on the following described property; Approximately 103 acres and building located east of Parkersville School. Purchase price, $21,500. Terms 1/2 down payment in cash, balance to be arranged by loan.

Between June 23, 1949 and July 22, 1949, the purchaser paid to the broker various sums totalling $11,500 without the knowledge or consent of the sellers. The buyers brought suit for specific performance, tendering balance of $9,500. Sellers demanded balance of $21,000. The court said,

> There is nothing in the language itself, 'Terms: 1/2 down payment in cash, balance to be arranged by loan' implying authority of the broker to receive such down payment . . . it was the duty of the purchaser to make the payments direct to the sellers rather than to the broker, and when they turned the money over to the broker, they did so at their own risk.

---

[128] Slusser v. Brillhart, 159 N.E.2d 480 (Ohio 1958).

[129] Mecklenborg v. Neihaus, 85 Ohio App. 271 (1948).

[130] Wartman v. Schockley, 154 Pa. Superior Ct. 196 (1943).

[131] Gerig v. Russ, 200 Ore. 196 (1954).

DISAGREEMENT OVER PROPERTY DESCRIPTION

In the sale of farmland or a ranch, a difference is to be observed whether the sale is "in gross or by the acre." The difference is defined in 55 Am. Jur. Vendor and Purchaser, Sec. 127:

> A contract of sale by the acre is one wherein a specified quantity is material. Under such a contract the purchaser does not take the risk of any deficiency and the vendor does not take the risk of any excess. A contract of sale by the tract or in gross is one wherein boundaries are specified, but quantity is not specified, or if specified, the existence of the exact quantity is not material; each party takes the risk of the actual quantity varying to some extent from what he expects it to be. Citing *Carrell v. Lux*[132]

In the case if *Witmer v. Bloom*,[133] which involved the question of whether the contract was for a sale of land in gross, or a sale by the acre. The agreement read, "Consisting of 26.6 acres more or less." The contract also provided "subject to survey of said property, to be made by buyer within 30 days . . ." The survey showed slightly less than 21 acres. The court said,

> A sale in gross, sometimes called a 'contract of hazard,' where specified designated parcels of ground are sold as whole and there is no warranty, expressed or implied, as to quantity. (2 Words and Phrases, Third Series page 446.) In determining whether a sale is by the acre or in gross as in other contracts, the intentions of the parties is controlling and must be given effect.

In this case, the court reversed the lower court and held the sale was by the acre and the purchaser could rescind the deal.

A purchaser of land in gross (more or less) will not be granted relief, when the purchaser can look at the boundaries of the property, bases his decision to buy upon that view, and it later develops that the measurements are not what the purchaser thought. He is bound to take the property, because he received substantially what he thought he was buying.[134]

In general the courts have held that a contract calling for "x" acres of land or square feet *more or less* is considered to be gross sales. In a 1987 Maryland Case, which was described as "16,000 sq. ft more or less," the court ruled that it *was not* a sale in gross.[135]

On actual survey the property was found to contain 22,047 sq. ft or about 40 percent more than the seller thought. When the seller sued the buyer for the additional value the court ruled "the seller had intended to enter into a gross sale contract, but not to assume the risk of extreme variation in quantity." Based upon the principal equity, the seller was due relief.

---

[132] Carrel v. Lux, 101 Ariz. 430 (1966).

[133] Witmer v. Bloom, 288 A.2d 323 (Md. App. 1972).

[134] Liddycoat v. Ulbricht, 556 P.2d 99 (Ore. 1976).

[135] Goette v. Steel, 526 A.2d 626 (1987).

DISAGREEMENT OVER WHAT IS PERSONAL PROPERTY

The true test for determining whether an article, fixture, or piece of equipment or machinery is realty or personalty is the *intention* which the article is attached or affixed to the property, considered in light of what is fair and reasonable under the surrounding circumstances. In other words, each case must stand upon its own particular facts, but the main feature is "the intention" as disclosed by the words or conduct of the owner when the installation was made, with due regard given to existing custom, if established. Custom plays an important part in determining what articles are realty and which are personalty. Most persons would be greatly surprised if the seller should detach and remove the chandeliers and radiators in a house. Yet, in Europe this is expected. We have come to look upon such fixtures as an essential part of the premises, as are doors and windows. It is a broker's obligation to prepare a comprehensive and satisfactory agreement defining what shall pass with the conveyance and the premises.

Chattels which are distinctly furniture, as distinguished from improvements, and not particularly fitted or fastened to the property with which they are used, remain personalty. Chattels which, although physically connected with the real estate, are so affixed as to be removable without destroying or materially injuring the fixtures or the property to which they are annexed become part of the realty or retain their character as personalty, depending upon the intention of the parties at the time of the annexation. Chattels which are so annexed to the property that they cannot be removed without material injury to the real estate or to themselves are realty even if there is expressed intention that they should be considered personalty.

In *Farmers & Merchants Bank v. Sawyer*,[136] a bathtub, built in ironing board and lights were held to be fixtures by reason of their mode of annexation to the realty and were not removable by the seller.

In an apartment building, refrigerators, wall-to-wall carpet, and gas and electric ranges in the various units are considered part of the realty. A sprinkler system in a factory or commercial structure is real estate.

The following tests are used by the courts to determine the real or personal nature of a fixture. They are:

• Annexation to realty; a built-in television set would be considered realty; likewise a roof antenna, a sprinkler system in a commercial building.

• Adaptability or application, as affixed to the use for which the real estate is appropriated; a theater sign or marques, specially constructed storm doors or screens for a particular dwelling; a built-in organ in a church.

---

[136]
Farmers & Merchants Bank v. Sawyer, 163 So. 657 (Ala. 1937).

- An intention of the parties to make the chattel a permanent part of the freehold; lighting fixtures, radiators, laundry tubs.

A trailer or mobile home, connected to a lot with which it is sold as a "package" would be considered realty, subject to taxation, as such. By being annexed to the land, the vehicle becomes real estate, although detached from the land, it would be personal.

SELLER'S ACTION AFTER BREACH BY BUYER

SUIT FOR DAMAGES

If the seller intends to sue the buyer for damages, resulting from the latter's breach, he should attempt to receive a bona fide offer for the same property from another buyer. He should then notify the defaulting buyer as to the best price offered and advise the buyer that unless he can get the seller a higher price, the property will be sold at that price and the buyer will be held responsible in damages for the difference between the defaulted contract price and the best price that the seller can obtain.

A clause often used in this connection reads,

> In the event of default by the Buyers, the Sellers may, at their option, elect to (a) Retain the earnest money deposit and all monies paid on account of the purchase price as liquidated damages, in which event this Agreement shall become null and void and both parties shall thereupon be released from further liability hereunder. It is hereby agreed that, without resale, the Seller's damages will be difficult to ascertain and that the earnest money deposit and all monies paid on account of the purchase price constitute reasonable liquidation thereof and not a penalty.

> In lieu thereof, Seller may elect either or both of the following remedies: (b) Apply the earnest money deposit and all monies paid on account of the purchase price and proceed with an action for specific performance; (c) Apply said monies towards Seller's loss on the sale of said property and proceed with an action at law for damages sustained by the Seller; Provided, however, that no such action of (b) or (c) shall be final or conclusive until full satisfaction shall have been received.

If the agreement of sale does not specify the damages available to the seller upon the buyer's default, the measure of damages would be the difference between the contract price and the market value of the property as of the date of the breach. It is not the difference between the contract price and the lower price obtained on a resale at a *later date*.[137]

---

[137]
MacRitchie v. Plumb, 245 N.W.2d 582 (Mich. App. 1976).

If the damages flowing from the breach are readily ascertainable at the time the contract is made, the clause relating thereto is a *penalty,* and unenforceable. If the damages are not so ascertainable, the clause is then considered one of liquidated damages, and enforceable. Keep in mind that if the amount of the damages agreed upon is unconscionable, the courts may relieve against the forfeiture.[138] In *Hook v. Vomar,*[139] the Court held that a loss of $30,000 deposit on a $95,000 contract of sale was unconscionable; forfeiture of a $3,000 deposit in a $30,000 transaction would be proper.

The liquidated damage amount must be fair and reasonable.[140] In the case of *Bremer v. Myers,*[141] vendors brought an action against the purchasers to recover damages for a breach of contract on the purchase of real estate. The agreement provided, "In the event Purchaser is the defaulting party, Seller shall have the right to retain said cash deposit as liquidated damages for the breach of this contract." The deposit was $200. The court held that the vendors were limited to the $200 as liquidated damages, and did not have the *option* to recover actual damages.

In the case of *Wegg v. Henry Broderick, Inc.,*[142] the plaintiff buyers signed an earnest money agreement for the purchase of an apartment building in Seattle at $240,000, payable $40,000 cash, and the balance in monthly installments of $1,500. Subsequently, due to a Boeing lay-off, rent strike, and other problems, the buyers were in financial difficulties. The purchasers were under the impression that their liability was limited to the money they had paid the seller. The seller insisted upon payment of the entire balance due on the contract. A settlement was negotiated. The buyers then sued the broker for the loss sustained. The Court sustained a verdict in favor of the purchasers, based on uncontradicted expert testimony that the broker has a duty to explain to the buyers that upon default on the contract, a buyer does not have a right to return the property to the seller and terminate all liability, but that the seller can sue for specific performance of the contract. The broker failed to do this.

In the case of *Bando v. Cole,*[143] the purchaser sued to recover a $12,000 deposit, paid on account of the purchase of a farm for $80,000. The agreement provided that in event of the purchaser's default, the seller had the option to forfeit all payments made. On the same day the agreement was signed, the buyer also signed an "Option to Purchase Real Estate" form, prepared by the Farmers Home Administration, for the purpose of obtaining a mortgage loan. This instrument provided that if a loan could be obtained, any down payment would be refunded. The purchaser was never able to obtain financing and the seller refused to refund the deposit.

---

[138] Hutchison v. Tompkins, 259 So. 129 (Fla. 1972).

[139] Hook v. Vomar, 320 F.2d 536 (Fla. 1968).

[140] Simmons v. Urban Redevelopment, 497 S.W.2d 705 (Ky. App. 1973).

[141] Bremer v. Myers, 545 S.W.2d 235 (Tex. App. 1976).

[142] Wegg v. Henry Broderick, Inc. 557 P.2d 861 (Wash. App. 1976).

[143] Bando v. Cole, 250 N.W.2d 651 (Neb. 1977).

The Court held that the agreement of sale was completed and the option agreement was intended only as an *accommodation* to the buyer to obtain financing through Farmers Home Administration. The purchaser could not recover.

TENDER AND DEMAND

Unless the buyer expressly waives tender of deed by the seller, in the agreement of sale, the latter, upon the buyer's failure to consummate the deal, should make a tender of the executed deed and demand the balance of the purchase price. This can be done by the broker, for the seller, or by the attorney for the seller. This is necessary in order to establish that the seller is free from default and that he is ready and willing to perform. Tender may be excused where the buyer has expressed unequivocally an intention of renouncing the agreement. This is known as anticipatory repudiation. A buyer ready, willing, and able to perform is held equivalent to a tender.[144]

A vendor is entitled to retain an earnest money deposit upon purchaser's anticipatory repudiation of agreement of sale, despite the absence in the agreement of a clause authorizing such retention.[145]

In the case of *Ward v. Doucette*,[146] the court held that a letter from the buyer, through his attorney, to the seller that he was prepared to pay the balance due and requested that a deed be executed for delivery to him, did not constitute a legal tender. Accordingly, the defendant seller was not in default.

BUYER'S ACTION AFTER BREACH BY SELLER

Where the seller breaches an agreement of sale, the buyer's measure of damages depends upon whether the seller is guilty of fraud in the breach. If no fraud is present, the buyer can recover only his down payment and actual expenses. Where a borough ordnance is discovered, which provides for widening of the street upon which the property abuts, the buyer could rescind his contract to purchase and recover the deposit money and actual expense. The same result would follow where a lot is of less width than contracted for, even though slight, and the buyer viewed the premises. False statements of value, or cost of the building, or the seller's arbitrary refusal to perform would constitute fraud and the buyer could then recover the full value of his bargain.

Usually, where a seller refuses to consummate the agreement of sale, the buyer will sue for specific performance to compel the seller to execute and deliver a general warrant deed to him. Plaintiff, in this case, must be free from default.[147]

---

[144]
Ricchio v. Oberst, 251 N.W.2d 781 (Wisc. 1977).
[145]
Pruett v. LaSalceda, 359 N.E.2d 776 (Ill. 1977).
[146]
Ward v. Doucette, 301 N.E.2d 256 (Mass. 1973).
[147]
Menke v. Foot, 261 N.W.2d 635 (Neb. 1978).

OPTIONS TO PURCHASE

A contract of sale is bilateral in its obligations, in that it binds both parties. An option, on the other hand, gives the second party a mere privilege to purchase the property, *if he chooses.*[148]

An option is a contract and may be defined as an agreement, in writing, whereby the owner (optionor) gives to another (optionee) the exclusive right for a limited time to purchase (or lease) his real estate upon certain terms and conditions.[149] The option requires a consideration to support it, or it may be under seal. The consideration may be nominal, as low as $1. If the option recites $1 consideration, that is sufficient, even though it has not actually been paid. *Time is the very essence of an option agreement.* If it is not exercised prior to its expiration date, it automatically expires.[150]

Unlike an agreement of sale, there is no grace for performance beyond the expiration date. Where the owner is married, the wife's signature should be obtained on the option agreement of sale so that, if the optionee elects to exercise his option, the wife can be compelled to join in the sale. Death of the owner during the term of the option would not affect the optionee's rights under the agreement. Where the option is extended or renewed for an additional period of time, there *must* be additional consideration for the added term.

An option is assignable in the same manner as an ordinary agreement of sale. The purpose of the option is to give the holder, in return for a consideration paid, a period of time to make up his mind whether he will elect to purchase the property in question. During the specified time, the property is withdrawn from other purchasers. If the optionee does not exercise his option, the money paid to the optionor is forfeited. The option may specify, however, that if the option is exercised, the money paid for the option shall be credited to the purchase price of the property.

Any rents paid during the period of the option belong to the owner, until such time as the option is exercised and the deed passed.

A letter from the optionee to the owner, during the option period, that he desired to exercise the option, within the next ten days, to purchase the property as therein set forth without tendering the purchase price, prior to the expiration date of the option, was fatal to the optionee's cause.[151]

In the case of *Waterway Gas 'N Wash., Inc, v. Sandbothe et al.,*[152] the plaintiff

---

[148] Rooney v. Dayton-Hudson Corp., 246 N.W.2d 170 (Minn. 1976).

[149] Johnson v. Worcester Business Development Corp., 302 N.E.2d 575 (Mass. 1973).

[150] Mattco, Inc. v. Manton Radio Ass'n., Inc. 246 N.W.2d 222 (N.D. 1976).

[151] Adams v. Swift, 500 S.W.2d 437 (Tenn. 1973).

[152] Waterway Gas 'N Wash, Inc. v. Sandbothe et al., 550 S.W.2d 617 (Mo. App. 1977).

brought suit to recover $2,500 paid for an option to buy land. The option provided for refund of the deposit, if the optionee used its best efforts to obtain rezoning, but failed. The plaintiff (optionee) filed a picture of the proposed site and its legal description with the County Planning Commission. The Commission requested additional information, which the optionee never furnished. The application was refused. Since the court found that the plaintiff had not employed diligence to secure rezoning, a refusal was denied to the plaintiff.

Where a lease is signed by two lessees, one of the lessees alone, could not exercise an option to renew the lease.[153]

When an option is executed, it is a good precaution to prepare and attach the proposed agreement of sale, spelling out the terms upon which the option is to be exercised.

Where the last day for giving written notice for exercise of an option was October 21, 1974, written notice mailed on October 21, 1974 and not received by the optionor until after that date, was held too late.[154]

THE RULE OF "CAVEAT EMPTOR" APPLIED TO SALES AGREEMENTS

The ancient rule of "Caveat Emptor" (let the buyer beware) is fast being eroded, as court authorities take a broader view of a new social philosophy oriented towards consumer protection. Under the doctrine of caveat emptor, the buyer was supposed to examine the property he was purchasing to satisfy himself that it was fit, suitable and satisfactory for his purpose. Not so today.

The reason why the rule has been so much eroded in modern times has been well stated in the case of *Mayo v. Wilbrite*[155] as follows:

> The rule of caveat emptor . . . is a statement of the mores of medieval times through nineteenth century England (and America), apparently worked well in agricultural societies, as evidenced by its centuries of acceptance. However, the sale of farm acreage (with) simple residence - the type of transaction to which caveat emptor originally addressed itself - is very different from the sale of a modern home with complex plumbing, heating, air conditioning, and electrical systems, which is possibly built on ground considered unsuitable for construction until recent years.

The case involved a septic tank, which overflowed during rainy weather and which the seller had never been able to repair. The Court pointed out that the

---

[153] Kleros Bldg. Corp. v. Ballagalia, 109 N.E.2d 221 (Ill. App. 1952).

[154] Salminen v. Frankson, 245 N.W.2d 839 (Mich. App. 1976).

[155] Mayo v. Wilbrite, 232 S.E.2d 141 (Ga. App. 1976).

purchaser agreed to buy a house which appeared to be in normal working order. The seller "had knowledge of the condition and surely knew the information concerning the defective condition would have significantly influenced the buyer's decision." This, the court termed *passive concealment*.

In the case of *Beavers v. Lamplighters Realty, Inc.,*[156] the court makes pertinent reference to an earlier case, *Prescott v. Brown,*[157] stating:

> which (opinion) featured a remarkably lucid no-nonsense (stand), executing a powerful assault on one of the less admirable hand-me-downs of our Anglo-Saxon common law heritage of caveat emptor, a doctrine that exalted deceit, condemns fair dealing and scorns the credulous.

In the case at issue, a prospect made an offer of $34,500, which was rejected. Still wanting the house, he called a broker. He was told, "If you are going to do anything, you had better do it pretty quick, because I've got a buyer for it at $37,000." The prospect offered $37,250, which was accepted. It developed that there was no offer at $37,000. The prospect sued to rescind the contract and was successful. The Court said,

> It is as much a actionable fraud wilfully to deceive a credulous person with an improbable falsehood as it is to deceive a cautious and sagacious person with a plausible one. The law draws no line between falsehoods.

The case of *Rotherberg v. Oleno,*[158] involved a new house under construction. A year after taking possession the buyers discovered that the structural defects had appeared in the foundation. The walls were cracking and bulging . . . nor was the foundation properly waterproofed which aggravated the damage to the foundation walls. The floors were uneven and hazardous and not finished in a workmanlike manner . . . the defendant relied upon the ancient doctrine of caveat emptor. The court said,

> The crucial question here is whether the doctrine of caveat emptor applies to the sale of a new house by a builder-vendor and it must be resolved on the basis of the particular facts presented in the case.

The court cited an English case, *Miller v. Cannon Hill Estate Ltd.,*[159] where the defendant told the plaintiff that he would use the best materials and perform the work in the best workmanlike manner, but this was not in the written agreement. Some time after the plaintiff took possession, excessive dampness penetrated the house, due to faulty construction. The court decided in favor of the plaintiff, holding that where the purchaser buys a dwelling under construction, there is an *implied*

---

[156] Beavers v. Lamplighters Realty, Inc., 556 P.2d 1328 (Okla. 1976).

[157] Prescott v. Brown, 120 P. 991 (Okla. 911).

[158] Rotherberg v. Oleno, 262 A.2d 461 (Vt. 1970).

[159] Miller v. Cannon Hill Estates Ltd., 2. K.B. 113 (1931).

warranty that upon completion, the dwelling will be for for the purpose intended and habitable. The Vermont court also cited a South Carolina case, *Rogers v. Scyphers*,[160] where the court said,

> While most courts still adhere to the proposition that in the usual, normal sale of land and old buildings, the ancient doctrine of caveat emptor, with respect to the vendor, who is also the builder of a new structure, the decided trend of modern decisions is to make a distinction. Where the vendor is also the builder he is today, by weight of modern authority, held liable for damages and injuries occurring after the surrender of title and possession, based on the theory of an implied warranty or an imminently dangerous condition caused by negligence in construction.

Other jurisdictions have adopted the implied warranty theory in *Vanderschrier v. Aaron, Glisan v. Smolenske, Jones v. Gatewood, Weck v. A.M. Sunrise Construction Co., Staff v. Lido Dune, Inc., Bethlahmy v. Bectel, and Humber v. Morton.*[161] The Vermont court said,

> The law should be based upon current concepts of what is right and just and the judiciary should be alert to the never ending need for keeping common law principles abreast with the times. Ancient distinctions, which make no sense in today's society and tend to discredit the law should be readily rejected as they appear to have been step by step in the cases cited . . . we find no rational doctrinal basis for differentiating between a sale of a newly constructed house by the builder-vendor and the sale of an automobile or any other manufactured product.

A Colorado Appellate Court held that the implied warranty doctrine does not apply when the house is bought from the previous owner, who is not the builder. In the case before the court, the defendants bought the house new and lived in it for 15 years. The house was represented to the buyers in July 1969 as in "good condition." In September of 1969, when the buyers attempted to operate the furnace, they found it defective and they had to install a new furnace at a cost of $525. The appellate court reversed the lower court and found in favor of the seller.[162]

It may be said that implied warranty is the antithesis to caveat emptor. Under the wave of consumerism, it is the seller who must beware.[163]

In a Louisiana case, the Supreme Court held that the buyer of a used home

---

160

Rogers v. Scyphers. 161 S.E.2d 81 (1968).

161

Vanderschrier v. Aaron, 140 N.E.2d 819 (Ohio 1957); Glisan v. Smolenske, 387 P.2d 260 (Colo. 1943); Jones v. Gatewood, 381 P.2d 158 (Okla. 1963); Weck v. A.M. Sunrise Construction Co., 181 N.E.2d 728 (Ill. 1966); Staff v. Lido Dune Inc., 262 N.Y.S.2d 544 (1965); Bethlahmy v. Bechtel, 415 P.2d 698 (Idaho. 1966), and Humber v. Morton, 426 S.W.2d (Tex. 1968).

162

Gallegos v. Graff, 508 P.2d 798 (Colo. App. 1973).

163

Pollard v. Saxe and Yolles Dev. Co., 525 P. 88 (Cal. 1974).

could recover cost of repairs due to *hidden* defects, even though the seller was unaware of the defect. There is no obligation on the part of a purchaser to inspect the property with *expertise,* particularly in regard to termite damage.[164]

In the case of *Pywell v. Haldave,*[165] the plaintiffs purchased a house from the owners, through a broker, who represented the house to be in good and sound condition. Later, the house was found to be damaged by termites and the buyers brought suit for damages. The appellate court held the broker's representation that the house was in sound condition was merely the expression of an opinion and not a representation of material fact. The court said,

> Such a description of the premises, quite common in the parlance of sales, was so vague and general as to be incapable of particular application. The words were but indefinite generalities so plain that they cannot be supposed to have deceived any rational person.

OTHER AGREEMENT CONSIDERATIONS

BLANK VENDEE IN AGREEMENT

Where the vendor knowingly signs an agreement of sale, with the name of the vendee not filled in, he impliedly gives the agent (broker) the authority to fill in the name of the vendee. When the vendee signs the agreement, upon terms set by the owner therein, it becomes an enforceable contract. If the vendor is interested in the identity of the vendee, he should make inquiry as to his identity. If he signs the agreement first, without such inquiry, he cannot refuse to perform his contract, after it is signed by the undisclosed vendee.[166]

ASSIGNMENT OF LEASES

If possession is to be given by assignment of leases, the leases should be checked for parties, terms, and *expiration* date(s) before the agreement of sale is signed. A provision should be incorporated in the agreement stating the expiration date(s) of the lease(es). The leases should be properly assigned to the grantee at the closing, as well as any insurance policies which are to be assumed by the new owner, and the consent of the companies to the transfer endorsed thereon.

ASSIGNABILITY OF AGREEMENTS

Ordinarily, an agreement of sale is assignable by the vendee without any special notation to that effect. Very often a purchaser engages to buy property with

---

[164] Lorio v. Kaiser, 277 So.2d 633 (La. 1973).

[165] Pywell v. Haldave, D.C. Court of Appeals (1962).

[166] McCrystall v. Connor, 331 Ill. 107 (1928) and Oliver v. Wyatt, 418 S.W.2d 403 (Ky. 1967).

out any intent of taking title, but with the expectation the he will be able to sell (assign) the agreement at a higher price to a new buyer and pocket the difference. This is common where new homes are in short supply and buyers are chosen by lot.

The seller cannot refuse to deed property to the new purchaser unless he has agreed to take back a mortgage from the original buyer in part payment of the purchase price, or unless the original buyer has assumed and agreed to pay an existing mortgage. This is based on the theory that a person has a right to select his debtor. It may make considerable difference to the seller whether the vendee, a person of financial stability, is indebted to him, or whether he must look to the vendee's assignee, a person financially irresponsible, for payment. If the owner desires to deal exclusively with the original buyer in any event, then he should stipulate that "rights under the within agreement of sale are not assignable."

In the case of *Brady v. Hoeppner, Melrose Realty & Inv. Co., 3rd Party Pltf.*,[167] an agreement of sale was negotiated by the broker for the sale of a property to Brady at $185,000, to be paid $24,200 in cash and the remainder by assumption of the balance due under Brady's purchase contract. Brady, in turn, negotiated a sale to Bishop. The defendant owner refused to consent to the assignment even though the contract of sale provided, "This is not assignable unless the prior written consent of the seller is first obtained, provided however, that said consent shall not be unreasonably withheld." The Court held that consent was not unreasonably withheld by the seller. Nor could the broker recover a commission.

SUNDAY CONTRACTS ARE NOT NECESSARILY ILLEGAL

The mere carrying out of negotiations on a Sunday does not invalidate an agreement of sale which is completed on a secular day.[168] It is also true that when a broker carried out a negotiation on a Sunday, and his listing contract was executed on a weekday, a claim for a commission would not be prejudiced.[169]

In the case of *Chadwick v. Stokes*,[170] the court observed that in 1946, following WWII, there was a severe housing shortage. On August 1, 1946, the plaintiff, an officer in the U.S. Army, received orders to leave Atlanta that same day and report to Ft. Dix, N.J., no later than August 5, 1946, for separation from service. On August 3, 1946, he located a house in Lansdale, Pa., which was suitable

---

[167] Brady v. Hoeppner, Melrose Realty & Inv. Co., 3rd Party Pltf., 558 P 2d 1009 (Colo. App. 1977).

[168] Heckel v. Burtchaell, 72 A.2d 794 (N.J. App. 1950).

[169] Mercner v. Fay, 177 A.2d 481 (N.J. 1962).

[170] Chadwick v. Stokes, 162 F.2d 132 (1947).

for his family, which included three children, ten-, five-, and three-years-old. A contract of sale was signed the next day, Sunday.

The court concluded that the sale was not within the prohibition of the Sunday law, for two reasons:

1. Procuring a home was not a worldly employment.

2. It constituted performing a work of necessity.

7

The Closing and Property Transfer

THE CLOSING AGENCY

Responsibility for closing the deal varies from state to state. In Pennsylvania the closing must be through a land title company. In Texas only lawyers may close a deal, while in Utah the closing is the responsibility of the broker. However, in practice, few brokers close their own deals preferring to have a title company do the accounting and leg work for a small fee which is usually shared by the buyer and seller.

The closing process is rather involved and requires a lot of research and accounting work. Here are a few of the responsibilities of the closing agency:

• Obtain a preliminary title report of the property to be closed. This will reveal the status of the title, indicate any liens, judgments, outstanding mortgages and restrictions on the use of the property.

• Notify the current mortgage holder to determine the current status of the mortgage, balance through the last payment and if it is to be assumed, the agreement to allow assumption, terms and conditions. The mortgagee will also furnish the current balance of the impound (escrow) account which represents mortgagor credits.

• If liens or other encumbrances are found, the closer must determine the amount required to clear these items at the closing date.

• Where the buyer does not desire to purchase his own insurance, the closing agent must acquire an insurance binder and pay the premium at closing.

• Check the status of taxes and if any arrears are found, determine the cost plus penalties to bring this account up to date.

• Prepare the closing statements for the buyer, seller, and his own agency.

- After closing the agent must pay-off all liens and encumbrances to include outstanding mortgages and record releases for each of these.

- Prepare the deed of transfer from buyer to seller and record it after closing.

- Obtain the required mortgage papers from the new lender to include deeds of trust and record these after closing.

- Prepare checks for payment of insurance, old mortgage pay-off, pay-off to lien holders, insurance agencies, state and local tax collectors, broker commissions, and seller's equity.

- Prepare a bill of sale for any personal property being transferred with the real estate.

In the process of preparing the closing papers, the closing agent has no alternative other than to follow the escrow instructions contained in the agreement of sale. He may not modify or change any of the conditions without the agreement of all parties concerned. This was firmly established in the *Pippin v. Kern-Ward*[1] case.

A typical set of closing statements (Figures 7-1-1 through 7-1-3) indicates the accounts of the buyer, seller and the closing agency. Important aspects of these statements are discussed in some detail below.

Example: Marshall P. and Myrna L. Smith have purchased the residence of Chess E. and Golda Ludlow for $120,000. The agreement of sale states that the buyers will pay $20,000 down and finance the remainder with an F.H.A. mortgage of $100,000. The sellers have agreed to pay the two-point discount required to obtain the loan. The buyers have deposited $5,000 as earnest money with Allied Realtors.

The Ludlow's have an existing mortgage with the 1st Security Bank, with a balance of $32,320.44 as of the last payment on January 31, 1992. The interest rate on this mortgage is 7.5 percent per annum. Escrow impounds for taxes and insurance total $425.50 as of the last payment.

The Smiths have been approved for a 30-year F.H.A. loan in the amount of $100,000 at 8.5 percent for 30 years. Payments are to be made on the 1st of each month. The new mortgagee, Big Bank Inc. will require escrow impounds to include two months taxes and insurance in advance plus seller prorated taxes due to date of closing.

The closing is scheduled for February 15, 1992 at XYZ Title company. Closing cost of $150 will be shared equally between buyer and seller. The title policy, to be purchased by the seller will cost $388.00 and the Alta policy to cover the Big Bank mortgage will be $162.00 additional, to be paid by the buyer.

The property has not been assessed for 1992. The seller's portion of 1992 taxes will be prorated based on the 1991 rate of $1,428.00. The Ludlows will cancel

---

[1]

Pippin v. Kern-Ward Bldg. Co., 8 Ohio App. 3rd 196, 456 N.E. 2d 1235 (1982).

their old insurance policy, after the closing, as the Smiths have acquired their own coverage through Farmers Insurance Co. at a cost of $386.00 per year.

The following documents will be required to be recorded:

- Release of old mortgage from 1st Security Bank
- Trust Deed from Big Bank
- Deed from Ludlows to Smiths

Recording fees are $2.00 per page.

Prepare a closing statement for the Buyer and the Seller, and a summary of the closing transaction by XYZ Title Company.

SELLER'S STATEMENT

The first significant item in the seller's statement, Figure 7-1-1 (page 213), is the selling price as shown. Next is the existing mortgage pay-off figure which is obtained from the current mortgagee. The figure furnished is typically as of the last payment which requires the closing agency to calculate and collect interest due up to the day of the pay-off. This total is then reduced by the amount of the mortgagor's impounds for taxes and insurance which have been collected as a part of monthly payments. These are the buyer's funds which will no longer be required.

The next items are those expenses of the seller, which include taxes from the first of the year to the closing date, cost of the title policy furnished the buyer, a recording fee to record the mortgage pay-off and clear the title, the selling commission, one half of the closing cost and mortgage points, which the seller agreed to pay to allow the buyer to obtain an FHA mortgage.

When the credits and debits are totaled, the difference is the amount due the seller at closing.

BUYER'S STATEMENT

The buyer's statement, Figure 7-1-2, begins with a debit in the amount of the purchase price agreed upon between buyer and seller. He is then credited for his earnest money deposit, usually held in the selling broker's trust account, and his new mortgage; in this case $100,000. From this new mortgage certain expenses and impounds are deducted from the check forwarded to the closing agency. These deductions typically include two months taxes and insurance in advance. These advance payments are to ensure that the mortgagee has the necessary funds, well in advance of the time that payments will be made. It will also be noted that the buyer is charged for a full year of insurance, this assumes that he has not already paid his insurance agent for the policy and has only brought a binder to the closing. The subject of insurance will be more fully discussed in later paragraphs.

It will also be noted that the buyer is paying mortgage interest in advance. Most lenders prefer certain dates for submission of monthly payments, in the example this is assumed to be the first of the month. Since the closing is on 2-15,

interest is collected to the end of the month so that the buyer's first payment will
not be due until March 1.

As in the seller's statement certain additional charges are applicable. Here we
find a recording fee of $4.00 to record the deed and the mortgage trust instrument.
The largest closing cost is normally the fee charged for the loan origination; in this
case 1.5% of the $100,000 mortgage. It will also be noted that a charge for a title
policy is made to the buyer. This is the American Land Title Association policy
(ALTA), issued in conjunction with the seller furnished policy, to insure the lender.
This charge is less than the cost of the policy furnished the buyers, since it is
basically the same and issued at the same time.

When the total credits and debits are added, we find that an additional amount
of $17,755.36 will be required to close the deal. This represents the agreed $20,000
down payment and closing costs.

CLOSING AGENCY STATEMENT

The closing agency statement, Figure 7-1-3, is prepared primarily for the
closing agency records but a copy is normally provided to the selling broker for his
records. Basically this statement is no more than a listing of all of the moneys paid
in and paid out. It is a double check on the accounting to determine if the other two
statements are correct.

The agreement of sale normally provides that the balance of the consideration
price shall be paid in cash at settlement. The seller usually can refuse a personal check
of the buyer as such check may not be honored at the bank because of insufficient funds,
or the buyer might die before the check clears the bank on which it is drawn. A cashier's
check is always acceptable, as is a certified check. Under extenuating circumstances a
personal check may be acceptable. For instance, an attorney gave his personal check,
for the buyer, at a Saturday settlement, when the bank was closed and he could not get
it certified. The tender of the check was proper.[2]

Checks payable to the seller and the selling broker are usually held by the
closing agency until the deed has been recorded and a last minute check of
indebtedness on the property is verified. If this process was not followed it would
be possible for the seller to arrange a loan on his property and wait until after the
selling close and then close the new loan, leaving the new buyer with an encumbrance of which he was unaware.

One of the most important jobs of the closing officer is the reviewing of all
closing papers and assuring that each participant fully understands what he is about
to sign. One of the most important items to be reviewed is the preliminary title
report showing the status of the title to include any items which will remain after
the transfer of the deed. These items usually related to right-of-ways easements and
so on.

---

[2]
Southgate, Inc. v. Ecklini, 207 N.W. 2d 729 (Minn. 1973).

SELLER'S CLOSING STATEMENT

Closing Date: 2-15-92

Seller: Chess E. & Golda Ludlow

Buyer: Marshall P. & Myrna L. Smith

		Debits	Credits
Selling Price:			$120,000.00
Old Mortgage Pay-Off:			
Balance as of: 1-31-92	$32,320.44		
Interest due: To: 2-15	92.66		
Less: Escrow Acct.:	(425.50)		
Seller Expenses		$31,994.56	
Taxes: 1-1-92 to 2-15-92	178.50		
Title Policy:	388.00		
Recording Fees:	2.00		
Selling Comm: @6%	7,200.00		
½ Closing Cost:	75.00		
Points Payable:	2,000.00		
		9,843.50	
Total Debits & Credits		41,838.06	$120,000.00
Due Seller at Closing		78,161.94	
Totals		$120,000.00	$120,000.00

Figure 7-1-1

BUYER'S CLOSING STATEMENT

Closing Date: 2-15-92

Seller: Chess E. & Golda Ludlow

Buyer: Marshall P. & Myrna L. Smith

	Debits	Credits
Purchase Price:	$120.000.00	
Earnest Money Deposit:		5,000.00
New Mortgage: Big Bank Inc.		100,000.00
Charges to Buyer:		
Escrow Account		
2 Mos.Insurance: 64.33		
2 Mos. Taxes 238.00		
Buyer Expenses 302.33		
1 Yr. Insurance: (Farmers) 386.00		
Title Policy: 162.00		
½ Closing Cost: 75.00		
Recording Fees: 4.00		
New Mtg. Int. to: 3-1-92 326.03		
Mtg. Fee: @ 1.5% 1,500.00	2,755.36	
Total Debits & Credits	$122,755.36	$105,000.00
Due From Buyer At Closing		17,755.36
Totals	$122,755.36	$122,755.36

Figure 7-1-2

"XYZ" TITLE COMPANY
CLOSING STATEMENT

Closing Date: 2-15-92

Seller: Chess E. & Golda Ludlow

		Debits	Credits
Buyer: Marshall P. & Myrna L. Smith			
Cash At Closing			17,755.36
New Mortgage:	$100,000.00		
Less:			
2 Mos. Ins.:	66.33		
2 Mos. Taxes:	238.00		
Seller Pd. Tax:	178.50		
Mtg. Fee:	1,500.00		
Interest To: 2-25-92	326.03		
Pts. Pd. By Seller:	2,000.00		
		4,306.86	95,693.14
1 Year Insurance:		386.00	
XYZ Title Costs			
Closing:	150.00		
Title Pol.:	388.00		
Alta Pol.:	162.00		
Recording Fees:		700.00	
Old Mtg. Pay-Off:		2.00	
Deed & New Mtg.		4.00	
Sales Comm.: @ 6%	$7,200.00		
Less Ernest Money Held:	5,000.00		
		2,200.00	
Total Debits & Credits		$ 35,286.56	$113,448.50
Due Seller at Closing		78,161.94	
Totals		$113,448.50	$113,448.50

Figure 7-1-3

REAL ESTATE INSURANCE

All lenders require the closing officer to assure that the mortgaged property is properly insured prior to disbursement of funds. In most states this minimum insurance is the HO-2 policy. Specific coverage of this policy is listed below.

HO-1: This named peril policy provides coverage for:

a. Fire and Lightening
b. Windstorm and Hail
c. Explosion
d. Riot or civil commotion
e. Vehicles
f. Smoke
g. Vandalism and Malicious Mischief
h. Theft
i. Breakage of glass (usually with a stated dollar deduction)

HO-2: This policy adds the following coverage to those contained in the HO-1 policy:

a. Falling objects
b. Weight of Ice, Snow and Sleet
c. Collapse of a building or any part
d. Accidental overflow or discharge of water or steam
e. Sudden and accidental tearing apart or bulging of heating, air-conditioning, or hot water systems
f. Freezing of plumbing, heating, air conditioning systems, or household appliances
g. Sudden and accidental damage from artificially generated electrical current

HO-3: Covers all risks except those specifically listed.

HO-4: This is renter's insurance covering renters personal possessions.

HO-5: This is the homeowner's broadest coverage available.

HO-6: This is similar to the HO-2 except the coverage is for condominiums.

All HO policies usually provide additional coverage for personal property (usually 50 percent of face value), limited liability coverage, and medical payments.

Regardless of the type of insurance policy purchased, it must be recognized that the policy covers only the *insured* person(s) at the designated property, not all owners of the property.

Example—Mr. B and his wife owned a home in Joint Tenancy. They separated and the husband took out a policy in his name only. The property was lost and Mr. B collected only the amount of his loss. The wife could not collect for her loss on *his* policy.[3]

Similarly, persons having a lien cannot collect nor can a city collect insurance proceeds to apply to pay delinquent taxes.[4]

> In the absence of an agreement that the owner should carry insurance for his benefit, the holder of a mechanics or supplier lien on property is not entitled to a lien on the proceeds of fire or other property damage insurance taken out thereon by the owner and made payable to himself.[5]

THE TRANSFER OF TITLE TO REAL ESTATE

The title to real estate, the evidence of ownership, passes in several ways: (1) By purchase, through delivery of deed, (2) by decent, through a will or by inheritance, (3) through adverse possession, and (4) by eminent domain.

It is a fundamental concept that the extent of the right which a person acquires in property can be no greater than that enjoyed by his predecessor in title. This means that one cannot buy more from the former owner that the latter had, despite the fact he may give what purports to be a valid deed. If an owner gives a deed for a tract of land 110 feet in depth, but he only owned 100 feet, it follows that the buyer obtains title to only 100 feet. Thus, in order to determine the exact extent of the rights of a present owner of property, a diligent and thorough search must be made in order to ascertain the rights which were handed down to him through a long line of former owners, and in many cases it is necessary to trace the title back to its origin so as to ascertain the extent of the original grant which was made. This general principle, of course, is subject to certain modifications, due to the passing of many laws intended to cure or remedy defects in titles produced through carelessness or blunders. Title to a property has a very long life, extending back to the beginning of private ownership.

Technically, titles emanate from a foreign power or government, the exact source varying in different parts of the United States. For example, in New Jersey and Delaware, it is Lord Baltimore; in New York, it is the Duke of York, or his successor; in Pennsylvania, it is William Penn. In Kansas and Nebraska, it is the United States Government, which secured title to the Great Western Domain through grants made by the 13 original states, and subsequent negotiations with France for the purchase of the Louisiana Territory. A prudent investor of land, anywhere, will insist upon an Abstract

---

[3] Russell v. Williams, 374 P. 2d 827 (Cal. 1962).

[4] Shelton v. Providence Washington Insurance Co., 131 SW 2d 330 (Tex. 1939)

[5] 9 ALR 2d 307.

of Title and opinion of title, or better still, have the title insured by a land title company. This ensures the new owner as to the quality of title to the land purchased or otherwise acquired.

QUALITY OF TITLE

The grantee is entitled to what quality of title which will enable him to sell the property without objection or difficulty. Good title is said to be a be such title, free from encumbrances and clouds, which a court would compel a purchaser to accept. The doctrine of "doubtful title" is that a purchaser of land is entitled to a title that will not get him involved in litigation.[6] Title to the property need not be perfect, but a purchaser has the right to require that the title shall be of such character the he will not be exposed to the dangers of litigation as to its validity. If the facts throw a cloud on the title, rendering it dubious in the minds of reasonable men, it is not merchantable.[7]

TITLE TRANSFER BY DEED

The law has always regarded the transfer of real estate as one of the most solemn acts in which an individual can engage and thus a great deal of formality attends its execution. In the early days of land tenure, transfer was accomplished by "livery of seizin," which literally, means transfer of possession. The seller and buyer would go upon the land in question and there, in the presence of witnesses, the seller would take a clod of turf or a twig from a tree and hand it over to the buyer as a symbol or token of transfer. The transfer was then made a matter of record by having the scrivener (the person in the community who could write) write out a transfer upon parchment or other durable matter, in order to prevent erasure or alteration; the scrivener wrote the names of the grantor (seller), and the latter affixed his personal seal.

With the development of education, the emphasis has shifted, so that the signature is the all-important feature in the execution of the deed and the seal is only incidental, usually printed upon the deed form. Although a deed is a contract between the grantor (seller) and the grantee (buyer), it is not necessary for the latter to sign it. In fact, this would be unusual. The acceptance of the deed consummates the contract. It should be kept in mind that a deed is a contract and, therefore, all the essential elements of a valid contract must be present. It is also necessary to have special formality—that is the deed must be in writing. There can be no such thing as an oral transfer of real estate. Under

---

[6] Baldwin v. Anderson, 161 N.W. 2d 553 (Wisc. 1968).

[7] Ewing v. Plummer, 308 Ill. 585 (1923).

Spanish law, an oral deed, coupled with transfer of possession, was effective to pass title. A deed represents the formal completion of the agreement of sale previously executed by the parties.

In construing a deed, every attempt should be made to carry out the intent of the grantor, and *substance* rather than *form* should control.[8]

The primary rule in interpreting a deed is that it be taken as a whole, with the intention of the grantor controlling.[9] However, ambiguous reservations are construed against the grantor.[10]

Where there is ambiguity of construction of a deed, it should be construed most favorably to the grantee, since the grantor prepared it.[11]

ESSENTIAL PARTS OF THE DEED

DEFINITION

Blackstone defines a deed as a "writing or instrument under seal, containing some contract or agreement, and which has been delivered by the parties." Thus the word *deed* in a legal sense may mean any sealed contract or instrument, such as a lease, mortgage, or bond. The popular sense of the word confines it to the conveyance of property. A deed may be defined as a writing by which lands, tenements, and hereditaments are conveyed, which writing is signed, sealed, and delivered by the parties. The ordinary common warranty deed contains a number of clauses that have an important bearing upon the rights of the parties. A present day definition of a deed is of a similar tenor.[12]

For purposes of study, a deed may be divided into three component parts: (1) the Premises, (2) the Habendum, and (3) the testimonium. The premises includes the date, the parties, consideration, granting clause, description, recital, and appurtenances. The Habendum et Tenendum (to have and hold clause) includes this clause and the Under and Subject to or Mortgage clause. The Testimonium clause includes the Warranty and "In Witness Whereof." In the following paragraphs, the various parts of the deed are discussed.

DATE

The date usually comes first but is not essential to the validity of the deed. When inserted, it indicates the time when the title passed; that is, when the deed

---

[8] Shulansky v. Michaels, 484 P. 2d 14 (Ariz. App. 1971).

[9] Guido v. Baldwin, 360 N.E. 2d 842 (Ind. App. 1977).

[10] Besing v. Ohio Valley Coal Co., Inc. of Kentucky, 293 N.E. 2d 510 (Ind. App. 1973) and Pfeffer v. Lebanon Land Dev. Co., 360 N.E. 2d 1115 (Ill. App. 1977).

[11] Jones v. Johnson, 307 N.E. 2d 222 (Ill. App. 1974).

[12] Williams v. Board of Education, 201 S.E. 2d 889 (N.C. 1974).

was delivered. Actually this is only prima facie evidence of delivery and the presumption of delivery can be rebutted by convincing testimony to the contrary. A deed dated on Sunday and delivered on a weekday is good. A deed without a date or a date subsequent to the acknowledgement affidavit would not be void, but the party accepting the deed would have the burden, in case of litigation, of proving when the deed was actually delivered. If the date of the acknowledgement antedates the date in the deed, a technical examiner may require a new acknowledgement and recordation. If the grantor is dead or cannot be located, difficulty in this connection is readily apparent. Great care should be exercised to examine the dates in the deed in order to avoid difficulty at a later date. If the date is inserted, the grantee would have the presumption in his favor that the deed was delivered on the date specified and the burden would then be upon the opponent of the deed to prove otherwise.

PARTIES

The names and residences of the parties to the deed immediately follow the date. The party selling the property is known as the *grantor;* The purchaser of the property is known as the *grantee.* Any uncertainty as to the persons intended would render the deed void. Where the parties have a middle initial, it should be inserted. A deed must be made to some certain person or else it is void. A deed to a fictitious person or unincorporated community or corporation which has no legal existence, is void. Thus a deed to the Ajar Printing Company, which is a partnership consisting of two members, is void. The deed should have been made in the names of the two partners. A deed to "the employers of the school at Plumb Creek" would also be invalid. Where a corporation is a party to a deed, a slight mistake in setting out its name will not vitiate the deed, if it is clearly apparent from the face of it that one certain corporation was intended. Thus a deed written in the name of Boulevard Land and Development Company, Inc. would be upheld where the name of the corporation was Boulevard Land Development Company, Inc. However, in the case of *Alton Evening Telegraph v. Doak,*[13] the word "Co." was omitted from the name. The court held that the action failed. Likewise in *Arrow Ambulance v. Davis,*[14] failure to include "Inc." in the action was held fatal. A corporation, not legally constituted, cannot hold title to property, even though it later becomes a legal corporation.[15]

TYPES OF DEEDS

Deeds are classified as: (1) warranty deeds, bargain and sale deeds, and quit claim deeds. Warranty deeds may be in the standard form or in the form of a

---

[13] Alton Evening Telegraph v. Doak, 296 N.E. 2d 605 (Ill. 1973).

[14] Arrow Ambulance v. Davis, 306 N.E. 2d (Ill. 1974).

[15] Piedmont and Western Invest. Corp. v. Carnes-Miller Gera Co., 384 S.E. 2d 687 (N.C. App. 1989).

"Special Corporate Form Warranty Deed" which adds a section in which the signer certifies that his corporation board of directors has authorized him to execute the deed on behalf of the corporation.

WARRANTIES, WHAT DO THEY MEAN?

A seller, in conveying property, makes certain representations to the purchaser. He *warrants* that he has a fee simple title, that he has the right and power to convey it and that there is no lien or encumbrance against the property that has not been revealed. The seller is placed in the position where he personally guarantees the truthfulness of these statement and may be held personally responsible for them in case any of the statements are later proven in error. Under the covenants of warranty the grantee may hold the grantor for any damage he has sustained. The three covenants of title relating to the ownership of a fee simple are: (1) the ownership of the property is in fee, (2) the right to convey, and (3) the property is free of encumbrances, known as covenants *in praesenti* (as of the present). The grantor also warrants that the grantee will enjoy quiet enjoyment and that the grantor will make further assurances. These enjoyment warranties are known as covenants *in futuro* (as of the future). The quiet enjoyment warranty means that the grantees will not be ousted by someone under a paramount title to his grantor. The further-assurances warranty provides that the grantor—if it is discovered at any time that, through oversight or mistake in the deed, the grantee's title is imperfect—will voluntarily execute such instruments as are necessary to give the grantee the title which he thought he was receiving and which it was intended that he should receive. For example, a deed is improperly executed by the grantor. The grantee there requests a properly signed new deed. The grantor cannot take the position that he is "through" with the deal and refuse to do anything more, unless remunerated for doing so. Under the particular warranty the purchaser could enlist the aid of the court to compel the seller to execute the necessary corrections.

THE WARRANTY DEED

The most commonly used form is the warranty deed, in which the grantor warrants the title and covenants to protect his grantee against any claimant. In a *general warranty deed* the grantor agrees with the grantee that he will "forever warrant and defend the property against every person or persons whomever lawfully claiming the same, or any part thereof." In other words he agrees to protect or defend the buyer against the entire world.

The covenant of special warranty is not so sweeping in its grant. A person may not care to defend the title of a property against everyone. He may feel that he should be required to guarantee the title only against himself or anyone claiming under him. A *special warranty* is a promise or covenant on the part of the grantor to defend the grantee against all claims which may be brought against the grantor or his heirs, assigns, or anyone claiming under the grantor. The general warranty clause can be made into a special warranty by inserting the few words "by, from, through, or under him." If there are plural grantors, then use "them, or nay of them." A purchaser of real estate has no right to expect a covenant of general warranty in his deed unless he bargains for it in the agreement of sale. He cannot refuse to take the deed merely because it contains a special warranty. Trustee deeds and deeds given in pursuance of an order of court are special warranty deeds. Where no warranty is expressed, the court will hold there is an implied special warranty in favor of the grantee.

In actual modern practice, the considerations of warranty discussed above are more or less negated by the issuance of title insurance, which is provided at the grantor's expense. Thus, any problem in the future falls upon the land title insurance organization, which must defend the title against all comers and, in the even of an error or omission determination, reimburse the parties who have suffered a loss as a result of such errors or omissions.

THE QUIT CLAIM DEED

A quit claim deed is used to clear clouds upon the title as in the case of a recorded agreement of sale or the release of a life estate or a contingent remainder. It is also often used in the case of minor boundary adjustments which are mutually agreed between adjacent land owners. A quit claim deed may be used to extinguish a recorded sale agreement. The vendee (purchaser) would be the grantor in this case. The grantee in the quit claim deed may already have or may claim a complete title to the premises and the grantor has a *possible* interest that might constitute a cloud upon the title. A deed of *conformation* is similar, in effect, to a quit claim deed. The operative words are "remise, release, and quit claim." The warranty is omitted entirely, and the grantor forever quits whatever interest he might have in the property. A wife who has not joined in the bargain and sale deed, may subsequently sign a quit claim deed barring her potential dower right in the property. A quit claim deed conveys only such interest as the grantor possessed at the time of the conveyance.[16]

It would be theoretically possible for anyone to legally quit claim the deed to New York Kennedy Airport to some party. For in so doing, he is merely stating that whatever interest he has at that time is being deeded to the grantee. The fact that he had no interest at that time is of no consequence.

DEED OF BARGAIN AND SALE—CONSIDERATION

A deed of bargain and sale, which is the instrument adopted in most states to transfer real estate, requires consideration for the deed, although it need not be necessarily expressed. Consideration in the deed may be either good or valuable.

---

[16]
Chatham Amusement Co. v. Perry, 216 Ga. 445 (1961).

A good consideration proceeds from love and affection or the like, and has no pecuniary value. A valuable consideration is money or its equivalent, or anything capable of being measured by a monetary standard. The practice of inserting a dollar as consideration is sufficient for the requirements of the law. Courts do not inquire into the adequacy of the consideration. The slightest consideration will support the transfer of property worth $1,000,000. If the title is being transferred to a relative without any cash consideration, as from father to son, the deed should recite for "1.00 and other good and valuable consideration." A deed made by an insolvent owner to a close relative or friend with the intent to disturb, delay, hinder or defraud creditors is void against a creditor.[17]

Under statutes dealing with transfer of real estate by an insolvent debtor, or made with actual intent to defraud, the burden of proof is initially upon the one seeking to set aside the conveyance.[18] Deeds from fiduciaries, such as trust companies, should recite the true consideration price rather than a nominal consideration. An error in stating the true consideration will not affect the validity of the deed.

DEEDS IN CONSIDERATION OF OR IN EXCHANGE FOR SUPPORT

A support deed, as the term implies, is when the grantor deeds real estate to the grantee in *consideration* of the grantee's agreement "to provide care, shelter, and maintenance for and during the term of the natural life of the grantor."[19] This clause in the deed is important.

If the grantee merely makes a verbal promise, and the promise is not kept, the grantor is in serious difficulties.

An aged parent, in return for support and shelter from a son, may deed the home to him. Later on, differences arise between the two, and sad to relate, the son orders the father from the home. Soon thereafter, the son sells the property to a bona fide purchaser. Unless the deed from the father to son recites that the conveyance to the son was made in consideration of support during the father's lifetime, the conveyance to the third party will be upheld.[20]

Where a parent has deeded a property to a child, other members of the family will often challenge the validity of the instrument on the grounds that undue influence was exercised. Where the deed recites a consideration of maintenance

---

17
Patterson v. Hopkins, 371 A. 2d 1378 (Pa. Super. 1977).

18
Sparkman & McLean Co. v. Derber, 481 P. 2d 585 (Wash. App. 1971) and Isabella Bank & Trust Co. v. Pappas, 261 N.W. 2d 558 (Mich. App. 1977).

19
Shook v. Bergstrosser, 51 A. 2d 681 (Pa. 1946).

20
Wood v. Swift, 428 S.W. 2d 77 (Ark. 1968); Kinney v. Kinney, 150 So. 2d 671 (La. 1963) and Mitchell et al. v. Wilcox et al., 139 N.W. 2d 203 (Neb. 1966).

and support and the deed is contested later on grounds of *failure* of consideration, the circumstances will be carefully scrutinized to ascertain whether the parent was imposed upon because of age, poor health or fraud, in making the deed.

The relationship of child to parent, does not, per se, raise a presumption of undue influence, duress or fraud.[21] "Love and affection" is "sufficient consideration" so far as the immediate parties are concerned, but it is not a "fair consideration" where the conveyance of real property is made to delay, defraud, or hinder creditors of the grantor.[22]

A niece's deception to her uncle that she and her cohabiter were married is sufficient ground for cancellation of a deed, which conveyed a life estate to them, as husband and wife.[23] In a deed from a 94-year-old uncle to his nephew, a presumption arises that the deed was invalid and burden of overcoming presumption was upon the nephew.[24]

If a parent conveys his property to a child in consideration of the child's promise to support the parent, and the child fails to carry out his promise, then equity will presume that the child had a fraudulent intent, and will allow the parent to rescind the deed transfer.[25]

Undue Influence—Undue influence is a mixture of fraud and force. Sometimes a person will enter into a contract in order to get rid of a persistent salesman. The mere fact that consent was obtained through nagging and importunity is insufficient to avoid the consequences of a contract. However, where the mind is enfeebled by old age, disease or great distress, undue influence may be readily proved. Force is opposed to freedom. Free consent is the essence of every agreement. The question to be determined is whether either party was deprived of the exercise of his free will power.

In order to establish undue influence as a basis for setting aside a deed from parents to son, the law requires more than an opportunity to exert undue influence or suspicions on part of those who feel aggrieved.[26]

OTHER COMPONENTS OF THE DEED

GRANTING CLAUSE

The words used in the deed that transfer the estate from the grantor to the grantee constitutes the granting clause and are termed the "operative words." These

---

[21] Prentice v. Cox, 547 S.W. 2d 744 (Ark. 1977).

[22] Jahner v. Jacob, 252 N.W. 2d 1 (N.D. 1977).

[23] Harrel v. Branson, 334 So. 2d 604 (Fla. App. 1977).

[24] Gross, Adm., etc. v. Allen, 345 So. 2d 1315 (Miss 1977).

[25] Kendall v. Kendall, 360 N.E. 2d 1242 (Ill. App. 1977).

[26] Hotchkiss v. Werth, 483 P. 2d 1053 (Kan. 1971); Gallegos v. Garcia, 480 P. ed 1002 (Ariz. 1971); and Hensley v. Stevens, 481 P. 2d 694 (Mont. 1971).

words are generally "grant and convey" or "grant, bargain, and sell." They usually precede the description but may be placed in any part of the deed. The necessity for technical words is no longer felt, and any words indicating the intention to convey will operate to transfer title. Following the grant and immediately preceding the description of the property are the words of limitation denoting the quantity of estate intended to be granted. The words ordinarily employed to pass a fee simple title are "heirs and assigns." A fee simple estate is the greatest estate which may be held in property, and at common law the words "heirs and assigns" were absolutely essential to pass a fee. Without the words "heirs" only an estate for life passes. It would not suffice to say that the "grantee is to have and to hold for ever" or "to grantee and his assigns forever," for this does not mean that the issue of the grantee acquire any vested interest in the land. The word "heirs" is said to be a word of limitation, rather than a word of purchase, and indicates a complete title of perpetual duration with power to sell to anybody; it does not give the issue or heirs of the grantee any right to the property after the owner's death. Today, the operative words in a deed "grant and convey" or either if them will generally be held to be effective to convey a fee simple title if the grantor had such title.

PROPERTY DESCRIPTION

The purpose of the description in the deed is to accurately describe the property to be transferred. No deed will be operative which does not contain a description sufficient for an exact identification. The description need not be technically exact but must be sufficiently precise to enable a surveyor to locate the boundaries. If the description is not sufficiently full, the deed will fail; verbal testimony will not be admitted to supply the deficiency unless such definition is the result of fraud, accident or mistake, in which case the courts permit a reformation of the deed description.

The parole evidence rule generally applies. The rule is that verbal testimony cannot be introduced to vary, contradict, add to, or subtract from a written instrument, or to change its legal import, unless fraud, accident, or mistake is pleaded. However, should the deed refer to some other instrument, such as a previous deed, which accurately describes the premises, the new deed will be valid.

A deed description calling for "about 8 acres to a lake" and "about 6 acres to a stake at road," without identifying stakes and giving beginning and ending points, was so indefinite as to be void.[27] The words "more or less" raise a presumption of sale by the acre.[28]

In the case of *Sabine Investment Co. v. Stratton*,[29] the vendee sued for specific

---

[27] Grand Lodge of Independent Order of Odd Fellows v. City of Thomasville, 226 Ga. 4 (1970).

[28] Witmer v. Bloom, 288 A. 2d 323 (Md. App. 1972) and Allen v. Youngblood, 200 S.E. 2d 758 (Ga. 1973).

[29] Sabine Investment Co. v. Stratton, 549 S.W. 2d 247 (Tex. App. 1977).

performance upon a sales agreement, which described the tract as "Lot 5, in the Donald McDonald Survey, Subdivision in Sabine County, Texas, according to a Plat recorded in the County Clerk's office of such county, or legal description as follows: 3.7 acres more or less." The County Clerk's Office showed no such recorded plat. The description was held wholly inadequate and specific performance refused.

Property descriptions in deeds should be liberally construed to sustain rather than defeat a conveyance. In the Louisiana case of *Placid Oil Co. v. Young*,[30] the grantor conveyed "acres in S.W. corner of N.E. of S.W. 1/4" of designated section, which was the same tract acquired by grantor under a partition agreement; the court held the description valid.

A real estate contract describing land only as "all that tract of Land Lot 112 of the 5th Dist. of Clayton County, Ga. being 36 acres on New Hope Road,: was void and unenforceable for uncertainty.[31]

A call for an established corner prevails over a call for distance.[32]

PROPERTY DESCRIPTION METHODS

There are four types of descriptions generally used in the United States. These are:

1. Rectangular survey descriptions
2. Lot number or plot and map
3. Metes and bounds description
4. Monuments

RECTANGULAR SURVEY

The rectangular survey method was adopted by Congress as early as May 20, 1785, and is used outside of the original thirteen states. In the *Real Estate Primer*, issued by the State of Iowa[33] the rectangular survey is explained and illustrated as follows:

The rectangular survey refers to a grid of north and south (meridians) and east and west (parallels) lines surveyed by the government. Identification of property is east or west so many ranges or vertical rows of checks from north and south line called "principal meridian" and so many horizontal rows of tiers or townships north of an east west line called the "base line." Ranges run north and south and townships run east and west.

Distance between the parallels and meridians is 24 miles and the area contained

---

[30] Placid Oil Co. v. Young, 246 So. 2d 306 (1971).

[31] Wallace v. Adamson, 201 S.E. 2d 479 (Ga. 1973).

[32] Jordan v. Tinnin, 342 So. 2d 748 (Ala. 1977).

[33] Permission of C.R. Galvin, Director.

therein is called a check. In this area are 16 townships and the townships are further divided into 36 sections of a mile square each. The section is further divided into halves, quarters, and smaller subdivisions.

Fractional sections on the north and west side of a township are due to corrections made in the survey lines for the curvature of the earth. This results in these sections having more or less 640 acres, depending upon the corrections. In describing these sections, the words "fractional sections" should be used.

Figure 7-2 shows a portion of the north part of a check with 4 tiers north of the base line and 4 ranges east and west of the principal meridian. Figure 7-3 shows a township consisting of 36 sections of 640 acres each. Each section is 1 mile by 1 mile in size. Note the section numbering, which begins in the upper right-hand corner and ends with section 36 in the lower right-hand. Figure 7-4 shows a subdivided section with some of the possible types of subdividing. Actually, these sections may be subdivided in any way that a line can be drawn.

We often find designations such as the SE of the SE of the SE of Section 20, Tier 2W, Salt Lake Base and Meridian. The question then asked is how many acres does it contain. If a section contains 640 acres, then the SE would contain $640 \div 4$ or 160 acres. If this portion is once again quartered, the size is 40 acres. If quartered once again, as in this example, the size is 10 acres. There is a much easier method of determining the size from the above description. One only has to multiply the denominators to determine the portion of the section; thus, $1/4 \times 1/4 \times 1/4 = 1/64$ of a section or 10 acres. Similarly 1/2 of 1/2 of a section is a 1/4 section or 80 Acres.

SUBDIVISION OF A CHECK

6 mi.			T2N R1W				
Tier	3	No.	T3N R1W				
			T4N R1W				
T1N R4W	T1N R3W	T1N R4W	T5N R1W	T1N R1E			

24 Miles   Base Line

5th Principal
Meridian

Figure 7-2

SUBDIVISION OF TOWNSHIP INTO SECTIONS

6	5	4	3	2	1
7	8	9	10	11	12
18	17	16	15	14	13
19	20	21	22	23	24
30	29	28	27	26	25
31	32	33	34	35	36

Figure 7-3

SUBDIVISION OF A SECTION

	W½	E½
NW ¼	80	80
160 Acre	Acres	Acres
	160 Rods	
40		
10A.		
Acres		

Figure 7-4

LOT NUMBER

The lot number system is used in large urban areas where there has been extensive development of the land. A property is transformed from farmland into a subdivision which is laid out in numbered lots. The plan, if approved by the municipality is then recorded. Specific properties, henceforth, could be referred to as Lot #25, Southland Subdivision as recorded in the office of the County Clerk or other appropriate agency. Subdivisions or "Surveys" are often divided into blocks and the blocks then subdivided into lots. A designated property, in this latter case might read Lots 22 & 24, Block 5, Big Field Survey.

METES AND BOUNDS

One of the oldest methods of land description is the metes and bounds method. *Metes* are measurements of length, normal recorded in feet, chains, or rods. *Bounds* are artificial and natural boundaries such as streets, streams, roads, and adjoining farms. Such a description will begin with a designated point, clearly identified, and then continue, side by side in a clockwise direction, for certain distances and directions until returning to the point of beginning. Directions are indicated as compass points designated in degrees, minutes, and seconds.

Example: Beginning at a point which is 80.0 rods east and 40 rods north of the NE corner of Section 25, Tier 3 North, Range 4 East, Salt Lake Base and meridian and proceeding N 21°33'44"E 120.0 ft. thence ..... and thence .....to the point of beginning.

The principle is well established that the courses and distances in a deed always give way to the boundary markers found on the ground or supplied by proof of their former existence when the marks or monuments are gone. Thus, a deed description "from said point, 40° 30" west a distance of 220 ft to the Revolutionary chestnut tree" would give the purchaser 230 ft, if that was the actual distance to the tree in question. This rule is to be used only in reconciling discrepancies.

MONUMENTS

In rural areas, descriptions by monuments are still frequently used. At the end of the description it is customary to insert "containing 64 acres, more or less." The description by monuments does not lend itself readily to an examination of the title, particularly for one not familiar with the locale of the property. A description conveying "10 acres more or less" of other lands, and not locating the particular 10 acres, would be void, owing to uncertainty.

FENCES

When the owners of adjoining land have acquiesced in the location of a fence for a length of time required by the statute of adverse possession, they are thereafter precluded from saying that the fence is not the true line. It then becomes immaterial to inquire whether the fence is on the original boundary line.

ROADS

It is a general rule of law, well established by authority, that a conveyance of lands bounded by a highway gives the grantee title to the middle of the road if the grantor had title and did not expressly or by clear implication reserve the bed of the road for himself. This right to the middle of the road is always subject to the right of the public. Ownership becomes important only if the road is later abandoned. Few state and local governments are comfortable with this type of ownership. Where such exists and improvements are planned, the governmental agency will normally require the owner to deed the right-of-way to that agency. Since the owner is unable to utilize the land anyway, there is no reason to not transfer the property in turn for the benefit of an improved roadway.

STREAMS

Where a nonnavigable stream is given as a boundary, the grantee takes to the middle of the stream as in the case of a street. In the case of a navigable stream, the grantee takes absolutely to the high water mark and, in a qualified sense, to low water mark. That is to say, in the area between the high water mark and the low, his rights are subject to the rights of the public for navigation purposes, which include all privileges for such purposes. A navigable stream in law is one which is navigable in fact. The land between the high water mark and the low is known as flat land. A description in a deed read "five acres of marsh meadow *bounded by the river S.*" The value of the farm land *by the river* carried with it the adjacent flat land. The fact that the description states that the land is bounded "by" a stream or that it runs "along" a stream and names a monument on the shore does not necessarily show an intention to exclude the stream, and in this regarded merely as a statement of the point at which the boundary strikes the stream. It is impractical to place a marker in the stream proper.

The right of navigation is the dominant right and superior to the right of fishing, but duty to exercise care rests on both parties. Where both rights can be enjoyed freely and fairly, the right of navigation has no authority to trespass upon and injure the right of fishing.[34] In the cited case the court held that a crab fisherman could recover loss of crab pots if destruction resulted from failure of the vessels with log tows to use reasonable care.

An individual property owner has no absolute riparian rights of ownership in a navigable stream and to the land *below* high water mark, nor does he have littoral rights of ownership to land covered and uncovered by the flow and ebb of the sea

---

[34]

Van Deursen v. Dunlap Towing Co., 562 P. 2d 666 (Wash. App. 1977).

tides. It has been held by the United States Supreme Court that even the State of California has no title to the submerged lands between the shoreline and the three-mile limit, but that title is in the Federal Government.[35] This question is highly important due to the valuable underlying oil deposits.

When a map, plan, or other survey is referred to in a deed, it becomes a material and essential part of the conveyance and is to have the same force and effect as if copied into the deed.[36] Where there is a deed reference to a map of a highway to be dedicated in the future, there are two opposing rules: (1) The New York rule holds that such a reference to an unopened highway raises a presumption of an intention to convey the land to the middle of the proposed highway as if the highway actually existed; (2) The Massachusetts rule, on the other hand, states that the roadbed of the proposed highway is not included and the boundary is fixed at the side of the proposed highway. In Pennsylvania, the law seems to be that where the street is merely plotted upon the plan, the grantee takes only to the edge of the street, but where the street is open, the grantee's title jumps to the middle of the street.

LINES ON THE GROUND

Calls in a deed are always controlled by lines on the ground. If the sale is made by lines staked and marked on the ground, such lines on the ground govern, if in conflict with the deed restriction.

THE DEED RECITAL

The recital is a statement of facts interesting, or necessary, for persons examining the title to know. It tells how the grantor acquired title, or the reason why the deed is made, or some other explanatory remark. It usually follows the description, although when long, such as a trustee's or executor's deeds made under an Order of the Court, it usually comes after the names of the parties and commences with the words "Whereas." It can hardly be regarded as an essential part of the deed unless it contains something of a contractual nature between the parties to the instrument.

APPURTENANCES TRANSFERRED WITH THE LAND

The deed may contain the phrase "with the appurtenances and all the estate and right of the party of the first part (grantor) in and to said premises."

The right to the appurtenances goes with the property, as a matter of law, so

---

[35] United States v. California, 332 U.S. 19 (1947).

[36] Segaro v. Cornell, 196 S.E. 2d 341 (Ga. 1973).

there is no real reason for the above clause. All easements, rights and incidents, which belong to the property conveyed and necessary to its full enjoyment, pass as "appurtenances" without any mention of them. What is merely convenient to the enjoyment does not. These include alleyways, water courses, light and air. Thus the deed should specify "together with" followed by a description of the rights intended to pass. What is appurtenant to a piece of land is appurtenant to every part thereof. Where a right-of-way is granted as appurtenant to a tract of land and the tract is later subdivided into smaller lots, each of the lot purchasers would be entitled to the same right-of-way. Also, where a property, bounded by a private alley, is sold and the alley is necessary to the premises sold, the right to use it passes as an appurtenance to the property unless there is something in the conveyance restricting the use solely to the grantor or expressly excepting the alley from the grant.[37]

THE HABENDUM CLAUSE

The habendum or "have and to hold" clause, where used, operates to define the quantity of estate which the grantee is said to have in the property granted. The habendum is not absolutely necessary. The estate granted may be limited in the earlier part of the deed and if the habendum contradicts the earlier limitation, it will have no effect. If the two can be reconciled, then the effect will be given to both. Where the limitations in the premises are in general terms, as to Jones and his heirs generally, and the habendum limits the estate to Jones for and during the term of his natural life, the grantee takes a life estate.

SIGNATURE(S)

The object of the signature(s) is to authenticate the genuineness of the document. It is not essential that the grantor himself sign the deed. His mark, where he cannot write, or even where he can, if intended as a signature, will be sufficient. Signature by mark would appear as:

(His
John   ×   Steel
mark)

A signature by mark must be witnessed by two persons. Where the signing is done by a third party in the *presence* of the grantor and *at the direction* of the grantor, it amounts to a compliance with the requirements of the law. The ordinary situation is for property to stand in the name of one person. It is usual, however, where the title is in the name of the husband alone, to have the wife join in the execution of

---

[37] Westland Nursing Home, Inc. v. Benson, 517 P. 2d 862 (Colo. App. 1974).

the deed. This joining is for the purpose of extinguishing any claim which she may later have through her dower interest in the property.

A forged deed, unlike one procured by fraud, deceit, or trickery, is void from inception. In the latter even, the deed is voidable as between the parties thereto, but not as to a bona fide purchaser for value.[38]

The deed may also be executed by proxy under a power of attorney. A power of attorney is defined as "an instrument, in writing, under seal, by which the party executing it appoints another to be his attorney and empowers the second party to act for him, either in all general matters of business or especially to do some specified act or acts, in his name and on his behalf." The power of attorney must be acknowledged so that it can be recorded in the county where the property is located; it must be recorded so that a purchaser may know that the particular execution was properly authorized. Death of the person executing the power of attorney automatically revokes the power of attorney even if the agent has no notice of the death. An attorney-in-fact has no right to delegate his authority unless the instrument by which he is appointed expressly authorizes the substitution. The signature by an attorney-in-fact should read as follows:

> "John Steel
> By Adam Taylor
> his Attorney-in-fact"

The attorney or agent need not sign his own name. The name of the principal is adequate. In actual practice, however, the signature of the agent is usually included.

Where a grantor signs a deed, he is presumed to have read it and to be familiar with its contents. Illiteracy is no defense to the validity of the instrument. If a person cannot read, the burden is upon him to have someone read the deed to him. A grantor cannot complain at a later date that the transaction has turned out differently from the way he anticipated, or that he was unaware of the full import of the deed, because he could not read. Where the illiterate grantor has been imposed upon and the deed content misrepresented to him, equity will grant relief and set the transfer aside.

In most states it is not necessary to have the deed witnessed. In Georgia, the law requires two witnesses in order to record a deed, but without witnesses, the deed is valid between the grantor and grantee. It is good precaution in the event a dispute arises, for the subscribing witnesses to be procured to testify as to the deed execution. The witness attests nothing but the signing and delivery of the deed. The date and other contents of the deed are matters which he does not attest and to which he seldom attends.

In the Florida case of *Wickes Homes v. Moxley,*[39] the court decided that "there

---

[38] Harding v. Ja Laur Corp., 315 A. 2d 132 (Md. 1974).

[39] Wickes Homes v. Moxley, 342 So. 2d 839 (Fla. App. 1977).

is no longer a requirement under the new Constitution for a mortgage of homestead realty to be signed in the presence of two attesting witnesses.

ACKNOWLEDGEMENT OF THE DEED

In addition to signing, sealing, and witnessing a deed, it is customary for grantor to acknowledge it. The acknowledgement is a formal declaration made before a notary public, justice of the peace, alderman, or other official empowered to perform the service, affirming the genuineness of the signature on the deed. The acknowledgement accomplishes two things: (1) it establishes the deed as *prima facie* evidence in any legal proceeding; that is, the deed will be accepted as evidence without any further proof of its genuineness; and (2) *it permits the recording of the deed.* The acknowledgement contains the venue or county in which it is executed— "State of Illinois, County of Cook"—the date, the name of the grantor(s) and the signature, seal, and expiration date of the commission of the officer taking the acknowledgement. It should state, that the affiant is personally known or satisfactorily proved to the subscriber. The grantor's marital status should also be indicated—John Steel, unmarried," or "John Steel and Mary Steel, his wife." In some states, such as Alabama, Texas, and North Carolina, separate acknowledgements must be taken and the wife's must be taken apart from her husband, where she must state that the signing is of her own free will and done voluntarily. This is a procedure carried over from the days when the husband might gamble away the homestead, but provided a way for the wife to stop the transfer. In North Carolina, a separate acknowledgement is necessary in a conveyance from a wife to her husband.

SPECIAL PROBLEMS OF DEEDS BY MARRIED WOMEN

In some states, where a married woman owns or inherits property in her name alone, the husband must join in a conveyance of the wife's land, or in an agreement to sell such land. This is required to extinguish his curtesy rights.

In some states such as Arkansas, Hawaii, Tennessee and the District of Columbia, a wife can convey title to her real property without joinder of her husband.

For cause shown, as where a husband has deserted the wife or is a profligate, the court, upon application of the wife, may declare her a feme sole, as if she were unmarried. She could then execute a valid deed by her signature alone. In Arkansas, Oklahoma and other states, a married woman can convey her separate property without the joinder of her husband. Care should be exercised, in these instances, to assure that the property, once separate, has not become community property through the addition of community assets over the years. For instance a business, inherited by the wife, and operated as a proprietorship or in partnership with her husband, may have profits from the joint efforts plowed back to expand the operation over a number of years. The profits, being community property, may have rendered the former separate property a community asset.

Where property is owned by a single woman who enters into an agreement of sale and, before the consummation of the sale, marries, the purchaser can compel the wife and the newly acquired husband to join in a valid deed. Since the married woman, prior to marriage, had contracted to sell the property, she retained only the bare legal title after the agreement of sale was signed, and her marriage was ineffective to enlarge her interest or to impinge upon the equitable title obtained by the purchaser under the agreement.

DELIVERY OF THE DEED—AN ESSENTIAL ACT OF THE TRANSFER

Delivery is one of the most important steps in the transfer of title to real estate. A deed, signed, sealed, witnessed, and acknowledged does not pass title until it is delivered by the grantor to the grantee, or to a third person for him.[40] A deed is presumed to have been delivered on the date which the deed bears.[41]

In the case of *Scroggins v. Roper,*[42] the court said,

> No particular form of words or action is necessary to constitute delivery of a deed, but manual delivery is not necessary; a deed may be delivered by words without acts, by acts without words, or by both. An intention to give present effect to an executed conveyance is sufficient.

In *Fiori v. Fiori,*[43] a deed was executed in 1940. It was not recorded until 1957. The grantor died in 1942. The court found that the grantor, at no time, told the grantee, or any member of his family, about the deed. The grantor controlled the property until his death. The court held that there was no presumption of delivery. An unrecorded deed, found by a grantee among the grantor's papers, after grantor's death, does not pass title, although the grantee had said that it belonged to the grantee.[44]

As between the parties to a deed, it is necessary that there be delivery to the grantee. Validity of the delivery depends upon the intentions of the grantor.[45] When the deed is not "handed over" questions of delivery arises. If delivery may be presumed from the circumstances, then title will pass. The question to be deter-

---

[40] Murphy v. Traylor, 289 So. 2d 584 (Ala. 1974).

[41] Doyl v. Carter et al., 362 N.E. 2d 214 (Mass. App. 1977).

[42] Scroggins v. Roper, 548 S.W. 2d 779 (Tex Civ App. 1977).

[43] Fiori v. Fiori, 405 Pa. 303 (1961).

[44] Willingham v. Smith, et a;., 106 S.E. 117 (Ga. 1921); 1st National Bank of Gainsville v. Harmon, 199 S.E. 223 (Ga. 1938) and Algood v. Algood, 196 S.E. 2d 888 (Ga. 1973).

[45] Proctor v. Forsythe, 480 P. 2d 511 (Wash. 1971).

mined is the *intention* of the grantor. An executed deed, recorded by the grantor, would raise strong presumption of delivery. Ordinarily, it may be said that retention of the deed by the grantor raises a strong presumption against delivery and possession by the grantee creates a presumption in favor of delivery. In both cases only a presumption is raised and is subject to rebuttal by proof.

Deposit of a deed with a third party to be turned over to the named grantee, upon death of the grantor, constitutes "delivery," only if the grantor surrenders all control over the deed, and conveys a present interest in the property. Intentions can be construed through conversations and acts at the time the deed was delivered to the third person.[46]

Where the decedent supplies purchase money for land, but took title in the name of her cousin, who did not know of the deed to him, title did not pass to him after the death.[47]

Delivery Absolute—There are two kinds of delivery, delivery absolute and delivery in escrow. Delivery absolute occurs when made to a grantee or his agent without any conditions or stipulations attached. This is the normal situation.

Delivery in Escrow occurs when a deed is delivered to a third party and will take effect only upon the performance of some condition by one of the parties or the happening of some event. In an escrow delivery, the grantor loses all control over the deed, and he is powerless to recall it.[48] The condition of the escrow must be stated *at the time* the deed is turned over to the escrow holder and not at some later date. The *time* for performance of the escrow condition as well as what happens if the condition is not performed should be definitely stated. Otherwise the delivery will be considered absolute and the escrow holder as agent for the grantee. The escrow holder should require that the conditions of delivery be in writing and signed by the interested parties. A deed delivered to escrow will pass no title if it is stolen or otherwise fraudulently procured by the grantee or if delivered to him without fulfillment of the escrow condition, but a bona fide purchaser from the grantee, without notice, will obtain good title.

It should be remembered that the escrow holder must be some disinterested or impartial third party and the principals or their legal counsel are not such disinterested parties within the contemplation of the law. Nor is a broker a disinterested third party, because he is the agent of the owner from whom he receives compensation for his services in the form of a commission. A bank, title company or other escrow company should preferably be used as the escrow holder. A deposit of earnest money with a real estate broker should not be confused with an escrow.

---

[46] Cain v. Morrison, 512 P. 2d 474 (Kan. 1973).

[47] Caron v. Wadas, 305 N.E. 2d 853 (Mass. 1974).

[48] Fike v. Harshberger, 317 A. 2d 859 (Md.1924).

RECORDING THE INSTRUMENT OF TRANSFER

When the deed has been signed, sealed, and delivered, the transfer of title is complete. Recordation is of no importance as far as passing of title is concerned between grantor and grantee.[49] However, in order for the purchaser to protect himself in the ownership, the law requires him to take one additional step. This consists of recording or registering his deed in the office of the Recorder of Deeds, Registrar, or Registrar of Deeds in the county in which the property is located. The recording of a deed consists in having it transcribed in a proper book and indexed, so that the public at large may have notice of the transfer of title. The deed should be recorded promptly in order to protect the grantee against a subsequent conveyance of the same property by his grantor, or against a mortgage or judgment entered against the same grantor.

> *Example*—Green delivers a deed to White on December 6, 1991 which is not recorded until March 21, 1992. A judgment entered against Green on February 21, 1992 would be a lien against the real estate in question. So also, a bona fide purchaser of the same land from Green would have a preferred claim to the property if he had no actual or constructive notice of the transfer to White. Actual notice is express or direct knowledge gained in the course of the transaction.

Once a deed is recorded, all persons are presumed to have constructive notice of the contents of the recorded instrument.[50] Constructive notice is notice given by public records. If a deed has been recorded in the proper office of the county, this is constructive notice to the public. A deed recorded outside of the chain of title does not constitute "constructive notice" under the Recording Act.[51]

Suppose that Black is purchasing property from Stone, and knows that Stone at one time had mortgaged the property to Chase. That fact would not be notice, per se, to Black, unless he learned about it in the course of negotiations for the property with Stone. Notice of the existence of the mortgage would be *presumed* under the circumstances. These circumstances would make a prudent person suspicious and cautious and evoke further inquiry. Also, if the land is not in possession of the person claiming ownership, but is occupied by the holder of a *prior* deed, a little inquiry from the party of possession would reveal the duplicity of the original owner.

Actual Notice—In *Weddell v. City of Atlanta*,[52] the court held that the actual possession of the realty by a wife and children was sufficient to put all who might purchase from the husband on notice and on inquiry as to what interest or claim that they might have.

---

[49] Huntington City v. Peterson, 518 P. 2d 1246 (Utah 1974).

[50] American Medical Intern, Inc. v. Ortez, 111 Cal. Rptr. 617 (1974).

[51] Sabo v. Horath, 559 P. 2d 1038 (Alaska 1976).

[52] Weddell v. City of Atlanta, 172 S.E. 2d 862 (GA. 1970).

INDEXING OF THE DEED

The buyer or his attorney should make sure that the deed is properly indexed in the Recorder's Office. If the deed is not properly indexed, a grantee may suffer serious consequences, by entry of a judgment, a mortgage, or even a subsequent recorded deed, against the grantor. This situation points up the advisability of obtaining title insurance.[53]

THE TORRENS SYSTEM OF LAND REGISTRATION

A system of land registration was introduced in Australia in 1858 by Sir Robert Torrens. The system provided for a permanent method of title registration with an assurance fund out of which losses due to title defects would be paid. Once the title is registered by the owner, subsequent transfers of the certificate of title registration could be readily effected at slight expense. The original Torrens system has not made any great inroads into the recording system in this country due to the initial expense involved, certain substantial objections inherent in the system, and the opposition of title companies. Although adopted in varying forms in a number of states—California and repealed in 1955, Colorado, Georgia, Illinois, Massachusetts, Mississippi, Minnesota, Nebraska, New York, North Carolina, North Dakota, Ohio, Oregon, South Carolina, South Dakota, Tennessee, Utah, Virginia, and Washington—searches are, in the main, still required. In Massachusetts and Illinois have the most satisfactory applications of the Torrens system. Adaptations of the Torrens system require the registration of title ownership through court proceedings. The certificate of title passed by court authorization is conclusive insofar as the character of the title is concerned.

PROPERTY TRANSFER BY OTHER THAN DEED

ADVERSE POSSESSION

Ordinarily an owner of property depends upon a "paper" title to establish ownership; that is, by deed from his predecessor, which when traced back shows a continuity of ownership to the source of title in the particular state. An examination of the public records establish "chain of title" upon which the occupier of land relies to prove ownership. Technically, the title emanates from a sovereign power or government, the exact source varying in the different sections of the country. However, a resident of land may claim title to property without any deed or color of title at all. He may rely on *adverse possession*. Such title may be superior to that of the holder of "paper" title if certain statutory requirements are met. This is known as title by adverse possession. The law governing adverse possession is now universal, being enforced in practically every state of the country. The purpose of

---

[53]
Adams v. United States, 76 U.S. Ct. No. 1333, S.D., N.Y. 1976.

these laws is identical. They are prompted, in the first place, by the demands of public policy which hold that a statute of this kind is necessary to prevent the abandonment of any portion of the territory.

The law provides that where an occupier holds land and maintains actual, continuous, hostile, notorious, distinct, and visible possession for the required period of time, he is deemed to have the legal title as against the one who holds a deed to the land. The required period of such possession varies from 7 to 30 years. In Arkansas and Utah, 7 years is the statutory period; Mississippi, Missouri, Nebraska, and Oregon specify 10 years; Connecticut, Kansas, Kentucky, Minnesota, and Oklahoma require 15 years; and in Louisiana the period prescribed is 30 years.

The adverse possession acts, in a sense, as a statute of limitations in that it bars the legal owner from asserting his claim to land where he has remained silent and done nothing to oust the adverse occupant during the statutory period. It is almost impossible to succeed in claiming adverse possession against a cemetery, even those deemed to have been inactive for a long period of time. In the *Forest Home Cemetery Association v. Dardanella Financial Corp.*,[54] the court stated that the land is deemed possessed in a way it was intended to be possessed and there can be no exclusive possession by an intruder.

The theory of adverse possession law is that "no person ought to be permitted to lie by while transactions can be fairly investigated and justly determined, until time has involved them in uncertainty and obscurity, and then ask for an inquiry." An adverse claimant may petition the court for a decree to perfect his title. A party claiming adverse possession bears a heavy burden of proof.[55]

ACTUAL POSSESSION

Incidents which help establish actual possession include building a dwelling or other structure, clearing brush, sowing crops, pasturing cattle, erecting fences, cutting timber, irrigating land, constructing drainage ditches, planting orchards, and paying taxes. The very acts of excluding intruders, cleaning of brush and other acts of domination may be indicative of adverse possession.[56]

Payment of taxes by an adverse possessor of land is not the controlling factor to establish title. In Florida, taxes must be paid by such adverse claimant for the requisite 7-year period, unless he has some color of title, i.e., some written instrument or court decree.[57] However, in the Texas case of *Garcia v. Placios*,[58] the

---

[54]
Forest Home Cemetery Association v. Dardanella Financial Corp., 329 N.W. 2d 895 (S.D. 1983).

[55]
Kerrigan v. Thomas, 281 So. 2d 410 (Fla. App. 1973).

[56]
Herriot v. Lewis, 35 Wash. App. 496,668, P. 2d 589 (1983).

[57]
Meyer v. Law, 287 So. 2d 37 (Fla. 1973).

[58]
Garcia v. Placios, 667 S.W. 2d 225 (Tex. App. 1984, writ ref. n.r.e.)

appellate court reversed the trial court and indicated that a failure to pay taxes on the contested property does not necessarily preclude adverse possession.

Payment of taxes alone, without actual residence and dominion over the property, would be insufficient to prove adverse possession. Payment of taxes is entitled to some weight in proving the adverse claim, but it is a contributing factor, not the controlling one.[59]

Just what is meant by *actual possession*?

By actual possession is meant such possession of the property as leaves no doubt in the mind of the ordinary person as to the nature of its occupancy. The law insists that a claimant must show the performance of adequate acts amounting to an open denial of the title of the recorded owner. It must not be inferred, however, that he is required to exercise forces, as the law does not insist that a man should provoke a quarrel in order to demonstrate his ownership. Evidence of actual possession is to be taken from such facts as cultivating land, erecting improvements upon it, fencing in the property, and payment of taxes. It has been said that the adverse claimant must "unfurl his flag on the land, and keep it flying, so that the owner may see, if he will, that an enemy has invaded his domains, and planted the standard of conquest ..." The owner is, of course, chargeable with knowledge of what is openly done on his land and therefore calculated to attract attention. But a mere passive possession without intending to claim property, is insufficient, regardless of the length of time it continues, or however open, notorious, or exclusive it may have been.[60]

Adverse possession, in the case of a platted property, had an unexpected conclusion in the Washington case of *Halverson v. City of Bellview*,[61] where a property owner filed a subdivision plat in 1978. In 1979, and prior to approval of the plat, a claimant filed a Lis Pendens and sued to quiet title by adverse possession to a strip of land in the platted property. The claimant notified the city; however, the plat was approved. The claimant then sued to invalidate the plat. The city claimed that the claimant had only a contingent ownership interest until adverse possession was adjudicated and made a matter of record. The court held that the plat was invalid as the state plat stature required signatures "of all parties having an ownership interest." Further, under law, adverse possession creates an ownership interest automatically after 10 years. Court action merely confirms it.

An old (1889) Oregon precedence case,[62] which held that the vendee under an executory land contract was precluded from holding adversely until the final payment was made, was forever changed by the 1984 case of *Owens v. Bartuff*.[63] The court held that the executory status of the land contract does not preclude

[59] Davis v. Mayweather, 504 S.W. 2d 741 (Ark. 1974); Talmadge v. Adams, 240 S.E. 2d P. 9 (Ga. 1977); and Kerrigan v. Thomas, supra. (substantial enclosure by fence).

[60] 1 R.C.L. section 7, 693.

[61] Halverson v. City of Bellview, 41 Wash. App. 457, 704, P. 2d 1232 (1985).

[62] Anderson v. McCormick, 18 Or. 301, 22 P. 1062 (1889).

[63] Owens v. Bartuff, 297 Or. 610, 687 P. 2d 1072 (1984).

achieving adverse possession. In this case, the defendants purchased lots 6 and 7 from the plaintiff pursuant to a land contract. While occupying lots 6 and 7 and paying for them they also entered into adverse possession of parts of lots 8, 9, and 10. The plaintiff claimed that occupancy could not be hostile until final payments were made on the contracts for lots 6 and 7 and relied upon the 1889 case. The reversal of the former precedence case would indicate the growing recognition of the contract buyer's ownership status.

Title by adverse possession, in the absence of color of title, cannot extend beyond the boundaries of land which is actually used and occupied. In the Michigan case of *Rozamarek v. Plamondon*,[64] it was shown that the plaintiff's lot was adjacent to the defendant's lot. Plaintiff had maintained actual, visual, notorious, exclusive, continuous, and uninterrupted possession *of a part* of the defendant's lot for at least 15 years. After that time the plaintiff attempted to negotiate a purchase of the record title to the contested lot without success.

The trial court awarded the contested lot to the plaintiff, and the Court of Appeals reversed, finding the attempt to purchase was evidence plaintiff did not believe he had obtained title by adverse possession and that a rail spur across the contested lot was for the defendant's use, which demonstrated the lack of exclusive use by the plaintiff.

The court of appeals was reversed and the case remanded to the trial court. The plaintiff gained title by adverse possession, but only to the part actually possessed. The court also held that purchase negotiations after the running of statutory time are not inconsistent with title by adverse possession.

In a wooded area, indistinct markings, which consisted of a few strands of barbed wire, tacked to trees, but not on the claimed boundary line, would not give notice of an adverse claim.[65]

A tenant could never claim title by adverse possession no matter what improvements he might make nor how long he might be in possession, because he acknowledges the superior title of his lessor from the beginning. Similarly, where a party occupies property under a permissive use, he cannot claim title by adverse possession.[66]

In order to satisfy statutory requirements of possession of government lands under claim of color of title, an applicant must establish a chain of title based upon a document which, on its face, purports to convey title to the claimed land.

An essential element of the color-of-title claim is the good faith requirement. Good faith, under the Color of Title Act mandates that an applicant and his predecessors honestly believed that they were vested with title. In order to determine whether a claimant or his predecessor honestly believed that he was seized

---

[64] Rozamarek v. Plamondon, 419 Mich. 287, 351 N.W. 2d 558 (1984).

[65] Wales v. Lester, 517 P. 281 (Or. 1973).

[66] Burns v. Owens, 357 S.W. 2d 520 (Ark. 1962) and Dimmick v. Dimmick, 374 P. 2d 824 (Cal. 1962).

with title, the Department of Interior may consider whether such belief was unreasonable in light of facts actually known. Knowledge of Federal ownership of the land negates the requisite good faith.

In addition the claimant must show that he and his predecessor were in possession of the land at least 20 years and that there was no break in such possession. Lately, the applicant must have made valuable improvements to the land or reduced it to cultivation.

In a 1989 court decision a New Jersey court ruled that private citizens may not gain adverse possession title to tax foreclosed property.[67] It was pointed out that municipalities, who acquire property through tax foreclosures are not able to monitor the uses of numerous parcels so acquired. The adverse possession claim was denied.

CONSTRUCTIVE POSSESSION

It is not to be inferred that actual possession of a particular tract or area will cover a larger tract in its entirety. It is a well recognized principle in the United States that a person having a "color of title" which serves to define the extent of the claim, no matter how imperfect the paper title, is to be regarded in constructive possession of the whole tract although he is actually resident of only a part of it. The entry of the owner would be barred to the entire tract after the lapse of the statutory period. This rule is founded on the theory that a person claiming adverse possession under "color of title" has a notorious possession by reason of the written instrument. A realistic interpretation of this doctrine must be made.

It is doubtful whether possession of a few acres out of a thousand purported to be conveyed by the invalid deed would be held to be constructive possession of the whole. The rule concerning constructive possession applies when possession is taken, first, under a conveyance which is invalid either for want of title or capacity of the grantor or for want of proper formalities in the execution of the instrument, and second, under a void or voidable decree of the court. However, if the paper title under which a person claims is a nullity, the adverse occupier acquires title only to so much of the land as has been actually occupied. One who enters into possession of a part of a tract of land under color of title is immediately, by construction of the law, in actual possession of the whole tract. But one who enters without color of title is a trespasser and acquires title only to the area actually occupied. In some states, where there is color of title, the period of adverse occupancy is materially reduced.

CONTINUOUS POSSESSION

An additional requirement for adverse possession is that the claimant must have exercised continuous and uninterrupted possession for the statutory period.

---

[67] Devins v. Borough of Bogota, 568 A. 2d 903 (N.J. Super. 1989).

Any abandonment of the property would defeat the title. A man claiming title to a wood lot by adverse possession will be defeated if he shows that the only occupancy of the property has been an occasional visit to it for the purpose of cutting firewood or for fence material. Likewise, a man cannot claim title by adverse possession to a coal mine to which he made only sporadic visits for a supply of coal. In the case of farmland, where the rigors of winter prevent its cultivation and the claimant temporarily abandons it to follow his trade so that he can obtain funds for the purchase of necessary far implements, the continuity of his possession is not broken.

TACKING

Where the possession has been continuous for a number of years and has been handed down from one to another without any break or interruption, for a valuable consideration, or by decent from parent to child, it is in some measure respectable. The right which the adverse occupier has in the property, although it has not ripened into title, may be sold. The purchaser can "tack" his seller's period of occupancy to his own possession in computing the necessary statutory period. The possession is *connected* by privity of contract or by decent. For example, Adams takes possession of certain lands in 1945 and sells his interest to Bell in 1953. Bell remains in possession until 1968. Bell can claim title to the land through the necessary period of adverse possession.

In order to take advantage of "tacking" it is advisable to indicate in the deed that the grantor is transferring all rights to any portion of the tract claimed by adverse possession to the grantee. Such a clause might read:

> The parties of the first part hereby convey any title by adverse possession to any property adjacent to the above described premises.

In the case of *Lewkowicz v. Blumish*,[68] a dispute arose between adjoining property owners as to their respective use of a driveway. The defendant claimed a prescription right by adverse possession. The Pennsylvania requirement for adverse possession is 21 years. The defendant, who acquired title to his property only three months earlier, could only establish 12 years' use by his grantor. Tacking on the 12 years to his 3 months' use was far short of the 21-year requirement.

A party, who had been in possession of a tract since 1945, when he purchased it could not tack on possession of his ancestor, to satisfy the 30-year requirement, since the ancestor's possession was not hostile to plaintiff's claiming ownership.[69]

---

[68] Lewkowicz v. Blumish, 442 Pa. 369 (1971).

[69] Thibodeaux v. Quibodeaux, 282 So. 2d 845 (La. App. 1973).

HOSTILE OR NOTORIOUS POSSESSION

In a claim of adverse possession, the claimant must show that his possession has been hostile to the holder of the paper title, and not subordinated to it. The adverse possessor "must keep his flag flying" which means that he must exercise all the acts of dominion over the land, not only against the outside world but also against the owner in case the opportunity presents itself. If he recognizes the claim of the owner as superior to his own, he defeats his own claim because the element of hostile possession is lacking. Where the owner is absent or cannot be found, the question of hostility is purely one of invention. It may be said that hostile merely means occupation *foreign* to the paper title.

The doctrine of hostility, however, varies in the various states. The Connecticut rule, frequently cited in other states, is that where the two owners had located a line between their properties in an inaccurate manner, under an honest belief or mistake as to the exact boundary, with the result that one of them occupied a strip of land which was, in reality, the property of the other, for the statutory period, and without interruption. He should be given title to it even though there had been no intention to do wrong, or to exercise hostile possession against his neighbor. The courts have decided, in effect, that *ground occupied under a mistaken belief is necessarily a hostile possession.* Other states have followed the rule laid down in Iowa. Under the same facts, as above, the decision would be that the adverse possession would not begin to run until the mistake was discovered by the one encroaching. The *intention* of the party who took it and occupied the ground was the controlling factor. The intention could not arise until the mistake was discovered.[70]

VISIBLE POSSESSION

Possession must be visible. This requirement would preclude adverse possession to coal where the entrance took place beneath the surface and the entry was not readily noticeable to the owner or the public at large.

DISTINCT POSSESSION

The final requirement of a claim of adverse possession is that the possession must be distinct. He cannot establish a claim to the ground unless he has laid claim to and exercised control over a definite piece of ground, which can be sharply defined. He must exercise *exclusive* occupancy over it. Joint occupancy would not satisfy the requirements.

---

[70]
Warren v. Collier, 559 S.W. 2d 927 (Ark. 1978).

EXCEPTIONS TO THE RULES OF ADVERSE POSSESSION

The statute of adverse possession will not run against a remainderman, until the termination of a precedent estate, such as a life tenant. One owner in common could not claim adverse possession against a co-owner.[71] Neither will the statute run against the state, against land owned by the United States government, nor against any land used for public purposes.

Property held in a proprietary capacity can be diverted to adverse possession. In the case of *Srejack v. City of Baltimore*,[72] it was revealed that a railroad purchased, in 1860, a narrow strip of land, 700 feet in length by 75 feet wide. When the railroad attempted to make use of the land in 1911, it was found to be in possession of one Jones. An ejectment action was brought to recover possession. In the trial of the case, the plaintiff railroad showed *paper* title to the land in question. The defendant, in reply, set up a claim of adverse possession in himself and his predecessors for more than 21 years. The pivotal question was whether title to land purchased by a railroad company for future railroad purposes outside of its right of way can be acquired by adverse possession. Ordinarily, land used by a railroad as a right of way and for public purposes cannot be subject to title by adverse possession. The same would be true insofar as land similarly used by any public utility. It is not true, however, where the land lies outside of the right of way. The railroad could not be heard to say, more than 40 years after the purchase, that it bought the land intending some day to use it for railroad purposes, but had not actively exercised this use. It was significant too, that the land in dispute was acquired by purchase rather than in the company's right of eminent domain. The fact of condemnation, indicates a public use, whereas in the case of purchase, it indicates nothing and establishes nothing but title to the purchaser.[73]

PRESENT-DAY SIGNIFICANCE OF ADVERSE POSSESSION STATUTES

Adverse possession statutes have contemporary significance through many cases where fences and markers have been improperly located and the mistakes not discovered for the period described in the statutes. This is particularly true in urban areas, formerly farmlands of small value, but now highly desirable residential or commercial properties. Older surveying methods, which began from different benchmarks, often introduced considerable errors in the location of boundary lines. Suddenly, the land is valued in double digit figures per square foot and any error represents significant amounts of money to the rightful owner.

Where the statutory period has expired, the claimant's subsequent abandonment of the property would not defeat his ownership unless some new occupier took over and maintained occupation, in turn, for the necessary period.

---

[71] Iverson v. Iverson, et al., N.W. 2d 708 (S.D. 1973).

[72] Srejack v. City of Baltimore, 313 A. 2d 843 (Md. 1974).

[73] Delaware Lackawanna R.R. v. Tobyhanna Co., 228 Pa. 487.

OTHER TRANSFER METHODS

DEDICATION

Dedication is the voluntary setting aside of private property for public use and acceptance by the municipality of the tract for public use. It may be intended as a parklet, a sports area, a beach or for improvement of public streets and highways. The dedicated property may be intended for general public use, or in a subdivision, it may be for the use of owners of the subdivision. If intended for public use and accepted by the municipality, the owner is exempt from taxes and other liabilities. As an alternative to dedication, the tract may be deeded to the municipality.

In order to constitute a dedication of a public road by implication, there must exist clear and unequivocal intention to do so by the landowner *and* acceptance by the public.[74] Where property is acquired through private dedication, the deed is strictly construed.[75] Courts guard zealously the restrictive covenants in donations of property for public use.

The offer of dedication may be withdrawn or revoked until the offer has been accepted by the donee, or estoppel has arisen by intervening rights. Payment of taxes upon a subject land was not deemed to effect a revocation of dedication offer.[76]

In the case of *Baird v. City of Altoona*,[77] Kenyon Road, Altoona, Pennsylvania had been dedicated to and accepted by the city of Altoona. Later the city passed an ordinance vacating the street but reserving to itself an easement for utilities which extending its length and width. The question before the court was whether the created easement and reservation in the ordinance was valid. The court held that once the street was abandoned, the city could not "tack on" a further use. The easement was invalid.

From the beginning of the development of this country, it has been assumed that one who buys land abutting navigable or unnavigable waters has the right to enjoy the beach as his private domain. Recently, the courts have decided more in favor of public beach use. In a 1973 California case, an implied dedication to the public was ruled when a landowner did not object to public use for a period in excess of 5 years. The referenced case, *County of Orange v. Chandler-Sherman Corp.*,[78] was most significant in that it dealt with the beach area *above* the high water mark, where the public are normally assumed to have no rights.

---

[74] Hudson v. Gains, 501 S.W. 2d 734 (Tex. 1973).

[75] Big Sur Properties v. Mott, 132 Cal. Rptr. 835 (1976).

[76] Smith v. Black, 547 S.W. 2d (Tenn. App. 1976).

[77] Baird v. City of Altoona, 361 A. 2d 458 (Pa. 1976).

[78] County of Orange v. Chandler-Sherman Corp., 126 Cal Rptr. 765 5 S.W.U. Rev 48 (1973).

PROPERTY ACQUIRED BY EMINENT DOMAIN

The subject of eminent domain, or the exercise of the police power of the state has been covered in considerable detail in Chapter 2 and no further discussion is necessary here except to remind the reader that this is one other method of land transfer and is considered an involuntary act of the property owner.

HOMESTEAD

Under the Federal Homestead Acts, properties belonging to the United States Government were made available for homesteading. The parties, desiring to acquire these properties, were required to live upon the land for specific periods of time, after which a deed would be granted to the homesteader. Under these acts, thousands of acres of Western properties were acquired by individuals. Today, there is little land left for homesteading, except in the state of Alaska and other remote U.S. possessions.

8

Financing the Purchase

MORTGAGES

Mortgages constitute a very important facet in the growth and development of home ownership in the United States. They provide long-term credit which makes home purchases possible for the normal wage earner. The function of mortgage-lending is said to promote the economic, social, and financial welfare of the community and has become one of the leading indicators of economic conditions within the country. During an economic slow-down an increase in the mortgage lending rate is said to be a strong indicator of an overall economic upturn within the following six months. On the other hand, a slowdown in the housing industry can indicate possible economic problems in the near future. The health of the mortgage industry is deemed a dominant factor in the development of city and rural communities through promotion of home, farm, commercial, and industrial ownership.

TYPES OF MORTGAGES

The following brief discussion of mortgage types will serve to introduce the reader to the various types of mortgages which are available from time to time.

ARMS

In Adjustable Rate Mortgages (ARMs) the lender sets a rate of interest for the first year and then has the right to adjust the rate up or down in accordance with some well known financial index, such as the cost of living. These mortgages usually specify a maximum percentage allowable per period and a maximum rate for the entire loan life. ARMs are usually quoted a few points below the fixed mortgage rate, since the lender is taking less risk. Borrowers who anticipate a interest rate reduction in the future would probably be wise to select this type of mortgage in lieu of a fixed rate.

RAM

The Reverse Annuity Mortgage (RAM) is a rather new type of mortgage being experimented with in several areas. This type of mortgage is for the person(s) who have a home fully paid for, but require additional income without having to sell their residence. This would be particularly advantageous for retired persons.

In this type of mortgage, the lender pays the property owner a stipulated amount each month for a lifetime or a number of years. The amount of the monthly payments is based upon the age of the annuity recipient and the value of the property. This type of mortgage is quite similar to the purchase of a basic annuity, except the value in the home is used in lieu of cash.

GPM

The Graduated Payment Mortgage (GAM) is very popular with the young professionals, who can expect a growing income over the coming years. This mortgage begins with a very low monthly payment, sometime less than necessary to cover the interest, and then increases a small percentage each year for a few years (usually about five years) after which the payments are stabilized at a fixed rate for the remainder of the mortgage term.

There can be problems with this type of mortgage if the mortgagor is forced to move during the first few years of the mortgage lifetime. It is entirely possible that the pay-off amount, at the end of 2 to 3 years will be greater than the face amount of the mortgage in the beginning. The low payments, in the first year or two, would produce a negative equity build-up as the interest alone exceeded the required payments.

SEM

The Shared Equity Mortgage (SEM) is one in which two parties, say parents and children, share the equity build up in the mortgaged property for a stated number of years. In this type of mortgage, a young couple who desire to buy a more expensive home than justified by their available down payment, receive a cash contribution from the parents. This additional down payment permits the mortgage payments to be at a level which the young couple can afford. At some stipulated time in the future, the home is appraised and refinanced, with the equity build-up being shared by the parents and children on a 50-50 basis. At the same time the parents initial contribution is returned to them. Hopefully, their share of the equity build-up will compensate them for their loss of interest on their money initially provided.

GEM

The Growing Equity Mortgage (GEM) is not too popular as there are other methods of accomplishing the same objective without having to be forced to pay a higher monthly payment. In this type of mortgage, the monthly payments are increased by a stipulated percentage each year. The increased amount is applied to the principal payments and result in a 12-20 year pay-off of a 30 year loan.

This same objective can be achieved by making additional principal payments from time to time, which more quickly amortizes the loan. In this method, the mortgagor is not *forced* to make additional payments over and above the normal amount, but can do so when and if he is able.

CONSTRUCTION LOANS

Construction loans can be made to the property owner or to a builder with the property owner's permission. The mortgage is usually a single-payment pay-off at the time the conventional long-term loan is made on the finished property. The amount to be advanced for construction is set but is not paid out except as work is completed, at which time the funds are disbursed to the contractor and/or his subcontractors. Payments require the signing of lien waivers by the contractors, who certify that the work being paid for has been completed. Lenders usually make periodic inspections of the construction site to verify completions of various phases of the project.

Construction loans command a higher interest rate, since the loan is riskier. The security is an unfinished structure and depends upon future events. If the structure is late, poorly constructed, or not completed at all, the lender may find himself with inadequate security for the funds advanced. The lender must assure himself that funds advanced are actually applied to prompt payments of subcontractors and materials people. These concerns are particularly acute in regards to the payment of "soft" costs —those related to legal fees, permits, accounting services, and so on. In some cases the lender will limit his payments to hard costs only. Even in those situations where loans are limited to only hard costs, the variance therefrom will not invalidate the loan.[1]

DOCUMENTATION

When a construction loan is approved by a lender, three documents are usually signed:

1. A promissory note as bond,

2. A construction loan mortgage or deed of trust, and

3. The construction loan agreement.

This latter document spells out the method for the disbursement of funds, events which will constitute default and the lender's remedies in event of default. The agreement will also include complete plans and specifications, a budget for each phase of the project and the date upon which the project will be completed.

---

[1]
Sharp Lumber Co. v. Manus Homes Inc., 189 N.E. 2d 447, 90). L.A. 421 (Ohio App. 1961).

The two most common methods of fund disbursement are; (1) the progress payment method in which the agreement spells out how much will be paid, when it will be paid, and the percentage of completion required to receive payment, and (2) the voucher/lien waiver method in which the lender dispenses funds upon receipt of actual bills of materials and subcontractor invoices. The checks, which are disbursed against the construction loan, may be made to the contractor or to his suppliers and subcontractors.

CONSTRUCTION BOND

Lenders usually require the contractor to furnish a performance bond to assure timely and proper performance, full payment of obligations, which if left unpaid would result in liens against the finished project. Utah law requires private contracts in excess of $2,000 in value to be covered by a performance bond.[2]

The bonding company which underwrites the performance bond agrees to make good in the event the contractor's default. The following are typical ways that a contractor may default upon his construction contract:

- Serious delays in the work schedule.
- Deviation from contract plans and specifications.
- Failure to pay for labor and materials in order to keep the property lien free.

The bonding company's liability is limited to the bond's penal amount.

MECHANICS LIENS

Mechanics and material people's liens are created by statute as a means of assuring the payment of contractors, workers, and material people, through a security interest in the real estate upon which they have improved or furnished materials.

The concept or inception of the lien law had its beginning in 1791 with the passage of acts by the Maryland General Assembly.[3] The passage of this legislation was based on a need to establish and improve the city of Washington, D.C. Thomas Jefferson and James Madison urged the passage of an act "Securing to Master Builders, a lien, on houses erected and land occupied."

Today every state of the union has enacted lien legislation. The laws vary from state to state so widely that it is not possible to discuss their complexities in this work. In 1932, a proposed "Uniform Mechanics Lien Law" was drafted by the commission on Uniform State Laws, but it was adopted only by the State of Florida and withdrawn in 1943.

---

[2] Utah Code Ann. 14-2-1.

[3] C.45 10 (1791).

PARTIES TO THE MORTGAGE

There are essentially two parties in a mortgage transaction; (1) the *mortgagor,* who is the borrower and the owner of the property and who executes a mortgage upon the property as security for payment of his debt, and (2) the *mortgagee,* who is the lender of the money and the creditor, who receives the mortgage.

In many states, the obligor (mortgagor) also executes a judgment note (cognovit note), in the amount of the indebtedness, as evidence of his obligation. Upon default, the creditor-mortgagee proceeds to obtain judgment on the note and then forecloses the mortgaged property, at sheriff's sale, to obtain satisfaction on the judgment. Should the mortgagor die, judgment could not be entered upon the note, but the property could be sold through court proceedings upon the mortgage.

A mortgage is a contract and the law of contracts is generally applicable. The same care that is taken in the preparation of a deed should also be exercised in the case of a mortgage. The mortgage instrument is comprised of two parts; (1) the conveyance of the property, and (2) the defeasance. The latter clause provides that if the debt is repaid and the other covenants are performed by the mortgagor, then the conveyance to the mortgagee shall be null and void.

The existence of a mortgage does not prevent the property from being sold by the debtor-owner and he does not have to obtain the consent of the mortgagee-creditor, unless the buyer desires to assume the obligation. The mortgagee can look to the property as security for the debt no matter who owns it, so long as the debt remains unpaid.

Most modern mortgages contain a "due-on-sale" clause which provides that upon transfer of the property, the mortgage debt shall thereupon, become due and payable. The acceleration of debt on encumbrance or transfer is more fully discussed in following paragraphs.

DEFINITION AND HISTORY OF THE MORTGAGE

A mortgage is a pledge of real estate as collateral for the repayment of money or the performance of some act. The term "mortgage" comes from the French *mort* (dead) and *gage* (pledge). Since early days the practice of pledging property for repayment of a debt has been prevalent. The mortgage grew out of the pledges of land for debt by the Anglo-Saxons. The early encumbrances operated in a very summary manner. If the debtor failed to meet the debt upon the exact day due, the pledged land became the absolute property of the creditor. The wide difference between the value of the land and the amount of the debt was of no consequence. This resulted at times in such injustice and hardship that the courts began to interfere. The legal principal, Equity of Redemption, was then developed which permitted the debtor, within a statutory period, to repay the debt together with a penalty in the form of interest and reclaim the property.

The pendulum of justice then swung to the other extreme, and a creditor, taking property for nonpayment of debt found it more difficult to dispose of the same, because a purchaser is reluctant to buy or improve the property, since the debtor may turn up and demand the return of his property. Once again the courts stepped in and allowed the creditor to file a bill to foreclose the debtor's equity of redemption, and a day was fixed on or before which the debtor was required to pay up or suffer his property to be lost.

CLOGGING THE EQUITY OF REDEMPTION

When the courts of equity created the "equity of redemption principle," they changed the basic intention of the parties to the mortgage transaction. Redemption allows the mortgagor to regain his property by performing the obligation, *after the legal title has vested absolutely in the mortgagee—according to the express language of the parties in the mortgage deed and the effect that the law gives that language and understanding.*

The equity courts have developed the doctrine prohibiting the clogging of the mortgagor's equity of redemption. The first use of the term "clogging" was in 1639 in the case of *Bacon v. Bacon.*[4] The doctrine states, in effect, that the courts will not enforce attempts of the mortgagee to have the mortgagor, at the beginning of the mortgage transaction, waive his rights to be foreclosed in the event of default. Various attempts to circumvent the doctrine have included:

- Limiting the time available to cure the default
- Making time of the essence in the agreement
- Specifying that the mortgagor or other specified person are the only ones who may redeem
- Allowing the mortgagee to keep a part of the property.

An example of such attempts to circumvent the principle was when an escrow was attempted, in which the mortgagor executed a deed at the time the loan and mortgage were given and deposited in escrow to be delivered to the mortgagee in payment of the debt in event of default. The court held in *Plummer v. Ilse* and *Kartheison v. Hawkins,*[5] that the mortgagor still had the right of redemption and that the arrangement violated the prohibition against clogging.

Exceptions to the clogging doctrine have been made by the courts in complex business transactions when both parties are represented by council and are aware of the consequences of their actions. In one Florida Supreme Court decision,[6] a seller-mortgagee who sold some land to a mortgagor for a subdivision and provided financing to construct sewer and water systems, also took back an option to

---

[4] Bacon v. Bacon, Tot. 133-4.

[5] Plummer v. Ilse, 41 Wash. 5, 82 P. 1009, 2 L.R.A., N.S. 627 (1905) and CF Kartheison v. Hawkins, 98 Nev. 237, 645 P. 2d 967, 1982.

[6] MacArthur v. North Palm Beach Utilities, Inc., 202 So. 2d 181 (Fla. 1967).

purchase the system for the construction costs. Later the mortgagee sought specific performance of the option and the mortgagor refused. Even though the option was not tied to any loan default, the trial court and district court applied the clogging principle. The Supreme Court reversed the decision and held that the option was a part of a complex transaction in which both parties were represented by council and aware of what they were doing.

The same approach is reflected in the Uniform Land Transactions Act (ULTA), under section 3-211, and the 1983 amendment to ULTA, which states, "An option to purchase granted to a mortgagee incident to a mortgage loan transaction is generally enforceable *if the right to exercise the option is not dependent upon the occurrence of default."*

SOURCES OF MORTGAGE FUNDS

Mortgage funds are made available through primary and secondary lenders. A primary lender is defined as "the person or organization who originates a mortgage loan and provides funds from his own sources." Principal primary lenders consists of banks, savings & loans, mortgage companies, insurance companies, and pension plans. One government organization can also be added to this primary lender pool, the Farm Home Administration, which makes direct loans for rural housing. Some of these primary lenders such as savings and loans, banks, and mortgage companies, would have a limited ability to provide funds unless their supply of funds could not be replenished by other than their own depositors or stockholders. Thus, the requirement for a secondary mortgage market.

The secondary mortgage market is defined as "a market for the purchase and sale of *existing* mortgage loans." The secondary market consists of some primary lenders, such as insurance companies and pension plans, which are supplemented by government and quasi-government organizations, which were created to expand the availability of mortgage funds. These organizations consists of The Veteran's Administration (VA), the Federal Housing Administration (FHA), Government National Mortgage Association (GNMA), Federal Home Loan Mortgage Corporation (FHLMC), and the Federal National Mortgage Association (FNMA). These government and quasi-government secondary markets are, in turn, supplemented by private organizations such as limited partnerships and syndicated equity pools.

Because of the strict regulations and control of interest rates provided by the VA and FHA, many people are of the opinion that these organizations are lenders. Actually, they are organizations set up to guarantee loans made by primary lenders and do not, except in rare instances, directly provide funds for loans. In the recent recession years of the 1980s and 1990s, the FHA and VA have been forced to provide direct funding in order to dispose of their large inventories of repossessed properties.

In the case of the VA loan, the loan is made by a primary lender under VA regulations, and the issuing debt is guaranteed by the Veterans Administration. No guarantee fee is paid by the veteran mortgagor. When an FHA mortgage is granted by a primary lender under FHA rules and regulations, the borrower is assessed an insurance fee, which goes to the FHA to defray operating expenses and losses.

Both FHA and VA mortgage rates are strictly controlled and are adjusted, from time to time, to more or less reflect the going cost of money. Usually the allowable rate is less than the real cost of borrowing, in which case the primary lender charges "points" to make up for the loss of interest. One point is 1 percent of the loan amount. Points, by VA and FHA regulations, are paid by the seller.

The Government National Mortgage Association, better known as Ginnie Mae, is a government-owned corporation of the Department of Housing and Urban Development (HUD), which assists federally aided housing projects, guarantees securities issued by private lenders and backs FHA, VA, and Farm Home Administration loans.

The Federal Home Loan Mortgage Corporation, better known as Freddie Mac, is a *government sponsored corporation*, whose stock is owned by the thrift industry and other stockholders. The purpose of the organization is to expand the source of mortgage funds by providing a ready market for existing mortgage loans. These loans are then packaged into large bundles and resold as securities (bonds).

The Federal National Mortgage Association, better known as Fannie Mae, is a private corporation sponsored by the United States Government, to provide funds to primary lenders. The association is authorized to issue and guarantee securities (packaged loans) backed by a portion of its mortgage portfolio.

THE MORTGAGE LOAN PROCESS

MAKING APPLICATION FOR THE LOAN

Once the agreement of sale has been signed, the buyer normally begins the search for financing. Once a potential lender is found, the buyer submits a copy of the sales agreement together with all of the personal information required by the lender.

In connection with the loan process, attention is called to a rather extensive and dangerous practice in real estate circles. It is the use of dual contracts (sales agreements). It is the use of dual contracts, sometimes referred to as "kiting" or "ballooning." This is the situation where the purchase contract is executed by the buyer and seller for the true consideration price, where the buyer requires a mortgage of an amount more than justified by the sales price. A second set of purchase contracts is then executed by the seller and buyer at a fictitious consideration well above the true price. It is this higher priced agreement that is submitted to the lender for a loan. Very often the dual agreements are suggested by the real estate broker, who is anxious to make a sale, and states, "It's done all of the time."

Not only is this practice considered unethical and violative of the REALTORS® Code of Ethics, but it constitutes a material violation of the license law and is a criminal offense as well. The broker, buyer and seller as well as the lending institution officer are all subject to criminal prosecution. Texas and Colorado make such a practice a misdemeanor under state law. The Federal Act of June 25, 1948 makes it a federal crime for any person to make a false statement in applying for an FHA mortgage insurance, or "to aid or abet" such action. The seller, buyer, and even the mortgage lender, who are participants in a dual contract arrangement, are vulnerable to a criminal charge.[7]

TRANSFER OF TITLE - LIEN - DEED OF TRUST

In some states a mortgage is actually a *transfer* of title to real estate upon condition, as security for the payment of the debt. Between property owner and mortgagee, it is a conveyance of real estate; as to third parties, it is a lien. In other states, a mortgage is considered and treated strictly as a lien. A lien is a hold or claim which a person has upon the real property of another, as security for some debt or charge. A lien is an encumbrance and a person purchasing real property, encumbered by a mortgage, takes the property subject to the lien. In both cases of transfer of title or lien, possession of the premises remains with the owner-debtor.

In a number of states, a deed of trust is used in lieu of a mortgage instrument. Arizona, California, Colorado, Idaho, Indiana, Minnesota, Mississippi, Missouri, New Mexico, North Carolina, Tennessee, Texas, Utah, Virginia, West Virginia, and the District of Columbia are "Trust Deed" states. A "deed of trust" is in legal effect, a mortgage with power to sell upon default.[8]

The Trust Deed—Trust deeds have the same function as a mortgage on real estate. There are three parties to the trust deed; (1) the debtor, (2) the lender, and (3) the trustee to whom the property is conveyed, as security for the accompanying promissory note of indebtedness. The note is a direct obligation from the debtor to the creditor. The primary difference between the trust deed and a mortgage is in the method of foreclosure.

Upon payment of the debt, the lender, who is also known as the beneficiary, completes a form "Request for Full Conveyance," the canceled note and other instruments relating to the loan transaction. If the mortgage debt is payed off at or before maturity, the debtor-grantor will ask for a "Request of Reconveyance." This is an authorization by the beneficiary to the trustee to reconvey to the grantor, or other parties entitled thereto (a purchaser from the grantor). The Trustee then makes the necessary conveyance, and the deed is recorded. A lending institution, such as a savings and loan association, a bank authorized to conduct trust business, title insurance, or an abstract company is usually selected as the Trustee.

In the deed of trust, the parties are: (1) the Trustor, who is the debtor-owner, who conveys the subject premises by a trust deed, as security for payment of the debt; (2) the Beneficiary, who advances the money (creditor), for whose benefit the Deed of Trust is executed; and (3) the Trustee, a third person, to whom the

---

[7] United States v. Hawkins et al., 205 F. 2d 837 (Ky. 1961) and State Real Estate Commission v. Bongiorno, 45 D & C 392 (Pa. 1968).

[8] Johnson v. Snell, 504 S.W. 2d 397 (Tex. 1973).

"naked" title to the real estate is transferred by the Deed of Trust. In form the Deed of Trust resembles the warranty deed to the extent that it contains such operative or granting words as "grant, bargain, sell, and convey" with the limitation "to the Trustee, in trust, with power to sell," in event of default or breach by the grantor (debtor), to reconvey the premises to the party entitled thereto. The grantor (owner), who has borrowed the money, also executes a promissory note in the amount of the debt. The note is evidence of the debt and the deed of trust is security for the debt. Figure 8-1 shows a typical Deed of Trust used in the state of Utah.

PRINCIPAL METHODS OF FORECLOSURE

Judicial Foreclosure—Judicial foreclosure in equity is available in every state and in some states it is the only method permitted. The judicial foreclosure method continues to be employed in many states under various conditions and situations. Of all of the methods available to the mortgagee, this method is the most time-consuming and costly. This fact can be most easily understood by a review of the required steps in the process. These are:

1. Preliminary title search is made to determine all parties having an interest in the property.

2. Filing of a bill of complaint and a lis pendens notice.

3. Service of the process.

4. A hearing, usually before a Master of Chancery, who reports his findings to the appropriate court.

5. The court issues a decree of judgment.

6. A notice of sale is published in accordance with state law.

7. Actual sale and issuance of a Certificate of sale.

8. A report of sale is made, after which the rights to any surpluses is determined by the court.

9. The state required time for redemption must pass before the buyer's title is good.

10. If the sale failed to satisfy the outstanding debt and costs, the mortgagee requests a decree of deficiency. (See discussion on Deficiency Judgments later in this chapter.)

Nonjudicial Foreclosure—Nonjudicial foreclosure or "Power of Sale" is usually vested in a public official such as the County Sheriff. If a Deed of Trust has been employed, the power of direct sale is vested in the Trustee, who holds the Deed of Trust.

Upon the grantor's failure to comply with the terms of his indebtedness, the Trustee may foreclose the mortgaged property by newspaper advertisement and sale, following the prescribed statutory requirement, such as 120 days of notice of default (may vary from state to state), before the sale takes place.

SPACE ABOVE THIS LINE FOR RECORDER'S USE

DEED OF TRUST

THIS DEED OF TRUST ("Security Instrument") is made on ......April..29,...1992..............................,
19.......... The grantor is .....Charles..T..&..June..A...Brown..
.... ("Borrower"). The trustee is .....Big..Bank..Incorporated......
.... ("Trustee"). The beneficiary is
......Altamont..Mortgage..Company..Inc..., which is organized and existing
under the laws of ....State..of..Utah............................., and whose address is ..111..E...Main..St...........
.....Salt..Lake..City,..Utah..84105... ("Lender").
Borrower owes Lender the principal sum of ...One..Hundred..Thousand......and..00/100...........................
.... Dollars (U.S. $100,000.00.......). This debt is evidenced by Borrower's note
dated the same date as this Security Instrument ("Note"), which provides for monthly payments, with the full debt, if not
paid earlier, due and payable on ....April..29,...2107..
This Security Instrument secures to Lender: (a) the repayment of the debt evidenced by the Note, with interest, and all
renewals, extensions and modifications; (b) the payment of all other sums, with interest, advanced under paragraph 7 to
protect the security of this Security Instrument; and (c) the performance of Borrower's covenants and agreements under
this Security Instrument and the Note. For this purpose, Borrower irrevocably grants and conveys to Trustee, in trust,
with power of sale, the following described property located in ....Salt..Lake..County...................... County, Utah:

All of Lot 23, Appleblossom Estates, No. 3

which has the address of ......7239..S...Appleblossom..Lane.,......Salt..Lake..City,..Utah.............,
                                                            [Street]   [City]
Utah ....84117................................... ("Property Address");
              [Zip Code]

TOGETHER WITH all the improvements now or hereafter erected on the property, and all easements, rights,
appurtenances, rents, royalties, mineral, oil and gas rights and profits, water rights and stock and all fixtures now or
hereafter a part of the property. All replacements and additions shall also be covered by this Security Instrument. All of the
foregoing is referred to in this Security Instrument as the "Property."

BORROWER COVENANTS that Borrower is lawfully seised of the estate hereby conveyed and has the right to grant
and convey the Property and that the Property is unencumbered, except for encumbrances of record. Borrower warrants
and will defend generally the title to the Property against all claims and demands, subject to any encumbrances of record.

THIS SECURITY INSTRUMENT combines uniform covenants for national use and non-uniform covenants with
limited variations by jurisdiction to constitute a uniform security instrument covering real property.

UTAH—Single Family—FNMA/FHLMC UNIFORM INSTRUMENT   Form 3045 12/83

Figure 8-1

UNIFORM COVENANTS. Borrower and Lender covenant and agree as follows:

1. Payment of Principal and Interest; Prepayment and Late Charges. Borrower shall promptly pay when due the principal of and interest on the debt evidenced by the Note and any prepayment and late charges due under the Note.

2. Funds for Taxes and Insurance. Subject to applicable law or to a written waiver by Lender, Borrower shall pay to Lender on the day monthly payments are due under the Note, until the Note is paid in full, a sum ("Funds") equal to one-twelfth of: (a) yearly taxes and assessments which may attain priority over this Security Instrument; (b) yearly leasehold payments or ground rents on the Property, if any; (c) yearly hazard insurance premiums; and (d) yearly mortgage insurance premiums, if any. These items are called "escrow items." Lender may estimate the Funds due on the basis of current data and reasonable estimates of future escrow items.

The Funds shall be held in an institution the deposits or accounts of which are insured or guaranteed by a federal or state agency (including Lender if Lender is such an institution). Lender shall apply the Funds to pay the escrow items. Lender may not charge for holding and applying the Funds, analyzing the account or verifying the escrow items, unless Lender pays Borrower interest on the Funds and applicable law permits Lender to make such a charge. A charge assessed by Lender in connection with Borrower's entering into this Security Instrument to pay the cost of an independent tax reporting service shall not be a charge for purposes of the preceding sentence. Borrower and Lender may agree in writing that interest shall be paid on the Funds. Unless an agreement is made or applicable law requires interest to be paid, Lender shall not be required to pay Borrower any interest or earnings on the Funds. Lender shall give to Borrower, without charge, an annual accounting of the Funds showing credits and debits to the Funds and the purpose for which each debit to the Funds was made. The Funds are pledged as additional security for the sums secured by this Security Instrument.

If the amount of the Funds held by Lender, together with the future monthly payments of Funds payable prior to the due dates of the escrow items, shall exceed the amount required to pay the escrow items when due, the excess shall be, at Borrower's option, either promptly repaid to Borrower or credited to Borrower on monthly payments of Funds. If the amount of the Funds held by Lender is not sufficient to pay the escrow items when due, Borrower shall pay to Lender any amount necessary to make up the deficiency in one or more payments as required by Lender.

Upon payment in full of all sums secured by this Security Instrument, Lender shall promptly refund to Borrower any Funds held by Lender. If under paragraph 19 the Property is sold or acquired by Lender, Lender shall apply, no later than immediately prior to the sale of the Property or its acquisition by Lender, any Funds held by Lender at the time of application as a credit against the sums secured by this Security Instrument.

3. Application of Payments. Unless applicable law provides otherwise, all payments received by Lender under paragraphs 1 and 2 shall be applied: first, to late charges due under the Note; second, to prepayment charges due under the Note; third, to amounts payable under paragraph 2; fourth, to interest due; and last, to principal due.

4. Charges; Liens. Borrower shall pay all taxes, assessments, charges, fines and impositions attributable to the Property which may attain priority over this Security Instrument, and leasehold payments or ground rents, if any. Borrower shall pay these obligations in the manner provided in paragraph 2, or if not paid in that manner, Borrower shall pay them on time directly to the person owed payment. Borrower shall promptly furnish to Lender all notices of amounts to be paid under this paragraph. If Borrower makes these payments directly, Borrower shall promptly furnish to Lender receipts evidencing the payments.

Borrower shall promptly discharge any lien which has priority over this Security Instrument unless Borrower: (a) agrees in writing to the payment of the obligation secured by the lien in a manner acceptable to Lender; (b) contests in good faith the lien by, or defends against enforcement of the lien in, legal proceedings which in the Lender's opinion operate to prevent the enforcement of the lien or forfeiture of any part of the Property; or (c) secures from the holder of the lien an agreement satisfactory to Lender subordinating the lien to this Security Instrument. If Lender determines that any part of the Property is subject to a lien which may attain priority over this Security Instrument, Lender may give Borrower a notice identifying the lien. Borrower shall satisfy the lien or take one or more of the actions set forth above within 10 days of the giving of notice.

5. Hazard Insurance. Borrower shall keep the improvements now existing or hereafter erected on the Property insured against loss by fire, hazards included within the term "extended coverage" and any other hazards for which Lender requires insurance. This insurance shall be maintained in the amounts and for the periods that Lender requires. The insurance carrier providing the insurance shall be chosen by Borrower subject to Lender's approval which shall not be unreasonably withheld.

All insurance policies and renewals shall be acceptable to Lender and shall include a standard mortgage clause. Lender shall have the right to hold the policies and renewals. If Lender requires, Borrower shall promptly give to Lender all receipts of paid premiums and renewal notices. In the event of loss, Borrower shall give prompt notice to the insurance carrier and Lender. Lender may make proof of loss if not made promptly by Borrower.

Unless Lender and Borrower otherwise agree in writing, insurance proceeds shall be applied to restoration or repair of the Property damaged, if the restoration or repair is economically feasible and Lender's security is not lessened. If the restoration or repair is not economically feasible or Lender's security would be lessened, the insurance proceeds shall be applied to the sums secured by this Security Instrument, whether or not then due, with any excess paid to Borrower. If Borrower abandons the Property, or does not answer within 30 days a notice from Lender that the insurance carrier has offered to settle a claim, then Lender may collect the insurance proceeds. Lender may use the proceeds to repair or restore the Property or to pay sums secured by this Security Instrument, whether or not then due. The 30-day period will begin when the notice is given.

Unless Lender and Borrower otherwise agree in writing, any application of proceeds to principal shall not extend or postpone the due date of the monthly payments referred to in paragraphs 1 and 2 or change the amount of the payments. If under paragraph 19 the Property is acquired by Lender, Borrower's right to any insurance policies and proceeds resulting from damage to the Property prior to the acquisition shall pass to Lender to the extent of the sums secured by this Security Instrument immediately prior to the acquisition.

6. Preservation and Maintenance of Property; Leaseholds. Borrower shall not destroy, damage or substantially change the Property, allow the Property to deteriorate or commit waste. If this Security Instrument is on a leasehold, Borrower shall comply with the provisions of the lease, and if Borrower acquires fee title to the Property, the leasehold and fee title shall not merge unless Lender agrees to the merger in writing.

7. Protection of Lender's Rights in the Property; Mortgage Insurance. If Borrower fails to perform the covenants and agreements contained in this Security Instrument, or there is a legal proceeding that may significantly affect Lender's rights in the Property (such as a proceeding in bankruptcy, probate, for condemnation or to enforce laws or regulations), then Lender may do and pay for whatever is necessary to protect the value of the Property and Lender's rights in the Property. Lender's actions may include paying any sums secured by a lien which has priority over this Security Instrument, appearing in court, paying reasonable attorneys' fees and entering on the Property to make repairs. Although Lender may take action under this paragraph 7, Lender does not have to do so.

Any amounts disbursed by Lender under this paragraph 7 shall become additional debt of Borrower secured by this Security Instrument. Unless Borrower and Lender agree to other terms of payment, these amounts shall bear interest from the date of disbursement at the Note rate and shall be payable, with interest, upon notice from Lender to Borrower requesting payment.

If Lender required mortgage insurance as a condition of making the loan secured by this Security Instrument, Borrower shall pay the premiums required to maintain the insurance in effect until such time as the requirement for the insurance terminates in accordance with Borrower's and Lender's written agreement or applicable law.

8. Inspection. Lender or its agent may make reasonable entries upon and inspections of the Property. Lender shall give Borrower notice at the time of or prior to an inspection specifying reasonable cause for the inspection.

Figure 8-1-2

9. Condemnation. The proceeds of any award or claim for damages, direct or consequential, in connection with any condemnation or other taking of any part of the Property, or for conveyance in lieu of condemnation, are hereby assigned and shall be paid to Lender.

In the event of a total taking of the Property, the proceeds shall be applied to the sums secured by this Security Instrument, whether or not then due, with any excess paid to Borrower. In the event of a partial taking of the Property, unless Borrower and Lender otherwise agree in writing, the sums secured by this Security Instrument shall be reduced by the amount of the proceeds multiplied by the following fraction: (a) the total amount of the sums secured immediately before the taking, divided by (b) the fair market value of the Property immediately before the taking. Any balance shall be paid to Borrower.

If the Property is abandoned by Borrower, or if, after notice by Lender to Borrower that the condemnor offers to make an award or settle a claim for damages, Borrower fails to respond to Lender within 30 days after the date the notice is given, Lender is authorized to collect and apply the proceeds, at its option, either to restoration or repair of the Property or to the sums secured by this Security Instrument, whether or not then due.

Unless Lender and Borrower otherwise agree in writing, any application of proceeds to principal shall not extend or postpone the due date of the monthly payments referred to in paragraphs 1 and 2 or change the amount of such payments.

10. Borrower Not Released; Forbearance By Lender Not a Waiver. Extension of the time for payment or modification of amortization of the sums secured by this Security Instrument granted by Lender to any successor in interest of Borrower shall not operate to release the liability of the original Borrower or Borrower's successors in interest. Lender shall not be required to commence proceedings against any successor in interest or refuse to extend time for payment or otherwise modify amortization of the sums secured by this Security Instrument by reason of any demand made by the original Borrower or Borrower's successors in interest. Any forbearance by Lender in exercising any right or remedy shall not be a waiver of or preclude the exercise of any right or remedy.

11. Successors and Assigns Bound; Joint and Several Liability; Co-signers. The covenants and agreements of this Security Instrument shall bind and benefit the successors and assigns of Lender and Borrower, subject to the provisions of paragraph 17. Borrower's covenants and agreements shall be joint and several. Any Borrower who co-signs this Security Instrument but does not execute the Note: (a) is co-signing this Security Instrument only to mortgage, grant and convey that Borrower's interest in the Property under the terms of this Security Instrument; (b) is not personally obligated to pay the sums secured by this Security Instrument; and (c) agrees that Lender and any other Borrower may agree to extend, modify, forbear or make any accommodations with regard to the terms of this Security Instrument or the Note without that Borrower's consent.

12. Loan Charges. If the loan secured by this Security Instrument is subject to a law which sets maximum loan charges, and that law is finally interpreted so that the interest or other loan charges collected or to be collected in connection with the loan exceed the permitted limits, then: (a) any such loan charge shall be reduced by the amount necessary to reduce the charge to the permitted limit; and (b) any sums already collected from Borrower which exceeded permitted limits will be refunded to Borrower. Lender may choose to make this refund by reducing the principal owed under the Note or by making a direct payment to Borrower. If a refund reduces principal, the reduction will be treated as a partial prepayment without any prepayment charge under the Note.

13. Legislation Affecting Lender's Rights. If enactment or expiration of applicable laws has the effect of rendering any provision of the Note or this Security Instrument unenforceable according to its terms, Lender, at its option, may require immediate payment in full of all sums secured by this Security Instrument and may invoke any remedies permitted by paragraph 19. If Lender exercises this option, Lender shall take the steps specified in the second paragraph of paragraph 17.

14. Notices. Any notice to Borrower provided for in this Security Instrument shall be given by delivering it or by mailing it by first class mail unless applicable law requires use of another method. The notice shall be directed to the Property Address or any other address Borrower designates by notice to Lender. Any notice to Lender shall be given by first class mail to Lender's address stated herein or any other address Lender designates by notice to Borrower. Any notice provided for in this Security Instrument shall be deemed to have been given to Borrower or Lender when given as provided in this paragraph.

15. Governing Law; Severability. This Security Instrument shall be governed by federal law and the law of the jurisdiction in which the Property is located. In the event that any provision or clause of this Security Instrument or the Note conflicts with applicable law, such conflict shall not affect other provisions of this Security Instrument or the Note which can be given effect without the conflicting provision. To this end the provisions of this Security Instrument and the Note are declared to be severable.

16. Borrower's Copy. Borrower shall be given one conformed copy of the Note and of this Security Instrument.

17. Transfer of the Property or a Beneficial Interest in Borrower. If all or any part of the Property or any interest in it is sold or transferred (or if a beneficial interest in Borrower is sold or transferred and Borrower is not a natural person) without Lender's prior written consent, Lender may, at its option, require immediate payment in full of all sums secured by this Security Instrument. However, this option shall not be exercised by Lender if exercise is prohibited by federal law as of the date of this Security Instrument.

If Lender exercises this option, Lender shall give Borrower notice of acceleration. The notice shall provide a period of not less than 30 days from the date the notice is delivered or mailed within which Borrower must pay all sums secured by this Security Instrument. If Borrower fails to pay these sums prior to the expiration of this period, Lender may invoke any remedies permitted by this Security Instrument without further notice or demand on Borrower.

18. Borrower's Right to Reinstate. If Borrower meets certain conditions, Borrower shall have the right to have enforcement of this Security Instrument discontinued at any time prior to the earlier of: (a) 5 days (or such other period as applicable law may specify for reinstatement) before sale of the Property pursuant to any power of sale contained in this Security Instrument; or (b) entry of a judgment enforcing this Security Instrument. Those conditions are that Borrower: (a) pays Lender all sums which then would be due under this Security Instrument and the Note had no acceleration occurred; (b) cures any default of any other covenants or agreements; (c) pays all expenses incurred in enforcing this Security Instrument, including, but not limited to, reasonable attorneys' fees; and (d) takes such action as Lender may reasonably require to assure that the lien of this Security Instrument, Lender's rights in the Property and Borrower's obligation to pay the sums secured by this Security Instrument shall continue unchanged. Upon reinstatement by Borrower, this Security Instrument and the obligations secured hereby shall remain fully effective as if no acceleration had occurred. However, this right to reinstate shall not apply in the case of acceleration under paragraphs 13 or 17.

NON-UNIFORM COVENANTS. Borrower and Lender further covenant and agree as follows:

19. Acceleration; Remedies. Lender shall give notice to Borrower prior to acceleration following Borrower's breach of any covenant or agreement in this Security Instrument (but not prior to acceleration under paragraphs 13 and 17 unless applicable law provides otherwise). The notice shall specify: (a) the default; (b) the action required to cure the default; (c) a date, not less than 30 days from the date the notice is given to Borrower, by which the default must be cured; and (d) that failure to cure the default on or before the date specified in the notice may result in acceleration of the sums secured by this Security Instrument and sale of the Property. The notice shall further inform Borrower of the right to reinstate after acceleration and the right to bring a court action to assert the non-existence of a default or any other defense of Borrower to acceleration and sale. If the default is not cured on or before the date specified in the notice, Lender at its option may require immediate payment in full of all sums secured by this Security Instrument without further demand and may invoke the power of sale and any other remedies permitted by applicable law. Lender shall be entitled to collect all expenses incurred in pursuing the remedies provided in this paragraph 19, including, but not limited to, reasonable attorneys' fees and costs of title evidence.

Figure 8-1-3

If the power of sale is invoked, Trustee shall execute a written notice of the occurrence of an event of default and of the election to cause the Property to be sold and shall record such notice in each county in which any part of the Property is located. Lender or Trustee shall mail copies of such notice in the manner prescribed by applicable law to Borrower and to the other persons prescribed by applicable law. Trustee shall give public notice of the sale to the persons and in the manner prescribed by applicable law. After the time required by applicable law, Trustee, without demand on Borrower, shall sell the Property at public auction to the highest bidder at the time and place and under the terms designated in the notice of sale in one or more parcels and in any order Trustee determines. Trustee may postpone sale of all or any parcel of the Property by public announcement at the time and place of any previously scheduled sale. Lender or its designee may purchase the Property at any sale.

Trustee shall deliver to the purchaser Trustee's deed conveying the Property without any covenant or warranty, expressed or implied. The recitals in the Trustee's deed shall be prima facie evidence of the truth of the statements made therein. Trustee shall apply the proceeds of the sale in the following order: (a) to all expenses of the sale, including, but not limited to, reasonable Trustee's and attorneys' fees; (b) to all sums secured by this Security Instrument; and (c) any excess to the person or persons legally entitled to it or to the county clerk of the county in which the sale took place.

20. Lender in Possession. Upon acceleration under paragraph 19 or abandonment of the Property, Lender (in person, by agent or by judicially appointed receiver) shall be entitled to enter upon, take possession of and manage the Property and to collect the rents of the Property including those past due. Any rents collected by Lender or the receiver shall be applied first to payment of the costs of management of the Property and collection of rents, including, but not limited to, receiver's fees, premiums on receiver's bonds and reasonable attorneys' fees, and then to the sums secured by this Security Instrument.

21. Reconveyance. Upon payment of all sums secured by this Security Instrument, Lender shall request Trustee to reconvey the Property and shall surrender this Security Instrument and all notes evidencing debt secured by this Security Instrument to Trustee. Trustee shall reconvey the Property without warranty and without charge to the person or persons legally entitled to it. Such person or persons shall pay any recordation costs.

22. Substitute Trustee. Lender, at its option, may from time to time remove Trustee and appoint a successor trustee to any Trustee appointed hereunder. Without conveyance of the Property, the successor trustee shall succeed to all the title, power and duties conferred upon Trustee herein and by applicable law.

23. Request for Notices. Borrower requests that copies of the notices of default and sale be sent to Borrower's address which is the Property Address.

24. Riders to this Security Instrument. If one or more riders are executed by Borrower and recorded together with this Security Instrument, the covenants and agreements of each such rider shall be incorporated into and shall amend and supplement the covenants and agreements of this Security Instrument as if the rider(s) were a part of this Security Instrument. [Check applicable box(es)]

- [X] Adjustable Rate Rider
- [ ] Condominium Rider
- [ ] 2–4 Family Rider
- [ ] Graduated Payment Rider
- [ ] Planned Unit Development Rider
- [ ] Other(s) [specify]

BY SIGNING BELOW, Borrower accepts and agrees to the terms and covenants contained in this Security Instrument and in any rider(s) executed by Borrower and recorded with it.

Charles T. Brown ....(Seal)
—Borrower

Jane A. Brown ....(Seal)
—Borrower

——————————————— [Space Below This Line For Acknowledgment] ———————————————

Figure 8-1-4

The proceeds of a Trustee sale are first applied to the expenses of the sale, to the obligation secured by the Trust Deed, other liens of record and the balance, if any, to the original grantor or owner at the time of foreclosure.

Strict Foreclosure—Strict foreclosure is rarely used except in Connecticut, Vermont, and Illinois.[9]

The chief advantages to the lender is the short period necessary for foreclosure. This is important since it is an incentive to an out-of-state lending institution to make funds available for financing in a particular state. Availability of considerable funds, obviously, is a benefit to the borrower as it tends to lower interest rates through competition. The procedure under the Trust Deed also protects the debtor against the possibilities of a deficiency judgment, and the right to cure a default at any time prior to the sale, by making the indebtedness current. The subject of deficiency judgments is covered in more detail later in this chapter.

Where the note secured by a trust deed contains provision that if default is made in any installment, holders can declare all indebtedness due on default in any payment.[10]

In some states such as Alabama and Florida, a seller has a vendor's lien for the balance of the unpaid purchase price. A vendor's lien is the right of the seller to subject the land as security for the unpaid purchase price. The lien may be enforced by a bill in equity to sell the property for the amount due. It is not good against subsequent creditors or purchasers, unless they have actual notice of it, or reference to the lien is contained in the recorded deed from seller to buyer.

Power of Sale Foreclosure—The power of sale foreclosure is authorized by the Uniform Land Transaction Act (ULTA); however it has not been adopted in part or in whole by any of the various states. The Act outlines the following steps:

1. After default, a minimum of 5 weeks must expire before the mortgagee notifies the mortgagor of his intent to foreclose.

2. An additional three weeks of grace must pass before the mortgagee informs the mortgagor of which default remedy he plans to use.

3. If the mortgagee chooses the power of sale, he must mail a notice to the debtor and all parties who have been found to have an interest in the property and would be cut off by the foreclosure.

4. If the mortgagor is a "protected individual" (owner/occupant of a residence), certain additional steps must be taken.

Most states authorize a power of sale to various parties under stipulated

---

[9] Conn. Gen Stat. Ann. 49-15 (1975) and Abacus Mortgage Insurance Co. v. Whitewood Hills Development Corp., 2 Conn. App. 460, 479 A. 2d 1231 (1984).

[10] Long v. Manning, 455 S.W. 2d 496 (Mo. 1970).

conditions. Where authorized, most mortgagees prefer the advantages of the power of sale, for the following reasons:

1. It accomplishes the same purpose as the judicial sale but in a shorter time.

2. It terminates all interests junior to the mortgage being foreclosed and provides the purchaser with a good title identical to that which the mortgagor held at the time the foreclosure began.

3. The process is less expensive.

Basically the mortgagee has two methods of collecting the debt:

1. He may sue and obtain a judgment against any/all debtor property, or

2. Foreclose on the property.

The two above options are usually concurrent. In some states, where the mortgagee has both options, once he elects one option the other is dismissed or stayed.

Many states impose strict notice requirements and statutory time limits. Failure to comply will inflict serious injury to the mortgagee.

THE DEFICIENCY JUDGMENT

During the depression years, 1931-1938, the mortgagee was entitled to a deficiency judgment for the difference between the sale price at the foreclosure sale and the mortgaged debt. Very often the property was sold to the plaintiff mortgagee at a nominal price (cost and taxes) as there were no other bidders and the deficiency judgment was considerable.

The legislatures and courts, motivated by a social consciousness, recognizing the unfairness of this situation that permitted a mortgagee to acquire property and to obtain a judgment for practically the entire debt as well, decreed that a debtor should have credit for the fair market value of the property at the date of the foreclosure sale as an offset to the debt. Thus, today, if the property is sold to the plaintiff mortgagee for a nominal bid, the debtor would be liable only if the amount of the debt were in excess of the fair market value of the property. But the possibilities of a deficiency judgment, in some amount, is still very real. This is particularly true in times of a real estate market slump such as in the late 1980s and early 1990s.

The mortgagee can look to the original owner for this deficiency, no matter through how many hand the property may have passed, because the original owner (mortgagor) is liable upon his contract obligation to pay the debt. Under the so called short form clause the mortgagee has no right of action against the purchaser of the mortgaged premises, as there is no privity of contract, i.e., relationship between the mortgagee and the purchaser of the property. The only way that the original mortgagor could be relieved of all personal liability would be for him to insist that his purchaser do his own financing and have the original mortgage paid off and satisfied and the accompanying note returned and cancelled. If the original mortgagor actually pays the judgment entered against him by the mortgagee, he would have the right of *indemnification* against his purchaser, but not otherwise.

Under the long-form clause, the mortgagee is considered a third party or creditor beneficiary under the deed contract between the owner and purchaser and would have the right to sue the purchaser of the mortgaged premises for the deficiency, proceed against the original debtor, or both. The principle of the law has been stated to be:

> where the contract is purely one of indemnity, the indemnitee (seller) cannot recover until he has suffered actual loss or damage; the mere incurring of liability gives him no such right; but where the contract is to protect against liability, the indemnee may recover as soon as liability has become fixed and established even though he has sustained no actual loss or damage at the time he seeks to recover.

Where the buyer takes over the existing mortgage, the protection of the seller requires the use of the long form clause in the deed. Since the deed is the formal consummation of an agreement of sale previously entered into, it behooves the broker or attorney preparing the agreement of sale to exercise adequate care in drawing the mortgage clause in the sales agreement.

Short and Long Form Mortgage Clauses—As stated previously, the short-form clause is usually as follows: "Under and subject, nevertheless, to a certain mortgage in the present unpaid amount of $50,000, given by John Steel, the grantor herein to the City National Bank, dated June 16, 1991 and recorded in the Recorder's Office of Piedmont County in Mortgage Book Vol. 2117, page 216." The long-form mortgage reads exactly the same, with the following addition: "which mortgage, the grantee expressly assumes and agrees to pay as part of the consideration herein." It must be remembered that the property is always liable for the debt. But it frequently happens, particularly in times of a depressed real estate market, that the values at a foreclosure sale are less than the mortgaged indebtedness.

SPECIAL MORTGAGE CLAUSES

Due on Sale Provisions—Where an existing low-interest loan can be assumed, during a period of high interest rates, the seller is often able to sell his property more expeditiously and/or command a higher price for it. For example, in the case of *Williams v. First Federal Savings & Loan Association,*[11] the court suggested that real estate nominally valued at $100,000 would bring $115,000, if the buyer was permitted to assume a $50,000 30-yr. loan with a fixed interest rate of 10 percent (27 years remaining) at a time when the going rate for a new mortgage was 15 percent.

In recent times lending institutions have taken steps to prevent the assumption of fixed interest loans, except with their approval, an increase in the prescribed interest rate, or other requirements. Naturally, these actions brought

---

[11] Williams v. First Federal Savings & Loan Association, 651 F. 2d 910 (4th Cir. 1981).

a plethora of cases to the courts challenging the legality of the due-on-sale clauses.

Most attempts to circumvent these clauses took the approach that they were restraint on alienation. Most judicial decisions have held that the due-on-sale clause, per se, is not unlawful as a restraint on alienation. Under predominant judicial understanding the due-on-sale clause is reasonable *unless the borrower can show that the lender engaged in unconscionable conduct.*[12]

In so ruling the courts appear to have recognized the desirability of protecting the mortgagee from the ups and downs of interest rates. In most cases the mortgagee need not establish the validity of the due-on-sale clause—it is usually enforced.

Several of the states including Arizona, Colorado, Iowa, New Mexico, Minnesota, and Utah have enacted laws which limit the conditions in which the due-on-sale clause may be enforced. Most of these laws require the mortgagee to:

1. Show impairment of security.

2. Require and/or allow an assumption fee.

3. Allow a modest increase in the interest rate—usually no more than 1 percent.

Some lenders have begun using a mortgage clause that will allow the lender to declare an acceleration of the debt upon the borrower's failure to occupy the property. These clauses have been held valid.[13]

Some lenders have inserted an interest-increase-clause in the event of assumption. The courts have usually upheld these restrictions.[14]

Unlike the due-on-sale clause, the increase in-interest-on-transfer clause does not allow the mortgagee an absolute right to accelerate the mortgage debt upon transfer of the mortgaged property, thus it gives the lender little protection against the transfer to a potential uncreditworthy buyer. In these cases there will be grounds for a declaration of default only if the transferee fails to pay the increase in the interest rate.[15]

Garn-St. Germain Act[16]—This act broadly preempts state laws that restrict enforcement of due-on-sale clauses, thereby making most clauses found in modern contracts enforceable. Many aspects of this law are yet to be tested in the courts, including the question as to whether Congress has the power to regulate intrastate transactions.

---

[12]
    Income Realty & Mortgage Inc. v. Columbia Savings and Loan Association, 661 P. ed 257, 265 (Colo. 1983) and Tierce v. APS Co., 382 So. 2d 485, 487 (Ala. 1979).

[13]
    Investors Savings and Loan Association v. Ganz, 416 A. 2d 918 (N.J. 1980).

[14]
    O'Connell v. Dockendorff, 415, So. 2d 35, 36-37 (Fla. 1982); Miller v. Pacific First Federal Savings & Loan Association, 86 Wm 2d 401, 406-07, 545 P. 2d 546, 549 (1976).

[15]
    O'Connell v. Dockendorff, 415 So. 2d 35,36 (Fla. App. 1982).

[16]
    12 U.S.C.A. 1701j-3.

Due on Encumbrance Restriction—Some lenders have attempted to cause the debt to be accelerated in the event the mortgaged property is further encumbered. These clauses are similar to the following:

> If the grantor further encumbers the premises by any mortgages, loans or security deeds, securing loans made to grantor without notice to and prior written permission from the grantee (mortgagee), such will constitute an event of default.[17]

MORTGAGE FORMS SPECIFIED BY GOVERNMENT SPONSORED SECONDARY MARKET

The mortgage forms specified for lenders, who sell mortgages to the Federal National Mortgage Association (FNMA) and the Federal Home Loan Mortgage Corporation (FHLMC), on the secondary mortgage market specifically exclude some restrictions on further encumbrances. The suggested wording normally appearing in these agreement is:

> If all or part of the property or an interest thereon is sold or transferred by the borrower without lender's prior consent, excluding (a) the creation of a lien or encumbrance subordinated to this mortgage .... Lender may, at the lender's option, declare all sums secured by this mortgage to be due and payable.

EXCEPTIONS TO THE DUE-ON-SALE RESTRICTIONS

In spite of the apparent universal acceptance of the legality of the due-on-sale clause, most courts have agreed that some exceptions should be allowed. These include:

1. Transfer to a spouse who become a co-owner.

2. Transfer to a spouse as a part of a property settlement on the dissolution of a marriage.

3. Transfer to an inter vivoce trust of which the mortgagor is the beneficiary.[18]

4. Mortgagor sells part of the mortgaged property, but retains title thereto and continues to live on the other part.

5. Transfer of property from a corporation to a sole share holder. An exception is made where all shares of the stock are transferred to a third party in which case the due-on-sale clause is triggered.[19]

---

[17] Chilivis v. Tumlin Woods Realty Associates, Inc. 250 Ga. 179, 279 S.E. 2d 4, (1982).

[18] Mills v. Nashua Federal Savings and Loan Association, 121 N.H. 722, 433 A. 2d 1312, 1316 (1981) and Powell v. Phoenix Federal Savings and Loan Association, 434 So. 2d 247, 253 (Ala. 1983).

[19] United States v. Med O Farm, Inc. 701 F. 2d 88 (9th Cir. 1983).

CONCEALMENT OF PROPERTY TRANSFER

In one court decision, it was suggested that the due-on-sale clause does not impose an obligation on the mortgagor to notify the mortgagee of a property transfer.[20] Regardless, the mortgagee usually finds out about the transfer through one or more of the following means:

• The insurance provider notifies the mortgagee that the insurance on the property has been cancelled, which signals the possibility of a new policy by a new owner.

• The result of periodic inspections of mortgaged property and a name change on the mailbox.

• The receipt of mortgage payments from a new person or source.

• Tax notices sent to the mortgagee by the local taxing authority, since they have been designated as the official escrow agent responsible for payment of taxes on the property.

The notification of insurance cancellation can be avoided by continuing the insurance in the name of the original owner with a side agreement with the new owner which assigns the beneficial interest to the new owner.

Buyers and sellers of mortgaged property continue to attempt to conceal the transfer of properties. This is particularly true in those states that enforce the due-on-sale provisions. Attempts to conceal take various ingenious ways but most generally follow one of the following approaches:

• The transaction is not recorded, and

• A third party is utilized to make payments in the name of the mortgagor.

Concealment Problems for the Transferee—Actual possession of the property in some jurisdictions constitutes "constructive notice" of a property transfer and should protect the transferee's interests in the property against the claims of lien holders and others attempting to encumber the former owner's assets. In other jurisdictions possession is not deemed as constructive notice, and even if it is, litigation would probably be required to establish the existence of such possession.

Concealment Problems for the Transferor—If and when the lender discovers the transfer, he would have a good case for recovery of any additional interest charges and other damages suffered as a result of the unauthorized transfer. In fact, the original borrower might be subject to two suits: (1) by the lender to recover the lost interest, and (2) by the new owner for increased interest charges and/or loss of the property, where he could not afford the increased interest rate.

---

[20] Medovoi v. American Savings and Loan Association, 89 Cal. App. 3rd 244, 152 Cal. Rptr. 572 (1979).

Where the parties to the unauthorized transfer decide to transfer the property without notifying the lender, the seller would be wise to include in the sale agreement a statement by the transferee that he acknowledges the risks of future loan acceleration and agrees to hold the seller harmless in the event the acceleration process occurs.

Such side agreements are normally prepared at the suggestion of the buyer's or seller's attorney. There continues to be a mixed opinion as to whether an attorney should provide advice to a client in methods to avoid notification. Most authorities agree that the American Bar Association Code of Professional Responsibility does not apply to such advice on a contract and is applicable when referring to criminal conduct.

A lender is precluded from accelerating a loan where the lender had knowledge of a prohibited conveyance more than 4 years prior to the attempt to accelerate the loan. In this case he was prevented from exercising the authority granted by the lending agreement.[21]

It is probably safe to say, that at the present time, any attempt of the lender to accelerate a loan payment in accordance with the terms of the loan agreement, will be upheld if challenged in the courts. The following cases are representative of many attempts which have failed.

In the case of *Gunther v. White,*[22] the mortgagor alleged that the acceleration clause was an illegal restraint on his right of alienation to sell his land upon his best possible terms. The court held the acceleration clause valid—see also.[23]

In an earlier case of *Peoples Savings Association v. Standard Industries, Inc.,*[24] the Ohio Court of Appeals held that the due-on-sale clause of acceleration was not illegal, inequitable or contrary to public policy.

Somewhat different is the California case of *LaSala v. American Savings and Loan Association.*[25] The mortgage, in addition to the acceleration clause, also included a restriction against encumbering the property. In this case, the mortgagor gave a second mortgage on the property and the mortgagee claimed that there was a default and the debt could be accelerated to the full amount. The Appellate Court held that the subject clause was not an illegal restraint upon alienation.[26]

21
Cooper v. Deseret Federal Savings and Loan Ass'n, 757 P. 2d 483 (Utah Ct. App. 1988).

22
Gunther v. White, 489 S.W. 2d 529 (Tenn. 1973).

23
Crockett v. First Federal Savings and Loan Association of Charlotte, 224 S.E. 2d 580 (N.C. 1976).

24
Peoples Savings Association v. Standard Industries, Inc. 257 N.E. 2d 35 (1970).

25
LaSala v. American Savings and Loan Association, 489 P. 2d 1113 (1971).

26
Mutual Federal Savings and Loan Association v. Wisconsin Wire Works, 239 N.W. 2d 20 (Wisc. 1976).

In *Miller v. Pacific Federal Savings and Loan Association*,[27] the Court held that a mortgage clause, permitting the mortgagee to increase the interest rate upon transfer of the mortgaged property, was not invalid.

In the case of *Peoples Savings Association v. Standard Industries*,[28] the mortgage contained a clause accelerating the due date of the note in the event of a sale of the premises without the prior consent of the mortgagee. The mortgagee instituted mortgage foreclosure proceedings against the buyer on the grounds that the violation of such acceleration clause constituted a default, permitting foreclosure. The purchaser contended that the provision for acceleration based on change of ownership was void as against public policy.

The court held that the right of the mortgagee to protect its security by maintaining control over the identity and financial responsibility of the purchaser is a legitimate business objective, and is not illegal, inequitable or contrary to public policy.

There have been a few minor exceptions to the situation. In the case of *Demey et al. v. Jonjon Roche et al.*,[29] the court held that where there was a proposed resale, with the essential elements of a land contract, an attempt to enforce the "due on sale" acceleration clause in the deed of trust was illegal and improper. When this type of question first arose,[30] the court held that there was a difference in an outright sale and a sale when the mortgagor continued to hold the deed and the vendor's legitimate interest was not threatened. Later, the California Supreme Court rejected the distinction between installment and outright sales on policy grounds.[31]

Due-on-sale provisions are justified because such provisions are necessary to a lender's security, as well as on the basis of sound economics.[32] Where an agreement for deed failed to mention an acceleration of debt upon default in making monthly payments, default did not warrant acceleration of debt.[33] In the case of *Tucker v. Lassen Savings and Loan Ass'n.*,[34] the Supreme Court held that

---

27
Miller v. Pacific Federal Savings and Loan Association, 86 Wash. 2d 401 (Wisc. 1976).
28
Peoples Savings Association v. Standard Industries, 275 N.E. 2d 406 (Ohio 1970).
29
Demey et al. v. Jonjon Roche et al., App. 133 Cal. Rptr. 570 (1976).
30
Tucker v. Lassen Savings and Loan Association, 12 Cal. 3rd. 629, 116 Cal. Rptr. 633, 526 P. 2d 1169 (1974).
31
Wellencamp v. Bank of America, 21 Cal. 3rd 943, 950, 148 Cal Rptr. 379, 383, 582 P. 2d 970, 974 (1978) and Income Realty & Mortgage, Inc. v. Columbia Savings & Loan Association, 661 P. 2d 257, 260 (Colo. 1983).
32
Medovoi v. American Savings and Loan Ass'n., 133 Cal Rptr. 63 (1976).
33
Adkinson v. Nybert, 344 So. 2d 614 (Fla. App. 1977).
34
Tucker v. Lassen Savings and Loan Ass'n., 526 P. 2d 1169 (Cal. 1974).

the due-on-sale clause could not be automatically invoked, accelerating the debt, when the mortgagor-owner sold the mortgaged property on an *installment land contract*. However in *Medovoi v. American Savings and Loan Ass'n.*,[35] the appellate court held otherwise.

Even though the motive of the mortgagee may be only to secure an increase in the rate of interest, this is not fatal to the exercise of the acceleration clause in the mortgage.[36]

In the case of *J.M. Realty Investment Corp. et al. v. Stern*,[37] the Appellate court held that the mortgagee-vendor could foreclose for the entire balance due, including amount due on the first mortgage, where the wrap-around mortgage included a balance due mortgagee, as vendor of subject property, as well as a balance owned on the first mortgage. Mortgagor's default in making payments as required by the wrap-around mortgage entitled the mortgagee to do so.

PREPAYMENT PENALTIES

Contrary to most popular beliefs, there is no common law right to pay off a mortgage debt prior to maturity. The courts have long held that if a mortgagor was allowed to pay off his mortgage at any time, such action could seriously effect the mortgagee.[38] It is generally agreed that the mortgagee has the right to refuse early payments of principal and interest in all except one circumstance, where the Pennsylvania Supreme Court took the approach that "where the mortgage note is silent to the right of repayment, there arises a presumption that the debt may be repaid."

In actual practice most lenders do allow prepayments, but the privilege is somewhat limited and/or requires a prepayment penalty. A typical mortgage note would include words somewhat as follows:

Additional payments on the principal may be made at any time without penalty, except any payments that exceed twenty percent (20%) of the original principal amount of this loan, during any twelve- (12) month period beginning with the date of this note. The undersigned agree to pay, as consideration for the acceptance of such payment, six months (6) advance

---

35
Medovoi v. American Savings and Loan Ass'n., 133 Cal. Rptr. 631 (1976).
36
Century Federal Savings and Loan Ass'n. v. Van Glaun, 364 A. 2d 558 (N.J. 1976).
37
J.M. Realty Investment Corp. et al. v. Stern, 296 So. 2d 588 (Fla. App. 1974).
38
14 L.J. (N.S.) Ch. 167, Chancery (1845).

interest on that part of the aggregate amount of all prepayments in excess of the said twenty percent (20%).

The Federal Home Loan Bank Board (FHLBB) regulations limit prepayment penalties for payment of the entire amount due to a maximum of six (6) months interest. These regulations also require penalty-free payments of up to twenty percent (20%) of the balance of the mortgage amount in any one twelve (12) month period.[39]

It is interesting to note a recent California court decision[40] found that:

> The lender has a justifiable interest in imposing the penalty to cover his costs due to a potential time lag and administrative processing prior to making a new loan.

Prepayment penalties do not apply where the lender elects to accelerate the debt.[41] This decision was based on the fact that acceleration, by definition, advances the maturity date so that the payment is, in effect, made on the maturity date.

Prepayments from fire insurance proceeds are not applicable although the court[42] recognized that in such cases both the mortgagee and the mortgagor suffer. The decision was based on the fact that the court felt that "the mortgagor suffered the most." Prepayment penalties also would not apply in the case of condemnation.[43]

Prepayment penalties which amount to a substantial fixed lump sum or are calculated as a percent of the balance of the loan are usually not upheld, when challenged.[44] Where the prepayments are more modest, say in the range of 1 to 1 1/2% of the installment due, and set to compensate the lender for administrative costs and lost interest,and where the payments have been timely, the penalties are usually upheld as in the case of *Fox v. Federated Department Stores, Inc.*[45]

RIGHTS OF THE MORTGAGOR AND MORTGAGEE

The rights of the mortgagor and mortgagee depend, in the main, upon the provisions of the mortgage contract. Even under the conveyance theory of mortgages, the mortgagor is regarded as the real property owner of the premises. As such, he has certain fundamental rights in the property. The most important, of which, is the right of possession and the accompanying right to sell the property subject to the mortgage. He may lease the premises and is entitled to the rents,

---

[39] 112 CFR 545.6-112 (b).

[40] Sacramento Savings & Loan Association v. Superior Court, 137 Cal. App. 3rd 142, 186 Cal Rptr. 823 (1982).

[41] LHD Realty Corp., 726 F. 2d 327, 330-331 (7th Cir. 1987).

[42] Chestnut Corp. v. Bankers Bond and Mortgage Co., 395 Pa. 153, 149 A. 2d 48 (1959).

[43] DeKalb County v. United Family Life Insurance Co., 235 Ga. 417,219, S.E. 2d 707 (1979) on remand 136 Ga. App. 822,222, S.E. 2d 644 (1975).

[44] Sybron Corp. v. Clark Hospital Supply Corp., 76 Cal. App. 3rd 896, 143 Cal. Rptr. 306 (1978).

[45] Fox v. Federated Department Stores, Inc. 156 Cal Rptr. 893, 94 Cal. App. 3rd 867 (1979).

profits and revenue arising from the property. He may dispose of the property by will, subject to the mortgage. Where the mortgagee has taken possession, the mortgagor is entitled to an accounting during his stewardship.

Usually the mortgagee is not entitled to possession so that his rights in the property are few. He is entitled to payment of interest and installments of principal as they become due.

MORTGAGEE IN POSSESSION

Where the property is income producing, the creditor may, upon default, exercise his right of *mortgagee in possession*. This is accomplished simply by notifying the tenants in possession that the mortgage is in default and demanding payments of future rents to the mortgagee. A tenant will be protected against any claim of his lessor-owner by payment to the mortgagee. If the lease antedates the mortgage, the mortgagee, in those states subscribing to the conveyance theory on mortgages, can compel the tenant to pay future rents to the mortgagee and upon the tenant's refusal can issue a landlord's levy to collect rent. Upon subsequent foreclosure of the property, the purchaser at the sale takes the property subject to the prior lease. If the mortgage antedates the lease, the tenant cannot be compelled to pay rent during the mortgagee's tenure in possession. Should the tenant refuse the mortgagee's demand for rent, the latter's only recourse would be to foreclose the property and thereby terminate the lease. Even if the lessee attorns to the mortgagee, the plaintiff mortgagee, upon foreclosure at a later date, could nevertheless void the lease. His status as a mortgagee in possession is separate and independent from his status as owner as a result of the foreclosure proceedings.

The duty of the mortgagee in possession is that of a provident owner. This means responsibility for management and preservation of the property.[46]

A mortgagee in possession may also become liable for damages to a person injured on or about the mortgaged premises. If the mortgagee takes over control and dominion of the property as to supplant the owner, then he also assumes tort liability to third persons. Mere receipt of rentals is insufficient, but actual control and possession are necessary to make a mortgagee liable. Courts in Kentucky, New York, and Pennsylvania have so held. "Actual control and possession" means collecting rents, negotiating leases, paying taxes, and authorizing repairs. In short it is necessary to establish that the mortgagee exercised those acts of dominion over the property which any owner of a similar property would do under the circumstances.[47]

---

[46] Essex Cleaning Contractors, Inc. v. Amato, 317 A. 2d 411 (N.J. 1974).

[47] Miners Savings Bank v. Thomas, 140 Pa. Super Ct. 5 (1940).

MORTGAGE TRANSFERS AND ADMINISTRATION

Assignment—Just as the mortgagor-owner can sell the premises subject to the mortgage, so the mortgagee can sell the mortgage. This is effected by assignment. The purchaser of the mortgage (assignee) acquires the same title and interests in the mortgage which his assignor had, but no better title. The assignee is said to stand in the shoes of his assignor. Any claim, demand, or setoff which the mortgagor had against the mortgagee can be set up against the assignee. Thus, if the mortgagor had paid the mortgagee $1,000 upon a $5,000 mortgage debt, which the mortgagee had sold to the assignee for $5,000, the mortgage purchaser could recover only $4,000 from the debtor.

Assignment of mortgages is a standard practice by lenders, who usually are able to maintain possession of a fraction of the mortgages generated. In order to obtain additional funds for new mortgages, sales are necessary. The mortgagor may not be aware that his mortgage has been sold, if the original lender continues to service his loan. It is not unusual for a mortgage lender to service thousands of loan, which he originated but no longer owns. Fees from assignees for mortgage servicing provide a major portion of the income of many lenders. If the loan is to be service by the new owner, the mortgagor will be advised and requested to send future interest and principal payments to the new mortgage owner.

Mortgagors, who have been notified that their mortgage has been sold to another institution should make sure that their records are up to date and that the amount of the indebtedness sold agrees with their own records. They should also confirm that their records of escrows and impounds are accurate.

Certificate of No Defense, Declarations of No Setoff and Estoppel Certificates—In order to protect himself against the possibility that payment records are incorrect, the purchaser of a mortgage should obtain a statement from the mortgagor acknowledging the indebtedness due. This is known as a Certificate of No Defense, and Estoppel Certificate, or a Declaration of No Setoff, by which the mortgagor admits that he owes the debt and must pay it in full at maturity. The Certificate or Declaration also serves notice and acknowledgment of notice upon the debtor of the transfer of the mortgage. Otherwise, he would be protected in continuing payments to the original creditor.

The assignee of a mortgage should also require the mortgagee to turn over to him the mortgage instrument, the accompanying note, fire insurance policy, and any other papers relating to the mortgage transaction.

Assumption of Mortgage—Where an existing mortgage is being assumed with the permission of the mortgagee, a person preparing the sales agreement should be fully cognizant of the legal effects of several clauses used. Let us assume that Adams is selling a property to Black for $100,000 and there is at present a mortgage against the property for $70,000, executed by Adams to the mortgagee, Crane, three years earlier.

From Adam's viewpoint it is to his advantage to insist the buyer, Black, pay all cash or provide his own financing so that Adam's mortgage to Crane can be paid and satisfied. This is the only certain way that Adams can be relieved of any further obligation under the mortgage. If Black is to take the property, subject to the mortgage, caution must be exercised to see that the buyer, Black, not only takes the premises subject to the existing mortgage in favor of Crane, but also that he *assumes and agrees to pay it*. If a short form clause—such as "Under and subject, nevertheless, to a certain unpaid mortgage in the amount of $70,000 given by Adams to Crane, which mortgage dated July 1, 1991, is recorded in the office of the Recorder of Deeds of Blank County in Mortgage Book Vol. 2139 P. 422"—is used, the buyer is simply purchasing whatever equity there is in the property over and above the mortgage debt. If the property should subsequently be sold for default of mortgage, Black would lose what money he has already paid on the property and no more.

Should the property at foreclosure sale be sold for less or be less valuable than the amount of Crane's claim, Black would be liable for the deficiency to the mortgagee. Crane would have to look to Adams alone for payment. On the other hand, if the clause referring to the mortgage read exactly as it appears above, with this addition, "which mortgage vendee expressly assumes and agrees to pay as part of the consideration herein," Crane in the event of a deficiency judgment, could look to Adams or Black, or both for payment. If Crane collected the full deficiency from Adams, then Adams in turn, could look to Black for reimbursement, by reason of the mortgage *assumption* clause. Of course it is necessary that the same clause be inserted in the deed from Adams to Black.

The Voluntary Deed—It frequently happens that a mortgagor, in order to avoid foreclosure and the possibility of a deficiency judgment against him, will agree to convey the property voluntarily to the mortgagee in settlement and satisfaction of the mortgage. It is important that the deed recite that the conveyance is *intended* as a satisfaction of the debt, as the deed, per se will not have that effect. The debtor should insist that the mortgagee satisfy the mortgage of record and return the mortgage and any other evidence of the debt to him. The mortgagee, in accepting a voluntary deed for the property, should have the record examined to make sure that he is acquiring the property free and clear of any judgment or other liens. Under a voluntary conveyance, the mortgagee would acquire no better title that the mortgagor had, whereas through foreclosure proceedings, he could divest liens and judgments entered of record subsequent to his mortgage.

Release and Postponement—Where a property is released from the lien of a mortgage, the rights of the creditor are forever barred insofar as the tract of land which he has released is concerned.

It is preferable for such creditors to postpone the lien of his judgment, rather than release it. Suppose A has a judgment for $1,000 against B, who owns three tracts of land. A's judgment is a lien against all three tracts. B desires to build on tract No. 3 and requires a $50,000 mortgage. A bank will be unwilling to make a lone since its mortgage will not be a first lien. Thus B may persuade A to postpone the lien of his judgment in favor of the bank's first mortgage as to tract No. 3. A may have ample security as tracts 1 and 2 are still subject to his lien. Or, A may be required to make a partial payment on his judgment for the accommodation.

Blanket Mortgages and Partial Releases—Where a mortgage covers more than one property, the loan is known as a "blanket mortgage." This is usually the case of new developments in which each all lots are covered under one mortgage taken out to provide development funds. The mortgagee cannot be required to release any one parcel from the blanket mortgage upon a prorata share of the mortgage debt, unless specifically provided for in the mortgage agreement.

Subordination Agreements—Subordination agreements are drafted in order to alter the relative priorities that the law would otherwise give a mortgage (move it from first to second priority). A mortgagee must personally agree to be subordinated.

In California, where much of the litigation relating to subordination agreements has occurred, the courts have been very sympathetic to the seller, who is generally regarded as an unsophisticated party in need of protection. The California courts have held that "an enforceable clause must contain terms that will define and minimize the risk that the subordinating lien will impair or destroy the seller's security."

In a subordination agreement, the terms of repayment can be supplied by the lender or custom, but the contract is not valid if the terms of repayment are left for future agreement between the parties.[48]

A mortgage taken out to provide development funds for water systems, sewers, streets, sidewalks, and other improvements is usually set up on a lot release basis. The mortgagee agrees that he will release any lot sold by the developer for a specific dollar amount. Thus the developer is able to provide free and clear deeds to his developed lots without having to pay the entire indebtedness.

Acknowledgement of the Mortgage—It is necessary for the mortgage to be acknowledged by the mortgagor, and like a deed, it should be immediately recorded by the mortgagee. In the case of *Insurance Co. of America v. Holliday*,[49] a mortgage was executed and acknowledged by only one of three owners of the real estate. It was signed by a second owner, but not acknowledged. The court held that it was entitled to be recorded.

Escrows (impounds)—In making a loan, the lender usually requires the borrower to make an initial deposit into the escrow account sufficient, when added to normal monthly payments of interest and principal, to provide enough money to pay taxes and insurance premiums when due. To prevent lenders from demanding excessive escrow amounts the Real Estate Settlement and Procedures Act (RESPA)[50] limits the initial payments to that just described plus a two-month cushion.

Several theories have been developed to justify having mortgagees account

[48] Stockwell v. Lindeman, 229 Cal. App. 2d 750 Cal Rptr. 555 (1964).

[49] Insurance Co. of America v. Holliday, 214 N.W. 2d 273 (Neb. 1974).

[50] 12 U.S.C.A. 2609.

for profits from the use or investment of escrow funds. Most attacks have been judicial challenges that have proved ineffective.

Several states have enacted legislation regulating escrow accounts that generally requires mortgagees to pay interest to mortgagors on escrow funds. States with this type of regulation are Connecticut, Massachusetts, Minnesota, New Hampshire, Nebraska, and New York. In most cases the amount of interest payable to mortgagors is nominal and in the range of 1 to 2 percent. FNMA and FHLMC forms expressly negate the payment of escrow interest, unless there is expressed agreement to the contrary. There is no federal law requiring mortgagees to pay interest. The Federal Home Loan Bank Board (FHLBB) authorizes federally chartered institutions to pay interest *only* on loans made after June 15, 1975 and then only in those state which require such payments.

CHATTEL MORTGAGES

There has been some activity for a "package mortgage," which will include not only the real estate but also the refrigerator, laundry equipment, furniture, and even the family car. Most states provide for mortgaging of personal property by a *chattel mortgage,* which is generally used to finance the purchase price of furniture, household appliances, and commercial equipment. The chattel mortgage, like the real estate mortgage, is recorded. Title is transferred to the purchaser, and he in turn can convey title to the article in question to any buyer, but the title is subject to the balance due under the chattel mortgage. In the examination of the title to real estate, search should also be made for chattel mortgages. A chattel mortgage differs from a conditional sale, in that, while possession passes in both cases to the buyer, title, in a conditional sale, remains in the seller until the last installment is made.

SELLER FINANCING

THE PURCHASE MONEY MORTGAGE

The purchase money mortgage is like a mortgage from a standard lending institution with the exception that the processing is easier and the seller becomes the mortgagee. In times of high interest rates or scarcity of funds from normal lenders, a seller may find it very expeditious to offer financing to a qualified buyer. Usually such financing is at a lower rate than is obtainable from conventional lenders. While the conventional lender has restrictions on the amount of money he may lend on a property (usually 80 to 90 percent of value), the seller-lender may lend as much as he may dare and at any rate he can get.

Sellers, financing their own sales, should be guided by the same principles of good business as conventional lenders. They should require a credit report on the buyer to ascertain his creditability and require sufficient down payment to assure that the buyer will not skip out leaving the seller with a badly worn and dilapidated property requiring substantial repairs in order to put it back on the market.

Purchase money mortgages may be first liens or second liens. In the case of second liens, it is necessary that the first mortgage not have a due-on-sale clause which would require the full payment of the existing mortgage. The financing arrangement in the case of a first lien, which will not be paid off at closing takes one of two forms: (1) The purchaser assumes the first mortgage obligation and gives a second mortgage for the balance due, or (2) the financing agreement is a wrap-around type in which one payment is made to the seller sufficient to make the first mortgage payments plus an additional sum to amortize the second mortgage.

In the latter case, the purchaser giving a purchase money second mortgage on property should take precautions to assure that his payments to the seller are applied first to the first mortgage and second to the seller-financed second mortgage. Otherwise, he may find that after he has paid his indebtedness, a first lien still remains on the property due to the original owner's failure to keep those payments up-to-date. Or worse still, he could have the property repossessed by the first lien holder.

A satisfactory solution to this problem is in the use of an escrow agent who receives the monthly payments, makes the first mortgage payments and pays the balance over to the former owner. When the purchaser's obligations are liquidated (usually the first mortgage and later the second), the escrow agent is instructed to provide the purchaser with appropriate mortgage releases and satisfaction pieces.

It is widely accepted that a purchase money mortgage executed at the same time as the deed of purchase, or as a part of one transaction, takes precedence over any other claim or lien attaching to the property through the vendee/mortgagor.[51] The purchase money mortgage will prevail over a claim of dower, community property or homestead.[52]

THE INSTALLMENT LAND CONTRACT

An installment land contract is also referred to as a contract for deed, or a conditional sales contract. It evidences a sale of land and an obligation of a vendor to convey the land of the purchaser to pay the purchase price in installments over a period of time. It is essentially a security instrument, taking the place of a purchase money mortgage.[53]

A purchaser, under a land contract for deed, or even in an agreement of sales,

---

[51]
Hursey v. Hursey, S.C. 326 S.E. 2d 178 (1985).

[52]
Associates Discount Corp. v. Gomes, 338 So. 2d 552 (Fla. App. 1976); Davidson v. Click, 31 N.Mex. 543, 249 P. 100, 47 A.L.R. 1016 (1926) and Martin v. First National Bank of Opelika, 279 Ala. 303, 184 So. 2d 815 (1966).

[53]
Hand L. Land Co. v. Warner, 258 So. 2d 293 (Fla. 1972).

is not required to sign the instrument. His *acceptance* of the instrument, signed by the seller, accompanied by the payment of a deposit, makes the contract bi-lateral.[54]

In the promotion of subdivision tracts, many lots are sold on the installment basis. A modest down payment is made and then periodic monthly payments are made until the full consideration price is liquidated, at which time the deed is delivered.

Considerable improved real estate is also sold in this manner. Should the buyer default in his payments, he forfeits the payments already made. In the alternative method, the seller could also elect to hold the buyer to his contract.

Remedies available to the vendor under defaulted land contracts include:

- Action for breach of contract.
- Ejectment, eviction, foreclosure and recision.
- Peaceful repossession.
- Suit for purchase money or specific performance.
- Summary proceedings and action to quiet title.

Election of one remedy barred pursuing an inconsistent remedy. For example, having elected the remedy of forfeiture and claim of possession, vendors could not seek judicial foreclosure and deficiency judgment.[55]

The more or less standard contract usually provides that in the event the purchaser defaults, the balance of the purchase price, at the option of the seller, shall become payable forthwith. A clause may even be included which would permit the seller to confess judgment against the buyer for the full amount unpaid.

The law in the area of default of the installment contract is not clearly defined. Not only does it vary from jurisdiction to jurisdiction, but also within the states, depending upon the type of actions brought, the exact terms of the contract and the facts of the particular case. It is very difficult to predict the outcome of any one case as to whether the buyer's interest will be forfeited upon default. While these forfeitures are still occasionally enforced,[56] it is safe to say that in no jurisdiction today will a vendor be able to assume that forfeiture provisions in the contract will be enforced as written.

Even in those states that enforce forfeitures, the courts may require the vendor to provide notice of interest to forfeit and a reasonable time period in which to cure the default, even though such actions are not spelled out in the contract itself.[57]

In many states legislative action has been taken to ease the impact of

---

[54] Stachnik v. Winkel, 213 N.W. 2d 434 (Mich. 1973).

[55] Gruskin v. Fisher, 245 N.W. 2d 427 (Mich. App. 1976).

[56] Hammer v. Rock Mountain Lake, Inc., 451 So. 2d 249 (Ala. 1984) and Bill v. Coots, 451 So. 2d 268 (Ala. 1984).

[57] Martinez v. Martinez, 101 N.Mex 88, 678 P. 2d 1163 (1984).

automatic forfeiture. A good example is in Iowa[58] where the statute prescribes a specific procedure which includes:

- A vendor must provide written notification to the vendee and to the person in possession of the property.
- The notice must identify the real estate, specify the contract terms that are in default and inform the vendee that he has 30 days in which to correct the default.

The most informative view that a land contract should be deemed a mortgage for remedy purposes after the default was noted in the Kentucky case of *Sebastian v. Floyd*,[59] in which the Kentucky Supreme Court reversed a trial court forfeiture determination where the vendee had paid nearly 40 percent of the principal balance on a contract for the sale of a house. The court required the vendor to seek judicial sale of the property. the court was of the opinion:

> that a ruling treating the seller's interest as a lien will best protect the interest of the buyer and seller.

The Utah courts have refuse outright forfeiture, in cases where the vendee could not or would not redeem and where outright forfeiture would be "unconscionable"—this often means that the vendee would suffer a substantial loss if the no restitution was ordered.[60] In some Utah cases, where vendee payments exceeded the vendor's damages, the courts approved restitution to the vendee of the excess paid over the vendor's damages.[61]

The purchaser's restitution remedy is well developed in California. Under the California rule of *Venable v. Harmon*,[62] a California vendor cannot receive a deficiency judgment regardless of his loss.

A vendor cannot exercise an option to accelerate the balance due and foreclose after the purchaser has made a valid, although late tender of the delinquent payment(s).[63]

Where the vendors wrongfully rescinded a conditional sales contract for a motel property, the buyers were entitled to recover principal payments, as well as interest from the date of wrongful ejectment. The vendors were not entitled to a

---

58
Iowa Code Ann. 656.1-6.

59
Sebastian v. Floyd, 585 S.W. 2d 381 (Ky. 1979).

60
Kay v. Wood, 549 P. 2d 709 (Utah 1976).

61
Morris v. Sykes, 624 P. 2d 681 (Utah 1981) and Kay v. Wood, 549 P. 2d 709 (Utah 1976).

62
Venable v. Harmon, 233 Cal App. 2d 297, 43 Cal Rptr. 490 (1965).

63
Sindlinger v. Paul, 404 N.W. 2d 212 (1987).

setoff in amounts of rents and profits accruing to buyers while they were in possession.[64]

In default of a land contract, consideration should be given to the ability of the purchaser to redeem his state of solvency. Value of the land and the likelihood of refinancing are deemed relevant facts. Also taken into consideration are the size of the vendee's equity and the length of default. The courts will attempt to do equity between the parties.[65] However, in the case of *Cooper v. Jefferson Investment Co.,*[66] the court held that in a land contract, an acceleration clause, upon default by the vendee, requires no preliminary notice of intent to foreclose. Suit can be instituted for the full amount.

In a California case, a vendee, under a land contract, became delinquent in his monthly payments during 1963. In 1966, the vendor started an action to quiet title. The vendee then offered to pay the entire balance due, plus interest. The vendor refused to accept payment. The vendee next sued for specific performance. The court decided in favor of the vendee, treating the land contract as a mortgage. The vendee had the right to redeem the property.[67]

The mere fact that a seller has permitted the curing of previous defaults is not an end unto itself to cure future defaults of the same nature.[68]

Where there is a "time is of the essence" clause in the land contract, it may be waived by the conduct of the vendor in accepting payments at irregular intervals. Where a land contract contained a "time is of the essence" clause for prompt payment of installments, the vendor is deemed to have waived the clause by accepting, without complaint, delay in making payments for six months.[69] The "time is of the essence" clause can be revived by the vendor by giving the purchaser a warning notice that strict compliance with the contract would be insisted upon in the future.[70]

---

[64] Smeekins v. Bertrand, 302 N.E. 2d 502 (Ind. 1973).

[65] Kallenbach v. Lake Publications, Inc., 142 N.W. 2d 212 (Wisc. 1966).

[66] Cooper v. Jefferson Investment Co., 246 N.W. 2d 311 (Mich. App. 1976).

[67] MacFadden v. Walker, 488 P.2d 1353 (Cal. 1971)

[68] Rogers v. Newton, 340 So. 2d 768 (Ala. 1976).

[69] Farmer v. Groves, 555 P. 2d 1252 (Or. 1976).

[70] Kirkpatrick v. Petreiksi, 358 N.E. 2679 (Ill. App. 1976).

9

Landlord and Tenant

The relationship of the landlord and tenant arises from a contract, expressed or implied, by which one person occupies the real property of another with his permission and in subordination to his rights. The occupant is known as the *tenant* and the person in subordination to whom he occupies is the *landlord*.[1] This relationship is created by a lease. The two parties to a lease are the lessor, who is the owner and the lessee, who obtains possession of the premises for a specified period of time. The term landlord is used interchangeably with the term lessor, and the same is true of the lessee, who is more often referred to as the tenant. While the tenant's interest is a temporary possession, the lessor's interest is the reversion of the property at the end of the lease. If the tenant sublets a portion of the premises to another person, he becomes the landlord and the sublessee is the tenant.

A lease is a nonfreehold, or as it is often stated, it is less than a freehold estate, legally referred to as a *leasehold*. It is an estate for a specified period of time and upon the expiration of the period, the leasehold estate terminates.

The lease contract, voluntarily entered into by the parties, largely determines the law by which the parties are governed. The lease contract may be *verbal* or in writing. A verbal lease is just as binding and of as great legal efficacy as a written contract, provided the term does not exceed the period prescribed by resident state Statute of Frauds. The Statute of Frauds requires certain contracts to be in writing, particularly those relating to real estate. Thus, a lease for more than one year, in most states, must be in writing in order to be enforceable.

Where the lessee occupies the premises under an oral lease fixing no duration, either lessor or lessee can terminate the lease at the expiration of any month, by giving written notice.[2]

The lease must be definite and free from ambiguity.[3] An agreement to contract

---

[1]
McNeill v. McNeill, 456 S.W. 2d 800 (Mo. App. 1970).

[2]
Branch v. Watkins Realty Corp., 289 So. 2d 381 (La. App. 1973).

[3]
Russell v. Valentine, 376 P. 2d 548 (Utah 1962).

for a lease in the future must be definite and specific as to the terms of the lease, otherwise it is unenforceable. A contract to lease which did not fix rental, and which was conditioned upon obtaining financing and adequate parking facilities (which were not met), was ruled unenforceable.[4]

The essence of a lease is the payment of rent. A lease may be defined as a contract, oral or written, for the *possession* of lands and tenements in return for recompense of rent or other income.

A license, on the other hand is a personal privilege. It is not an estate in land, and it is not usually assignable. In deciding whether a writing was a lease or a license for pinball machines, the court held that the test is whether exclusive possession of premises is given or merely possession to use.[5] A license may be termed a tenancy at will, which can be terminated at any time.

In an action to collect rents under a three-year lease for property in California, signed only by the lessee, the court held that the lease violated the Statute of Frauds in that a lease for more than one year must be in writing and signed by the party to be charged (lessor). The lessee, a resident of Oregon, where the suit was brought, could not recover.[6] The period runs from the date when the contract is entered into, rather than from the date the lease term commences. In Pennsylvania, a lease in excess of three years must be in writing. For obvious reasons, a written lease is preferred to an oral one. The tenure of human life is uncertain, and one or both parties to the contract may die during its term. In the case of controversy or litigation, the surviving party would not be permitted to testify as he is a party in interest, and the other party is deceased.

TENANT ESTATES

When a tenant-landlord relationship comes into being, the law will classify the tenant's estate as:

- An estate at sufferance,
- An estate at will,
- A periodic estate, or
- An estate for years.

These classifications are important in that each is terminated in a different manner.

ESTATE AT SUFFERANCE

This estate arises when one rightfully takes possession of property as a lessee but remains in possession *after* termination of the lease and without the consent of

---

[4] Kapetan v. Kelso, 481 P. 2d 24 (Wash. App. 1971).

[5] Timmons v. Cropper, 172 A. 2d 757 (Dela. 1961).

[6] Palmer v. Wheeler, 481 P. 2d 68 (Ore. 1971).

the landlord. In most states, such as Utah, no notice is required to terminate an estate at sufferance; however, the landlord may not personally dispossess the tenant. The lessor/landlord must obtain a court order to evict, after which the police or other authority will evict the tenant.

A tenant at sufferance is legally no tenant at all since he holds over without the consent of the landlord, which is essential to the landlord/tenant relationship. He is a wrongdoer and the lessor may bring action in ejectment to recover possession.[7]

ESTATE AT WILL

An estate at will occurs when a person takes possession of a property with the landlord's consent, but without entering into an oral or written lease. At this point the tenant owns an estate at will. In the case of *Evershed v. Berry*,[8] the Court said,

> If nothing more is shown than payment and receipt of rent, the result in common law is the creation either of a tenancy at will or at most one from year to year.

An estate usually occurs when it is agreed that the tenant may move in and there is an understanding that a lease will be negotiated at a later date. In most states a tenancy at will can be terminated by the landlord with very little notice—as little as 5 days.

A lease that provides that the tenant may terminate at a date of his choice creates a life tenancy and prevents the landlord from terminating the lease at will.[9]

PERIODIC ESTATE

This estate occurs when the parties agree on the conditions of the lease but do not specify its term or length. For example, the parties might agree on a rent of $15 per day payable monthly in advance. In this agreement there is a clear implication that the parties expect the lease to continue for longer than one month, yet neither has stipulated an ending date. This estate continues for the length of the payment period (one month in this case) and is automatically renewed unless one of the parties gives the other adequate notice of termination. Usually the notice period, in most states is specified as the period of payment. The advantage of this type of estate is the flexibility afforded to both parties.

ESTATE FOR YEARS

This estate arises from a lease in which the parties agree upon the ending date of the lease. It is somewhat of a misnomer in that the lease does not have to be for

---

[7] Kilbourne v. Forester, 464 S.W. 2d 770 (Tex. 1971).

[8] Evershed v. Berry, 20 Utah 2d 203, 436 P. 2d 438 (1968).

[9] Garner v. Gerrish, 63 N.Y. 2d 575, 473 N.E. 2d 223, 483 N.Y.S. 2d 973 (1984).

a calendar year but may be for any period such as one week, one month or 10 years. In the estate for years, neither the lessee nor the lessor may terminate the relationship prior to the date established in the lease. A lessee, who fails to remain in possession for the entire period of the lease, may be liable for the remaining rent to the end of the lease. The liability is limited as the landlord must use every effort to re-lease the premises and if successful, the former tenant is liable for only the period in which the property was not rented. If the landlord is unable to obtain the full amount of rent as specified in the lease, the former tenant would be liable for the difference in rent. Under Florida law, the tenant may, in fact, be liable for double rent.[10]

In the case of *Housing Authority of Pittsburgh v. Turner*,[11] the termination of a month to month lease by the Housing Authority, without giving any reason, was held no abuse of due process. Whereas, in the case of *Custis v. Klein*,[12] involving a month to month lease, the court held that notice given in April to vacate the premises on April 30 was defective and the lessee was entitled to possession for the full month of May.

HOLDOVER TENANTS

It is not unusual for a tenant to remain in possession after the termination of the estate. When this occurs, the landlord has a choice of several remedies. For instance, he may have the tenant physically evicted by the sheriff. If the landlord elects to keep receiving rents, which the tenant is liable for during the holdover period, the estate for years will probably be transformed into a periodic estate for the length of the payment period.

In agricultural leases, if the tenant holds over for 60 days or more, most states rule that the tenant is entitled to hold over for one additional year at the same terms and conditions as the original lease. Generally, when a lease for a certain term expires, a lessee is not entitled to crops planted at such time that they do not mature before the expiration of the lease; however, a lessee is entitled to the crops where the lessor knew the crop could not mature during the term of the lease and still consented to the lessee's planting and cultivating.[13]

In the Ohio case of *Zanetos v. Sparks*,[14] the court held that a rent payment, nine days late, does not constitute a technical breach of the lease. The case showed that the plaintiff requested his rent on July 6th and received a check, dated July 7th, which was several days late. On July 9th the plaintiff served notice to vacate and the court granted judgment, which was reversed on appeal.

---

[10] Nelson v. Grower's Ford Tractor Co., 282 So.66 (Fla. App. 1973).

[11] Housing Authority of Pittsburgh v. Turner, 191 A. 2d 869 (Pa. 1963).

[12] Custis v. Klein, 127 A. 2d 268 (D.C. 1962).

[13] Beken v. Elster, 503 S.W. 2d 408 (Tex. 1973).

[14] Zanetos v. Sparks, 13 Ohio App. 3rd 242, 468 N.E. ed 938 (1984).

PARTIES TO THE LEASE

The names of the parties are inserted in the lease primarily for purposes of identification. A mistake or omission in setting forth the parties, if it is not material or does not cast doubt upon the parties intended, will have very little effect upon the validity of the contract. Generally speaking, anyone who is capable of making a contract is capable of making a lease. A lease may be executed by the owner of the property himself or by a properly authorized agent acting in his behalf. If the lease must be in writing under the Statute of Frauds, then the *agent's* authority to execute the lease must be *in writing*. A lease signed and sealed by an agent in his own name alone would be wide open to attack by the lessor or lessee. The execution of a lease by an agent must be carefully made. An agent may execute a lease, *as agent,* for an undisclosed principal, in which case the agent is considered as the lessor. It would be signed "John Steel, agent." The best execution, from the standpoint of the agent is to include the name of the lessor as,

Adam Taylor
by John Steel, agent.

An agent who is appointed merely to collect rents, such as an apartment house manager, has no authority to negotiate a lease for the owner.

If a *minor* leases land, the same rules apply as in the case of any other contract executed under the same conditions. Such a lease, in other words, is not void but only voidable by the minor, and may be disaffirmed by him during his minority or within a reasonable time after attaining his majority. A *guardian* of a minor stands, however, in the same place that he would stand had he himself owned the property, so far as his power to lease is concerned. He has been appointed for the purpose of administering the affairs of the minor, and consequently possesses all of the power which may be necessary for executing a lease.

In a similar way, a *trustee* may grant leases which are unimpeachable so long as the trustee has remained within the powers granted to him by the deed of trust. The trust instrument should be examined to ascertain the extent of the trustee's authority. An *administrator* cannot lease. He has been appointed for the purpose of winding up the estate and has nothing to do with the renting of real estate. An *executor,* for the same reason, unless he has also been appointed a trustee of the real estate, cannot lease any of the estate property.

A *married woman* has full capacity to execute a lease on property owned by her. Where the property is owned by the entireties, in the names of husband and wife, either spouse can execute a valid lease upon the property owned by both. The lease benefits enure to both spouses.

It is important to note that a wife is for all practical purposes a co-beneficiary of the lease. An owner in common has no authority to bind his co-owners by a lease. In order to bind all, the lease must be executed by *all* the owners.[15]

---

[15]
Needleman v. American Clothing Co., Inc., 63 A. 2d 201 (Vt. 1949).

DESCRIPTION OF THE PROPERTY

In making a lease, it is not necessary to insert a minute description of the premises which are the subject of the property lease. The lease should provide that the premises are leased "as is" that is to say, in their present condition. If the premises are in good repair, a statement to that effect should be included. In the case of commercial or industrial property, a full description should be used. In renting a furnished house, it is important to have a list of the furniture and other articles which are to pass with the house, attached to the lease. After the lessee has verified the existence of all of the articles on the list and has inspected them, he should be requested to initial each page of the form to certify that the equipment was there on the day of possession. A clause should also be inserted giving the lessor the right to make an examination of the articles in order to ascertain the condition of the furniture, which the tenant is to preserve in good order, except for fair wear and tear.

COMMERCIAL LEASES

Commercial leases are almost identical to those for other properties with the exception of the payment of certain items such as taxes, insurance, and maintenance. A typical commercial lease may be referred to as a double-net or triple-net lease, written "net[2]" or "net[3]" leases. The double-net lease refers to the fact that the lessee is responsible for the payment of taxes and insurance, whereas in the triple-net lease the lessee is responsible for taxes, insurance, and maintenance. These provisions are included for convenience of the parties. Instead of saying, "The lessee is responsible for any increases in taxes and insurance assessed during the term of the lease," the lessee just pays the bill. Similarly, if the plumbing needs repair, in a triple-net lease the tenant would just have the work performed and pay for it. This would save time in communicating the problem through the owner to the plumber as the tenant could just call him directly and authorize the work.

The particular commercial use to which the leased premises are to be put should be spelled out with clarity. While courts will not make contracts for the parties, they will lend their aid in ascertaining the *intentions* of the parties for the language in the lease agreement.

Just as in the case of a sale of property, the broker should be familiar with zoning laws applicable to an intended lease by a prospective lessor. In the case of *Hoff v. Sander*,[16] the lessor and lessee both believed that the leased property could be used for boarding horses, dogs, and other pets. The city zoning ordinance, in

---

[16] Hoff v. Sander, 497 S.W. 2d 651 (Mo. App. 1973).

fact, did not permit that use. The court held that the parties were charged with knowledge of zoning applicable and could not procure a rescission of lease or damages on account of a mutual mistake. Contracting parties are presumed to know the law and have it in mind when drawing their agreement.[17]

In the case of *Anderson v. Busoda*,[18] the lease prohibited the use of the premises "for any other purpose than laundry service." The tenant, after several months on the premises, added a dry cleaning service. He changed the name from "Normandy Laundry" to "Astro Laundry and Cleaners." The court held there was a violation of the lease pointing out that, "In ordinary and popular usage there is a vast distinct difference between laundry service and dry cleaning service, both in the methods used and the results accomplished." It is obvious that the "use" clause in a lease in shopping centers is very important. Restrictions, such as those just discussed, are often placed on tenants to protect the business of other tenants in the same shopping area.

RETAIL STORE AND SHOPPING CENTER LEASES

Most retail store leases are of the percentage-lease type, in which a minimum lease price per period is specified together with a percentage of the gross sales. This percentage decreases as the gross volume increases. The purpose of this type of lease is to be able to offer properties at the lowest possible figure, consistent, with a profitable operation, to encourage the establishment of new businesses. As the business prospers and the sales increase, the landlord takes an increasingly larger rent to compensate for his low initial rent. A percentage lease might read, "5 percent of Gross Sales, up to Gross Sales of $100,000, but not less than $1,000 per month; 3 percent of Gross Sales from $100,001 to $500,000, and 1 1/2 percent of Gross Sales there over." Thus the beginning rent with few sales would be $1,000 per month. When sales reached $200,000, the rent would be:

$$5\% \times \$100,000 = \$5,000.00$$
$$3\% \times (\$200,000 - \$100,001) = \underline{2,999.97}$$
$$\text{Total} \quad \$7,999.97$$

In order to promote harmony among the tenants, the retail lease will probably embody necessary rules as to days and hours of operation, parking for employees, types of fronts allowed on the stores, outside displays, deliveries, and trash collection. Usually the policing of the rules and regulations and the changes required from time to time are administered by a Merchant's Association, consisting of all merchants in the shopping center or area.

---

[17] Dill v. Pondexter, 451 S.W. 2d 365 (Mo. App. 1970).

[18] Anderson v. Busoda, 180 A. 2d 130 (D.C.).

RESTRICTIVE COVENANTS REGARDING COMPETITION

Restrictive covenants in a lease barring competition from a similar business are strictly construed.[19]

A shopping center leased a store for a retail bakery, donut shop, and snack bar. The lease contained a prohibition against a lease for similar use within a designated distance. The lessee, later, received permission to sell sandwiches and other allied items usually sold. Subsequently, an adjoining vacant store was leased for a Mexican-type restaurant. The court held that the restaurant use violated the first lease.[20]

COVENANTS, CONDITIONS, AND WARRANTIES IN A LEASE

When parties enter into a lease agreement, there are numerous promises flowing from the landlord and the tenant. For example, the landlord promises to deliver the premises on a certain date and the tenant promises to pay a cleaning deposit by the end of a specified period. In most states a breach of a promises in a lease can be classified covenants and conditions. In most states a breach of a condition automatically gives the other party the right to not perform his obligations. In contract, a breach of a covenant does not eliminate the obligation of the injured party to perform. It merely gives him the right to sue for damages caused by the breach of the covenant. In some states, the landlord has the right to evict the tenant for breach of *either* a covenant or condition.

Upon the execution of a lease, there is an implied warranty that the conditions of the premises described in the lease will remain the same between the time of the execution of the lease and the beginning of the term. If a material change takes place in the premises, the tenant is not bound to take possession, for the premises tendered are not those described in the lease. For example, where a landlord rented a city property, and, before the lessee took possession at the beginning of the term, the landlord allowed a third party to dump earth on the premises, thereby changing the character of the leasehold, without the consent of the tenant. The landlord could not recover in an action for rent.

A lessee should require the lessor to covenant that the tenant will obtain possession of the premises at the commencement of the term, or otherwise the tenant can recover only damages for the delay in obtaining possession. It is not unusual for a lessee to be unable to take possession because of the unlawful holding over of the prior tenant. In a commercial establishment, this may result in considerable damage to the new tenant. Whether the new tenant can consider the breach sufficient to terminate the lease depends upon the particular circumstances of the

---

[19] Howard D. Johnson Co. v. Parkside Development Corp., 384 N.E. 2d 656 (Ind. 1976).

[20] Anderson v. Blondo Plaza, Inc., 186 N.W. 2d 114 (Neb. 1971) and Carousel Snack Bars v. Crown Construction Co., 439 F. 2d 280 (Pa. 1971).

situation. For example, Adam's lease of a dairy store premises from Brown had a 90-day sales clause. Brown sold the property to Clement, who immediately leased the premises to Denton for a dairy store at a considerably higher rental. The lease term was for five years, beginning on February 15, 1978. Adams leased other premises about a half-block away but could not get possession until May 1, 1978. On April 1, 1978, Denton notified Clement that he would not honor the lease because of Clement's inability to give him possession. Denton claimed that he suffered irreparable harm since he could not take possession until after Adams was able to enter into active competition with him. Denton expected to obtain a considerable portion of Adam's present trade, which *induced* him to sign the lease and was, in a sense, a condition precedent. Here possession on February 15th was distinctly understood as a material element in the contract and Clement could not hold Denton to the lease. Clement could have protected himself from this situation by a lease provision that:

> lessor or his agent shall not be liable in damages or otherwise, for failure to deliver possession of the demised premises to the lessee at the commencement of the term, where such failure is due to the unlawful holding over by a prior tenant or occupant; this lease shall, nevertheless, remain in full force and effect, with an abatement of rent to the lessee until the date of possession is made available to him.

In the case of *Hartwig v. 65 Realty Co.,*[21] an eight-month delay in giving the tenant possession, due to a failure to complete the building, permitted the tenant to rescind the lease.

IMPLIED COVENANTS AND CONDITIONS

In general implied covenants and conditions favor the landlord. Consequently most tenants would be wise to insist on executing a very detailed lease. Where not specifically covered in the terms of the lease, many states place the burden and duty to repair upon the tenant. This stems from common law obligations on all, who temporarily occupy realty, to not allow the property to waste. If the landlord's conduct causes the defect, he is obligated to repair and failure to do so may result in *constructive eviction,* in which case the tenant would be able to move out and pay no further rent. For instance, the failure to repair a furnace in an apartment building during a cold winter would justify the tenant's moving out even though he had an additional period on his lease. Similarly, a Texas court ruled that a tenant had been constructively evicted by the failure of the landlord to prevent harassment by third parties. The case involved a tenant-doctor who practiced medicine of a nature not approved by some of his neighbors.[22]

---

[21] Hartwig v. 65 Realty Co., 324 N.Y.S. 2d 567 (1971).

[22] Fidelity Mutual Life Ins. Co. v. Kaminsky, 768 S.W. 2d 818 (Tex Ct. App.- Houston [14th Dist]. 1989).

THE IMPLIED WARRANTY, A GROWING TREND

The implied warranty doctrine as a principle of law is growing in a number of jurisdictions, to apply to the leasing of dwellings and apartments. The emphasis of these decisions is upon the assertion that the leased premises *must* be habitable. The opinion of Justice Tobriner, in the case of *Green v. Superior Court of the City and County of San Francisco*,[23] gives a very clear and comprehensive discussion for the justification of the implied warranty of habitability for residential leases. The opinion states,

Under traditional common law doctrine, long followed in California, a landlord was under no duty to maintain leased dwellings in habitable condition during the term of the lease. In the past several years, however, the highest courts of a rapidly growing number of states and the District of Columbia have reexamined the basis of the old common law rule and have uniformly determined that it no longer corresponds to the realities of the modern urban landlord/tenant relationship. Accordingly, each of these jurisdictions has discarded the old common law rule and has adopted an implied warranty of habitability for residential leases.[24] On June 1972, the California Court of Appeal reviewed this emerging out-of-state precedent in the case of *Hinson v. Delis*,[25] and persuaded by the reasoning of these decisions, held that a warranty of habitability is implied by law in residential leases in California. We granted a hearing in the instant case, and a companion case, to consider the Hinson decision and to determine whether the breach of such implied warranty may be raised as a defense by a tenant in an unlawful detainer action.

For the reason discussed below, we have determined that the Hinson court properly recognized a common law warranty of habitability in residential leases in California, and we conclude that the breach of such warranty may be raised as a defense in an unlawful detainer action.

First, as the recent line of out-of-state cases comprehensively demonstrates, the factual and legal premiss underlying the original common law rule in this area have long ceased to exist; continued adherence to the time-worn doctrine conflicts with the expectations and demands of the contemporary landlord/tenant relationship and with modern legal principles in analogous fields. To remain viable, the common law must reflect the realities of present day society; an implied warranty of habitability in residential leases must be recognized.

Second, we shall point out that the statutory "repair and deduct" provisions of

---

[23] Green v. The Superior Court of the City and County of San Francisco, 517 P. 2d 1168 (Cal. 1974).

[24] See Pines v. Perssion, 1961 14Wis. 2d 590, 111 N.W. 2d 409; Lemle v. Breeden, (1969) 51 Haw. 426, 462 P. 2d 470; Javins v. First National Realty Corp., (1970) 138 U,S. App. D.C. 369, 428 F. 2d 1071, cert. den. 400 U.S. 925, 91 S. Ct. 186, 27 L.Ed. 185; Marini v. Ireland, (1970) 56 N.J. 130, 265 A. 2d 526; Kline v. Burns, (1971) 111 N.H. 87, 276 A. 2d 248; Jack Spring, Inc. v. Little, (1972) 50 Ill. 2d 351, 280 N.E. 2d 208; Mease v. Fox, (1972) Iowa, 200 N.W. 2d 791; and Boston Housing Authority v. Hemmingway, (1973) Mass. N.E. 2d 831.

[25] Hinson v. Delis, (1972) 26 Cal. App. 3d 62, 102 Cal. Rptr. 661.

Civil Code section 1941 et seq. do not preclude this development in the common law, for such enactments were never intended to be the exclusive remedy for tenants but have always been viewed as complementary to existing common rights.

Finally, we have concluded that a landlord's breach of this warranty of habitability may be raised as a defense in an unlawful detainer action. Past California cases have established that a defendant in an unlawful detainer action may raise any affirmative defense which, if established, will preserve the tenant's possession of the premises. As we shall explain, a landlord's breach of the warranty of habitability directly relates to whether any rent is "due and owing" by the tenant; hence, such breach may be determinative of whether the landlord or tenant is entitled to possession of the premises upon nonpayment of rent. Accordingly, the tenant may properly raise the issue of warranty of habitability in an unlawful detainer action . . .

In the case of the lease of an apartment, it is interesting to note that the New Hampshire Supreme Court also pronounced principles, which represent a radical departure from the common law. In the case of *Kline v. Burns,*[26] a tenant brought an action against his landlord to recover rent paid during his occupancy of an apartment on the ground that the premises were in violation of the City Housing Code. The landlord, in turn, brought an action for possession and to recover the unpaid rent. The language of the Supreme Court is significant. The court said:

The following are factors to be considered in the appraisal of the legal principles to be applied to the present day relationship of landlord and tenant: (1) Our legislature has recognized (RSA ch. 48-1) that the public welfare requires that dwellings offered for rental be at the beginning, and continue during the tenancy to be, in a safe condition and fit for human habitation. (2) Common experience demonstrates that the landlord has a much better knowledge of the condition of the premises than the tenant. Furthermore housing code requirements and violations are usually known or made known to the landlord. *Marini v. Ireland,* 56 N.J. 130, 142, 265 A. 2d 526, 533 (1970); 44 Denver L.Q. 387, 398 (1967); *see* RSA 48-A:3(III) (supp.). It follows that the landlord is in a better position to know of latent defects, such as some of those involved in this case, which might go unnoticed by the tenant who rarely has sufficient knowledge or expertise to see or discover defects in wiring, fusing, or venting of gas appliances or furnances. *See Reste Realty Corp. v. Cooper,* 53 N.J. 444, 452, 251 A. 2d 268, 272 (1969). (3) It is Appropriate that the landlord who will retain ownership of the premises and any permanent improvements should bear the cost of repairs necessary to make the premises safe and fit for human habitation. 1 American Law of Property s. 3.78, at 347-48 (1952). In today's housing market, the landlord is usually in a much better bargaining position than the tenant which results in rental of poor housing in violation of public policy. A. B. Foundation, Model Residential Landlord-Tenant Code 9 (Tent. Draft 1969); 50 B.U.I. Rev. 24, 38, 39 (1970).

In our opinion the above considerations demonstrate convincingly that in a rental or an apartment as a dwelling unit, be it a written or oral lease, for a specified time or at will, there is an implied warranty of habiltability by the landlord that the apartment is habitable and fit for living. . . . *Marini v. Ireland,*

26

Kline v. Burns, 276 A. 2d 248 (N.H. 1971).

56 N.J. 130, 144, 265 A. 2d 526, 533 (1970); *Javins v. First Nat'l Realty Corp. supra; Lemle v. Breeden,* 51 Hawaii 426, 433, 462 P. 2d 470, 474 (1969); *Lund v. MacArthur,* 51 Hawaii 473, 475, 482 P. 2d 461, 463 (1969). The warranty of habitability which we hold exists in such a case is imposed by law on the basis of public policy. It arises by operation of law because of the relationship of the parties, the nature of the transaction, and the surrounding circumstances. . .

The Colorado Supreme Court rejected the trend of *implied* habitability in the case of *Blackwell v. Del Bosco,*[27] indicating that tenant relief should come from the legislature, rather than from the courts. Implied warranty of habitability does not apply to commercial buildings.[28]

In the case of *Winchester Mgt. Corp. v. Staten,*[29] 80 new tenants in an apartment complex refused to pay rent because of failure of the landlord to provide adequate heat and air conditioning during the winter and summer months, respectively. Under Housing Regulations of a municipality, the Court held it may take cognizance of such complaints, and allow setoff against rent for failure to provide agreed-upon services.

In an action by a landlord for unpaid rent, a tenant may defend and setoff the landlord's breach of his continuing obligation to maintain an adequate standard of habitability. The case of *Park Hill Terrace Associates v. Glennon,*[30]J. App. 1977). involved the failure of an air-conditioning unit to function—and whether air conditioning was an amenity or an element of habitability. Here the appellate court held that the air-conditioning failure affected the habitability of the premises, and the tenant was entitled to an abatement of rent.

HABITABILITY VS MINOR TENANTABLE REPAIRS

While the above discussions have established the requirement for the landlord to maintain the premises in a habitable condition, the question of repairs is less clear. The tenant is generally *required* to make tenantable repairs, but he cannot be forced to make lasting and general repairs to the structure which would put the overall property in a better condition than it was when he took possession. The general rule is that there is an *obligation* of the tenant to pay rent and a *covenant* by the landlord to make repairs, each of which are separate and independent. The failure of the landlord to make promised repairs does not automatically discharge the obligation of the tenant to pay rent, unless the landlord evicts the tenant, even partially. If the tenant remains in possession, liability for rent continues.[31]

---

[27]
Blackwell v. Del Bosco, 558 P.2d 568 (1977).

[28]
Granford Realty Corp., v. Valentine, 337 N.Y. 2d 160 (1972).

[29]
Winchester Mgt. Corp v. Staten, 361 A. 2d 187 (D.C. 1976).

[30]
Park Hill Terace Associates v. Glennon, 369 A. 2d 938 (n

[31]
Zion Industries, Inc. v. Loy, 361 N.E. 2d 605 (Ill. App. 1977).

A tenant cannot be bound to make good such deterioration as arise from necessary wear and tear incident to the proper and ordinary use of the property.[32] Most standard lease forms require the tenant to keep the premises in good repair and, at the expiration of the term, "to deliver up the said premises in as good order and condition as the same are now, reasonable wear and tear, and damage by fire or other casualty, not occasioned through Lessee's negligence, excepted."

In the case of *Scott v. Prazma,*[33] the owner leased a 30-year old building, in some disrepair, for 10 years. The lease contained the usual clause in regard to keeping the building in good repair and returning it in a similar condition. After the second year of the lease, the municipality served notice that considerable repairs should be made to the structure for it to comply with the safety code. These repairs would cost a substantial sum. The tenant refused to pay further rent, claiming constructive eviction had occurred. The Court held that the landlord was obligated to make major repairs and that the tenant was justified in moving from the premises.

A LEASING BROKER IS HELD ACCOUNTABLE FOR REPRESENTATIONS

In negotiating a sale of an investment property, the broker is held accountable for any representations made to induce the sale. In the case of *Neff v. Bud Lewis Co.,*[34] the selling broker had managed the apartment building before the sale and had caused the owners to make repairs to the heating and cooling system. He assured the buyers that the repairs had been made and that the system was soundly constructed. After the sale, tenants complained as to inadequate service and the new owners were obliged to make repairs, at a considerable cost. The court held the broker liable, stating that the buyer had a right to rely on the negligent representations of a fiduciary.

Ordinarily there is no obligation upon the landlord to make repairs. If, due to an existing defect, the tenant, a member of his family or an invitee is injured, does the injured party have a right of action against the owner. The general rule of law is that a landlord who is entirely out of possession and control is not liable for an injury sustained by the tenant or by one visiting the tenant, if the defect responsible for the accident was a patent one. The principle of law is well established that, where a tenant rents the entire premises, the owner is not liable for any injury to the tenant or his invitees by reasons of any dangerous condition existing at the time the tenant took possession. "The lessee's eyes are his bargain" and he takes the

[32] Lensing v. Carlisle Motor Sales, Inc. 189, A. 2d 307 (Pa. 1963).

[33] Scott v. Prazma, 555 P. 2d 591 (Wyo. 1976).

[34] Neff v. Bud Lewis Co., 548 P. 2d 107 (N.Mex App. 1976).

property "as is" with all of its existing faults. However, the landlord may be liable depending upon the circumstances in the particular case under an implied warranty of habitability, as heretofore discussed.

A landlord's duty of reasonable care in maintaining property that he controls extends to all lawful visitors on his premises, including the lawful visitors of his tenants.[35] However, he is not required to protect tenants from criminal action by unidentified outsiders or to so secure the premises that no accident can happen—he must exercise due care. Such due care may extend to a tenants dog. In *Strunk v. Stolanski*,[36] a landlord was held responsible for a dog bite by a tenant's dog. The case indicated that the property owner knew of the vicious propensities of the tenant's dog when he leased to him but failed to take reasonable care to protect others on the property. The court stated that it was not holding the landlord to the strict standards which is imposed on the dog's owner, only a duty of *reasonable care*.

A landlord is responsible where he conceals or fails to disclose a dangerous condition of which he has knowledge and one which a tenant was not likely to discover upon examination. A hidden, or latent, defect does impose a liability upon the landlord. He is also liable when he leases premises in a dangerous condition for a public use and he has reason to believe the tenant will not first correct the defect. The lease of a theater or a stadium is in this classification. In other words, where an owner leases public premises which constitute a nuisance, then, whether he is in or out of possession is immaterial insofar as relieving himself of liability is concerned.[37]

A department store or a public garage would not fall in the described category. Although a landlord may not be required to make repairs, if he undertakes repairs voluntarily, he becomes responsible for any accident occasioned by the negligent manner in which the work is performed. Where a landlord has covenanted to repairs and fails to do so, and someone is injured as a result of such failure, the agreement to repair does not operate as a resumption of control by the landlord and he is not liable for the injury.

Of course in an action of assumpsit on the contract, the landlord would be liable for damages suffered by the tenant. He would not be liable in a tort action for negligence. Where a landlord has promised to make repairs as an inducement to the execution of the lease, the tenant should insist that the repairs be written into the lease contract. If verbal only, and if the landlord later refuses to perform, the tenant would run into difficulty in compelling performance under the parol evidence rule.

---

[35] Lindsey v. Massios, 360 N.E. 2d 631 (Mass. 1977); Kosin v. Shero, 360 N.E. 2d 572 (Ill. App. 1977); and Noble v. Worthy, 378 A. 2d 674 (D.C. App. 1977).

[36] Strunk v. Stolanski, 62 N.Y. 2d 572, 468 N.E. 2d 13, 479 N.Y.S. 2d 175 (1984).

[37] Folkman v. Laver, 244 Pa. 605 (1914) and Webel v. Yale University 7A Fd. (Conn. 1939).

LIABILITY DEPENDS UPON POSSESSION

Who is responsible for accidents upon the premises? An owner, out of control and possession is not liable. An owner who rents out a portion of the premises or who rents out separate parts to different tenants is held to remain in possession and control of the sidewalk, stairways and corridors and is, therefore, responsible if any injury occurs in these areas.[38] Where the municipality notifies the owner to repair a sidewalk and an injury occurs before the repairs are made, the owner would be liable.

A mortgagee in possession, who exercises control and dominion over the leased premises is held to occupy the same role as an owner. In order to recover damages, the injured party must establish the existence of a dangerous condition and that the owner *had notice of it.* The claimant must also be free of contributory negligence.

Dangerous conditions include accumulations of ice and snow, a missing brick, an elevation or depression causing an uneven surface, an accumulation of debris concealing an uneven pavement or gutter, an accumulation of oil causing a slippery surface, a hole in the sidewalk, and faulty position of basement outlets or doors to the pavement.[39]

In the case of *Richardson v. Weekworth,*[40] the landlord agreed to repair a broken sidewalk. He failed to do so for several months. The tenant fell, suffering serious injuries. The tenant sued. The landlord's defense was that the defective sidewalk had been in existence for one year, the tenant knew it and, therefore, the tenant assumed the risk, and was guilty of negligence. The landlord was held liable for the tenant's injuries.

Where an owner is sued for injuries, the owner must have had notice of the defective condition. Notice to the owner can be *actual* or *constructive.* Actual knowledge is defined as knowledge of the owner through observation or proximity. Constructive notice is where the defect has existed for such a long time that it will be presumed that the owner saw it or could have seen it with a reasonably frequent inspection of the property. Since the municipality owes a duty of protective safety to its citizenry, the person injured will usually sue the city in the first instance. The city will then bring in the property owner as an additional defendant. The owner, in turn, may bring in the tenant as an additional defendant, if the responsibility appears to lie with the tenant.

COMMERCIAL PROPERTY ADDITIONS, ALTERATIONS, OR IMPROVEMENTS

An important covenant contained in business property leases is one which provides that all alterations, additions and improvements made by the lessee upon

---

[38] Leary v. Lawrence Sales Corp., 442 Pa. 389 (1971).

[39] Geise v. Lee, 519 P. 2d 1005 (Wash. App. 1974).

[40] Richardson v. Weekworth, 509 P. 2d 1113 (Kan. 1973).

the property shall remain until the end of the lease, at the *option* of the lessor. It is frequently also provided that the lessor will have the option of requiring the tenant to restore the premises to their original condition.

The meaning of the terms additions, alterations and improvements have been the source of much friction between lessor and lessee. It is practically impossible to lay down hard and fast rules which would be applicable in all circumstances. The conflicts usually arise between the parties over machinery and other fixtures annexed to the freehold. The tenant claims that such equipment is personalty, trade fixtures, and so on, which may be removed by him at the expiration of the lease term. The landlord contends that such equipment is included in the phrase "alterations, additions, and improvements."

For example, if a tenant leased a store and installed shelving at considerable expense, the landlord would be within his rights in maintaining that such shelving constituted additions, alterations and improvements, and in requiring that it be left upon the premises at the expiration of the lease. On the other hand, if the shelving installed was of little value and would cost more to remove than it is worth, the landlord could insist that the tenant restore the premises to their original condition, in accordance with the terms of the covenant in the lease.

TRANSFER OF THE LEASEHOLD ESTATE

In the absence of a contrary agreement between the parties and incorporated into the lease, the lessee is generally has the legal right to transfer his right of possession to another. Where this power exists, the landlord has little control of who the next tenant will be. Therefore it is often provided that "transfer of the lease is subject to the lessor's approval." Maryland and other states hold that a lease can *absolutely* prohibit assignments and subletting by a "freely negotiated provision" in the lease. However, if the lease does allow such assignments or subletting with the landlord's permission, that approval must be reasonable.[41]

While landlords dislike the lessee's power to transfer his interest, it must be recognized that such power can be very valuable, particularly during an inflationary period. If the tenant sublets his/her interests, the fee may be higher than that called for in the original lease. Thus the original lessee gets an override of the difference in rental paid by the sublessee and the rental called for in the original.

Where the override is substantial and the remaining period relatively long, the lessee may actually gain a substantial "leasehold" interest in the property. For example:

Jones leases a manufacturing building from Smith for a period of 20 years at a monthly rental of $1,000. Five years into the lease Jones'

---

[41] Julian v. Christopher, 575 A. 2d 735 (Md. App. 1990); Robinson v. Weitz, 370 A. 2d 1066 (Conn. 1976); and Stern v. Taft, 361 N.E. 2d 279 (Ohio App. 1976).

business has grown to the point that the facilities are no longer adequate. He subleases the building to Brown for $2,000 per month, which provides him with an override payment of $1,000/mo. Assuming money is valued at 8 percent per annum, the 15 years remaining on the lease would be valued at:

Present Value of $1,000/mo for 15 years @ 8%
or $104,640.59

This Present Value might well exceed the owner's equity in the building.

Transfers of tenant interests can either be assignments or subletting. The rights of the parties vary considerably, depending upon which method of transfer is elected. They are so distinct that some courts will permit an assignment but prohibit subletting. Where the lease prohibits assignment or subletting, the landlord may forfeit his right if he/she accepts rent from the party to whom the property has been assigned or sublet. In order for a tenant to assign his interest in realty, he must transfer *all* of his interest for all of the time remaining. Subletting occurs when a tenant transfers the right to exclusive possession to another for a period shorter than the remaining term of his lease. It is the presence of the tenants reversion that distinguished subletting from assignment.

One should not forget that the owner/landlord has the right and legal power to transfer his interest in rented property. In general, the new owner takes the property subject to the existing lease and rights of the tenants. The new owner is bound by the old leases because, in most cases, he has knowledge of the leases from the presence of the tenants on the property. If the tenants are not on the property, and the buyer is unaware of the lease, when he becomes the new owner, he is usually not bound by the lease agreements.

To prohibit subletting entirely, it is important to provide "or any part thereof." Since the lessor usually prepares the lease instrument, any ambiguities, are most strongly construed against the lessor. A tenant, in subletting, should see to it that the subtenant's rights do not rise higher than his own.

In the case of *Kroger v. Chemical Securities Co.*,[42] a long-term lease between the owner and tenant contained no restriction on assignment or subletting. At the end of the primary term, the tenant sublet the premises to a retail establishment. The landlord preferred to relet the premises to another grocery, or to have Kroger continue in the grocery operation. The trial court and the Court of Appeals held that there was an implied covenant of continual occupation by the tenant. The Supreme Court reversed, holding an implied covenant of continual occupancy was not warranted since there were no specifics covering the lease assignment. The Court also noted that the original lease was negotiated by an expert real estate broker.

---

[42]
Kroger v. Chemical Securities Co., 526 S.W. 2d 468 (Tenn. 1975).

TERMINATION OF THE LEASE

There are several methods of terminating a lease. The most common method, of course, is by performance, that is, the lease expires at the termination date. The lease may also be terminated by a breach of the agreement or by mutual agreement. If terminated, before the end of the lease, the termination is known as *surrender.* Where the landlord is guilty of a violation of the lease, such a breach is termed an *eviction,* which is a violent assertion of a right of the landlord as opposed to the rights of the tenant. In other words, it is an unwarrantable ousting of the tenant by the landlord. Of course the tenant can be legally removed by the court for a breach of his agreements or covenants. Such removal is legally termed an *ejectment.* The distinction between eviction and ejectment rests primarily upon the point of whether the removal was justified. An eviction is a *wrongful* dispossession of the tenant, whereas the action of ejectment is used to establish title to real estate.

EVICTION

In the case of eviction, it must be remembered that the act complained of must be committed by the landlord or an agent representing the landlord or acting for him. The only ground on which a tenant can plead eviction by a third party is when the one whose act he complains of was exercising a right that he secured under a *paramount title to that of the landlord.* For example, if Jackson leased to Finch and afterward it turned out that the title was not vested in Jackson but in Chase, and Chase should proceed to dispossess Finch, the action of Chase would amount to eviction. If, however, the party whose acts were complained of proceeded under a questionable or defective title, the tenant could not plead immunity on the grounds that an eviction has occurred. An overt act committed by a third party is not an eviction in contemplation of law.

Anderson, the owner of a building, had leased the upper wall of the building, for advertising purposes, to Brown for a period of three years. Brown had erected an advertising sign upon the wall which could be seen by people passing in the vicinity. At the expiration of one year, Chambers, the owner of an adjoining building, erected an addition on his building in such a way that the view of Brown's wall was completely hidden and its value for advertising purposes destroyed. Consequently, Brown refused to pay rent on the grounds that an eviction had occurred, but the court disallowed the claim on the grounds that the injury had been inflicted neither by the owner nor by one having paramount title to the wall upon which the advertisement was displayed, but by a third party, over whose action Anderson had no control.

Entry by the city, or repairs ordered by a municipality, would not constitute an eviction. Eviction by the State, under the power of eminent domain, would not sustain a cause of action against the landlord.

Fisk leased certain premises to Martin. They were part of a double house. Crum, the owner of the other half of the dwelling, had the party wall torn down after complying with legal requirements. Martin claimed an eviction and refused to pay rent since he only had three walls on the leased premises. The tenant was held liable for rent.

In another case, Appleby owned certain premises subject to a mortgage in favor of Eastman. Appleby then leased the premises to Crane for five years. Regretting his bargain, and seeking to get rid of Crane, Appleby purchased the mortgage from Eastman and took an assignment in the name of a "straw" party. The assignee then foreclosed and sought to eject Crane from possession. Appleby lost sight of the fact that under his lease to Crane the covenant of quiet possession protected the tenant if the mortgagee asserts his rights to put the tenant out of possession. If the lessor becomes the holder of the mortgage, his exercise of the right of possession would at the same time subject him to a liability for so doing. The same result would follow if he brings action in the name of another (straw party).

A mortgagee in possession must be cognizant of the fact that the mortgagor might pay off the debt during the term of a lease given by the mortgagee to the tenant. In order to avoid this possibility, a mortgagee in possession, when leasing property owned by the mortgagor, should include a provision in the lease as follows:

> The lessee herein understands and agrees that the lessor is executing this lease under rights as mortgagee in possession of said premises and does not in any way or manner, covenant, agree, promise or otherwise guarantee to the lessee, his heirs or assigns, possession, quiet enjoyment or otherwise as against any person having a paramount title or interest in the within leased premises, anything contained in the written lease to the contrary notwithstanding.

However, if the lessee entertains any doubts or suspicions as to the lessor's legal right to lease the premises, he should insist upon a provision that states:

> The lessor hereby certifies and represents that he has full right and authority to make and execute this lease and further certifies and represents that the demised premises are at the time of entering into this lease, free and clear from any mortgage, lien, or other encumbrance, which if proceeded upon, might or could divest this lease.

TENANT'S RIGHTS IN EVICTION

If an actual or constructive eviction occurs and the tenant chooses to terminate the agreement, all of the rent which is past due and payable becomes an obligation which must be settled by the tenant on demand. This action on the part of the tenant terminated any right which the landlord has to demand rent after the date of the eviction. It is important to note that if the landlord should evict a tenant from a portion of the property, the tenant could, on this ground, evade the duty of paying rent on the portion which still remains to him. An eviction by a landlord from part of the premises, is in the eyes of the law, an eviction from all of the property.

An important modification of this rule exists in the case where a tenant is evicted from part of the premises by a paramount title invoked by a third party. In this case, the rent would be apportioned so that he would have to pay rent for that portion of the premises which still remain to him. If, however, the tenant takes the property with knowledge of the defective title of the lessor, it is then impossible for him to plead eviction as a defense against paying rent. After an eviction has occurred and the tenant remains in possession of the premises and takes no action which would indicate that he intends to hold the landlord responsible for the overt act, his continued occupation would constitute a waiver of the injury.

When an eviction occurs, the tenant should promptly assert his rights in the manner. There are two courses which he may pursue: (1) He may terminate the contractual relationship between himself and the landlord by moving out and bringing suit for damages which he has sustained; or (2) he may remain in possession of the premises, and after notifying the landlord of the injury suffered and stating that he will hold the landlord responsible for the damage, he may bring suit for the amount he claims have been lost. In this event, however,it is necessary for him to continue to pay rent in exactly the same manner as though no breach had occurred.

ABANDONMENT OF PREMISES

In the case of *Condor Corp. v. Arlen Development Co.*,[43] the question involved was whether, upon abandonment of the premises by the tenant, the landlord acted in a reasonable manner in his efforts to relet the premises and mitigate the tenant's damages.[44] While reasonable efforts to mitigate the tenant's damages are required, no hard and fast rule applies. Each case depends upon its particular facts as to the extent of the landlord's efforts to find a tenant and the nature of the property involved, including the terms of the lease.

SURRENDER OF PREMISES

Whether a tenant is liable for damages caused by fire, the elements, an act of God, or an inevitable casualty depends upon the language in the lease. If he agrees to return the premises, at the expiration of the lease, reasonable wear and tear alone excepted, he must restore the premises if damaged by fire or other accident. If fire is excepted, the tenant would still be responsible for damages by flood, tornado or other "act of God" or by inevitable accident.

In legal terms, acts of God and inevitable accidents are not synonymous. Even if the cause is sufficiently comprehensive so as to exclude a liability for rebuilding, the tenant would still be liable for the payment of rent, unless there was a clause abating rent. This is the common law rule, but it has been modified by statute in

---

[43] Condor Corp. v. Arlen Development Co., 529 F. 2d 87 (Minn. 1976).

[44] Sommer v. Kridel, 738 A. 2d 767 (N.J. 1977).

some states to the effect that the rent ceases until the property is repaired by the lessor. However if the premises are only partially destroyed by fire and the tenant remains in possession, the rent does not abate. It is not uncommon in a commercial lease to include provision for the abatement of rent due to destruction of the leased premises as follows:

> It is understood and agreed by and between the parties hereto, that if during the term of this lease and any renewal thereof, the building is damaged by fire, act of God, or other casualty so that the demised premises are rendered unfit for occupancy to the extent that said premises cannot be repaired within ninety (90) days from the happening of such injury, then this lease shall cease and determine from the date of the injury. In such case, the tenant shall pay the rent apportioned to the time of injury, and shall immediately surrender the leased premises to the Lessor, who may enter upon and repossess the same. If any such injury can be repaired within ninety (90) days thereafter, Lessor shall enter and repair, and this lease shall not be affected except that the rent shall be apportioned and suspended while such repairs are being made; but if said premises shall be so slightly injured by fire, act of God, or other casualty, so as not to render same unfit for occupancy, then the Lessor agrees that the same shall be repaired with reasonable promptitude, and in that case the rent accrued or accruing shall not cease or determine.

Where the lessee has made extensive repairs at his own expense preparatory to taking possession, his investment should be protected by adequate fire insurance and a clause relative thereto, incorporated into the lease. The lease provision should read, "The proceeds of any fire insurance carried in both the Lessor's and Lessee's names and paid for by the Lessee, shall inure to the sole benefit of the Lessee."

SURRENDER OF THE LEASE

The parties may mutually agree to terminate the lease before the expiration date. This is called *surrender*. It is not necessary that such an agreement be in writing or in any particular form, and no consideration need be included in order to make the contract binding on both parties, the presumption being that the advantage accruing to both parties is sufficient to give full force and effect. In order to make a surrender completed, it is necessary that it be specifically accepted by the landlord.

In the case of *Estate of Wm. O. Barnes, Deceased*,[45] the court held that turning over keys to the superintendent of the building did not constitute a surrender. Proof of acceptance must be clear and explicit.

A lease may be terminated by breach of condition. Where one of the parties violates some important covenant in the lease, the other party may plead such act as grounds for the termination of the contract.

---

[45]
Estate of Wm. O. Barnes, Deceased, 37 N.Y. Misc. 2d 833 (1962).

Gray, owner of a commercial building, operated a shoe store. He later sold the stock and fixtures to Dean, leasing the store to Dean for five years. Dean was unsuccessful in operating the business after six months, and decided to quit. He sold the stock and Gray agreed to buy the fixtures, cash register, and the like, on July 1, 1968. At the end of the day, Dean placed the keys in the cash register and abandoned the premises. Three months later, Gray sued Dean for the intervening month's rent. The court held there was a surrender of the lease since the owner used the premises to store the fixtures.[46]

FORFEITURE

Whereas the tenant has the right to terminate the lease by reason of a landlord's breach of covenant, the landlord has a corresponding right to terminate the lease in the case of a tenant's violation of a material covenant. This is known as forfeiture.

Under the common law, if the tenant should disclaim, disaffirm, or impugn the landlord's title by some positive act, he thereby forfeits all rights under the contract. The reason for this is obvious. If the landlord could not terminate the contractual relationship, it might be possible for the tenant to work great harm against the property, not only by violating the spirit and letter of the agreement but also by going so far as to claim title to the property by adverse possession after continuous occupation for the statutory period. The law, therefore, provides that the landlord has the option of declaring the lease forfeited upon the breach of any material covenant by the tenant. The landlord then has the right to enter and take possession of the property unless it can be shown that he has by some acts waived the breach which has occurred. Suppose for example, that the landlord should accept rent from the tenant for a period subsequent to the acts in controversy; in this case, he would have waived his right to declare the contract forfeited by permitting the tenant to continue in possession. The most usual breach by the tenant is nonpayment of rent.

It is important to note that in this connection that distraint instituted for rent in default constitutes a *technical waiver* of the forfeiture which has occurred and permits the tenant successfully to maintain his right of possession under the terms of the lease. A landlord's levy is one of statutory enactment entirely. Under the common law, the landlord had no lien on the chattels of the tenant on leasing the premises or to the crops raised thereon. They were absolutely property of the tenant. It is in statutory law that the landlord has a method by which he can secure a lien upon the chattels and goods of the tenant. The right to distrain, however, exists in favor of the landlord only upon a claim for rent due and accrued.

---

[46] Sanden v. Hanson, 201 N.W. 2d 404 (N.D. 1972).

Distraint may therefore be defined as the right of the landlord to levy upon a tenant's goods and chattels for rent in arrears. The right does not reside in the landlord until there has been a default in rent, but he can bring this action the day after the rent is due. The case of *Phillips v. Guin and Hunt Inc.*,[47] emphasizes the importance of following exact requirement in an action of distraint. A diligent search and inquiry must be made for personal service, rather than merely posting notice on the premises.

LANDLORD ENTRY IN TENANT'S ABSENCE

Sometimes a landlord or his agent, in the tenant's absence, will change the locks on a dwelling or apartment to prevent the tenant for obtaining reentry. Even though the rent may be delinquent, the landlord cannot take the law into his own hands. In the case of *Edwards v. Investment Co.*,[48] the lease contained a clause that in event of the tenant's default in rent or other provisions of the lease, the landlord may, without notice or demand, terminate the lease and remove, store, or dispose of the tenant's property at the risk and expense of the tenant. The court held that the clause was against public policy and therefore, void. A landlord must resort to law and legal methods, and not resort to self help, to obtain possession of premises, when the tenant fails to make payments.[49]

Where a tenant is temporarily away from the premises, the landlord takes a grave risk when he padlocks the premises and prevents the tenant's re-entry.[50]

SPECIAL CONSIDERATIONS IN APARTMENT LEASING

It is not unusual in leasing a unit in an apartment building to implement the lease contract by a set of rules and regulations, which by reference to them, become a part of the lease proper. The rules are intended to prevent a tenant from becoming obnoxious or a nuisance to other tenants or to the public.

One prohibition, in particular, prohibits the maintenance of any domestic or wild animal in or about the premises except with the written consent of the lessor. In the case of *Margolin et al. v. Richards,*[51] confession for possession was entered against a tenant who kept a small dog in his apartment in a recently completed building. Several tenants complained. The lessee contended that before he signed a lease, the building manager told him that "he might surreptitiously bring the dog in and out the cellar door." The court held that, "There was nothing to indicate the

---

[47] Phillips v. Guin and Hunt Inc., 344 So. 2d 568 (Fla. 1977).

[48] Edwards v. Investment Co., 272 N.E. 2d 652 (Ohio 1971).

[49] Bass v. Boltel & Co., 217 N.W. 2d 804 (Neb. 1974).

[50] Pittman v. Griffith, 200 S.E. 2d 760 (Ga. 1973).

[51] Margolin et al. v. Richards, 70 D & C 380 (Pa. 1949).

manager had any authority to waive any provision in the lease, and, furthermore whatever oral agreements or conversations were made before the signing a contract are merged in the written agreement."

The importance of a lease of an apartment is not to create a tenurial relationship, but rather to arrange the leasing of a habitable dwelling. This means that there are no latent defects in facilities vital to the use of the property for residential purposes and that these essential facilities will remain during the entire term in a condition which will make the property livable.[52] The very object of letting was to furnish the defendant with quarters suitable for living purposes. This is what the landlord at least implied (if not expressly) when he represented he had available what the tenant was seeking. "The warranty of habitability which we hold exists in such case is imposed by law on the basis of public policy. It arises by operation of law because of the relationship of the parties, the nature of the transaction, and the surrounding circumstances."

Adoption of this view makes available to the tenant the basic contract remedies of damages, reformation, and rescission.[53] The tenant can obtain relief by instituting action for breach of warranty or by offsetting his damages against a claim made against him by the landlord.

RENT

One of the characteristics that distinguishes a lease from a license is the payment of rent. Rent may be payable not only in money but in provisions, chattels, or labor. When no time is fixed for the payment of rent in a lease for a term, such as a year, the rent is not payable until the end of the term. If a specified time is provided, the rent is due and payable on that date.

In most cases, the lease contains a clause stipulating that the rent shall be paid monthly in advance. It is considered good practice to insert an express covenant in the lease by which the tenant binds himself to pay the amount agreed upon. This is valuable because of the fact that while an implied agreement can be presumed in all cases for the tenant to pay the agreed rental, yet if there is an express covenant and the tenant should subsequently assign the lease, even with the lessor's consent, the first tenant would be liable for the rent. The only way in which he can be relieved from this responsibility is by the formal release by the landlord of the tenant.

This practically amounts to the cancellation of the first lease and the creation of a second agreement with the new tenant. If the tenant is of questionable financial responsibility, a landlord can protect himself by insisting that the tenant provide a satisfactory surety to guarantee the terms of the lease; or the landlord may require the tenant put up a substantial sum of money as evidence of good faith, which shall be applied to the rent for the last several months of the lease term.

In the case of *Martinique Realty Corp. v. Hull*,[54] tenant had made advance

---

[52] Marini v. Ireland, 265 A. 2d 526 (N.J. 1970).

[53] Lemle v. Breeden, 51 Hawaii 426 (1969).

[54] Martinique Realty Corp. v. Hull, 166 A. 2d 803 (N.J. 1960).

payment of rent for the full term. The property was sold during the term. The court held that it was the duty of the purchaser to ascertain the lease arrangement, and that he was bound by the prepaid rentals.

It is also good practice to insert a clause in the lease of an apartment or furnished house, that all or part of said deposit may be used by the lessor to compensate home for any damage caused by the lessee to the furniture or premises during his occupancy.

A landlord may estop himself from insisting upon the punctual payment of rent where he has indulged a tenant in accepted rent after the due date. Suppose the lease from Adams to Brown provides for the payment of rent on the first day of every month during the term of the lease from May 1990 to April 30, 1991. Brown pays the May rent on the first day, but after that he makes his rent payments anywhere from the 15th to the 25th of the month. In October 1990, Adams could not distrain for the months rent on October 2, because of his previous conduct in accepting the rent late. The doctrine of estoppel could be invoked against him. In order to insert his right to punctual payment of rent, it would be necessary for Adams to notify Brown of his intention to hold him to punctual payment of rent in the future.

The lessee need not tender payment in money when he has on previous occasions tendered a check which was accepted as payment. If the landlord desires to insist upon payment in cash, the lessee is entitled to notice. Where rent is delinquent and the tenant makes a partial payment, the payment generally will be applied to the rent which first accrued. Rent paid "on account" will not give rise to the presumption that it was paid for the current period. The lessor may apply it to the most delinquent rent. This rule, of course, may be modified by agreement between the parties.

Where lessee paid all overdue rent before receipt of notice to quit, lessor had no right to terminate the lease for failure to make timely payment of rent.[55]

SECURITY DEPOSITS

It is a general practice in urban areas for the landlord to require the tenant to pay a full month's rent as a security deposit upon signing a lease for an apartment. This deposit is in addition to a month's rent, which the landlord may require as a guarantee for payment of rent during the term of the lease. The security deposit is normally applied to the last month's rent. The security deposit is held by the landlord until the tenant vacates the apartment. It is intended to reimburse the landlord for any damage to the premises during the tenant's occupancy. The tenant

---

[55] Village Development Co. Ltd. v. Hubbard, 214 N.W. 2d 178 (Iowa 1974).

will also be charged, as an offset to the deposit, for any expenses incurred by the landlord in "cleaning up" the premises or in obtaining a new tenant during the unexpired term of the lease.[56] It also acts as an incentive to the tenant to keep the premises in good order, reasonable wear and tear excepted.

In Utah renters of residential properties are protected by a law that restricts the landlord's use of cleaning and security deposits.[57] Landlords using a written lease may not treat any portion of the deposits as nonrefundable, unless the tenant is given written notice at the time the deposit is taken. In addition, the landlord who retains a portion of the deposit for damages to his property above normal wear and tear, or for other expenses, is required to give a written itemization of the deductions to the tenant. A lessor who fails to give the itemization within 30 days of termination will usually be required to return the full deposit.

The question arises—who is entitled to interest on the security deposit held by the landlord during the term of the lease, which may be renewed from year to year? The Illinois law provides that the lessee is entitled to four percent interest upon the deposit money held for more than six months. The New Jersey law provides that interest be paid to the tenant, less one percent to the landlord for administration expense. In the absence of a statute, the lease should contain a provision as to which party is entitled to the interest on the deposit money.

OPTION AND FIRST RIGHT OF REFUSAL CLAUSES

Where a lease contains an "option" clause, the lessee has the privilege of purchasing the leased premises at a *specified* price, during the term of the lease. The lessee knows exactly what price he must pay. In a lease with a "right of first refusal" clause, the lessee has the right to meet any bona fide offer made by a third party for the purchase of the leased premises. It differs from an option in that the lessee does not know what the price offered will be.[58]

In an option the time element is the very essence of the contract. An option *expires* if not exercised within the time limit. In the case of *Cities Service Oil Co. v. National Shawmut Bank of Boston, Adm. et al.*,[59] the lessee had an option to purchase leased property during the 10-year term, expiring August 31, 1959. A letter purporting to exercise the option was mailed to the lessor in Boston from

---

[56]
    Pyrimid Enterprises, Inc. v. Amadeo, 294 N.E. 2d 713 (Ill. App. 1973).

[57]
    Utah Code Ann. 57-17-1 to 57-17-4 (Supp. 1981).

[58]
    King v. Dalton Motors, Inc. 109 N.W. 2d 51 (Minn. 1961); LoCicero v. Demers, 186 N.E. 2d 604 (Mass. 1962) and Hamel v. Altman, 317 N.Y.S. 2d 722 (1971).

[59]
    Cities Service Oil Co. v. National Shawmut Bank of Boston, Adm. et al., 172 N.E. 2d 104 (Mass. 1961).

New York on August 31, 1959, at 8:30 P.M. It was received by the lessor on September 1, 1959. The court held that the mailing in New York "at such a late hour was not a proper giving of notice." The court held in effect that it is the majority rule that notice to exercise an option is effective only upon its *receipt* by the parties to be notified, unless the parties agree otherwise (citing numerous cases).

In *Schlussberg v. Rubin et al.,*[60] the court held that a lease provision, giving the lessee first refusal to renew the lease at a price *to be agreed upon,* or meet a bona fide offer, was not definite and certain, and was, therefore unenforceable. A case of similar tenor is *Playmate Club Inc. v. Country Clubs, Inc.*[61] In accord, was *Milles v. Bloomberg.*[62]

EFFECT OF BANKRUPTCY ON A COMMERCIAL LEASE

A forfeiture clause in a commercial lease, because of the tenant's bankruptcy, was declared unenforceable in the case of *Queens Blvd. Wine and Liquor Corp. v. Blum.*[63]

EFFECT OF A MORTGAGE ON A LEASE

Where a lease antedates a mortgage, the mortgagee takes the property subject to the lease if the mortgage is foreclosed at a later date. The lease cannot be terminated. In order for the mortgage to have precedence, it would be necessary to stipulate in the lease that it is subject and subordinate to any mortgage or record or which may at any time be placed on the property. The tenant should have the right to pay any delinquency on the mortgage and apply such payments to the rent obligation.

Ordinarily, a mortgage placed upon the premises before the execution of a lease would have priority through foreclosure. This is true even though the mortgagee accepts rents from the tenant during a period prior to foreclosure, when the former was mortgagee in possession. In other words, his rights as *owner* are separate and independent from his rights as *mortgagee in possession.*

LIMITATIONS ON THE LANDLORD'S RIGHTS

Under former landlord authority, which still applies to other than residential properties, the landlord was free to select his own tenants, renew their leases or

---

[60] Schlussberg v. Rubin et al., 435 S.W. 2d 226 (Tex. 1971).

[61] Playmate Club, Inc. v. Country Clubs, Inc., 462 S.W. 2d (Tenn. 1970).

[62] Milles v. Bloomberg, 324 N.E. 2d 207 (Ill. App. 1975).

[63] Queens Blvd. Wine and Liquor Corp. v. Blum, 503 F. 2d 202 (N.Y. 1974).

refuse to renew and to evict tenants whose tenancy was terminated. Modern court decisions are placing some restrictions on these rights.

For instance in the case of *Colon v. Tompkins Square Neighbors, Inc.,*[64] it was held that a landlord cannot reject a tenant on the sole ground that the tenant was a welfare recipient.

Where any public body is the landlord, the tenant's tenancy cannot be terminated without a hearing and inquiry into the reasonableness of the termination.[65]

THE RISE OF TENANT UNIONS

Because one tenant has little bargaining power with the landlord, tenant unions have been formed in some areas of Florida and other highly urban areas. These organizations engage in collective bargaining with landlords, much in the same manner as labor unions with their employers.

Tenant goals in organizing usually include such items as:

- Negotiations of new leases for individual tenants.
- Development of grievance procedures and plans for arbitration of disputes.
- Recognition of the unions as sole bargaining agents for the tenants.
- Participation of tenants in decisions on rent increases.
- Security within the areas.

Where these unions are properly organized and operated, they can be of benefit to the landlords as well as the tenants. From the tenants' viewpoint, they have some authority to negotiate with their landlord on points of interest. From the landlord's viewpoint, tenant participation is most likely to foster better landlord-tenant relations.

---

[64] Colon v. Tompkins Square Neighbors, Inc., 294 F. Supp. 134.

[65] Thorpe v. Housing Authority, 393 U.S. 268.

10

Valuation and Appraisal of Real Property

PROPERTY VALUATION, THE HEART OF THE REAL ESTATE INDUSTRY

Accurate and professional property evaluation is considered the very heart of the real estate industry. Financing for sales is dependent upon a healthy and vigorous financial market, which in turn depends upon professional appraisers to protect the investments of financial institutions as mortgagees. The training and certification of these professional appraisers in the past was primarily assumed by various professional appraisal organizations who established their own training procedures and requirements for member designations. Some of these organizations were very meticulous in setting their requirements, courses of study and experience for award of designations. Others, were more lenient and awarded their designations based only on as little as an expression of interest in the profession along with the necessary fee. Almost none of the states required a state license to practice the art of real estate appraising, and control of the practitioners was left entirely to the industry itself.

Although most banks, mortgage companies and savings and loans demanded that their carefully selected appraisers meet the training and experience qualifications of the recognized appraisal organizations, the work of these professionals lacked any form of government supervision. Lenders, who were anxious to put their cash to work, were often guilty of hiring less qualified appraisers or those who were relied upon to provide "numbers" which would justify a desired loan.

The savings and loan crisis in the mid-1980s and the resultant congressional attention to the problem revealed some rather embarrassing statistics. A brief summary of a report of the Committee on Government Operations, entitled "Impact of Appraisal Problems on Real Estate Lending, Mortgage Insurance, and Investment in the Secondary market," September 25, 1986, will serve to highlight the situation. The report stated in part:

> Faulty and fraudulent real estate appraisals have become an increasingly serious national problem. Their harmful effects are widespread, pervasive, and costly. They have seriously damaged and contributed directly to the insolvency of hundreds of the Nation's financial institutions and have helped cause billions of dollars in losses to lenders, private mortgage insurers, investors and Federal insurance funds.
>
> Hundreds of savings and loans chartered by the FHLBB or insured by the FSLIC have been severely weakened or declared insolvent because faulty and fraudulent real estate appraisals provided documentation for loans larger than justified by the collateral's real value.
>
> Two thrifts studied in depth by the subcommittee—the Sunrise Savings and Loan Association of Florida and the Community Savings and Loan of Maryland—were found to have failed in a large part due to appraisal problems and abuses, with resultant appraisal-related losses estimated at more than $300 million.

Several private appraisal organizations recognized that legislation was inevitable and, deeming themselves best qualified to assist the Congress in enacting efficient and workable solutions, formed The Appraisal Foundation, a self-funded nonprofit organization consisting of seven of the leading appraisal trade organizations. Their goal was to assist members of the Congress in the drafting and passing of appropriate legislation, which became Title XI of the Financial Institutions Reform, Recovery and Enforcement Act (FIRREA). This act was signed into law by President George Bush on August 9, 1989.

Due to the excellent work of the foundation's various Committees and the confidence of the Congress in the foundation's ability to assist in regulating the appraisal profession, The Appraisal Foundation was given a leading role in implementation of FIRREA.

The following brief summary of Title XI as implemented throughout the United States is as follows:

THE APPRAISAL FOUNDATION

A nonprofit organization of the appraisal industry consisting of seven private appraisal trade organizations (The Appraisal Institute,[1] American Society of Appraisers, American Society of Farm Managers and Rural Appraisers, International Association of Assessing Officers, International Right of Way Association, National Association of Independent Fee Appraisers, and National Society of Real Estate Appraisers) and six real estate-related organizations. It is directed by a Board of

---

[1]
   An organization formed by the merger of the American Institute of Real Estate Appraisers and the Society of Real Estate Appraisers, effective January 1, 1991.

Trustees, which appoints two independent boards: the *Appraisal Standards Board* (ASB) and the *Appraiser Qualifications Board* (AQB). Title XI of the Financial Institutions Reform, Recovery and Enforcement Act (FIRREA) delegates to the Foundation the authority to:

(1) promulgate appraisal standards for State certified and licensed appraisers,

(2) promulgate appraisal qualifications for state certified and licensed appraisers, and

(3) issue or endorse an examination for state certified appraisers.

The act also requires federal financial institutions to adopt appraiser qualifications criteria and appraisal standards that are at least equivalent to those promulgated by the Foundation or higher.

In accordance with the provisions of FIRREA, Title XI mandates that "...real estate appraisals utilized in connection with federally related transactions ... (be)... performed in writing, in accordance with uniform standards, by individuals whose competency has been demonstrated and whose professional conduct will be subject to effective supervision." It is estimated that this requirement will affect 85 percent of all real estate transactions.

Legislation, as of this time, has been passed in all of the 50 states; however, the time for implementation by all states has been extended to July 1, 1992. Under these legislation, two levels of appraiser qualification are established:

STATE CERTIFIED APPRAISER

State certified appraiser is an individual who has satisfied the requirements for state certification in a state whose certification program has been approved by the Appraisal Subcommittee of the Financial Institutions Examination Council, which is responsible for administering the Federal Appraiser's Act. Such programs must provide for qualifications criteria (education, experience, and so on) appraisal standards, and certification examinations at least equivalent to hose promulgated the Appraisal Foundation. The State Certified Appraiser is entitled to perform appraisals of all types of real estate, regardless of size or complexity in federally related transactions.

STATE LICENSED APPRAISER

A state licensed appraiser is an individual who has satisfied the requirements for state licensing in a state whose licensing program has been approved by the Appraisal Subcommittee of the Financial Institutions Examination Council. State licensed appraisers are not subject to the qualifications criteria promulgated by the Appraisal Foundation, but the Subcommittee must approve the adequacy of the state licensing requirements in order for state licensed appraisers to be eligible to be included on the Federal Registry. A State licensed appraiser is entitled to perform, in federally related transactions, appraisals of single family residential properties consisting of 1-4 units (unless the size and complexity of the appraisal requires a state certified appraiser), and any other properties which the Appraisal Subcommittee may, by rule, prescribe.

Although requirements for state licensing do not include membership in any of the various appraisal trade organizations, past experience of most lenders, in selecting their appraisers, tends to give heavy weighting to those *who have been awarded the coveted designations* of Appraisal Foundation members.

APPRAISAL DESIGNATIONS

It is not possible to discuss the various roles of all of the members of the Appraisal Foundation, their requirements for designations and various designations awarded; however, a brief discussion of The Appraisal Institute is in order.

The Appraisal Institute was formed on January 1, 1991 by the merger of the Society of Real Estate Appraisers (SRA), originally organized in 1935 and the American Institute of Real Estate Appraisers (AIREA), organized in 1928. Prior to the consolidation of the AIREA and the SRA the following designations were in effect:

AIREA—Residential Member (RM)
Member of the Appraisal Institute (MAI)

SRA—Senior Real Estate Appraiser (SRA)
Senior Real Property Appraiser (SRPA)
Senior Real Estate Analyst (SREA)

Awarding the RM, SRPA and SREA designations ceased as of the effective date of the merger, January 1, 1991. Former RM members were awarded the designation SRA, SRPA members with over three qualified years of experience were awarded the MAI designation, while SRPA members with less than three years experience continue to hold the SRPA designation for the next 10 years or until they qualify as MAIs. SREA members who received their designations prior to April 30, 1989 were awarded the MAI designation.

The designation of SRA indicates that the recipient has attended all of the designated courses of instruction and successfully passed the required examinations, and in addition has acquired the actual experience necessary to appraise residential properties up to and including 4-unit structures. The SRPA and MAI designations indicate the holder is fully qualified to appraise *all* real properties. These are the Institute's highest designations.

PROFESSIONAL STANDARDS OF THE APPRAISAL FOUNDATION

The Uniform Standards of Professional Appraisal Practices, as adopted by the Appraisal Foundation is the Standards of the Appraisal Institute, with the following supplemental standards:[2]

1. The Uniform Standards of Professional Appraisal Practice shall apply to all activities of a Member Candidate involving analysis, opinion, or conclusion relating to the nature, quality, value, or utility of specified interests in, or aspects of, identified real estate.

2. The form of certification used by a Member or Candidate in a written report that contains an analysis, opinion, or conclusion relating to the nature, quality, value, or utility of specified interests in, or aspects of, identified real estate must include a statement indicating compliance with the Code of Professional Ethics and Uniform Standards of Professional Appraisal Practice and a statement advising the client and third parties of the Appraisal Institute's right to review the report. The form of certification used by a member or Candidate in a written report that contains an analysis, opinion or conclusion relating to the nature, quality, value or utility of specified interests in, or aspects of, identified real estate must be include a statement indicating the current status of the Member under the Appraisal Institute's continuing education program.

BASIC CONCEPTS OF VALUATION

Even though they may not qualify as expert appraisers, brokers and salespeople should be familiar with the theoretical concepts of value, the forces which influence values and the methods by which such values may be best estimated. Such knowledge is essential in arriving at a logical solution as to the most profitable use of the property.

Almost on a daily basis, the real estate broker is asked by clients about the fair market value, a fair price, a fair rental, a fair basis of trade, or proper insurance coverage for their property. The real estate practitioner needs to know how to answer these questions intelligently. In fact, he cannot be successful in his business unless he can determine whether he can profitably spend his time in trying to sell a property at a listing price suggested by the owner. In this regard, he must keep in mind that in accepting a listing he obligates himself to put forth his best efforts to find a buyer for the property.

In the following discussions of valuation concepts, it is assumed that the reader is familiar with most of the technical jargon used. For those readers who are less familiar with these terms, most of these terms are briefly defined in Appendix A.

2
Extracted from: *Final Plan Of Unification Of The American Institute Of Real Estate Appraisers And The Society Of Real Estate Appraisers, October 15, 1989.*

VALUE DESIGNATIONS

There are many kinds of value. They may, however, be divided into two main classifications: (1) *Value in Use* or that special value to the owner or user (usually referred to as the *subjective value*) and (2) *Market Value* or the value in exchange. This is the value at which a property can be sold or exchanged at a given time or place as a result of the balancing of market forces. It is primarily based on the "willing buyer" and "willing seller" concept. This is truly an *objective value*.

Generally, when the term property value is used, the reference is to what is called "Market Value" or "Fair Market Value". Fair Market Value is defined as:

> The most probable price a property will bring in a competitive and open market under all conditions requisite to a fair sale. This would include the buyer and seller each acting prudently, knowledgeably, and the assumption that the price is not affected by undue stimulus. Implicit in this definition is the consummation of a sale as of a specific date and the passing of title from seller to buyer under conditions whereby:
>
> a. Buyer and seller are typically motivated;
> b. Both parties are well informed or well advised, and are each acting in what he/she consider his/her best interests;
> c. A reasonable time is allowed for exposure in the open market;
> d. Payment is made in terms of cash in U.S. dollars or in terms of financial arrangements comparable thereto; and
> e. The price represents the normal consideration for the property sold unaffected by special or creative financing or sales concessions granted by anyone associated with the sale.[3]

Among the other various types of value that are used from time to time are book value, tax value, cash value, capital value, speculative value, par value, true value, exchange value, insurance value, investment value, rental value, and cost value.

Value can be distinguished from cost as well as from price. The principal differences may be explained as follows:

a. Value has to do with the combined factors of present and future anticipated enjoyment or profit. The value sought in an appraisal of property may be said to be the present worth of all desirable things (benefits) which may accrue from a skillful use of it. A conclusion in regard to these things will clearly be a matter of opinion—an intelligent estimate based on the thorough analysis of all available influencing factors and on reasonable and more or less warranted assumptions.

b. Cost represents a measure of past expenditures of labor, materials, or sacrifices of some nature. While cost may be, and frequently is, a factor upon which value is partially based, it need not be, as it does not control present and future value. An example of this is an oil well, which in one case may prove to be a big

---

3

Blankenship, Frank J., *Prentice Hall Real Estate Investors Encyclopedia,* Prentice Hall, Englewood Cliffs, N.J., 1989, p 195.

producer and of great value, while in another case may prove to be a dry hole and of no value, although both may have cost the same to develop or drill.

c. Price is what one pays for a commodity. Usually it is considered to be the amount of money involved in the transaction. Whether we receive in value more or less than what we pay for it will depend on the soundness of the judgment in appraisal of value, or upon fortuitous future developments. Under an efficient market structure, prices will usually tend to equal values, varying only as buyers and sellers have unequal knowledge or economic strength.

FACTORS INFLUENCING VALUE

In the valuation of real property, the appraiser must consider a number of factors in reaching his final estimation. These include:

1. *Directional Growth*—In an estimate of value attention must be paid to the city's directional growth. The city directional growth refers to the manner and direction in which the city tends to grow. Properties in the direction of growth tend to increase in value with time, especially if the growth is steady and rapid.

2. *Location*—This includes access. This factor of valuation in commercial property is often measured by traffic counts, which in turn, have to be interpreted in purchasing power as well as volume of traffic. A property *must* have access by street, right-of-way, easement, alley or other means to have value. And old REALTOR® saying is that the three most important factors affecting the value of a residence are: (1) location, (2) location, and (3) location.

3. *Utility*—This is the capacity to satisfy a need or desire. This important factor involves judgment as to the best use to which a given property may be put, considering codes, zoning, and other public restrictions which affect its utility.

4. *Size*—This includes width and depth as well as overall size. Two properties of equal size may not have the same utility. A square lot might have many uses, whereas a long thin commercial lot might have use only for an arrow factory or a one-lane bowling alley as salespeople laughingly say.

5. *Shape*—Not only width and depth but overall shape is important. Parcels of land with irregular shapes cannot usually be developed as advantageously as rectangular parcels.

6. *Thoroughfare Conditions*—The width of streets, traffic congestion, condition of pavement, divided, lanes and location vs. traffic flow are important. For instance, convenience stores prefer the "going home" side of the street to make it easy for the driver to stop off for a needed commodity.

7. *Business Character of the Area*—Cities tend to develop enclaves of similar businesses. The character of the area will tend to limit the usefulness to some occupations.

8. *Social Atmosphere*—The quality of the neighborhood is important in both commercial and residential neighborhoods. It is a paramount consideration in residential.

9. *Plottage*—This is the added value of several parcels of land when brought together under one ownership making it possible to achieve a higher utility than when separately owned. This is synergism at work.

10. *Character of the Soil*—This is all important in agricultural property but also may be important as a consideration in construction costs.

11. *Grades*—Another important factor in cost of construction or limitations on types of buildings that can be constructed.

12. *Obsolescence*—A form of depreciation. It consists of two major types "Economic" and "Functional." Functional obsolescence is caused by changes in materials, designs, and interior arrangement. Economic obsolescence is due to factors outside the property itself. While functional obsolescence may be curable at some price, economic obsolescence is rarely curable.

13. *Appreciation*—A trend of rising costs, labor, materials, and land which cause the value of the property to increase at a rate which exceeds depreciation.

THE FOUR GREAT FORCES INFLUENCING VALUE

The value of real estate is created, maintained, modified, and destroyed by the following four great forces. These determinants are interdependent and in a constant state of change.

1. *Social Ideas and Standards*—Examples of social forces include: population growth and decline, marriage, birth, divorce, and death rates, attitudes towards education, recreation and other instincts and yearnings of mankind.

2. *Economic Adjustments*—Examples of economic forces include: natural resources, industrial and commercial trends, employment trends, wage levels, availability of money and credit, interest rates, price levels, tax loads, and so on.

3. *Political Climate*—Examples of political forces include: building codes, zoning laws, public health measures, fire regulation, government guaranteed loans, government housing, credit controls, and so on.

4. *Physical Forces*—Examples of physical forces include: climate and topography, soil fertility, flood control, mineral resources, soil erosion, subsurface conditions, and so on.

THE APPRAISAL FORMAT

Depending upon the type of property being appraised, the purpose of the appraisal and the property value, one of two formats is selected by the appraiser: (1) the simple form appraisal, or (2) the narrative type. By far the largest percentage of the appraisals are prepared on the various residential forms.

The Uniform Appraisal Report—An example of a residential appraisal utilizing this form, known both as Freddie Mac Form 70 and Fannie Mae Form 1004, is shown as Figure 10-1 (page 322). It utilizes some concepts of the three major approaches to value—cost, market, and income—but places its main emphasis on the market comparison portion of the report. In prior years the appraiser typed required information onto a blank form and then submitted the required number of copies to his employer. Today, almost all appraisers are utilizing computers, computer software, and laser printers which allow the appraiser to call up the form on his screen, fill in the necessary data and conclusions and then print both form and data on the laser printer. Normally included with the form appraisal are floor plans of the residence, three pictures (front, back and street scene), and the appraiser's certificates and other supplemental data.

While many organizations have their own forms, most tend to follow the basic outline of the forms shown in Figures 10-1 and 10-2. Usually the differences are noted in additional data required for that organization's special considerations.

The Narrative Report—Wherever the appraisal will require a more detailed report than that possible with the fixed form, the narrative report is used. These may vary in length from 10 to as many as 100 or more pages, depending upon the complexity of the data to be considered. The narrative form usually follows the following outline:[4]

- Purpose of the Appraisal
- Limitations of the Appraisal
- Identification of the Subject Property
- Owners of Record
- Statement of Highest and Best Use
- Ownership Plat
- Regional, City and Neighborhood Data
- Site Data
- Location Map
- Market Approach to Value
- Cost or Replacement Approach to Value
- Income Approach to Value

---

[4] Blankenship, Frank J., *The Prentice Hall Real Estate Appraisal Deskbook,* Prentice Hall, Englewood Cliffs, N. J., 1986, pp. 270-290.

- Reconciliation and Final Estimate of Value
- Assumptions and Limiting Conditions
- Certifications
- Appraiser Qualifications and Experience
- Appraiser's Status under the Institute's Continuing Education Program
- Property Photos

The appraisal is usually permanently bound to prevent unauthorized duplication and is accompanied by a letter of transmittal and invoice of services rendered.

DEFINITION OF AN APPRAISAL

To appraise means to arrive at an estimate of the "value of the property", as defined by the appraiser, of a parcel of real property as of a specific date and for a specific purpose. It is a conclusion which results from the analysis of *facts*.

Real estate appraising is slowly becoming more standardized by virtue of the experience and approved practices followed by those, in all parts of the country, who encounter the same types of valuation problems, and who follow approved procedures in the process, to arrive at logical conclusions, based upon the facts and the appraiser's experienced analysis. The appraisal of real estate is part science and part art. If it was all science, one would expect no difference in two appraisals of the same property. In practice it is quite natural that differences of opinion exist as to the value of a particular parcel of real estate; however, it is rather amazing that two or more appraisers, with similar experience and training, and utilizing different market data, will arrive at quite similar values.

METHODS OF APPRAISING PROPERTIES

It is generally accepted that there are three methods or approaches to a value estimate. These three methods or types of approaches are:

1. *The Comparison or Market Data Approach* in which a comparison of the subject property is made with a number (at least 3) of similar properties recently sold. The selling price is adjusted for differences, plus and minus, with the subject to arrive at a comparable value.

2. *The Cost Approach* in which the present-day cost to reproduce the subject property is calculated, after which a deduction is made for accumulated depreciation to date and the resulting value added to the current land value, which is determined by the market or other recognized approach.

3. *The Capitalization or Income Approach* where value is estimated on the basis of its relationship (capitalization rate) to the net income which the property produces or ought to produce.

If at all possible, the skilled appraiser will utilize all three approaches in appraising a given property. No single approach, by itself, can always be depended upon to produce reliable results. The appraiser will give different weighting to each of the values obtained based upon his understanding of which approach is most likely to provide the most accurate answer. The type of property being appraised and the availability or lack of certain pertinent data may well eliminate one or more approaches that would otherwise be the dominant or best choice selections for properties of the type being appraised. In other instances, proper procedures may call for a partial or appropriate full discounting of conclusions drawn from some data.

Each method or approach is used independently to reach an estimated value. In most appraisals, all three methods will have something to contribute. Normally, it can be expected that one approach will be most highly weighted in the determination of *the* value.

As a final step, by applying to each separate value a weight proportionate to its merits in the particular instance, a logical conclusion can be reached as to the most likely true value. This analysis and weighting is known as the correlation and final estimate of value, and it is in this final step that the experience and training of the appraiser is most evident.

THE MARKET APPROACH

This approach is most generally adaptable for use by real estate brokers and salespersons, who have ready access to current sales and statistics, published by the various multilist organizations. This approach lends itself well to the appraisal of land, residences, and other buildings that exhibit a high degree of similarity and normally have a ready market. It also serves as an excellent check on values obtained by other methods of appraising all types of properties in which the market value is the end result being sought.

The mechanics of the process involves the use of market data of similar properties sold compared to the subject property being appraised. The sources of such data are actual verified sales prices, listings and other pertinent data together with an analysis of social and economic factors affecting marketability.

This information is obtained directly from sellers, the statistics of REAL-TOR® multilisting networks, official records, the appraiser's own collection of current sales data and the sharing of statistical data among appraisers in the local area.

Listing data is useful in indicating the top value, which can be expected, while bid prices may indicate the possible lowest values. Offers are more likely to approach market values than listings, which only indicate "what we would like to get" rather than actual values. Listings are often only an attempt to test the market.

Property Description & Analysis — **UNIFORM RESIDENTIAL APPRAISAL REPORT** — File No. ABC010192

Property Address	1234 S. American Avenue
Census Tract	1035

SUBJECT

City	Salt Lake City
County	Salt Lake
State	UT
Zip Code	84115
Legal Description	Lot #3, USA Sub No. 1
Owner/Occupant	Jane Doe
Map Ref.	7160-184
Sale Price $	48,000	Date of Sale	March, 1992
Loan charges/concessions paid by seller $	
R.E. Taxes $	480.00	Tax Year	1991	HOA $/Mo.	n/a
Lender/Client	XYZ Mortgage Services
	#1 State Street Plaza/Salt Lake City, UT 84000

PROP RIGHTS APPRAISED: X Fee Simple / Leasehold / Condominium (HUD/VA) / De Minimus PUD

LENDER DISCRETIONARY USE

Sale Price	$
Date	
Mortgage Amount	$
Mortgage Type	
Discount Points and Other Concessions	
Paid by Seller	$
Source	

NEIGHBORHOOD

LOCATION	X Urban	Suburban	Rural	
BUILT UP	X Over 75%	25-75%	Under 25%	
GROWTH RATE	Rapid	X Stable	Slow	
PROPERTY VALUES	Increasing	X Stable	Declining	
DEMAND/SUPPLY	Shortage	X In Balance	Over Supply	
MARKETING TIME	Under 3 Mos.	X 3-6 Mos.	Over 6 Mos.	

PRESENT LAND USE %		LAND USE CHANGE	PREDOMINANT		SINGLE FAMILY HOUSING		
Single Family	65	Not likely	X OCCUPANCY		PRICE $(000)	AGE (yrs)	
2-4 Family	20	Likely	Owner	65% X	30 Low	25	
Multi-family	13	In process	Tenant	35% X	75 High	90+	
Commercial		To:	Vacant (0-5%)	X	Predominant		
Industrial			Vacant (over 5%)	X	50-60 40-50		
Vacant	2						

NEIGHBORHOOD ANALYSIS:

	Good	Avg.	Fair	Poor
Employment Stability		X		
Convenience to Employment		X		
Convenience to Shopping		X		
Convenience to Schools		X		
Adequacy of Public Transportation		X		
Recreation Facilities		X		
Adequacy of Utilities		X		
Property Compatibility		X		
Protection from Detrimental Conditions		X		
Police & Fire Protection		X		
General Appearance of Properties		X		
Appeal to Market		X		

Note: Race or the racial composition of a neighborhood are not considered reliable appraisal factors.

COMMENTS: Subject is located in an older residential neighborhood of Salt Lake City about 2-3 miles southeast of downtown. This area has adequate schools w/public busing provided as reqd, has a good selection of parks and churches, and is within minutes of all the cultural and shopping amenities of downtown. Zoning allows up to low-density apartments.

SITE

Dimensions	57.1 x 67.5 (plat attached)
Site Area	3,854 sf / 0.09 acres
Corner Lot	no
Zoning Classification	Residential R-3A / apts
Zoning Compliance	yes
HIGHEST & BEST USE: Present Use	yes	Other Use	
Topography	flat/street grade
Size	typical/see plat
Shape	rectangular
Drainage	appears adequate
View	typical neighbrhood
Landscaping	mature/typical
Driveway	concrete
Apparent Easements	usual utility
FEMA Flood Hazard	Yes* / No XX
FEMA* Map/Zone	490105 0033 A/C

UTILITIES	Public	Other	SITE IMPROVEMENTS	Type	Public	Private
Electricity	X		Street	paved asphalt	X	
Gas	X		Curb/Gutter	concrete	X	
Water	X		Sidewalk	concrete	X	
Sanitary Sewer	X		Street Lights	mercury vapor	X	
Storm Sewer	X		Alley	none	O	

COMMENTS (Apparent adverse easements, encroachments, special assessments, slide areas, etc.): Flood Map dated 8-1-83/excerpt att/in Zone C/minimal flooding hazard. No apparent adverse easements/encroachments, usual utility easements. Small fenced back yard with mature landscaping, detached single-car garage.

IMPROVEMENTS

GENERAL DESCRIPTION

Units	1
Stories	1
Type (Det/Att)	detached
Design (Style)	bungalow
Existing	yes
Proposed	
Under Construction	
Age (Yrs.)	apx 60 yr
Effective Age (Yrs.)	30 years

EXTERIOR DESCRIPTION

Foundation	concrete
Exterior Walls	fr/vinyl
Roof Surface	asph shng
Gutters & Dwnspts.	aluminum
Window Type	wood DH
Storm Sash	none
Screens	partial
Manufactured House	no

FOUNDATION

Slab	
Crawl Space	
Basement	yes/shelf
Sump Pump	no
Dampness	none obs
Settlement	typical
Infestation	inspect
	minor/typical settling obsv

BASEMENT

Area Sq. Ft.	522 sf
% Finished	none
Ceiling	no finish
Walls	no finish
Floor	no finish
Outside Entry	no
	basement has low overhead no finish

INSULATION

Roof	
Ceiling	unk
Walls	unk
Floor	
None	
Adequacy	avg
Energy Efficient Items:	newer furnac
	avg/typical

ROOMS

ROOMS	Foyer	Living	Dining	Kitchen	Den	Family Rm	Rec. Rm.	Bedrooms	# Baths	Laundry	Other	Area Sq. Ft.
Basement									1	stg		522
Level 1	rear	1	kitchen	1				2	1			989
Level 2												

Finished area above grade contains: 4 Rooms; 2 Bedroom(s); 1 Bath(s); 989 Square Feet of Gross Living Area

INTERIOR

SURFACES	Materials/Condition
Floors	cpt/vinyl/avg
Walls	plaster/wlltex
Trim/Finish	paint/avg
Bath Floor	vinyl/avg
Bath Wainscot	ceramic/avg
Doors	l-panel/paint
	all items in average condition

HEATING	
Type	WFA
Fuel	gas
Condition	new
Adequacy	good
COOLING	
Central	none
Other	none
Condition	

KITCHEN EQUIP	
Refrigerator	O
Range/Oven	X
Disposal	O
Dishwasher	O
Fan/Hood	O
Compactor	O
Washer/Dryer	O
Microwave	O
Intercom	O

ATTIC	
None	
Stairs	X
Drop Stair	
Scuttle	X
Floor	
Heated	
Finished	
	no finish

IMPROVEMENT ANALYSIS

	Good	Avg.	Fair	Poor
Quality of Construction		X		
Condition of Improvements		X		
Room Sizes/Layout		X		
Closets and Storage		X		
Energy Efficiency		X		
Plumbing - Adequacy & Condition		X		
Electrical - Adequacy & Condition		X		
Kitchen Cabinets - Adequacy & Condition		X		
Compatibility to Neighborhood		X		
Appeal & Marketability		X		

Fireplace(s): mirror/antiqe 1

AUTO

CAR STORAGE:

Garage	X
No. Cars	1
Condition	avg
Carport	
None	
Attached	
Detached	X
Built-in	

Adequate	X House Entry
Inadequate	Outside Entry
Electric Door	Basement Entry

Estimated Remaining Economic Life: 30-35 Yrs.
Estimated Remaining Physical Life: 35-40 Yrs.

Additional features: Wood shutters in living room, levelor-type blinds in other rooms, mirrored fireplace with antique cover in living room, wall coverings, new gas forced-air furnace. Laundry facilities in shelf basement which is unfinished.

COMMENTS

Depreciation (Physical, functional and external inadequacies, repairs needed, modernization, etc.): Subject is in average condition with no significant amounts of deferred maintenance/minor settling noted. House is a typical older but livable floor plan located in an older but still desirable residential neighborhood, no functional or locational inadequacies noted.

General market conditions and prevalence and impact in subject/market area regarding loan discounts, interest buydowns and concessions: MLS statistics indicate local market activity is up 13-18% above previous year, is expected to remain strong if interest rates continue at current moderate levels. Houses in area mostly financed with FHA/conventional loans. See att sheet for rates/points charged by sample of local lenders.

Freddie Mac Form 70 10/86 — "TOTAL" appraisal software by a la mode, inc. 1 (800) 328-6825 — Fannie Mae 1004 10/86

Figure 10-1

Valuation Section   **UNIFORM RESIDENTIAL APPRAISAL REPORT**   File No.

Purpose of Appraisal is to estimate Market Value as defined in the Certification & Statement of Limiting Conditions.

COST APPROACH	

BUILDING SKETCH (SHOW GROSS LIVING AREA ABOVE GRADE)
If for Freddie Mac or Fannie Mae, show only square foot calculations and cost approach comments.

(See attached sheet for floor plan sketch of main and basement levels)

MAIN LEVEL: 25.0 x 36.5 =   912.50 sf
            2.5 x 7.5 =   18.75
            4.0 x 14.5 =   58.00
         Total (rounded):   989 sf

ESTIMATED REPRODUCTION COST - NEW - OF IMPROVEMENTS		
Dwelling	989 Sq. Ft. @ $ 42.00	$ 41,538
bsmt	522 Sq. Ft. @ $ 10.00	5,220
Extras floor coverings/appl		2,700
fireplace		1,200
Special Energy Efficient Items	included	
Porches, Patios, etc.		600
Garage/Carport	242 Sq. Ft. @ $ 14.00	3,388
Total Estimated Cost New		$ 54,646
Less	Physical	Functional	External
Depreciation	16,394		1,639	$ 18,033
Depreciated Value of Improvements		$ 36,613
Site Imp. "as is" (driveway, landscaping, etc.)		$ 2,000
ESTIMATED SITE VALUE		$ 10,000
(If leasehold, show only leasehold value.)		
INDICATED VALUE BY COST APPROACH		$ 48,613

(Not Required by Freddie Mac and Fannie Mae)

Does property conform to applicable HUD/VA property standards?   ☐ Yes   ☐ No

If No, explain:

Construction Warranty	☐ Yes ☒ No
Name of Warranty Program	none appraiser is aware of
Warranty Coverage Expires	n/a

The undersigned has recited three recent sales of properties most similar and proximate to the subject and has considered these in the market analysis. The description includes a dollar adjustment, reflecting market reaction to those items of significant variation between the subject and comparable properties. If a significant item in the comparable property is superior to, or more favorable than, the subject property, a minus (-) adjustment is made, thus reducing the indicated value of subject; if a significant item in the comparable is inferior to, or less favorable than, the subject property, a plus (+) adjustment is made, thus increasing the indicated value of the subject.

ITEM	SUBJECT	COMPARABLE NO. 1		COMPARABLE NO. 2		COMPARABLE NO. 3	
Address	1234 S. American Ave Salt Lake City	500 E Cleveland Ave 1440 South		1500 South 600 East		500 E. Kensington Avenue/1505 South	
Proximity to Subject		2 blocks E		4 blocks SE		2 blocks SE	
Sales Price	48,000		55,600		46,900		55,500
Price/Gross Living Area	48.53	54.19		58.19		48.68	
Data Source	Inspection	MLS closed sale		MLS closed sale		MLS closed sale	
VALUE ADJUSTMENTS	DESCRIPTION	DESCRIPTION	+ (-) $ Adjustment	DESCRIPTION	+ (-) $ Adjustment	DESCRIPTION	+ (-) $ Adjustment
Sales or Financing		FHA sale		FHA sale		FHA sale	
Concessions		no concessns		no concessns		no consessns	
Date of Sale/Time	March, 1992	12-30-91		10-10-91		2-10-92	
Location	E SL City/av	E SLC/eql		E SLC/eql		E SLC/eql	
Site/View	0.09 ac/avg	0.15 ac/eql	-1,000	0.17 ac/eql	-1,500	0.10 ac/eql	
Design and Appeal	bungalow/avg	bungalow/eql		bungalow/eql		bungalow/eql	
Quality of Construction	fr/vinyl/avg	brick/eql		fr/asbestos	+2,000	brick/eql	
Age	apx 60 yr	apx 60 yr		41 years/eql		apx 60 yr/eq	
Condition	good/avg	good/avg/eql		good/avg/eql		good/avg/eql	
Above Grade	Total : Bdrms : Baths	Total : Bdrms : Baths		Total : Bdrms : Baths		Total : Bdrms : Baths	
Room Count	4 : 2 : 1	5 : 2 : 1		4 : 2 : 1		5 : 2 : 1	
Gross Living Area	989 Sq. Ft.	1,026 Sq. Ft.	-700	806 Sq. Ft.	+3,700	1,140 Sq. Ft.	-3,000
Basement & Finished	522 sf	1026 sf	-2,500	806 sf	-1,500	700 sf	-1,000
Rooms Below Grade	no finish	bedroom	-500	BR/FR	-1,000	bedroom	-1,000
Functional Utility	avg/typical	avg/typ/eql		avg/typ/eql		avg/typ/eql	
Heating/Cooling	WFA/new	WFA/new/eql		WFA/newer		WFA/evap ac	-500
Garage/Carport	garage/det/1	garage/det/1		gar/1/cpt/1	-500	carport/2/eq	
Porches, Patio, etc.	porch	porch/eql		prch/cov pto	-500	porch/eql	
Pools, etc.	landscp/fnce	lndsc/fnc/eq		lndsc/fnc/eq		lnd/fnc/spkl	-500
Special Energy	avg/typical	avg/typ/eql		avg/typ/eql		avg/typ/eql	
Efficient Items	ceiling fan	storm windw	-500	eql extras		eql energy	
Fireplace(s)	fireplace/1	fireplace/1		fireplace/1		fireplace/1	
Other (e.g. kitchen equip., remodeling)	ORDsp minor update	eql appl eql updates		eql appl eql updates		eql appl eql updates	
Net Adj. (total)		☐+ ☒- $	5,200	☒+ ☐- $	700	☐+ ☒- $	6,000
Indicated Value of Subject			$ 50,400		$ 47,600		$ 49,500

Comments on Sales Comparison   All sales located in older Salt Lake City neighborhoods within 4 blocks of subject, all adjusted within guidelines. Superior interior of #3 is offset by condition of its roof which will soon need to be replaced. All 3 sales are valid indicators of value

INDICATED VALUE BY SALES COMPARISON APPROACH			$ 48,500
INDICATED VALUE BY INCOME APPROACH (If Applicable) Estimated Market Rent $	n/a /Mo. x Gross Rent Multiplier	n/a	= $ n/a

This appraisal is made ☒ "as is" ☐ subject to the repairs, alterations, inspections or conditions listed below ☐ completion per plans and specifications

RECONCILIATION	

Comments and Conditions: Appraisal made as-is, subject is in good/avg condition/no repairs reqd. There is insufficient rental data in area/price range to support income approach.

Final Reconciliation: In the local market the cost approach tends to set the upper limit of value. In this instance the cost approach valuation is nearly the same/strongly supports the value conclusion of the direct sales comparison approach which is most reliable indicator of value.

This appraisal is based upon the above requirements, the certification, contingent and limiting conditions, and Market Value definition that are stated in

☐ FmHA, HUD, &/or VA instructions.
☒ Freddie Mac Form 439 (Rev 7/86)/Fannie Mae Form 1004B (Rev 7/86) filed with client   attached 19

I (WE) ESTIMATE THE MARKET VALUE, AS DEFINED, OF THE SUBJECT PROPERTY AS OF   March 20,   19 92 to be $ ☒ attached   48,500

I (We) certify: that to the best of my (our) knowledge and belief the facts and data used herein are true and correct; that I (we) personally inspected the subject property, both inside and out, and have made an exterior inspection of all comparable sales cited in this report; and that I (we) have no undisclosed interest, present or prospective therein.

APPRAISER(S)	REVIEW APPRAISER
Signature	Signature (If applicable)
Name Joe Jones, Fee Appraiser	Name

                 ☐ Did ☐ Did Not Inspect Property

Freddie Mac Form 70 10/86   Fannie Mae 1004 10/86

Figure 10-2

The actual procedure for application of the market approach is basically:

- A collection of actual sales data of properties similar to, closely comparable, and in the same general area as the subject.
- Selection of a number of the best comparables for use in the final evaluation.
- Adjustment of each comparable for differences plus and minus that of the subject.
- Selection of the most likely fair market price from the adjusted values of the selected comparables.

THE ADJUSTMENT PROCESS

The adjustment process can be best explained by the following example. The appraiser is attempting to determine the market price of a frame residence of 1000 s.f., located in an area of similar homes built by the same builder 25 years ago. He has determined that a home, 2 lots from the subject, has recently been sold for $45,000. This home is quite similar to the subject property with the following exceptions:

1. The sold property has a 2-car garage located on the rear of the lot, whereas the subject has only a 1-car garage.

2. The sold property has only 1 bathroom, whereas the subject has 1 and 3/4 baths.

The rule for adjusting a sold property to compare with the subject is "make the comparable look like the subject." This means that the larger garage, of the sold property, must be price-reduced (a negative adjustment) to compare with the subject and the subject's extra 3-4 bath must be added (a positive adjustment) to the sold value of the comparable. The appraiser determines that the extra garage space is valued at $1,500 and the extra 3/4 bath is valued at $1,000. The adjustments to the sold property are:

Garage	−1,500
Bath	+1,000
Net Adj.	− 500

The adjusted value of the sold property is therefore $45,000 − $500 or $44,500.

Referring to Figure 10-1, we see in the Sales Comparison Analysis that this appraiser has made several adjustments to each of his selected comparable sales with the resultant adjustment for the three properties of -5,200, +700 and -6,000. When these adjustments are applied to the actual sales prices, the results are adjusted values of $50,400, $47,600, and $49,500. The appraiser's opinion, based on these three sold adjusted properties is that the fair market value of the subject is $48,500.

Where did the appraiser get this number? It is slightly less than the average of the three adjusted sales ($49,167), slightly more than the adjusted #2 sale, but less than the #3 adjusted sale. Here the appraiser's experience, knowledge of the local area, and examination of current offerings in the area are combined to determine the opinion of value. There is no cut and dry method of value determination. All we can say from looking at the data is that the subject property cannot be valued higher than $50,400 (#1 Value) or less than $47,600 (#2 Value). The actual and best number obviously lies somewhere between these two extremes.

The above simplified explanation of the market approach tends to hide the great expertise required to make accurate adjustments, to select those adjustments that actually make a market price difference and to selectively omit those items that do not make a difference. Also, the dollar evaluation of these differences requires much knowledge and experience. The difference on new properties is easy to determine from actual cost data, but older attributes are far more difficult to evaluate accurately.

Some of the advantages of the market comparison approach are:

• It is the simplest of the various methods to learn and to use. The factor of economic obsolescence of the neighborhood is more or less automatically included in the use of nearby comparables.

• It is particularly applicable for appraisal purposes involving the sale, exchange, and loan transactions of single family residences. These make up the great bulk of real estate sales. It is a valuable check against the values obtained by other methods.

Some of the disadvantages of the market approach are:

• Its reliability can be greatly reduced by the lack of suitable comparisons. These must be adequate in number, reliable as to source and sufficiently current to justify reasonable conclusions.

• Scattered comparisons may exaggerate or disregard special influences that have an effect on market value.

• Individuals using this approach frequently neglect to make comprehensive inspections to get a true comparison of values among the properties used in the comparison and the subject being appraised.

THE COST APPROACH

In the cost approach only the improvements on the land are involved in the calculations. The value of the land must be obtained by other methods. In estimating the cost of reconstruction of the improvements, on the date of the appraisal, the appraiser may estimate either the reproduction or replacement costs. There are advantages and disadvantages to both methods.

Reproduction cost is the cost of faithfully reproducing the improvements precisely as they are. However, due to changes which constantly occur in methods of construction, materials, and design, since the subject building was erected, reproduction cost will usually include a measure of functional obsolescence, which must be considered in estimating overall depreciation. The older the building, the more obsolescence of this type will occur.

Replacement cost, on the other hand, is the cost of replacing the building being appraised with one having equivalent utility and amenities. It is the cost of erecting a building of its type, using the design, materials, and construction methods normally in use as of the date of the appraisal. Substituting modern construction features for the obsolete ones in the building being appraised eliminates the need for estimating functional obsolescence. On the other hand, it is open to criticism that, although it does represent how this building would be erected on the date of the appraisal, it is not the actual building being evaluated. This criticism is particularly applicable if the building being appraised has considerable age.

The replacement method may be the only one of the two cost methods possible. If one were to appraise a 100-year-old cathedral, it would be impossible to utilize the reproduction cost approach. Even though the original plans were available, the original materials and construction methods would not.

The important fact to remember in the use of one of these two methods is that the value obtained must reflect the principle that people will not ordinarily pay more for a property than it would cost to duplicate in its present condition on the date of the appraisal.

The appraisal procedure using the cost approach is as follows:

• The value of the land is determined, usually by the market comparison approach. This value is always the current market value of the land, considered as vacant and available for improvement to its highest and best use. The value is seldom related to the actual cost when purchased.

• The value of the improvements can be determined, from available data, by either the "component method" or the "value in place." The component method takes into account the cost of each component part—walls, roofs, installed utility systems, and so on— in order to determine the total value, whereas the value in place uses figures representing the total value per square or cubic foot for the class of building being appraised. Obviously the latter method is simpler to use, however certain aspects of the component method must be utilized to adjust for differences in the "standard" building and the subject. For instance, the standard building might include refrigerated air conditioning, where as the subject employed the evaporative type of cooling. The difference in the two costs would be used as a negative adjustment to the subject property.

Cost figures are obtainable from local contractors or from any of several appraisal services such as Marshall and Swift[5] or the Boeckh Manual, published by Boeckh Publications.[6] Most professional appraisers prefer to use the professional publications as they are adjusted monthly and for each local area in the U.S.

---

[5] Marshall & Swift Publications Company, 1617 Beverly Blvd., Los Angeles, Ca. 90026. (213-624-6451).

[6] Boeckh Publications, a Division of American Appraisal Associates, 525 E. Michigan Ave., Milwaukee, Wisconsin, 53201 (414-271-7240).

The nominal yearly charges for these publications are far less than the expense of maintaining locally acquired figures.

- Determine the accrued depreciation from all causes, physical, economic, and functional. This figure must be subtracted from the cost calculations in order to obtain the current value. A value, determined by the cost approach is no more accurate than the estimate of accrued depreciation. There is no justification for assuming that the improvements have depreciated in direct relation to age. In this respect it is interesting to note that buildings rarely depreciate in a straight line method. We are reminded that buildings with an expected lifetime of 50 years may often have considerable utility left at the end of that time period.

Depreciation is estimated in "effective" age rather than "chronological" age. We have all seen homes that are 10 years old that look like they are 30 years old and others that are 30 years old that look 10. Good preventive maintenance and tender loving care (TLC) go a long way in reducing effective depreciation.

The cost approach is particularly appropriate for appraising newly build structures, where depreciation is nominal. It is also appropriate for public service properties, such as schools, churches, hospitals, and libraries. These have no active market and there is no income, actual or potential, upon which an income or capitalization approach could be based.

THE INCOME APPROACH

The income approach is concerned with the present worth of future benefits of property. This method is particularly important in the valuation of income producing property, although it can rarely be used as the only approach. The value obtained is usually measured by the net income which a fully informed person is warranted in assuming the property will produce during its remaining useful life. An exception to this method is where gross income may be used in lieu of net in the appraisal of multifamily residences by use of the gross-rent multiplier. We will discuss more about this method later in the chapter.

The procedure used in the capitalization or income approach is basically three steps.

1. A net income is derived, preferably over a number of years, by deducting total expenses from gross income. Unless the income has been rather constant, it is important that the trend in income and expenses be taken into account in forecasting future income. The existence of currently excessive income would indicate the possibility of real competition in the early years and some reduction in the future.

2. A selection or calculation of an appropriate capitalization rate or present worth factor. This is all important and critical to an accurate value computation.

The rate is dependent upon the return that the average investor would demand on an investment of the required amount and type of risk. The risk is two-fold: (1)

the risk of whether the capital will be returned, and (2) the risk of a proper return on the investment. A small error in estimating the capitalization rate will result in a large error in the value, where the formula is:

$$\text{Value} = \text{Income} \div \text{Rate}$$

3. The calculation of the property value, using the previously calculated net income and capitalization rates.

> *Example*—A certain property is found to have a net annual income of $50,000 per year. If a capitalization rate of 10 percent (.10) is assumed the value is $50,000 ÷ .10 = $500,000. However, if a rate of 9 percent (.09) was assumed in error, the value of the property would be shown to be $50,000 ÷ .09 = $555,555. If the rate was assumed to be 11 percent (.11) the value would be $50,000 ÷ .11 or $454,545. In summary, an error of 1 percent plus or minus would result in a price deviation of $555,555 − $454,545 = $101,010.

It will not be possible to discuss the methods of calculating capitalization rates as they are quite complicated and often utilize the concepts of present and future values of money. Regardless of the value utilized by the appraiser, the appraisal reviewer should carefully analyze the methodology of computation, the reasonableness of assumptions used, and the source of data used. An appraisal by the income approach which uses a capitalization rate, which is not supported by current market data is suspect, to say the very least. Too often, an inexperienced appraiser will just select a rate, which when divided into the income, produces an approximate value as that found by some other method.

An important element in the capitalization rates is the provision for a return *of* and as well as a return *on* the investment. The return of the investment is called "recapture." It may be provided for by straight-line depreciation, which recovers an equal amount each year for the useful life of the property or by other methods such as sinking funds.

In the hands of those who are familiar with its use, the capitalization technique may be helpful in determining the underlying land value "land residual process" or the building value "building residual process." Where the overall value of the property is known and either the land value or building value determined, the missing item (land value or building value) may be calculated.

An error frequently committed by even the experienced appraiser is the failure to realize that the land parcel is larger than that required to sustain the income calculated. Where this situation exists, the excess land should be separately evaluated and its value added back to the value obtained by the income approach. This correction assumes that if the excess land were sold, the building and remaining land would continue to produce the same income as before the sale.

Errors are also frequently made in the calculation of the net income, where the appraiser fails to realize that the expense figures, usually furnished by the owner, fail to include such items as accurate vacancy factors, on-site management expenses, lack of reserves for future redecoration and equipment replacement and a failure to charge the project for owner-furnished maintenance and management time. On the plus side of the ledger, owners often forget to include miscellaneous income derived from coin-operated laundry equipment or rental of excess parking spaces.

GROSS MULTIPLIERS

In the evaluation of small rental properties, such as duplexes and 4-plexes, it is often impossible to get reliable net income data on market sales; however, the gross income and sales figures are usually quite reliable. Gross income multipliers are calculated by dividing comparable property sales prices by their gross annual or monthly income to obtain a *gross multiplier.* Where this procedure is done for a reasonably large number of recent sales and the average value of these gross multipliers calculated, that multiplier times the subject property's income will produce a very good estimate of market value.

Example—In evaluating a duplex the appraiser found that 10 duplex buildings were sold in the local area in the past three months. The gross annual income multipliers are calculated as a low of 9.1 to a high of 10.5 with the average multiplier being 9.8. The subject property, being appraised has an annual rental income of $12,000. The estimated value is therefore:

$$\$12,000 \times 9.8 = \$117,600$$

DEPRECIATION

Depreciation includes all of the influences that reduce the property value below its new replacement cost. The principal influences which affect the property value are often grouped under three general headings as follows:

1. Physical deterioration, resulting from:
   a. Wear and tear from normal use.
   b. Negligent care (deferred maintenance).
   c. Damage by dry rot, termites, and so on.

2. Functional obsolescence, resulting from:
   a. Poor or obsolete architectural design and style.
   b. Out-of-date equipment.
   c. Lack of modern facilities.

3. Economic obsolescence, resulting from:
   a. Misplacement of improvements.

b. Zoning and/or legislative restrictions.
c. Detrimental influence of supply and demand.
d. Change of locational demand.

The first two groups are considered to be inherent within the property itself. The third group of influences consists of economic and social influences which are extraneous to the property itself.

Accrued depreciation may be classified as either curable or incurable. The latter classification includes those instances that would require complete replacement or excessive repair costs, thus making correction of depreciation uneconomical. Accrued depreciation may be estimated in three ways: (1) the observed method in which the total depreciation is usually determined by establishing the total cost to make all required repairs to correct curable physical deterioration and functional obsolescence, plus the estimated loss in value due to incurable physical deterioration and functional economic obsolescence; (2) the age-life method, based on depreciation tables, such as that shown in Figure 10-3.[7] (These tables have been developed to reflect age-life experience in the depreciation of structures of various types and uses, assuming average care and maintenance); and (3) a method used by appraisers as a by-product of the capitalization approach to value, known as the building residual technique (previously discussed).

ACCRUAL OF DEPRECIATION

Future depreciation or recapture is the loss in value, which has not occurred but will come in the future. It is of significance in the capitalization of income method. In the income approach, accrued depreciation in based on the remaining economic or useful life during which time provisions are made for the recapture of the value of the improvements. It is the return "of" investment as differentiated from the return "on" investment (interest and profits). Under the income approach the depreciation is measured by one of two methods. These are:

Straight-Line Depreciation, in which a definite sum is deducted from the income each year during the total economical life of the building, which will provide funds to replace the capital investment.

Sinking-Fund Method, which also includes a fixed annual deduction from income, but at a slightly lesser amount than the straight-line method. These yearly reserves are assumed to be invested at a compound interest rate, at which the total future value will exactly equal the amount required to replace the capital investment. This method is more sophisticated than the straight-line method in that it recognizes that annual deductions for depreciation can be invested to produce additional income. In short, it is the amount, deposited each year at interest, which will grow to the value of the improvement at the end of its useful life.

---

[7]
Blankenship, Frank J., *The Prentice Hall Real Estate Appraisal Deskbook,* Prentice Hall, Inc., Englewood Cliffs, N. J., 1986, p. 197.

DEPRECIATION —
COMMERCIAL PROPERTIES

EFFECTIVE AGE IN YEARS	70	60	55	50	45	40	35	30	25	20
				DEPRECIATION – PERCENTAGE						
1	0	0	0	0	1	1	1	2	2	3
2	0	1	1	1	1	2	2	3	5	7
3	0	1	1	1	2	3	4	5	7	10
4	1	1	1	2	3	4	5	7	10	14
5	1	1	2	3	4	5	6	9	13	18
6	1	2	2	3	4	6	8	11	16	22
7	1	2	3	4	5	7	10	14	19	26
8	1	2	3	5	6	8	11	16	22	30
9	2	3	4	5	7	10	13	18	25	35
10	2	3	4	6	8	11	15	21	29	40
11	2	4	5	7	9	13	17	24	32	45
12	2	4	6	8	10	14	19	26	36	50
13	2	5	6	9	12	16	22	29	40	55
14	3	5	7	10	13	18	24	32	44	60
15	3	6	8	11	14	20	26	35	48	65
16	3	7	9	12	16	22	28	39	52	69
17	4	7	10	13	18	24	31	42	56	73
18	4	8	11	14	19	26	34	46	60	76
19	4	9	12	16	21	28	36	49	64	78
20	5	9	13	17	23	30	39	53	68	79
21	5	10	14	18	25	32	42	57	71	80
22	6	11	15	20	27	35	45	60	73	
23	6	12	16	21	29	37	48	63	75	
24	7	13	17	23	31	40	52	66	77	
25	7	14	19	25	33	43	55	69	79	
26	8	15	20	27	35	46	58	72	80	
27	9	16	21	28	37	49	61	75		
28	9	17	23	30	40	52	64	77		
29	10	18	24	32	42	54	68	78		
30	11	20	26	34	45	57	72	79		
32	13	22	30	38	50	62	75	80		
34	15	25	34	43	55	68	77			
36	17	28	38	48	61	73	79			
38	19	32	42	53	67	77	80			
40	21	35	46	59	72	79				
42	25	39	51	65	75	80				
44	28	43	56	70	77					
46	31	48	60	74	78					
48	34	53	64	77	79					
50	38	58	68	79	80					
55	48	67	75	80						
60	57	74	78							
65	65	78	80							
70	71	80								
75	75									
80	78									

Figure 10-3

Recapture of depreciation is recognized as a proper charge against the income of investment property, used in trade or business. Such deductions are not authorized by IRS regulations for residential property, unless such property is used for rental income. The rate of depreciation authorized varies from time to time as well as the method of depreciating the property. Depreciation is calculated in several different ways, straight-line, sum-of-the-digits, double-declining-balance, and so on. Normally, the investor will choose the authorized method that returns the most money as fast as possible. Depreciation for tax purposes is more fully covered in Chapter 11.

RECONCILIATION AND FINAL ESTIMATE OF VALUE

In this final part of the appraisal, the appraiser brings under consideration all of the value estimates that he has made by the various approaches and draws his final conclusion as to the market value of the appraised property as of the date of the appraisal. All three major appraisal approaches do not lend themselves to all property types. Some property, such as land, can only be appraised by the market approach or by the land residual method if the total property value is known or can be calculated as well as the improvement value. Income properties, such as office buildings may be appraised by all three methods; however, it is recognized that the income and market values are most accurate. Public use properties, however, may be best appraised by the cost approach.

The appraiser's thinking may be best understood in the following example:

The appraiser has just completed his calculations of value for a one-year old 12-unit apartment house. He has obtained the following values by the various approaches:

Cost of Replacement	$450,000
Market	$430,000
Income	$440,000

He recognizes that the income approach must be quite accurate as he was able to obtain very reliable information in regards to income and expenses. His capitalization rate was derived from a large number of recent local sales of similar properties. He is also quite confident of the market value that he arrived at, since it was based on very reliable market sales data.

He mentally rejects the cost value obtained, since he was cognizant that it was possible to err in his assumptions of accumulated depreciation. But most of all, he knows that in the current real estate market, no one is likely to pay much more than the going market rate, even though the subject apartment has considerable appeal due to its location and design.

His consideration is now basically one of deciding whether the market value or the income value is *the value*. Since he feels equally confident in the accuracy of his market and income calculations, he concludes that the current Fair Market

Value lies somewhere between these two numbers and sets the value at the average of the two—$435,000.

USING THE PROFESSIONAL APPRAISER

Professional appraisers are used in a variety of real estate related tasks. The following is a partial list of those types of tasks which may require their services:[8]

LOANS
1. First and second mortgage.
2. Construction loans.
3. Mortgage buy-back and defaults.

INSURANCE
1. Acquisition of hazard insurance.
2. Damage assessment covered by insurance.

BUSINESS
1. Purchase evaluations.
2. Buy-sell agreements between partners/associates.
3. Employee transfer assistance.
4. Transfer of properties between closely held corporations and principals.

ESTATE PLANNING AND TAXATION
1. Establishment of living trusts.
2. Gifts of property and gift tax calculations.
3. Estate taxation and probate.

LITIGATION
1. Condemnation actions.
2. Property damage due to action of others.
3. Contract disputes.
4. Land boundary problems.

PROPERTY SALES
1. Listing of properties.
2. Proposed trades.
3. Sales subject to appraisal.

GOVERNMENT OPERATIONS
1. Tax assessments.
2. Purchases for public use.

---

[8] Blankenship, Frank J., *The Prentice Hall Appraisal Deskbook,* Prentice Hall, Inc., Englewood Cliffs, N. J., 1986, pp. 257-258.

A brief review of the above list would indicate that all appraisers, even though highly qualified, are not qualified to make all of these types of appraisals. One would scarcely dare to hire an excellent real estate appraiser to represent him in a condemnation proceeding, if that appraiser had little or no court experience. Similarly, one would question the ability of a good real estate appraiser to do an adequate job at small business evaluation. He might do a good job on the property, but can he evaluate the company's equipment and the good will developed over the years? To do a good job, he will need to have extensive training in accounting as well as appraising.

Appraisers are more likely to be generalists than specialists. If your job is a specialized one, make sure that the appraiser selected is:

- a state certified appraiser (the highest license),
- a designated member of one of the better appraisal trade organizations,
- a specialist in your type of job, and
- able to provide client references—make sure you check them.

SUMMARY

In concluding this chapter in concepts, valuation, and appraisal techniques, let us wave three warning flags. It is to be noted that there is no real difference between the words *valuation* and *appraising*. The first is broader in concept, tends to be economic in origin and emphasizes theory; where as the latter refers more to practice, methods, and techniques. Anybody can make an appraisal, even a layperson, but the worth of an appraisal report is determined by the experience, qualifications, and the motives of the person behind it. And finally, let us not be deceived by any broad statements that appraising is an exact science. It is a science tempered with the artistry of the appraiser. It perhaps could be classed as a *social science,* but people and property cannot be appraised with the exactness and accuracy reached by the mathematical and physical sciences.

Recently REALTOR® organizations and the real estate industry in general have frowned upon the use of the term *appraisal* when performed by anyone other than a licensed appraiser. The recommended term for evaluations performed by real estate personnel is Market Analysis.

11

Finance and Tax Considerations

THE VALUE OF MONEY

Before beginning to plan for the future, you must have an understanding of the present and future concepts of money as applied to the consideration of compound interest. Compound interest is nothing more than interest on interest. For instance, if you deposit $1 in a bank at 8 percent per annum compound interest, that dollar will grow to $1.47 at the end of five years. Similarly $1 deposited at the beginning of each year at 8 percent per annum compound interest will grow to a value of $5.87 during the same period.

However, if you are expecting to receive $1 five years in the future and the interest rate is 8 percent per annum, the present value of that future receipt is only $.68. Stated another way $.68 at 8 percent compound interest will grow to $1 in five years.

The values of various sums deposited or received in the future at various interest rates is easily calculated with any of the numerous financial calculators now available at minimum cost. The only problem with their use is where you put in a wrong number, the answer is wrong and you really won't know the difference unless you thoroughly understand the principles of present and future values.

This chapter will give the reader a good understanding of the basics. To more easily explain the uses, we will utilize tables rather than calculators. In that way, you will be able to see just what happens from year to year, within the limitations of the tables, of course. Four basic tables are required:

- Figure 11-1: the Present Value of $1 received at the end of various periods.
- Figure 11-2: the Present Value of $1 per period received at the end of those periods.
- Figure 11-3: the Future Value of $1 received at the end of the period.

- Figure 11-4: the Future Value of $1 per period received at the end of various periods.

Financial calculators provide us with thousands of tables. We can have any percentage, and any time period. We are not limited to the few periods and percentages shown in our demonstration tables.

PRESENT VALUE OF $1 RECEIVED AT THE END OF A PERIOD

Looking at Figure 11-1 we find that interest rates from 2 percent to 28 percent are listed across the top of the table and the period from 1 to 45 is listed on the left. To find a value, say 12 percent at the end of 5 years, one merely enters the 12 percent column and comes down to the 5 period to find a factor of 0.567. We say "factor" because it is just that. The table percentages are actually "percentage of interest per period" and the period is the number of times the money is compounded. In our example, we will assume that the period is years (compounded once per year) and the interest is per annum. If the money to be received is $1 and the factor we found was 0.567, then the factor is $1 × 0.567 or about 57¢. Had we wanted to compound twice a year at a 12 percent per annum rate, we would use (2 × 5) or 10 periods and (12% ÷ 2) = 6% in which case the factor would be 0.558 or about 56¢.

The important concept about $1 *received in the future* is:

- The higher the interest rate the less valuable the future receipt is at present, and

- The longer we must wait (time period), the less valuable the future receipt is at present.

Since money is always worth something to us (interest rate), the longer we wait and the more valuable it is the less a receipt in the future is worth. Again looking at Figure 11-1 we find that $1 received 10 years from now with money valued at 10 percent is worth only 39¢. In this case the "bird in the hand" is worth almost three in the bushes (10 years hence).

PRESENT VALUE OF $1 PER PERIOD RECEIVED AT THE END OF EACH PERIOD

Figure 11-2 is a useful tool for calculating the value of a number of payments to be received at the end of several periods. This would be represented by a promise of someone to pay a certain amount at the end of each year for a number of years. While $10 at the end of each year for 10 years sounds like $100. It isn't near that if we are able to earn, say 8 percent per annum on our investments. Referring to Figure 11-1, we find that the factor for $1 per period at 8 percent interest is only 6.710 × $10 = $67.10. Once again note what happens in the table:

PRESENT VALUE OF $1
Received at the End of the Period
PV1 p-%

PERIOD	2%	4%	6%	8%	10%	12%	14%	16%	18%	20%	24%	28%
1	0.980	0.962	0.943	0.926	0.909	0.893	0.877	0.862	0.848	0.833	0.807	0.781
2	0.961	0.925	0.890	0.857	0.826	0.797	0.770	0.743	0.718	0.694	0.650	0.610
3	0.942	0.889	0.840	0.794	0.751	0.712	0.675	0.641	0.609	0.579	0.525	0.477
4	0.924	0.855	0.792	0.735	0.683	0.636	0.592	0.552	0.516	0.482	0.423	0.373
5	0.906	0.822	0.747	0.681	0.621	0.567	0.519	0.476	0.437	0.402	0.341	0.291
6	0.888	0.790	0.705	0.630	0.565	0.507	0.456	0.410	0.370	0.335	0.275	0.227
7	0.871	0.760	0.665	0.584	0.513	0.452	0.400	0.354	0.314	0.279	0.222	0.178
8	0.854	0.731	0.627	0.540	0.467	0.404	0.351	0.305	0.266	0.233	0.179	0.139
9	0.837	0.703	0.592	0.500	0.424	0.361	0.308	0.263	0.226	0.194	0.144	0.108
10	0.820	0.676	0.558	0.463	0.386	0.322	0.270	0.227	0.191	0.162	0.116	0.085
11	0.804	0.650	0.527	0.429	0.351	0.288	0.237	0.195	0.162	0.135	0.094	0.066
12	0.789	0.625	0.497	0.397	0.319	0.257	0.208	0.168	0.137	0.112	0.076	0.052
13	0.773	0.601	0.469	0.368	0.290	0.229	0.182	0.145	0.116	0.094	0.061	0.040
14	0.758	0.578	0.442	0.341	0.263	0.205	0.160	0.125	0.099	0.078	0.049	0.032
15	0.743	0.555	0.417	0.315	0.239	0.183	0.140	0.108	0.084	0.065	0.040	0.025
16	0.728	0.534	0.394	0.292	0.218	0.163	0.123	0.093	0.071	0.054	0.032	0.019
17	0.714	0.513	0.371	0.270	0.198	0.146	0.108	0.080	0.060	0.045	0.026	0.015
18	0.700	0.494	0.350	0.250	0.180	0.130	0.095	0.069	0.051	0.038	0.021	0.012
19	0.686	0.475	0.331	0.232	0.164	0.116	0.083	0.060	0.043	0.031	0.017	0.009
20	0.673	0.456	0.312	0.215	0.149	0.104	0.073	0.051	0.036	0.026	0.014	0.007
25	0.610	0.375	0.233	0.146	0.092	0.059	0.038	0.025	0.016	0.011	0.005	0.002
30	0.552	0.308	0.174	0.099	0.057	0.033	0.020	0.012	0.007	0.004	0.002	0.001
35	0.500	0.253	0.130	0.068	0.036	0.019	0.010	0.006	0.003	0.002	0.001	–
40	0.453	0.208	0.097	0.046	0.022	0.011	0.005	0.003	0.001	–	–	–
45	0.410	0.171	0.073	0.031	0.014	0.006	0.003	0.001	–	–	–	–

(-) Number less than 0.001
Where 4th decimal place is 5 or greater, 3rd. decimal rounded up.
Table prepared utilizing Hewlett-Packard 38-C calculator.

PRESENT VALUE OF $1 PER PERIOD
Received at the End of Those Periods
$PV1/P_{p-\%}$

PERIOD	2%	4%	6%	8%	10%	12%	14%	16%	18%	20%	24%	28%
1	0.980	0.962	0.943	0.926	0.909	0.893	0.877	0.862	0.848	0.833	0.807	0.781
2	1.942	1.886	1.833	1.783	1.736	1.690	1.647	1.605	1.566	1.528	1.457	1.392
3	2.884	2.775	2.673	2.577	2.487	2.402	2.322	2.246	2.174	2.107	1.981	1.868
4	3.808	3.630	3.466	3.312	3.170	3.038	2.914	2.798	2.690	2.589	2.404	2.241
5	4.714	4.452	4.212	3.993	3.791	3.605	3.433	3.274	3.127	2.991	2.745	2.530
6	5.601	5.242	4.917	4.623	4.355	4.111	3.889	3.685	3.498	3.326	3.021	2.759
7	6.472	6.002	5.582	5.206	4.868	4.564	4.288	4.037	3.812	3.605	3.242	2.937
8	7.326	6.733	6.210	5.747	5.335	4.968	4.639	4.344	4.078	3.837	3.421	3.076
9	8.162	7.435	6.802	6.247	5.759	5.328	4.946	4.772	4.607	4.303	3.566	3.184
10	8.983	8.111	7.360	6.710	6.145	5.650	5.216	4.833	4.494	4.193	3.682	3.269
11	9.787	8.761	7.887	7.139	6.495	5.938	5.453	5.029	4.656	4.327	3.776	3.335
12	10.575	9.385	8.384	7.536	6.814	6.194	5.660	5.197	4.793	4.439	3.851	3.387
13	11.348	9.986	8.853	7.904	7.103	6.424	5.842	5.342	4.910	4.533	3.912	3.427
14	12.106	10.563	9.295	8.244	7.367	6.628	6.002	5.468	5.008	4.611	3.962	3.459
15	12.849	11.118	9.712	8.560	7.606	6.811	6.142	5.576	5.092	4.676	4.001	3.483
16	13.578	11.652	10.106	8.851	7.824	6.974	6.265	5.669	5.162	4.730	4.033	3.503
17	14.292	12.166	10.477	9.122	8.022	7.120	6.373	5.749	5.222	4.775	4.059	3.518
18	14.992	12.659	10.828	9.372	8.201	7.250	6.467	5.818	5.273	4.812	4.080	3.529
19	15.679	13.134	11.158	9.604	8.365	7.366	6.550	5.878	5.316	4.844	4.097	3.539
20	16.351	13.509	11.470	9.818	8.514	7.469	6.623	5.929	5.353	4.870	4.110	3.546
25	19.524	15.622	12.783	10.675	9.077	7.843	6.873	6.097	5.467	4.948	4.147	3.564
30	22.397	17.292	13.765	11.258	9.427	8.055	7.003	6.177	5.517	4.979	4.160	3.569
35	24.999	18.665	14.498	11.655	9.644	8.176	7.070	6.215	5.539	4.992	4.164	3.571
40	27.356	19.793	15.046	11.925	9.779	8.244	7.105	6.234	5.548	4.997	4.166	3.571
45	29.490	20.720	15.456	12.108	9.863	8.283	7.123	6.242	5.552	4.999	4.166	3.571

Where 4th place decimal is 5 or greater, 3rd. place rounded up.
Table prepared utilizing Hewlett-Packard 38-C calculator.

Figure 11-2

- The higher the percentage the less valuable is a series of future payments, and

- The longer the wait, the greater the value, but only because *more* payments are received.

THE FUTURE VALUE OF $1 RECEIVED AT SOME TIME IN THE FUTURE

This is probably the simplest of the concepts to understand, as we are all familiar with the deposit of money to grow at interest. Obviously we know:

- The longer we let it grow the bigger it will be, and
- The higher the interest rate the faster it will grow.

Looking at Figure 11-3, we see that the above is certainly true. At 10 percent interest, $1 will grow to $2.59 in 10 years. At 12 percent interest it would grow to $3.11.

FUTURE VALUE OF $1 PER PERIOD RECEIVED AT THE END OF VARIOUS PERIODS

Once again referring to a table, this time Figure 11-4, we see that:

- The longer we wait the more payments we will receive and the more those deposits will grow, and
- The higher the interest rate the faster they will grow.

Looking at tables is not very interesting, but the practical applications of such concepts, expressed by the tables are most useful to the real estate investor. For instance, lets assume you value money at 8 percent (the average return you are getting on your present investments). You have just purchased a building with a remaining economic life of 25 years. If the building is now valued at $100,000, how much depreciation would you need per year to exactly return the investment at the end of the 25 years?

Or asked another way, what dollar amount would you have to deposit each year at 8 percent interest so that at the end of 25 years you would have $100,000?

Putting this as a formula, the question is:

Dollar amount (A) times the Factor for 8 percent for 25 years (B) equals $100,000.

or

$$A \times B = \$100,000$$

B can be found in Figure 11-4. Go down the 8 percent column to the 25 years line: the Factor is 73.105.

FUTURE VALUE OF $1
Received at the End of the Period
FV1p-%

PERIOD	2%	4%	6%	8%	10%	12%	14%	16%	18%	20%	24%	28%
1	1.020	1.040	1.060	1.080	1.100	1.120	1.140	1.160	1.180	1.200	1.240	1.280
2	1.040	1.082	1.124	1.166	1.210	1.254	1.300	1.346	1.392	1.440	1.538	1.638
3	1.061	1.125	1.191	1.260	1.331	1.405	1.482	1.561	1.643	1.728	1.907	2.097
4	1.082	1.170	1.263	1.361	1.464	1.574	1.689	1.811	1.939	2.074	2.364	2.684
5	1.104	1.217	1.338	1.469	1.611	1.762	1.925	2.100	2.288	2.488	2.932	3.436
6	1.126	1.265	1.419	1.587	1.772	1.974	2.195	2.436	2.700	2.986	3.635	4.398
7	1.149	1.316	1.504	1.714	1.949	2.211	2.502	2.826	3.186	3.583	4.508	5.630
8	1.172	1.369	1.594	1.851	2.144	2.476	2.853	3.278	3.759	4.300	5.590	7.206
9	1.195	1.423	1.690	2.000	2.358	2.773	3.252	3.803	4.436	5.160	6.931	9.223
10	1.219	1.480	1.791	2.159	2.594	3.106	3.707	4.411	5.234	6.192	8.594	11.805
11	1.243	1.540	1.898	2.332	2.853	3.479	4.226	5.117	6.176	7.430	10.657	15.111
12	1.268	1.601	2.012	2.518	3.138	3.896	4.818	5.936	7.288	8.916	13.214	19.342
13	1.294	1.665	2.133	2.720	3.452	4.364	5.492	6.886	8.599	10.699	16.386	24.758
14	1.320	1.732	2.261	2.937	3.798	4.887	6.261	7.988	10.147	12.839	20.319	31.691
15	1.346	1.801	2.397	3.172	4.177	5.474	7.138	9.266	11.973	15.407	25.195	40.564
16	1.373	1.873	2.540	3.426	4.595	6.130	8.137	10.748	14.129	18.488	31.242	51.923
17	1.400	1.948	2.693	3.700	5.055	6.866	9.277	10.761	12.467	16.672	22.186	38.740
18	1.428	2.026	2.854	3.996	5.560	7.690	10.575	12.375	14.462	19.673	26.623	48.038
19	1.457	2.107	3.026	4.316	6.116	8.613	12.055	16.776	23.214	31.948	59.567	108.89
20	1.486	2.191	3.207	4.661	6.728	9.646	13.743	19.460	27.393	38.337	73.864	139.37
25	1.641	2.666	4.292	6.849	10.834	17.000	26.461	40.874	62.668	95.396	216.54	478.90
30	1.811	3.243	5.744	10.062	17.449	29.959	50.950	85.849	143.37	237.37	634.81	1645.5
35	2.000	3.946	7.686	14.785	28.102	52.800	98.100	180.31	328.00	590.67	1861.1	5653.9
40	2.208	4.801	10.285	21.724	45.259	93.050	188.88	378.72	750.37	1469.7	5455.9	19246.
45	2.438	5.841	13.765	31.920	72.890	163.99	363.68	795.44	1715.7	3657.3	15995.	66750.

Last decimal number rounded up if next number was 5 or more.
Table prepared utilizing Hewlett-Packard 38-C calculator.

Figure 11-3

$$A \times 73.105 = \$100,000$$
$$A = \$1000 / 73.105$$
$$A = \$1,367.86$$

Thus, a deposit of $1,367.86 each year for 25 years will grow to $100,000 in 25 years.

Another example might be a situation in which you desire to receive $2,000 semi-annually for 10 years after your retirement some 10 years hence. If money can be invested to earn 12 percent per annum (6 percent per period), how much cash will you need at retirement to provide those payments?

Again in formula style we can say:

$$\$2,000 \text{ times Factor} = (?)$$

Referring to Figure 11-2, we find the factor for 20 periods @ 6 percent = 11.470

Restating the formulation above:

$$\$2,000 \times 11.470 = \$22,940$$

Now that you understand the power of compounding, which of the following situations would you choose? Fast sum-of-the digits depreciation or the slower straight-line? Obviously, you would choose the fast method which would allow you to invest it at interest for the longest possible period.

TAX CONSIDERATIONS

INCOME TAXES

As a real estate investor, you should do two things: (1) Become personally knowledgeable of the income tax laws applying to investment real estate, and (2) consult a tax specialist before you agree to buy, sell, or trade real property. Even though you become quite well informed on tax matters, often subtle changes in the IRS regulations could be very expensive if you are unaware of the change. Your CPA should always be consulted where large amounts of money are involved.

The Tax Reform Act (TRA) of 1986 has complicated the income tax structure while at the same time effectively reducing the overall rate for many persons. Prior to 1986 we were concerned with long-term gains and short-term gains. Under the revised regulations *everything* is just income; however, income has now been divided into three categories:

1. Earned income from labor and services.

2. Investment income, received from dividends and interest on investments, and

3. Passive income, received from the ownership of real estate or business in which the taxpayer is not materially active.

FUTURE VALUE OF $1 PER PERIOD
Received at the End of Various Periods
$FV1/P_{p-\infty}$

PERIOD	2%	4%	6%	8%	10%	12%	14%	16%	18%	20%	24%	28%
1	1.000	1.000	1.000	1.000	1.000	1.000	1.000	1.000	1.000	1.000	1.000	1.000
2	2.020	2.040	2.060	2.080	2.100	2.120	2.140	2.160	2.180	2.200	2.240	2.280
3	3.060	3.122	3.184	3.246	3.310	3.374	3.440	3.506	3.572	3.640	3.778	3.918
4	4.122	4.246	4.375	4.506	4.641	4.779	4.921	5.066	5.215	5.368	5.684	6.016
5	5.204	5.416	5.637	5.867	6.105	6.353	6.610	6.877	7.154	7.442	8.048	8.700
6	6.308	6.633	6.975	7.336	7.716	8.115	8.536	8.977	9.442	9.930	10.980	12.135
7	7.434	7.898	8.394	8.923	9.487	10.089	10.730	11.413	12.141	12.915	14.615	16.553
8	8.583	9.214	9.898	10.636	11.435	12.299	13.232	14.240	15.327	16.499	19.122	22.163
9	9.755	10.582	11.491	12.487	13.579	14.775	16.085	17.518	19.085	20.798	24.712	29.369
10	10.950	12.006	13.180	14.486	15.937	17.548	19.337	21.321	23.521	25.958	31.643	38.592
11	12.168	13.486	14.971	16.645	18.531	20.654	23.044	25.732	28.755	32.150	40.237	50.398
12	13.412	15.025	16.868	18.977	21.384	24.133	27.270	30.850	34.931	39.580	50.894	65.510
13	14.680	16.626	18.882	21.495	24.522	28.029	32.088	36.786	42.218	48.496	64.109	84.852
14	15.973	18.291	21.015	24.214	27.975	32.393	37.581	43.672	50.818	59.195	80.496	109.61
15	17.293	20.023	23.276	27.152	31.772	37.279	43.842	51.659	60.965	72.035	100.81	141.30
16	18.639	21.824	25.672	30.324	35.949	42.753	50.980	60.925	72.939	87.442	126.01	181.86
17	20.012	23.697	28.212	33.750	40.544	48.883	59.117	71.673	87.068	105.93	157.25	233.79
18	21.412	25.645	30.905	37.450	45.599	55.749	68.394	84.140	103.74	128.11	195.99	300.25
19	22.840	27.671	33.760	41.446	51.159	63.439	78.969	98.603	123.41	154.74	244.03	385.32
20	24.297	29.778	36.785	45.762	57.275	72.052	91.024	115.37	146.62	186.68	303.60	494.21
25	32.030	41.645	54.864	73.105	98.347	133.33	181.87	249.21	342.60	471.98	898.09	1706.8
30	40.568	56.084	79.058	113.28	164.49	241.33	356.78	530.31	790.94	1181.8	2640.9	5873.2
35	49.994	73.652	111.44	172.32	271.02	431.66	693.57	1120.7	1816.7	2948.3	7750.2	20189.
40	60.402	95.025	154.76	259.05	442.59	767.09	1342.0	2360.7	4163.2	7343.8	22728.	69377.
45	71.893	121.03	212.74	386.51	718.91	1358.2	2590.6	4965.3	9531.6	18281.	—	—

(-) number too large for table

Figure 11-4

It is no longer possible to deduct passive losses from other income. Passive losses are only deductible against passive gains, or carried forward to future years. The principal effect of this tax change is to make each property stand on its own in profitability—no longer operate at a tax loss to wipe out other income. This has had a very depressing effect on the sale of limited partnerships, where in the past, losses were just as good as gains. Prior to 1986, if you were in the 50 percent tax bracket $1 of loss was worth 50¢ in tax savings, whereas $1 of income, less taxes, was also worth 50¢. A real estate investor didn't care whether his project lost money or made money, because Uncle Sam paid 50¢ on the dollar in either case.

The new law cracks down on the old techniques of income splitting, a device used by high-bracket income parents to cut the overall family income tax bill. Income splitting was achieved by transferring income-producing assets to the lower-income children. This mechanism was eliminated by Sec. 1(j) of the code and was effective for the tax years beginning after the date of enactment. Under the new law, *net unearned income* of children under 14 years of age is taxed at the parents' rate. If the child is over the age of 14, at the end of the taxable year, his income is taxed at his own rate.

The new law does more than prevent income splitting between parents and children. It also requires many parents to file income tax reports for their children. Also, beginning in 1987, parents were required to include the child's social security number on the parents' return and the child's return must also include the parents' social security numbers.

CAPITAL GAINS TAXES

Capital gains taxes are payable on the sale gain of a property over its basis (book) value. For example, Mr. Brown buys a warehouse for $100,000 in 1980. He makes capital improvements of $50,000 and depreciates the improvements each year. At the end of 4 years, he has accumulated depreciation of $50,000 at which time he sells the building for $125,000 after payment of REALTOR® fees and other selling costs. What is his taxable gain?

Purchase Cost	$100,000
Capital Improvements	+ 50,000
Base Cost	150,000
Less: Accumulated Depreciation	−50,000
Book Value	$100,000

His capital gains would then be the $125,000 selling price less Book Value of $100,000 = $25,000, taxable as ordinary income in the year of the sale. Perhaps he should have considered a contract sale in which only a portion of the gains would be taxed each year. Although if he believes that taxes are likely to rise above the current rate, maybe he should just sell for cash and pay his taxes now. These are the considerations on which only a qualified tax consultant, knowing your tax situation, can give advice.

Capital losses are deductible against capital gains, but only to the extent of your capital gains. The net loss can be deducted against $3,000 of ordinary income. Any additional loss must be carried forward to future years.

It should also be noted that where accelerated depreciation has been taken for tax purposes, and the property is sold prior to full depreciation, the difference in actual depreciation taken and straight-line depreciation is recaptured.

Taxpayers have been on a roller coaster ride, when it comes to allowable depreciation on investment property. Property placed in service prior to 1981 was depreciable over its useful life. The recovery period dropped down to 15 years for property placed in service after 1980, moved up again to 18 years for property placed in service after March 15, 1984, and went to 19 years if placed into service after May 8, 1985. Effective for property placed in service after the end of 1986, the new law boosted the recovery period to 27.5 years for residential rental property and to 31.5 years for non-residential. The net effect is less depreciation and therefore less profit, since depreciation on investment property is an expense of doing business.

ESTATE TAXES

Estate taxes are those federal taxes paid on the decedent's taxable assets held at the time of his death. This includes the value of all cash, bonds, other investments, real estate holding, cash proceeds from life insurance policies owned by the decedent, and businesses. Assets are taxable regardless of how the title is held or how the assets are scheduled, by the will, to be distributed. Persons living in separate property states may hold title in there own name. If they guess correctly which partner will die first, taxes can be saved. For instance, suppose Mr. Black died and was the joint owner of a parcel of land. One-half of this value would be included in calculating his estate value. Had he guessed correctly, at the time he took title, he would have had his wife purchase the land with her separate funds. Thus when he died, the value of the land would not be in his estate. As a practical matter, it is difficult to plan that well.

Here we will assume that a will exists. Every person, regardless of the amount of his wealth or lack thereof needs a will. If not, his assets will be distributed in accordance with the will provided by the state, higher expenses will be involved in settling the estate and the assets may not go to the person or persons the decedent desired to receive them.

In the case of married couples, the first death does not present a big tax problem, unless the estate is exceptionally large, since the surviving spouse is deemed to have been the owner of 1/2 of all of the jointly owned assets. It is upon the second death that the big tax occurs. Assuming that the survivor has lived primarily off of the income from the invested assets, the total estate is taxable on the second death. The use of trusts and other tax reduction measures, such as gifts, can greatly reduce the total estate taxes paid at the two deaths. Once again it is advised that your tax attorney and CPA be advised of your financial situation and your desires as to the estate's distribution. He may well recommend yearly and one-time gifts and other measures to reduce this burden.

GIFT TAXES

Gift taxes are taxes payable by the donor on gifts made to others during his/her lifetime. IRS regulations classify all transfers of cash or property (assets) without adequate compensation as gifts. Most gifts, with the exception of charitable gifts, are taxable in the year the gift is made. All gifts in excess of $10,000 per year to any one individual (annual exclusion) must be reported on the gift-tax form and are taxable on a cumulative basis—the more that is given, the higher the tax bracket.

Gifts from married persons are considered as coming 1/2 from each marital partner. Thus a man and wife can give any one child only $10,000 tax free per year. However, the same gift may also be made to the wife/husband of the child or to each of their children. People are very reluctant to give away their hard earned assets, their thinking being, "I may need it later." It is possible to have your cake and eat it too. Gifts can be made to a nonrevocable trust, controlled by the parents, who receive the income from the trust during their lifetime. This procedure will avoid most of the tax but not all.

Although gifts to others are an excellent way of reducing estate taxes, any gifts made in contemplation of death (three years prior) are taxable in the estate of the decedent.

Don't make the mistake of just quitclaiming a property to someone to avoid estate taxes. Such a procedure is a failure to make a gift tax return, and has subsequent problems. Most who use this procedure are either dishonest and hope they don't get caught, or unaware of the tax laws and their consequences.

INHERITANCE TAXES

Inheritance taxes are *state* taxes paid by the person receiving the inheritance. Actually, the Administrator or Executor of the estate being probated, calculates each heir's taxes due and pays them on behalf of the heir before giving the heir his money.

State inheritance taxes vary from state to state and are usually based on a sliding scale—the larger the inheritance the greater the tax rate. Each beneficiary of the estate is taxed on the basis of what he/she receives. While inheritance taxes in the various states are much less than the federal bite from the estate, they can still be substantial. Proper estate planning can go a long way in reducing this tax burden.

12

Land Use

BACKGROUND AND HISTORY

Land use law has moved through various stages of development, primarily in the state courts. In the early days the courts were hostile to the ideas of *zoning*. This attitude ended after the Supreme Court of the United States upheld comprehensive zoning in the 1926 Euclid Case.[1]

In the Euclid case a zoning ordinance, which restricted the plaintiff's land to residential use, imposed a four-fold loss on the value of the property, which the plaintiff desired to put to commercial use. The complaint alleged that the zoning ordinance destroyed a "great part" of the land value, but the owner did not pursue this point. His major complaint was that the law was unconstitutional. For this reason the Euclid case is considered a due process and equal protection case rather than one of property taking. The Court specifically pointed to the action which threatened enforcement of the zoning ordinance.

The second stage of land use law development was marked by a two-tiered approach to land use problems:

1. The courts usually upheld most zoning regulations, and

2. The courts generally reserved discretion to review the validity of zoning as applied to individual properties.

This presumption of legality usually protects zoning from successful attacks, but the courts may disregard this presumption if they decide to hold against the local government. A zoning law's constitutionality is more likely to be upheld when applied to an individual land owner's property.

The latest stage in land use law development had its beginning in the mid-1960s with cases involving exclusionary zoning of large lots. The *National Land and Investment Co. v. Kohn*,[2] was a major landmark case. In the Kohn case,

---

[1] Village of Euclid v. Ambler Realty Co., 277 U.S. 365 (1926).

[2] National Land and Investment Co. v. Kohn, 215 A. 2d 597 (Pa. 1965).

a small municipality in the Philadelphia area adopted a four-acre lot size minimum that applied to 30 percent of the area. A developer challenged the four-acre requirement which he claimed reduced the value of the land. The Court noted that, at that time, there was no market for four-acre lots. It applied a balancing test that weighed the purpose of the four-acre zoning against the loss in value suffered by the land owners. The zoning was held to be unconstitutional.

In much later cases, involving the constitutionality of agricultural zoning, the courts have held that ordinances protecting the residents of a municipality from the "ill effects" of urbanization are legitimate. The courts have upheld the lot size requirements, even though the owners have believed that their land was unjustly taken (i.e., value reduced) by the zoning regulation (see "Zoning May Be Considered a Taking" later in this chapter).

A good example is *Cordorus v. Rodgers*,[3] in which the court held that a 50-acre lot size requirement did not violate due process even though it reduced the value of property by up to two-thirds.

In some of these later cases, social concerns have been addressed in such questions as, "What is a family?" Two 1983 cases drastically revised the former definitions of *the family*. In New York, the establishment of a residence for eight mentally disabled adults, under the provisions of Sections 41.33 and 41.34 of the Mental Hygiene Law, was unsuccessfully contested on the grounds that ground covenants limited use of the premises to "single-family" dwellings.[4] Again in Ohio the court stated that if a structure is maintained as a private residence, even though occupied by persons unrelated by consanguinity, but who live together as a single household unit, the covenant is not violated.[5] Even later the courts obtained greater control on zoning in some states by holding that zoning must be consistent with a *Comprehensive Master Plan*.

The very latest stage of land use development had its beginning in the 1980s, when the United States Supreme Court decided a large number of land use cases. The courts adopted a more rigorous *taking doctrine* and held that successful plaintiffs, in taking cases, may secure compensation for a temporary taking and struck down a special permit denial for a group home for the mentally retarded. The court also applied the Federal Antitrust Act to land use regulations and free-speech protection.

In June 1987, the U.S. Supreme Court announced two of the most significant land use decisions of the last 50 years: *First English Evangelical Church v. County of Los Angeles*[6] and *Nolland v. California Coastal Commission*.[7] These cases

[3] Cordorus v. Rodgers, 492 A. 2d 73 (Pa. Commw. 1985).

[4] Crane Neck Association v. N.Y.C./Long Island County Service Group, 92 App. Div. 2d 119, 460. N.Y.S. 2d 69 (1983).

[5] Beres v. Hope Homes, Inc., 6 Ohio App. 3rd 71, 453 N.E. 2d 1119 (1983).

[6] First English Evangelical Church v. County of Los Angeles, 107 S. Ct. 2378 (1987).

[7] Nolland v. California Coastal Commission, 107 S. Ct. 3141 (1987).

shifted court opinion to favor property owners in the never ending battle between the state's right to regulate land use to benefit health, safety and public welfare and the power of private owners to use their lands as they prefer. Although these cases chose new direction, the future of land use planning is still uncertain.

THE FIRST ENGLISH CASE

In the First English case, a land use regulation supposedly denied the land owner of all economic use of his land. Considering these facts, the Court determined by a 6 to 3 vote that the regulation was invalid, and that the constitution requires the payment of compensation for the *temporary* taking of property.

The English case resulted from a 1978 storm run off which totally destroyed the church's retreat center for handicapped children. In 1979, the Los Angeles County enacted an interim ordinance that prohibited the redevelopment of the area. The church filed a complaint saying that the ordinance denied them the use of their land and demanded compensation. Both the California Superior Court and the Court of Appeals rejected the church's cause, citing the California Supreme Court opinion in *Agins v. City of Tiburon*,[8] which held that a landowner may not maintain a reverse condemnation suit, but must seek the invalidation of the ordinance instead. In the First English Supreme Court decision, the court carefully side-stepped the question of whether deprivation must be a total taking in order to be entitled to monetary recovery.

THE NOLLAND CASE

Two weeks after the First English decision, the Supreme Court announced its decision in *Nolland v. California Coastal Commission*, which resulted in a controversial 5 to 4 vote. The Court concluded that the California Coastal Commission could not require property owners to provide public access to beaches in return for private property permit approvals.

The Nolland case resulted when the Nollands acquired an option to purchase a parcel of Ventura County Coastline property, upon which a small run-down bungalow was situated. They applied to the Coastal Commission for a permit to demolish the existing structure and replace it with a two-story building, encompassing approximately three times the square footage of the older building. Over the Nolland's protest, the Commission granted the permit, but required them to grant a lateral easement which would allow the public to pass alongside the ocean, across *their* beach in the area between their seawall and the historic high tide line. The easement would have entailed public use of a substantial portion of the Nolland's property.

---

[8] Agins v. City of Tiburon, 598 P. 2d 25 (Cal. 1979).

HISTORICAL BACKGROUND TO BEACH RIGHTS

From the beginning of the development of the United States, it has been assumed that one who buys land abutting navigable waters or unnavigable waters has the right to enjoy the beach as his private domain. In lands abutting tidal waters, this right usually stops at the high-water mark. Beyond that mark, the public is normally assumed to have no rights.[9] Recently the Courts have decided more in favor of public beach use. For example, in California an implied dedication to the public was ruled, when a landowner did not object to the public use for a period in excess of five years. The referenced case, *County of Orange v. Chandler-Sherman Corp.*,[10] was most significant in that it dealt with the beach area *above* the high-water mark.

A further erosion of the original assumed owner rights is contained in the Massachusetts Public Trust Rules, which provide that land *below* the high water mark, even though sold by the state, remains subject to public rights of fishing and navigation.[11]

POWER OF THE STATE

Under the United States system of government, it is held that government has four inherent rights over private property. Two of these concern land use: (1) Police Power, or the right to regulate private property for the public interest, convenience or necessity; and (2) Eminent Domain, or the right to take property in the public interest upon payment of just compensation. As we have seen from the above discussions, zoning in some case may be considered a taking with compensation due the private property owner, and in other cases zoning may result in damages to private property, justifying possible compensation, even when that property is not taken per se.

Under the inherent right of Police Power, cities may enact *zoning codes* that regulate property use. If the Police Power is exercised, normally the property owner is due no offsetting compensation or payments from the local agency exercising the power. However, the exercise of these inherent powers often poses a question as to whether the action was a "taking" under the power of eminent domain or was it a simple case of the exercise of police power, in which no compensation is due.

In 1887 The Supreme Court, in the case of *Mugler v. Kansas*,[12] decided that a state prohibition law which forced the closing of a brewery was not a "taking" but an exercise of police power to protect the community. This very early interpretation of taking has undergone many changes throughout the years and has been

---

[9] Re Opinion of Justices, 313 N.E. 2d 561 (Mass. 1974)

[10] County of Orange v. Chandler-Sherman Corp., 126 Cal. Rptr. 765, 5 S.W.U. Rev 48 (1973).

[11] In Re Opinion of the Justices, 313 N.E. 2d 561 (Mass. 1964).

[12] Mugler v. Kansas, 123 U.S. 623 (1887).

expanded to include government actions, which do not result in the *physical taking* of property, but these actions may include:

- a reduction in the value of land.
- temporary restricted use of the land., or
- restriction on the use of land due to adjacent land use.

This latter situation has spawned a new legal term, "Reverse Condemnation." *Black's Law Dictionary*[13] defines Reverse Condemnation as:

> An action brought by a property owner seeking just compensation for land taken for public use, against a government or private entity having the power of eminent domain. It is a remedy peculiar to the property owner and is exercisable by him where it appears that the taker of the property *does not intend* to bring eminent domain proceedings.

Examples of reverse condemnation can be found in the previously discussed Nolland Case and *Ossman v. Mt. States Telephone and Telegraph Co.*[14] Another possible example would be where the use and value of property adjacent to a new airport or freeway is materially diminished.

DISGUISED EMINENT DOMAIN

To avoid the problem of paying just compensation as required under the power of eminent domain, some governmental agencies have attempted to acquire control of the property by limiting the highest and best use through zoning. Where land is contemplated to be needed for public purposes in the future, it can be zoned for a nonproductive use[15] and future request for rezoning, which would permit a more economic use can be denied. The land can be designated as lying in the bed of a street, or a park site. Any requests for permits inconsistent with these designations would then be granted on condition that the requested improvement be excluded from compensation in *any* subsequent taking.

Generally the practice of using police power to save on condemnation costs has been rebuked by the courts. The use of the police power in aid of condemnation is not recognized as a valid purpose and therefore is not a proper objective.[16] In the case of *City of Plainfield v. Borough of Middlesex* previously cited, the court said that no matter how desirable for public purposes the contemplated project may be, the state cannot use the police power to depreciate the value of the property for the purpose of purchasing it at a lower price.

---

[13] *Black's Law Dictionary, 6th Ed.* 1990, West Publications Co., St. Paul, Minn.

[14] Ossman v. Mountain States Telephone and Telegraph Co., 32 Colo., App. 230, 511 P. 2d 519.

[15] City of Plainfield v. Borough of Middlesex, 69 N.J. 136, 137, 173 A. 2d 785 (1961) and Robyns v. City of Dearborn, 341 Mich. 495, 67 N.W. 2d 718 (1953).

[16] Kissinger v. City of Los Angeles, 161 Cal. 2d 454, 327 P. 2d 10 (1958) and Robertson v. City of Salem, 191 F. Supp. 604 (D. Ore. 1961).

On a theoretical basis, the use of the police power to condemn is contrary to constitutional principles. On a practical basis, even though the courts have not openly legitimized the use of police power in the aid of condemnation, many practices have developed which permit the tandem use of these two powers.

ZONING MAY BE CONSIDERED A TAKING

In the 1981 case of *San Diego Gas and Electric Co. v. City of San Diego*,[17] the gas company purchased a property as a possible site for a nuclear power plant. The city rezoned a part of the property, which reduced the size available for commercial use. The company brought an action of reverse condemnation. The result was:

- The Superior Court awarded damages.
- The California Supreme Court reversed and transferred it to the Court of Appeals.
- The Court of Appeals reversed the damage award and suggested that the case be retried on a basis of invalidating the ordinance.
- The U.S. Supreme Court reviewed the case to determine the status of the California decisions and the result was a mixed decision which indicated that *if* the case had come before the court for a decision, it was *possible* that the court would have awarded damages for the inverse condemnation, if the landowner could have proven that a taking had occurred. In effect, it appears that the Court had reasserted what it had previously held: A very strict regulation of land can constitute a taking.

SPECIAL CONSIDERATIONS IN CONDEMNATION

A lessee may be entitled to damages due to the taking of leased property, unless he has previously waived that right by lease agreement or otherwise. In commercial leases, especially where long-term, provisions for protection of the lessee in the event of condemnation should be provided. It is not unusual for the lessee to have a greater interest in the condemnation than the land owner. In the case of *State of Tennessee v. Burkhart et al.*,[18] the verdict awarded the lessee ten times as much as the owners. However, the lease may provide, as in the case of *Sugarman v. City of Baltimore et al.*,[19] that:

> In the event that condemnation proceedings are instituted against the premises hereby demised, and title taken by any Federal, State or Municipal body, then the lease shall become null and void, and the lessee shall not be entitled to receive any part of the award which may be received by the Lessor.

---

[17] San Diego Gas and Electric Co. v. City of San Diego, 28 U.S.C. 1259.

[18] State of Tennessee v. Burkhart et al., 370 S.W. 2d 411 (Tenn. 1963).

[19] Sugarman v. City of Baltimore et al., 191 A. 2d 240 (Md. 1963).

EXCESS CONDEMNATION

Excess Condemnation, as the name implies, is the taking of land in larger amounts than is actually necessary for the improvement proper. Special constitutional authority is necessary for exercising this extraordinary right. The earlier court decisions have held that statutes for excess condemnation, enacted under the general constitutional provisions, were invalid. Recent social philosophy may well influence the judicial view that public use, liberally interpreted, may often permit excess condemnation. For instance, a street is laid out and land on each side of the proposed street is taken in excess of the area actually confined to the street itself. The control of the excess part by the municipality, whether in the case of a street, park, or other development, ensures the usefulness of the improvement and is conducive to the better channeling of municipal growth. Better city planning is bound to ensue.

Title taken under the right of eminent domain ordinarily carries with it a fee simple title to the land, so that the condemnor has as absolute a title as if it were acquired by purchase, but land taken for roads is usually a base fee and is governed by statute.

Under a base, or qualified fee, when the use for which the property has been taken is abandoned, title to it reverts to the original owner or his heirs. In other takings of land, a fee simple title is acquired.

ZONING CLASSIFICATIONS

Municipalities follow different zoning classes, depending upon their requirements and the size of the municipal area. All ordinances have classifications of residential, industrial and commercial zones. A higher classification is usually permissible in a lower use classification; i.e., residential use would be permitted in an apartment zoned area. In urban areas, industrial areas are usually subdivided into "light" and "heavy." Even in the heavy industrial classified zones, some businesses may be prohibited. Such prohibitions might include abattoirs, manufacture of animal fertilizers, explosive manufacturing, stockyards, and so on. These types of operations are considered offensive and are usually limited to outside of city limits or to special industrial areas.

Commercial districts may also be subdivided to permit various classifications of commercial use such as retailing, medical centers and offices.

Residential zoning is usually subdivided into several categories, such as single-family, multifamily up to four units, apartment complexes with more than four units. Residential zoning regulations usually are concerned with living aspects other than the size or type of the building allowed. Residential areas are designed also to control the minimum amount of green-area that must be provided, the height of buildings, minimum sizes of lots, side-yards, rear-yards and front set-back. Specific requirements for sidewalks, curbs and gutters, and type of utility installations permitted are also provided in the residential zoning regulations.

ZONING ORDINANCES ARE NOT ENCUMBRANCES

While the restrictions placed on the use of property may be considered as a limitation on its use, it is not *an encumbrance,* within the strict meaning of that term; however, a title policy will except any zoning ordinance from the title insurance coverage.

It is the selling broker's responsibility to inform a potential buyer of the existing zoning of property offered for sale and assure himself that the buyer's intended use is permissible under current zoning. If the buyer indicates that he plans to request a variance or a change in zoning, that plan should be made a "subject to" provision of the sales contract.

A situation may arise where a buyer purchases a tract of land on the strength of existing zoning, obtains a building permit, and makes development expenditures, to find that the zoning code, in the mean time, has been amended to prohibit his intended use of the land. Such a situation arose in the case of *Gulf Oil Co. v. Fairview Township Board of Supervisors,*[20] where the Court laid down the following rule quoted in *Penn Township v. Yecko Bros..*[21]

> A property owner who is able to demonstrate (1) that he has obtained a valid building permit under the old zoning ordinance, (2) that he had obtained it in good faith (without "racing"), to get it before a proposed change is made in the zoning ordinance, and (3) that in good faith he spent money or incurred liabilities in reliance on his building permit has acquired a vested right and need not conform with the zoning ordinance as changed.

EXCLUSIONARY ZONING

Another important United States Supreme Court case holds that zoning laws are not exclusionary in effect, if they are not enacted with an intention to discriminate against low-income groups and were not motivated by racial discrimination.[22] However a zoning ordinance that provided for apartment construction in only 80 acres of the 11,589 acres in the township was held invalid, as exclusionary.[23]

---

[20] Gulf Oil Co. v. Fairview Township Board of Supervisors, 438 Pa. 457 (1970).

[21] Penn Township v. Yecko Bros., 217 at 2d A. 171 (1966).

[22] Village of Arlington Heights v. Metropolitan Housing Development Corp., 97 S. Ct. 555 (1977).

[23] Township of Willistown v. Chesterdale Farms Inc., 341 A. 2d 466 (Pa. 1975).

13

Special Property Ownership Types

PLANNED UNIT DEVELOPMENTS (PUDs)

Planned Unit Developments are relatively high-density single-family structures designed for maximum land utilization. Lot sizes may be as small as 2,000 s.f. with zero-lot line construction authorized. Although there may be some facilities, such as tennis courts and swimming pools, which are shared among the property owners of the development, the PUD differs from the condominium in that each residence is usually free-standing, has its own legally described lot and all of the other characteristics of single-family housing.

A special designation "De Minimis PUD" is applied to those units in a planned-unit development, in which the value of commonly owned facilities or other amenities are incidental to the total value of the unit itself.

The PUD typically consists of garden type apartments, or free standing residential units. A PUD may be of all one type of building or a mixture of several types. The advantage of the PUD is its ability to provide living space in an area of relatively high-cost land but at a reasonable price. This is due to the use of common areas and facilities and the higher density of units than are typically allowed for normal single-unit construction.

The PUD is created by the recording of a subdivision plat which shows the lots, common facilities and provides a declaration of covenants, restrictions and conditions which govern the day-to-day operation of the project. The recorded declaration sets out the rules governing the property, creates an ownership association, in which all owners are members and establishes voting rights, right of use of common facilities and the authority to set and collect assessments to provide for the maintenance of the common facilities and common areas. Assessments are legally liens on the units assessed until paid.

CONDOMINIUMS

Condominiums are legal organizations which provide individuals with many of the benefits of private ownership in multiple-unit buildings and developments, particularly housing developments. Only recently have states enacted legislation to permit nonresidential condominium properties.[1] As applied to residential projects, the ownership of a "unit" means an apartment in a multifamily project. The owner of a unit is also a member of the condo association or organization which is responsible for the management of commonly owned areas and the maintenance of the exteriors of the various buildings and other facilities.

The condominium, traces its origins back to antiquity, but today is essentially a creature of statute. Its method of organization and operation and its essential characteristics are expressly defined in legislation. Without legislation, it could not be successfully adapted to the complex requirement of mortgage financing, FHA insurance, title insurance, taxation, and many other facets of modern large-scale real estate development.

One particular characteristic of the condominium is that, unlike conventional rental apartment buildings or cooperative housing buildings, there is no one owner to whom public authorities, creditors, occupants or third parties can look for enforcement of rights and liabilities. Absent a statutory solution, there would be no generally acceptable formula for integrating the total operation of the condominium so that it can be accommodated to established commercial practices.

Each owner of a unit in a multiple development has exclusive title to his own unit and he is generally free to deal with it as though it were a private dwelling. Only the common elements of the condominium are under the control of a common manager, and absent a statutory requirement, even this responsibility could take any form which the unit owners saw fit to select.

The ownership of a unit includes a fee title ownership of the specific unit purchased plus a pro-rata share interest in the common facilities. Voting rights in the association's elections of management and other decisions may be apportioned on the basis of unit size. The association, in accordance with its established by-laws, has the power to assert a lien on an owner's individually owned unit to enforce his obligation to pay his apportioned share of association expenses for management, maintenance, and other authorized expenses. In the Brickyard Homeowner's Association Management case,[2] the condo management committee was assured of standing (i.e., the legal right) to sue owners on behalf of the association and a liberal interpretation of the enabling statutes.

Condominium owners cannot withhold association payment assessments in protest of an aggrievance as indicated by the *Newport West Condo Association v. Veniar*,[3] case. The Veniar family purchased a condominium and agreed to pay

---

[1] U.C.A. §10103 (25) 1980.

[2] Brickyard Homeowner's Association Management Committee v. Gibbons Realty Co., 668 P. 2d 535 (Utah 1983).

[3] Newport West Condo Association v. Veniar, 134 Mich. App. 1, 350 N.W. 2d 818 (1984).

monthly fees to cover operation, management and maintenance. In setting up the annual budget, the association board of directors was required to provide for an adequate "reserve fund" to cover depreciation and obsolescence of capital assets. The defendants withheld a portion of their monthly fee due to a dispute over the reserve fund. The association placed a lien on the Veniar condominium, which was upheld by the court which reiterated that the withholding of association fees is not one of the remedies available to the condominium owner.

A second peculiar aspect of condominium ownership is that the traditional rules of real estate law and conventional financial techniques are not easily adapted to multiple unit ownerships in a common structure, particularly in high-rise buildings where an "air-lot" must be treated as a private dwelling. To overcome these limitations, statutes prescribe in some detail how the condominium must be organized and operated, so that the rights and duties of all persons associated with, or dealing with, the condominium can rely on a functional entity with its essential elements defined. Under these statutes, the basic "charter" of the condominium is established by the filing of the "condominium declaration. The declaration commits the signers to submit the property to the provisions of the statute, and describes, among other things, the land, the buildings and improvements, the number and location of each unit, the common elements and the intended use of the units. It also contains unit designations conforming to official tax lot numbers.

As an owner of any other type of real estate, the owner of a condominium unit can mortgage his property essentially as he would if he owned a private detached residence. He thus has the option to buy his unit unencumbered by a mortgage or he can raise money to purchase the unit through first mortgage financing. Significantly, mortgage loans on condominiums are generally considered to be legal investments for banks and other fiduciaries. On the other side of the coin, however, the sponsor or manager of the condominium enterprise retains no interest to support a blanket mortgage on the entire project, after completion of construction and the sale of all units.

TAX CONSIDERATIONS

Since each condominium unit is separately owned, it is separately billed for local tax purposes. Default in payment of taxes by the owner of one of the units does not jeopardize the owners or the other units.

The condominium owner is entitled to deduct mortgage interest and real estate taxes from his federal tax return since the condominium falls within the normal tax provisions governing real estate. The condo owner is also entitled to the benefit accorded persons 65 years and older who sell their principal residence.

MAINTENANCE

The condominium project (common areas and exterior of buildings) are maintained by the condominium association with funds assessed monthly to each unit owner. The interior maintenance of individual units is the responsibility of the unit owner.

Every jurisdiction in the United States has enacted condominium statutes that regulate the development and operation of projects within its jurisdiction. Most of the laws were enacted in the 1960-1970 period. Most are heavily based upon FHA regulations then in effect. In 1977 the Commission on Uniform Laws produced the Uniform Condominium Act, which was amended in 1980. Many states have adopted this act in part or in toto.

In the early period of condominium development in the United States, developers exempted themselves for payment of operating expenses on unsold units. This practice was ended by two cases brought before the courts in 1984.[4] Now developers are required to pay their share of assessments on all unsold units.

COMMERCIAL CONDOMINIUMS

The recent development of commercial condominium projects has proven to be far less acceptable to the public than residential unit developments, however this type of project has several advantages for the buyer. These advantages are:

• Fixed expense of ownership, although it must be recognized that the association costs for operation and maintenance are subject to change.

• Guaranteed occupancy for as long as the ownership applies.

• Potential for capital gains on the investment.

• The same tax savings as available for other types of ownership.

• The synergistic effect of owning property in close association with other businesses.

The commercial condo also has some disadvantages. These are:

• Loss of flexibility in acquiring or eliminating additional space as the business changes.

• A commitment of assets which otherwise could be applied to the needs of the business and its growth.

• Lost time for participation in owner association activities.

Adapting the condominium to commercial purposes normally requires greater flexibility than is currently allowed under state laws. Present laws, for example, frequently do not permit condominium buildings on leased lands. Their provisions governing unit ownership, allocation of percentages of interest in common elements, sharing of profits and expenses, allocation of and tax responsibility and the order of lien priorities are too rigid for some types of commercial applications.

---

[4] Hatfield v. LaCharmant Home Owner's Association, 469 N.E. 2d 1218 (2d App. 1984) and Kelley v. Astor Investments Inc., 123 Ill. App. 3rd 593, 462 N.E. 996 (1984).

TIME-SHARING CONDOMINIUMS

During the 1970s a new type of condominium ownership emerged, primarily in the resort areas. These units were known as time-sharing condominiums. The prime motivation for the development of this type of unit was two fold:

1. The developer could sell occupancy time-slots to many buyers. The high-season slots were sold at premium prices and the off-season at substantial reductions. The total selling price of the units far exceeded the price which a full-time ownership would command.

2. Buyers could obtain units for vacation or limited use at lower prices than for total ownership of comparable units, while enjoying the tax advantages associated with other types of second homes.

The basic premise of time ownership is that a buyer purchases the right to occupy a unit of a selected type (not necessarily the same unit each year) for a selected calendar period each year. In most cases the buyer is allowed to rent his space, through on-site management, in the event he elects to not use his time slot for that year. He may also trade his occupancy for another at another location, where the developer is a member of a time-sharing network or has additional units in other locations. Thus, an owner owning a 30-day slot for January might spend one vacation in Florida, the next in Hawaii, and the next in Palm Springs. Although the sales pitches are most interesting, the limitations on switching ability often preclude desired location switching at will.

Time sharing ownership falls into three general classes:

1. *Tenancy-in-Common* which consists of a tenancy-in-common undivided interest together with a side agreement for the use of a designated time period by each owner of the undivided interest. The disadvantage of the tenancy-in-common is the inherent right of partition held by owners of an undivided interest. This is usually solved by the use of a waiver or covenant against partition which also binds future purchasers in the property.

2. *Interval Ownership* which is a conveyance of an estate for years followed by a remainder over as tenant in common (usually 40 years or more after the first sale). This revolving estate for years lasts for the expected lifetime of the project, after which all owners become tenants in common of the entire project. The developer normally retains title to the project.

3. *Floating Time Ownership* which operates on a hotel-type reservation basis. A purchaser is bound by the reservation rules and procedures which cover items such as; (a) reservation priorities, (b) seasonal restrictions, and (c) timing of requests. When a request for a reservation is made for a specific time period, the resort will confirm it if available, or if not, will attempt to provide alternative choices.

Time sharing ownership is effectively an interval ownership, where the owner is granted an estate for years for an agreed time period each year.

Due to numerous problems and scams that have been perpetrated upon the public, many states have enacted legislation to authorize and regulate time sharing development and operation. A good example of this type of law is the one in force in Florida.[5]

When considering the possible purchase of time sharing units, the buyer should carefully examine the official declaration with particular attention to:

- Use and service periods of interest in common facilities.
- Exclusive right to use provisions.
- Methods of collection of costs directly attributable to occupants use; i.e., phone service, repairs and maintenance, expendable supplies, and so on.
- Any waivers of rights of ownership.

COOPERATIVES

The cooperative differs from the condominium primarily in its method of ownership. The cooperative is usually owned by a nonprofit corporation. Purchasers of units do not receive fee titles to those units but two other evidences of ownership:

1. a property lease indicating the right of possession, and

2. a stock certificate which indicates a share of ownership of the corporation, which holds title to the entire project.

In a cooperative development, the corporation owns the entire project. The purchaser of a unit does not become an owner of real estate; instead he becomes a stockholder in the corporation which owns the land and buildings. The number of shares he receives is essentially based on the value of his unit in relationship to the value of the entire project. His stock holding entitles him to a long-term proprietary lease of the unit he "purchases."

The stock holding and the leasehold ownership must reside in a common owner; the interests cannot be disposed of separately. As a shareholder, he has the right to vote annually for the Board of Directors who conduct the affairs of the corporation and supervise the operation of the building. The co-op owner's interest in the stock and the lease is recognized for many purposes as personalty, not realty.[6]

---

[5] Fla. Stat. Ann. §718.103.

[6] Categorizing co-op ownership as "realty" or "personalty" for various legal purposes has lead to unrealistic results at times and has created dilemmas for those who must determine whether to apply the fundamental different bodies of law governing each category. See Miller's Estate, 130 N.Y.S. 2d 295 (1954), holding that a co-op apartment passes under an estate as personal property; Silverman v. Alcoa Plaza Associates, 323 N.Y.S. 2d 39, (1971) holding that upon default by purchaser of co-op, seller corporation could not retain down payment, applying Uniform Commercial Code provisions applicable to personalty. Justice Steuer, dissenting, points out however, that the Courts have recognized co-ops as real estate for some purposes. See also, In Re Pitts Estate, 218 Cal. 184, 22 P. 2d 694 (1933) and Matter of State Tax Comm. v. Shor, 53 N.Y. App. Div. 2d 814(8), (1976).

TAX CONSIDERATIONS

The co-op corporation is assessed and taxed as an entity, and in the event of default by the corporation, the individual unit owner's interests could be foreclosed.

Since most cooperatives are corporations, they do not require statutory implementation to give them organizational identity. Conventional corporate practices provide many of the organizational solutions dealt with in the condominium statutes. Specific state legislation, where it exists, usually deals with specialized problems of the cooperative. A few states have adopted legislation dealing generally with cooperative organization, but the purpose of such organization is to provide a local equivalent of the federal securities laws, viz, to protect the public against fraudulent or misleading public offerings of cooperative shares. In most states such protection of investors is afforded through the normal operation of the so-called "blue-sky" laws.

In New York, for example,[7] a person is prohibited from taking part in a public offering or sale of "cooperative interests in realty," unless and until there shall have been filed with the appropriate public authority, an *offering statement* or *prospectus,* containing designated information and representations and the Attorney General has issued to the issuer or other offerer a letter stating that the offering has been filed. This legislation was upheld in the case of *160 West 87th Street Corp. v. Lefkowitz,*[8] in which a challenge to the power of the Attorney General to withhold approval of a co-op plan without notice and hearing as a deprivation of property without due process, was over ruled and the law sustained.

Since the mortgage on a cooperative project, usually a blanket mortgage, is in the name of the corporation, rent paid by the tenants must be sufficient to pay all debt servicing costs, management, maintenance, taxes, and other authorized expenses. IRS regulations[9] allow cooperative owners to deduct monthly payments for taxes and interest (the largest portion of their rent payments) in the same manner as owners of condominiums or private residences. The principal requirement of the IRS regulation requires that a minimum of 80 percent of all of the cooperative income be from tenant-stockholders.

Since the co-op corporation retains title to the land and buildings, notwithstanding the leasing of units to tenant/shareholders, it can and usually does, place a blanket mortgage on the entire project. The tenant/shareowner, however, ordinarily cannot obtain a mortgage on the basis of his stock and proprietary lease, because: (1) the nature of his holding—whether real estate or personalty—for mortgage purposes is uncertain; (2) the underlying mortgage on the entire project renders his mortgage less secure, and (3) transfers of tenant/shareholder's interests, upon foreclosure, are complicated by the usual co-op requirements that a new tenant/shareholder be approved by the Board of Directors of the corporation.[10]

---

[7] N.Y. Gen. Bus. Law, Sec 353(e). This statute also applies to condominium sale offerings.

[8] 160 West 87th Street Corp. v. Lefkowitz, 350 N.Y.S. 2d 957, (1974).

[9] I.R.C. §6.216

[10] New York specifically authorizes banks and savings and loan associations to grant loans on cooperatives: Ch. 376, McKinney's 1971, amended by Chap. 596, McKinney's 1972, Session Laws of New York, and liberalized by L. 1976, Chap.534, s.1.

MAINTENANCE

Tenant/shareholders in a co-op pay their assessments for repairs and maintenance in the form of rent. Should it become necessary to raise abnormally large sums for repairs and improvements, the co-op corporation, as owner of the property, may in principal have more flexibility than the condominium, since it may have access to mortgage financing or other secured borrowing, in addition to the right to assess tenant/shareholders.

REAL ESTATE SYNDICATIONS

Real estate syndications had their beginnings in the mid-1960s and by the early 1970s were being sold at the rate of more than $1 billion per year in the interstate market. Many additional billions were probably marketed through private offerings in intrastate sales, which were not required to be registered with the Securities and Exchange Commission.

The term "Real Estate Syndicate" has no precise legal significance. Generally the term has come to mean a specialized form of ownership venture, which is structured so as to produce certain tax advantages for passive investors whose invested funds are employed to acquire and develop real estate projects under an experienced partner.

Syndications are most usually organized in the form of "limited partnerships" because their characteristics lend themselves most readily to compliance with tax laws and other objectives of syndication. The limited partnership is a form of partnership in which one or more partners are *general partners,* i.e., partners who manage the business and assume unlimited liability, and any number of additional *limited partners,* i.e., partners who do not participate in the management of the business and whose liability is limited to their respective contributions to the overall partnership capital. *The limited partner is essentially a passive investor or silent partner.*

The inherent distinction between a limited partner and a general partner provides a natural and flexible vehicle for achieving a variety of objectives sought by each type of partner. The entrepreneur—the general partner—is able to organize the venture, obtain the funds for acquisition of the investment property from the limited partners, and manage the enterprise for compensation. He may also take an interest as a limited partner if he so desires. The limited partner has an opportunity to participate in a large or diversified investment which might not otherwise be available to him without any management responsibility. This type of opportunity is particularly attractive to doctors, dentists, professional athletes, and others who have large sums to invest but little time for investment management.

For the general partner, there is an opportunity to reap a substantial bonanza from the project. These entrepreneurs are most often real estate brokers who are paid a commission for the sale of the land to the limited partnership, paid a management fee for the management of the finished project, and again paid a commission on the listing and sale of the project at a later date. He may also demand and receive a limited partnership interest of 10 to 20 percent for putting the deal together.

THE SYNDICATION PROCESS

There are many types of syndications. A representative example might be as follows:

The syndicator, probably a REALTOR®, locates a property which has the appropriate economic characteristics to produce the benefits he seeks for himself and for his potential investors. After satisfying himself of the validity of his appraisal and forecasts and the propriety of his proposed tax plan for distribution of income and losses among the partners, he makes a binding commitment (usually a option to buy)for the purchase of the property, which he will later on convey to the syndicate. He then formally establishes the syndicate with several joint venturers and associates. The limited partnership is organized under the state statutes which are generally based on the Uniform Limited Partnership Act.

Before offering interests to prospective investors, he determines whether he is subject to the requirement of the federal security laws or state "blue sky" laws regulating the offering of securities. Depending on the nature of the offering and the proposed investor clientele to be offered partnership interests, he begins his solicitation of investors through a prospectus and offering circular or similar document.

The prospectus or offering circular spells out in detail the nature of the proposed investment, the anticipated economic and tax benefits, the essential provisions of the partnership agreement and all other relevant information. These offering pieces also include an application form inviting investors to join the syndication as a limited partner.

The subscription of the limited partnerships supply the minimum cash needed to purchase the equity in the property subject to a mortgage which the syndicator has previously had committed. The syndicate then purchases the property.

There are countless variations on the above described process as the syndication may involve construction of new buildings on acquired property, the purchase of going projects or the purchase of a number of projects of similar type. The syndicate may be a closed-end organization in which a stated and limited number of partnerships are offered or it may be open-ended, allowing for the continuous solicitation of partners in order to provide additional funds for continued investment as worthwhile projects are identified.

TAX ASPECTS

Unlike corporations, which are subject to income tax, the limited partnership, like any other partnership, pays no income tax as a legal entity. Each partner is taxed on a pro-rata basis of distributed income or loss the partnership enterprise.

The ability of the partners to share in the syndication losses was the key incentive for the investor. Prior to the tax change in 1986, investors could use syndicate tax-losses to offset income from other sources, such as from professional income. Also, prior to the 1986 tax reform, the upper tier of the income tax schedule was 50 percent or higher, depending upon the overall income. Thus a dollar of loss could offset a dollar of earnings and was worth a tax savings of 50%. In fact a dollar of losses was worth the same as a dollar of earnings (after taxes).

The change of law most adversely affecting the limited partnerships was the new definitions of income, which are now divided into three categories:

1. earned income from labor and services,

2. passive income from investments in which the participant did not actively participate in the management and operation, and

3. investment income such as interest, dividends, and so on.

Since all income or losses passed through limited partnerships are now classed as "passive income and losses," passive losses can only be used to offset passive income or carried forward to future returns. In effect the tax change makes each syndication project rise and fall on its own merits. If it isn't projected to be profitable, no one is interested. The net effect has been to drastically reduce limited partnership and real estate investment trust offerings and to make those previously offered difficult to resell.

THE REAL ESTATE INVESTMENT TRUST (REIT)

The real estate investment trust is a special kind of syndication with the following requirements:

- It must be managed by one or more trustees or directors.
- Must have transferable shares of ownership. (REIT shares are freely transferable on stock exchanges, like corporate stock; this is not true of limited partnerships because of the tax rules applicable).
- Must have at least 100 beneficial owners and five or fewer persons may not own more than 50 percent of its total shares.
- Must be a legal entity, which would be taxable as a domestic corporation except for the special provisions of the IRS code.
- Must make a formal election to be taxed as a REIT (similar to the Subchapter "S" election for small corporations).
- Must meet prescribed tests on asset values and income sources to insure that its investment are essentially in real estate.
- The REIT is not allowed to engage in the real estate business of buying and selling , managing or construction—the 1986 provisions ease this somewhat (see page 365).

The Tax Reform Act of 1986 made several changes in REIT taxation. The following are some of the more important changes:

• The law eases some of the qualification requirements for REITs. REITs have been relieved of certain shareholder and income asset requirements for the first year that an entity otherwise qualifies as a REIT.

• The law made some important changes in the definition of rents from real property. The modification in the new law enables REITs to perform services what would not result in the receipt of unrelated business income. It also includes in the definition of rents from real property, and the definition of interest, rent or interest that is based on the net income of the tenant or debtor.

• The new law grants some relief from the required distribution of certain types of income that are not accompanied by the receipt of cash, although the REIT must pay tax on the amounts not distributed.

• There is an expansion of the safe harbor granted REITs under which sales by a REIT may not be treated as a prohibited transaction.

• To qualify as a real estate investment trust, 75 percent or more of the trust's income must come from real property. Under the new law, a REIT receiving equity capital which is invested in stock or bonds, may consider the interest, dividends or gains from the sale of investments, as income for the purposes of the 75 percent requirement.

• A REIT may be charged 100 percent tax on net income from "prohibited transactions." However, there are a number of "safe harbors" that permit avoidance of this tax. Under the new law, the number of property sales that a REIT may make within the safe harbor is increased from five to seven or the adjusted base of all sales which are not more than 10 percent of the adjusted bases of all assets as of the beginning of the tax year.

REAL ESTATE MORTGAGE INVESTMENT CONDUITS (REMICs)

The 1986 tax reform act created a special tax vehicle for entities which issue multiple classes of investor interests, which are backed by a pool of mortgages. The new vehicle is generally a conduit for tax purposes. It is intended to be the exclusive vehicle for issuing multiple-class mortgage-backed securities (bonds). Where the complex qualification rules are met, any corporate, partnership, trust or similar entity is granted pass-through REMIC status.

The operation is basically as follows:

• The operating entity acquires a large pool of mortgages or mortgage-backed securities (Large-valued FNMAE or GNMAE bonds) and issues smaller denomination (usually $1000 par value) securities.

• Income from the underlying mortgages or large mortgage-backed securities is passed through to the holder.

• REMIC security holders report income received on their personal tax forms.

A REMIC qualifies as such only if it meets two tests:

1. Substantially all assets at the close of the forth month ending after "start up" day and each quarter ending thereafter must consist of qualified mortgages and permitted investments, and

2. All investor interests in the REMIC must consist of one or more classes of regular interests and a single class of residual interests.

WHEN IS REAL ESTATE A SECURITY?

Traditionally, the federal securities laws have dealt with public offerings which involve typical securities, such as corporate stocks, bonds and debentures. Real estate transactions seemed a far cry from the reach of the security laws. But with the explosive growth of real estate syndications and other forms of sophisticated real estate transactions in recent years, recurring litigation has established the offerings to the public of interests in real estate does indeed constitute an offering of securities more often than the conventional wisdom supposed.

One reason why securities law enforcement has been slow to reach interests in real estate is the fact that federal securities laws make no specific reference to real estate. They do, however, define *security* to include undertakings which are frequently associated with real estate transactions, including "evidence of indebtedness," "certificates of interest or participation in any profit-sharing agreement," and "iinvestment contract."

How, then, does one determine when a real estate offering is a security offering under the federal securities laws? A three-prong test, laid down in the U.S. Supreme Court in *SEC v. Howey Co.*,[11] has provided the basic guideline for determining whether a real estate transaction is an *investment contract*, the category of security into which most real estate transactions fall. To qualify as an investment contract an arrangement must be a scheme whereby:

1. a person invests his money in a common enterprise

2. he is led to expect profits, and

3. the expectation of profit is solely from the efforts of the promoter or a third party.

In the Howey case, the sale of large units in a large Florida citrus grove, coupled with an offer by the developer to cultivate and market the fruit and to remit

---

[11]
SEC v. Howey Co., 328 U.S. 293 (1946).

the net proceeds to the investors, was held to constitute a security offering. Similarly, where the sale of condominium units was coupled with an arrangement whereby the purchasers of the units were to derive fixed guaranteed annual return from rentals managed by the sellers or a third party, the offer was a security.[12]

The Howey opinion emphasized the need for flexibility in determining whether ". . . the countless and variable schemes devised by those who seek the use of money of others or the promise of profits . . ." constitute an investment contract. This flexibility has resulted in unpredictable application of the Howey test.[13]

On December 6, 1973, the SEC filed a test case in the Federal Court in San Francisco to compel six corporations, which operate Pajaro Dunes, a 400-unit condominium, to register their offerings of units as securities.[14] On March 1, 1974, it issued "Proposed Guide 60: Preparation of Registrations Statements Relating to Interests in Real Estate Limited Partnerships," which prescribes certain disclosures that must be made in registration statements.

STATE "BLUE SKY" LAWS

The solicitation or sale of securities has also been regulated by the various states under the so-called "blue sky" laws, which aim at preventing deceit and fraud in the sale of securities. All of the states have enacted laws of this kind and 31 states have adopted, without modifications, the Uniform Securities Act as approved by the National Conference of Commissioners on Uniform State Laws.

Offerings of real estate interests may fall within the purview of either federal or state securities regulations, or both. As in the case of federal securities laws, the trend has been in the direction of bringing transactions involving real estate interests within the scope of Blue Sky regulations. As recently as 1970, State Courts held uniformly that shares of cooperative housing corporations were not securities. Since that date, courts have modified their position and treated such shares as

---

12
SEC v. Marasol Properties, F. Supp. -(DC 1973) and Kahn v. Kaskel, 367 F. Supp. 784 (1973).
13
See, Nash & Associates, Inc. v. LUM'S of Ohio, Inc. 484 F. 2d 393 (6th Cir. 1973). E.G. "Co-op offerings" are both "stock" and "investment contracts" within the Securities Act of 1933; 1950 Tenants Corp. et al. v. Jakobsen et al, 365 F. Supp. 1171 (S.D. N.Y. 1973), July 8, (Ca 9) (1975) and owners of S.W. 8 Real Estate v. McQuaid, 513 F. 2d 558 CA 9) (1975). There must be an expectation of profit, however. Thus a state subsidized and supervised nonprofit housing co-op does not offer "securities"; tax benefits, reduced rental and benefits from the leasing of commercial facilities do not constitute an expectation or profit per se: United Housing Foundation, Inc. v. Forman, 421 U.S. 837 (1975), reversing Forman v. Community Services, 500 F2 1246 (Ca. 2) (1974). See also, Grenader v. Spitz, 537 F2 612 (CA 2) (1975); AMR Realty Co. v. State Bureau of Securities, 373 A. 2d 1002 (Super. Ct., N.J. App. Div.) (1977).
14
SEC v. Hare, Brewer & Kelley, Inc. et al., SEC Docket, Vol 3, No. 5, Dec 18, 1973.

securities within the meaning of state laws. Specific regulations, moreover, have been adopted by some states regulating the sale of certain forms of interests in real estate.

THE INTERSTATE LAND SALES FULL DISCLOSURE ACT[15]

The Interstate Land Sales Full Disclosure Act regulates the interstate sale or lease by developers of fifty or more unimproved lots in a subdivision as part of a common promotional plan. When such sales are direct sales of real estate, that would normally fall within the protection of the securities laws. The Act therefore provides a method of registration with the Department of Housing and Urban Development (HUD) which is analogous to registration under the Securities Act. No such lot may be sold or leased unless a "statement of record" containing detailed information concerning the property and the plan filed with HUD.[16]

The Act provides the following exemptions from the Act's registration requirements, among others:

• The plan offers less than 50 lots or lots consisting of at least five acres each.

• The lots contain an existing building on improved land or the seller is obligated to erect such building within 2 years.

• The lots are purchased for the purpose of constructing residential, commercial or industrial buildings by a professional builder, or

• The lot is free and clear of all liens and encumbrances at the time of the sale and the purchaser has personally inspected the property.

The office of Interstate Land Sales Regulation of HUD has adopted elaborate regulations pursuant to the Act. Among other disclosures, the developer must provide audited financial statements, reports on environmental factors including unusual conditions affecting habitability, assurances on the developer's commitments to provide promised improvements, and the availability of utilities and sewage facilities.

In order to lighten the burden on developers with limited resources, the agency has provided a "Limited Offering-Intrastate Exemption" for subdivisions which contain less that 300 lots and which are offered and advertised intrastate to residents of the state where the subdivision is located (except that 5 percent or less of sales in any one year may be made to residents of another state). Qualification for this exemption, however, must be granted expressly by HUD.

In 1973, the state of Utah passed the Utah Uniform Land Practices Act, which

---

[15] 15 USC 1701 et seq, Pub L. 90-448, August 1, 1968.

[16] See Gladys Husted v. AMREP Corp, et al., 429 F. Supp. 298 (S.D. N.Y. 1977) for interpretation of various key provisions of the ILSFDA. See also Bryan v. AMREP Corp. 429 F. Supp. 313 (S.D. N.Y. 1977) for class action involving ILSFDA.

implements the Federal Act. The most important aspect of the act, besides details of implementation, was the provision for stiff fines and/or imprisonment for violation. Section 16 states:

> Any person who willfully violates any provision of this act or of a rule adopted under it or any person who willfully, in an application for registration under this act or under the Federal Act, makes any untrue statement of material fact or omits to state a material fact may be fined not less than $1,000 or double the amount of gain from the transaction, whichever is larger, but not more that $50,000; or he may be imprisoned for not more than two years; or both. No indictment or information may be returned or complaint filed under this act more than five years after the alleged violation. . .

APPENDICES

Appendix A
DEFINITIONS OF
REAL ESTATE TERMS[1]

Abandonment

A conveyance of a recorded instrument used to terminate a homestead.

Abrogate

A legal term meaning to cancel or annul.

Absolute Fee Simple Title

One that is unqualified; it is the best title one can obtain.

Abstract of Title

A condensed history of the title, consisting of a summary of the various links in the chain of title, together with a statement of all liens, charges, or encumbrances affecting a particular property.

Acceleration Clause

A clause in a mortgage, land purchase contract or lease stating that, upon default of a payment due, the balance of the obligation should at once become due and payable. See also Due on Sale Clause.

Access Right

The right of an owner to have ingress and egress to an from his property.

Accretion

Addition to the land through natural causes —usually by change in water flow.

Acknowledgment

A formal declaration before a notary public or other person empowered to perform the service, by the signatory to the instrument, as to the genuineness of the signature.

Acre

An area of 43,560 square feet, 160 square rods, or 4,840 square yards.

---

[1]
Additions to the tenth edition are from Blankenship, Frank J., *Real Estate Investor's Encyclopedia,* (Englewood Cliffs, N.J.: Prentice Hall Inc., 1989).

Acre-Foot

A water quantity measurement equal to one acre in area and one foot deep.

Actual Possession

The physical possession or occupation of a land parcel by which a claimant attempts to obtain good title by means of adverse possession.

Administrator

A person appointed by the court to administer an estate of a deceased person who left no will (i.e., died intestate).

Advance Fee

A fee paid in advance of any service rendered in the sale of property or in obtaining a loan.

Ad Valorem

A tax according to a fixed percentage of value.

Adverse Possession

The right of an occupant of land to acquire title against a real owner, where possession has been actual, continuous, hostile, visible, and distinct for the statutory period.

Affiant

A person who has made an affidavit.

Affidavit

A statement of declaration reduced to writing, and sworn or affirmed to before some office who has authority to administer an oath of affirmation.

Agent

One who represents another from whom he has derived authority.

Agreement of Sale

A written agreement whereby the purchaser agrees to buy certain real estate and the seller agrees to sell upon terms and conditions set forth therein.

Air Rights (Easement)

The ownership of the right to use, control, or occupy the air space over a designated property.

Alienation

The transfer of real property by one person to another.

Alluvion

Also Alluvium. Soil deposited by accretion; increase in land on shore or bank of a river due to change in flow of a stream.

American Land Title Association (ALTA)

An organization dedicated to the improved practices and standards in the examination of titles to land.

Amenities

The satisfaction or enjoyable living to be derived from a home; or a beneficial influence arising from the location of the property.

Amortization

The liquidation of a financial obligation on the installment basis.

Anchor Tenant

A major tenant, who is well known to the public, who is expected to draw shoppers and other tenants to a developed area.

Annuity

A sum of money or its equivalent that constitutes one of a series of periodic payments.

Appellant

The party who takes an appeal to a higher court.

Appellee

The party against whom the appeal is taken to a higher court.

Appraisal

An estimate of quantity, quality, or value. The process through which a conclusion of property value is obtained; also refers to the report setting forth the estimate and conclusion of value.

Appraisal by Capitalization

An estimate of value by capitalization of productivity and income.

Appraisal by Comparison

Comparability to the sales price of other similar properties.

Appraisal by Cost

An estimate of value calculated by summation of the costs of all components of the property.

Appraisal by Summation

The adding together of parts of a property, separately appraised, to form the whole.

Appraisal Institute

A professional organization of real estate appraisers formed in 1990 by a merger of the Institute of Real Estate Appraisers and the Society of Real Estate Appraisers.

Appurtenance

That which belongs to something else; something that passes as an incident to land, such as a right of way.

Arbitrage

The difference between the interest of a wrap-around mortgage and the prime mortgage.

Architect

A member of the American Institute of Architects, whose profession is designing buildings, drawing plans, and generally supervising construction.

Arpen

French measurement term, being 7/8 of one acre.

Assessed Valuation

Assessment of a real estate unit by a unit of government for taxation purposes.

Assessment

A charge against real estate made by a unit of government to cover the proportionate cost of an improvement, such as a street or sewer.

Assessment Lien

A lien against real estate, placed by a unit of government, to indicate an unpaid assessment.

Assignee

The person to whom an agreement or contract is assigned.

Assignment

The method or manner by which a right, a specialty, or contract is transferred from one person to another.

Associate Broker

A person who is qualified and licensed as a real estate broker, but works for another broker. See also Associate REALTOR®.

Associate REALTOR®

A person who is qualified and licensed as a real estate broker and a member of the local, state, and NATIONAL ASSOCIATION OF REALTORS®, but works for another REALTOR®.

Assumption Agreement

An agreement between two parties whereas the party of the second part agrees to assume a debt or other obligation primarily resting with the party of the first part.

Attestation

The witnessing of a signature to an instrument at the request of the person who signed it.

Avulsion

Removal of land from one owner to another when a stream suddenly changes its channel.

Backfill

The replacement of excavated earth into a hole or against a structure.

Balloon Payment

A lump sum payment due on a mortgage or other obligation in addition to the regular periodic payment.

Balustrade

A handrail supported by small posts or columns.

Bargain and Sale Deed

A deed which conveys the property for valuable consideration.

Barge Board

A wide trim board placed on the ends of a gable roof.

Base and Meridian

Imaginary lines used by surveyors to find and describe the location of lands by the Rectangular Survey Method.

Baseboard

The board skirting the walls of a room at the floor line. Also referred to as shoemold.

Basement Floor

The lowest floor level in a building, usually below the ground level.

Bench Marks

A location indicated on a durable marker by a surveyor.

Bilateral Contract

Both parties expressly enter into a mutual agreement (reciprocal).

Bill of Sale

An official document transferring personal property to another.

Binder

An agreement to cover a down payment for the purchase of real estate as evidence of good faith on the part of the purchaser; in insurance: a temporary agreement given to one having an insurable interest, and who desires insurance subject to the same conditions which will apply if, as, and when a policy is issued.

Blanket Mortgage

A single mortgage which covers more than one piece of real estate.

Blight

A reduction in value of real property due to a variety of causes, which have a harmful effect upon the appearance of the property area affected.

Block-Busting

An attempt to persuade persons to sell or move out by creating or exploiting fears of racial change in the neighborhood; prohibited by federal law.

Blue Sky Laws

Laws enacted by the various states to regulate the sale of securities.

Board Foot

A lumber measurement; one foot long by one foot wide by one inch thick.

Board of Equalization

The official organization within a county or parish which sits to hear appeals of property owners who feel their property has been incorrectly assessed.

Bona fide

In good faith, without fraud.

Bond

Any obligation under seal. A real estate bond is a written obligation, usually issued on security of a mortgage or trust deed.

Bridge Loan

An intermediate loan to provide funds on a temporary basis for new construction.

Bridging

Small wood or metal pieces used to brace floor joists.

Broker

One employed by another, for a fee, to carry on any of the activities listed in the license law definition of the word.

B.T.U.

British thermal unit. The quantity of heat required to raise the temperature of one pound of water one degree Fahrenheit.

Buildable Units

The total number of living units which can be legally constructed on a land parcel.

Building Code

The sum of municipal ordinances which regulate the construction of buildings within that municipality.

Building Line

A line fixed at a certain distance from the front and/or sides of a lot, beyond which no building can project.

Bundle of Rights

Establishes real estate ownership; consists of right to sell; to mortgage or lease; to will; to regain possession at end of a lease (reversion); to build and remove improvements; to control use within the law.

Business broker

A licensed broker who negotiates the sale of a mercantile business for another for a fee.

Buyer's Market

A market in which there is an excess number of properties for sale in relation to the number of buyers. See also seller's market.

Cadastre

A public record of the extent and value of land for taxation purposes.

Capitalization rate

The percentage rate by which the net income is divided to determine value in the formula $V = I \div r$.

Caveat Emptor

"Let the purchaser beware": the principle by which the buyer is duty-bound to examine the property he is purchasing to the best of his ability, and he assumes the conditions which are readily ascertainable upon view.

Certificate of Eligibility

A certificate issued by the Veterans Administration stating that the veteran applicant is qualified for a VA loan.

Certificate of no defense

An instrument issued by a mortgagor, upon the sale of the mortgage, to the assignee, as to the validity of the full mortgage debt.

Certificate of Reasonable Value

A written statement issued by the Veterans Administration as to the maximum value of the property.

Certificate of Release

A certificate issued by a lending institution certifying that a mortgage has been paid in full. Also known as satisfaction of mortgage.

Certified check

A check drawn by a depositor, in which the bank certifies as to the amount drawn, and against which the depositor cannot stop payment.

Certiorari

A writ obtained from an appellate court, directing a lower court to send up the record for review and determination, or for trial by the lower court.

Cestui Que Trust

The person who has a beneficial interest in an estate, the legal title to which is vested in another person.

Chain

A unit of land measurement—66 feet.

Chain of Title

A history of conveyances and encumbrances affecting the title of a property.

Chattel

Personal property, such as household goods or removable fixtures.

Chattel Mortgage

An encumbrance upon personal property. Usually held by the vendor until paid for by the purchaser.

Check

A negotiable instrument issued in payment of an obligation.

Chimney cap ·

The finishing course or courses at the top of a chimney.

Chronological Age

Actual age of a structure, as measured by the calendar.

Civil Law

A derivation of Roman law which forms a basis for real estate law in some of the states. See also Old Spanish Law.

Cleaning deposit

A deposit made with a landlord by a tenant to guarantee that on lease termination the property will be left in a clean and sanitary condition.

Closing Statement

An accounting of funds in a real estate sale made by the broker or other closing agency to seller and buyer, respectively. See also Escrow.

Cloud on the title

A record of a claim or encumbrance which, if valid, would affect or impair the owner's title; a judgment, or dower interest.

Code of ethics

A set of rules by a professional organization, prescribing standards of ethical conduct which its members are bound to obey.

Cognovit note

A note authorizing a confession of judgment.

Co-insurance

A usual insurance policy provision, which requires the insured to carry insurance in an equal amount of 80 percent of the property replacement value; also, where two or more insurance companies carry risk in certain proportional amounts, upon large commercial properties.

Collateral

Security given for the fulfillment of a debt or obligation.

Color of title

That which appears to be good title, but as a matter of fact, is not good title.

Commingle

To mingle or mix client's (trust) funds in the broker's personal or operating account; also the mixing of separate and community property in those states recognizing these designations of ownership.

Common law

A body of law which grew from custom and decided cases (English law) rather than from codified law (Roman law).

Community property

Property accumulated through joint efforts of husband and wife living together.

Compass call

A surveyors term indicating direction in degrees, minutes, and seconds, by which a property line extends from one point of beginning or turning.

Competent party

A person fully competent by age, position, and mental capacity to enter into a legal contract with others.

Completion bond

A surety bond posted by a developer or contractor to guarantee that the work will be performed in accordance with specifications and/or time.

Compound interest

Interest paid on the original principal and also on the accrued and unpaid interest; interest on interest.

Condemnation

The taking of private property for public use, with compensation to the owner, under the right of eminent domain.

Condominium

Individual ownership of units in a multifamily structure or project, combined with joint ownership of common areas and facilities.

Conduit

A pipe or channel for conveying fluids or wires; also methods or procedures for the transfer of funds.

Confession of judgment

An entry of judgment upon the debtor's voluntary authority to an attorney to do so in his behalf.

Construction loan

Provides for progressive payments of the loan proceeds during the erection of a building.

Constructive Eviction

Breach of a covenant of warranty or quiet enjoyment; for example, the inability of a purchaser or lessee to obtain possession by reason of a paramount outstanding title.

Constructive notice

Notice given by public records.

Constructive possession

When title to property is transferred, the owner is said to have constructive possession; actual possession may or may not have actually occurred.

Contract rent

The rental price agreed upon between lessor and lessee.

Contract sale

A contract to purchase land where the owner becomes the mortgagor in effect. Also known as Land Sales Contract.

Contractor's lien

A lien recorded by a contractor or sub-contractor against a property for unpaid services rendered.

Conveyance

The means or medium by which title to real estate is transferred.

Cornice

An ornamental projection at the top of a wall.

Corporate deed form

A modified warranty deed form used to transfer property from a corporation. The form provides a place for the signature of a corporate officer who certifies that the transfer has been authorized by the corporation. Also known as a Special Warranty Deed.

Cost plus contract

A construction contract which requires an owner to pay the cost of labor and materials plus a fixed percentage of the total cost to the builder as his profit.

Co-tenant

Property ownership by more than one person creates a co-ownership and the owners are said to be co-tenants.

Counter offer

A rejection of an offer to purchase or sell and replaced with another offer.

Covenant

An agreement between two or more persons, by deed, whereby one of the parties promises the performance or non-performance of certain acts, or that a given state of things does or does not exist.

Coverture

The status of a married woman.

Creative financing

A method of financing a real estate purchase by other than cash or a standard mortgage arrangement.

Cubage

Width of a building multiplied by length multiplied by height.

Culinary water

Water fit for drinking or cooking.

Cul-de-sac

A passageway with one outlet; a dead end.

Curtesy

The right which a husband has in his wife's estate at her death.

Curtilage

Area of land actually occupied by a building, its yard and outbuildings, which is actually enclosed or considered enclosed.

Damnum Absque Injuria

A loss which does not give rise to an action for damages against the person causing it.

Date of possession

The effective date of transfer of ownership of property. Possession may be actual or constructive.

Dba

Abbreviation for Doing Business As.

Debt Service

The cash required each month to cover the mortgage or contract debt payments, taxes, and insurance.

Declaration of no set-off

See Certificate of no defense.

Decree of Foreclosure

A decree issued by a court upon the completion of foreclosure of a mortgage, lien, or contract.

Dedication

An appropriation of land by an owner to some public use together with acceptance for such use by or on behalf of the public.

Deed

A writing by which lands, tenements, and hereditaments are transferred, which writing is signed, sealed, and delivered by the grantor.

Deed of Distribution

A deed provided by a fiduciary transferring ownership of property from a decedent to another person. See also Executor's deed.

Deed of Restriction

A limitation in a deed of conveyance in which future owners of the property are denied full ownership.

Default

The nonperformance of a duty, whether arising under a contract or otherwise; failure to meet an obligation when due.

Defeasance

An instrument which nullifies the effects of some other deed or of an estate.

Deficiency judgment

The difference between the indebtedness sued upon and the sale price of market value of the real estate foreclosure sale.

De Minimis PUD

A unit in a planned unit development, in which the value of the commonly owned facilities and amenities is incidental to the total value of the unit itself.

Demise

A conveyance of an estate or interest in real property by lease or will.

Depreciation

Loss in value, brought on by deterioration through ordinary wear and tear, action of the elements, or functional or economic obsolescence.

Depth table

Tabulation of factors representing the rating value per front foot between selected "standard" depths (usually 100 feet) and other lots of greater or lesser depth.

Devise

A gift of real estate by will or last testament.

Direct deduction mortgage

A mortgage which requires periodic payment reductions upon the principal.

Discount

A loan placement charge made by a lending institution to the buyer or seller, by increasing the yield on the investment (known in the trade as points, a point usually being 1 percent of the loan).

Discounted paper

Notes, mortgages, and other written evidence of debt which are sold for less than face value thereby increasing the yield to the buyer.

Discrimination

Prejudice or refusal to sell or rent to a person because of race, color, or national origin.

Dispossess

To deprive one of the use of real estate.

Distinct possession

A requirement for a claim of adverse possession in which the property claimed must be sharply defined and controlled.

Domicile

The place of one's permanent residence and usually the place where he is registered to vote.

Dower

The right which a wife has in her husband's estate at his death.

Due on Sale Clause

A clause in modern mortgages which requires full payment at the time the property is transferred or sold. See also Acceleration clause.

"Dummy Purchaser"

The purchase of a property in the name of one financially irresponsible in order to conceal the identity of the true purchaser. Also known as straw man.

Duplex

A structure designed for two-family occupancy.

Duress

Unlawful constraint exercised upon a person, whereby he is forced to perform some act, or sign an instrument, against his better judgment or will.

Dutch roof

A roof design incorporating two slopes, the lower one being steeper than the first.

Earnest money

Down payment made by a purchaser of real estate as evidence of good faith.

Easement

The right, liberty, advantage, or privilege which one individual has in the lands of another.

Economic life

The period over which a property may be profitably or usefully utilized.

Economic rent

The rent a property will command on an open market at the time of the evaluation.

Egress

The right to return from a tract of land. See also ingress.

Ejectment

A form of action to regain possession of real property, with damages for the unlawful retention.

Emblements

The right of a tenant to harvest and remove, after his tenancy has ended, such annual products of the land, as have resulted from his own labor and care; also known as "way growing crop."

Eminent Domain

The right of the people or government to take private property for public use upon payment of compensation. See also condemnation.

Encroachment

A building, part of a building, or obstruction which intrudes upon or invades a highway or sidewalk or trespasses upon property of another.

Encumbrance

A claim, lien, charge, or liability attached to and binding upon real property, such as a judgment, unpaid taxes or a right of way; defined in law as any right to, or interest in, land which may subsist in another to the diminution of its value, but consistent with the passing of the fee.

End Loan

Also called "Take Out" financing, whereby the lender, who provides financing during the construction period of a building project, will also provide permanent financing for the ultimate purchaser.

Entity

A thing that has individual existence; a corporation is a legal entity.

Equitable title

A beneficial title to property obtained as a result of court action or signing of a contract to sell.

Equity

The interest or value which an owner has in real estate over and above the mortgage against it; system of legal rules administered by courts.

Equity of Redemption

Right of original owner to reclaim property sold through foreclosure proceedings on a mortgage, by payment of debt, interest, and costs.

Equity vehicles

A form of business arrangement between joint owners used to finance the project or syndication.

Erosion

The wearing away of land through the process of nature as by streams and winds.

Escalator clause

A clause in a mortgage or lease, which provides for increase in rent or interest based upon fluctuations in certain economic indices, costs, or taxes.

Escheat

Reversion of property to the sovereign state owing to lack of heirs capable of inheriting.

Escrow

A deed delivered to a third party for the grantee to be held by such party until the fulfillment or performance of certain conditions; used in the trade as the process of closing the deal.

ESOP

An employee stock ownership plan.

Estate

The degree, quantity, nature, and extent of interest which a person has in real property.

Estate at sufferance

Property possessed by a tenant after the expiration of a lease and without consent of the landlord.

Estate at will

A landlord-tenant relationship in which the tenant is in possession of the landlord's property without a lease.

Estoppel certificate

See Certificate of no defense.

Et al.

An abbreviation for *et alii* (and others). Also used in an abbreviation for *et alius* (and another).

Ethics

That branch of moral science, which treats of the duties which a member of a profession or craft owes to the public, to his client and to other members of his profession. See also Code of ethics.

Et ux.

Abbreviation for *et uxor*, meaning "and wife."

Eviction

A violation of some covenant in a lease by the landlord or tenant which severs the landlord-tenant relationship and returns the property to the landlord's possession.

Excess rent

The amount of rent payable over and beyond economic rent.

Exchange

The trading of one property for another, with or without additional monetary consideration.

Exclusive agency

The appointment of one real estate broker as sole agent for the sale of a property for a designated period of time.

Exclusive right to sell

A real estate listing which pays the listing agent a commission regardless of who sells the property.

Execution

A writ issued by a court to the sheriff directing him to sell property to satisfy a debt.

Executor (Executrix)

A person named in a will to carry out its provisions.

Executor's deed

A deed in which the grantor is the executor of an estate in probate. See also Deed of distribution.

Ex officio

By virtue of his office. Example: in Iowa and Nebraska, the Secretary of State is ex officio chairman of the Real Estate Commission.

Extender clause

A clause in an exclusive listing contract, which carries the original exclusive period over for an additional period, to protect the broker, if a sale is made to the broker's prospect who was obtained during the original listing period.

Exculpatory clause

A clause in an agreement of sale, freeing the broker from any blame in the transaction.

Facia board

A vertically faced board covering the lower ends of roof rafters and, together with the soffit, forming the lower roof trim.

Fair market value

The best price which a property would bring upon the open market to a willing seller, not compelled to sell, from a willing buyer, not compelled to buy.

"Fannie Mae"

Trade name for the Federal National Mortgage Association. See FNMA.

Farm Home Administration

An agency of the Department of Agriculture that grants loans for the purpose of providing rural housing.

Farm lease

A farm lease in which the tenant usually pays a rental based on a crop sharing basis.

FNMA

A secondary market which provides a market for mortgages held by private lenders, such as banks, savings and loan associations, and mortgage companies and provides the primary market with a ready market, so as to permit a greater turn over of money for loans.

Fee-tail estate

An estate of inheritance given to a person and the heirs of his body. If the grantee dies without leaving an issue, the estate terminates and reverts to the grantor.

Fee simple

The largest estate of ownership in real property; also known as fee simple absolute.

Federal Home Loan Bank

Composed of 12 regional banks, which provide credit reserves for savings and loan financing institutions.

F.H.A.

Federal Housing Authority; an agency of the federal government that insures real estate loans.

FSLIC

Federal Savings and Loan Insurance Corporation, an agency of the federal government, which insures bank depositors accounts up to $100,000.

Financing charge

A fee charged by a lender at the time a mortgage loan is made.

Finder's fee

A fee paid to a broker for obtaining a mortgage loan for a client or for referring a mortgage loan to a broker. It may also refer to a commission paid to a broker for locating property.

Fixture

An article that was once personal property, but has become real estate by reason of its permanent attachment in or to a property improvement.

Firm commitment

A commitment made by a lender to provide a mortgage on a specified property in a stated amount and at a guaranteed interest rate.

Flashing

Strips of material placed around a roof opening to provide water tightness.

Floating rate loan

A loan in which the interest varies in accordance with some designated economic bench mark or index.

Force majeure

In Roman law, an act of God; frequently found in construction contracts to exonerate a builder from liability for delay due to an act of God or other unavoidable delay.

Forcible entry and detainer

A legal action to recover possession of premises which are unlawfully held.

Foreclosure

A court process instituted by a mortgagee or lien creditor to defeat any interest or redemption which the debtor-owner may have in a property.

Foreshore

Land between high-water mark and low-water mark.

Foundation

The walls of a building below the first or ground floor; also a legal entity established to provide funds or support for general public benefit.

Fraud

The intentional and successful employment of any cunning, deception, collusion or artifice, used to circumvent, cheat, or deceive another person, whereby that person acts upon it, to his detriment, loss, or disadvantage.

Freehold

An estate in fee simple for life.

Front foot

A standard of measurement of a lot; one foot in length measured along the fronting street property line.

Fructus industriales

Land products produced by the labor of the occupant. See also Emblements.

Fructus naturales

Products of the land produced by nature alone.

Future sweat

A payment made on a property purchase by a trade of the buyer's work for the cash value thereof; sometimes referred to as "sweat equity."

Future value of one

The value to which one dollar will grow in a designated time period at a specified interest rate.

Future value of one per period

The value to which a payment of one dollar per period will grow in a designated time and a specified interest rate.

Gable roof

A pitched roof with sloping sides.

G.I.

A member or veteran of the United States military services.

G.I. loan

A loan guaranteed by the Veterans Administration under the Servicemen's Readjustment Act of 1944, as amended from time to time.

General mortgage

A pledge of a mortgagor in which all properties owned are pledged as security for a new loan. See also Blanket loan.

General warranty

A covenant in the deed whereby the grantor agrees to protect the grantee against the world.

Gradient

The slope, or rate of increase or decrease in elevation, of a surface, a road or pipe, expressed in inches of rise or fall per horizontal foot.

Graduated lease

One in which the rent will increase or decrease after the initial period.

Graduated payment mortgage

A mortgage in which payments begin at a lower than normal rate and increase in steps over stipulated periods of time. See also Adjustable rate mortgages.

GNMA

Government National Mortgage Association. A government owned corporation of the department of Housing and Urban Development (HUD), which assists federally aided housing projects, guarantees securities issued by private lenders, and backs FHA, VA and Farm Home Administration Loans.

Grandfather clause

A clause in a new rule or regulation which exempts prior actions from the new rule or regulation.

Grantee

A person to whom property is conveyed; the buyer.

Grantor

A person who conveys real estate in a deed; the seller.

Gray water waste

Water from toilets and other noxious activities which are considered hazardous to watershed areas.

Greenbelt tax classification

Valuable property, which is adjacent to metropolitan areas, taxed as farmland, which if not so designated would be taxed at a higher fair market value.

G.R.I.

Graduate Realtor's Institute, a component of the NATIONAL ASSOCIATION OF REALTORS®; a designation awarded to a REALTOR® or REALTOR ASSOCIATE® who successfully completes the necessary courses and experience requirements.

Gross lease

A lease of property whereby lessor is to meet all property charges regularly incurred through ownership.

Ground lease

A long term lease of ground upon which a building is erected by the tenant.

Ground rent

A rent reserved by a grantor to himself, his heirs and assigns in conveying land in fee.

Habendum clause

The "To Have and to Hold" clause which defines or limits the quality of the estates granted in the premises of the deed.

Hand money

See Earnest money.

Hazard insurance

Insurance which protects the owner in the event of loss by designated hazards—fire, windstorm, falling aircraft, and so on.

Hectare

A metric measurement of surface area (2.471 acres).

Hereditaments

The largest classification of property; included lands, tenements, and incorporeal property, such as right of ways.

Highest and best use

The fundamental concept of value which implies maximum profitability or utilization of an asset.

Holdover tenant

A tenant who remains in possession of leased property after the expiration of the lease term.

Holographic will

A will written in longhand by the testator.

Homeowner's association

The administrative body charged with the management of a condominium project.

Homestead

Real estate occupied by the owner as a home; the owner enjoys certain special benefits such as tax reduction, protection against liens, and so on.

Horizontal property act

Law relating to condominiums.

Hostile possession

Possession of another's property without his consent.

Housing for the elderly

A project designed especially for older persons, which provides living unit accommodations, common social and activity space, and facilities for health and nursing services.

H.U.D.

Department of Housing and Urban Development.

HVAC

Heating, ventilating, and air conditioning.

Hypothecate

To pledge an asset without giving up possession of it.

Implied easement

An easement which is apparent by past and continued use, but is not officially recorded.

Implied warranty or covenant

The law, by judicial power, will supply a guaranty of assurance, if the circumstances in the case warrant.

Impounds

Funds held in a trust account by a lender to assure payment of taxes, insurance, and other fees.

Inchoate

Not yet vested or completed; example: rights to dower is inchoate until the husband dies.

Indenture

A formal written instrument made between two or more persons in different interests; name comes from the practice of indenting or cutting a deed on the top or side in waving lines.

Industrial park

A land parcel developed for multitenant or multiowner use and zoned for industrial utilization.

Ingress

Access to enter a tract of land; See also egress.

Injunction

A decree of a court of equity to restrain and enjoin a defendant from doing an act which is deemed inequitable or unjust.

Installment land contract

Purchase of real estate upon an installment basis; usually the seller acts as lender of financing.

Insulation "R" value

A quantitative measure of insulation effectiveness. The higher the number the better the insulation.

Inter alia

Among other things.

Inter vivoce trust

A trust established during the lifetime of the trustor.

Ipso facto

By the fact itself.

Irrigation district

A quasi-political district created under special laws to provide water services for property owners in the district.

Irrigation water

Water provided by an organization for agricultural use.

Jalousie

A kind of blind or shutter made by slats fixed at an angle.

Joint and several liability

A debt incurred by two or more persons "jointly and severally" whereby one action may be brought against all of the parties or against one party for the entire debt.

Joint tenancy

Property held by two or more persons together with the distinct character of survivorship; also known as Joint Tenancy with Right of Survivorship.

Judgment

A decree of court declaring that one individual is indebted to another and fixing the amount of the indebtedness.

Judgment d.s.b.

D.s.b. is the abbreviation for the Latin *debitum sine brevi*, which means "debt without writ." It is a judgment confessed by authority of the language in the instrument.

Jumping signs

The replacement of a "for sale" sign upon a property with another "for sale" sign of the offending broker or salesperson.

Junior lien

A recorded encumbrance against a property which is subordinate to another recorded indebtedness.

Junior mortgage

A mortgage second in lien to a previously recorded mortgage.

Kicker

A gift of interest in a project to a lender as a bonus for granting a mortgage loan.

Laches

Delay or negligence in asserting one's rights.

Lanai

A porch, usually in the tropics.

Land Contract

A contract for the purchase of real estate upon an installment basis; upon payment of the last installment, the deed is delivered to the purchaser. See also Creative financing and Installment Land Contract.

Land economics

The branch of science of economics which deals with the classification, ownership, and utilization of land and buildings erected thereon.

Land/ground lease

An agreement for the use of land; sometimes secured by a building erected on the land by the lessee. See also Ground lease.

Land locked

A property having no access to a public road or way without trespassing upon another owner's land.

Landlord

One who rents property to another.

Lands, tenements, and hereditaments

A term used in early English law to express all types of real estate.

Late payment charge

A penalty charge payable on late periodic payments of contracts and mortgages.

Lease

A contract, written or oral, for the possession of lands and tenements on the one hand and a recompense of rent or other income, on the other hand.

Leasehold

An estate in realty held under lease.

Leasehold insurance

Insurance that compensates a landlord for losses resulting from a lease cancellation occasioned by fire or other natural peril.

Leasehold value

The difference in economic rent less contract rent, capitalized at the investor's required yield on investment and for the remaining period of the lease.

Legal description

A description recognized by law, which is sufficient to locate and identify the property without oral testimony.

Lessee

A person to whom property is rented under a lease.

Lessor

See Landlord.

License

A privilege or right granted by the state to operate as a real estate broker or salesman. An authority to go upon or use another person's land or property without possessing any estate therein.

License year

The period specified in license law for license; often different from the calendar year or in some cases a multiyear authority.

Lien

A hold or claim which one person has upon another's property as security for a debt or charge; judgments, mortgages, and taxes.

Life estate

An estate or interest held during the term of some person's life.

Life estate pur autre vie

A special type of life estate in which the property is granted by "A" to "B" for the life of "C".

Limited partnership

A special kind of partnership in which participants (limited partners) share in the profits and losses of a venture, which is operated and managed by a general partner.

Lis Pendens

Suit pending; usually recorded so as to give constructive notice of pending litigation.

Listing

Oral or written employment of a broker by an owner to sell or lease property.

Littoral

Belonging to shore of sea or Great Lakes; corresponds to riparian rights.

Loan broker

An organization or person who specializes in arranging loans from his/her client lenders to qualified borrowers.

Loan ratio

The loan amount divided by the appraised value of the property and expressed as a percentage. Also known as Loan to Value ratio.

Loan window

A long-term loan with provisions for interest renegotiation at the end of specific periods or windows, such as every five years.

Lock-in mortgage

One without provision for prepayment, with or without interest; may also provide for full interest payment to maturity in order to permit refinancing.

Locus sigilli

Place of the seal.

Lot line

A legally defined line dividing one tract of land from another.

Lot release system

A method of acquiring development property for resale with minimum down payment. The entire development tract is purchased on a contract basis with the owner providing a clear deed to specific lots as payments are received.

Louver

A roof ventilation opening, usually located in the gable end of the roof; also may be located as many small openings in the soffit.

MAI (Member, Appraisal Institute)

The highest designation awarded to members of the Appraisal Institute.

Mansard roof

A roof with two slopes on each of the four sides, the lower slope being steeper than the higher.

Manufactured housing

Residential housing units built in a factory for transportation in either a knock-down or completed condition. Also known as pre-fab.

Marginal land

Land which has little productivity or value, due to access, terrain, or blight, until better land is available for economic use.

Market data approach

An appraisal technique utilizing a comparison of sales of comparable properties.

Market value

See Fair Market Value.

Marketable title

A title such as a court would compel a purchaser to accept; it is free from any encumbrances or clouds.

Marshalling

Where a creditor has two or more funds out of which to satisfy a debt, he cannot so elect as to deprive another individual, who has but one fund, of his security.

Master plan

The guideline established by a municipality for the orderly zoning and development of properties within that municipality.

Mechanics lien

A species of lien created by statute which exists in favor of persons who have performed work or furnished materials in the erection or repair of a building.

Meeting of minds

A mutual intention of two persons to enter into a contract affecting their legal status based upon agreed terms and conditions.

Merchantable title

See Marketable title.

Meridian

A principal north-south line of a government survey.

Messuage

Dwelling house and adjacent land and outbuildings.

Metes and Bounds

A method of land identification which begins at a designated point and continues with a series of distances and compass calls to identify the various boundaries. The last compass call and distance returns to the point of beginning.

Mill rate

The measure used to state the property tax rate. One mill = 1/10th of a cent.

Mobile home

A single family housing unit constructed of aluminum or other lightweight materials, which is designed to be pulled from site to site or semi-permanently installed on a mobile park pad.

Mobile home park

A development designed and built for rental to mobile home or manufactured home owners. A mobile home site is called a pad.

Monument

An artificial or natural landmark used to anchor a property description by the metes and bounds method.

Moral turpitude

An act of baseness, vileness, or depravity in the private and social duties which a man owes to his fellow man, or to society in general, contrary to the accepted and customary rule of right and duty between man and man.

Moratorium

An emergency act by a legislative body to suspend legal enforcement of contractual obligations.

Mortgage

A conditional transfer of real property as security for the payment of a debt or the fulfillment of some obligation.

Mortgage company

A company which processes loan applications and closes loans, all or a majority of which are sold on the secondary mortgage market.

Mortgage constant

The periodic payment required to pay off one dollar of debt to include interest on the constantly declining balance.

Mortgage note

The legal instrument which requires the borrower to pay the debt, regardless of what is offered as security.

Mortgagee

A person or institution to whom property is conveyed as security for a loan made to such person (the creditor).

Mortgagee in possession

A mortgage creditor who takes over the income from a mortgaged property upon default on the mortgage by the debtor.

Mortgagor

An owner who conveys his property to a mortgagee as security for a loan (the debtor).

Multiple dwelling

A residence structure designed to accommodate two or more families.

Muniments

Written or other evidences of title.

Multiple listings

An arrangement among real estate board members whereby each broker brings his listings to the attention of other members. If a sale results, the commission is divided between the listing broker and the selling broker on a prearranged or advertised basis.

Mutual savings bank

Institutions mutually owned by the depositors. Mutual savings banks are primarily chartered in the eastern states, with 75 percent of their assets in New York and Massachusetts.

NAR

NATIONAL ASSOCIATION OF REALTORS®, the professional organization for people in the real estate business.

Necessity easement

An implied easement, where the intent is clear and strictly necessary to provide access to dominant land, to support adjoining buildings, partition walls or party driveways.

Net lease

A lease under which the lessor receives a fixed rental and the lessee pays taxes, insurance, and other specified operating expenses, such as interior maintenance of the facility.

Net listing

A price, which must be expressly agreed upon, below which the owner will not sell the property and at which the broker will not receive a commission; the listing broker typically receives the excess over and above the net listing as his commission.

Nonconforming use

Use made of property before the last zoning or zoning change, which is not in conformity with the latest authorization. See grandfather clause.

N.S.F. check

Not sufficient funds; check not honored by the bank upon which it is drawn.

Nonapparent easement

Intangible easements, such as scenic sights.

Notorious possession

The open holding or possession of real property in direct opposition to one or more additional claimants. This is the first step in a claim for adverse possession.

Novation

The substitution of a new agreement for an existing one.

Nudum pactum

"Naked pact"—no contract.

Nunc pro tunc

Now for then; the court allowing an act to be done after the time it should have been done, with retroactive effect.

Nuisance rent raise

An artificially high rent increase imposed on a tenant at the end of a lease period for the purpose of causing the tenant to move voluntarily.

Nuncupative will

An oral will.

Obsolescence

Impairment of desirability and usefulness brought about by physical, economic, fashion, or other changes.

Offset statement

A statement(s) of owner of property or owner(s) of lien against the property, setting forth the present status of liens against the property.

Old Spanish law

A property law practiced in some western states. It recognizes property obtained by inheritance or prenuptial acquisitions as separate and as distinct from community property.

One-party listing

A listing contract with a real estate broker which limits his or her right to sell and receive a commission to one potential and designated buyer.

Open-end mortgage

A mortgage, which after the principal amount has been reduced by payments, can allow the borrower to increase the debt level to the original amount or some other prescribed amount.

Open listing

An oral or general listing.

Option

The right to purchase or lease a property at a certain price for a certain designated period, for which right a consideration is paid.

Overage rent

Rental payments over and above the minimum rental specified in the lease. Overage rents usually occur in commercial leases which specify minimum rentals plus a percentage of gross sales or other sweeteners. See also Percentage lease.

Overhang

The part of the roof extending beyond the walls.

Over-improvement

An improvement which exceeds the highest and best use of the site on which it is placed by reason of size or cost.

Owner's equity

The difference between appraised fair market value and the existing indebtedness on the property.

Package mortgage

One which includes certain personal property within the lien of the mortgage.

Parole evidence rule

A judicial principal which prohibits oral testimony in a court action attempting to explain or clarify a real estate contract which is considered the complete and final agreement between the parties.

Partition

A division made of real property among those who own it in undivided shares.

Party wall

A wall erected on the line between two adjoining properties, belonging to different persons, for use of both properties.

Passive income

An Internal Revenue Service designation of income received from rental or investment property, where the owner is not actively managing the property.

Patent

Conveyance of title to government land.

Percentage lease

A lease of property in which the rental is based upon a percentage of the volume of sales made, over a stated minimum amount. See also Overage rent.

Percolation test

A soil test to determine if a septic system will operate satisfactorily.

Periodic estate

A tenant-landlord relationship in which the tenant has permission to occupy the landlord's property for a stated period of time.

Personalty

All property that is not real estate.

Pi

A symbol (π) designating the ratio of the circumference of a circle to its diameter. $\pi \approx 3.1416$.

Piggy-back loan

A loan from a conventional lender which is supplemented by a second mortgage, provided by a private lender. Payments are usually made to the piggy-back lender who makes the first mortgage payments and retains the remainder of the debtor payment as payment on the second mortgage.

Plaintiff

One who initiates a request for redress from the courts.

Plat book

A public record of various recorded plans in the municipality or county. Records may be in the form of drawings, text, or as computer data.

Plottage

Increment in value of a plot created by assembling smaller ownerships into one ownership.

Pocket license card

Evidence of licensure, which should be carried at all times by licensed brokers and agents.

Points

See Discount.

Police power

The inherent rights of a government to pass legislation as may be necessary to protect the public health and safety and/or promote the general welfare.

Postponement of lien

The subordination of a presently prior lien to a subsequent judgment or mortgage.

Present value of one

The discounted value of $1 to be received at a designated time in the future and at a specified interest rate. Value is less than $1.

Present value of one per period

The value of $1 deposited now and at each period in the future for a number of periods and at a designated interest rate. Value is greater than the sum of the deposits.

Prepayment penalty

A lender charge if the loan is paid before it is due.

Prima facie evidence

Evidence considered in law to be sufficient to establish fact, if not contradicted.

Principal

The employer of an agent; the person who is ordinarily liable primarily.

Principal meridian

A north-south line projected through a prominent landmark established under the Governmental Survey system.

Principal note

The promissory note which is secured by the mortgage or trust deed.

Principle of anticipation

This principle affirms that a value is created or destroyed by expectations of benefits to be gained or lost in the future.

Principle of Balance

This principle requires the investor and/or appraiser to consider the proper economic balance between types and locations of properties in the subject area to assure that value will be sustained by the population.

Principle of change

This principle of property evaluation considers that nothing remains the same and that all things are subject to constant and inevitable change.

Principle of competition

This principle of appraising requires the evaluator to consider that when net income is greater than the average return on labor, capital, management, and land, the excess tends to breed competition.

Principle of conformity

This principle considers how compatible the subject property is with surrounding properties.

Principle of contribution

This principle of value requires the appraiser to consider the property based on its contribution to income.

Principle of substitution

A principle which states that when several commodities are available to satisfy a need, the one with the lowest price will have the greater demand.

Principle of demand

This basic principle considers the economic factors of supply and demand. A surplus property will reduce the price that a seller can expect (buyer's market), whereas scarcity can inflate the price expectations of the seller (seller's market).

Principle of surplus productivity

Surplus productivity is defined as the income remaining after payment of labor, capital, and management—income attributable to land.

Private mortgage insurance (PMI)

Mortgage insurance for the lender which is furnished by other than a government agency.

Property

The right or interest which an individual has in lands and chattels to the exclusion of all others.

Prospectus

A printed advertisement for a new enterprise, such as a limited partnership. Most states require that a buyer read and sign a prospectus before the sale can be concluded.

Public policy

That principle of law that holds that no person can lawfully do that which has a tendency to be injurious to the public or against the public good.

Public trustee

A person appointed or required by law to execute a trust.

PUD

A planned unit development; usually consisting of housing units located on limited ground space with or without commonly owned facilities. See also De minimis PUD.

Purchase money mortgage

A mortgage given by a grantee to the grantor in part payment of the purchase price of real estate. See also Contract sale.

Quadrangle

A tract of land in the U.S. Government Survey System measuring 24 miles on each side of the square; sometimes referred to as a check.

Quasi contract

An obligation for a party to do something, which is imposed by law.

Quiet enjoyment

The right of an owner to use the property without interference of possession.

Quiet title

A court action brought to establish title and to remove a cloud on the title.

Quit claim deed

A deed given when the grantee has, or claims to have, complete or partial title to the premises and the grantor has a possible interest that otherwise would constitute a cloud upon the title; the deed cannot transfer more than the grantor has.

Quit notice

A notice to a tenant to vacate rented property.

Quotient

The number obtained when one number is divided by another.

Range

A strip of land six miles wide determined by Government Survey and running in a north-south direction. Ranges are numbered as East or West of a principal meridian.

Ratification

Giving approval by act or conduct of something done by another, without authority.

REALTOR®

An active member of the local, state, and NATIONAL ASSOCIATIONS OF REAL-TORS®.

Recovery fund

An assessment paid by licensed real estate agents and brokers to provide a fund for reimbursing complainants who have suffered a financial loss due to the wrongful acts of licensees.

Redemption rights

The right of a mortgagor to redeem the property by paying the debt after the expiration date; the right of an owner to reclaim his property after a sale for taxes.

Redlining

A prohibited practice of lending institutions which refuse to grant loans in certain urban areas, especially in those fast becoming racially integrated.

Reduction certificate

A certificate showing the balance due on a mortgage at the time of closing the sale.

Reformation

An action to correct a mistake in a deed or other instrument.

Regulation "Z"

A government regulation which requires a lender to disclose certain facts to the borrower.

Release

The relinquishment of some right or benefit to a person who already has some interest in the property.

Release of lien

The discharge of certain property from the lien of a judgment, mortgage, or other claim.

Reliction

The term refers to land created by the gradual and imperceptible withdrawal of water from land. The withdrawal must be permanent in order for the property to be claimed by the adjoining property owner.

Remainder estate

An estate in property created at the same time and by the same instrument as another estate and limited to arise immediately upon termination of the other estate.

Remaining economic life

The time remaining in which a property improvement will continue to produce income and provide for the recapture of the investment.

Reproduction cost

Normal cost of exact duplication of a property, as of a certain date.

Res gestae

Attendant facts and circumstances to the issue involved.

Res judicata

A matter judicially decided.

Respondeat superior doctrine

"Let the master answer." A principal is liable for the wrongful acts of his agent.

Restriction

A device in a deed limiting the use of the property conveyed for a certain period of time.

Reverse Mortgage

A modern technique of removing equity from a property in the form of an annuity.

Reversion

The residue of an estate left to the grantor, to commence after the determination of some particular estate granted out by him.

Rider

A supplemental memorandum in the nature of an amendment, attached to, and made a part of a contract.

Right of way

An easement over another's land—also used to describe a strip of land used as a roadbed by a railroad or other public utility for a public purpose.

Riparian

Pertaining to the banks of a river, stream, or waterway.

Riparian owner

One who owns land bounding upon a river or water course.

Rod

One fourth of a chain or 16.5 feet.

Rule of 1 1/4

A rule of thumb in investing which states that rental rates should not exceed one fourth of the income of the typical tenant.

Rule of 5

A developer's rule that states that an improved single-family building lot should sell for approximately five times the raw land value.

Rule of 78s

A quick method of calculating the amount of interest payable each month on a one-year note, where the interest is computed as simple interest on the previous month's balance.

Running with the land

An easement which inures to the benefit and advantage of subsequent owners of the land, for which it was originally created.

Sale-buyback

A provision of a sale which states that the owner can repurchase the property at the end of the lease.

Sale-leaseback

The sale of a property with the simultaneous leasing back of the facility to the seller.

Sales price

The true price paid by the buyer for the property; not necessarily the amount reported as received by the seller. Example: Reported sales price of $100,000 in which the seller paid three FHA points ($3,000) making the true sales price $97,000.

Salvage value

The value of the property improvements left on the land at the end of the economic life of the property.

Sandwich lease

A lease held by one who subleases the property to another; the original lessee is in the middle (sandwiched) between the property owner interest and the current occupant's interest.

Sanitary sewer

A municipal or developer owned underground pipeline for the collection of waste water products.

Security deposit

Money paid by the lessee to the lessor to ensure payment of rent and/or return of the premises in satisfactory condition at the end of the lease.

Seizin

Possession of real estate by one entitled thereto.

Seller's market

A economic period in which there are fewer properties offered for sale than there are buyers for that type of property.

Separate property

Property owned by a husband or wife which is not community property; acquired by either spouse prior to marriage or by gift or devise after marriage.

Septic tank system

A private sewage disposal system consisting of a septic tank and a pipe field to provide for disposal of the effluent by soil absorption.

Servient tenement

The real property, which bears the burden of an easement.

Setback

The distance from the curb or other established line, within which no building may be erected. See also Building line.

Severalty ownership

Real property owned by one person only; sole ownership.

Sheriff's deed

A deed to property sold for nonpayment of taxes or foreclosure of mortgage. The deed to the property is subject to the redemption rights of the former owner; also known as marshall's deed.

Shoreline

The edge of the body of water at ordinary high level.

Siding

The finish covering on the outside wall of a structure.

Simple listing

A listing of property with a broker for sale or rent other than through exclusive agency or exclusive right-to-sell contract; usually verbal.

Simple proportion

The relationship between four quantities in which the quotient of the first, divided by the second, is equal to that of the third, divided by the fourth.

Sinking fund

A fund set aside from property which, with accrued interest, will eventually pay for replacement of improvements; also funds to redeem bonds or other debt obligations.

Sky lease

A long-term lease of space above a piece of real estate. See also air rights.

Soffit

The horizontal portion of an eave, sometimes containing vents for attic ventilation.

Special assessment

A one-time tax assessment made against property owners for the purpose of providing property improvements, such as paving, curbs and gutters, sidewalks, or street lighting.

Special warranty deed

A special form of the warranty deed providing for signature of the corporate officer authorized to grant and another who certifies that the sale or disposition of the property has been authorized by the board of directors or other corporate authority.

Specific performance

A remedy in court compelling the defendant to carry out the terms of the agreement or contract which was executed.

Spot zoning

Occurs when a piece of property is singled out for different treatment from adjacent and other properties in the area. The zoning may or may not conform with the municipality master plan.

Squatter's rights

Occupancy of land by virtue of long use against the recorded title owner.

Statute of frauds

Requires certain contracts relating to real estate, such as agreements of sale, to be in writing, in order to be enforceable.

Statute of limitations

The law which provides that an action is barred unless suit is brought within the statutory period.

Stick built home

Construction which utilizes wooden stud walls, usually placed on 16-inch centers, together with wooden rafters or trusses.

Straight-line depreciation

A method of depreciation in which an equal amount is charged as an accounting expense each year against income.

Subdivision

A tract of land divided into lots suitable for home-building purposes.

Subletting

A leasing by a tenant to another, who holds under the original tenant.

Subordination clause

A clause in a mortgage or lease, stating that the rights of the holder shall be secondary or subordinate to a subsequent encumbrance.

Subpoena

A legal order or writ commanding the named individual to appear and testify in a legal proceeding.

Subpoena duces tecum

A subpoena "to bring with you" certain specified records or writings in the possession of the person named.

Sufferance lease

The retention of property possession after termination of the lease and without the landlords permission; also known as Estate at sufferance.

Sump pump

An automatic water pump used in a basement to raise water to sewer level.

Surface water

Diffused storm waters, in contrast to concentrated flow within a stream.

Surrender

The cancellation of a lease by mutual consent of lessor and lessee.

Survey

The process by which a parcel of land is measured and its area ascertained; also the process by which the legal description is located upon the ground.

Syndication

A specialized form of partnership venture, structured to produce certain tax advantages and other benefits for the investor.

Syndicated equity pools

An organization of multiple owners (usually limited partnerships) formed for the purpose of raising equity to invest in real estate.

t/a

Abbreviation for trading as.

Tax

A charge assessed against persons or property for public purposes.

Tax deed

A deed for property sold at public sale by a political subdivision, such as a city, for nonpayment of taxes by the owner.

Tax-free trades

Investor trades for like property, which delays the payment of capital gains on the property that was traded. Capital gains realized are used to adjust the cost basis of the new property acquired in the trade.

Tenancy at will

A license to use or occupy lands and tenements at the will of the owner.

Tenancy in common

A form of real estate held by more than one person, each of whom is considered as being possessed of the whole of an undivided part.

Tenant

A person who holds real estate under a lease (lessee).

Tenant at sufferance

One who comes into possession of lands by lawful title and keeps it afterwards without any title at all.

Tenement

Everything of a permanent nature which may be holden.

Termites

Antlike insects which destroy woodwork in a building.

Terre tenant

One who has actual possession of land.

Three-party blanket

A deal involving a buyer, a seller, and a third party who furnishes collateral to secure the paper carried back by the seller.

Tidelands

The lands over which the tides ebb and flow; such lands may be developed if it does not conflict with rights of the public.

Tier

A strip of land six miles wide and running in an east-west direction, as determined by Government survey. See also Range.

Time sharing ownership

Joint ownership of real estate which permits an owner to possess and occupy the property for a specific time period or number of days during the calendar year.

Title

Evidence of ownership, which refers to the quality of the estate.

Title by adverse possession

Land acquired by occupancy and recognized as against the property owner.

Title insurance

A policy of insurance which indemnifies the holder for any loss sustained by reason of defects in the title not excepted in the policy.

Topography

The contour and slope of land, hills, valleys, streams, and so on.

Tort

An actionable wrong.

Township

A territorial subdivision, six miles long and six miles wide, and containing 36 sections, each one mile square.

Trade fixture

An item of personal property upon the premises, as under a commercial lease, in connection with the tenants business; usually, removable by the tenant at the end of the lease term.

Triple net lease

A lease of property in which the tenant is responsible for taxes, insurance, and maintenance—a type of net lease.

Trust deed

A form of mortgage by which the borrower conveys title to a trustee, who holds title for protection of the lender, as security for the loan debt.

Trustee

A person in whom an estate, interest, or power, in or affecting property, is vested or granted for the benefit of another person.

Trustor

One who deeds his property to a trustee.

Twenty-four contingency clause

A clause contained in an earnest money agreement of sale which accepts an offer with a contingency and allowing the buyer a 24-hour time period after the occurrence of a stipulated event (usually the seller receipt of another offer) to remove the contingency, before a second offer is accepted by the seller.

Ultra vires act

A contract entered in excess of the corporation's express or implied powers according to its charter.

Undue influence

Taking a fraudulent or unfair advantage of another's weakness of mind, distress, or necessity.

Unearned increment

An increase in value of real estate due to no effort on the part of an owner; often due to an increase in population or other economic factor.

Unilateral contract

One in which one party makes an express undertaking, without receiving in return any promise of performance from the other.

United States Governmental Survey System

Also known as the Rectangular Survey System; a method of describing or locating real property by reference to government survey.

Unlawful detainer

The statutory proceedings by which a landlord removes a tenant who holds over after his lease has expired or after his tenancy is terminated by notice or after default in payment of rent or other obligation.

Useful life

See economic life.

Useful square footage

The space contained in a structure which is useful for production of income—rentable space.

Usufructuary right

The right of use and full enjoyment of another's property, with provision that the use and enjoyment be without alteration or damage beyond fair wear and tear.

Utility value

Something that has the ability to satisfy a human need or desire.

V.A. loan

See G.I. loan.

Value in use

A value concept which is based upon the productivity of economic good to its owner-use.

Vara

A Spanish term of measurement equal to 33 1/2 inches.

Vendee

The purchaser of real estate under an agreement.

Vendor

The seller of real estate, usually referred to as the party of the first part in an agreement of sale.

Vendor's lien

A lien placed on real estate for nonpayment of materials or supplies delivered to the construction site. See also Mechanic's lien.

Vertical revitalization

The rehabilitation of existing high-rise structures or the development of air space above the existing structure.

Visible possession

Possession of property which is visible to the owner and the world in general; a necessity for an adverse possession claim.

Void contract

A contract that is no longer in force.

Voidable contract

A contract that can be voided by one or both parties under conditions agreed to in the basic agreement.

Warranty deed

A deed that contains a covenant that the grantor will protect the grantee against any claimant.

Waste

Willful destruction of any part of land or improvements, so as to injure or prejudice the estate or mortgagee, landlord, or remainderperson.

Water master

A person assigned the duty of directing the flow within an irrigation system.

Water table

The normal elevation of available underground water in a given area.

Well permit

Authorization to drill a water well, issued by the federal or state authority which controls the use of ground water.

Will of decent

State laws that direct the disposition of the assets of a person who died intestate.

Window sill

The lower base framing of a window opening.

White water waste

Water that has been used for human bathing and other washing activities.

Without recourse

Words used in endorsing a negotiable instrument to denote that the endorser will not be liable to a future holder, in event of nonpayment.

Wrap-around mortgage

A method of refinancing, whereby a mortgage or deed of trust secures a loan, which includes the balance due on an existing mortgage, and the additional amount advanced by the warp-around mortgagee. The latter makes the payment due on the existing mortgage.

Writ of eviction

A court order, obtained by the landlord, which directs a tenant to vacate a rented property.

Writ of execution

A writ which authorizes and directs the proper officer of the court (usually the sheriff) to carry out the judgment of the court.

Yield

The annual percentage rate of return on an investment in real estate, stocks, or bonds.

Yield on equity

Net income after debt service plus equity loan payments, divided by owner equity. Also known as equity dividend rate.

Yield on value

Net income divided by the current fair market value; may also be modified to reflect income taxes paid. Sometimes referred to as overall return.

Zero down technique

A method of buying real estate with no money down—100 percent financing.

Zero lot line

A zoning provision allowing construction of buildings on or approximately on the boundary line. Normal zoning requires specific building set-back distances.

Zone

The area set off by a governing body for specific use; such as residential, commercial, or manufacturing.

Zoning

An area in a municipality, restricted by ordinance, for a particular use.

Zoning ordinance

The exercise of police power of a municipality in regulating and controlling the character and use of property.

Zoning variances

Authorized use of land which does not conform to the specific zoning of the parcel or area.

Appendix B
LEGAL REFERENCES
LISTED BY SUBJECT

(Number on left of first line is page number where case(s) is(are) discussed more fully.)

ETHICAL AND HONEST BEHAVIOUR

5   Mason v. Kierks Lumber and Coal Co., 94 Ark. 107; Hutter v. Weiss, 132 Ind. App. 244

By intentional misrepresentation, misleading conduct, or wrongful concealment of facts, a person may be precluded from asserting legal title to land or from enforcing an encumbrance on, or maintaining an interest in, real estate.

STATE LICENING AND SUPERVISION

7   Roman V. Lobe, 243 N.Y. 51, 152 and Watson v. Muirlsead, 57 Pa. 161 (Pa.1868)

The legislature acts within its lawful powers when it establishes a system of licenses for real estate brokers with annual renewals.

9   Riley v. Chambers, 185 P. 855 (1919)

The right of the states to restrict the right to engage in the real estate business to those who possess certain educational and character qualifications

was upheld.

10   Lee v. Delman, 66 So. 2d 252 (Fla. 1953)

A rule requiring real estate persons to devote full time to the profession was held invalid.

10   Carlson v. Real Estate Commission of Hawaii, 38 Haw. 9 (1949)

Requirement for real estate examination declared void based on current Hawaiian law. Law ammended the following year to provide for the exam requirement.

10   Real Estate Commission v. Roberts, 271 A. 2d 246 (Pa. 1970); Shapiro v. U.S., 355 U.S. 1 (1948) and United States v. Morton Salt Co., 338 U.S. 632

Government agencies have the right to inspect records without a supoena —"even if one were to regard the request for information ....as nothing more than curosity, nevertheless law inforcing agencies have a legitimate right to satisfy themselves that (appellant's) behavior is consistent with the law and the public interest."

10   Real Estate Commission v. Roberts, 271 A. 2d 246 (Pa. 1970)

A state can revoke a broker's license if he fails to keep adequate earnest money deposit records or prevents inspection thereof.

12   Southern Ry. Co. v. Greene, 216 U.S. 400, 417, 54, L.Ed. 536.

Certain exemptions granted by licensing laws to certain individuals "must be based upon some real and substantial distinction, bearing a reasonable and just relation to the things in respect to which such classification is imposed."

12   Firpo v. Murphy, 236 P. 968, (1925)

Commission was denied due to the fact that the plaintiff broker had employed an unlicensed agent.

9   State v. Hurlock, 49. S.W. 2d 611; Riley v. Chambers, 185 P. 855 (1919); Breechen v. Riley 187 Cal. 121; Cyphers v. Allen 142 Conn. 699; Shelton v. Florida Real Estate Commission 121 So. 2d 711; Sims v. Reeves 261 S.W. 2d 812; Zerlin v. Louisiana Real Estate Board 103 So. 528; State v. Spears 75 N.M. 400; Groetzinger v. Forrest Hills Terrace Corp. 205 N.Y.S. 125; State v. Warren 114 S.E. 2d 660; Hall v. Geiger-Jones Co. 242 U.S. 539; Young v. Dept of Public Instruction 105 Pa. Sup. 153 (1932); Davis v. Halley 227 S.W. 1021; State v. Jackson 120 W. Va. 521; and Payne v. Volkman 198 N.W. 438.

Cases are representative of Courts sustaining the rights of states to regulate the real estate industry.

PERSONS EXEMPT FROM LICENSE LAW

13   State v. Bodner, 99 So. 2d 582 (Fla. 1956)

While acting as an attorney for the estate of a decedent, he is exempt from meeting educational requirements for a salesperson's examination.

13   Tobin v. Courshon, et al., 155 So. 2d 785 (Fla. 1963)

Lawyers, who are not licensed as Real Estate Brokers, may not collect a commission for their real estate activeties.

13   Haas v. Greenwald, 196 Cal. 236,237 P. 38 (1925) and Bratton v. Chandler, supra, in United States Supreme Court: 72 L. Ed. 415.

Persons engaging in only one transaction are not exempt from the license law provisions.

13   Trentman Co. et al. v. Brown, 176 La. 854 (1933)

One who is engaged in the business of real estate brokerage cannot be exempt solely because of his holding of a power of attorney.

13   Riley v. Chambers, 181 P. 589 (Cal.)

Trustees, selling under a deed of trust, are exempted from licensing law requirements.

15   North Carolina Real Estate Licensing Board v. Rentex, 228 S.E. 2d 493 (N.C. App. 1976), State v. Warren, 114 S.E. 2d 660 (S.C. 1960) and Minnesota, etc. v. Beslanowitch, d/b/a Rental Directory.

The Supreme Courts held that licensing statutes do not contemplate persons who merely compile and publish information about rental vacancies.

14   Real Estate Commission v. Phares (Homefinders), 268 Md. 344 (1973)

Decision against the commission required a change in Maryland law to amend the definition of a real estate broker. A later suit brought by the defendant also failed as the new law was considered to "bear a rational relationship to legitimate state objectives."

15   People v. Schomig, 239 P. 413 (1925)

A challenge to the real estate act on grounds that different penalties are prescribed for individuals than corporations was over ruled by the District Court of Appeals—hearing denied by the Supreme Court.

OUT OF STATE LICENSING

17   Aronson v. Carobine, 222 N.Y.S. 721 (1927) and Tillman v. Gibson, 44
      Ga. App. 440, 161 S.E. 630 (1931)

A broker selling property in another state to a party in his own state is entitled to a commission and is not required to be licensed in the property state—Lex loci contractus governs.

17   Land Co. v. Fetty, 15 Fed. 2d 942 (1926)

A lumberman hired to sell one tract of land is not a broker.

16   State v. Rose, 122 So. 225 (1929)

States may not deny (qualified) persons of another state the right to do business in their state.

17   Talbot v. Jones, 288 So. 2d (La. 1974) and Frankel v. Allied Mills, 369
      Ill. 578, 17 N.E. 2 570 (1938)

An unlicensed broker cannot recover a fee for mortgage assistance in those states requiring mortgage brokers to be licensed. Latter case cited as precedence.

18   Webster v. Rushing, 304 So. 2d. 66 (La. App. 1974)

In states requiring Mortgage Brokers to be real estate licensed, no commission can be collected by those who are not so licensed.

17   Moore v. Burdine, 174 So. 279 (1937)

A broker, licensed in one state, but performing in another must be licensed in the state of performance—an exception to the Lex loci contractus rule.

STATE LICENING AUTHORITIES ARE AUTHORIZED TO SUPERVISE & DISCIPLINE

20   Haller v. Real Estate Commission, 253 N.W. 2d 280 (Neb.1977)

The right of real estate commissions to discipline licensees for the benefit of the public was upheld.

20   Lee v. Real Estate Commission, 516 P. 2d 1342 (Okla. 1973) and Wilcox
      v. Reynolds, 36 P. 2d 488

Suspension upheld. Latter case quoted, "An obligation of agent to his principal demands the sincerest integrity, good faith and most faithful service."

21   Rifkin v. Florida Real Estate Commission, 345 So. 2d (Fla. 1977)

Where license law provides for revocation or suspension if the licensee is found guilty of certain named offenses, the commission may not discipline a licensee absent a finding of guilt by a court of competent jurisdiction.

20   Flagg v. Layman, 517 P. 2d 329 (Or. App. 1973)

A license law tribunal, upon its own initiative, or upon complaint filed, may for cause, refuse, suspend or revoke a license.

20   Handelsman v. Real Estate Commission, 244 A. 2d 131 (N.J. 1968)

Suspension up held based on broker plead of *nolo contendere* to charge of violation of FHA regulations. License law provision of "similar offense" embraced the charged offense.

21   McKnight v. Florida Real Estate Commission, 202 2d 199 (1967); Fibus
            c. Real Estate Commission, 7 Pa. Com. Ct. 74 (1973); McKnight v.
            Florida Real Estate Commission, 202 So. 2d 420; Boineau v. South
            Carolina Real Estate Commission, 230 S.E. 2d 440 (S.C. 1976) and State
            Real Estate Commission v. Tice, 190 A. 2d 188 (Pa. 1963)

Revocation upheld for broker transgressions in dealing for himself—the law requires licensee to be honest, trustworthy, truthful, and of good character and reputation.

22   Williams v. Florida State Real Estate Commission, 232 So. 2d 239
            (1970)

A commissions right to discipline applies to actions out of state, where actions relate to a good reputation for fair dealings.

LICENSE FEES

22   Texarkansas v. Hudgins Products Co., 164 S.W. 739; William Coltin
            and Co. v. Manchester Savings Bank, 197 A. 2d 208 (N.H. 1964) and
            C. Dan Blackshear, et al., v. G.W. Hogan, et al., File No. C-22561 - Civil
            action, Fulton County Superior Court, Ga., 1977

License fees are not for revenue raising but for administration of license law. Excessive fees are not allowed.

23   Maury v. State, 93 So. 802 (1922)

States have a right to charge a license tax on persons engaged in buying, selling, or renting real estate for a commission.

FINDERS FEES VS COMMISSIONS

23   Consolidated Oil & Gas, Inc. v. Roberts, 425 P. 2d 282 (Colo. 1967),
            Shoenfeld v. Silver Springs, U. S. Dist. Court Eastern Div. (Wisc. 1971)
            and Brakhage v. Georgetown Associates, Inc., 523 P. 2d 145 (Colo. App.
            1974)

Court decisions are not in harmony on the practice of finders fees, but most refer to local laws regarding licensing requirements to share in commissions.

24   Brakage v. Georgetown Associates, 523 P. 2d 145 (Colo. App. 1974)

Case involves plaintiff who sold stock in a corporation that owned and sold real estate. Commission denied to this unlicensed person.

24   Sorice v. DuBois et al., 167 N.Y.S. 2d 227 (1966) and Carey v. Borden
            Co., 386 P. 2d 585 (Colo. 1963)

Finders fee to an unlicensed person denied where the sale was principally real estate.

24   Sullivan v. Collins, 435 F. 2d 1128 (1970)

Finders fee awarded in this California case, where the plaintiff was shown to have contributed far more than introduction of buyer to seller.

24   Evans v. Riverside International Raceway, 237 Cal. App. 2d 666 (1965)

The distinction between finder and broker was decided on basis of work performed. Finders normally have no involvement in price negotiations or any other terms of the transaction.

24   Parr v. Asaff, 322 So. 313 (La. 1975)

Finder's fee as incentive bonus denied since plaintiff was an unlicensed agent in Louisiana.

OTHER STATE LAWS AFFECTING REAL ESTATE

25   Weitz v. Davis, 4 Ariz. App. 209, 419 P. 2d 113, Aff'd Ariz. 40, 424 P. 2d 168 (1966)

Instant case established the formula for assessment for street improvements based on front footage.

25   Citizens for Underground Equality v. Seattle, 6 Wash. App. 338, 492 P. 2d 1071 (1972)

Property owners may be assessed for placement of under ground utilities.

POWER OF THE STATES TO REGULATE LAND USE THROUGH ZONING

26   Christopher v. Mathens, 362 Mo. 242 (1951) and Tennison v. Shomette, 379 A. 2d 187 (Md. App. 1977)

Spot zoning is allowed under certain special circumstances.

27   Norton Realty & Loan Co., Inc. v. Gainsville, 224 Ga. 166 (1968); Walworth County v. Hartwell, 214 N.W. 2d 288 (wis. 1974); Seattle, 573 P. 2d 359 (Wash. 1978); and Boise City v. Blaser, 352 P. 2d 892 (Idaho 1977)

Zoning laws have no application to the location of properties or their use prior to the enactment of the zoning measure. This is known as nonconforming use.

27   Goldfarb v. Dietz, 506 P. 2d 1322 (Wah. App. 1973)

Where a property was converted to multi-family use prior to the ordnance passing, it could not be rebuilt if destroyed by fire.

27   Braschi v. Stahl Assocs. Co., 544 14 N.Y.S. 2d 784 (1989)

The family redefined to include those living together but not necessarily blood related; i.e., gays, fraternities and possibly half-way houses.

27   Village of Belle Terre et al., v. Bruce Boraas et al., (No. 73-191 AprIl 1, 1974)

The word *family* was defined as one or more persons related by blood, living and cooking together as a single-housekeeping unit. Six unrelated college students did not meet this requirement.

27   Halverson v. City of Bellview, 41 Wash. App. 457, 704, P. 2d 1232 1985)

Plat approvals require the signatures of all, who have an interest in the property.

28   Nickola v. Township of Grand Blanc, 209 N.W. 2d 803 (Mich. 1973)

Court refused redress based on verbal representations of city official regarding potential for rezoning.

28   City of East Lake, et al. v. Forest City Enterprises, Inc., 96 S. Ct. 238,
            L. Ed. 2d 132 (1976)

Referral of a proposed zoning ordnance to a referendum was held legal by the Supreme Court citing:

"(1) the referendum decision could not properly be characterized as a deligation
of power, and (2) the referendum rezoning decision was properly reserved to
the people under the Ohio Constitution."

STATE RIGHTS TO CONDEMN PRIVATE PROPERTY

29   Pennsylvania Coal Co. v. Mahore, 260 U.S. 393 (1922)

The Dimenitization of Value Test in a municipal taking under eminent domain.

29   Just v. Marienette Co., 56 Wisc. 2d 7, 201 N.W.2d 761 (1972)

Instant case established the "Harm-Benefit Test"

29   LaSalle National Bank v. County of Cook, 60 Ill. App. 2d 39, 208 N.E.
            2d 430 (1965)

Above case cited as example of balance of public benefit against private loss test.

29   Arvene Bay Constr. Co. v. Thatcher, 278 N.Y. 22, 15 N.E. 2d 587 (1938);
            Schere v. Freehold, 119 N.J. Super. 433, 292 A. 2d 35 *Cert. denied, 410
            U.S. 93* (1972).

The reasonable use test in condemnation.

30   Town of Halle v. City of Eau Claire, 471 U.S. 34, 105, S.C.T. 1713, 85
            L.Ed. 2d 24 (1985)

Municipalities are exempt from Clayton Act if it shows anticompetitive actions were taken pursuant to a clearly articulated zoning plan.

30   Town of Hallie v. City of Eau Claire, 471 U.S. 34, 105, S.C.T. 1713, 85
            L. Ed. 2d 24 (1985)

Municipalities need only show active supervision to be exempted from liability under the Clayton Act.

31   Pittsburg W & K.R. Co., 8 S.E. 453 (W.Va.)

Eminent domain denied as the benefits would accrue to a second party and the railroad, not the public as a whole.

COMPENSATION FOR THE TAKING

31   Armstrong v. U.S., 364 U.S. 40,49 (1960)

The principle of just compensation was designed to bar Government from forcing some people alone to bear public burdens.

32   Harwell v. United States, 316 F. 2d 791

Just compensation is normally defined by market value.

32   United States v. Cors, 337 U.S. 325, 69 S. Ct. 1086

The courts have not established firm rules for evaluation, but remain somewhat flexible.

33   Missouri Public Service Co. v. Garrison, 454 S.W. 2d 628 (Mo. App. 1969)

Unsightliness of farm property caused by construction of transmission lines was held to be a proper element of damages.

33   State of Lousiana v. Carmouche, 155 So. 2d 451 (La. 1963)

Factors considered in total taking of a dwelling are comparative data and reproduction costs.

32   Defnet Land and Dev. Co. v. State, ex re Herman 480 P. 2d 1013 (Ariz. App. 1971) and State Highway Commission v. Crooks, 282 So. 2d 232 (Miss. 1973)

Where only a part of property is taken, the measure of severance damage is the difference between market value of the remainder before and after the taking.

33   Pozin v. State Department of Transportation, 281 So. 2d 73 (Fla. App. 1973) and Levit v. State Department of Transportation, 248 So. 2d (Fla. App. 1971)

Owners are not entitled, as an element of compensation, to the increase in value of property prior to the taking and attributable to the proposed improvement. The later case limited the former as follows:

"Such enhanced value is generally peculiar only to land lying adjacent to the improvement and within close proximity to the interchange exits and entrances leading to and from the intersecting roads and highways."

33   Behlman v. City of Florissant, 548 S.W. 2d 619 (Mo. App. 1977)

Damages caused by a municipality in changing the level of streets from their natural level to an newly established grade is compensable.

33   Seaboard Coast Line R.R. v. Harrelson, 202 S.E. 2d 1 (S.C. 1974)

The existence of valuable deposits of sand, gravel and limestone is a proper element in ascertaining value of land.

34   Kayo Oil Co. v. State, 340 So. 2d 756 (Ala. 1976) and State of Alaska v. Hammer, 550 P. 2d 820 (Alaska 1976)

Compensation for loss of business due to the taking of land is normally not compensable; however in the latter case the court held such loss of profits was compensable, and "not dammun absque injuria (injury without damages).

34   State of Alaska v. Ness, 516 P. 2d 1212 (1973)

Generally a condemnee is not entitled to compensation for personalty used in land taken; however, depreciation in value of personalty in addition to physical damage should be allowed.

33   Restaurants, Inc. v. City of Wilmington, 274 A. 2d 137 (Del. 1971)

The loss of a business license (liquor) is not compensable.

33   Public Service Co. of Indiana v. Morgan County Rural Elec. Membership Corp., 360 N.E. 2d 1022 (Ind. App. 1977)

Losses of intended uses of property to arise in the future are not compensable.

34   Dept. of Public Works, etc. v. Greenwell, 359 N.E. 2d 780 (Ill. 1977)

Where a condemnee suffered no loss of direct access to an existing road but required circuitry of travel for 800 feet, no compensation was allowed.

34   Frank v. Mercer County, 186 N.W. 2d 439 (N.D. 1971)

In eminent domain proceedings, the burden is upon the property owner to establish that public use is the direct and proximate cause of the damage for which the complaint is based.

35   United States v. 50.8 Acres of Land, 149 F. Supp. 749, 752.

Appraisers are required to consider the probability and possibility of higher use and value when estimating fair market value for condemnation.

35   Babinec v. State, 512 P. 2d 563 (Alaska 1973)

A property owner is entitled to severable damages, if it is shown that the property taken is a part of a larger tract, which has been adversely affected by the taking.

35   United States v. 147.47 Acres of Land, 352 F. Supp. 1055 (Md./Pa. 1972)

For compensation for the taking of raw land as *subdivided land* the subdivider must have taken forward steps to make the change by the time of the taking.

35   State Dept. of Highways v. Miltenberger, 344 So. 2d 705 (La. App. 1977)

Trees and shrubbery are not appraised independently of the land, unless they have some unique value in addition to the fair market value of the land.

LESSEE RIGHTS IN CONDEMNATION

36   Barnini et al. v. Sun Oil Co., 283 A. 2d 158 (Conn. 1971); State Highway Commission v. Samborski, 463 S.W. 2d 896 (Mo. 1971) and County of Gennepin v. Holt, 297 N.W. 2d 723 (Minn. 1973)

If the lease does not foreclose the lessee's right to damages, all elements affecting the value of the household must be determined.

36   Wessels v. State of Alaska, 562 P. 2d 1042 (Alaska 1977)

The right of a lessee to compensation for property taken may be waived or contracted away by terms of the lease.

37   Pillar of Fire v. Denver Urban Renewal Authority, 509 P. 2d 1250 (Colo. 1973)

Church property is private property, which can be taken in eminent domain.

ENVIRONMENTAL CONCERNS

38   United States v. Bliss, 667 F. Supp. 1298 (E.D. Mo. 1987) United States v. Motalo, 629 F. Supp. 56 (D. N.H. 1984) City of Philadelphia v. Stepan Chemical Co., 544 F. Supp. 1135, 1140 (E.D. Pa. 1982)

Brokers may expose themselves to CERCLA liability by arranging for property clearance.

38   New York v. Shore Realty, 759 F. 2d 1032 (2d Cir. 1985)

Corporate officers may be liable for torts of the corporation.

39   Ecodyne Corp. v. Shal, 718 F. Supp. 1454 (N.D. Cal 1989)

Prior owners, who did not own the land at a time that hazardous substances were introduced, are not liable for CERCLA clean-up costs.

39   Reardon v. U.S., First U.S. Circuit Court of Appeals, Boston, 90-1319, 1991.

The government may not place a cleanup lean against property without a hearing to justify the action.

39   United States v. Fleet Factors Corp., 901 F. 2d 1550 (11th Cir. 1990)

Lenders may be CERCLA liable even though they have not operated the facility or been directly involved in decisions of disposal.

41   Kohl v. United States, 91 U.S. 367, 23 L.Ed. 449 (1875)

The right of the Federal Government to exercise the power of eminent domain was firmly established.

ANTI-DISCRIMINATION LAW

43   Jones v. Mayer Co. 392 U.S. 409 (decided June 17, 1968)

Congressional Act of 1866 forbade racial discrimination in the sale or rental of housing in the United States. The Act contains no exemptions as in the 1968 Act and it lacks federal enforcement machinery and other remedies contained in the 1968 Act.

44   Clark v. Universal Builders, Inc., 501 F. 2d 324 (7th Circuit), 88 Harvard Law Rev. 1610 (1975); Boyd v. Lefrak Organization, 509 F. 2d 1110 (N.Y. 1974) and Evening Sentinel v. National Organization of Women, 357 A. 2d.498 (Conn. 1975)

Open housing laws are designed to prevent discrimination due to age, sex, religion, race, color, national origin, or ancestry.

44   Chicago Real Estate Board v. City of Chicago, 224 N.E. 2d 793 (Ill. 1967)

Instant case establishes the right of cities to adopt a Fair Housing Ordinance.

44   People, etc. v. Betts Realtors, Inc. et al, 361 N.E. 2d 581 (Ill. 1977)

Acts established to eliminate "Blockbusting" are legal.

REAL ESTATE DEFINED

45   Butler v. Frontier Telephone Co., 186 N.Y. 486, 491 (1906)

Space above the land is real estate the same as the land itself.

45   Am. Jur. 2d 618, 2 Blackstone Commentaries 18 (1836)

He who owns the soil owns it to the heavens.

PROPERTY RIGHTS

49   Glassman v. Weldin Farms, 359 A. 2d 669 (Del. Ch. 1976) and Tyler v. Vanelst, 512 P. 2d 760 (Wash. App. 1973)

An upper property owner cannot interfer with the natural drainage of surface water so as to increase the area of flooding to the land of lower owners—some exceptions in Western states where diversion is permissable and protects the first appropriation as a recognized proprietary right. A valid appropriation consists of three elements: (1) intent to appropriate the water to some beneficial use existing at the time or contemplated in the future; (2) an actual diversion from the natural channel by means of a ditch, canal or other conduit; and, (3) the practical application of the water within a reasonable time to some useful purpose.

50   Solomon v. Solomon, 546, S.W. 2d 129 (Tex. 1977)

Child support arearages cannot be levied against a homestead.

TITLE TO REAL ESTATE

50   Solomon v. Solomon, 546 S.W. 2d 129 (Texas 1977)

Homesteaded property, like property held by the entireties, cannot be sold to satisfy a judgment against one of the spouses.

51   Gibbons v. Gibbons, 287 So. (Miss. 1974)

A life tenant is entitled to the benefits of the property, but he cannot suffer the property to go into disrepair or waste.

51   Fabianski v. Boutin, 371 A. 2d (N.H. 1977)

Mere nonuse is insufficient to void a life estate.

51   Drees Farming Ass'n. v. Thompson, 246 N.W. 2d 883 (N.D. 1976)

A life tenant cannot make a lease beyond his life estate.

50   Heard v. Mathis, 344 So. 2d 651 (Fla. App. 1977)

The test for a "family" for homestead purposes, which must be met singly or in combination, are: (1) a legal duty arising out of the relationship, and (2) a continuing communial living by at least two individuals, where one is regarded as the person in charge.

54   Yannopoulos v. Sophos, 365 A. 2d 1312 (Pa. 1976)

A property owned by brother and sister as joint tenants, with right of survivorship, was sold but the brother died prior to closing. The court ruled that the signing terminated the joint tenancy and created a tenancy in common with the dead brother's estate entitled to one half of the proceeds of the sale.

53   Zomisky v. Zomisky, 449 Pa. 239 (1972)

Where a grantor conveys a parcel of land to himself and a son as joint tenant with right of survivorship, the son is entitled to the property at the death of the father.

54   Tenhet v. Boswell, 133 Cal. Rptr. 10 (1976)

Where one of two owners leases the property so held, the tenancy is not severed.

54   Heatter v. Lucas, 397 Pa. 296 (1951)

A deed to a single man and to another man and his wife produces a problem of ownership interpretation in which the court held that the single man owned 1/2 and the man and wife the other one half.

55   Ballard v. Farley, 226 S.W. 544 (1920)

In those states recognizing titles of "estates by the entireties" a deed to a man and wife (unnamed) was sufficient to create an estate by the entireties.

55   Sawada v. Endo, 561 P. 2d 1291 (Hawaii 1977)

In most states a judgment against one spouse would not be a lien against jointly held property, unless the debtor spouse survived, thus becoming the sole owner.

55   Scweitzer v. Evans, 63 A. 2d 39 (Pa. 1949)

Where property is held as an estate in the entireties and the man and wife are separated, neither party may convey or lease without the joinder of the other.

56   Zanzonico v. Zanzonico, 124 N.J. Eq. 477 and Martose v. Martose, 134 N.Y.S. 2d, 831 (1954)

In New York and New Jersey, where property is held by the entireties, both parties share equally in rents and profits and each spouse can compel an accounting in this connection, except where one of the parties uses a residence as a home.

56   Garner v. Pierce, 134 A. 494 (Pa. 1926)

Lease payments to either of the parties of property, held by the entireties, is legal payment of the obligation.

57   Michael v. Lucas, 152 Md. 512 (1927) and Adams v. Foster, 466 S.W. 2d 706 (Mo. 1971)

Properties held by parties as estate in the entireties, and not married, enures to the survivor as though married.

57   Singer v. Singer, 342 So. 2d 861 (Fla. App. 1977)

Owners in common have a mutual obligation to pay charges upon the property and the equity of one owner should not be enlarged by the expenditures made by the other party.

58   Wilcox v. Penn Mutual Life Ins. Co., 357 Pa. 581 (1947)

Instant case declared the community property law invalid in Pennsylvania. This institution legally exists in Cal., La., N.Mex., Tex., Ariz., Nev., Idaho., Wash., Okla., Hawaii, Mich., Neb., Ore., and Pa.

58   176 Cal. Reptr. 132 (1981)

Oral contracts about distribution of assets as payment for sexual favors are illegal.

58   176 Cal. Rptr. 132 (1981)

Homosexual claim on assets of deceased partner.

58   Marvin v. Marvin, 557 P. 2d 106 (Cal. 1976)

Adults may contract regarding sharing of earnings and assets so long as the agreement does not rest upon illicit considerations.

59   Re Marriage of Baragry,73 Cal App. 3rd 444

A man living with a single woman may incur a liability to that woman as well as his legal wife.

RESTRICTIONS ON PROPERTY USE

60   Witt v. Sternwehr Development Co., 400 Pa. 609 (1960)

Restrictions may arise by: (1) express covenants, or (2) by implication in the deed wording, or (3) by conduct of the parties.

60   Weber v. Les Petite Academies, 548 S.W. 2d 847 (Mo. App. 1976)

The law favors the unrestricted use of property. Restrictive covenants are strictly construed and every doubt is resolved against the existance of the restriction.

64   Park County Rod & Gun Club v. Dept. of Highways, 517 P. 2d 353 (Mont. 1973)

An implied easement provides access to main roads over another's property, where the highways and properties have been improperly laid down.

60   Hunt v. Collo, 317 A. 2d 545 (del. 1974)

Restrictions on former property deeds effect future deeds.

61   Beech Mountain Property Owner's Ass'n v. Current, 240 S.E. 2d 503 (N.C. App. 1978)

Any owner of a lot on which restrictive covenants apply may enjoin the violation by any other lot owner.

61   Amason et al. v. Woodman et al., 498 S.W. 2d 142 (Tex. 1973)

Release of restrictive covenants is not effective unless all persons who own property in a restricted subdivisions join in the release.

60   Burgess v. Putnam, 464 S.W. 2d 698 (Tex. Civ. App. 1971 and Foro v. Deutsch, 320 N.Y. 2d 778 (Sup. Ct. 1971)

Oral representations of the developer was admissable to establish a restriction.

61   Wallace v. St. Clair, 127 S.E. 2d 742 (W.Va. 1962)

Some states do not strictly construe restrictive covenants because they are said to protect the land owner and the public rather than land use.

64   Soltis v. Miller, 444 Pa. 357 (1971)

Where property is conveyed, so that access to it cannot be had except by passing over the grantor's land, an implied easement is created.

61   Shea v. Sargent, 499 S.W. 2d 871 (Tenn. 1973)

Restrictive covenants are strictly construed and will not be extended by implication to anything not clearly and expressly prohibited.

64   Camp v. Milain, 277 So. 2d 95 (Ala. 1973) and Burrow v. Miller, 340 So. 2d 779 (Ala. 1976)

An easement by necessity is an exception. The prerequisites are: (1) that the properties in controversy must come from a common source, (2) there must be a necessity for the creation, and (3) it must be the only practical means of ingress and egress.

65   Porter v. Griffith, 543 P. 2d 138 (Ariz. App. 1975)

Easement denied as there was no common grantor.

64   Oliver v. Ernel, 178 S.E. 2d 393 (N.C. 1971) and Soltis v. Miller, 444 Pa. 357 (1971)

An easement was granted against a grantor, where the land conveyed was land-locked and grantee had no other access to a public road.

64   Burrow v. Miller, 340 So. 2d 779 (Ala. 1976)

An easement by necessity requires a common source and a reasonable necessity for its creation—the only practical means of ingress and egress.

66   Garam v. Bender, 55 A. 2d 353 (Pa. 1947); Fristoe v. Drapeau, 215 P. 2d 729 (Cal. 1950); Ragonaud v. Dimmagio, 249 N.Y.S. 2d 705 (1964) and Westland Nursing Home, Inc. v. Benson, 517 P. 2d 862 (Colo. App. 1974)

As long as the use of property, is confined to those who are holders of any part of the original property, the courts will not intervene to release the servient tenement.

66   McDonald v. Bemboom, 694 S.W. 2d 782 (Mo. App. 1985)

Both dominant and servient tenants who utilize an easement are liable for repair and maintenance costs.

66   McDonald v. Bemboom, 694 S.W. 2d 782 (Mo. App. 1985)

Where the dominent tenant and the servient tenant jointly use a right of way, maintenance and repair is a joint responsibility.

67   Bunn v. Offutt, S.E. 2d 522 (Va. 1976)

An easement in gross does not pass with the sale since the easement fails to include the essential words "his heirs and assigns."

67   DeShon v. Parker, 361 N.E. 2d 457 (Ohio App. 1974)

An easement in gross terminates when the person, for which the easement was created, dies or sells the property.

67   Fisher v. Grinsbergs, 252 N.W. 2d 619 (Neb. 1977; Pitts v. Roberts, 562
                P. 2d 231 (Utah 1977) and Union Hills Cemetary Ass'n. v. Camp Zoe,
                Inc., 547 S.W. 2d 196 (Mo. App. 1977)

A permissive use cannot be ripened into an easement by perscription.

PRESCRIPTIVE EASEMENTS

67   George v. Dickinson, 504 S.W. 2d 658 (Mo. App. 1974)

Uninterrupted use of a roadway over farmland creates an easement by prescription.

67   Dickinson v. Pike, 201 S.E. 2d 897 (N.C. 1974)

To acquire prescriptive rights, the use must be open and notorious.

68   Flynn v. Korsack, 175 N.E. 2d 397 (Mass. 1961); Whytock v. Green,
                383 P. 2d 628 (Okla. 1963) and Stewart v. Bittle, 370 S.W. 2d 132 (Ark.
                1963)

A fence between properties for more than 30 years was sufficient to establish a prescriptive easement.

67   Shultz v. Atkins, 554 P. 2d 205 (Utah 1976)

The establishment of an easement by prescription requires use in such a way as to constitute "some actual infringement or invasion of the right to the owner or subservient party."

68   Taxman v. McMahan, 124 N.W. 2d 68 (Wis.1963)

A party wall constitutes an encumbrance, where there is a covenant to maintain and rebuild the wall.

68   Rice v. Reich et al., 186 N.W. 2d 269 (Wis. 1971)

Relief from a sales agreement for property in which there was an *open, visable, permanent and continuous* easement was denied.

62   Jones v. Park Lane Home for Convalescents, 120 A. 2d 535 (Pa. 1856)

Prohibition of construction of a commercial structure will not operate to prevent the use of a residence for commercial purposes.

63   Albino v. Pacific First Federal Savings & Loan Ass'n., 479 P. 2d 760
                (Ore. 1971)

Radical changes of conditions and resulting rezoning can neutralize restrictions.

63   McBride v. Behrman, 272 N. E. 2d 181 (Ohio 1971)

A house trailer or mobile home was defined as a "temporary structure."

63   Burgess v. Putnam, 464 S.W. 2d 698 (Tex. Civ. App. (1971)

Restrictions may be created in a number of ways; (1) set forth in the deed; (2) In separate instruments; or by estoppel through oral representations.

69   Toms v. Settipane, 317 A. 2d 467 (Conn. 1973)

Nonuse, no matter what the period of time, cannot extinguish an easement.

63   Kent v. Koch, 333 P. 2d 411 (Cal. App. 1958)

A developer has no right to enjoin the violation of a restrictive covenant in a subdivision in which all lots have been sold.

ZONING RESTRICTIONS

69   Village of Euclid, Ohio v. Ambler Realty Co., 272 U.S. 365

Zoning restrictions are closely allied to building restrictions, which result from voluntary agreement of the parties.

69   City of Oakdale v. Benoit, 342 So. 2d 691 (La. 1977)

Zoning restrictions must be strictly construed in favor of the property owner; however, it should be enforced when its provisions are clear, unambiguous and no valid legal grounds exist to prevent it.

69   First National Bank of Des Plains v. Cook County, 360 N.E. 2d 1377
            (Ill. App. 1977)

Every property owner has the right to use his or her property in any way, subject only to the restraint necessary to secure the public welfare.

70   Hackett v. Gale, 179 A. 2d 451, the New Hampshire Supreme Court,
            1962.

Real Estate Brokerage is a business rather than a profession.

70   Beres v. Hope Homes, Inc., 6 Ohio App. 3d. 71, 453; N.E. 2d 1119
            (1983)

The definition of a family appears to have changed to non-blood-related persons meeting certain conditions.

70   Crane Neck Association v. N.Y.C./Long Island County Service Group,
            92 App. Div 2d 119, 460; N.Y.S. 2d 69 (1983)

The definition of a family appears to have been changed to non-blood-related persons meeting certain conditions.

REALTOR® MULTI-LISTING SERVICES

71   Collins v. Main Line Board of Realtors®, 304 A. 2d (1973)

This Pennsylvania case ruled that an MLS cannot refuse a licensed broker admission to the multi-list service; however, the 1974 California Case, Marin County Board of Realtors® v. Palson would appear to provide for cause as a legal reason for such exclusion.

71   Oates v. Eastern Bergen Multilist, 273 A. 2d 795 (N.J. 1971)

This early case held that exclusion from the Realtor® multilist service was in restrain of trade.

71 Barrows v. Grand Rapids Real Estate Board, 214 N.W. 2d 532 (Mich. 1974)

Exclusion of part time Realtors® from multilist service is proper where it can be shown that nonmembers are able to compete in the market.

72 Supermarket of Homes, Inc. v. San Fernando Valley Board of Realtors, 786 P. 2d 1400 (9th Cir. 1986)

Members of multilist organizations, who have legal access to publications cannot use them for commercial purposes.

72 Oglesby and Barclif, Inc. v. Metro MLS, Inc. CCH TRR Section 61, 064 (Va.1976)

Case establishes the illegality of Realtor® Board listing fee fixing. Boards now allow individual members to establish their own fee and advertise that to other board members.

72 O'Horo v. Ohio Real Estate Commission, 4 Ohio App. 2d 75 (1964)

In most states it is illegal for a broker to attempt to sell a property known to be listed by another broker and without that broker's permission. It is also counter to the code of Ethics of the NATIONAL ASSOCIATION OF REALTORS®.

BROKERAGE

73 Meerdink v. Krieger, 15 Wash. App. 540 (1976)

A broker normally acts for the seller or buyer but not both.

73 Hughes v. Robbins et al., 164 N. E. 2d 469 (Ohio 1959); Investment Exchange Realty v. Hillcrest Bank, Inc. et al, 513 P. 2d 282 (Wash. 1973) and Ornamental and Structural Steel, Inc. v. BBT Inc., 500 P. 2d 1053 (Ariz. 1973)

A broker may operate in a dual agency capacity but only with the full disclosure and consent of all parties.

75 Holbert v. Block-Meeks Realty Co., 297 S.W. 2d 924 (1957)

A listing for the period "till 8/15/55" was deemed valid through that date.

75 Roy Annett, Inc. v. Kellin, 112 N.W. 2d 497 (Mich 1961)

A property sold to the broker's client during the extender period, but by another broker, failed on the terms of the listing which stated "sold by the owner." The listing should have stated "by whomsoever sold."

75 Beerland, Reiss, Murphy & Mosher, Inc. v. Schmidt, 261 N.W. 2d 540 (Mich. App. 1977); Richter v. First National Bank of Cincinnati, 82 Ohio App. 421 (1947) and Roudebush Realty Co. v. Toby, 135 N. E. 2d 270 (1955)

A property owner may revoke a broker's authority at any time, particularly if that broker fails to perform.

76 Romine v. Green, 13 N. J. Super. 261 (1951); Kennedy & Kennedy v. Vance, 202 P. 2d 214 (Okla. 1949); Hartig v. Schrader, 190 Ky. 511 (1921) and Hawks v. Moore, 27 Ga. App. 555 (1921)

Where multiple brokers are employed and the seller negotiates a sale very soon after the revoking of a listing, the seller must show that he was the procuring cause of the sale and that such sale was not to a party being worked by a broker at the time the authority to sell was revoked.

77   Schechter v. Voltz, 179 Pa. Superior Ct. 119 (1955)

Listings for a period "until sold" are not valid except for a "reasonable time."

77   Blank v. Borden, 524 P. 2d 127 (Cal. 1974); Buckaloo v. Johnson, 537
            P. 2d 865 (Cal. 1975)

A seller may not cancel a broker's authority and then sell to that broker's client in order to avoid payment of a commission.

78   Phoenix Title and Trust Co. v. Grimes, 416 P. 2d 979 (1966)

Where the employment of a broker is coupled with an interest in the property, such employment is irrevocable even after death.

78   Rucker & Co. v. Glenman 130 Va. 511 (1921) and (1921)

The question as to whether a broker has an interest in the listed property must be decided on factors other than *interest in a commission.*

78   Barnard v. Gardner Investment Co., 129 Va. 346 (1921)

The question as to whether a broker has an interest in the listed property must be decided on factors other than an interest in a commission.

79   Gray v. Kohlhase and Lines, 502 P. 2d 169 (Ariz. 1973); Beazell v.
            Schrader, 381 P. 2d 390 (Cal. 1963)

In most states requiring a listing to be in writing, the commission must be stated in the listing. It cannot be agreed at a later time. In California it is permissible to provide the commission by parol if there is sufficient evidence to show a fact of employment.

81   Brown v. Miller, 360 N.E. 2d. 585 (Ill. 1977) and Flynn v. LaSalle
            National Bank, 9 Ill. 2d 129 (1958)

Above cases define Exclusive Right to Sell and Exclusive Agency contracts.

81   Nance v. McDougald, 211 Ark. 800 (1947); Barry Norman Agency, Inc.
            v. Elias, 245 A. 2d 80 (N.J. 1971); Jenkins v. Vaughn, 197 Tenn. 578
            (1955) and Sinden v. Loabs, 30 Wisc. 2d 618 (1966)

Where a listing is terminated by the owner prior to expiration, the owner may be liable for damages assessed on a basis of what the broker had done until that time.

82   Covino v. Pfeffer, 160 Conn. 212 (1970)

Where the owner is aware that a purchaser has agreed to buy prior to the expiration of the listing, a subsequent sale after the expiration does not exempt the owner from payment of a commission.

82   Hutchinson v. Dobson-Bainbridge Realty Co., 31 Tenn. App.490 (1946)

If a broker has a bona fide purchaser prior to cancellation of the listing contract, he should receive a commission on the sale if made to that buyer.

83   Ferris v. Meeker Fertilizer Co., 482 P. 2d 523 (Ore. 1971)

The expiration date of a listing may be waived with the seller's knowledge and encouragement of the broker to continue his efforts.

85   Chamberland v. Grisham, 230 S.W. 2d 721 (1950)

An owner may not cancel a bilateral agreement between the broker and himself without an obligation to reimburse the broker for his efforts and expenses.

85   Samuels v. Firestone Tire and Rubber Co., 342 So. 2d 661 (La. 1977)

A written listing may be changed orally.

85   Dorman Realty and Insurance Co. Inc., v. Stalvey, 212 S.E. 2d. 591 (S.C. 1975)

An oral listing, assumed to be an exclusive right to sell rather than an exclusive agency. It is difficult to support in the courts.

86   Givens v. Dougherty, 671 S.W. 2d 877 (Tex. 1984)

A written listing agreement cannot be canceled orally.

87   Yurgelin v. Emery, 282 Mass. 571 (1933)

An inquiry as to how much a broker would charge for his services is insufficient to indicate employment.

87   Sackett v. Ford, 1 Tenn.506 and Hunger v. Judy, 194 Kan 159 (1965)

A broker inquiry as to a seller's asking price does not constitute a listing agreement and no commission is payable, even though the broker assisted in the transaction.

87   Young v. Zimmer, 56 (Ill. App. 2d 298 1965)

A statement to a broker regarding the price desired is not sufficient to employ the broker. The broker must act with the consent of the owner.

87   Corpus Juris Secundum, 32 Section 12

"... the mere leaving of a description of the property at the office of a broker, by the owner or his agent, with the request that the broker sell the property at a designated price and upon designated terms, amounts to an employment of the broker; but the mere fact that a broker asks and obtains from the owner the price at which he is willing to sell does not in itself establish the relation of principal and agent between them."

87   Morton v. Barney, 140 Ill. App.333 (1908)

A broker may not effect a contract of employement by his own letter to a seller or buyer—it take two to contract.

87   Reeve v. Shoemaker (Iowa) 205 N.W. 742, 43 A.L.R. 839

Where a broker approaches a seller regarding sale of his property and no promise is made to pay a commission, the owner may assume that the broker is representing himself or another client.

BROKER COMMISSIONS

88   Tucker v. Green, 96 Ariz. 371 (1964)

Where multiple brokers are employed, liability for a commission depends upon seller's knowledge of the broker's involvement *prior* to his consummating the sale.

88   O.L. Hamilton v. Booth, 332 S.W. 2d 252 (1960)

A printed form indicating "Sold through—Realty" is insufficient evidence of a written listing contract which was required in the subject state.

BROKER LIABILITY

89   Levittown Norse Associates v. Joseph P. Day Realty Copr., 541 N.Y.S. 2d 421 (App. Div. 1989).

Broker statements of opinion are not actionable in court.

89   Edwards v. Cobb, 451 So. 2d 1271 (La. App. 1984)

Brokers who exceed their authority may be liable for seller losses.

89   Liftus v. American Realty Co., 334 N.W. 2d 366 (Iowa Ct. App. 1983)

Responsibilities outlined in a personal service contract (listing) are not assignable. Broker is liable for any subcontractor errors or omissions.

90   Crogan v. Metz, 303 P. 2d 129 (Cal. 1956); Petersen v. Quvel, 552 P. 2d 538 (Or. 1976) and Wegg v. Broderick, Inc. 557 P. 2d 861 (Wash. App. 1976)

Even though the broker's first responsibility is to his principal (seller), he also owes a high ethical duty to the purchaser. He may not missrepresent the seller's intended selling price or omit other factors.

WHO MAY LIST PROPERTY FOR SALE

90   Sylvester v. Johnson, 110 Tenn. 392 (1903)

Defendants daughter authorized a broker to sell her father's property and a for sale sign was erected without objection by owner. Broker recovered a commission.

91   Virginia M. Pepper appellant v. J. C. Chatel, Appellee, No. 30561, Municipal Court of Appeals for the District of Columbia (1962)

Appellant listed property owned by her prior to marriage. A subsequent sale failed to close as appellant's husband refused to join in. Since the broker was unaware of the appellant's marriage, commission was due.

91   Ginn v. MacAluso, 310 P. 2d 1034 (N.M. 1957)

A marital relationship does not make one of the parties an agent for the other. The broker failed to collect as he should have been aware of the need for both parties consent.

91   Cohen v. Garlick, 344 Mass. 654 (1962)

An auctioneering firm was hired to sell property. The firm advertised that broker participation would be allowed. The successful participating broker failed to collect a commission as the court held that the auctioneering firm had no right to bind the seller.

LISTING TIME EXTENSIONS

92   Snyder v. Schram, 547 P. 2d 102 (Ore. 1976)

When the owner encourages the broker to continue his efforts after the expiration of the listing, there is an implied extension of the listing time.

BROKER EMPLOYMENT

92   Snyder v. Schram, 547 P. 2d 102 (Or. 1976)

An implied extension of the listing agreement exists where the broker continues with his efforts to consumate a sale and keeps the owner fully advised, and the said owner fails to notify the broker to cease his efforts.

92   Williams v. Brittingham, 38 D.& C. 342 (Pa. 1965)

Failure to include a bold statement, "The broker earns a commission on the sale by whomever made, including the owner" will negate a claim for commission.

93   Svoboda v. DeWald, 159 Neb. 594 (1955)

Court held that the brokers name on the agreement of sale constituted a listing and commission was payable.

93   Mid-Continent Properties, Inc. v. Pflug, 249 N.W. 2d 476 (1976)

A statement in the sales contract that a broker is due a commission is a sufficient substitute for a written listing.

93   Kelley v. J.R. Rice Realty Co., 235 Ky. 643 (1930)

An owner's signature on his card authorizing the sale of property was held to be a "written" listing.

93   Sherman v. Bratton, 497 S.W. 2d (Tex App. 1973)

In states requiring a written listing agreement, a commission may not be collected, based on other than a written agreement.

94   Lancaster Farmers National Bank, 219 A. 2d 647 (1966); Lanard and Axilbund v. Thompson Printing Co., 84 Pa. Super. 199 (1924) and Levit v. Bowers, 2 Ill. App. 2d 343 (1954)

General notices to brokers, indicating property for sale, do not constitute contracts of employment.

95   Lacalusa Inv. Co. v. Hesse, 273 P. 766 (Cal. 1929)

Commission lost since officer of corporation was shown to be acting outside of his scope of authority.

95   Barker v. Great Southern Dev. Co., Inc. 249 Miss. (1973) and McCabe v. Howard, 281 So. 2d 362 (Fla. App. 1973)

Above cases establish need for a broker to ascertain that corporate officers have the authority to act.

95   Tierney v. American Urban Corporation, 365 A. 2d 1153 (Conn. 1976)

A general manager of a company is assumed to have power to negotiate with a broker. A commission was due and payable.

95   McGarry Realty Co. et al. v. McCrone, et al. 97 Ohio App. 543 (1954)

An agent cannot profit by his failure to do his job—in this case he failed to ascertain if the funds from a relative were available.

95   Simon v. Porter, 180 A. 2d 227 (Pa.1962)

Case involved an officer of a corporation who instructed a broker to prepare sales papers. Later, the corporation refused to pay a commission as the officer was not empowered to list the property. The court awarded a commission since the officer's actions, the eyes of the broker, were deemed to be apparently within his scope of authority.

EARNING THE COMMISSION

96   Harkey v. Gahagan, 338 So. 2d 133 (La. App. 1976)

For a broker to claim a commission, he must show that he is the procuring cause of the sale through continuous actions that eventually lead to a sale.

96   Sharp v. Long, 283 So. 2d 567 (Fla. App. 1973); Gopher State Bus. Opportunities, Inc. v. Stockman, 121 N.W. 2d 613 (Minn. 1963)

An able purchaser is defined as a substantual party who is financially able to close the transaction.

96   Mehlberg v. Redlin, 96 N. W. 2d 399 (S.D. 1959)

A jury determination of whether the broker was the procuring cause of the sale must consider the effectiveness of the effort not how much effort.

97   Wheaton v. Ramsey, 436 P.2d 248 (Idaho 1968); Reilly v. Maw, 146
            Mont. 145 (1945) and Iusi v. Chase, 169 Cal. App. 2d 83 (1959)

State law prohibits fee splitting with a broker, not licensed in the state and who conducts operations within the nonlicensed state. Had the out of state broker not conducted any of his actions within the state, he could legally collect a finder's fee.

98   Thorpe v. Ross J. Carte, 250 A. 2d 618 (Md.) 1969

Agreeing to have the buyer pay a commission to avoid the legal problem of fee splitting with a nonbroker is illegal.

98   Sutton v. Transcontinental, 222 N.Y.S. 2d 778, 1961.

A broker is due a commission on a sale of out-of-state property, if all of his work was performed within the state of his licensing.

99   Kemmerer v. Roscher, 100 N.W. 2d 314 (Wis), 1960 & Payne v.
            Volkman, 183 Wis. 412, 198 N.W. 438, 1924

Where an action is begun by two associated brokers, one licensed and the other unlicensed, the contract being invalid as to the unlicensed broker, the contract is invalid in toto. In the first cited case the broker was licensed but his company was not.

98   Smirlock v. Potomac Development Corp., 200 A. 2d 922 (Md. 1964)

A broker armed with a power of attorney can perform one real estate act without being licensed.

99   Rosenthal et al. v. Art Metals, Inc. et al. 101 N.J. Super. 156, 1968;
            Certified Realty Co. v. Reddick, 456 P. 2d 502 (Oregon) 1969; Bendell
            v. Dominicis,167 N.E. 452, 1929

The court stated succinctly that a broker must be properly licensed in the state in which he seeks to gain a commission, "Otherwise an unlicensed broker might negotiate sales with impunity up to the point of a complete agreement and then obtain his license for the purpose of recovering his commission on the execution of the formal contract. The law is not so toothless."

100   Quickshops of Mississippi, Inc. v. J. Bruce, 232 So. 2d 351.1970;
            Weingast v. Rialto Pastry 693 (New York) 1926; Rockmatt Corp. v.
            Ehrlich, 294 So. 2d, 412 (Fla. 1974)

Subject cases refer to commissions collectable on sale of a business. In the first case the court awarded a commission on the sale of personal property sold as a part of the business even though the broker was not licensed to sell real estate. In the second case the incidental use of real estate forms did not deny the unlicensed broker of his commission on the business sale. In the third case a real estate commission was denied since the broker received a 10 percent commission on the entire business sale.

99   Schreibman v. L.I. Combs and Sons Inc., et al., 377 F. 2d 410, 1964

The plaintiff broker was licensed in New York at the time he received the listing. He obtained a license in Indiana after he received the listing in Indiana and was duly licensed at the time the sale was made. The Federal Circuit Court ruled that the plaintiff was licensed at the time the cause of action arose (when the agreements were signed). The case was returned to the district courts for a hearing on its merits.

100   Houston v. Williams, 200 P. 55; Davis v. Chapman, 282 P. 992; Wise v.
            Radis, 242 P. 90; Pound v. Brown, 140 N.W. 2d 183, 1966

The above cases cited as precedence were rejected as the language of the Illinois licensing law requires a plaintiff broker to be licensed "prior to the time of offering to perform any such act or service or procuring any promise or contract for the payment of compensation for any such contemplated act or service."

100   Weingast v. Rialto Pastery Shop, 152 N.E. 693 (New York 1926)

An unlicensed broker may collect a commission on the sale of a business despite the fact that some real estate is included in the sale.

100   Rockmatt Corp. v. Ehrlich, 294 So. 2d 412 (Fla. 1974)

A unlicensed salesman selling a business containing real estate cannot collect a commission on the real estate.

100   Abrams v. Guston, 243 P. 2d 109 (1952)

Broker selling personal property which is only of value if it includes the real estate, requires a license.

100   Marks v. McCarty, 205 P. 2d 1025 (Cal. 1949)

When personal property and real estate are priced separately, even within one deal, the unlicensed broker may collect a commission on the personal property only.

101   Cohen v. Scola, 90 A. 2d 643 (N.J. 1951)

An unlicensed person was denied a commission on the sale of stock, fixtures and good will as well as real estate.

101   Hanks v. Hamilton, 339 So. 2d 1123 (Fla. 1976)

An unlicensed real estate salesperson was denied a commission share even though the sales agreement called for it.

11   Farragut Baggage and Transfer Co. v. Sharon Realty Inc., 501P. 2d 88, 1972

In the case cited the commission was denied as the agent's work to obtain a lease was begun while he was employed by another broker, but subsequently had his license transferred to the plaintiff broker. During the lease negotiation the agent was unlicensed for a period of time while the transfer of license was being made.

101   Mammen v. Snodgrass, 13 Ill. App. 2d 538 (1957)

If a broker has clearly abandoned his effort to sell to a party, he may not collect a commission where the sale is later made by his principal or another broker. However, the fact that a sale was made on different terms than those which he offered does not defeat his right to a commission.

102   Jackson v. Northwestern Life Insurance Co., 133 F. 2d 111 (1943)

A broker is not entitled to a commission if he fails to consumate a sale and abandons his efforts.

MULTIPLE BROKERS

103   Cannon v. Bates, 115 Va. 711

Where a seller lists his property with multiple brokers, each aware of the other's listing, he may sell to the first party produced by one of the brokers and only that broker is entitled to the commission.

103   Watts v. Barker, 275 Ky. (1938)

Where multiple brokers are employed, the seller is liable for only one commission. The winner is the one who can show that he is the procuring cause of the sale.

104   Carney v. John Hancock Oil Co., 187 Minn. 293

Where multiple brokers are employed and a question arises as to who contributed to the sale, the seller cannot be held liable for multiple commissions. Only the agency deemed to be the procuring cause is due a commission.

103   Averill v. Hart & O'Farrell, 101 W.Va. 411 (1926); Dobson v. Wolf, 54 N.W. 2d 469 (S.D., 1952)

In the case where multiple brokers are employed and more than one participate to some degree in finding a buyer, the courts have ruled that the broker judged to be the "procuring cause" is the one entitled to the commission.

104   Vreeland v. Vetterlein, 33 New Jersey 247 (1969); Julius Heller Realty Co. v. Jefferson Gravoco Bank, 144 S.W. 2d 174,176 (Mo. 1940)

Where it is difficult to determine which of several brokers was the procuring cause of the sale and thus due a commission, the courts must decide, based on facts presented.

104   Nichols v. Pendley, 331 S.W. 2d 673 (Mo. 1960)

A listing stating commission payable for a sale to a person "submitted" during the listing period hangs on the word "submitted." In this case a buyer was brought through the property while the owners were there, thus satisfying the term submitted.

104   Nichols v. Pendley, 331 S.W. 2d 673 (Mo. 1960); Brennan v. Roach, 47 Mo. App. 290 (1891)

A principal has the right to revoke a broker's authority to sell, while that broker is yet unsuccessful. A second broker, if successful in selling to the first broker's client must show that he is the procuring cause of the sale. The court stated, "It is the broker that shakes the tree not the one who runs up and picks the apples who is entitled to the commission."

104   Hunt v. Judd, 255 Ill. App. 395 (1922); Kennedy v. Vance, 201 Okla. 80 (1949) and Dindo v. Capeletti, 77 A. 2d 840 (Vt. 1951)

A number of courts have held that where multiple brokers are employed a sale by one automatically terminates the authority of the others, even though they have no notice of the sale.

105   Lee C. Richards, Inc. v. Brewer, 548 S.W. 2d 196 (Mo. App. 1977); Realty Marts International, Inc., v. Barlow, 348 So. 2d 63 (Fla. App. 1977)

A failure of the broker to inform his principal of all of the names of persons shown the property, which is sold during the term of the listing, does not extinguish his right to a commission.

106   Trent Trust Co. v. MacFarlane, 21 Hawaii 435 (1913)

This case is considered as establishing the general rule of law which states that where multiple brokers have been employed, a broker who has failed and thus abandoned his effort, cannot collect a commission if another broker finally succeeds in making a sale to the same client.

106   Walker v. Randall, 85 Pa. Super. 443 (1925)

In multiple broker claims, payment to one broker is not admissable as evidence in another broker's suit for commission.

106   Essres Realty & Insurance Inc. v. Zeif, 512 P. 2d 650 (Colo. App. 1973)

A broker must bring a buyer and seller together while the property is on the market. A later sale with no additional broker effort is insufficient to earn a commission.

107   Bass Investment Co. v. Banner Realty, Inc. 436 P. 2d 894 (Ariz. 1968)

A broker is entitled to a commission if a property is sold to his prospect even though the selling price is different than the listed price—higher or lower.

108   Blake Realty Inc. v. Gilligan, 547 N.Y.S. 2d 930 (N.Y. App. Div. 1989)

A broker may earn a commission to a buyer with whom the seller had previously negotiated if the listing agreement is mute to this point.

108   Adams and Leonard, Realtors v. Wheeler, 493 P. 2d 436 (Okla. 1972)

A management contract, containing a provision for an exclusive listing if the managed property is sold, is not enforceable unless the listing agreement is completed to include the rights and obligations of the seller if/when the property is sold.

107   Reap Realty v. Hadlock, 181, N. E. 2d 732 (Ohio 1961)

In deciding if a commission is due, the deciding factor is how effective was the broker's efforts, not what did he do.

109   Wolfenberger v. Madison, 357 N.E. 2d 656 (Ill. App. 1976)

A broker is entitled to a commission if he obtains a buyer on seller's terms but seller refuses to sign.

108   Bell v. Warren Development Corporation, 319 A. 2d 299 (N.H. 1974)

A broker's right to a commission stands or falls upon terms of the offer made by the prospective purchaser. If the terms vary in any material degree from those specified by the vendor, no commission is payable, unless the seller agrees.

109   Ellsworth Dobbs, Inc. v. Johnson (owner) and Iarussi (buyer), 50 N. J. 528 (1967)

The Supreme Court ruled in the referenced case that the mere procurement of a buyer ready and willing to buy does not earn a commission until the deal is closed. In this case the buyer was found liable for the commission since he failed to conclude the transaction without a valid reason.

110   Hersh v. Kelman, 104 N.E. 2d 35 (1951)

Where the broker fails to comply with special provisions of the listing contract, no commission is due.

110   Stabb v. Messier, 264 A. 2d 790 (Vt. 1970); Brown v. Grimm, 481 P. 2d 63 (or. 1971) and Tristram's Landing Inc. v. Wait, 327 N.E. 2d 727 (Mass. 1975)

Above cases all cite Ellsworth Dobbs, Inc v. Johnson 50 N.J. 528 (1967) as precedence.

110   Jones v. Palace Realty Co., N.C. 303 (1946)

A broker cannot recover a commission if the agreement says he is to be paid out of the sales price and the deal does not close.

111   Stewart Realty v. Brock, 60 N.M. 216 (1955)

Where the deal is not closed between buyer and seller, for a cash stipulation payment to the seller, the agent is due a full commission.

110   Bechtel Properties, Inc. v. Blanken, 299 F. 2d 928 (D.C. 1962)

Where commission is due at the close of the sale and the sale is not consumated, by mutual agreement between buyer and seller, the agent should not be deprived of his commission.

111   Nelson et al. v. Rosenblum Inc. 182 N.W. 2d 666 (Minn. 1970); Fink v. Dougherty, 90 Pa. Super. 443 (1927)

In those states in which a net listing is allowed, the broker cannot collect a commission if the selling price does not produce the minimum net-to-seller specified in the listing contract.

112   Nelson v. Rosenblum Co., 182 N. W. 2d 666 (Minn. 1970)

Where a broker produces a buyer ready willing and able to buy, and who is accepted as such by the seller, and no condition on commission payment specified, such as "commission due on closing," the commission is payable.

112   Campbell v. Grange, 23 D&C 2d 344 (1961)

A broker board member, acting as a subagent for the listing broker, has no right to sue the principal.

112   Oglesby v. Barclif, Inc. v. Metro M.L.S., Inc., CCH, TRR, Sec 61,064 (Va. 1976)

The same MLS commission for all brokers is illegal. Each must set their own rate and percentage payable to other brokers selling their listing.

113   Wheeler v. Waller, 197 N. E. 2d 585 (Iowa 1972)

A broker invited to assist another broker in the sale cannot deny the first broker a share of the commission received by the second broker.

113   J.A. Carter & Associates, Inc. v. Devore, 281 So. 2d 245 (Fla. App. 1973) and Fowler v. Taylor, 554 P. 2d 205 (Utah 1976)

An agreement for fee spliting between broker and another broker and/or broker and salesperson need not be in writing—the Statute of Frauds does not apply.

113   Fowler v. Taylor, 554 P. 2d 205 (Utah 1976)

An agreement to share a commission between brokers need not be in writing.

113   DeBenedictis v. Gerechoff, 339 A. 2d 225 (N.J. 1975)

Instant case involves question of commission due an ex-agent who was the procuring cause of a later sale. The court awarded a 50 percent commission.

114   Pitt v. Kent, 179 A. 2d 626 (Conn. 1962)

The question of a former partner sharing in a deal after the partnership was disolved was settled in favor of the ex-partner. It was shown that a prior interest existed.

113   Clair v. Kall and Kall Inc., N. Y. Misc. 2d (1960)

Case involved payment of commission to an ex-agent. Court awarded commission based on extensive work of agent before his departure.

114   Turnblazer v. Smith, 379 S.W. 2d 772 (Tenn. 1964)

Case established precedence that only a broker may sue for a commission. In the instant case the broker refused to sue and the agent attempted to collect. Commission was denied.

115   Kulp Real Estate v. Randolph Favoretto et ux., 316 A. 2d (N.J. 1974);
House v. Erwin, 501 P. 2d 1221 (Wash. 1974)

A buyer's forced forfeiture of his earnest money payment may not be legal, where it can be shown that the buyer was unaware of the legal language in the sales agreement and where it had not been explained to him by the selling broker.

115   Barry Norman Agency, Inc. of Morris County v. Elias, 285 A. 2d 80 (N.J. 1971); Ellsworth Dobbs, Inc. v. Johnson, 236 A. 2d 843 (1967)

Where circumstances of the situation give the edge to the professional, the court ruled that the broker is due damages, but not necessarily his entire commission.

116   Haymes v. Rogers, 319 P. 2d 339 (Ariz. 1950)

Broker lost a commission when it was shown he stated to the buyer that he believed the owner would take less than the listed price. Mr. Justice Udall issued a strong dissenting opinion saying, "...it would be a most naive purchaser who would not know or assume that the owner of realty might sell for less than the original asking price."

116   Dail Realty v. Vodicka, 237 N.W. 2d 7 (S. Dak. 1975)

If a broker knows of nay defect in title of a property listed and a subsequent sale fails because of that defect, he may not collect a commission.

116   Jones v. Del Anderson and Associates, 539 S.W. 2d 348 (1976)

Brokers are expected to know and comply with all State real estate laws or forfeit their commissions.

116   Heard, et al., v. Miles, 32 Tenn. 410 (1949)

Case involved activeties by two brokers the second who had negotiated a lease agreement saying in effect "commission due on any future sale." Second broker lost since it was shown he failed to point out this provision of the lease to the owner at the time of signing.

116   Wolf v. Casemento, 185 So. 537 (1939)

Instant case opposes Arizona decision of Haymes v. Rogers, 319 P. 2d 339 (Ariz 1950).

117   Hughey v. Rainwater Partners, 661 S,.W. 2d 690 (Tenn. App. 1983)

Brokers must reveal the form and quality of the earnest money or down payments.

117   Thompson v. Hoagland, 242 A. 2d 642 (N.J. 1968) and Brotonari v. Rollofo, 246 N.W. 2d 368 (Mich. App. 1976)

Broker failed to notify his principal that he was to personally share in the action of the purchase.

117   Brotonari v. Rollofo, 246 N.W. 2d 368 (Mich. 1976)

A broker must advise his principal if he is to be a purchaser of the listed property.

122   Everson v. Phelps, 115 Oregon 523 and Schmidt Inc., v. Brock, 97 Ohio App. 469 (1953)

Where the listing does not contain a hold-over statement, the seller may negotiate with prospects introduced by the broker after the expiration of the listing without obligation to pay a commission.

117   Aeschlimann v. Rosbach, 558 P. 2d 1231 (Or. 1977)

A sale by a broker to a corporation, in which the broker has no interest, can recover a commission.

118   Croughaw v. Gerlach, 68 S.D. 93 (1941)

An agent (attorney) hired to dispose of ot of state property, has a right to hire a subagent at the owner's expense. Custom would assume that an attorney, so acting, would have owner authority to hire a broker in the property state. Where the owner knew of the appointment and failed to object, a commission would have been payable.

OFFERS AND ACCEPTANCE

119   Kerdyk v. Hammock Oakes Estates, Inc., 342 So. 2d 833 (Fla. App. 1977)

A seller cannot reject an offer for less that the net amount specified in the listing and then sell to another for that same lower price, without paying a broker's commission on the sale.

120   Gaynor v. Laverdure, 291 N. E. 2d 617 (Mass. 1973)

Even though the listing contract calls for specific and special performance by the broker, the broker cannot be denied a commission if the sale fails due to the seller's fault.

120   Quality Home Builders v. Harrick, 173 S.E. 2d 846 (Va.1970)

A broker who produces a buyer at a price, that does not equal or exceed the net to seller specified, is not entitled to a commission.

121   Kostan v. Glasier, 60 N. W. 2d 283 (1953); Amies v. Wesnofske, 174 N. E. 436 (N.Y. 1931); Tristam's Landing, Inc. v. Wait, 327 N.E. 2d 727 (Mass. 1975) and Dixon v. Andres Tile Mfg. Corp. 357 A. 2d 667 (Pa. 1976)

In all of the above cases written requirements for completion of specific event which did not occur relieved the seller of obligation to pay a commission.

121   Stovall Realty & Insurance Co., Inc. v. Goff, 159 S.E. 2d 467 (Ga. 1968)

Where the sales agreement calls for certain conditions to be met, the broker cannot collect a commission if those conditions are not fulfilled.

121   Dixon v. Andres Tile & Mfg. Corp., 357 A. 2d 667 (Pa. 1976) and Richard v. Falletti, 13 N. J. Sup. 534 (1951)

Specific events or provisions, whether written or oral requirements, must be satisfied in order for a commission to be payable.

121   Chamberlain v. Porter, 562 A. 2d 675 (Me. 1989)

Brokers generally earn a commission upon presentation of a client ready, willing, and able to buy; however, the listing agreement may modify this standard.

122   Broadway Realty & Trust, Inc. v. Gould, 136 Ariz.236, 555 P. 2d 580 (1983)

Broker/Client agreements for commissions on future sales must be specific as to the commission payable.

122   Advance Realty Co. v. Spanos, 348 Mich. 464 (1957)

The requirement to "negotiate a sale" to earn a commission was held to mean "produce a purchaser."

122   Bonn v. Summers, 249 N.C. 357 (1950)

Where a hold-over period is stated in the listing, the broker must inform the seller within three days of the expiration, of all prospects with which he has negotiated.

123   E.M. Boerke, Inc. v. Williams, 137 N.W. 2d 489 (Wis. 1965)

A requirement to inform the seller of all prospects *prior* to expiration of the listing was held to mean "prior to the actual date of the listing expiration." Any ambiguity as to "expiration date" is to be resolved against the broker, who prepared the listing.

123   McGuire v. Sinnett, 158 Ore. 390 (1938)

A broker is due a commission on a sale to a prospect made within the listing extender period if:

1. He found a buyer ready willing and able to purchase
2. He placed the buyer in touch with the seller either during the term of the listing or extension period, or
3. He was the procuring cause of the sale.

124   United Farms of Wisconsin, Inc. v. Klasen, 112 Wisc. 2d 634, 334 N.W. 2d 110 (1983)

The term "with whom the broker negotiated" in a listing agreement is accepted on its broadest interpretation.

124   Kalna v. Fialko, 125 N.E. 2d 565 (1955); King v. Dean, 238 N. E. 2d 828 (Ohio 1968) and Jessup v. La Pin, 150 N.W. 2d 342 (Wis. 1967)

The term "In touch with" is insufficient. To earn a commission on property sold after the termination of the listing, the broker must show that the client was "one with which he was negotiating." Negotiating is not a single act but a series of communications and actions.

125   Fleetham v. Schneekloth, 52 wash. 2D 176 (1958) and Williams v. Brittingham, 38 D & C 342 (Pa. 1965)

Failure to include certain statements in a listing or failure to provide the seller with a copy of the listing will not void a broker's right to a commission.

125   Cunningham v. Aeschliman, N.E. 2d 326 (Ill. 1973) and Anthony v. Enzler, 132 Cal. Rptr. 553 (1976)

A commission was due the broker who negotiated a lease with an option during the terms of the listing even though the option was exercised later, but during the term of the negotiated lease.

125   Dean v. King Service, 249 N.E. 2d 45 (Ohio 1969)

A broker is required to advise his principal of any prospects shown the listed property during a listing extender time. Failure to do so may result in loss of commission, where the property is subsequently sold to that same buyer after the listing expiration.

126   Percy Galbreath & Son, Inc. v. Dehyco Co., Inc. et al, 548 S.W. 2d 664 (Tenn. App. 1976)

Commissions on future leases must specify the exact commission to be paid.

127   Rosenfeld v. Cadence Industries Corp., 348 N.Y.S. 2d (1973)

Lease agreements calling for a commission on all lease payments must be paid for the full term of the lease, if the landlord voluntarily cancels the contract.

127   Richard B. Herman and Co. v. Stern, 419 Pa. 272 (1965) and W.D. Nelson & Co. v. Taylor Heights Development Corp., 207 Va. 386 (1966)

Collection of a commission is possible, where there is a statement in a lease agreement, which is a logical substitute for an additional agreement between lessor and broker normally required.

128   Hussey v. Stephens, 194 S.E. 2d 243 (S.C. 1973); Larkin v. Richardson, 502 P. 2d 1156 (Ore. 1972)

Where the sales agreement calls for commission payments as principal installment payments are received by the seller, no commission is due in the future, where the deal fails to be completed.

128   Heymann v. Electric Service Mfg. Co., Inc. 194A. 2d 429 (Pa. 1963); Baird & Wagner, Inc. v. Ruud, 359 N. E. 2d 745 (Ill. App. 1976); Lyons v. Stevenson, 135 Cal. Rptr. 457 (1977)

Where real estate is transferred for stock in a corporation, the broker is due a commission on the sale, even though he may not be a securities broker—the stock transfer being incidental to the sale of the real property.

129   Jones v. Howard, 234 Ill. (1908)

A broker who contracts to buy a property he lists, if not sold by a certain date, can collect a commission on the sale of that property as well as the new one purchased by the seller.

129   Lundstrom, Inc. v. Nikkei Concerns, Inc. 788 P. 2d 561 (Wash. Ct. App. 1988)

For purposes of earning a commission, condemnation is not considered a sale.

132   Dimmitt-Rickhoff-Bayer Real Estate Co. v. Finnigan, 179 F. 2d 882 (Mo.) 1950

Salespeople who are not required to keep specific hours are not employees.

133   Bidwell v. Iowa Employment Security Commission (1973); Dimmitt-Rickhoff-Bayer Real Estate Co. v. Finnegan, 179 F. 2d 882 (Mo. 1950); Dept. of Employment v. Bake Young Realty, 560 P. 2d 504 (Idaho 1977); California Employment Stabilization Commission v. Morris, 172 P. 2d 497; (1946); Moore v. Idaho Employment Security Agency, 367 P. 2d 291 (1961); Realty Mortgage and Sales Co. v. Okla. Employment Security Commission, 169 P. 2d 761 (Okla. 1946)

The broker, who is obligated to pay a commssion to the salesperson when received in the office is not an employer subject to payment of contributions under state employment security laws.

134   Hughes v. Industrial Commission, 551 P. 2d 962 (Ariz. App. 1976)

The right of the broker to control the agent, rather than the actual exercise of control, establishes the employee/independent agent status.

134   Marin County Board of Realtors® v. Palson, 549 P. 2d 833 (1976)

California's Cartwright Anti-trust law forbids exclusion of part time brokers from Realtor® board multilist service. They may be excluded for cause, however.

134   Guadango v. Mount Pleasant Listing Exchange, Inc. CCH TRR Section 61, 065 (N.Y. 1976)

Membership requirements which include residency time limits are not in violation of N.Y. General Business Law.

BROKER ETHICS

136   Yerkie v. Salisbury, 287 A. 2d 498 (Md. 1972) and 8 Am. Jur. Sects. 89, 152.

Broker owes full loyalty to his client and may not have a secret interest in the transaction.

136   Blakely v. Bradley et al., 281 S.W. (2d) 835 (1955); King v. Pruitt, 288 S.W. 2d 923 (1956) and Curroto v. Hammack, 241 S.W. 2d 897 (Mo. 1951).

A broker may not buy property listed by himself unless all facts are made known to his principal.

136   Batson v. Strehlow, 305 P. 2d 686 (Cal. App. 1957), Cox v. Bryant, 347 S.W. 2d 861 (Mo. 1961) and Nutter, Appellant, v. Becktel, 433 P. 2d 993 (Ariz. 1967)

Referenced cases establish precedence that a broker or salesman may not act for himself without full knowledge of all facts given to the seller/principal.

137   Gallagher-Smith-Feutz Realty Inc., v. Circle Z Farma, Inc. et al., 545 S.W. 2d 395 (Mo. App. 1976)

A broker who knows of a better offer at the time he attempts to influence his principal to sell to another is guilty of a breach of duty.

137   Cochrane v. Wittbold, 102 N.W. 2d 459 (Mich. 1960)

A broker or salesman may not purchase for his own use through a straw party without full disclosure to the principal.

137   Case v. Business Centers, Inc., N.E. 2d 47 (Ohio App. 1976)

A broker must inform his principal of any knowledge he may have regarding a planned resale of the property being purchased.

138   Martin v. Hutton, 90 Neb. 34 1912)

A person is justified in relying on a representation where it is a positive statement.

139   In re Isaacs, 181 N.Y.S. 403; Maple Hill Farm v. New Jersey Real Estate Commission, 170 A. 2d 789 (1961); McKnight v. Real Estate Commission, 122 So. 2d 420 (Fla. 1976); Real Estate Commission v. Tice, 190 A. 2d 188 (Pa. 1963); Boineau v. S. C. Commission, 230 S.E. 440 (1976) and Blank v. Black, 512 P. 2d 1016 (Or. App. 1973)

Brokers acting for themselves as sellers are held to an especially high standard as regards missrepresentation, "puffing of goods" and other considerations of dishonesty and lack of professionalism.

139   Simone v. McKee, 298 P. 2d 667 (Cal. 1956), E. A. Stout Agency v. Wooster, 99 A. 2d 689 (Vt. 1955)

It is the duty of a broker (agent) to report all activeties to his principal, whether he thinks them worthy or not.

139   Simone v. McKee, 298 P. 2d 667 (Cal. 1956)

A broker is bound to disclose any second offers he is aware of.

140 M.S.R. Inc., v. Lish, 527 P. 2d 912 (Colo. App.1974)

Failure of broker to disclose that a sale was to a corporation in which he had substantial interest cost him a commission.

140 Sylvester v. Beck, 406 Pa. 607 (1962)

A broker may buy for his own portfolio if his principal is aware of all facts. A resale by the broker shortly thereafter and at a profit may suggest a questions of ethics.

140 Sylvester v. Beck, 406 Pa. 607 (1962)

The court found nothing wrong with a sale to a broker for his own profit potential, where all facts were made known to the principal during the sale.

141 Earle v. Lambert et al., 205 Cal. App. 2d 452 (1962)

Broker held liable for damages to principal due to change in price of a property traded without his principal's knowledge or authority.

141 Jackson v. Williams, 510 S.W. 2d 645 (Tex App. 1974)

Broker held financially liable for a deposit returned against specific instructions of his principal.

142 Cryder Well Co., v. Brown et al., 136 N.W. 2d 519 (Iowa 1965)

A broker's listing and authority "to sell" does not authorize him to allow possession before closing.

142 Peek v. Meadors, 500 S.W. 2d 333 (Ark. 1973)

Where the agent does not exceed his authority, or where his representation is a repetition, in good faith, of a statement authorized by his principal, the agent cannot be found liable.

142 Gallegher v.Jones, 129 U.S. 195, 9 Ct. 335, 32 L Ed 658, 660 and Quinn v. Phipps, 113 So. 419

In the absence of any special agreement, it is the principal's judgment and not the agent's that is to control.

143 Wilson v. Hisey, 305 P. 2d 686 (Cal. App. 1957)

A broker who fails to provide competent guidance to his client can be held liable.

143 Goodwin v. Glick, 139 A. Ca. Supp.958 (1956)

A broker and/or agent for a seller may request assistance of other board members but cannot deligate his agent-client responsibility.

143 Zwick v. United Farm Agency, Inc. 556 P. 2d 508 (Wyo. 1976)

A broker cannot be held liable for a mistake in judgment that results from other than a failure to know what a prudent person would do in similar circumstances.

144 Wise v. Dawson, 353 A. 2d 207 (Del. 1975)

The agent/subagent relationship of board members does not create an agent/subagent relationship, where the subagent commits a fraud or other tort.

145 Orr v. Woolfolk, 250 Ky. 279 (1933)

Where multiple brokers are employed, the seller cannot avoid payment of a commission to one broker by using a third party to make the purchase. The court also stated that a commission cannot be denied when a sale is made by a broker's client influencing another to buy.

145   Beogher v. Clark, 81 Kan 250 (1909) and Gresham v. Lee, 152 Ga. 829 (1921)

A broker cannot be deprived of a commission by another stepping in to make a sale to the first broker's customer.

145   Beougher v. Clark, 81 Kan. 250 (1909); Greshman v. Lee, 152 Ga. 829 (1921)

A broker cannot be deprived of a commission on a sale to a client who he has found, by another agent stepping in to make the sale.

146   McCue v. Deppert, 21 N.J. Sup. 591 (1952) and Schlesinger v. Zeilengold (Ohio 1952)

In the case of Exclusive Listings, a buyer cannot by his own wrongful or deceitful acts prevent a broker from earning a commission; i.e., going direct to the seller to avoid commission payment.

147   Hayman v. Ross, 22 N.C. App. 624 (1974); Fleming v. Romero, 342 So. 2d 881 (La. App. 1977)

Contracts for real estate must be in writing to be enforceable.

EARNEST MONEY, OFFERS, AND ACCEPTANCE

148   Cowman v. Allen Monmuments, Inc. 500 S.W. 2d 223 (Texas 1973)

It is not necessary for a consideration to be paid at the time of signing as the promises of the parties are deemed sufficient consideration.

148   City of Roslyn v. Hughes Construction Co., 573 P.2d 385 (Wash. App. 1978)

Offer and acceptance means there must be a "meeting of the minds."

149   Riley v. Stoves, 526 P. 2d 747 (Ariz. 1974)

An infant may disaffirm his voidable contract. State laws indicate the legal age of consent.

150   Pepper v. Chatel (D.C. No. 3056 1962)

A contract made by a married woman prior to her marriage is binding upon the husband, who is compelled to join in the deed.

151   Watson v. Alford, 503 S.W. 2d 897 (Ark. 1974)

Vendor's physical condition and an inadequacy of price are sufficient to prove incompetence.

150   Star Realty, Inc., v. Bower, 169 N.W. 2d 194 (Mich.1969)

Mental capacity to contract is defined as, "whether the person in question possesses sufficient mind to understand, in a reasonable manner, the nature and effect of the act in which he is engaged."

151   Roy S. Ludlow Inv. Co. v. Taggart, 509 P. 2d 818 (Utah 1976)

A buyer cannot profit from an error in the sales agreement, which he knew to be wrong at the time of signing.

151   Ryan v. Brady, 366 A. 2d 745 (Md. App. 1976)

To avoid a contract on the grounds of a mistake, the error must be mutual and substantial.

152   Johnson v. Geer Real Estate Co., 720 P. 2d 660 (1986)

A broker can be liable for seller's misrepresentations where, as a professional, he should have known better.

152   Hoffman v. Connall, 746 P. 2d 242 (1987)

A broker cannot be held liable for "innocently and nonnegligently conveying a seller's misrepresentations; however, he is held to a standard of reasonable care and professionalism.

153   Haddock Construction Co. v. Snedigar Dairy, 510 P. 2d 752 (Ariz. App. 1973)

Contracts for real estate must be in writing to be enforceable.

154   Bokelheide v. Snyder, 71 S.D. 470 (1947)

A brief memorandum and receipt of earnest money is insufficient data to inforce specific performance.

153   Zaborski v. Kutyla, 185 N.W. 2d 586 (Mich. App. 1971); Walker v. Walker, 448 S.W. 2d 171 (Tex. 1969); Brotman v. Brotman, 353 Pa. 570 (1946) and Harris v. Potts, 545 S.W. 2d 126 (Texas 1976)

The requirement for a contract to be in writing may be exempt from the statute of frauds if: (1) Earnest money has been deposited, (2) the purchaser has gone into possession, or (3) improvements have been made to the property. The last cited case states "all three events must have occurred."

153   Ripps v. Mueller et al., 517 P. 2d 512 (Ariz. 1973) and Kenimer v. Thompson, 196 S.E. 2d 363 (Ga. 1973) and Davison v. Robbins, 517 P. 2d 1026 (Utah 1973)

An agreement to make an agreement is not enforceable.

153   Harris v. Potts, et al. 545 S.W. 2d 126 (Tex. 1976)

Specific performance on an oral agreement was denied.

153   Kenimer v. Thompson, 196 S.E. 2d 363 (Ga. 1973)

A check with a brief notation "For lot 100 Earnest Money" is not enough to satisfy the requirements that a contract be in writing.

154   Tompkins v. France, 2I. App. 2d 227 (1959)

Where a preliminary agreement calls for a future agreement to be prepared on a *specified form,* that form must be utilized.

155   Cook v. Barfield, 162 S.E. 2d 417 (Ga. 1968)

An agreement calling for three equal payments and without dates is unenforceable.

154   Colrodas v. Russell, 289 So. 2d 55 (Fla App. 1974) and Kenimer v. Thompson, 196 S.E. 2d 363 (Ga. 1973)

An enforceable agreement must be in writing and not partially in parol. It must also be complete to be enforceable.

154   Klymshyn v. Szarek, 185 N. W. 2d 820 (Mich. App. 1971)

A brief memorandum of agreement stating deposit amount, property to be purchased and the selling price and signed by the seller is sufficient to satisfy the contract provisions of the statute of frauds.

155   Lalone v. Modern Album and Finishing Co., Inc., 331 NYS 2d 889 (1972)

A contract of sale need not be contained in one written instrument, if the instruments are connected by the internal nature of the subject matter.

155   Goren v. Royal Investments, Inc., 25 Mass. App.Ct. 137, 516 N.E. 2d 173 (1987); Blomendale v. Imbrescia, Mass. App. Ct. 144, 516, N. E. 2d 177 (1987)

A signed memorandum may or may not constitute a final agreement.

156   Picard v. Burroughs, 304 So. 2d 455 (Fla. App. 1974)

A binder by itself is insufficient to force performance, since it is too ambiguous.

156   Huber v. Gerahman, 300 S.W. 2d 501 (Mo. 1957)

Although the sales agreement is a contract between buyer and seller, the broker has an interest where it indicates him as procuring cause of the sale. If later, the deal is mutually receneded, the broker is entitled to his full commission.

156   Herman v. Stern, 419 Pa. 272 (1965); W.D. Nelson & Co., Inc. v. Taylor Heights Development Corp., 207 Va. 386 (1966) and Mid-Continent Properties Inc. v. Pflug. 249 N. W. 2d 476 (Neb. 1977)

Sales contracts are between buyer and seller but broker may have a commission interest if it mentions him as the one negotiating the deal.

157   Real Equity Diversification, Inc. v. Coville, 744 P. 2d 756 (Colo. Ct. App. 1987)

Even though the purchaser's broker may derive his commission from the seller, he has no fiduciary responsibility to the seller.

157   Haldeman v. Gosnell Development Corp. 748 P. 2d 1209 (Ariz. Ct. App. 1987)

A seller's broker has no obligation to explain the terms of a contract to the purchaser.

157   Yerkie, Jr. v. Salisbury, 287 A. 2d 498 (Md. 1972)

Problems occuring with a contract, prepared by a broker acting for his principal, will be resolved against the seller.

158   Security Aluminum Window Mfg. Co. v. Lehman Associates, Inc. et al., 108 N.J. Super. 137 (1970)

A broker and his agent can be held liable for compensatory and punitive damages where fraud or misrepresentation is involved.

159   Huber, Hunts & Nichols, Inc. v. Moore, 136 Cal. Rptr. 603 (1977)

An architect, acting for his principal, has rather broad authority of supervision but he cannot enlarge upon the contract agreement signed by his principal.

159   Peters v. Windmiller, 314 Ill. 496 (1925); Gallant v. Todd et al., 111 S.E. 2d 779 (S.C. 1960); Fleming v. Romero, 342 So. 2d 881 (La. App. 1977) and O. L. Hamilton v. Booth, 332 S.W. 2d 252 (Ky. 1960)

A broker, without special authority, cannot bind his principal to an agreement.

160   O.L. Hamilton v. Booth, 322 S.W. 2d 252 (Ky. 1960).

A broker has no authority to release a contingency condition without his principal's permission.

160   McDonald v. Cullen, 559 P. 2d 506 (Or. 1977)

A contingency release, furnished by the broker without authority of the seller, voids an action for specific performance.

161   Shay v. Schrink, 335 Pa. 94 (1939)

Authority given a broker to collect interest does not authorize him to also collect principal payments.

196   Mecklenborg v. Schockley, 154 Pa. Super Ct. 196 (1943)

Where a broker signs a receipt for earnest money which contains a notation "Check to be returned if mortgage is not obtainable," he is personally liable for return of the earnest money if the mortgage is not obtained.

170   Gaynes v. Allen 362 N.E. 2d 197 (N.H.)

A sales agreement subject to buyer's obtaining "Available Financing" is binding if *any* financing is available.

170   Gaynes v. Allen, 362 N.E. 2d 197 (N.H. 1976)

An agreement subject to obtaining available financing implies reasonable terms and conditions are acceptable.

170   Dillahunty v. Keystone Savings Ass'n., 303 N. E. 2d 750 (Ohio 1973)

The principal of Caveat Emptor applies to the sale of real estate relative to conditions open to observations.

170   S.G. Payne & Co. v. Nowak, 465 S.W. 2d 17 (Mo. 1971)

A closing statement may vary from the sales agreement in some respects if acceptable by buyer and seller.

171   Baker v. Leight, 370 P. 2d 208 (Ariz. 1962)

An owner must assure that his mortgage is assumable before he signs an agreement to allow the purchaser to assume it.

172   Beattie-Firth, Inc. v. Colebank et al., 143 W.Va. 740 (1958)

A seller is not required to sue for specific performance just to assure his realtor has earned a commission.

172   Beattie-Firth, Inc. v. Colebank et al., 143 W. Va. 740 (1958)

A listing agreement requiring that the sale be consumated, before a commission is payable, relieves the seller of the commission obligation if the buyer fails to close.

172   Reynolds v. Hancock, 53 Wash. 2d 682 (1959)

A buyer may revoke an offer at any time until accepted by the seller and the buyer notified.

173   Little v. Rohauer, 707 P. 2d 1015 Colo. (Colo. App. 1985)

When is a subagent considered to be an agent of the seller.

173   Little v. Rohauer, 707 P. 2d 1015 Colo. (Colo. App. 1985)

Acceptance by an authorized agent constitutes delivery.

173   Ardente v. Horan, 366 A. 2d 162 (R.I. 1976)

A counteroffer constitutes a rejection of the original offer and the initiation of a new one. Once rejected the original offer is dead forever.

173   Stearns v. Western, 252 N.E. 2d 126 (Ill. 1967) and Pravorne v. McLeod, 383 P. 2d 855 (Nev. 1963)

An offer to purchase, under certain stated conditions, entitles the buyer to a return of earnest money if the stated conditions cannot be met exactly as specified.

175   Perry v. Thorpe Bros., Inc. 267 Minn 29 (1963) and Gosslin v. Martin, 56 Ore. 281, 107 P. 957

If earnest money is paid to a broker and the contract broken by the seller, the broker is liable to the buyer for a full refund, regardless of whether he has a legitimate claim on his principal for a commission earned.

175   Cowman v. Allen Monuments, 500 S. W. 2d 223 (Texas 1973)

The size of the earnest money is not fixed but should normally be sufficient to cover the broker commission in event of buyer default. Deposits can be in more than one installment.

175   Hicks v. Howell, 203 Va. 32 (1961)

The broker may not keep an earnest money deposit as part of his commission in the even the seller is unable to provide a marketable title. The buyer is entitled to an immediate refund.

175   Somers Co. v.Pix, 134 P. 932 (1913)

A broker who return an earnest money deposit because of a seller objection to the title, which was not unmarketable, waived his right to a commission.

175   Polette v. Wall, 256 S.W. 2d 283 (Mo. 1953)

A broker cannot ignore the instructions of his principal. A broker exceeds his authority if he returns an earnest money deposit to the buyer without knowledge and consent of his principal.

176   Eggerling v. Cuhel, 246 N.W. 2d 199 (Neb. 1976)

A broker or salesperson cannot be held liable for return of commission paid by the seller from an earnest money deposit, if at a later date the deal was not consumated—there was no fraud or bad faith on the part of the broker and salesperson.

176   Mathis v. Yarig, 176 A. 2d 794 (N.J. App. 1961)

Where the seller refuses without cause to consummate a sale, the broker is required to return the earnest money deposit to the buyer.

177   Tieri v. Orbell, 192 Pa. Super. Ct. 612 (1960)

An agreement subject to obtaining a mortgage implies a loan with at least a 20-year maturity.

178   Ricchio v. Oberst, 251 N.W. 2d 781 (Wis. 1977)

If the date of closing is not made *the essence of the agreement,* both parties have a reasonable time to close after the specified date.

177   Simmons and Associates v. Urban Renewal Agency, 497 S.W. 2d 705 (Ky. 1973)

In the event of default by the buyer, the seller would be provided three remedies: (1) Sue the buyer for specific performance, (2) Resell the property and sue the buyer for any loss on the resale and (3) Retain the earnest money as liquidated damages. The third alternative was selected in the instant case.

178   Robinson v. Abren, 345 So. 2d 404 (Fla. App. 1977)

Time requirements for payments in "time is of the essence" agreements cannot be met by moneys paid to a broker, who is not specifically authorized to receive such payments.

178   Kimm v. Anderson, 313 A. 2d 46 (Me. 1974) and Smith v. Hues, 540 S.W. 2d 485 (Texas App. 1976)

An oral extension of time, negotiated by vendor of agreements containing a "time is of the essence" clause, need not be in writing—waiver may be shown by parole evidence by way of circumstances or course of dealing.

178   Tom Jones Realty Corp. v. Frick, 533 N.Y.S. 2d 995 (N.Y. App. Div. 1988)

An agreement which does not contain a "time is of the essence" clause may be turned to one that does, after notification of the buyer, who has not closed in a timely manner.

179   Ewing v. Plummer, 308, Ill. 585 (1923)

A cloud on a title which normal men regard as dubious makes the title unmarketable.

179   Bryan, Appellant v. Jack Justice, 287 So. 2d 331 (Fla. 1973)

Broker can recover commission where he did not know that seller was unable to provide good title.

LIENS AND JUDGMENTS

181   Mitchell v. Chastain, 233 S.E. 2d 829 (Ga. App. 1977)

A lien revived by a scire facias proceeding attaches only as of the date of the revival.

181   Robinson v. Varela, 136 Cal. Rptr. 783 (1977)

Taking default judgment on the first day on which defendant's answer was delinquent will set aside judgment.

181   Robinson v. Varela, 138 Cal. Rptr. 783 (Cal. 1977)

The law looks with disfavor upon a party who attempts to take advantage of a mistake, surprise, inadvertence, or neglect of his adversary.

182   Courville v. Southern Casualty Ins. Co., 304 So. 2d 93 (La. 1974)

A default judgment rendered without proof of the demand sufficient to establish a prima facie case must be set aside.

182   Kenne v. Wiggins, 138 Cal. Rptr. (Cal. App. 1977)

Judgment is granted only where there is no triable issue of material fact.

182   Freeman v. Augustine's Inc., 360 N.E. 2d 1245 (Ill. App. 1977); Kincaid v. Kingluen, 559 P. 2d 1044 (Alaska 1977) and Keene v. Wiggins, 138 Cal. Rptr. 3 (Cal. App. 1977).

A summary judgment should be granted, as a matter of law, where there is no genuine issue as to any material fact.

182   Cardinali v. Planning Board of Lebanon, 373 A. 2d 251 (Me. 1977)

A judgment on a cognovit instrument should be cautiously invoked.

183   Fishel v. Givens, 362 N.E. 2d 97 (Ill. App. 1977).

The purpose of a summary judgment is not to tray an issue of fact, but to ascertain whether there is a fact issue to be tried.

182   Lammert v. Lammert Industries, Inc., 360 N.E. 2d 1355 (Ill. App. 1977).

To vacate a default judgment, it is essential that the defendant show a meritorious defense.

182   Davis v. Thomas, 548 S.W. 2d 755 (Tex. Civ. App. 1977)

A default judgment should be set aside in any case where the failure of the defendant to answer was not intentional or the result of indifference.

183   Edwards v. Edwards, 481 P. 2d 432 (Colo. App. 1970

A petition to set aside a default judgment is addressed to the sound discretion of the court.

183   Bourough of Monroeville v. Effie's Ups and Downs, 315 A. 2d 342 (Pa. Cmwlth. 1974); Cardente c. Travelers Ins. Co., 315 A. 2d 63 (R.I. 1974) and Girkin v. Cook, 518 P. 2d 45 (Okla. 1973).

A summary judgment may not be entered where there is disputed question of fact.

183   Ute, Inc. v. Opfel, 518 P. 2d 156 (Nev. 1974)

If the judgment appears erronious upon its face, the proper proceeding is to strike it off by motion.

183   Williams v. N.C. Board of Education, 201 S.E. 2d 889 (1974).

A judgment can only be collected for the real debt due.

183   U.S. Supreme Court, 405 U.S. 191 (1972)

It is not unconstitutional to enforce the confession of judgment against those earning over $10,000.

183   Swarb. v. Lennox, 314 F. Supp. 1091 (1970); 405 U.S. 191)1972)

The confession clause was a violation of due process for persons having incomes less than $10,000.

183   Coronet Ins. v. Jones, 359 N.E. 2d 768 (Ill. 1977)

To vacate an ex parte judgment, a defendant must have a meritorious defense and show that he exercised due diligence.

183   Cashion v. Ammadi, 345 So. 2d 268 (Ala. 1977)

A factual issue precluded summary judgment.

185   Kilgust v. Kemp, 235 N.W. 2d 292 (Wis, 1975)

Delivery of materials to the owner or agent is sufficient to sustain a mechanic's lien.

186   Hostetter v. Inland Development Corp. of Montana, 561 P. 2d 1323 (Mont. 1977)

A purchaser of property under construction is charged with any lien that is attached to the premises.

185   Lenexa State Bank and Trust Co. v. Dixon, 559 P. 2d 776 (Kan. 1977)

A prospective mortgagee must make an inspection of property to ascertain whether there has been recent work that might constitute a prior lien.

185   Connoly Development, Inc. v. Superior Court of Merced County, 533 P. 2d 637 (Cal. 1976)

A mechanic's lien is subordinate to encumbrances recorded before commencement of work.

186   Hartford Fire Ins. Co. v. Balch, 350 P. 2d 514 (Okla. 1960)

Carpets loosely tacked to the floor are personalty.

186   United Benefit Life Ins. Co. v. Norman Lumber Co., 484 P. 2d 527 (Okla. 1971)

Carpets permantly fastened to the floor are lienable as fixtures.

186   Reuben E. Johnson Co. v. Phelps, 156 N.W. 2d 247 (1968)

Liens cannot be attached after preliminary work has begun on a property to which a mortgage is to be placed.

187   Holiday Development Co. v. Tobin Construction Co., 549 P. 2d 1376 (Kan. 1967)

A mechanic's or material mean's lien cannot be obtained based on a quasi contract.

187   Lambert v. Newman, 431 S.W. 2d 480 (Ark. 1968)

Work "to" the land and not "upon it" is insufficient to file a mechanic's lien.

187   Sears Roebuck & Co. v. Seven Palms Motor Inn, 530 S.W. 2d 695 (Mo. 1975)

Draperies affixed to the property is lienable. Bedspreads, which are removable are not.

188   McCausland v. Davis, 204 So. 2d 335 (Fla. 1967)

Cour defines *actual notice, implied notice, and constructive notice.*

188   Maddox v. Astro Investments, 343 N.E. 2d 133 (Ohio App. 1975)

A judgment becomes a lien when it is delivered for filing to the clerk.

188   Coral Gables, Inc. v. Kerl, 334 Pa. 441, 6 A. 2d 275 (1939)

It is not necessary that the name of a judgment debtor as docketed and indexed be letter perfect.

188   L.C. Russell Co. v. Pipeguard Corp., 504 S.W. 2d 596 (Tex. 1973)

A judgment is personal property and assignable in the same manner as a note or mortgage.

LOSSES PRIOR TO TRANSFER OF TITLE

189   Dubin Paper Co. v. Insurance Co. of North America, 361 Pa. 68 (1948) and Beatty v. Guggenheim Exploration Co., 225 N.Y. 380

In the case of property loss prior to deed transfer, the insurance proceeds belong to the buyer.

189   Good v. Jarrard, 76 S.E. 698 (S.C.); Oakes v. Wingfield, 95 Ga. App. 871 (1957); Insurance Co. of N.A. v. Erickson, 50 Fla. 419 (1905); Sanford v. Breidenbach, 173 N.E. 2d 702 (Ohio App. 1960) and Skendzel v. Marshall, 301 N.E. 2d 641 (Ind. 1973)

The weight of authority holds that an accidental loss, prior to deed transfer, falls on the purchaser who is the equitable owner.

189   Thompson v. Gould, 20 Pick. 134 (Mass. 1838); Libman v. Levenson, 128 N. E. 13 (Mass. 1920) and Durham v. McCready, 151 A. 544 (Me. 1930)

The minority view of loss prior to deed transfer holds there is a failure of consideration and the loss falls on the seller.

ZONING CHANGES AFTER OFFER IS MADE

190			Didonate v. Reliance Standard Life Ins. Co., 433 Pa. 219 (1969)

Zoning changes after the agreement signing is no difference than any other loss, which falls on the buyer who has equitable title.

190			White Realty & Ins. Co. v. Moreland, 259 A. 2d 461 (Pa. 1969); Wright v. City of Littleton, 483 P. 2d 953 (Colo 1971); Craig v. Presbyterian Church, 62 Mich. App. 617 (1975) and Gignilliat v. Borg, 205 S.E. 2d (Ga. App. 1974)

Agreements where seller "Warrants" property to be zoned for certain uses are deemed contracts which tend to interfere with the government's administration and are not enforceable—commissions are not payable in event of failure of the deal.

190			La Grave v. Jones, 336 So. 2d 1330 (1976)

An agreement subject to obtaining a variance may be waived by the buyer and require specific performance by the seller.

STATEMENTS MADE BY BROKER AND SELLERS

191			Wilson v. Caine, 366 A. 2d 474 (N.H. 1976)

Negligent misrepresentation by a broker or seller, which causes financial loss to the buyer, can be the basis of action for damages.

191			Colby v. Granet State Realty, Inc., 366 A. 2d 482 (N.H. 1976)

A buyer is justified in relying upon material statements of fact concerning matters peculiarly within the seller's knowledge.

191			Karan v. Bob Post, Inc., 521 P. 2d 1276 (Colo. 1974)

Fraud may arise where the seller witholds material facts, disclosure of which is a duty.

191			Lake v. Thompson, 366 Pa. 352 (1950)

An owner or broker must be circumspect in regards to statements he makes.

192			Peoples Furniture and Appliance Co., v. Healy, 113 N. W. 2d 802 (Mich 1962)

Instant case held that buyer was entitled to relief based upon broker's representation of "a slight possibility of flooding." The situation was such that the buyer was unable to obtain flood insurance.

192			Goggans v. Winkley et al., 465 2d 326 (Mont. 1970)

An agreement that buyer would pay for survey did not preclude cause of misrepresentation by broker.

192			Viebahn v. Gudim et al., 273 Minn 504 (166)

Seller's furnishing of accurate information prior to closing precludes complaint by buyer of missrepresentation by broker.

192			Isaacs v. Cox, 431 S.W. 2d 494 (ky. 1968) and Becker v. Lagerquist Bros. Inc., 348 P. 2d 423 (Wash. 1960)

The parole evidence rule prevents introduction of data which effects the terms of a contract but not in the case of accident, fraud, or mistake.

193   Ritz v. Mymor Houses, Inc., 213 N.W. 2d 470 (Iowa 1973) and Colby v. Granet State Realty, Inc., et al., 366 A. 2d 482 (N.H. 1976)

Exoneration or exculpatory clauses cannot exonerate a broker or his principal for any fraud or misrepresentation.

193   Becker v. Lagerquist Bros.Inc., 348 P. 2d 423 (Wash. 1960)

Parole evidence is admissable to show fraud or misrepresentation.

193   Webb v. Culver, 509 P. 2d 1173 (Ore. 1973) and Lawson v. Citizens and So. National Bank, 193 S.E. 2d 124 (S.C. 1972)

Fraud may also consist of concealment of a material defect of which there is a duty to disclose.

193   Bicknell v. Barnes, 501 S.W. 2d 761 (Ariz. 1973)

Where there is general agreement that the sales agreement is merged into the deed, reformation will not be prevented upon showing of misrepresentation, fraud, or mistake of fact.

194   Dillahunty v. Keystone Savings Association, 303 N.E. 2d 750 (Ohio 1973)

When the deed is accepted, no further action arises under terms of the sales agreement—the sales agreement is abrogated.

EARNEST MONEY OTHER THAN CASH

194   Witherspoon v. Pusch, 136 P. 2d 137 (Colo. 1960)

A check, given as earnest money, cannot be stopped without the permission of the seller.

195   Duncan v. Baskin, 154 N. W. 2d 617 (Mich. 1969)

A buyer who has given a check as earnest money and later stops payment can be sued by the holder (broker).

195   Staab v. Messier, 264 A. 2d 790 (Vt. 1970) and Ellsworth Dobbs, Inc. v. Johnson, 236 A. 2d 843 (N.J. 1967)

A broker who accepts a check as earnest money, in which the agreement states that the check be held for satisfaction of stipulated conditions, cannot sue for a commission if the sale fails.

196   Slusser v. Brillhart, 159 N.E. 2d 480 (Ohio 1958) and Mecklenberg v. Niehaus, 85 Ohio App. 271 (1948)

A broker who accepts a note as earnest money, but fails to inform his principal of this fact, cannot sue for a commission if the deal fails.

196   Wartman v. Schockley, 154 Pa. Superior Ct. 196 (1943)

A broker who accepts a check as earnest money, where the agreement stipulates a return if certain conditions are not met, is personally liable for return of the deposit if those conditions are not met.

196   Gerig v. Russ, 200 Ore. 196 (1954)

Sales agreements calling for specific payments of principal towards the purchase must be made to the seller, since the contract is between buyer and seller. The broker has the right to collect only earnest money. Principal payments to the broker are made at the buyers risk.

LAND DESCRIPTIONS IN THE AGREEMENT

197   55 Am. Jur. Vendor and Purchaser, Sec. 127 and Carrel v. Lux, 101 Ariz. 430 (1966)

The difference between sale of land "in gross" vs. "by acre" is defined.

197   Witmer v. Bloom 288 A. 2d 323 (Md. App. 1972) and Allen v. Youngblood, 200 S.E. 2d 758 (Ga. 1973)

Descriptive words such as *more or less* raise a presumption of sale by the acre.

197   Liddycoat v. Ulbricht, 556 P. 2d 99 (Ore. 1976)

A sale in gross may not be given relief if he observes the boundaries and bases his decision to buy upon that personal observation.

197   Goette v. Steel, 526 A. 2d 626 (1987)

Sales contracts indicating parcel size, followed by more or less, are not necessarily sales in gross.

REALTY AND PERSONALTY

198   Farmer's and Merchants Bank v. Sawyer, 163 So. 657 (Ala. 1937)

Items not easily removable by the seller are defined as fixtures (real estate).

DEFAULTS ON THE AGREEMENT

199   MacRitchie v. Plumb, 245 N.W. 2d (Mich. App. 1976)

Upon default the damages available to the seller is the *difference between contract price and the market value of the property as of the day of contract breach.*

200   Wegg v. Broderick, Inc. 557 P. 2d. 861 (Wash. App. 1976)

Where a missunderstanding exists between buyer and seller, brokers can be held liable for improperly explaining all factors to the parties involved. Failure of the buyer to fully perform on a contract of sale was unenforceable due to failure of seller to inform buyer of consequences of failure to perform.

200   Hutchison v. Tompkins, 259 So. 129 (Fla. 1972); Hook v. Vomar, 320 F. 2d 536 (Fla. 1968) and Simmons v. Urban Redevelopment, 497 S.W. 2d 705 (Ky. App. 1973)

If damages flowing from a breach are ascertainable at the time the contract is made, the clause is a penalty and unenforceable. If not, it is considered as one for liquidated damages which must be reasonable.

200   Bremer v. Myers, 545 S.W. 2d 235 (Tex. App. 1976)

Clauses allowing seller to "retain earnest money deposits as liquidated damages" limits damages to that amount.

200   Bando v. Cole, 250 N.W. 2d 651 (Neb. 1977)

A sales agreement specifying that the earnest money deposit would be forfeited in event of default is legal and enforceable.

201   Pruett v. LaSalceda, 359 N.E. 2d 776 (Ill. 1977)

Vendor is entitled to retain earnest money upon purchaser's anticipatory repudiation of agreement.

201   Riccio v. Oberst, N.W. 2d 781 (Wisc. 1977)

Unless waived by the buyer, seller must tender deed through his attorney or broker to establish fact seller is free of default.

201   Ward v. Doucette, 301 N. E. 2d 256 (Mass. 1973)

A letter through the buyer's attorney saying he is prepared to pay the balance due and requesting deed execution does not constitute legal tender.

202   Rooney v. Dayton-Hudson Corp., 246 N.W. 2d 170 (Minn. 1976)

An option is not a contract but provides the second party the priviledge of buying if he so desires.

201   Menke v. Foote, 261 N.W. 2d 635 (Neb. 1978)

Where the seller refuses to perform, the buyer may sue for specific performance. Plaintiff must be free from default.

202   Mattco, Inc. v. Manton Radio Association, Inc., 246 N.W. 2d 222 (N.D. 1976)

Time is of the essence of an option agreement and if not exercised by the expiration date automatically expires.

OPTIONS

202   Johnson v. Worcester Business Development Corp., 302 N.E. 2d 575 (Mass. 1973)

The Optioner gives the optionee the right for a limited time to purchase (or lease) upon certain terms and conditions.

202   Adams v. Swift, 500 S.W. 2d 437 (Tenn. 1973)

A letter of intent to exercise an option, sent within the option period, is insufficient. The option must be exercised within the option period.

202   Waterway Gas 'N Wash, Inc. v. Sandbothe et al., 550 S.W. 2d 617 (Mo. App. 1977)

Where the option agreement contains contingencies or conditions which must be satisfied or option fee is returnable, the optionee must use due diligence to satisfy the contingent condition.

203   Kelros Bldg. Corp. v. Ballagalia, 109 N.E. 2d 221 (Ill. App. 1952)

An option to renew a lease signed by two parties cannot be exercised by one party.

PRINCIPLE OF CAVEAT EMPTOR

203   Mayo v. Wilbrite, 232 S.E. 2d 141 (Ga. App. 1976)

The principal of Caveat Emptor is modified in the case of more complex conditions in which the seller may have exercised "passive concealment."

203   Salminen v. Frankson, 245 N.W. 2d 839 (Mich. App. 1976)

Written notice of intent to exercise an option, mailed within the option notice period but not received by the optioner during the period, is invalid.

204   Beavers v. Lamplighters Realty, Inc., 556 P. 2d 1328 (Okla. 1976) and Prescott v. Brown, 120 P. 991 (Okla. 1911)

The principal of Caveat Emptor was further eroded in the referenced cases where fraud or deceit were employed to influence the buyer to buy.

204   Rothenberg v. Oleno, 262 A. 2d 461 (Vt. 1970); Miller v. Cannon Hill Estate Ltd., 2 K.B. 113 (1931) and Rogers v. Scyphers, 161 S.E. 2d 81 (1968)

The application of the principal of Caveat Emptor, in the case of new construction, depends upon the basis of facts. Normally the courts have ruled that there is an implied warranty that the dwelling, when finished, will be suitable for the purpose intended.

IMPLIED WARRANTIES

205   Vanderschrier v. Aaron, 140 N. E. 2d 819 (Ohio 1957); Glisan v. Smolenske, 387 P. 2d 260 (Colo 1943); Jones v. Gatewood, 381 P. 2d 158 (Okla. 1963); Weck v. A.M. Sunrise Construction Co., 181 N. E. 2d 728 (Ill. 1966); Staff v. Lido Dune, INc., 262 NYS 2d 544 (1965); Bethlahmy v. Bechtel, 415 P. 2d 698 (Idaho 1966) and Humber v. Morton, 426 S. W. 2d 554 (Tex. 1968)

Cited cases have adopted the application of implied warranty under the principal of Caveat Emptor.

206   Lorio v. Kaizer, 277 So. 2d 633 (La. 1973)

There is no obligation on the part of a purchaser to inspect the property with *expertise*.

205   Gallegos v. Graff, 508 P. 2d 798 (Colo. App. 1973)

Implied warranty does not apply in the case where a seller is not the builder.

205   Pollard v. Saxe and Yolles Dev. Co., 525 P. 2d 88 (Cal. 1974)

Implied warranty is the antithesis of Caveat Emptor. It is the seller who must beware.

206   Pywell v. Haldave, D.C. Court of Appeals (1962)

A broker representation of a home "in good condition" and later found to be damaged by termites, cannot be construed as a representation of material fact.

206   McCrystall v. Connor, 331 Ill 107 (1928) and Oliver v. Wyatt, 418 S.W. 2d 403 (Ky. 1967)

Vendors, who sign sales agreements prior to inquiry as to identity of buyer, cannot refuse to perform.

207   Brady v. Hoeppner, Melrose Realty & Inv. Co., 3rd Party Pltf.,558 P. 2d 1009 (Colo. App. 1977)

Where a contract is nonassignable without the permission of the seller, even though it contains a clause "Permission will not be unreasonably withheld" is still not necessarily assignable.

SUNDAY CONTRACTS

207   Heckel v. Burtchaell, 72 A. 2d 794 (N.J. App. 1950); Mercner v. Fay, 177 A. 2d 481 (N.J. 1962) and Chadwick v. Stokes, 162 F. 2d 132 (1947)

Sunday contracts are not necessarily invalid.

CLOSING THE DEAL

210   Pippin v. Kern-Ward Bldg. Co., 8 Ohio App. 3rd 196, 456 N.E. 2d 1235 (1982)

An escrow agent must follow the agreements of the parties, attempts by one or more parties to unilaterally change the agreement must be disregarded.

212   Southgate, Inc. v. Ecklini, 207 N.W. 2d 729 (Minn. 1973)

Although payment to the seller is normally cash or a certified check, a check from the closing agent is considered legal.

INSURANCE PROCEEDS

217   Shelton v. Providence Washington Ins. Co., 131 S.W. 2d 330 (Tex. 1939)

Persons holding a lien nor cities owed back taxes cannot collect from insurance proceeds.

217   Russell v. Williams, 374 P. 2d 827 (Cal. 1962)

Insurance covers the insured person only, not all owners of the property.

THE PROPERTY TRANSFER

218   Baldwin v. Anderson, 161 N.W. 2d 553 (Wisc. 1968)

Grantee is entitled to that quality of title which will enable him to sell the property without objection or difficulty.

218   Ewing v.Plummer, 308 Ill. (1923)

Title need not be necessarily perfect but must be of such character that the buyer will not be exposed to dangers of litigation as to its validity.

219   Shulansky v. Michaels 484 P. 2d 14 (Ariz. App. 1971) and Guido v. Baldwin, 360 N.E. 2d 842 (Ind. App. 1977)

Where problems of interpretation are encountered every attempt should be made to carry out the intentions of the grantor; substance rather than form should control.

219   Bessing v. Ohio Valley Coal Co., Inc. of Kentucky, 293 N.E. 2d 510 (Ind. App. 1973); Pfeffer v. Lebanon Land Dev. Co., 360 N..E. 2d 1115 (Ill. App. 1977) and Jones v. Johnson, 307 N.E. 2d 222 (Ill. App. 1974)

Ambiguities in the construction of a deed should be construed most favorably to the grantee, since the grantor prepared it.

219   Williams v. Board of Education, 201 S.E. 2d 889 (N.C. 1974)

A deed is defined as a writing by which lands, tenements and hereditaments are conveyed, which writing is signed, sealed, and delivered by the parties.

ILLEGAL DEEDS/DEED PROBLEMS

220   Piedmont and Western Invest. Corp. v. Carnes-Miller Gear Co., 384 S.E. 2d 687 (N.C. A pp. 1989)

A corporation, not legally constituted, cannot hold title to property, even though it later becomes a legal organization.

220   Alton Evening Telegraph v. Doak, 296 N.E. 2d 605 (Ill. 1973) and Arrow Ambulance v. Davis, 306 N.E. 2d (Ill. 1974)

A deed to or from a fictitious organization which has no legal existance is void. Minor mistakes in setting out a name will not vitiate a deed.

223   Patterson v. Hopkins, 371 A. 2d 1378 (Pa. Super. 1977)

Deeds made with intent to disturb, delay, hinder, or defraud creditors are void.

223   Sparkman & McLean Co. v. Derber, 481 P. 2d 585 (Wash. App. 1971)

and Isabella Bank & Trust Co. v. Pappas, 261 N.W. 2d 558 (Mich. App. 1977)

Under statutes dealing with transfer of real estate by an insolvent debtor, or made with actual intent to defraud, the burden of proof is initially on the one seeking to set aside the conveyance.

223   Wood v. Swift, 428 S.W. 2d 77 (Ark. 1968); Kenney v. Kinney, 150 So. 2d 671 (La. 1963) and Mitchell et al. v. Wilcox et al., 139 N. W. 2d 203 (Neb. 1966)

Unless a deed from father to son recites that the conveyance is made in consideration of support during the father's lifetime, a further conveyance will be upheld.

224   Jahner v. Jacob, 252 N.W. 2d 1 (N.D. 1977)

Love and affection is sufficient consideration in a deed but it is not a fair consideration where the conveyance is made to delay, defraud, or hinder creditors of the grantor.

224   Harrel v. Branson, 334 So. 2d 604 (Fla. App. 1977)

A niece's deception to her uncle that she and her cohabitor were married, was sufficient to cancel a deed, which conveyed a life estate to them.

224   Prentice v. Cox, 547 S.W. 2d 744 (Ark. 1977)

The relationship of child to parent, does not, per se, raise a presumption of undue influence, duress, or fraud.

224   Gross, Adm., etc. v. Allen, 345 So. 2d 1315 (Miss. 1977)

In a deed from a 94-year-old uncle to a nephew in which there was a presumption that it was invalid, the burden of overcoming the presumption was upon the nephew.

222   Chatam Amusement Co. v. Perry, 216 Ga. 445 (1961)

A quit claim deed conveys only such interest as the grantor possessed at the time of the conveyance.

224   Kendall v. Kendall, 360 N.E. 2d 1242 (Ill. App. 1977)

Deeds made in consideration of future support are recindable in the event the grantee fails to carry out their promise.

224   Gallegos v. Garcia, 480 P. 2d 1002 (Ariz. 1971); Hotchkiss v. Werth, 483 P. 2d 1053 (Kan. 1971) and Hensley v. Stevens, 481 P. 2d 694 (Mont. 1971)

To establish undue influence as a basis for setting aside of a deed from parents to son, the law requires more than an opportunity to exert undue influence or suspicions.

225   Sabine Investment Co. v. Stratton, 549 S.W. 2d (Tex. App. 1977)

A description citing a lot and plat that were not recorded was inadequate.

225   Grand Lodge of Independent Order of Odd Fellows v. City of Thomasville, Ga. 4 (1970) and Wallace v. Adamson, 201 S.E. 2d 479 (Ga. 1973)

Weak or indefinite descriptions of property in a deed will void the transfer.

226   Placid Oil Co. v. Young, 246 So. 2d 306 (1971)

Property descriptions in deeds should be liberally construed to sustain rather than defeat a conveyance.

226   Jordan v. Tinnin, 342 So. 2d 748 (Ala. 1977)

A descriptive call for an established corner prevails over a call for distance.

231   United States v. California, 332 U.S. 19 (1947)

Land between the shore line and the three-mile limit is vested in the United States Government and does not belong to the state.

230   Van Deursen v. Dunlap Towing Co., 562 P. 2d 666 (Wash. App. 1977)

Where both navigation and fishing rights can be enjoyed freely and fairly, navigation has no authority to trespass or injure the right of fishing.

231   Segaro v. Cornell. 196 S.E. 2d 341 (Ga. 1973)

When a map plan or other survey is referred to in a deed, it becomes a material and essential part of the conveyance and is to have the same force and effect as if copied into it.

232   Westland Nursing Home, Inc. v. Benson, 517 P. 2d 862 (Colo. App. 1974)

Appurtenances pass with the deed unless the use was restricted to the grantor or there is something in the conveyance expressly excepting it from the grant.

233   Harding v. Ja Laur Corp., 315 A. 2d 132 (Md. 1974)

A forged deed is void from inception; however those procured by fraud, deceit, or trickery may be upheld in the case of a bona fide purchaser.

233   Wicks Homes v. Moxley, 342 So. 2d839 (Fla. App. 1977)

Witnesses to a homestead mortgage signing is no longer required.

DELIVERY OF THE DEED

235   Fiori v. Fiori, 405 Pa. 303 (1961); Willingham v. Smith, et al., 106 S.E. 117 (Ga. 1921); 1st Natn. Bank of Gainsville v. Harmon, 199 S.E. 223 (Ga. 1938) and Algood v. Algood, 196 S.E. 2d 888 (Ga. 1973)

An unrecorded deed found among grantor's papers, after the grantor's death, cannot be presumed to have been delivered and thus is invalid.

235   Murphy v. Traylor, 289 So. 2d 584 (Ala. 1974); Doyle v. Carter et al., 362 N.E. 2d 214 (Mass. App. 1977) and Scroggins v. Roper, 548 S.W. 2d 779 (Tex. Civ. App. 1977)

A deed does not pass title until delivered. A deed is presumed to have been delivered on the date the deed bears. In the last referenced case the court said:

"No particular form of words or actions is necessary to constitute delivery of a deed, but manual delivery is not necessary; a deed may be delivered by words without acts, by acts without words, or by both. An intention to give present effect to an executed conveyance is sufficient."

235   Proctor v. Forsythe, 480 P. 2d 511 (Wash. 1971)

Validity of the delivery depends upon the intentions of the grantor. Recording of the deed by the grantor raises a strong presumption of delivery. Retention of the deed by the grantor raises a strong presumption against delivery. In any case the presumptions are subject to rebuttal by proof.

236   Fike v. Harshbarger, 317 A. 2d 859 (Md. 1924)

A delivery in escrow occurs when the deed is delivered to a third party and will take effect only upon performance of some conditions—in an escrow delivery, the grantor looses all control and cannot recall the deed.

236   Caron v. Wadas, 305 N.E. 2d 853 (Mass. 1974)

A decedent who supplies purchase money but deeds the property to another without their knowledge did not deliver the deed. The property did not pass to the named grantee.

236   Cain v. Morrison, 512 P. 2d 474 (Kan. 1973)

The deposit of a deed with a third party and with surrender of all control constitutes delivery.

237   Huntington City v. Peterson, 518 P. 2d 1246 (Utah 1974)

When the deed has been signed, sealed, and delivered the transfer of title is complete.

237   American Medical Intern, Inc. v. Oritz, 111 Cal. Rptr. 617 (1974)

Once a deed is recorded, all persons are presumed to have constructive notice of the contents of the recorded instrument.

237   Sabo v. Horvath, 559 P. 2d 1038 (Alaska 1976)

A deed recorded outside the chain of title does not constitute "constructive notice."

237   Weddell v. City of Atlanta, 172 S.E. 2d 862 (Ga. 1970)

Actual possession by a wife and children was sufficient to put the public on notice of possible interest in the property.

238   Adams v. United States, 76 U.S. Ct. No. 1333, S.D., N.Y. (1976)

Constructive notice is not given where the recorded deed is not properly indexed in the records and may result in serious consequences to the grantee.

ADVERSE POSSESSION

239   Herriot v. Lewis, 35 Wash. App. 496,668, P. 2d 589 (1983)

The acts of excluding intruders and other acts of dominion may be indicative of adverse possession.

239   Forest Home Cemetery Association v. Dardanella Financial Corp., 329 N.W. 2d 895 (S.D. 1983)

It is almost impossible to succeed in a claim of adverse possession against a cemetery. The land is deemed possessed in a way that it was intended to be possessed.

239   Kerrigan v. Thomas, 281 So. 2d 410 (Fla. App. 1973)

A party claiming title by adverse possession bears a heavy burden of proof.

240   Davis v. Mayweather, 504 S.W. 2d 741 (Ark. 1974); Talmadge v. Adams, 240 S.E. 2d P. 9 (Ga. 1977) and Kerrigan v. Thomas, 281 So. 2d 410 (Fla. App. 1973)

Payment of taxes is given some weight in proving adverse possession. It is a contributing factor, but not the controlling one.

239   Meyer v. Law, 287 So. 2d 37 (Fla. 1973)

A Florida claimant for title by adverse possession must have paid the taxes on the property for the requisite 7-year-period.

239   Garcia v. Placios, 667 S.W. 2d 225 (Tex. App. 1984, writ ref. n.r.e.)

A failure to pay taxes does not necessarily preclude adverse possession.

240   Anderson v. McCormick 18 Or. 301, 22 P. 1062 (1899) and Owen v. Bartuff, 297 Or. 610, 687, P. 2d 1072 (1984).

The court recognizes contract buyers ownership in adverse possession.

240   Anderson v. McCormick, 18 Or. 301, 22 P. 1062 (1889); Owen v. Bartuff, 297,,)r. 610,687 P. 2d 1072 (1984)

The 1889 case holding that a vendee was precluded from holding adversely was reversed by the 1984 case.

240   Halverson v. City of Bellview, 41 Wash. App. 457, 704, P. 2d 1232 (1985)

Adverse possession creates an ownership interest in 10 years. The court only confirms it.

241   Rozmarek v. Plamondon, 419 Mich. 287, 351 N.W. 2d 558 (1984)

Title by adverse possession, in absence of Color of Title, cannot extend beyond the boundaries of land which was actually used and occupied.

241   Dimmick v. Dimmick, 374 P. 2d 824 (Cal. 1962) and Burns v. Owens, 357 S.W. 2d 520 (Ark. 1962)

A party who occupies property, under a permissive use, cannot claim title by adverse possession.

241   Wales v. Lester, 517 P. 281 (Ore. 1973)

A few strands of barbed wire tacked to trees in a wooded area did not constitute adequate notice of an adverse claim.

242   Devins v. Burough of Bogota, 568 A. 2d 903 (N.J. Super. 1989)

Private citizens may not gain title by adverse possession to lands acquired by municipalities through tax foreclosures.

243   Lewkowitz v. Blumish, 442 Pa. 369 (1971)

In the instant case claimants, tacking of grantor's 12-year use to his own 3 months, was insufficient to meet Pennsylvania's requirement of 21 years possession.

243   Thibodeaux v. Quibodeaux, 282 So. 2d 845 (La. App. 1973)

Claimant could not tack on his ancestor's possession time to meet Louisana's 30-year requirement, since the ancestor's use was not hostile.

244   Warren v. Collier, 559 S.W. 2d 927 (Ark. 1978)

In the instant case it was ruled that hostile possession could not begin until the mistake in possession was discovered. Other states have ruled that an honest mistake in boundary location and possession for the requisite time, is sufficient to establish a claim.

245   Iverson v. Iverson, et al., 213 N.W. 2d 708 (S.D. 1973)

Exceptions to adverse possession claims do not run against a remainderman until termination of a precedent estate (Life estate), nor against the state or United States Government.

245   Srejack v. City of Baltimore, 313 A. 2d 843 (Md. 1974) and Deleware Lackawanna R.R. v. Tobyhanna Co., 228 Pa. 487

Normally a claim of adverse possession cannot be filed against a railroad or other property used for public purposes. In the instant case the railroad's case faltered, due to its failure to: (1) incorporate the purchased property into its right of way and (2) the fact that the property was purchased rather than acquired by eminent domain.

PROPERTY DEDICATION

246   Hudson v. Gains, 501 S.W. 2d 734 (Tex. 1973) and Big Sur Properties
               v. Mott, 132 Cal Rptr. 835 (1976)

The dedication of a property to the public by implication, must show that there exists a clear and equivocal intention by the land owner and acceptance by the public.

246   Smith v. Black, 547 S.W. 2d 947 (Tenn. App. 1976)

An offer of dedication may be withdrawn or revoked until the offer has been accepted by donee, or estoppel has arisen by intervening rights. Payment of taxes was not deemed to effect a revocation of the offer.

246   Baird v. City of Altoona, 361 A. 2d 458 (Pa. 1976)

The vacating of a street and reservation of an easement for utilities was held invalid as regards the easement. The court said, "Once abandoned, the city could not tack on a further use."

246   County of Orange v. Chandler-Sherman Corp., 126 Cal Reptr. 765, 5
               S.W.U. Rev 48 (1973)

An implied dedication to the public exists when a landowner does not object for a period in excess of five years.

MORTGAGE LOANS

251   Sharp Lumber Co. v. Manus Homes Inc., 189 N.E. 2d 447, 90, O.L.A.
               421 (Ohio App. 1961)

Even where construction loans are limited to "hard costs" only, the variance therefrom will not invalidate the loan.

254   Plummer v. Ilse, 41 Wash. 5, 82 P. 1009, 2 L.R.A., N.S. 627 (1905); Cf.
               Kartheison v. Hawkins, 98 Nev. 237, 645 P. 2d 967 (1982)

A signed deed held by the mortgagee as security for the debt violates the prohibition against clogging.

254   Bacon v. Bacon, Tot. 133-4 (1639)

The first use of the term "Clogging of Equity."

254   MacArthur v. North Palm Beach Utilities, Inc., 202 So. 2d 181 (Fla.
               1967)

Some exceptions to the prohibition against clogging are made in complex cases, where both parties are represented by council.

257   United States v. Hawkins et al., 205 F 2d 837 (Ky. 1961) and State Real
               Estate Commission v. Bongiorno, 45 D & C. 392 (Pa. 1968)

Dual contracts, prepared to assist in obtaining financing, is a federal crime and usually a state offense as well.

257   Johnson v. Shell, 504 S.W. 2d 397 (Tex. 1973)

A deed of trust is, in legal effect, a mortgage with the power to sell upon default.

263   Long v. Manning, 455 S.W. 2d 496 (MO. 1970)

Lender requires short period for forclosure where note, secured by trust deed, contained provisions against default in installment payments.

263   Conn. Gen. Stat. Ann. 49-15 (1975); Abacus Mortgage Insurance Co. v. Whitewood Hills Development Corp., 2 Conn. App. 460, 479 A. 2d 1231 (1984)

Strict foreclosure, which is still used in Conn., Ver. and Ill. is a rarely used procedure.

265   Williams v. First Federal Savings & Loan Association, 651 F. 2d 910 (4th Cir. 1981)

Property bearing a low interest assumable loan is more valuable in times of high going interest rates.

ACCELERATION OF THE DEBT

266   Investors Savings and Loan Association v. Ganz, 416 A. 2d 918 (N.J. 1980)

Failure of the borrower to occupy the property can be used to accelerate the debt.

266   Income Realty & Mortgage Inc. v. Columbia Savings and Loan Association, 661 P. 2d 257, 265 (Colo. 1983); Tierce v. APS Co., 382 So. 2d 485, 487 (Ala. 1979)

The due on sale clause is usually held as reasonable unless the borrower can show that the lender engaged in unconscionable conduct.

266   O'Connell v. Dockendorff, 415, So. 2d 35, 36-37 (Fla. 1982); Miller v. Pacific First Federal Savings & Loan Association, 86 Wm 2d 401, 406-07, 545 P. 2d 546, 549 (1976)

Mortgage lenders can legally insert an "interest-increase" clause covering assumptions. The buyer can be held in default only if he fails to pay the increased interest rate.

267   Mills v. Nashua Federal Savings and Loan Association, 121 N.H. 722,433, A. 2d 1312, 1316 (1981); Powell v. Phoenix Federal Savings and Loan Association, 434 So.2d 247, 253 (Ala. 1983)

Transfer of mortgaged property to an inter vivos trust will not accelerate the debt.

267   Chilivis v. Tumlin Woods Realty Associates, Inc., 250 Ga. 179, 279, S.E. 2d 4, 4 (1982)

Lenders are precluded from foreclosing based on a further encumbrance of the property.

267   United States v. Med O Farm, Inc., 701 F. 2d 88 (9th Cir. 1983)

Transfer of property from a corporation to a sole shareholder will not accelerate the debt, unless all shares are transferred to a third party.

268   Medovoi v. American Savings & Loan Association, 89 Cal. App. 3d 244, 152 Cal. Rptr. 572 (1979)

The mortgagor has no obligation to notify the lender of a transfer of property.

269   Cooper v. Deseret Federal Savings and Loan Ass'n, 757 P. 2d 483 (Utah Ct. App. 1988)

Where the lender has known for a number of years of the transfer of the mortgaged property, he cannot exercise his otherwise right of acceleration of debt.

269   LaSala v. American Savings & Loan Association, 489 P. 2d 1113 (1971)

Acceleration clauses are not enforceable upon initiation of secondary financing.

269   Gunther v. White, 489 S.W. 2d 529 (Tenn. 1973); Crockett v. First Federal Savings and Loan Association of Charlotte, 224 S.E. 2d 580 (N.C. 1976) and Peoples Savings Association v. Standard Industries, Inc. 257 N.E. 2d 35 (1970)

An acceleration clause in the mortgage was upheld.

269   Mutual Savings and Loan Association v. Wisconsin Wire Works, 239 N.W. 2d 20 (Wisc. 1976)

Acceleration clause including restriction against further encumberance of property upheld.

270   Miller v. Pacific Federal Savings and Loan Association, 86 Wash. 2d 401 (Wisc. 1976)

Acceleration clause allowing mortgagee to increase interest rate upon transfer of property upheld.

270   Peoples Savings Association v. Standard Industries, 275 N.E. 2d 406 (Ohio 1970)

Acceleration clauses are enforceable upon resale.

270   Demey et al. v. Jonjon Roche et al., App. 133 Cal. Rptr. 570 (1976); Tucker v. Lassen Savings and Loan Ass'n., 526 P. 2d 1169 (Cal. 1974) and Medovoi v. American Savings and Loan Ass'n, 133 Cal. Rptr. 631 (1976)

In first two cases courts held that acceleration clause does not apply when property is sold on installment land contract; however, acceleration clauses are justified to protect lender's security. Third case held otherwise.

270   Adkinson v. Nybert, 344 So. 2d 614 (Fla. App. 1977)

Where agreement for deed failed to mention acceleration of debt upon default of monthly payment, default did not warrant acceleration of debt.

270   Wellencamp v. Bank of America, 21 Cal. 3d 943,950, 148 Cal. Reptr. 379, 383, 582 P. 2d 970, 974 (1978); Income Realty and Mortgage, Inc., v. Columbia Savings & Loan Association, 661 P. 2d 257, 260 (Colo. 1983)

The distinction between an outright sale and a sale by land contract was upheld on policy grounds.

270   Tucker v. Lassen Savings and Loan Association, 12 Cal. 2d 629, 116 Cal. Rptr. 633, 526 P. 2d 1169 (1974)

The instant case held that there was a difference in sale by contract and outright sale. This position was later rejected by the California Supreme Court in Wellencamp v. Bank of America, 1978.

271   Century Federal Savings and Loan Ass'n. v. Van Glaun, 364 A. 2d 558 (N.J. 1976)

Even though the motive of the acceleration clause may be to secure an increase in interest rate, it is not fatal to the exercise of the acceleration clause.

EARLY PAYMENT PENALTIES

271   14 L.J. (N.S.) Ch. 167 Chancery (1845)

If mortgagors were allowed to pay off loans early, the mortgagee would be seriously harmed.

271   J.M. Realty Investment Corp. et al. v. Stern, 296 So. 2d 588 (Fla. App. 1974)

Mortgagee-vendor can foreclose for entire balance due, including amount due on first mortgage, where the wrap-around mortgage included balance due mortgagee, as vendor of the subject property.

272   Sacramento Savings and Loan Association v. Superior Court, 137 Cal. App. 3d 142, 186 Cal. Reptr. 823 (1982)

A lender has a justifiable interest in imposing the penalty to cover his costs due to a potential lag time and administrative processing prior to making a new loan.

272   LHD Realty Corp., 726 F. 2d 327, 330-331 (7th Cir. 1984)

Prepayment penalties do not apply where the lender elects to accelerate the debt.

272   Fox v. Federated Department Stores, Inc. 156 Cal. Rptr. 893,94 Cal. App. 3d 867 (1979)

Penalties for early payment, which are modest and compensate the lender for administrative costs and lost interest are usually upheld.

272   DeKalb County v. United Family Life Insurance Co., 235 Ga. 417,219, S.E. 2d 707 (1979) on remand 136 Ga. App. 822, 222 S.E. 2d 644 (1975)

Prepayment penalties do not apply in the case of condemnation.

272   Chestnut Corp. v. Bankers Bond & Mortgage Co., 395 Pa. 153, 149 A. 2d 48 (1959)

Prepayments from fire insurance proceeds are not applicable although the courts recognize that both the mortgagor and mortgagee suffer.

272   Sybron Corp. v. Clark Hospital Supply Corp., 76 Cal. App. 3d 896, 143 Cal. Reptr. 306 (1978)

Prepayments which amount to substantial fixed lump sums or are calculated as a percent of the balance of the loan are normally not upheld.

MORTGAGEE IN POSSESSION

273   Miner's Savings Bank v. Thomas, 140 Pa. Super. Ct. 5 (1940)

A mortgagee in possession may also be liable for injury to a person injured on/about the mortgaged premises.

273   Essex Cleaning Contractors, Inc. v. Amato, 317 A. 2d 411 (N.J. 1974)

The duty of a mortgagee in possession is that of a provident owner to protect the mortgagor.

MORTGAGE SIGNATURE REQUIREMENTS

276   Stockwell v. Lindeman, 229 Cal. App. 2d 750 Cal Reptr. 555 (1964)

In a subordination agreement, the terms of repayment can be supplied by the lender or custom, but the contract is not valid if the terms of repayment are left for future agreement between the parties.

276 Insurance Co. of America v. Holliday, 214 N.W. 2d 273 (Neb. 1974)

Mortgages signed and acknowledged by any one of three owners is sufficient to allow recording.

VENDOR LENDERS

278 Associates Discount Corp. v. Gomes, 338 So. 2d 552 (Fla. App. 1976); Davidson v. Click, 31 New Mex. 543, 249 P. 100, 47 A.L.R. 1016 (1926); Martin v. First National Bank of Opelika, 279 Ala., 303. 184 So. 2d 815 (1966)

The purchase money mortgage will prevail over a claim of dower, community property, or homestead.

279 Stachnik v. Winkel, 213 N.W. 2d 434 (Mich. 1973)

Purchasers, under land contracts for deed, need not sign the agreement—acceptance of the owner signed instrument together with payment of deposit makes the contract bilateral.

278 Hursey v. Hursey, S.C. 326 S.E. 2d 178 (1985)

A purchase money mortgage, which is executed at the same time as the deed of purchase, takes precedence over any other claim or lien attached to the property through the vendee/mortgagor.

278 Hand L. Land Co. v. Warner, 258 So. 293 (Fla. 1972)

The land contract is essentially a security instrument, taking the place of a purchase money mortgage.

279 Gruskin v. Fisher, 245 N.W. 2d 427 (Mich. App. 1976)

Election of one of many remedies upon default precludes the exercise of another remedy.

280 Sebastian v. Floyd, 585 S.W. 2d 381 (Ky. 1979)

A land contract should be deemed a mortgage for remedy purposes after default.

279 Martinez v. Martinez, 101 N.Mex. 88, 678 P. 2d 1163 (1984)

Even in those states which allow land contract forfeitures, the vendor is required to give notice of interest to forfeit and a reasonable time period in which to cure the default.

279 Hammer v. Rock Mountain Lake, Inc. 451 So. 2d 249 (Ala. 1984 and Bill v. Coots, 451 So. 2d 268 (Ala. 1984)

Forfeiture provisions in land contracts are rarely upheld.

280 Venable v. Harmon, 233 Cal. App. 2d 297, 43 Cal. Reptr. 490 (1965)

A California vendor cannot receive a deficiency judgment regardless of his loss.

280 Morris v. Sykes, 624 P. 2d 681 (Utah 1981) and Kay v. Wood, 549 P. 2d 709 (Utah 1976)

In some Utah cases, where vendee payments exceeded the vendor's damages, the courts approved restitution to the vendee of the excess paid over vendor's damages.

280 Kay v. Wood, 549 P. 2d 709 (utah 1976)

The Utah courts have refused outright forfeiture, in cases where the vendee cannot or will not redeem and where outright forfeiture would be unconscionable.

280   Sindlinger v. Paul, 404. N.W. 2d 212 (1987)

A vendor cannot exercise an option to accelerate the balance due after the purchaser has made a valid, although late, tender of the delinquent payment(s).

281   Kallenbach v. Lake Publications, Inc., 142 N.W. 2d 212 (Wisc. 1966)

The remedy of strict foreclosure on a land contract foregoes the owner's right to collect the full amount. Courts must decide the amount due based on several facts.

281   Cooper v. Jefferson Investment Co., 246 N.W. 2d 311 (Mich. App. 1976)

An acceleration clause in a land contract requires no notice of intent to foreclose—suit can be instituted for the full amount.

281   Smeekens v. Bertrand, 302 N.E. 2d 502 (Ind. 1973)

Vendors wrongful recision of a conditional sales contract are required to return principal payments and interest—a setoff agains buyer's rents and profits during possession is not allowed.

281   Farmer v. Groves, 555 P/ 2d 1252 (Ore. 1976) and Kirkpatrick v.
             Petreikis, 358 N.E. 2679 (Ill. App. 1976)

Time is of the essence clause in a contract may be waived by the vendor in accepting payments at irregular intervals. The clause may be revived by giving the purchaser a warning notice that strict compliance will be expected in the future.

281   Rogers v. Newton, 340 Ao. 2d 768 (Ala. 1976)

The mere fact that seller has permitted the curing of previous defaults is not an end into itself to cure future defaults.

281   Kirkpatrick v. Petreikis, 358 N.E. 2679 (Ill. App. 1976)

The time is of the essence clause, regarding payments, can be revived by the vendor of a land contract , by the vendor's giving notice to the purchaser that strict compliance will be insisted upon in the future.

281   McFadden v. Walker, 488 P. 2d 1353 (Cal. 1971)

A vendor may not refuse to accept payment after an action to quite title. The courts treat the land contract as a mortgage with full right to redeem the property.

LANDLORD/TENANT

283   McNeill v. McNeill, 456 S.W. 2d 800 (Mo. App. 1970)

The relationship between landlord and tenant is that which arises from a contract, expressed or implied.

283   Russell v. Valentine, 376 P. 2d 548 (Utah 1962)

A lease must be free from ambiguity.

283   Branch v. Watkins Realty Corp., 289 So. 2d 381 (La. 1973)

Oral leases with no fixed duration can be terminated by either lessee or lessor at the expiration of any month by giving written notice.

284   Kapetan v. Kelso, 481 P. 2d 24 (Wash. App. 1971)

An agreement to contract for a lease in the future must be definite and specific as to terms of the lease.

284   Timmons v. Cropper, 172 A. 2d 757 (Del. 1961)

The test for deciding if a writing is a lease or license is whether exclusive possession of premises is given or merely possession to use—A license may be terminated at any time.

284   Palmer v. Wheeler, 481 P. 2d 68 (Ore. 1971)

California requires that a lease for more than one year be in writing and signed by the party to be charged (lessor).

285   Evershed v. Berry, 20 Utah 2d 203, 436 P. 2d 438 (1968)

An estate at will can be established with no more than payment and receipt of rents.

285   Kilbourne v. Forester, 464 S.W. 2d 770 (Tex. 1971)

A tenant who holds over without the landlords permission is no tenant at all but a wrongdoer. The lessor may bring action in ejectment to recover possession.

285   Garner v. Gerrish 63. N. Y. 2d 575, 473 N.E. 2d 223, 483 N.Y.S. 2d 973
            (1984)

A lease which provides for a tenant to vacate at a date of his choosing creates; (1) A life tenancy, and (2) Prohibits a landlord from terminating the lease at will.

286   Custis v. Klein, 127 A. 2d 268 (D.C. 1962)

In a case of lease for month to month, landlord notice given to a tenant during the month requiring he vacate at the end of the month is defective.

286   Nelson v. Growers Ford Tractor Co., 282 So. 66 (Fla. App. 1973)

A tenant who holds over after the expiration of a lease, is liable for reasonable rent—in some states he may be liable for double rent.

286   Housing Authority of Pittsburg v. Turner, 191 A. 2d 869 (Pa. 1963)

Termination of a month to month lease without reason is valid.

286   Beken v. Elster, 503 S.W. 2d 408 (Tex. 1973)

Crops not harvestable during the term of a lease are property of the lessee except, where the lessee acquiesces to the lessor's planting of crops, knowing they cannot be harvested during the term of the lease.

286   Zanetos v. Sparks, 13 Ohio App. 3rd 242, 468 N.E. ed 938 (1984)

Rent payments, nine days late, does not constitute a technical breach of the lease.

287   Needleman v. American Clothing Co. Inc., 63 A. 2d 201 (Vt. 1949)

A wife is a co-beneficiary of a lease. An owner in common has no right to bind his co-owners by a lease, thus to bind all, the lease must be signed by all owners.

289   Anderson v. Busoda, 180 A. 2d 130 (D.C.)

Lessors are strictly held to the uses of property permitted by the lease.

288   Hoff v. Sander, 497 S.W. 2d 651 (Mo. App. 1973) and Dill v. Poindexter,
            451 S.W. 2d 365 (Mo. App. 1970)

In a lease, where mutual errors of assumptions have been made regarding legal uses of property, parties may not sue for damages and are presumed to be knowledgable of local laws.

290   Howard D. Johnson Co. v. Parkside Development Corp., 384 N.E. 2d
            656 (Ind. 1976); Anderson v. Blondo Plaza, Inc. 186 N.W. 2d 114 (Neb.
            1971) and Carousel Snack Bars v. Crown Construction Co., 439 F. 2d
            280 (Pa. 1971)

Restrictive covenants in a lease barring competition from a similar business are strictly construed.

291   Hartwig v. 65 Realty Co., 324 N.Y. S. 2d 567 (1971)

Failure to provide possession at agreed time, permits tenant to rescind the lease.

CONSTRUCTIVE EVICTION

291   Fidelity Mutual Life Insurance Co. v. Kaminsky, 768 S.W. 818 (Tex. Ct. App.-Houston [14th Dist.] 1989, no writ hist.)

A tenant who landlord failed to prevent harassment is guilty of constructive eviction.

292   Green v. The Superior Court of the City and County of San Francisco, 517 P. 2d 1168 (Cal. 1974); Hinson v. Delis, (1972) 26 Cal. App. 3rd 62, 102 Cal. Rptr.661; Pines v. Perssion, (1961) 14 Wis. 2d 590, 111 N.W. 2d 409; Lemle v. Breeden, (1969) 51 Haw. 426, 426 P. 2d 470; Javins v. First National Realty Corp., (1970) 138 U.S. App. D.C. 369, 428 F. 2d 1071, cert. den. 400 U.S. 925, pl S. Ct. 186, 27 L. Ed. 2d 185; Marini v. Ireland, (1970) 56 N.J. 130, 265 A. 2d 526; Kline v. Burns, (1971) 111 N.H. 87, 276 A. 2d 248; Jack Spring, Inc. v. Little, (1972) 50 Ill. 2d 351, 280 N.E. 2d 208; Mease v. Fox, (1972) Iowa, 200 N.W. 2d 791; and Boston Housing Authority v. Hemingway, (1973) Mass., 293 N.E. 2d 831.

Implied warranty of habitability was upheld and the prior common law doctrine over ruled.

292   Kline v. Burns, 276 A. 2d 248 (N.H. 1971); Reste Realty Corp., v. Cooper, 53 N.J. 444, 452, 251 A. 2d 268,272 (1969) and Lund v. MacArthur, 51 Hawaii 473, 475, 482 P. 2d 461, 463 (1962)

Implied warranty of habitability was upheld.

292   Marini v. Ireland, 265 A. 2d 526 (N.J. 1970) and Reste Realty Corp. v. Cooper, 53 N.J. 444, 452, 251 A. 2d 268, 272 (1969)

The warranty of habitability is imposed by law on the basis of public policy.

294   Blackwell v. Del Bosco, 558 P. 2d 568 (1977); Dawson Industries Inc. v. Godley Construction Co., Inc. 224 S.E. 2d 266 (N.C. 1976)

Implied warranty of habitability does not apply to commercial buildings. Relief of tenant is through the legislature not the courts.

294   Winchester Mgt. Corp. v. Staten, 361 A. 2d 187 (D.C. 1976)

Set off against rents due allowed due failure of landlord to provide adequate heat and air conditioning called for in the lease.

292   Lemle v. Breeden, 51 Hawaii 426 (1969)

Warranty of habitability makes available to the tenant the basic contract remedies of damages, reformation, and recission.

294   Mannie Joseph, Inc. v. Stewart, 335 N.Y. S. 2d 709 (1972); Granford Realty Corp. v. Valentine, 337 N.Y. 2d 160 (1972)

Tenants remedy for nonhabitability is vacating the premises.

294   Park Hill Terrace Associates v. Glennon, 369 A. 2d 938 (N.J. App. 1977)

Air conditioning was held as affecting habitability and set off against rent allowed.

295   Scott v. Prazma, 555 P. 2d 591 (Wyo. 1976)

Failure of the landlord to make repairs required by the municipality, to comply with safety and building codes, was ruled as constructive eviction.

294   Zion Industries, Inc. v Loy 361 N.E. 2d 605 (Ill. App. 1977)

Failure of the landlord to make repairs does not relieve the tenant of duty to pay rent unless the landlord evicts the tenant, even partially.

295   Lensing v. Carlisle Motor Sales, Inc., 189 A. 2d 307 (Pa. 1963)

Tenant is bound to make tenatable repairs but not such that he will put the premises in better condition than when first occupied. Required repairs do not include those required due to normal wear and tear.

295   Neff v. Budd Lewis Co., 548 P. 2d 107 (N.M. App. 1976)

Equipment repairs required to meet tenant needs, where the broker assured the new owner, during the purchase, that such repairs had been made, was the liability of the broker who made negligent representations.

LANDLORDS MUST PROTECT TENANTS & VISITORS

296   Strunk v. Stolanski, 62 N.Y. 2d 572, 468 N.E. 2d 13, 479 N.Y.S. 2d 175 (1984)

A landlord is held to a duty of reasonable care in protecting his tenants and visitors to the property.

296   Lindsey v. Massios, 360 N.E. 2d 631 (Mass. 1977); Kosin v. Shero, 360 N.E. 2d 572 (Ill. App. 1977) and Noble v. Worthy, 378 A. 2d 674 (D.C. App. 1977)

Landlord requirement to maintain property that he controls extends to all lawful visitors on the premises including visitors to his tenants; however, the landlord is not required to so secure the premises so that no accident can occur.

296   Folkman v. Laver, 244 P. 605 (1914) and Webel v. Yale University 7A Fd. (Conn. 1939)

Landlord is responsible where he leases a property with known dangerous conditions, or one which he has reason to believe the tenant will not first correct the defect(s). Liability applies whether landlord is in or out of possession.

297   Leary v. Lawrence Sales Corp., 442 Pa. 389 (1971)

Landlords who rent portions of a property to different tenants are held to be in possession of sidewalks, stairways and corridors and are held liable if injuries occur.

297   Geise v. Lee, 519 P. 2d 1005 (Wash. App. 1974) and Richardson v. Weckworth, 509 P. 113 (Kan. 1973)

Dangerous conditions, for which landlords are liable, include accumulations of snow or ice, a missing brick, an elevation or depression causing an uneven surface, an accumulation of derbis concealing a hazard, an accumulation of oil causing a slippery surface, a hole in a sidewalk, and faulty position of basement outlets or doors to the pavement—does not apply to snow and ice in a mobile home park unless landlord has assumed this liability.

297   Richardson v. Weckworth 509 P. 2d 1113 (Kan.), 1973

A landlord is liable for injury to a tenant due to the landlord's failure to repair the leased property.

ASSIGNMENT OF THE LEASE

298   Stern v. Taft, N.E. 2d (Ohio App. 1976)

Where the lease stated that "consent shall not be unreasonably withheld," refusal to sublease to a widow was held in violation of the lease terms.

298   Robinson v. Weitz, 370 A. 2d 1066 (Conn. 1976)

Where the lease simply provides that written consent to an assignment is required, the landlord may refuse consent, his reason is immaterial.

298   Julian v. Christopher, 575 A. 2d 735 (Md. App. 1990)

A lease can absolutely prohibit assignments and sub-letting by a "freely negotiated provision." If the lease allows such sub-letting or assignment with approval of the landlord, such approval must be reasonable.

299   Kroger v. Chemical Securities Co., 526 S.W. 2d 468 (Tenn. 1975)

Where the lease is mute as to allowable reassignment or subletting, an implied covenant of continual occupancy is not warranted.

LEASE SURRENDER

302   Condor Development Corp., v. Arlen Realty and Development Co., 529 F. 2d 87 (Minn. 1976) and Sommer v. Kridel, 378 A. 2d 767 (N.J. 1977)

Required and necessary actions by the landlord, where premises have been abandoned, is a decision of the courts and varies based on circumstances.

303   Estate of Wm. O. Barnes, Deceased, 37 N.Y. Misc. 2d (1962) and Sanden v. Hanson, 201 N.W. 2d 404 (N.D. 1972)

Mutual agreement to surrender a lease must include acceptance by the landlord or evidence of acceptance by landlord action.

LANDLORD REPOSSESSION

305   Phillips v. Guin and Hunt, Inc., 344 So. 2d 568 (Fla. 1977)

The right of distraint does not reside in the landlord until there has been a default in the rent.

305   Edwards v. Investment Co., 272 N.E. 2d 652 (Ohio 1971) and Bass v. Boltel & Co., 217 N.W. 2d 804 (Neb. 1974)

A landlord must resort to law and legal methods and not self-help to obtain possession of premises, when tenants fail to make rental payments. Entry in the tenants absence is not permitted.

305   Pittman v. Griffith, 200 S.E. 2d 760 (Ga. 1973)

Where a tenant is temporarily away from the premises, the landlord takes a grave risk when he padlocks the premises and prevents the tenant's re-entry.

305   Margolin et al. v. Richards, 70 D&C 380 (Pa. 1949)

Prohibitions of the keeping or maintenance of domestic or wild animals cannot be waived by managers, who have not been given specific authority to do so.

PREPAYMENTS

306   Martinique Realty Corp. v. Hull, 166 A. 2d 803 (N.J. 1960)

Prepayments of rents to a former owner are binding on the new purchaser. It is the duty of the purchaser to ascertain the provisions of existing leases.

302   Pyrimid Enterprises, Inc. v. Amadeo, 294 N.E. 2d 713 (Ill. App. 1973)

Security deposits are intended to protect the landlord for damages by the tenant, for cleaning if needed and for expenses of the landlord in obtaining a new tenant, during the unexpired term of the lease.

307   Village Development Co., Ltd. v. Hubbard, 214 N.W. 2d 178 (Iowa 1974)

Where lessee pays all overdue rent before receipt of notice to quit, lessor has no right to terminate the lease for failure to make timely payments.

OPTIONS/FIRST RIGHT OF REFUSAL

309   Schlussberg v. Rubin, et al., 435 S.W. 2d 226 (Tex. 1971); Playmate Club Inc., v. Country Clubs, Inc., 462 S.W. 2d 269 (Tenn. 1970) and Miles v. Bloomberg, 324 N.E. 2d 207 (Ill. App. 1975)

First right of refusal agreements with terms such as "to be agreed upon" and "to meet any bona fide offer" are indefinite and uncertain. The agreement is not enforceable.

308   King v. Dalton Motors, INc. 109 N.W. 2d 51 (Minn. 1961); LoCicero v. Demers, 186 N.E. 2d 604 (Mass. 1962) and Gamel v. Altman, 317 N.Y.S. 2d 722 (1971)

First right of refusal and option to purchase were defined.

308   Cities Service Oil Co., v. National Shawmut Bank of Boston, Adm. et al., 172 N.E. 2d 104 (Mass. 1961)

In an option, the time element is of the very essence of the contract.

309   Queens Blvd. Wine and Liquor Corp. v. Blum, 503 F. 2d 202 (N.Y. 1974)

In the case of bankruptcy, forfeiture clauses in commercial leases are unenforceable.

310   Colon v. Tompkins Square Neighbors, Inc., 924 F. Supp. 134.

A landlord may not reject a prospective tenant solely upon the basis he is a welfare receipient.

310   Thorpe v. Housing authority, 393 U.S. 268

A public housing tenant cannot be evicted without a hearing into the reasonableness of the action.

ZONING

347   Village of Euclid v. Ambler Realty Co., 277 U.S. 365 (1926)

Instant case ended the courts hostility to zoning.

347   National Land and Investment Co., v. Kohn, 215 A. 2d 597 (Pa. 1965)

This was the first instance involving exclusionary zoning of large lots.

348   Cordorus v. Rodgers, 492 A. 2d 73 (Pa. Commw. 1985)

Ordnance protecting the residents of a municipality from the "ill effects" of urbanization are legitimate.

348   Beres v. Hope Homes, Inc. 6 Ohio App. 3d 71, 453 N.E. 2d 1119 (1983)

A private residence may be occupied by persons unrelated by consanguinity.

348   Crane Neck Association v. N.Y.C./Long Island County Service Group, 92 App. Div. 2d 119, 460. N.Y.S. 2d 69 (1983)

Instant case established a new definition of "single family."

348 First English Evangelical Church v. County of Los Angeles, 107 S. Ct. 2378 (1987); Nolland v. California Coastal Commission, 107 S.Ct. 3141 (1987)

The most modern Supreme Court Decision protecting property owners against unlawful land use regulation.

349 Agins v. City of Tiburon, 598 P. 2d 25 (Cal. 1979)

Landowners may not maintain a reverse condemnation suit, but must seek invalidation of the ordnance. This has been drastically changed by the *First English and Nolland* cases.

350 Re Opinion of Justices, 313 N.E. 2d 561 (Mass. 1974)

Property owners have no rights to navigable or unnavigable waters beyond the high water line.

350 County of Orange v. Chandler-Sherman Corp., 126 Cal. Rptr 765 5. S.W.U. Rev 48 (1973)

An owner, who did not object to the public use of his beach for over 5 years had impliedly dedicated it to the public.

CONDEMNATION

350 Mugler v. Kansas, 123 U.S. 623 (1887)

The subject Supreme Court decision of "no taking" has been drastically changed in modern times.

351 Ossman v. Mt. States Telephone and Telegraph Co., 32 Colo. App. 230, 511 P. 2d 519.

A good example of reverse condemnation.

351 City of Plainfield v. Borough of Middlesex, 69 N.J. Super. 136, 173 A. 2d 785 (1961) and Robyns v. City of Dearborn, 341 Mich. 495, 67, N.W. 2d 718 (1953).

Governments may not use the police power of rezoning to ease the burden of just compensation in a future condemnation.

351 Kissenger v. City of Los Angeles, 161 Cal. 2d 454, 327 P. 2d 10 (1958) and Robertson v. City of Salem, 191 F. Supp. 604 (D. Ore. 1961)

The use of police power to aid condemnation is not recognized in legal opinions as a valid public purpose and not a proper objective.

352 San Diego Gas & Electric Co. v. City of San Diego (1981), 28 U.S.C. 1259

The courts appear to have reasserted, what it had previously held, an overly strict regulation of land can be construed as a taking.

352 State of Tennessee v. Burkhart et al., 370 S.W. 2d 411 (Tenn. 1963) and Sugarman v. City of Baltimore et al., 191 A. 2d 240 (Md. 1963)

Unless specifically exempted by terms of the lease, a tenant may be compensated by the condemnor according to his interests. Tenant interest may exceed those of the owner.

354 Village of Arlington Heights v. Metropolitan Housing Development Corp., 97 S. Ct. 555 (1977)

The Supreme Court upheld the decison that stated that zoning laws are not exclusionary if they are not enacted with any intention to discriminated against low income groups and were not motivated by racial discrimination.

354   Gulf Oil Co. v. Fairview Township Board of Supervisors, 438 Pa. 457 (1970) and Penn Township v. Yeco Bros., 217 at 2d A. 171 (Pa. 1966)

A property owner has obtained a vested right and need not conform with a zoning ordnance if he can demonstrate: (1) he obtained a valid building permit under the old ordnance, (2) he obtained it in good faith and without racing to beat a proposed change, and (3) that he spent money in good faith or incurred liabilities in reliance on his building permit.

354   Township of Williston v. Chesterdale Farms, Inc., 341 A. 2d 466 (Pa. 1975)

The setting aside of only 80 acres from 11,589 acres for apartment construction in a township was ruled exclusionary.

CONDOMINIUMS

356   Newport West Condominium Association v. Veniar, 134 Mich. App. 1, 350, N.W. 2d 818 (1984)

Assessment fees cannot be withheld due to an owner condominium disagreement.

356   Brickyard Homeowner's Association Management Committee v. Gibbons Realty Co., 668 P. 2d 535 (Utah 1983)

Homeowner associations have standing to sue on behalf of property owners the project.

358   Hatfield v. LaCharmant Home Owner's Association, 469 N.E. 2d 1218 (2d App. 1984); Kelley v, Astor Investments, Inc., 123 Ill. App. 3rd 593, 462 N.E. 2d 996 (1984)

Developers who have unsold condominium units are liable for their proportionate share of the association expenses.

COOPERATIVES

360   Miller's Estate, 130 N.Y.S. 2d 295 (1974)

A co-operative apartment passes under an estate as personal property.

360   Silverman v. Alcoa Plaza Associates, 323 N.Y.S. 2d 39 (1971)

Upon default by purchaser of a Co-op, the seller corporation could not retain the down payment, applying Uniform Commercial Code applicable to personalty.

360   Pitts Estate, in re, 218 Cal. 184, 22 P. 2d 694 (1933) and State Tax Commission v. Shor, 53 N.Y. App. Div. 2d 814(8) (1976)

In some instances courts have recognized Co-ops as real estate.

361   160 West 87th Street Corp, v. Lefkowitz, 350 N.Y.S. 2d 957 (1974)

Sustained the constitutionality of statute against challenge that the power of the Attorney General to withhold approval of a co-op plan without notice and hearing is deprivation of property without due process.

REAL ESTATE INVESTMENTS

366   SEC v. Howey Co., 293 (1946); SEC v. Marasol Properties, F. Supp,
              (D.C. 1973) and Kahn v. Kaskel, 367 F. Supp. 784 (1973)

Supreme Court guidelines for determining whether a real estate transaction is an "investment contract"

(1) A person invests his money in a common enterprise. (2) He is led to expect profits (3) The expectation of profit is solely from the efforts of the promoter or a third party.

367   United Housing Foundation, Inc. v. Forman, 421 U.S. 837 (1975);
              Grenader v. Spitz, 537 F. 2d 612 (Ca 2, 1975) and AMR Realty Co. v.
              State Bureau of Securities, 373 A. 2d 1002 Sup. Ct. of N.J. App. Div.
              (1977)

A state supervised and subsidized non-profit co-op does not offer "securities."

367   Nash & Associates, Inc. v. LUM'S of Ohio Inc., 484 F. 2d 393 (6th Cir.
              1973); 1050 Tenants Corp. et al. v. Jakobsen et al., 365 F. Supp. 1171
              (S.D. N.Y. 1973), Affirmed July 8, 1974, 503 F. 2d 1375 (1975) and
              Owners of S W 8 Real Estate v. McQuaid, 513 F. 2d 558 (Ca 9, 1975)

The trend is increasingly toward holding real estate investment offerings as "securities."

367   SEC v. Hare, Brewer, Kelley, Inc. et al., SEC Docket, Vol. 3, No. 5, Dec
              18, 1973

The Federal Court in San Francisco compelled six corporations to register their offerings of units as "securities."

INTERSTATE LAND SALE REGULATIONS

368   Bryan v. AMREP Corp. 429 Supp. 313 (S.D. N.Y. 1977)
Class action involving ILSFDA.

368   Gladys Husted v. AMREP Corp., et al., 429 F. Supp. 298 (S.D. N.Y.
              1977)

Key provisions of The Interstate Land Sales Full Disclosure Act (ILSFDA) defined.

Appendix C
A STUDY OF
BROKERAGE OPERATIONS

QUESTIONS AND ANSWERS

1. Name four ways by which the relationship between broker and owner can be terminated.

Ans.
Performance, death, recision, and bankruptcy.

2. An owner listed a property with a broker at $3,200,000 and agreed to pay a commission of $50,000, if sold. About three weeks later, the broker procured a prospect for $2,900,000. Later a letter from the broker to owner stated, "If a sale at a higher price than above, we will negotiate a reasonable and appropriate commission to be paid." The property was sold to the broker's prospect for $2,850,000. The broker sued for a commission of $50,000. Decide.

Ans.
In favor of the broker. The court held that the letter was not a waiver of the $50,000 in the listing agreement. There was no *new* consideration "to negotiate a reasonable and appropriate commission": *Guild Management Co. v. Oxenhandler,* 541 S.W. 2d. 687 (Mo. 1976).

3. Jackson has an *oral* listing in Nebraska for Stanton's property. He negotiates a sale to Crawford at the listed price. The agreement of sale contains a clause recognizing Jackson as the broker and acknowledges a commission to be paid to him by the seller. Later, Stanton refuses to pay. Can Jackson recover?

Ans.
Yes. Even though Jackson does not have the required written listing, Jackson can recover on the theory that the broker is a third-party beneficiary: *Mid-Continent Properties, Inc. v. Pflug,* 249 N.W. 2d. 476 (Neb. 1977).

4. What is the relationship between owner and broker?

Ans.
Principal (owner) and agent (broker) relationship.

5. In order to recover a real estate commission in court, what must a broker first aver in the complaint and prove?

Ans.
That he was a duly licensed broker.

6. Daisy Reston, single, lists property for sale on January 2, with Bennett Realty at $18,500. She marries Henry Boyd on February 28. Bennett obtains a cash offer of $18,500 on March 21. Henry refuses to sign the sales agreement. Can Bennett recover a commission from Daisy?

Ans.
Yes. The property was owned by Daisy alone when listed. The broker performed his part of the contract in full; the marriage, after the listing, has no effect.

7. C.D. Sloan owns a vacant commercial building in a downtown area. He places a large sign reading, "For Sale or For Rent, Call 261-1225 or "SEE YOUR BROKER." Randolph, a prospect, contacts a broker, Marlin, who calls Sloan and obtains the terms of sale. Later, a sale is made by Sloan to Randolph at $72,000. Marlin claims the usual 7 percent commission in that area. Can he recover?

Ans.
No. The statement "See Your Broker" does not establish a contract of employment between Sloan and Marlin. In states requiring a listing contract to be in writing, Marlin, of course, could not recover.

8. In how many ways may a broker establish a contract of employment?

Ans.
(1) By express contract; (2) by ratification of the owner, or (3) by conduct of the parties.

9. A county board of REALTORS® restricts membership in the multiple listing service to brokers "Primarily engaged in the real estate business." An application of a part-time broker for membership was refused on that account. The board was charged with violation of the states's anti-trust law. It was contended by the board that the exclusion promoted higher ethical and professional standards. Are the board's by-laws valid?

Ans.
No. The by-law against part-time brokers is invalid. It must yield to anti-trust laws where "the association has the power to shape and influence the economic environment of its particular market": *Marin County Board of Realtors v. Paulson*, 549 P. 2d 833 (Cal. 1976).

10. Adams employed the Boston Auction Company to sell his residence at auction. The auctioneer announced that "broker participation" would be allowed if the broker registered his client with "us" if his party was the successful bidder. A broker, Clark, registered the successful bidder with the auctioneer, who refused to pay a commission. Clark sued Adams. Can he recover?

Ans.
No. There was no privity of contract between Adams and Clark. The auctioneer had no authority to bind the owner.

11. Broker, Jones obtains an oral listing from seller, McDonald, to sell his house for $77,000; agreement to terminate in 30 days, commission to be 6 percent. Jones secures a buyer for the property at $77,000. The owner refuses to permit broker to complete the sale and completes it himself. Jones demands his commission. Can he recover?

Ans.

In those states which require a listing to be in writing, he could not recover. In the other states he could.

12. A broker is employed by a wife to sell her real estate; he secures a buyer on her terms; the husband refuses to sign the contract of sale and the deal falls through. Is the broker entitled to a commission from the wife?

Ans.

Yes. He has fully performed his contract of employment since he produced a purchaser, ready, willing, and able to buy. However, if he had good reason to believe that the husband would not join in the contract of sale the decision would be different.

An owner gives an exclusive listing to broker Abel for six months' period. During the exclusive period, he gives a nonexclusive listing to Kane, who produces a buyer. What is the owner's liability for commission?

Ans.

He is obligated to pay a full commission to both Kane and Abel.

13. A salesperson is assisted in a deal by another salesperson, employed by another broker. The first salesperson pays one-half of his commission to the salesperson who assisted him. Is this legal?

Ans.

No. The salesperson has no right to recognize anyone other than his employing broker. The latter should deal and recognize the other broker and not the other broker's salesperson.

14. Why does an exclusive right to sell listing contract afford the broker more protection than an exclusive listing?

Ans.

Full commission is assured the broker, regardless of who sells the property during the term of the listing.

15. If you have a property listed for sale and find a prospect who is willing to take an option on the same terms offered, are you entitled to your commission?

Ans.

No. An option does not bind the purchaser to buy, and the broker is entitled to his commission only if the option is exercised.

16. Name five methods by which an agency can be terminated.

Ans.

(1) By agreement between principal and agent; (2) By expiration of the term; (3) By extinction of subject matter; (4) By death of either principal or agent, and (5) By incapacity of either principal or agent.

17. A broker is employed by the son of A and B, husband and wife, to sell the parent's property. The mother has authorized the son to list the property but the father has not. The broker secures a buyer on the exact terms of the listing; the father refuses to sign an agreement of sale and the deal falls through. Can the broker recover a commission?

Ans.
The broker can recover from the mother since the son was her authorized agent. Or the broker can sue the son, who gave the listing, as he represented that he was duly authorized to do so. He could not recover from the father.

18. A broker claimed a commission for procuring a purchaser for the owner's property. He obtained a buyer. When the deal closed, title was taken in the name of the father of the purchaser and the property leased to the son. Can the broker recover a commission?

Ans.
Yes. The broker clearly made the deal and the arrangement for taking title would not defeat his earned commission.

19. The National Insurance Company owned a farm. Wilson, a broker offered to trade an apartment house, listed for sale, for the farm. He dealt with Alberts, treasurer of the Company. The treasurer stated, "We want a high class apartment property." The broker replied, "All right sir, I will see what I can do." An exchange was made though another broker. Can Wilson recover against National Insurance Company?

Ans.
No. There is no expressed or implied contract of employment. It would appear that plaintiff was representing the apartment building owner, since the insurance company had not listed the farm with him.

20. A property was listed with James, who was not licensed but obtained his broker's license before he rendered any services. Two days after he received his license he negotiated a real estate deal. Can he be prosecuted?

Ans.
Yes. Since James did not have a license when he obtained the listing he was acting in violation of license law.

21. Aiken listed property for sale with Benson, a broker, at $8,000, the broker to receive a commission of 5 percent. Benson procures a buyer who refuses to pay more than $7,500. Two months later the deal is made at $7,500 to that same buyer and Benson claims $375 as commission. Aiken refuses to pay, claiming the listing was at $8,000. Can Benson recover?

Ans.
Yes. The courts will not permit an owner to take advantage of a broker's efforts and then turn him "out of doors." The agent here was still the efficient and procuring cause of the sale.

22. Bowles, a broker, was employed by Archer to sell three lots for him. It was not an exclusive agency. Bowles procured Mrs. Crane who was acting for herself and her husband. Each purchased one lot, as did Drake, whom Mrs. Crane had informed that the lots in question were for sale. Bowles sued Archer for a commission on the sale of all three lots. Can he recover?

Ans.
Bowles can recover commissions only upon the sale of the two lots to the Cranes. The broker was in no way directly connected with the sale of the lot to Drake. The law deals only with proximate and not remote causes.

23. The plaintiff broker, Bender, "worked upon" one Collins and induced him to look at property owned by Allen, listed with Bender for sale. Collins finally decided not to buy himself, but upon Collin's advice, Collin's brother bought directly from the owner, Allen. Is Bender entitled to a commission on this sale?

Ans.
No. Absence of any collusion or fraud, the plaintiff was not the procuring cause of the sale to Collin's brother.

24. Jones gave Peters an exclusive listing upon his property for $9,000. The agreement was for a term of three months at 5 percent commission. The agreement provided for termination after the term of 30 days' written notice from the owner. "In default of such notice, this exclusive contract shall renew itself from term to term as an exclusive contract . . . until notice herein provided shall be given to terminate." The agreement was dated May 16th. The property was sold by the owner, Jones, on July 28. Is the broker entitled to a commission?

Ans.
Yes. Written notice of termination given May 16 was too late to terminate the contract during the term in which it was given. It operated to terminate the listing as of August 28. Inasmuch as the property was sold on July 26, Peters was entitled to a commission.

25. Smith, a minor, employs Jones to sell a piece of real estate which he owns. Jones, dubious as to Smith's age, makes inquiry. Smith represents his age to be 25 years. After Jones sells the property, Smith disaffirms the contract of employment and refuses to pay Jones any commission. Can Jones recover?

Ans.
No. Jones's suit in assumpsit (on contract) is against an infant upon a *voidable* contract. Smith cannot make himself of age by misrepresenting his age. He is still an infant in fact and the law permits him to plead infancy as a defense. An infant is liable for deceit, which is a tort (an actionable wrong) action. Jones could sue Smith in a trespass action on the tort.

26. Flynn, a broker, asks Dubbs, an owner, the price of his house, and introduces him to a client, who subsequently purchases it. Can he recover a commission?

Ans.
No. Even though he may have, to some extent, influenced the sale, he cannot recover, because he cannot prove an employment. "How much do you want for it?" does not constitute employment.

27. Arthur lists property with Blaine for $12,000. Blaine negotiates a sale to Clancy, who paid $1,000 down. After the agreement of sale is signed, Arthur obtains a memorandum from Blaine that "commission is to be paid at the time of settlement." Settlement is never made due to mutual releases by seller and buyer. Can Blaine recover from Arthur for commission?

Ans.
Yes. There was no legal consideration for the promise to wait for his commission until the date of settlement. The mutual releases do not absolve the seller from payment of a commission already earned.

28. Woods mails a description of his property to Talley, a broker, with a request that he sell it at $18,500 cash. Nothing is said about a commission. The broker obtains a buyer at $18,500 cash. There is an argument about paying a commission. Can Talley recover?

Ans.
Yes. There is an implied promise to pay the usual commission, since the broker obtained a satisfactory buyer upon the seller's terms. He could recover on a "quantum meruit" basis, what he deserves, would be the usual commission.

29. If a salesperson is considered an individual contractor, name two important advantages to the broker.

Ans.
(1) Broker would not carry workmans' compensation insurance, and (2) would not be required to make income tax and social security payments.

30. An extender clause in a listing contract required the broker to file the names of the prospects with whom the broker negotiated during the original term of the listing by December 29. The broker mailed the list of his prospects on December 24. Due to a delay in the postal service, the letter was not received by the owner until January 3. The property was sold to one of the broker's prospects on February 15. The broker sued for a commission. Can he recover?

Ans.
No. "Filing with" is not the same as "mailing to." The burden was on the broker to make sure that a list of his prospects reached the owner by December 29.

31. Name three events which determine how long a broker may hold deposit money.

Ans.
(1) Until the transaction is consummated, (2) Until the deposit is forfeited by the buyer, and (3) If the seller refuses to sell, deposit money must be returned.

32. A broker obtained an exclusive right to sell listing for six months from February 15. He did not advertise the property, nor did he make a diligent effort to obtain an interested buyer. On May 15, the owner terminated the listing by a written notice. Was this proper?

Ans.
Yes. The broker had a reasonable time to manifest his good faith intention to perform: *Atkinson v. Zarenich,* 80 P. 2d 110 (Cal. 1933); nominal damages only.

33. Benson, a broker, obtained an inquiry from Mann for certain industrial real estate, at a purchase price of $20,000. Benson had the same property listed with him by Ambers, the owner at $14,000. Benson informed Ambers that he himself would purchase the property at Amber's price. Agreements were signed and Benson assigned the agreements to Mann. Ambers sues Benson for $6,000. Can Ambers recover? Is Benson entitled to a commission on the $20,000 deal?

Ans.
Ambers can recover. Benson is not entitled to any commission. An agent is a fiduciary. He owes a high degree of loyalty to his principal. Since Benson offered to buy the property *after* he had a purchaser at a higher price, he forfeits his rights to a commission.

34. Peters gave Brent an exclusive agency to sell his real estate for $8,500. The contract is dated February 28th. It runs for six months and then indefinitely as an *exclusive agency* unless terminated by 30 days written notice by the owner. After procuring a few prospects in March, nothing is done by Brent upon the listing. Peters sells the property in July, through another broker, Kane, to whom he pays the usual commission. Can Brent collect a commission?

Ans.
Yes. Although his right would appear unconscionable, the exclusive listing "ran on" until Peters took the necessary steps to cancel it, by giving Brent written notice to that effect. If the license law, or Rule of the Commission, requires *definite* expiration date for the listing, Brent could not recover.

35. Name two persons to whom a broker can legally pay compensation for services in a real estate transaction.

Ans.
(1) His licensed real estate salesperson, and (2) a licensed real estate broker.

36. In obtaining a listing of a residence for sale, name several factors in regard to the property that a broker should include on the listing form.

Ans.
Lot size, building size, number of rooms and baths, heating and air conditioning, garage or carports, taxes, mortgage data, kitchen built-ins, and items of equipment to be included in the sale.

37. What is the legal terminology of the relationship between the owner and the broker?

Ans.
Agency

38. Broker Smith gives you information concerning one of his listings and you sell the property. Should you negotiate through Smith or directly with the owner? Why?

Ans.
With Smith because he has the only legally enforceable contract of agency employment.

39. What is the difference between a REALTOR® and a Real Estate Agent?

Ans.
A REALTOR® is a member of the local, state, and National professional association (NATIONAL ASSOCIATION OF REALTORS®).

40. Ash lists a property for sale with Burns on January 16. Ash leaves for a two-month vacation but dies while he is away. Burns, unaware of Ash's death, obtained a signed agreement for the property from Johnson upon Ash's terms. Ash's heirs refuse to honor it or pay a commission. Can Burns recover?

Ans.
No. Ash's death automatically canceled Burns' employment. The fact that Burns was unaware of Ash's death is legally immaterial.

41. Ahern lists his property for sale with Brown by telephone. Brown calls Foster's attention to the property by phone. Ahern and Brown are friends, and Foster has visited Ahern's home a number of times. When Brown calls Ahern's attention to Foster as a prospect, Ahern replies, "Oh, I talked to him about buying the property years ago." Later Ahern sells to Foster. Is brown entitled to a commission?

Ans.
Yes. He brought the parties to an agreement. Although his services, measured in time, are minimal, he was responsible for bringing the parties together, which resulted in an agreement of sale.

42. Weston employs Richter to sell his property. The listing makes no mention as to who shall hold the deposit money. Richter obtains a purchaser on Weston's terms. Weston refuses to sign the contract unless the deposit money is paid to him. Is his contention sound?

Ans.
Yes. The listing should authorize the broker to hold the deposit money in his escrow (trust) account.

43. What different types of listings are used in modern real estate practices?

Ans.
Exclusive, Exclusive right to sell, and Multiple listings. Some very few states authorize Open listings.

44. Which type of the above listings would give the owner the greatest chance of selling his property?

Ans.
Under the multiple listing, since all members of the multi-list association would be aware of the availability of the property and have the right to sell.

45. Is it legal for a broker to purchase a property listed by his agency?

Ans.
Yes, if the broker discloses all information to the owner, which might influence the owner's decision.

46. Does the law *require* a broker to obtain an earnest money deposit, in order to have a binding agreement?

Ans.
No, but the broker would be negligent if he did not *request* a deposit commensurate with the sales price.

47. A broker has been authorized by all parties involved to negotiate an exchange of certain properties. Would he be entitled to a commission on all of the properties in the transaction?

Ans.
Yes. His dual employment is known and recognized by all parties involved.

48. Jane Thomas, who generally conducted her father's (Tom Thomas's) affairs, gave Jones the sole agency for the sale of a lot. He placed a sign on it. This was done with the father's knowledge, and without his objection. Jane referred a prospect to the broker, stating that the matter was entirely out of her hands. Can Jones recover from Thomas upon a sale to the prospect?

Ans.
Yes. Under the doctrine of estoppel, the father is prevented from denying the authority of his daughter to list the property with the broker.

49. Allen employed Frye, a broker, to sell some investment property for him. Frye obtained Clay as a purchaser. At the time of the closing it developed that the property did not have the rental income claimed by Allen, whereupon Clay refused to complete the sale. Is Frye entitled to a commission?

Ans.
Yes. Frye has fully complied with his employment contract of employment with Allen.

50. Miss Agatha Vebler listed property, which she had inherited, with Smith-Jones Realty Company. The next day, the firm produced a purchaser and Miss Vebler signed the contract of sale. Prior to the closing, Miss Vebler married Anthony Taylor, who refused to join in the deed and the deal fell through. Can the plaintiff broker recover a commission?

Ans.
Yes. The broker acted in good faith. He procured a buyer ready, willing, and able to buy.

51. A principal directs a broker to sell his property for $50,000, but by collusion with the purchaser he sells it to him for $40,000 with the consent of the owner, who knows nothing about the collusive agreement and is anxious to sell at any price. The owner, later learning of the broker's infidelity, refused to pay him a commission. What are the rights of the parties?

Ans.
The broker cannot collect. The owner can collect from the broker any secret profit which the broker may have made on the transaction. The broker has violated his loyalty to his principal and forfeits any rights to any compensation.

52. Axford employs Bird, a licensed broker, to sell property for which he is to receive a specified sum as commission. Without informing Axford, Bird also acts for the buyer, who also promises him a commission. When Axford discovers that Bird is acting for both parties, he goes through with the deal but refuses to pay the broker's commission. Bird sues. Can he recover?

Ans.
No. A broker cannot serve two masters. The broker's employment by the buyer is incompatible with his similar employment by the seller.

53. Under what circumstances, if any, may a seller impose the condition on a broker that he is to receive a commission only in the event that the sale is consummated by the execution and delivery of the deed?

Ans.
Only if the condition is agreed upon before the broker has obtained a bona fide purchaser for the property and a properly executed agreement of sale.

54. Barnes, a broker employed by Arthur, procures an agreement of sale signed by Clark and upon the owner's terms of sale. However, the agreement, provides for closing the deal six months hence. Arthur has another purchaser of the property at the same price with the closing fixed for 30 days. Arthur refuses to sign Barns' agreement. Is Barnes entitled to a commission?

Ans.
No. Six months is an unreasonable time for closing, and Arthur is within his rights to refuse to sell.

55. An agreement of sale recites that the owner agrees to pay a broker commission of $9,000, pursuant to a listing agreement. In a suit where the buyer failed to consummate the deal, the trial judge instructed the jury that it was their duty "to determine" what amount of money was fair and reasonable to recompense the broker for his services." The jury awarded $1,000. Were the court's instructions proper?

Ans.
No. The broker was entitled to the commission agreed upon in the listing agreement. *Gaynor v. Laverdure,* 291 N.E. 2d 617 (Mass. 1973).

56. A real estate broker is forced to sue to collect a commission that is due him. In addition to the facts setting forth his cause of action, what facts does the License Law require him to allege in his complaint and prove on the trial of his case?

Ans.
That he was a *properly licensed* real estate broker at the time the cause of action arose.

57. In dealing with an officer of the corporate owners of commercial property listed for sale, what precautions should the broker take?

Ans.
The broker should assure that the officer has been duly authorized by the board of directors or other corporate authority to sell the property.

58. Jones, a broker, obtains an oral listing from Smith, to sell Smith's residence. Jones obtains a signed offer to purchase from Green and before presenting the offer to Smith, goes to Smith and obtains a written listing from him. Two days later, agreements are signed by Smith and Green. The sales agreement states that Smith owes Jones a 6 percent commission. Can Jones recover the commission?

Ans.
Yes. The post listing agreement, supported by the obligation of Smith to pay Jones a commission, would constitute ratification of Jones' employment.

59. A broker negotiated an option to purchase real estate, which expired on May 15. On July 1, the optionee exercised and purchased the property. The broker claims a commission. Can he recover?

Ans.
No. Since the optionee did not exercise his option prior to the expiration date, the option expired and the broker's rights terminated at the same time.

60. A contract for the sale of real estate provides as follows: "The seller agrees that John Doe brought about this sale and agrees to pay him a broker's commission of $500." Subsequently to the execution of the contract, John Doe, in a conversation with the seller, states that he will not claim a commission unless title is actually closed. Thereafter, and prior to the date set for the closing of the title, John Doe demands his commission from the seller who refuses to pay, claiming that John Doe was not entitled to a commission until the actual closing of title. Who will win?

Ans.
John Doe, the broker, will win as his commission was earned when he produced a purchaser ready, willing and able to buy upon the seller's terms upon the execution of the sales agreement. There was no consideration for Doe's promise to wait until the closing for his commission.

61. Bell listed his property for sale with Abbott on January 4 for a six-month period at $40,000, with commission at 7 percent. Three months later, the state condemned the property, but before condemnation was completed, and within the listing period, the state offered Bell $40,000 and he accepted. The broker is claiming a 7 percent commission. Decide if the broker can recover.

Ans.
The broker cannot recover. The broker was in no way responsible for the sale.

62. What protection does a written listing give the owner?

Ans.
The terms of the contract are clearly defined so that any controversy or litigation can be avoided.

63. A broker, Carroll, has an exclusive listing on certain property from an owner and receives an unsolicited bona fide offer from Broker Woodruff. He refuses to submit the offer to the owner on the grounds that his exclusive agency does not obligate him to deal with or through any other broker, and that the prospect must deal with him directly and not through another broker. Is he correct?

Ans.
No. The broker is obligated to submit any offer or information which he may have regarding the subject of the agency. While Carroll may refuse to split a commission, his duty to his principal requires him to divulge the offer through Woodruff. The owner may decide to pay each broker a full commission.

64. Abel listed his property with broker Berm at $15,500. Berm received an offer of $10,500 from a prospect. Should he ignore the offer or obtain a deposit from the prospect and communicate it to Abel?

Ans.
He should accept the deposit and advise Abel of *all* information which comes to his knowledge. It is up to the owner to accept or reject the offer.

65. If the broker or salesperson selling the property is the owner thereof or has an ownership interest therein, should that fact be disclosed to the purchaser before the latter obligates himself?

Ans.
Yes. A broker or salesperson is not permitted to act as an undisclosed principal in a real estate transaction, whether it be to the purchaser or seller.

66. A salesperson in the employ of a real estate broker put through a sale. He demanded commission on behalf of his firm and the seller refused to pay. His employing broker refused to be involved in litigation regardless of the merits of the claim. Thereupon the salesperson sued the seller in his own name. Can he recover?

Ans.
No. A salesperson usually has no standing in a court of law: an action for commission must be instituted in the name of the broker employed by the owner.

67. Jones gives you an exclusive listing on a home; you procure a buyer, ready, willing, and able. You now discover that Jones does not own the house but that his brother does. May you recover a commission from Jones?

Ans.
Yes. You have fulfilled the terms of your contract with Jones. By holding himself out as the owner, Jones is liable.

68. Harris, a broker, obtained a purchaser, and a $500 deposit, on an "open" listing. The listing was for $12,000 and the buyer agreed to pay $11,200. Before the owner, Grant, would sign the agreement, he had Harris write in "Commission to be paid when deal is consummated." The buyer moved to Detroit and defaulted. Grant sold the property through another broker. Can Harris recover?

Ans.
No. Failure of the buyer to close the deal, without any fault of the seller, relieved the seller under the special terms of the contract from liability for the commission.

69. Enumerate five duties which an agent owes to his principal.

Ans.
(1) Loyalty and trust, (2) must obey instructions, (3) must account for money and property, (4) must not be negligent, and (5) must act in person.

70. Under what circumstances, if any, may a broker recover a commission from both the buyer and seller?

Ans.
A broker may recover a commission from both parties when: (1) he is employed by both parties, (2) he merely brings the parties together, (3) nothing is left to his discretion, (4) no special confidence is reposed in him, and (5) the fact that he is acting in a dual capacity is known to both parties.

71. Who is a broker-salesperson?

Ans.
A broker-salesperson is one who holds a broker's license but is acting in the capacity of a salesperson for another licensed broker. He is often referred to as "Other Broker," "Associate Broker," or other such title.

72. The substance of a purchaser's complaint is: "Five months ago, I gave a broker a $1,200 deposit for the purchase of a home, which he owns. The deal was to be closed one month later. He is out when I call and never returns my calls. I have visited his office four times and I have waited an hour each time, but his secretary keeps telling me he is expected back any time. I think he is avoiding me. What should I do?

Ans.
Four avenues of relief are open: (1) file a complain with the real estate commission, (2) file a complaint with the Consumers Bureau, (3) sue him in a Justice of the Peace or similar tribunal, or (4) if he is a REALTOR®, file a complaint with the REALTOR BOARD.

73. A tenant in an apartment building obtained a tenant for a three-bedroom unit in the building, upon the owner's promise to pay him a $250 fee. After the lease was signed with the new tenant, the owner reneged on his promise. The tenant sued. Can he collect?

Ans.
No. Since the tenant was not licensed, this is a fatal bar to a recovery.

74. Thompson, a licensed broker, agreed to divide a commission with an attorney, who referred a prospect to him. Later the broker refused to pay and the attorney sued. Can he recover?

Ans.
No. Since the attorney does not have a real estate license, he cannot recover. Also the broker would jeopardize his license by paying a commission to an unlicensed person.

75. The listing contract provided for a six months' "carry over" clause—if property was sold for $65,000 to a buyer procured by the broker, in which case he would be entitled to a commission. During the six months period the property was sold by another broker for $45,000. It was established that plaintiff broker presented no offers to the owner, but he had submitted the property to the ultimate purchaser during the original term of the listing: but he did not offer $65,000. Can the broker recover?

Ans.
No. The broker did not *procure* an acceptable buyer. He cannot recover a commission for an independent sale at a later date to a prospect for a substantially lower amount than quoted by the owner.

76. Should a broker keep his commissions in his trust account at all times?

Ans.
No, only until the deal is closed.

77. What points should an exclusive listing cover?

Ans.
Property Description, price, terms, encumbrances, definite period for which the listing is binding, agreement to pay a specified commission in event of a sale, exchange, or lease.

78. David A. Stone lists his property for sale with Rogers & Co. at $14,500. The only offer Rogers receives is $7,700, cash for Adams. Rogers states, "It would be an insult to even submit such a ridiculous offer." Two months later, Stone sells directly to Adams at $7,700. When Rogers finds out, he sues for a commission. Can he recover?

Ans.
No. He was not the efficient and procuring cause of the sale. He was also negligent in not submitting the original offer to Stone.

79. Hill is looking for a commercial property in the retail district of Phoenix. He contacts the A.L. Weaver Company and promises to pay Weaver $5,000 if he can locate a satisfactory site. Six suitable properties are listed for sale with the Weaver Agency, including property of Wilson heirs. Shortly thereafter, a sale is made by the Wilson heirs, to Hill. Weaver demands the $5,000 from Hill, which he refuses. Can he recover?

Ans.
No. The employment of Weaver, by the Wilson heirs, precludes any recovery from Hill.

80. In question 79, can Weaver recover from the Wilson heirs?

Ans.

No. His attempt to collect two commissions on the same transaction impinges upon his duty of loyalty to either party.

81. An orange grove was listed by the owner, Margaret O'Neill, with the Citrus Realty Co. at $125,000. Citrus obtained a signed offer to purchase at that price, with a $2,500 earnest money deposit, from Home Fruit Company, a Florida Corporation. The agreement was signed on March 15. Home Fruit Company was unable to obtain financing, because of a bad credit rating and a bankruptcy proceeding in the prior year. Is the broker entitled to a commission?

Ans.

No. The broker must produce a purchaser of *substance*, or one able to command the necessary money to close the transaction.

82. Henry Colt was licensed in Texas as a real estate broker, as an attorney, and as an engineer. A Dallas property was listed with his office for sale. He negotiated the sale between seller and buyer. The seller refused to pay any commission since the listing was not in writing as required by Texas law. Can he recover?

Ans.

No. Since he was acting solely as a real estate broker, the listing had to be in writing.

83. How, if at all, should a broker go about negotiating a sale of property listed exclusively by another broker?

Ans.

Contact the listing broker and operate through him as a cobroker.

84. A broker fails to renew his license by July 1. He then continues to operate and does not renew his license until July 14. On July 5 he completes a transaction and retains his commission. The owner of the property demands that he receive the full amount including the portion retained by the broker for his commission. Can a broker collect a commission under such circumstances?

Ans.

No. He was not licensed and not legally operating as a licensed broker at the date the sale was made.

85. Smith, a broker, has a customer for a warehouse. He contacts an official of a manufacturing building and inquires if the company will consider the sale of one of its buildings. The officer replies in the affirmative and states a price of $30,000. Smith introduces his customer to the official and later a sale is made. Is the broker entitled to a commission?

Ans.

No. The broker is unable to establish that he was employed by the seller, which is a prerequisite to recovery; or, that the official was authorized to act for the corporation.

86. What is a listing?

Ans.
A detailed record of a property listed with a broker for sale or rent; the contract of employment between owner and broker.

87. A prospect desires to purchase property listed with a broker at $26,000 and proposes two offers: (1) $23,000, and (2) full price of $26,000. The second offer, however, is to be submitted only in the event the owner rejects the first offer. Should the broker take two offers in this manner?

Ans.
No. He must be loyal to his principal and instruct the buyer that he can only accept the $26,000 offer.

88. Why should a broker purchasing a property from an owner disclose his personal purchase?

Ans.
Acting as a principal is incompatible with a brokers employment as an agent in a fiduciary capacity.

89. Adams gives Blair a written exclusive listing for 30 days. Adams dies during the 30-day period. Is the agency canceled?

Ans.
Yes. Death automatically cancels the agency, unless it is coupled with an interest.

90. If the listing contract is ambiguous, how will the courts construe it?

Ans.
Most strongly against the broker, because he prepared it.

91. Kentucky requires a listing to be in writing. Plaintiff broker sued for a $750 commission and relied on a sales agreement signed by the seller and buyer, which contained a printed clause that the property was sold "through Bud Hamilton Realty Auction Co." Could the plaintiff recover on this writing as a contract?

Ans.
In the case of *Hamilton v. Booth,* 332, S.W. 2d 252 (Ky. 1960) the court held that the broker could not recover on this writing between seller and buyer.

92. Nebraska requires a listing contract to be in writing. A contract of sale contained a clause, "I further agree to pay the above named agent the cash commission agreed upon in the amount of $3,500." At the bottom lefthand side, underneath witness, broker signed "Bill B. Svoboda." Does the broker have a written contract of employment?

Ans.
The lower court held against the broker. The Supreme Court reversed: *Svoboda v. DeWald,* 159 Neb. 594 (1955). The appellate court found that the writing complied with the requirements of the Statute, in that (1) it was in writing, (2) contained a description of the property, (3) commission to be paid, and (4) it was signed by the parties.

93. Steiner owned a property upon which there was a mortgage, delinquent in a large amount. He gave an exclusive right to sell on the property to Stoner for 90 days, hoping to salvage something from the sale. During the 90-day period, the owner and the mortgagee resolved their differences by having the owner give the mortgagee a voluntary deed in return for a cash payment of $500. The broker claimed a commission on the value of the property (listing price). Could he recover?

Ans.
Yes. The court held that it was a voluntary sale based upon a valuable consideration, so that the broker was entitled to his commission.

94. Hoyle listed his property for sale with Doyle, a good friend, who was a member of a multilisting association. It was sold by Boyle, a fellow member. Upon Hoyle's refusal to pay a commission, Boyle sued him. Can he recover?

Ans.
No. There is no privity of contract (employment) between Hoyle and Boyle.

95. What is meant by "carry over" or "extender" clause in an exclusive contract?

Ans.
It is a clause which reads in effect, "If a sale or exchange is made within six months after the exclusive period has expired, to any person with whom the broker has been negotiating, he is entitled to a commission."

96. On or about April 26, the owner has listed his property for sale exclusively until "on or about the 15 of June" on which date the defendant anticipated moving with his family to Florida. Plaintiff advertised the property and showed it to several prospects. On May 20, it was sold through another broker. Is the plaintiff entitled to recover a commission?

Ans.
Yes. (*Werder v. Browne,* 78 Ga. App. 587.) The court held that the alleged date on which the contract was to come to an end was not so vague and indefinite as to render the contract void and unenforceable. The date of the planned move to Florida was a definite time capable of being sustained by proof.

97. Plaintiff broker sued for $2,625 commission in connection with the sale of a motor court on U.S. Highway, south of Savannah. The broker failed to plead that he was a licensed broker. Was this fatal to his claim?

Ans.
Yes. (*Lynes Realty Co. v. Mays,* 80 Ga. App. 4.)

98. Should a listing contract authorize a broker to sign a binding contract of sale for the owner?

Ans.
No. Except under very unusual circumstances. It would be better for the owner to give the broker a *Power of Attorney to sell* in addition to the listing contract.

99. A licensed broker sued an owner for a commission upon an employment contract that the seller was to "obtain $125,000 cash or better, or $125,000 with *reasonable* financing." The broker obtained a responsible buyer who was willing to pay $55,000 cash and execute a $70,000 mortgage, payable within 15 years, with interest at 5 percent. The seller refused to accept the deal. Is the broker entitled to his commission?

Ans.

Yes. The broker's deal would constitute reasonable financing.

100. Fred Lane signed an exclusive right to sell listing with the Rucker Agency on April 10 for a period of three months. During the exclusive period, Lane sells the property himself. Rucker sues for a commission. Lane defends on the grounds that it was verbally agreed between him and Rucker that if he sold the property himself during the exclusive period, no commission would be due Rucker. Is this a good defense?

Ans.

No. Under the Parole Evidence Rule, oral testimony cannot be introduced to vary or contradict a written instrument, except for fraud, accident, or mistake. Lane would have to allege and prove that the oral understanding was fraudulently omitted from the written listing.

101. Broker Hayes negotiated a deal between Stevens, seller, and Todd, buyer. After the agreements were signed, Hayes gave Todd permission to fill in some of the subject property, which was to be used for parking. The deal fell through and Todd sued Hayes for $725, cost of fill and paving. Can he recover?

Ans.

Yes. Hayes is a special agent, with only limited authority to obtain a buyer. He exceeded his authority when he authorized the buyer to fill in and pave the lot. He is personally liable for the buyer's expense.

102. Eaton lists his property for sale with Foster for $15,000. After some efforts, Foster is unable to sell the property and he then offers to buy the property for $14,000. Eaton agrees to sell at that price. Within three weeks, and before the deal is closed, Foster sells the property for $24,000. After both deals are closed, Eaton learns of the $24,000 deal, and sued Foster for the profit. He claims the broker made an unconscionable profit, was guilty of bad faith and breached his duty of loyalty to his principal. Can he recover?

Ans.

No. The parties acted as principals. So long as the agent did not conceal anything from his principal while he was acting as agent, he owes no duty to the former owner after he acquires ownership in good faith.

103. Alberts owned a vacant tract of land. He arranged with Bates, a broker, that the latter would have the engineering work done to lay out the land into a 40-lot subdivision. Bates was to have the exclusive sale of the lots for a three-year period. At the end of the first year, a few lots had been sold and Alberts desired to terminate the agency. Can he do so?

Ans.
No. The agency is coupled with an interest and cannot be revoked; even if Alberts died during the three-year period, the agency would continue.

104. What is the function of the real estate broker or salesperson?

Ans.
To bring about an agreement of sale between his principal, the owner, and a third party, the purchaser.

105. What is the difference between a "finder" and a "broker"?

Ans.
A "finder" merely brings a buyer to the attention of an owner, while a broker *negotiates* a sale to the buyer for the owner.

106. Is it necessary for a "finder" to have a state real estate license?

Ans.
No; if he "remains pure" in abstaining from any negotiations between owner and purchaser.

107. Must such an agreement between owner and "finder" be in writing in order to be enforceable?

Ans.
No.

108. Must there be an expressed contract between, oral or written, owner and "finder"?

Ans.
Yes; since any suit for "fee" would have to be based upon a contract.

109. Is there any difference between a "volunteer" and a "finder"?

Ans.
Yes. A volunteer negotiates between owner and prospect, but he cannot recover any commission, because he cannot prove he was employed. A "finder" locates a prospect for the owner, and does nothing more, but a sale is made. However, there must be an understanding (contract) between owner and "finder" for payment of a "fee."

110. Ideal Printing Company listed its plant for sale with Stan Weber, REALTOR®, at $180,000. Weber produced a buyer, Moore Mfg. Co., Inc. President for the firm was Frank Miller, who is a brother-in-law of Weber, and the general manager, James Collins, was married to Weber's mother. Weber did not disclose these facts to the officers of Ideal Printing Co. The transaction was made at $175,000. When Weber claimed a 6 percent commission, Ideal refused to pay and Weber sued. Decide who would win.

Ans.
In the absence of any bad faith, or undue pressure on the part of Weber, he would not have violated his duty of loyalty to his principal, and he would be entitle to a commission, based of the facts presented.

111. Why should the broker, who negotiates a sale, include a clause in the agreement of sale to the effect that his commission is due and payable by the seller?

Ans.
The broker is a third-party creditor-beneficiary and the clause would protect his claim for a commission, even if the listing is verbal.

112. Dorr listed his property for sale with Dawson Realty on February 1, for 60 days, at $45,000, with commission at 6 percent. The listing contains a clause that if the owner withdraws the listing before the expiration date, or transfers the property, he will be obligated to pay Dawson a commission. Dawson advertises the property immediately and shows it to four prospects who answer the advertisement. On March 2nd, Dorr called Dawson and told him to take the property off the market, as he had decided not to sell. Dawson sued. Can he recover?

Ans.
Yes. There has been partial performance by Dawson on the contract. It is too late for the owner to withdraw his listing. The owner's agreement to pay a commission upon prior withdrawal, obligates him to pay the broker the agreed commission.

113. What is the important factor in determining whether a licensed is an independent contractor or an employee of the broker?

Ans.
The amount of control the broker exercises over the salesperson. The potential for liability is great for both persons, a the resulting effect of damages in a negligence suit may be substantial. *Gipson v. Davis,* 215 Cal. App. 2d 190 (1963).

114. Property is owned by James and Charlotte Webster, by the entireties. Due to family discord, James moves and lists the property for sale with Steve Sands. Sands obtains a bona fide purchaser, who signs an offer to purchase at the listed price. Charlotte refuses to sign the sales agreement. Sands sued for a commission. Can he recover?

Ans.
No. Since Sands knew or should have known of the couple's marital difficulties, He should have had Charlotte sign the listing. Since she refuses to sign the sales agreement, Sands is precluded from recovering a commission.

115. Filbert lists his home for sale with Adams for $58,000, with a commission of 7 percent, upon sale. The listing is for 90 days. Adams has been unable to make a sale during the listing period, but has his mother-in-law buy the property one months later for $55,000. Three days after the closing, she deeds the property to Adams and his wife and moves in with them. Under these circumstances, can Filbert recover the commission paid to Adams at closing?

Ans.
Yes. Adams was duty bound to disclose all of the facts in the case to Filbert and he failed to do so.

116. Under the above facts, if Adams had told Filbert that he would buy the property himself if Filbert would reduce the price to $55,000, would Filbert have any action against Adams?

Ans.
No. The parties would have been dealing at "arms length" and Adams would have had no ulterior motive, such as reselling the property at a higher price to a prospective buyer, already obtained.

117. On November 6, Baer, a broker, negotiated the sale for $60,000, closing to be made on May 1 of the following year. The buyer, Cole, gave Baer a deposit check for $6,000. The broker deposited the check in an interest bearing savings account, which he opened at that time. Is the broker entitled to the interest?

Ans.
No. The broker is required to deposit the money is in his escrow or trust account. In the absence of any agreement between buyer and seller regarding this matter, the interest would belong to the seller.

118. If the listing agreement has a printed heading "EXCLUSIVE LISTING AUTHORIZATION," and in the body of the agreement a clause stating that the owner gives the broker "exclusive right to sell," could the broker recover a commission, if the owner himself sold the property during the term of the listing?

Ans.
No. The listing contract is ambiguous as to whether it is an exclusive listing contract or an exclusive right to sell contract. Since the broker prepared the listing, the ambiguity will be construed against him, and he cannot recover: *Bourgoin v. Fortier*, 310 A. 2d 618 (Main 1973). See also *Dorman Realty and Ins. Co. v. Stalvey*, 212 S.E. 2d 591 (S.C. 1975).

119. (a) Name three types of properties generally exempt from municipal and county taxation.
(b) Can a broker recover a commission upon the sale of exempted property?

Ans.
(a) Charitable institutions, educational institutions, and religious institutions.
(b) Yes.

True and False   **Answer**

1. The law of brokerage is a combination of the statute of frauds and the law of equity.   False

2. A sign "For Sale—See Your Broker," constitutes employment of nay broker who produces a prospect.   False

3. "Puffing the Goods" constitutes an actionable wrong.   False

4. Two or more persons must be involved together in an act of conspiracy.   True

5. Owner and buyer, to evade a broker's commission, could both be sued by the broker.   True

6. A salesperson who negotiates a sale has the right to sue the owner for his commission if not paid.   False

7. A salesperson who takes a listing should sign it, rather than the broker.   True

8. The salesperson who attends the closing is the one entitled to the commission. — False

9. Where salespersons from three different agencies negotiate with the same prospect, the one who obtains the buyer's signature to an agreement is usually the one entitled to the commission. — False

10. There is economic justification for a real estate broker. — True

11. In relation to a broker, the owner is the principal. — True

12. Preparation of a listing contract constitutes the unauthorized practice of law. — False

13. A broker's contract with a salesperson must be in writing. — False

14. A listing contract given by a husband to a broker for the sale of property owned by himself and his wife will be binding upon the wife. — False

15. Where a prospect answers a broker's advertisement and inspects the subject property, he is the broker's client. — False

16. Where a property is listed for sale with several brokers, under an open listing, and the property is sold by one broker, the owner must immediately notify the other brokers that the property is sold. — False

17. A broker obtains a buyer who negotiates an option on December 15 and signs an agreement to purchase the property on January 25, at which date the listing has expired. The broker can collect a commission on the sale. — True

18. An open listing can be given to more than one broker. — True

19. An exclusive right to sell listing for 30 days is preferable to an open listing for 90 days. — True

20. A selling broker is a subagent of the listing broker in a multilisting organization. — True

21. The first essential in a suit for a real estate commission is a real estate license. — True

22. A licensed broker may divide his commission with an unlicensed attorney, who cooperated in making the sale. — False

23. The broker generally pays for the advertising of a property for sale. — True

24. The contract giving employment of the broker is known as the listing contract. — True

25. The salesperson, who leaves a broker may take all of his listings to his new broker. — False

26. A licensed salesperson may divide his commission with another licensed salesperson with his broker's consent. — False

27. The principal in a listing contract is the seller. — True

28. The State Real Estate Board or Commission has authority to fix 6 percent as the rate of commission on real estate. — False

29. A broker is obliged to advise a seller of his responsibility to pay such loan discounts (points) as is imposed when the real estate contract calls for F.H.A. or V.A. financing. — True

30. "Earnest money" is the commission which a broker receives in the deal. — False

31. "REALTOR®" is the term used by a broker after he successfully negotiates a deal. — False

32. A contract between two brokers, who cooperate on a deal, need not be in writing. — True

33. A broker may pay compensation only to his own salesmen and another broker. — True

34. A listing contract is ended if the salesperson, who obtained the listing dies. — False

35. An exclusive listing is preferable to an open listing. — True

36. A broker is responsible for the closing of deals made by his salesperson. — True

37. A seller can refuse to pay a broker and earned commission when he discovers that the buyer is also paying the broker a commission. — True

38. A salesperson should understand the law of principal and agent. — True

39. A salesperson who solicits listings, but does not sell, is not required to have a license. — False

40. There is no statutory lien for a broker's unpaid commission. — True

41. A listing commission might be renewed after its expiration date. — True

42. A broker may not represent more than one party to a transaction unless he so advises both of them and has their consent. — True

43. A listing contract is terminated by the death of the owner. — True

44. The fact that the person who signed the listing did not own the property is no defense in an action for a real estate commission. — True

45. It is not important to specify the amount of commission to be charged for the sale of property because that is fixed by law. — False

46. Commissions for the sale of real estate is determined by agreement between the parties. — True

47. A broker, employed as a salesperson, should maintain a trust account for earnest moneys deposits paid to him. — False

48. An *extender* clause in a listing is the same as a *carry over* clause in a listing. — True

49. A Real Estate Board in a metropolitan area can fix the commission rate for its members to charge. — False

50. Where a broker becomes a member of a real estate board, the salespersons automatically become associate members. — False

51. An owner gave an exclusive listing to a broker. During the term of the listing, the property was sold by another broker. The owner is liable for two commissions. — True

52. It is unlawful for a salesperson to receive a commission from anyone other than the broker to which he is licensed. — True

53. A salesperson should advertise the sale of real estate in his own name. — False

54. Placing a *sold* sign on property sold by a broker is one of the best ways to obtain additional listings. — True

55. A salesperson, leaving a broker's employ, can recover from the broker commissions due, upon signed agreements, but not yet closed. — False

56. The law obligates every agent to act in and for the best interest of his employer. — True

57. A salesperson selling his own property or that of the broker by whom he is employed should inform a prospective buyer of that fact. — True

58. Employment of a broker to find a tenant for real estate need not be in writing to be enforceable. — True

59. A real estate broker is required to exercise due diligence to keep his employer informed of his actions in the course of his agency. — True

60. A salesperson's principal is the broker-employer. — True

61. An exclusive listing and a net listing are the same thing and the terms can be used interchangeably. — False

62. Where it is necessary to pay *points* in order to consummate a sale, the salesperson who made the sale should acquaint the owner with his obligation to pay the *points*. — True

63. A salesperson cannot collect a commission in his own name and then divide it with his broker. — True

64. A principal is the employer of the broker. — True

65. A broker's client and a broker's prospect are on and the same thing. — True

66. A defrauded client has no right of court action against a broker but must sue the surety company, if the broker is bonded. — False

67. If a broker has real estate for sale and finds a prospect willing to take an option to purchase the property at the price stated, the broker is entitled to a commission. — False

68. A salesperson licensed one broker may deal directly with another broker and obtain a commission from the second broker. — False

69. Under no circumstances can a broker collect a commission from a buyer. — False

70. From the owner's standpoint, an exclusive agency contract is preferable to an exclusive right to sell. — True

71. It is unlawful for a broker to give part of his commission to the buyer for the purchase of a new electric range. — True

72. A real estate broker under an agency acts in a fiduciary relationship to his principal. — True

73. The listing agreement between broker and owner need only be signed by the owner. — False

74. An agent is the *alter ego* of his principal. — True

75. It is unlawful for a broker to purchase property, listed by him, in the name of a straw man. — True

76. Real Estate Commissions, by Rule and Regulation, require the broker to give the owner a copy of the signed listing, *at the time of signing*. — True

77. If a salesperson's name is used in an advertisement for property for sale, the ad should also contain the name and address of the broker. — True

78. A real estate broker is entitled to a commission for the consummation of a sale of real property upon the asking price set by the seller even though he was in a position to obtain another purchaser willing to pay more than the asking price. — False

79. The price of the listed property determines whether the listing contract must be in writing. — False

80. A broker, upon expiration of the listing term, should always furnish the owner with the names of all persons to whom he submitted the property during the term of the listing. — True

81. When deposit money is received by the broker, he may use such money for his personal account up to the amount of his commission as soon as the agreement of sale is signed. — False

82. Brokers employing salespeople are relieved of all responsibility for the acts of the salespeople if they bonded. — False

83. All brokers are members of the NATIONAL ASSOCIATION OF REALTORS®. — False

84. In an estate by the entireties, either husband or wife may give a valid listing of the property to a broker and bind the other spouse. — False

85. One who takes and passes a real estate course, given by a real estate board, is entitled to use the title *Graduate Realtor's Institute*. — False

86. In order to prosecute a person for acting as a broker without license, it is essential to prove that he received or expected compensation. — True

87. A real estate listing can be taken in the name of the salesperson as long as the transaction is closed in the name of the broker. — False

88. A broker is entitled to a commission under an *exclusive right to sell listing*, if the owner sells the property himself during the term of the listing. — True

89. If owner and broker have not agreed upon a rate of commission, the broker is entitled to recover on a *quantum meruit* basis, if he makes the deal. — True

90. A property is listed for $100,000. The broker tells a prospect that he knows that the owner will accept $80,000, which is accepted by the owner. The broker has violated his duty to the owner. — True

91. Where an owner lists a property for sale by a broker "at a sale for not less than $50,000," the broker is entitled to a $10,000 commission if the property is sold for $110,000. — False

92. If an owner lists a property for sale with one broker, he cannot employ another broker to sell the same property unless the first broker withdraws. — False

93. An agency to sell real estate usually comes under the Statute of Frauds. — False

94. Where a property is listed for sale for $70,000 and then sold for $50,000, the broker is entitled to a commission. — True

95. Every real estate contract negotiated by a broker should have a clause recognizing the broker as the procuring cause of the sale. — True

96. A broker is the *efficient and procuring* cause of a sale when he procures a buyer, ready, willing, and able to buy. — True

97. A broker may file a lien against an owner's property for an unpaid commission. — False

98. A *postdated check* given for a deposit has the same effect as a N.S.F. check. — False

99. The broker who obtains the buyer's signature on the dotted line is the one entitled to the commission on the sale. — False

100. It is illegal for a broker to lend his commission to the buyer for an earnest money deposit. — True

101. A broker may collect a commission from both parties in an exchange deal with the knowledge and consent of both parties. — True

102. Where two or more brokers claim a commission for the sale of the same property, the owner should pay the money into the court. — True

103. A contract accompanied by deposit money is not *always* conclusive evidence that the broker is entitled to the commission. — True

104. In order to protect his commission, it is advisable for a broker to draw up a contract of sale. — True

105. Placing a "For Sale" sign on a vacant lot without the owner's permission constitutes unethical conduct. — True

106. In order to secure a listing of property to sale, it would be permissible to give a friend a $10 bill to assist you in securing the listing. — False

107. A broker is entitled to a commission if he produces a buyer ready, willing, and able to meet the terms proposed by the seller in the listing, even if the owner refuses to go through with the deal. — True

108. Where parties to a sales contract rescind the agreement, the broker cannot recover a commission. — False

109. Quantum meruit means the reasonable value of the broker's services. — True

110. An escrow company may be fined for paying a commission to an unlicensed person. — True

111. A broker may purchase property listed with him for sale if he informs the seller he is acting as principal. — True

112. After an agreement of sale is signed and the buyer sues the seller for some grievance, the broker should file an interpleader action to protect his commission. — True

113. An able buyer must be a buyer of financial *substance*. — True

114. In practice, in a multilist association, the listing broker always receives a larger portion of the commission than the selling broker. — False

115. A licensed broker, under the licensing law, cannot be employed as a salesperson by another broker. — False

116. A *foreign* broker usually refers to a broker licensed in another state. — True

117. Suit for a commission is an action assumpsit. — True

118. Hand money and earnest money are the same. — True

119. A broker is a nonproductive economic element in our society. — False

120. Inquiry of a seller as to price and availability for sale does not constitute a contract of employment. — True

121. A real estate broker's commission is deemed to have been earned by him at the time the closing of title. — False

122. A real estate broker holding a 60-day exclusive agency to sell a parcel of real estate should discontinue his efforts to sell the property if the owner dies during the period. — True

123. A "For Sale—See your broker" sign automatically gives another broker authority to sell the property. — False

124. All full time brokers are REALTORS®. — False

125. If a real estate broker failed to disclose the identity of his prospective   True
customer, and if the negotiation failed, and the purchaser sought out the
owner and consummated the deal direct, the broker would not be entitled
to a commission.

126. It is unethical for a licensee to advise that the selling price of the seller is   False
too high or too low.

127. A broker should not bother an owner by submitting an offer which the   False
broker considers ridiculously low.

128. A Real Estate Commissioner may sell real estate without a license.   False

129. "Puffing of Goods" as applied to real estate means extravagant statements   True
regarding the desirability of the property.

130. A gives Broker B an exclusive listing on March 21, 1992 for 90 days. B   True
dies on April 24, 1992. The listing is canceled.

131. A listing by a minor is voidable by him.   True

132. In a multilist association, the listing broker and the selling broker usually   False
receive an equal amount of commission.

133. "Caveat Emptor" relieves an owner or broker from any misrepresenta-   False
tion.

134. In a multilist association, the selling broker generally has no right to sue   True
the owner for a commission.

135. Dual contracts, prepared by a broker to assist in getting a loan, are illegal.   True

136. Brokerage is the most profitable segment of the ordinary licensee's   True
business.

137. An owner-builder of more than 20 homes requires a broker's license.   False

138. A person may call himself a REALTOR® once he passes the state   False
licensing examination.

139. Where a property, subject to a mortgage, is listed for sale by the owner,   False
the mortgagee must agree to the listing.

140. Where a property is leased, the broker must receive the consent of the   False
tenant, to a listing given him by the owner.

141. By-laws of a real estate board do not take precedence over the Rules and   True
Regulations of a Real Estate Commission.

142. A broker may rely on the seller's statement regarding the zoning of the   False
property he lists.

143. A broker may advertise State Approved Broker or REALTOR when he   False
receives his license.

144. The Graduate Realtor's Institute is a major step forward in attaining   True
professional acceptance by the public.

145. A salesperson owes the prospect the duty to disclose the lowest price the   False
seller will take, if it is considerably less that the listed price.

146. It is illegal for a broker to recommend that the seller allow the buyer credit   True
of $1,000 for the purchase of a $5 painting from the buyer, in order for
the buyer to obtain a higher mortgage.

147. A person who has passed the state broker's examination, amy advertise   False
real estate for sale.

148. A broker should know the zoning of a listed property.   True

149. Cities and villages may add their own licensing requirements to those established by the legislature.   False

150. Most states now have educational and/or apprenticeship prerequisites for a broker's license.   True

151. Brokerage is the "heart" of the real estate business.   True

152. A broker can advance a salesperson's commission from his escrow account only in a hardship case.   False

153. If a question relative to the validity of title should arise, it is necessary that the broker recommend that the buyer consult an attorney.   True

154. A listing agreement is always a bilateral contract.   True

155. A Georgia broker may take a listing on property for a vacant tract of land in Florida.   True

156. Representing that a seller is eager to sell because of ill health is merely "puffing of goods."   False

157. A listing should contain a statement over the owner's signature that the data furnished the broker is true and correct.   True

158. A broker may loan a purchaser the earnest money deposit, in return for a check payable in 30 days.   False

159. A real estate association by-law can deny membership to a part-time broker.   False

160. A multilist association of a real estate board cannot refuse membership to a nonmember of a board who is licensed.   True

161. A real estate board is required to admit to membership every licensee who makes application.   False

162. Many cannons of ethics of the NATIONAL ASSOCIATION OF REAL-TORS® are statutory grounds for disciplinary action by the Real Estate Commission.   True

163. The Court may strike down a commission contract where there is unequal bargaining power between broker and owner.   True

164. A clause in a listing contract which provides for payment of a commission if canceled by the owner prior to its expiration date is binding.   True

165. A real estate board can refuse membership to an applicant for cause.   True

166. Most Real Estate Commissioners are REALTORS®.   True

167. Exclusion of a part-time broker from multiple-listing service is an anti-trust violation.   True

168. Where an owner cancels an exclusive listing the next day after it was signed, the broker, per se, is entitled to the commission agreed upon in the listing.   False

169. A broker's knowledge of available properties is his "stock in trade."   True

170. Failure of a broker to disclose all offers to his owner may constitute grounds for disciplinary action.   True

171. A corporation and a partnership have the same advantages and disadvantages in operating a real estate business.   False

172. A property should be advertised at a higher price than the listed price, to include the broker's commission.   False

MULTIPLE CHOICE

1. City Industries Inc. posted a large sign on its six-story building which read:

> FOR SALE
> OR
> FOR RENT
> SEE YOUR BROKER

Adams, a licensed broker, talked to Lee, Executive Vice-President, City Industries Inc., about price, terms of sale, area, and possession. Adams next sent Lowell, a prospect to inspect the building. He was shown through the building by the building superintendent on a Sunday. Several days later, Lowell's firm bought the building. Under these circumstances:

Ans.
d.

   I. Adams can recover commission from City Industries Inc.
   II. Adams can recover a commission from Lowell's firm.
      a. I only.
      b. II only.
      c. Both I and II.
      d. Neither I or II.

2. Broker Haines, representing James, negotiated an option with Kane for the purchase of a tract of land for $210,000. The period of the option was from September 1, 1991 to December 1, 1991. Kane notified James on November 21, 1992, that he was exercising the option to purchase, according to its terms. Formal agreements were not signed until January 2, 1992 and payment made. Under these circumstances, Hanes is entitled to a commission.

Ans.
a.

   I. From James
   II. From Kane
      a. I only.
      b. II only.
      c. Both I and II.
      d. Neither I or II.

3. Abbott gave broker Bates an exclusive listing on his property October 1, 1991 for six months. Bates placed his "For Sale" sign on the property. On November 25, 1991, a severe wind storm loosened several slate shingles, which fell to the street. A neighbor reported this fact to Bates, who surveyed the damage but did nothing more. On January 19, 1992, a severe windstorm disrupted several more shingles, which struck and injured a pedestrian, Evans. Under these circumstances, Evans has a cause for action against:

Ans.
c.

   I. Abbott
   II. Bates
      a. I only.
      b. II only.
      c. Both I and II.
      d. Neither I or II.

4. Anderson lists his residence with Bailey, a licensed broker, at $120,000   Ans.
   for a 90-day period, expiring July 31, 1991. During this period, Bailey   c.
   shows the property to Charwick. On August 26, 1991, Bailey returns with
   Chadwick to see the Bailey home, but Chadwick says, "I don't want to
   see it again, I don't like the blue gable roof." That evening Chadwick and
   his wife, unbeknownst to Bailey, return to the Anderson property and
   purchase it for $5,000 less than the listed price. Chadwick dies not disclose
   that they ever say the property with Bailey. Under these circumstances:

   I. Bailey can recover a commission from Anderson.
   II. Bailey can recover from Chadwick.
      a. I only.
      b. II only.
      c. Either I or II.
      d. Neither I or II.

5. An exclusive right to sell listing is given by Jones to Gaines, a licensed   Ans.
   broker, for 90 days. It provides: "In consideration of $1.00 received by me   a.
   (the owner), I hereby list my property with (broker)." The $1.00 was not
   paid by the broker to the owner. The broker advertised the location of the
   property in a display advertisement and several prospects went to see the
   property. Ten days later, the owner canceled the listing and sold the
   property himself to his own prospect. The broker sued for a commission.

   I. The broker can recover a commission.
   II. The broker can only recover his expenses.
      a. I only.
      b. II only.
      c. Both I and II.
      d. Neither I or II.

6. Adams, unlicensed on March 21, 1991, negotiated a real estate sale on that   Ans.
   date from the owner, Bates, to Chase, a fellow employee of Adams. Bates   d.
   knew that Adams was going into the real estate business and told him, "I
   will take care of you." Agreements of sale were signed on March 24, 1991.
   The transaction was closed on June 24, 1991. At that time, Adams was a
   licensed salesperson for Donovan, a licensed broker. Bates and Chase
   refuse to pay a commission to anyone.

   I. Adams can recover from Bates on a quantum meruit basis
   II. Donovan can recover from bates.
      a. I only.
      b. II only.
      c. Both I and II.
      d. Neither I or II.

7. The average real estate broker finds commissions are earned mainly from   Ans.
   sales of: a.

      a. Dwellings.
      b. Commercial properties.
      c. Industrial properties.
      d. Investment properties.

8. A salesperson receiving a deposit should:
    a. Place it in his "special account."
    b. Place it in his broker's general account.
    c. Turn it over to his broker.
    d. Place it in the salesperson's trust account.

Ans. c.

9. In an exchange deal, a salesperson employed by broker A may receive a share of commission from:
    a. Broker B, who represents one of the principals.
    b. Salesperson C employed by B.
    c. Salesperson D employed by A.
    d. None of these.

Ans. d.

10. Upon the death of a broker, his listings may be taken over by:
    a. His widow.
    b. His son, who is of lawful age.
    c. A trust company.
    d. None of these.

Ans. d.

11. An oral agreement between two licensed brokers to divide a commission is:
    a. Void.
    b. Valid.
    c. Voidable.
    d. Must be approved by the seller.

Ans. b.

12. If a property consisting of 10 dwellings is listed at *not less that $650,000* to the owner, and after one year, the dwellings are sold separately, but in the aggregate, the sum realized is $650,000, the broker can recover, as his commission:
    a. The amount of deposit held in escrow at that time.
    b. 7 percent which is the going commission rate.
    c. On a quantum meruit basis.
    d. Nothing.

Ans. d.

13. A broker took a prospect to a listed property, but the prospect declined to inspect it. That evening, the prospect and his wife went to inspect the home, telling the owners that the wife had heard that it was for sale at a meeting of the wife's garden club that afternoon. The prospect purchased the property. Under these circumstances, the broker can sue:
    I. The sellers in an assumpsit action.
    II. The buyers in a trespass action.
    a. I only.
    b. II only.
    c. Both I and II.
    d. Neither I or II.

Ans. c.

14. The duty of the broker to keep the owner full informed as to negotiations with a prospect, is because the broker is:
    a. Cestui que trust.
    b. Fiduciary.
    c. Liable under the doctrine of respondent superior.
    d. Amicus curiae to the owner.

Ans. b.

15. In a multilist association, the selling broker, as between him and the listing broker, usually receives:

    a. One-half of the net commission paid.
    b. Less than one-half.
    c. More than one-half.
    d. The amount determined by the executive board.

16. A contract between Davis Realty Co. and Helen Miller, salesperson, provide in part, "No commission shall be considered earned, or payable to a salesperson, until the transaction has been completed and the commission collected by the company." Helen procured a buyer and agreements were signed. Before the deal was closed, she changed employers:

    a. She can recover her commission.
    b. She cannot recover her commission.
    c. She would first have to terminate her employment.
    d. She can sue the owner.

17. Two rival brokers claim a commission in a real estate deal. Broker A sues the owner. The owner should:

    a. Pay the broker with whom the property was listed.
    b. Pay the money into court (interpleader).
    c. Pay each broker one-half.
    d. Wait for the brokers to settle the matter between themselves.

18. An open listing is one that allows the broker:

    a. A reasonable time period to find a buyer.
    b. A definite time period within which to find a buyer.
    c. 90 days within which to obtain a buyer.
    d. The customary time to procure a buyer.

19. In a multilist association, a salesperson, who negotiates a sale, is directly responsible to:

    a. The listing broker.
    b. His employing broker.
    c. The multilist association.
    d. The seller.

20. Real estate practice dictates use of:

    a. An open listing.
    b. A net listing.
    c. Exclusive listing.
    d. An exclusive right to sell listing.

21. A proper recital of the commission to be paid in a whiten listing should read at:

    a. The rate usually charged in the area.
    b. Fixed percentage on the sales price, as negotiated between broker and seller.
    c. On a quantum meruit basis.
    d. The rate prescribed by law.

22. Real estate brokerage is governed by the law of:

    a. Statute of Frauds.
    b. Agency.
    c. The commercial code.
    d. Conveyancing.

Ans.
b.

23. Where a broker obtains a buyer, how many contracts are essential in order for the broker to establish a valid commission claim?

    a. One.
    b. Two.
    c. Three
    d. Four.

Ans.
b.

24. In listing property for sale, which item is *not* necessary for a valid exclusive listing?

    a. Date of listing.
    b. Address of property.
    c. Legal description.
    d. Listing period.

Ans.
c.

25. Another broker has a listing on a property you desire to show a prospect. Which one of the following should you do?

    a. Call the local Real Estate Board.
    b. Wait until the other broker's listing expires.
    c. Get in touch with the other broker and ask his permission to show the property.
    d. Show your prospect the property and then call the owner for a listing.

Ans.
c.

26. A real estate listing is:

    a. A list of all property held by the owner.
    b. A written list of all improvements on the property.
    c. A rendition of property for taxation.
    d. Employment of a broker by an owner to sell or lease certain property.

Ans.
d.

27. An agency coupled with an interest is one:

    a. That cannot be terminated before its expiration date.
    b. Where broker makes a secret profit at the expense of his principal.
    c. Where broker receives interest bearing notes in payment of his commission.
    d. Where suit is filed for commission, which constitutes a lien against the property.

Ans.
a.

28. Alberts negotiated a sale between his owner, Burrows, and a buyer, Champ. Later owner and buyer agree to call the deal off. The broker, Alberts, can:

    a. Recover a commission from Burrows.
    b. Recover a commission from Champ.
    c. Recover from Burrows and Champ.
    d. Recover from neither Burrows or Champ.

Ans.
a.

29. It is possible for an owner to have more than one agent endeavoring to sell his property. It is:

    a. An open listing.
    b. Multiple listing.
    c. A nonexclusive listing.
    d. A general listing.

    Ans.
    b.

30. The first step necessary for a licensed broker to recover a commission is to:

    a. Find a buyer.
    b. Find a seller.
    c. Have a contract of employment.
    d. Advertise the property for sale.

    Ans.
    c.

31. Norton listed his residence for sale with Todd at $100,000. Todd obtained a prospect, Hale, telling him to make an offer of $85,000, which he said the owner would very likely accept. Hale made the offer and Norton accepted. The transaction was closed. Later Norton ascertained that Hale would have paid $100,000. Norton sued Todd.

    I. Norton can recover the commission paid.
    II. Norton can recover the difference in price.
    a. I only.
    b. II only.
    c. Both I and II.
    d. Neither I or II.

    Ans.
    c.

32. A listing agreement which contains a rate of commission, fixed by a real estate organization, is:

    a. Valid.
    b. Void.
    c. Voidable.
    d. Subject to arbitration.

    Ans.
    b.

33. A licensed broker had a verbal listing of a property in a state that requires listings to be in writing. He negotiated a sale. The agreement of sale contained a clause which recognized the broker's right to a commission of 6 percent on the purchase price. The owner refused to pay and the broker sued.

    I. The broker can recover, as a third party creditor-beneficiary.
    II. The seller must pay, due to unjust enrichment.
    a. I only.
    b. II only.
    c. Both I and II.
    d. Neither I or II.

    Ans.
    a.

34. A valid listing on community property must be given by:

    a. Husband.
    b. Husband and wife.
    c. Seller and mortgagee.
    d. Broker and salesperson.

    Ans.
    b.

35. A prospect to whom a broker has shown a property, ordinarily has a right to rely upon the broker's representations as to:

    a. Title.
    b. Future prospects of income.
    c. All statements made by the broker regarding the property.
    d. Past rentals of the property.

Ans.
d.

36. Henry gave a listing to Fairview Realty on May 3 for 90 days. It provided for a commission to be paid "upon the sale or exchange" of the property. The broker obtains a prospect, Crawford, on July 31. On August 1, Crawford enters into a lease for one year, At $500 per month, with an option to purchase; any rent paid to apply to the purchase price. Under these circumstances:

  I. Fairview can recover a commission on the sale.
  II. Fairview can recover a commission on the rent paid.
    a. I only.
    b. II only.
    c. Both I and II.
    d. Neither I or II.

Ans.
a.

37. Miller, a broker, receives $5,000 from Gray, a buyer, upon the sale of Lee's home. Miller's commission is $1,750. The sale is not consummated because of a defect in Lee's title. Under these circumstances:

  I. Gray can recover the $5,000 from Miller.
  II. Gray can recover the $5,000 from Lee.
    a. I only.
    b. II only.
    c. Both I and II.
    d. Neither I or II.

Ans.
b.

38. Michael Martin negotiates a sale of a dwelling for Allen, a builder, at $95,000 and receives an earnest money deposit of $4,000. At the closing, the buyer, Phelps, claims that the builder has used second grade facing brick, contrary to specifications, and refuses to close the deal. Under these circumstances, the broker should:

  I. Refund the money to Phelps.
  II. Report the matter to the Real Estate Commission.
    a. I only.
    b. II only.
    c. Both I and II.
    d. Neither I or II.

Ans.
d.

39. A broker told a buyer that the house was connected to a township sewer, when it was serviced by a septic tank system. It cost the buyer $1,700 to change to the township system. The buyer seeks to recover this amount. Buyer can:

    a. Recover from the owner.
    b. Recover from the township.
    c. Recover from the broker.
    d. Recover from no one.

Ans.
c.

40. A property was listed for $185,000. A prospect told a broker that he wanted the property and would pay the listed price, but asked the broker to submit a signed offer for $165,000 and see if the owner would accept it. The owner agreed. Later the broker sued for commission.

Ans.
b.

    a. He can recover.
    b. He cannot recover.
    c. He can recover from the buyer.
    d. He can file a suit for "unjust enrichment," against the buyer.

41. A broker obtained an exclusive listing on a property for 30 days at $200,000. On the last day of the listing, the broker brought an offer to purchase the property signed by E. Gilligan. When asked who E. Gilligan was, the broker replied, "A client of our firm." The deal was closed. Actually the buyer was the mother-in-law of the broker and was a member of his household. Later, the seller brought action to rescind the transaction.

Ans.
a.

    a. The transaction will be rescinded.
    b. It will not be rescinded since the property was sold at the listed price.
    c. The transaction will not be rescinded but the broker will have to forfeit his commission.
    d. The buyer will own the property as trustee for the seller.

42. The state of Arizona requires that a listing be in writing. Wayne obtains a listing from King, but no mention is made of the commission to be charged. Wayne obtains a buyer whom King accepts. Later, Wayne tells King his commission is 6 percent. Under these circumstances:

Ans.
d.

  I. Wayne is entitled to 6 percent commission.
  II. Wayne can recover on a quantum meruit basis.
    a. I only.
    b. II only.
    c. Both I and II.
    d. Neither I or II.

43. Flynn and Filson are co-owners of a property. Flynn lists it for sale with Boulevard Realty, Inc. for $60,000, with commission at 6 percent. Boulevard obtains a bona fide purchaser at that price. Filson refuses to sign the agreement of sale. Boulevard Realty sues for commission.

Ans.
a.

  I. Boulevard can recover from Flynn.
  II. Boulevard Realty can recover from Filson.
    a. I only.
    b. II only.
    c. Both I and II.
    d. Neither I or II.

44. Lee has given an open listing to Aber and Co. and to Sweeney and Co. on March 18. Aber shows the property to a prospect, Clark on March 27. Sweeney negotiates a sale to clark on May 31. Lee pays Sweeney the commission.

Ans.
d.

I. Aber can sue for conspiracy against Lee and Sweeney.

II. Aber is entitled to one-half of the commission from Sweeney.

Under these facts, which of the following apply?

    a. I only.

    b. II only.

    c. Both I and II.

    d. Neither I or II.

45. Which of the following should *not* be placed in the real estate trustee account?   Ans. d.

    a. Earnest monies.

    b. Rental collections.

    c. Installment land contract collections.

    d. Insurance premiums.

46. A broker, Adams, listed Bigbee's property for sale at $125,000. He obtains a prospective purchaser, Clark at $145,000. Adams can: Ans. c.

    a. Report the sale to Bigbee at $125,000, and keep the excess as his commission.

    b. Obtain a "straw" party, Davis, at $125,000 and then resell to Clark for $145,000.

    c. Report the sale to Bigbee as $145,000 and collect a commission on the sale.

    d. Adams can buy in his own name for $125,00 and resell it to Clark for $145,000.

47. A broker is holding an earnest money deposit, equal to the amount of his commission. The seller, before the closing, not only refuses to pay the broker a commission but demands that the broker pay him the entire deposit money. The broker should: Ans. d.

    a. Refuse to permit the closing of the deal.

    b. Retain the earnest money as his commission.

    c. File a complaint with the Real Estate Commission.

    d. Pay the earnest money to the seller and then sue for his commission.

48. In the absence of a prior agreement as to when the broker's commission is earned, such commission is earned at: Ans. b.

    a. Consummation of the deal.

    b. Meeting of the minds of buyer and seller.

    c. The time the broker introduced the buyer to the seller.

    d. When the deed is delivered.

49. "In consideration of your efforts to obtain a purchaser, I hereby list with your for sale," etc. is a: Ans. b.

    a. Bilateral contract.

    b. Unilateral contract.

    c. Mutual contract.

    d. None of these.

50. A real estate broker must bring action in the courts to recover a real estate commission within:

    a. One year.
    b. Four years.
    c. Time fixed by law for suits on simple contracts (Pennsylvania is six years).
    d. Ten years.

Ans.
c.

51. A licensed New York broker, unlicensed in New Jersey, obtained a listing on an industrial plant in New Jersey owned by a Delaware corporation. He submitted full details of the property to a firm in New York. Two officers of the firm made their own inspection of the property, and agreed to buy it. The closing was in New York, since the property was in New Jersey, the owners refused to pay a commission to the New York broker. Under these circumstances, the broker can recover:

    I. From the seller.
    II. From the buyer.
    a. I only.
    b. II only.
    c. Both I and II.
    d. Neither I or II.

Ans.
a.

52. Adams listed his property for sale by Boyer at $400,000. The listing does not state that Boyer is to hold the earnest money in his escrow account. Boyer negotiates a deal at $400,000 to Clifton and receives an earnest money deposit of $10,000. Adams refuses to sign the agreement unless the $10,000 is paid to him. The agreement of sale recites "receipt of a deposit of $10,000 is hereby acknowledged on account and in consideration price." The deposit money should be:

    a. Paid to the seller.
    b. Retained by Boyer in his escrow account.
    c. An escrow account for the $10,000 should be opened in the joint name of Adams and Boyer.
    d. An escrow account should be opened in the joint names of Adams, Boyer, and Clifton.

Ans.
a.

53. Which one of the following will not cancel a principal-agent relationship?

    a. Insanity of either principal and agent.
    b. Death of the principal.
    c. Death of the agent.
    d. Change of business address of the principal.

Ans.
d.

54. A contract which provides for the payment of a commission to a broker even though the owner makes a sale without the aid of the broker is called an:

    a. Exclusive listing.
    b. Open Listing.
    c. Option.
    d. Exclusive right to sell.

Ans.
d.

55. When a broker and a salesperson have a dispute over the commission from a deal, they should:

    a. Complain to the owner.
    b. Bring action in court.
    c. File a complaint to the Commission.
    d. Compel arbitration.

56. An owner employs a broker to sell his property and promises to pay a commission; the broker brings about a sale on terms orally accepted by the owner so that a sale is fully consummated. Under such circumstances the broker's employment is:

    a. Valid.
    b. Void.
    c. Voidable.
    d. None of these.

57. If a broker receives more than one worthy, bona fide offer for the same property at approximately the same time, he should:

    a. Submit only the highest offer.
    b. Submit all offers to his owner.
    c. Submit only the one he considers is for the owner's best interest.
    d. None of these.

58. Adam Smith is 17 years of age, married, and owns a vacant lot in hi own name. He employs the Ajax Realty Company to sell the lot for $16,000. Mary Richards, a licensed salesperson, procures a buyer at the listed price and the deal is closed. Smith refuses to pay a commission on the grounds of infancy. Which of the following can recover a commission?

    a. Ajax Realty Company.
    b. Mary Richards.
    c. Ajax Realty and Mary Richards in joint action.
    d. No one.

59. The broker's fiduciary relationship with his principal requires that:

    a. He act as a responsible and prudent person.
    b. He discuss all angles of each deal with his salesmen.
    c. He act in the highest and best interest of his client.
    d. He act commensurate with his compensation.

60. To be enforceable a listing must be signed by:

    a. Broker.
    b. Seller.
    c. Buyer
    d. Tenant.

61. A broker receives an offer to purchase upon a form which states, "This offer shall remain open irrevocably for a period of five days." On the third day, the prospective buyer notifies the broker he does not want the property and requests the return of his earnest money deposit. The broker should:

    Ans.
    a.

    a. Return the deposit to the buyer.
    b. Inform the buyer he must wait the full five days to see if the seller accepts.
    c. Notify the buyer he must go through with the deal.
    d. None of these.

62. Ethics most nearly means:

    Ans.
    c.

    a. Observing usual closing hours of other businesses.
    b. Belonging to the proper civic clubs and community projects.
    c. Observing duties to his clients, colleges and public.
    d. None of these.

63. There are two ways of determining the amount of commission a broker is to receive. One of these is:

    Ans.
    e.

    a. By overage.
    b. By time and effort.
    c. By provision of the real estate license law.
    d. By diligence.
    e. By agreement.

64. The second way is:

    Ans.
    a.

    a. Upon a quantum meruit basis.
    b. Arbitration.
    c. Decision of the local real estate board.
    d. None of these.

65. A broker receives a deposit on a sale from the buyer. The deposit is held in the broker's escrow account. The seller was unable to convey good title. The buyer demanded a refund of his deposit, which is the same amount as the broker's commission and claimed by the broker, as his commission. Under these circumstances:

    Ans.
    c.

    I. The buyer can sue the seller and broker for his deposit.
    II. The broker should file an interpleader for his commission.
        a. I only.
        b. II only.
        c. Both I and II.
        d. Neither I or II.

66. Bright listed a vacant lot for sale with Boyd, who procured a social group, The Supreme Social Society, as buyer. Both the president and treasurer had criminal records. As a courtesy to his neighbors, Bright refused to sell. Boyd then produced Brown, who was introduced as a retired doctor, interested in building a medical clinic. After agreements were signed, Bright discovered that Brown was a "front" for Elite and refused to convey title. Boyd sued for his commission. Under these circumstances:

    Ans.
    d.

    I. Boyd can recover from Bright.

    II. Boyd can recover from Brown.

       a. I only.

       b. II only.

       c. Both I and II.

       d. Neither I or II.

67. Suit for a real estate commission can only be brought by:

       a. Salesperson of the listing broker, who made the sale.

       b. Cooperating broker, who produced the prospect.

       c. The listing Broker.

       d. The salesperson of the cooperating broker, who assisted in the necessary financing.

Ans. c.

68. Johns, a neighbor of Stone, a licensed broker, tells Stone on December 15, 1991, that his brother-in-law is interested in buying a home in the same neighborhood. Stone sells him a listed home within three days. In appreciation, Stone can:

    I. Offer the purchaser's wife $500, as a Christmas gift.

    II. Purchase a membership for the husband in a neighborhood tennis club.

       a. I only.

       b. II only.

       c. Both I and II.

       d. Neither I or II.

Ans. d.

69. A broker, upon showing a client's property to a prospect, should:

       a. Make an office memorandum.

       b. Confirm the interview by a memo to the buyer.

       c. Notify the seller of the prospect's identity.

       d. Wait until the prospect makes the deal with the owner.

Ans. c.

70. A net listing contract:

       a. Generally favors the owner.

       b. Generally favors the broker.

       c. Is void as against public policy.

       d. Usually prevents a sale of the listed property.

Ans. b.

71. Brown, a broker, represents to a young couple with two grade school children, that the grade school is only two short blocks away. Actually, the school is scheduled to be closed in September and become part of a grade school district, with the new school about 1 miles distant. The buyers learn this in August, after the deal is closed.

       a. The buyers have no remedy.

       b. The broker will be liable for transportation charges to and from school.

       c. The buyers can rescind the deal.

       d. Obtain a refund of part of the selling price.

Ans. c.

72. A salesperson, enroute to a sample house with a prospect, suffers injuries in an automobile accident. He is:

    a. Protected for injuries against his broker, under the workman compensation laws.
    b. He is not so protected.
    c. He can recover for his injuries under any accident policy he carries personally.
    d. He can recover unemployment compensation against his employer for the period he is unable to work.

Ans.
a.

73. The Winthrop Clinic offers to pay a commission to Neil Smith, if he could purchase an adjacent lot, which they desired for parking. Smith obtains a listing and a sale is made to Helen Miller, a secretary to the clinic's manager. Three days later she conveys the lot to the clinic. In a claim for commission:

    a. Smith can recover from the clinic.
    b. Smith can recover from the lot owner.
    c. Smith can recover from both the clinic and the lot owner.
    d. Smith can recover from no one.

Ans.
d.

74. Broker Stone showed a number of properties to Ann Simon. On seeing one of the properties, she told Stone that she had already seen the property with Broker Wolf. She contacted Wolf about three weeks later and signed an agreement of sale. Stone contacted Wolf and Mrs. Simon and demanded one-half of the commission.

    a. Stone can recover one-half of the commission from Wolf.
    b. Stone can recover one-half of the commission from Mrs. Simon.
    c. Stone can recover a full commission from the lot owner.
    d. Stone cannot recover from anyone.

Ans.
d.

75. Whether to keep the forfeited earnest money, resell the property, or sue the buyer for specific performance, where the buyer defaults, is a matter to be decided by:

    a. Broker
    b. Salesperson.
    c. Court.
    d. Seller.

Ans.
d.

76. The broker must obey all instructions made known to him by his principal. Should the principal instruct the broker to violate the law, the broker should:

    a. Do as instructed.
    b. Not do as instructed.
    c. Withdraw from the transaction.
    d. Sue the principal.
    e. Do nothing.

Ans.
c.

If an option is drawn, satisfactory to the seller, the broker is entitled to a commission of:

    a. 7 percent of the option price for the property.
    b. 10 percent of the option price for the property.
    c. 7 percent of the amount paid for the option.
    d. Nothing.

Ans.
d.

77. An owner converts a three-story dwelling into six apartments, in violation of the zoning law. The owner lists the property for sale with a broker for $125,000. Should the broker list the property?

    a. List the property at $125,000.
    b. Refuse to list the property.
    c. Suggest the owner list the property at $100,000.
    d. Obtain a buyer at $125,000 and have the owner apply for a variation permit from the Zoning Board or Board of Adjustments.

Ans.
b.

78. Broker Martin advertised a dwelling for rent at $240 per month. A prospect inquired and wanted to see the property immediately. Martin was too busy at the time, so he gave the prospect a key to the premises and demanded a $10 deposit for its return. Later, it was discovered that an air conditioning unit was missing, worth $350.

    a. Martin is liable for the loss.
    b. Martin is not liable for the loss.
    c. The loss will be made up out of the first two months rent.
    d. No commission will be due on any lease negotiated by Martin during the first year.

Ans.
a.

79. The terms of a written exclusive listing is 60 days, and calls for a 7 percent commission. At the expiration of the term, the owner at the request of the broker, orally extends its duration for one month. During that month, the broker brings a prospect, who purchases the property. The owner refuses to pay a commission, claiming that the extension was not in writing. Broker sues.

    a. The broker cannot recover.
    b. The broker can recover.
    c. The broker can recover on a quantum meruit basis.
    d. The broker can recover from buyer and seller.

Ans.
b.

80. If a net listing specifies the broker's commission, it is:

    a. Void.
    b. Voidable.
    c. Valid.
    d. Unenforceable.

Ans.
c.

81. An attorney in fact is the holder of:

    a. A certificate as an attorney at law.
    b. Power of attorney.
    c. Appointment by the court.
    d. Decree from a court.

Ans.
b.

82. Two rival brokers claim the commission in a real estate transaction. It should be paid to:

    a. The broker with whom the property was first listed.
    b. The broker who was the procuring cause of the sale.
    c. The broker who makes the first claim.
    d. None of these.

Ans.
b.

83. Horn, a salesperson, had access to a number of property listings during his employment by Denton. Upon leaving Denton's employ to work for Hartman, a competitor, Horn takes the listings to Hartman. Horn is guilty of:

    I. Conversion.
    II. Larceny.
        a. I only.
        b. II only.
        c. Both I and II.
        d. Neither I or II.

Ans. b.

84. Gold gives Silver, a broker, an oral listing on his residence. Silver obtains Brass, a buyer, upon Gold's terms. The agreement contains Silver's name as a witness to Brass' signature, and also a notation in the lower left hand corner "Silver" broker. The state of Nebraska requires a listing to be in writing. Silver sues for a commission. Can he recover?

        a. Yes.
        b. No.
        c. He can sue the buyer.
        d. He can sue seller and buyer.

Ans. a.

85. Helen Meyers gave an exclusive right to sell to Jack Erler, broker, on a farm property at $4,000 per acre, or on any terms acceptable to the owner. The listing was for three years with commission of 10 percent of the selling price. Two years later, the owner sold the property to Dawson, who had been shown the property by Erler 14 months earlier. The sale was at $3500 per acre. In the suit the court held:

        a. That the three-year listing was an unreasonable restraint on alienation.
        b. Erler could only recover his expenses.
        c. Erler could recover his full 10 percent commission.
        d. Erler could recover on a quantum meruit basis.

Ans. c.

86. A real estate salesperson may legally receive an extra commission on a difficult sale from:

        a. An appreciative seller.
        b. The broker-employer.
        c. The mortgage finance company.
        d. A thankful buyer.

Ans. b.

87. In accepting a note as a deposit from a buyer, the broker should:

        a. Assume personal responsibility for payment of the note.
        b. Place the note in a safety deposit box.
        c. State in the agreement that the deposit is in the form of a note.
        d. Discount the note with his bank to obtain cash.

Ans. c.

88. Salesperson Sloan is licensed under broker Klaus but wants to work for broker Fair, so he:

        a. May start selling for Fair as soon as he places his license on display in Fair's office.
        b. May start selling as soon as he notifies the Real Estate Commission of the change.
        c. May start selling if Klaus writes the Commission that he has no objections to the transfer.
        d. May start selling for Fair as soon as the Real Estate Commission has reissued his license to Fair.

Ans. d.

89. The REALTOR® Code of Ethics recommends an:

    a. Open listing.
    b. Exclusive listing.
    c. Net Listing.
    d. Parol listing.

Ans.
b.

90. A salesperson can buy property listed with his broker if:

    a. He takes title in the name of another person.
    b. He takes title in the name of his broker, in trust for the salesperson.
    c. He discloses his intentions to the seller.
    d. He notifies the Real Estate Commission in advance.

Ans.
c.

91. Under the usual employment contract, a broker is entitled to a commission when:

    a. The deal is consummated.
    b. He produces a ready, willing and able buyer, upon the seller's terms, even though the seller refuses to sign the agreement of sale.
    c. He produces a ready and willing buyer at the listing price, subject to a purchase money mortgage.
    d. None of these.

Ans.
b.

92. A broker owes certain duties to his principal. Which one of the following is not included:

    a. Loyalty to his principal.
    b. Must obey instructions.
    c. Maintain the property.
    d. Account for money and property.

Ans.
c.

93. A broker is asked to prepare an agreement of sale and deed for seller and buyer, for which he makes a charge of $35.00. The broker can legally:

    a. Charge the seller only.
    b. Charge the buyer only.
    c. Charge both buyer and seller.
    d. Charge neither buyer or seller.

Ans.
d.

94. A broker negotiates a sale, for which he is paid a commission. He prepares the deed and handles the closing. For these additional services, he may charge:

    a. The seller.
    b. The buyer.
    c. Both buyer and seller.
    d. Neither buyer or seller.

Ans.
d.

95. Ruth Stevens, owner, leased a property to the Sun Ray Oil Company, through Stone, a broker. The lease contained a "first right of refusal clause." Later she listed the property for sale with Stone, who procured a purchaser, Lemore, at $275,000. An agreement of sale was signed by the owner and the purchaser, Mr. Lemore, which provided that if Sun Ray exercised its right to purchase at the same price, the agreement with Lemore was to be null and void. Sun Ray exercised its right to purchase at $275,000. Stone sued for a commission:

Ans.
a.

a. Stone can recover from Stevens.

b. Stone cannot recover from Stevens.

c. Stone can recover from Stevens and Sun Ray.

d. Stone cannot recover from anyone.

96. A broker's listing may not be terminated by the owner before its expiration date, where:

Ans.
c.

a. The broker negotiated the sale to the owner.

b. The broker advertised the property.

c. The agency is coupled with an interest.

d. The owner desires to list the property with a more active real estate firm.

97. Awarding a bonus to the salesperson producing the highest volume of sales during the year is:

Ans.
b.

a. A violation of real estate law.

b. A good incentive.

c. Contrary to public policy.

d. Invalid if paid in cash.

Appendix D
A STUDY OF DEEDS

QUESTIONS AND ANSWERS

1. Allen conveyed a 200-acre farm to Bell in 1988, "reserving to himself, his heirs and assigns, a certain right of way over the rear of the farm." Allen never used the right of way, and upon his death in 1992, his farm, which adjoined the farm sold to Bell, was inherited by the son, John Allen. In 1992, John sold the inherited farm to Chester. When Chester attempted to use the right of way, he was stopped by Bell. Chester filed suit for an injunction. Decide who will win.

Ans.
Chester will win. Mere nonuse of an easement, created by a deed, however long continued, does not create an abandonment.

2. A grantor executed a deed to property to the Secretary of the Department of Housing and Urban Redevelopment. The deed was delivered to the grantor's attorney "to be held by him." The property was destroyed by fire, and the next day the deed was recorded, presumably by the grantor's attorney. In a suit to determine who is entitled to the insurance proceeds, who will win?

Ans.
The grantor since he was the owner of the property at the time of the fire. Delivery to the *grantor's attorney* did not constitute delivery to the grantee.

3. Discuss the nature or form of an encumbrance.

Ans.
An encumbrance can be in the nature of an easement or restriction, which affects the *title*, or it may be in the nature of an easement or restriction, which affects the physical condition of the property.

4. A grantor executed a deed but did not deliver it to the grantee. He told several neighbors and tradespeople that he had sold the farm. He referred several customers for farm produce to the grantee, as owner. Is the absence of delivery of the deed, in this case, fatal to transfer of the title?

Ans.
No. The statement he had made to so many people that he has sold the property, coupled with the execution of the deed to the grantee, showed an *intention* to transfer title: *Scroggins v. Roper,* 548 P. 2d. 779 (Tex. Civ. App. 1977).

5. The premises of a deed contain the names of parties, consideration, description, the "have and to hold" clause, and the recital clause. What element has been omitted?

Ans.

The operative clause (granting).

6. What words are required to create an appurtenant easement rather than an easement in gross?

Ans.

The words "his, (her, or their) heirs and assigns.

7. Earl Homes deeded his farm property to his son, Jon, on February 15, 1987. The deed was never recorded. Earl Homes died in 1989 and Jon died on May 16, 1988, leaving a will in which he devised the farm to his wife, Mary. Mary desires to sell the farm to Henry Simms. A question now arises, because the Earl Homes deed was never recorded. Can Mary give good title to Simms?

Ans.

Yes, in the absence of any recorded judgment or mortgage against the prior owners.

8. A light industrial use of property was established in 1979. In 1982, a zoning ordnance was enacted, changing the zoning to single or multiple family dwellings. In 1987, the building was destroyed by fire. In 1988, the owner decides to rebuild and use the factory. He applies to the city for a building permit, which is refused, He sues. Decide who will win.

Ans.

The municipality will win based on *Goldfarb v. Dietz*, 506 P. ed. 1322 (Wash. App. 1973). The nonconforming use is barred.

9. A certain subdivision contains a restrictive covenant, prohibiting structures of a temporary nature. A purchase bought a lot an attempted to install a mobile home upon concrete blocks, resting on three steel I-beams. The subdivider objected. Was this mobile home in violation of the restriction?

Ans.

Yes. The house was not actually attached to the foundation and could be moved. Accordingly, it was a temporary structure.

10. Is it necessary for the grantee to sign the deed?

Ans.

No. Acceptance of the deed by the grantee is sufficient.

11. What is meant by "curative statute" in reference to a deed?

Ans.

An act of the legislature to validate defective acknowledgements.

12. A deed is written with a life interest to Adam, and upon Adam's death, the property vests in Bennett. What is Bennett's interest in the property called?

Ans.

A remainderman.

13. Which is preferable—a general warranty deed or a special warranty deed?

Ans.
A general warranty deed, because the grantor protects the grantee against the world; whereas in a special warranty deed, the grantor limits his protection to anyone claiming under him or through him.

14. What kind of warrantee does a grantor make in a quite claim deed?

Ans.
None.

15. What does real property include?

Ans.
Lands, tenements, and hereditaments.

16. What is meant by tenements and hereditaments?

Ans.
Tenements include land and anything affixed permanently to the land such as a building. Hereditaments include lands, tenements, and things of an incorporeal nature, such as a right of way.

17. Do all titles emanate by patent from the U.S. Government?

Ans.
No. In the 13 original states, title originated from the Proprietor (Under grants from the King of England) or from the sovereign states.

18. Under a fee simple deed, what is the legal concept of land which a purchaser acquires?

Ans.
The surface land, to and indefinite extent upwards and down to the center of the earth.

19. How would you define a property right?

Ans.
The right to enjoy lands and chattels to the exclusion of all others.

20. Into what two classes is property divided?

Ans.
Real and personal.

21. Into what two classes can real property be divided?

Ans.
Corporeal (lands and buildings) and incorporeal realty such as easements and right of ways.

22. Name four ways in which good title to real property can be obtained.

Ans.
Deed, Will, Adverse Possession, and Eminent Domain.

23. What estate is of potentially indefinite duration and fully transferable and inheritable.

Ans.
Fee Simple.

24. What is meant by merchantable title?

Ans.
A title free of nay defects or clouds and one which a buyer is bound to accept.

25. Name four types of legal descriptions of land.

Ans.
(1) Rectangular survey, (2) metes and bounds, (3) monuments, and (4) recorded map—lot and block number.

26. Name at least three classifications of estates.

Ans.
(1) Inheritance, (2) life, (3) life, and (4) at will.

27. When real estate is held in the husband's name, why is it necessary for the wife to join the husband in deeding the property to another?

Ans.
To extinguish her dowry right.

28. What is meant by government patent?

Ans.
Original and initial conveyance of real property from the United States government to individuals, or from a state to an individual.

29. What defect is there in the following property description:
"Property next to Marvel Gasoline Station, City Limits, Andrews County, Texas, official records in Recorder's office of Andrews County, also known as 500 block on Main Street in the City."

Ans.
The name of the city does not appear.

30. Who are the parties to a deed?

Ans.
The grantor, and the grantee.

31. Real estate ownership is said to consist of a "bundle of rights." Name six rights.

Ans.
(1) To lease, (2) to sell, (3) to will, (4) to regain possession at the end of a lease—reversion, (5) to build thereon—destroy improvements, maintain, control use within the law, and (6) To mortgage.

32. What is a quit claim deed?

Ans.
A deed used to clear clouds on a title. The operative words are "remise, release, and quit claim."

33. What does the work "Title" mean when referring to property?

Ans.
Title is evidence of ownership in land.

34. Why is it necessary for a deed to be in writing?

Ans.
Statute of Frauds.

35. For what purpose is a special warranty deed generally used?

Ans.
It is the usual form for transferring a tax title. It is also used by fiduciaries or trustees in conveying real estate.

36. What are the principal types of deeds used in real estate transfers?

Ans.
General Warranty Deed, Quite Claim Deed, and Special Warranty Deed.

37. What are the two most common methods of title closing?

Ans.
Escrow and delivery of deed.

38. Is a date essential to the validity of a deed?

Ans.
No. It indicates the time when the deed was delivered. It is only prima facie evidence: i.e., appears to be sufficient to establish the time of delivery but may be rebutted by stronger proof.

39. Is a deed dated on Sunday void?

Ans.
Not if delivered on a weekday.

40. Is consideration necessary in a deed?

Ans.
Yes. Good or valuable consideration.

41. Is $1.00 or nominal consideration valid?

Ans.
Yes. Courts do not inquire into the adequacy or inadequacy of the consideration.

42. What parties have limited or qualified rights to a contract?

Ans.
Infants, insane persons, corporations, and aliens.

43. Is a deed from a husband to a wife valid where the husband has been made the defendant in a lawsuit involving substantial sums of money?

Ans.
No. Any conveyance made with the intent to disturb, delay, hinder, or defraud creditors may be set aside as fraudulent.

44. Is a joint estate the same as an estate by the entireties?

Ans.
An estate by the entireties, which may be held by husband and wife, enjoys advantages over joint tenancy. In some states, husband and wife hold as joint tenants, similar to estate by the entireties.

45. What are the "appurtenances" in a deed?

Ans.
Rights that pass as incidental to the premises—something necessary for the enjoyment of the land, for instance, a right of way.

46. What are the husband's rights in a wife's property called?

Ans.
Curtsey rights.

47. Is a deed by a married woman for her own property valid, void, or voidable?

Ans.
Valid in most states, but void in others, unless she has been declared a "femme sole."

48. Who is a "femme sole?"

Ans.
A single woman or a married woman who has been declared by court decree as such, where her husband has deserted her or is a drunkard, or there is other good cause.

49. What are the advantages of an estate by the entireties?

Ans.
(1) Upon the death of one party the property vests to the surviving spouse.
(2) No probate or court proceedings is necessary.
(3) Property is not subject to inheritance tax.
(4) A judgment against one spouse will not be a lien.

50. What is the difference in "joint tenancy" and "tenancy in common?"

Ans.
In joint tenancy, where one party dies, the property vests to the other. In tenancy in common, the parties are considered as being possessed of the whole of an undivided part, upon death of one, his interests goes to his heirs.

51. What are the purposes of the acknowledgement?

Ans.
(1) The deed will be accepted as prima facie evidence in any court proceeding.
(2) The deed may be recorded.

52. Jones conveys certain properties to Brown and Smith as joint tenants, and not as tenants in common. Subsequently, Brown dies, and Smith claims the property. Brown's son claims title to the same property. Who will win?

Ans.
Smith, the survivor. The deed to Smith and Brown expressly created a joint tenancy.

53. What is a tax deed?

Ans.
A deed issued for property which has been sold for taxes.

54. Is a title that is acquired by purchase at a treasurer's sale for unpaid municipal taxes, good and marketable?

Ans.
No. The owner still has the right of redemption.

55. White conveys property to Smith and Jones as joint tenants. Can Smith sell his interest to Green? If so, would Green become a joint owner with Jones?

Ans.
Smith can sell or alienate his interest in the property to Green. Green does not become a joint owner with Jones, but Jones and Green now hold the property as tenants in common. (Alabama, Indiana, North Carolina, Pennsylvania, and Texas)

56. Name three types of encumbrances which might cloud the title to real estate.

Ans.
Unpaid taxes, a judgment, or a right of way.

57. Where are deeds to real estate officially recorded?

Ans.
In the office of the Recorder of Deeds, or Register of Deeds.

58. Does an abstract of title guarantee a clear title?

Ans.
No. It merely gives a summary as to the conditions of the title and the abstractor's opinion.

59. What is the purpose of a correction deed?

Ans.
It corrects an error in a previously recorded deed. This is usually done with a quit claim deed containing explanations.

60. Is it correct to state that a lease on a property being sold constitutes an encumbrance?

Ans.
Yes.

61. What are the dangers in not having a deed recorded promptly?

Ans.
(1) The deed may be lost or destroyed.
(2) Judgments may be entered against the former owner, which would constitute a valid lien.
(3) The previous owner might mortgage the property to someone else, who by his recording would have priority.

62. What is included in the execution of a deed?

Ans.
The signing, sealing, witnessing, and acknowledgement of the instrument.

63. Is it necessary for the grantor, himself, to sign the deed?

Ans.
No. It can be signed by an attorney in fact.

64. If the grantor cannot write, how should the deed the deed be signed?

Ans.
The grantor should make his mark in the presence of witnesses and the grantor's name should be appended by someone for him. Two witnesses are required.

65. Can a grantor later repudiate a deed because he is illiterate and could not read the instrument?

Ans.
No. The burden is upon the grantor to have someone read the deed to him, unless fraud has been practiced on the grantor.

66. What information does the acknowledgement contain?

Ans.
The venue (State and County), the name of the grantor and his marital status, the signature of the person taking the acknowledgement and his official title, expiration of his office, and the office seal.

67. Must the grantor appear in person before the officer taking the acknowledgement?

Ans.
Yes.

68. When should a proxy or power of attorney be used?

Ans.
Only in rare circumstances, where the grantor does not want to sign the deed in advance of the closing. The attorney in fact, must be a person of high trust.

69. When does title to the property pass to the grantee or his agent?

Ans.
When the deed is delivered to the grantee or his agent.

70. What kinds of delivery are there?

Ans.
(1) Delivery absolute where the deed is given to the grantee or his agent.
(2) Delivery in escrow, where the deed is handed over to a third person to be held until performance of some act by one of the parties.

71. Arthur delivers a deed in escrow to Cox until certain items in the title are cleared up. The purchaser, Bell, turns over the consideration price at the same time to the escrow agent, Cox. Two days later Arthur notifies Cox to return Bell's money to Bell and return the deed to Arthur. Must Cox comply with these instructions?

Ans.

No. Once the deed is delivered to the escrow agent and the conditions of the delivery is specified, the grantor is powerless to recall it.

72. Anthony executes a deed to Burger and delivers it to Conway, to be delivered to Burger upon the death of Anthony. Will Burger get good title upon the death of Anthony?

Ans.

Yes. If the title does not pass until Anthony's death, it cannot do so at the death. This would seem to defeat Anthony's purpose. But the law comes to the rescue and considers the passing of title as "relating back to the date of delivery," which was, of course, prior to Anthony's death. This is known as the doctrine of relation. When finally delivered to the grantee, it operates from the date of the first delivery, which was prior to Anthony's death.

73. Jones executes a deed to Brown and Jones records it. Later Jones seeks to set aside the conveyance, claiming that there has been no delivery to Brown. Will he succeed?

Ans.

No. Delivery is presumed at recording.

74. Is it necessary to have the deed recorded?

Ans.

As grantor and grantee, the title passes upon delivery and it is not necessary to record it. However, in order to protect the grantee against a lien or subsequent deed by the grantor for the same property, the law requires the grantee to record the deed. This constitutes constructive notice.

75. Adams delivers a deed to Black on December 6, 1991, which Black records on January 21, 1992. Adams deeds the same property to Clark on January 14, 1992; Clark records the deed the same day. Who owns the property?

Ans.

Clark. The person who gets his deed recorded first is deemed the owner.

76. Williams owns two parcels of real estate. A house is built on one tract, with the cornice encroaching upon the other. Williams sells the other tract to James. Nothing is mentioned in the deed about the encroachment. Later James notifies Williams that he is trespassing by the encroachment and demands that he remove the objectionable cornice. Will James succeed?

Ans.
No. Williams has an implied easement in James' land to the extent of the encroachment. The condition was open, visible, continuous, and permanent at the time James purchased the property and accordingly, he takes it subject to the existing condition. If the house were destroyed by fire or other cause, Williams could not rebuild so as to continue the encroachment.

77. What are the granting words or operative clauses used in a deed to pass a fee simple title?

Ans.
Grant and convey.

78. Adams, without Clark's consent, uses a shortcut across Clark's farm. From time to time, Clark places an obstruction across the path, which Adams removes. The use, under these conditions, continues for 21 years. Clark now erects a cable fence across the path and Adams takes legal action to prevent Clark's interference with his use of the right of way. Who will win?

Ans.
Adams. In order to defeat the statute of adverse possession, Clark's interference or objection must be effective. Since the barriers during the 21-year period were not effective in preventing the use, Adams will win. Clark should have obtained a court decree enjoining the trespass.

79. In 1980, an owner made a contract with the owner of an adjoining residence for the joint use of an automobile driveway, half of which lay on each lot. In 1985, the owner made a contract to sell and convey his lot free of all encumbrances. When the title was searched, the joint user's agreement, which had been recorded, came to light. Under these circumstances, would the buyer have the right to refuse to go through with the deal?

Ans.
Yes. The joint driveway is an easement, constituting an encumbrance within the meaning of the term.

80. Adams, residing in Dade County, Florida, owns a lot in Broward County. Adams asks where he must legally record the deed to his lot.

Ans.
In Broward County. Recordation must be in the county where the property is located.

81. Harris conveys certain real estate to his son John "for and during the grantee's life." What kind of estate does John obtain?

Ans.
A life estate.

82. A deed is executed by Alfred Simms to the First Presbyterian Church, of which he is a member. The Church is not incorporated. Does the church obtain good title?

Ans.
No. The deed is void because the grantee is incapable of taking title to real estate.

83. What is meant by a "homestead?"

Ans.
The homestead consists of a dwelling in which the claimant resides, together with outbuildings and the land on which the same are situated. Declaration of homestead must be filed in the Recorder's Office.

84. What advantage accrues to homestead property?

Ans.
Such property is protected from execution and foreclosure sale against most creditors.

85. What claims will not be defeated by a homestead?

Ans.
(1) Judgments which become liens before the homestead is recorded.
(2) Mechanic's liens for work and materials furnished upon the premises.
(3) Mortgage and trust deeds recorded before the declaration of the homestead.
(4) Mortgages and trust deeds executed and acknowledged by husband and wife or by an unmarried owner.

86. How may a homestead be terminated?

Ans.
By conveyance or recorded instrument of abandonment.

87. What is the difference between (1) an abstract of title, (2) a certificate of title, and (3) a title insurance policy?

Ans.
(1) An abstract of title is a document setting forth a brief synopsis of all matters of record affecting the title to the real estate in question.
(2) A certificate of title gives the net results of the title examination, showing the name of the owner and the encumbrances and defects of title as of the date of the certificate.
(3) Title insurance insures the title in a given name, subject to noted exceptions and encumbrances listed in the policy, and renders the insurer liable to compensate the insured for loss arising from errors of search and legal interpretation, in an amount not exceeding that stated in the policy.

88. Helen is married to Michael. The property is in Michael's name only. Should Helen sign the agreement and deed?

Ans.
Yes. She should sign the agreement so that she is compelled to sign the deed. Signing the deed extinguishes her dower right.

89. What is the bulk sales law and what is its purposes?

Ans.
It is a law that requires the seller of certain personal property to give a list of the outstanding obligations prior to the completion of the sale and that creditors be notified of the sale. It is intended to protect the purchaser of certain types of personal property, such as merchandise purchased in bulk, and arises frequently in connection with the sale of businesses.

90. For the purpose of legal description of urban real estate, how is land usually divided?

Ans.
In lots, blocks and plan of lots or lots of recorded subdivisions listed by name.

91. Is the street address of a property one and the same thing as "legal description?"

Ans.
No.

92. Adams owns a tract of land which is traversed by a stream of water. The source of the stream is a spring-fed lake about two miles distant. Baker owns land between the lake and Adam's tract. Baker diverts the stream in order to make a pond about 1/4 mile away from the stream channel. Adams learns of Baker's diversion and gets an injunction against Baker prohibiting his action. Will the injunction stand?

Ans.
Yes. An upper owner merely has a usufructuary right. He may not divert the stream from its natural course so as to deprive a lower owner of his right of use.

93. An electric light company has the right of way to erect poles and run its lines along the rear five feet of a lot. What sort of property right is this?

Ans.
An easement.

94. A tract of land was settled by Miller, who lived on it for nine consecutive years. Due to conditions of health, he moved away for a six-year period. He then moved back to the same land and occupied it for six more years. At the end of this period, or 21 years from his first occupancy, he claimed title by adverse possession. Will he succeed?

Ans.
No. The possession must be continuous. Since he moved away for six years, the continuity is broker, which is fatal to his claim.

95. A deed of farmland describes the land as running from a certain defined point 900 feet to the Revolutionary chestnut tree. The tree in question has long been identified and known in the neighborhood as such. The actual distance to this tree is 987 feet. Is the purchaser entitled to 987 feet or 900 feet?

Ans.
987 feet. In reconciling distances in a deed with distances shown by monuments upon the ground, the latter govern.

96. Where a single woman owns real estate and sells the property after marriage, how should the deed refer to her as grantor?

Ans.
"Mary Steel," formerly "Mary Stone." The notarial acknowledgement should read the same.

97. If a warranty deed has been executed and delivered to a purchaser, is it necessary to have it recorded in order to make it a valid conveyance?

Ans.
No.

98. May a life estate be sold?

Ans.
Yes. The purchaser would hold during the life of the grantor (per autre vie).

99. Who is the legal owner of a piece of property when the deed to it is to be delivered but not recorded?

Ans.
The grantee (purchaser).

100. Is there a difference in making a deed "under and subject to a mortgage" and in making a deed "under and subject to a mortgage, which the grantee assumes and agrees to pay?"

Ans.
Yes. In the first case the grantee does not *personally* assume any obligation to pay the debt; in the second case, he does and would be personally liable for any deficiency judgment.

101. A deed is signed in blank by an owner and left with a broker, with the request that the broker make the best deal possible. The broker sells the property to a friend at a lower than market price. Is the deed valid?

Ans.
Yes. The deed is good unless there was some "connivance" between broker and buyer.

102. At a closing, a seller refuses to pay a broker's commission and demands that the deal be closed. Can the closing officer ignore the broker's claim and disburse the funds?

Ans.
Yes. The broker has only a collateral interest in the deal between buyer and seller.

103. What are five governmental limitations on land?

Ans.
(1) Police Power
(2) Eminent domain
(3) Zoning
(4) Taxation
(5) Escheat

104. Can a United States Consul in England, take an acknowledgement to a deed of property in the United States?

Ans.
Yes.

105. Why is it necessary to have an examination of title to a particular property?

Ans.
In order to ascertain if the owner received good title from his predecessor owner, and on back through previous ownerships. Also it is necessary to ascertain if there are nay clouds on the title.

106. What do you understand by ownership in fee simple?

Ans.
It is the highest and most complete ownership.

107. Adams purchased a property from Bell. The deed gave Bell, the seller, and his family use of a swimming pool. Later Adams sold the property to Crane, who notified Bell that his family could no longer use the pool. Crane now seeks injunctive relief to prevent Bell from using the pool. Will he succeed?

Ans.
Yes. Bell had only an easement *in gross*, which was personal to Bell's family, as long as Adams owned the property. Upon sale of the property to Crane, Bell's right to use the pool terminated.

108. What is the purpose of a lis pendens proceeding?

Ans.
It is to give effective notice to third parties of pendency of action affecting title to, or asserting mortgage or lien on, real property.

True and False   Answer

1. A deed that has been signed and delivered, but not acknowledged, does not pass title.   False

2. A remainderman and a life tenant are one and the same thing.   False

3. The optioner and the grantee in a real estate transaction are one and the same.   False

4. *Egress* means an exit from a tract of land.   True

5. A deed is recorded to give constructive notice to everyone.   True

6. A permitted license to use is an easement.   False

7. A life tenancy is a form of real estate ownership.   True

8. A wife does not have a dower right in property owned by her husband and another person, as joint tenants.   True

9. Real estate is more inclusive than real property.   False

10. Eminent domain is used more frequently in the 1970s than in the 1940s.   True

11. One party only signs the deed (grantor).   True

12. An oral deed coupled with possession and the making of improvements, is sufficient to pass title.   False

13. A marketable title is one free of liens and encumbrances.   True

14. Under a "government survey," a check is 24 by 24 miles on each side of a square.   True

15. In a tenancy in common, one person may own 1/5th interest and another person own a 4/5th interest.   True

16. When the tide water is a boundary in a deed, title to the ordinary high water mark is conveyed.   True

17. If Albert owns real estate, he can create a tenancy in common by conveying to Blake and undivided interest is such real estate.   True

18. Urban real estate is always described by sections.   False

19. A special warranty deed is preferable to a general warranty deed.   False

20. A quit claim deed may serve the same ends as a suit to quiet title. — False
21. Land with improvements thereon, is described as real property. — True
22. Fee simple is the greatest estate in real estate. — True
23. A deed signed on Sunday and delivered on Monday is invalid. — False
24. The original source of ownership for most land in the United States was in the form of a grant or patent. — True
25. In a recorded plan, a lot within the plan is usually described by metes and bounds. — False
26. There is no difference between a condominium and a co-operative apartment. — False
27. Delivery of a deed to the grantor's agent passes title to real estate. — False
28. A deed recites a consideration of $1.00; the actual selling price is $100,000. The deed is void because of fraud on the public in misrepresenting the selling price. — False
29. In joint ownership, if one of the parties dies, his interest goes to the surviving parties and not to the decedent's heirs. — True
30. A person under 21 years of age cannot hold title to real estate. — False
31. A deed takes effect only upon delivery. — True
32. In describing land by the metes and bounds method, a course described as being, "North 45° east" runs in a northeasterly direction. — True
33. Certain parts of a condominium ownership are held as tenants in common. — True
34. A typewritten signature to a deed is void. — True
35. In order to create a joint tenancy, there must be present four unities of time, title, interest, and possession. — True
36. A quit claim deed warrants and guarantees nothing. — True
37. A tenancy in common carries with it the right of survivorship. — False
38. A deed is recorded to give notice to the public that the party named in the deed has a vested right or interest in the property described. — True
39. A public utility company always has an easement in any property by act of the legislature. — False
40. It is proper to give a quit claim deed even though your interest in the property is negligible or questionable. — True
41. One who receives the deed is called the grantee. — False
42. Real estate taxes are levied only upon the owner's equity between the assessed value and the mortgage encumbrance. — False
43. The owner of real estate property becomes the grantor when he sells the property. — True
44. It is necessary to itemize in the deed all improvements affixed to the real estate being conveyed if they are to be sold with the property. — False
45. When a grantor faultily executes a deed, he can be compelled to sign a corrected deed. — True
46. A good title and a marketable title generally mean the same thing. — True
47. Metes and bounds is a system of land description by measure and direction. — True
48. A sheriff's deed is usually a warranty deed. — False
49. Real property in the name of the wife is presumed to be here separate property. — True

50. A deed to husband and wife creates an estate by the entireties.   True
51. Zoning restrictions and building restrictions are the same thing.   False
52. A habendum clause is essential in a deed in order to pass a valid title.   False
53. A deed need not be in writing if grantor and grantee appear before the   False
    County Recorder of deeds and swear that the transfer is voluntary and for
    consideration.
54. Joint tenants with rights of survivorship means literally that the building   False
    is being operated as a "joint" with police protection.
55. Title insurance guarantees the owner against all defects in title.   False
56. A judge of a court of record may take acknowledgements.   True
57. The law of caveat emptor has been strengthened through court decisions.   False
58. The recording of a deed to real property is the obligation of the grantee.   True
59. The full consideration in any real estate transaction must always be in legal   False
    tender.
60. A grantor impliedly warrants that he has a fee simple title to the property.   True
61. A purchaser at a foreclosure sale usually receives a bargain and sale deed.   False
62. Real property includes everything that is not personalty.   True
63. Tenements, in conveying title, refers to substandard structures.   False
64. The grantee in a deed is the same person that executes a mortgage on the   True
    property.
65. A septic tank system is a private sewage disposal system for individual homes.   True
66. Title by adverse possession is just as valid as a title by deed.   True
67. Real estate commissioners are authorized by the state licensing law to take   False
    acknowledgements.
68. A section of land contains 320 acres.   False
69. The consideration in an option is always applied to the purchase price, if   False
    the option is exercised.
70. Zoning regulations limit the uses of real estate.   True
71. A property may be transferred by a deed when the consideration is only   True
    love and affection.
72. A deed to partnership property sold by the partners need not have the   True
    joinder of the wives of the partners.
73. It is legal to describe a property by lot, block, and tract number if sold from   True
    a recorded plan.
74. The deed which is executed in a foreclosure sale is an Executor's Deed.   False
75. The ownership of real estate by two or more persons, each of whom has   True
    an undivided interest, without the "right of survivorship" is called a
    Tenancy in Common.
76. "Beneficiary," "Trustor," and "Trustee" are the legal designations of the   True
    parties to a trust deed.
77. A "conditional sales contract" on real property can be recorded only if it   False
    has been acknowledged by the buyer.
78. In a standard township, section 31 is located in the Southwest corner.   True
79. A deed must be recorded in the county where the property is located.   True
80. A grantor, who has improperly executed a deed, which has been recorded,   False
    cannot be required to execute a new deed.

81. Courts do not inquire into the sufficiency of the consideration price. True
82. A recital of title is essential to the validity of a deed. False
83. A deed executed in a foreign country should be acknowledged before a minister or consul of this country. True
84. Either parent, by operation of law, is duly authorized to execute a deed for a minor child. False
85. Building restrictions, as specified in a deed, are not encumbrances against the property. False
86. A corporation deed should always recite the resolution of the board of directors. True
87. A road through a private property used by another with the permission of the owner is an appurtenance. False
88. A sheriff's deed and a tax deed are the same as far as warranties are concerned. True
89. A covenant of seizin is the grantor's guarantee that he is the owner of the property and has the power to convey title thereto. True
90. Signing a deed does not transfer title. True
91. A fee simple estate and a fee simple absolute estate are the same thing. True
92. A quit claim deed by a husband need not be signed by the wife. False
93. Tenancy in common refers to ownership. True
94. Spot zoning is permissible in hardship cases. True
95. The habendum clause and the testimonium clause in a deed are similar and can be used interchangeably. False
96. A single man and a husband and wife may own property as joint tenants. True
97. Tenancy in common may be created by destruction of joint tenancy. False
98. Horizontal rows of townships are called tiers. True
99. Condominium ownership has greater safeguards to the individual owner than a co-operative apartment. True
100. Condominium ownership in this country is a relatively new type of ownership. True
101. An estate is the interest one has in property. True
102. A reconveyance deed is used in connection with a deed of trust. True
103. There are 20 acres included in the S 1/2 of the NW 1/4 of the SE 1/4 of a section of land. True
104. A devise of real estate may be changed by the maker of the will at any time before death. True
105. An oral gift of real estate to take effect after death, made in the presence of two disinterested witnesses, is valid. False
106. Delivery in escrow is where a deed to real estate is delivered to a third person pending the performance of some conditions. True
107. Harry Jones, a single man and Mary Jones, a married woman, may own property as joint tenants. True
108. The statute of frauds is the same as the truth in lending law. False
109. The grantor may impose restrictions as to the sale of real property to persons other than the Caucasian race. False
110. In recording a deed, it must be recorded in the city or town where the property is located. False

111. If you include the ancient grandfather's clock in the sale of your house, it becomes a part of the real estate.   False

112. Real property may be owned jointly by persons other than husband and wife.   True

113. A tax rate of one mill is the same as a rate of 1/10th of one percent of the assessed value.   True

114. Two or more persons may together own property in severalty.   False

115. A building permit, issued by a city, which violates a zoning law is a nullity.   True

116. A trust account serves the same purpose as an escrow account.   False

117. In an easement of a right of way, the servient tenement receives the benefit.   False

118. An easement in gross is appurtenant to the land.   False

119. An implied easement is enforceable.   True

120. An appurtenant easement offers more protection to a grantee than an easement in gross.   True

121. Constructive notice of ownership is given by the grantee's possession of the premises.   False

122. A single deed that contains a legal description of more than one property is invalid.   False

123. A landmark stated in a deed description would take precedence in reconciling a linear deed description.   True

124. Where three persons have acquired title to real estate and the deed does not state whether they are joint owners or tenants in common, the grantees would own the property equally, as tenants in common.   True

125. An estate by the entireties is real property owned by two members of the same family.   False

126. A deed to Henry Martin and Jane Martin, his wife, who are not actually married, always creates a tenancy in common.   False

Multiple Choice

1. There is an encroachment when the owner's property: Ans. c.

    a. Extends to the side area of adjoining property.

    b. Extends back a certain distance from the street line.

    c. Extends beyond the owner's survey lines.

    d. Contains more than 16 steps in the stairs to the basement.

2. Right to dower may be extinguished by: Ans. c.

    a. A subordination agreement.

    b. Deed in severance.

    c. Ante-nuptial agreement.

    d. Lease in perpetuity.

3. Zoning acts represent an exercise in police power of the state and are enacted in pursuance of: Ans. b.

    a. The common law.

    b. A state statute.

    c. A U.S. Supreme Court decision.

    d. A State Supreme Court edict.

4. A nonconforming use in zoning means which of the following:

    a. Not allowed to continue if the zoning ordnance is amended to prohibit its use.

    b. A continuing use for a certain number of years.

    c. Permitted to continue until use is abandoned, or building is destroyed.

Ans.
c.

5. Adams subdivided a tract of land into 40 lots. Each lot contained a reservation that no dwelling would be built costing less than $90,000. All lots have been sold and Adams is now subdividing a newly purchased tract of 40 acres, which will be restricted to $70,000 dwellings. Burns purchases a lot in the earlier subdivision, has made application for a building permit to erect a dwelling, costing $70,000. Under these circumstances:

    I. Adams can enjoin Burns in constructing the $70,000 home.
    II. Adams can collect damages for violation of the restriction.

        a. I only.
        b. II only.
        c. Both I and II.
        d. Neither I or II.

Ans.
d.

6. Three friends purchase a vacant tract of land for $100,000. Allen contributed $20,000, Blake contributed $30,000 and Clair contributed $50,000. The deed is made to George Allen, Frank Blake and William Clair. The three grantees are:

    a. Partners.
    b. Joint Tenants.
    c. Owners in common.
    d. Joint entrepreneurs.

Ans.
c.

7. Easement in gross is a:

    a. Privilege in the servient tenement.
    b. Personal privilege in land of another.
    c. One created by statute.
    d. Percentage of receipts paid as rent.

Ans.
b.

8. The United States Government Survey system is:

    a. Metes and bounds.
    b. Recorded plat.
    c. Rectangular survey system.
    d. None of these.

Ans.
c.

9. Bates conveyed a fee simple title to the Avon Baptist Church, by deed, to be use for church purposes only. Later the church abandons the property, due to environmental conditions. Title to the property will:

    a. Remain in the church.
    b. Escheat to the state.
    c. Revert to Bates.
    d. Be owned by the church and Bates as joint tenants.

Ans.
c.

10. Probate means an action to:

    a. Cure a defect by a quit claim deed.

    b. Prove title by adverse possession.

    c. Process a will, to establish its validity.

    d. Obtain access to a safety deposit box.

Ans. c.

11. The construction of a mobile home in a commercial use zone:

    a. Violates residential restrictions.

    b. Does not violate residential restrictions.

    c. Violates the city health code.

    d. Is a violation, per se.

Ans. b.

12. The voluntary transfer of title to real estate:

    a. Divestiture.

    b. Adverse possession.

    c. Alienation.

    d. Surrender.

Ans. c.

13. Trees on land become personal property when:

    a. Converted to lumber.

    b. The land is sold.

    c. Appropriated by eminent domain.

    d. Foreclosed on a mortgage.

Ans. a.

14. Which one of the following is not necessary for a valid transfer of title by real estate?

    a. Signing.

    b. Acknowledgement.

    c. Delivery.

    d. Recording.

Ans. d.

15. A man devised his residence to his widow and upon her death, it was to go to two of his three children. The widow received a:

    a. Life estate.

    b. Partial estate.

    c. Remainder estate.

    d. Leasehold.

Ans. a.

16. Real estate occupied as a home, by an owner, who enjoys special rights and privileges is:

    a. A freehold.

    b. A homestead.

    c. A joint tenancy.

    d. Unjust enrichment.

Ans. b.

17. The water table is the:

    a. Measure of water flow.

    b. Rate for cost of water.

    c. Depth where water is found.

    d. Average rainfall per month.

Ans. c.

18. An estate at will is: Ans.

    a. A form of co-ownership.   b.
    b. Tenancy of uncertain duration.
    c. Inheritance of property by will.
    d. Life estate.

19. Alice Nichols, a single woman, and Henry Steel, single, may not own real   Ans.
    estate as: c.

    a. Tenants in common.
    b. Joint tenants.
    c. Tenants by the entireties.
    d. Remainder devisee.

20. A conveyance is made to John Smith, his heirs, and assigns.   Ans.

    a. Smith has a life estate.   b.
    b. Smith has a fee estate.
    c. Smith's heirs have a remainder estate.
    d. Smith's heirs have a reversionary estate.

21. In order to record a deed, it must be in writing and: Ans.

    a. Signed by grantee.   c.
    b. Recite its actual purchase price.
    c. Acknowledged.
    d. Be free of all liens.

22. James Steel and Mary Steel, his daughter, buy a tract of ground for cash   Ans.
    and the property is deeded to them "with right of survivorship." James and a.
    Mary are:

    a. Joint tenants.
    b. Tenants by the entireties.
    c. Tenants in common.
    d. None of the above.

23. An estate of inheritance, or for life is known as: Ans.

    a. Freehold.   a.
    b. Less than a freehold.
    c. Greater than a freehold.
    d. None of these.

24. A wall erected on the line between two adjoining properties belonging to   Ans.
    different persons, which serves as an outside wall of both buildings is a: a.

    a. Party wall.
    b. Community wall.
    c. Line wall.
    d. Share wall.

25. A land description reading: The N 1/2 of the S 1/2 of the SW 1/4 of the   Ans.
    NW 1/4 contains: b.

    a. 15 acres.
    b. 10 Acres.
    c. 7 Acres.
    d. 20 Acres.

26. Land acquired by husband and wife by their labor after marriage in Arizona, California, Florida, and Texas is:

    a. Separate property.
    b. Real Property.
    c. Community property.
    d. None of these.

Ans. c.

27. The instrument which conditionally conveys title to real estate is a:

    a. Conditional bailment lease.
    b. Chattel mortgage.
    c. Mortgage.
    d. Land purchase contract.

Ans. c.

28. A means of acquiring title where the occupant has been in actual open, notorious, exclusive, and continuous occupation of property for the statuary period is known as:

    a. Reversion.
    b. Adverse Possession.
    c. Fee Simple.
    d. Fee absolute.

Ans. b.

29. The recording of a warranty deed:

    a. Passes title.
    b. Insures the title.
    c. Guarantees the title.
    d. Gives constructive notice of ownership.

Ans. d.

30. The four unities required for joint ownership are:

    a. Possession.
    b. Time.
    c. Husband and wife.
    d. Title.
    e. Location.
    f. Interest.

Ans. a, b, d & f.

31. The clause in a deed which sets forth or limits the extend of the interests in the title being conveyed is:

    a. The demising clause.
    b. The testimonial clause.
    c. The habendum clause.
    d. The indenture clause.

Ans. c.

32. A person who has property devised to him by a will is said to have acquired title by:

    a. Reversion.
    b. Inheritance.
    c. Adverse possession.
    d. None of these.

Ans. b.

33. A deed to be valid need not necessarily be:

    a. Signed.
    b. Written.
    c. Sealed.
    d. Delivered.

Ans. c.

34. By will, Calhoun devised his property to his daughter, Mary Calhoun, for
    life, and at her death to "her children." At Calhoun's death, Mary, 30 years
    of age and unmarried, deeds a fee simple estate to Davis. The title is:

    a. Valid.
    b. Invalid.
    c. Davis obtains a fee tail estate.
    d. Davis is a tenant.

    Ans.
    b.

35. The 1968 federal housing act relates to open housing and related
    mortgages. It deals with:

    I. Multiple listing associations.
    II. Racial discrimination.
    a. I Only.
    b. II only.
    c. Both I and II.
    d. Neither I or II.

    Ans.
    b.

36. A clause in a deed limiting the use and enjoyment of property is:
    I. A hereditament.

    II. A restriction.
    a. I only.
    b. II only.
    c. Both I and II.
    d. Neither I or II.

    Ans.
    b.

37. Describing land boundaries, setting forth the lines together with terminal
    points and angles, is termed description by:

    a. Acreage.
    b. Metes and bounds.
    c. Perimeter.
    d. Lot and block number.

    Ans.
    b.

38. A document which transfers possession of real property but does not
    transfer ownership is:

    a. A deed.
    b. A mortgage.
    c. A lease.
    d. A deposition.

    Ans.
    c.

39. The party to whom a deed conveys real estate is called:

    a. Grantee.
    b. Grantor.
    c. Beneficiary.
    d. Recipient.

    Ans.
    a.

40. The word "escrow" refers to:

    a. A young crow.
    b. Deposit of legal documents with a third party to be delivered upon
       the fulfillment of certain conditions.
    c. Deposits in a bank, subject to withdrawal by the depositor.
    d. Safe deposit box where a deed is placed.

    Ans.
    b.

41. An acquired legal privilege or right of use or enjoyment falling short of ownership which one may have in the land of another is known as:

    a. A devise.
    b. An abstract.
    c. An easement.
    d. A riparian right.

Ans.
c.

42. Property held in joint tenancy, upon the death of the other tenant, passes to the:

    a. Landlord.
    b. State.
    c. Heirs of the deceased.
    d. Surviving owner.

Ans.
d.

43. An absolute conveyance of property would be by:

    a. A quit claim deed.
    b. Assignment.
    c. Warranty deed.
    d. Deed of extinguishment.

Ans.
c.

44. Two persons, who contribute unequal shares of money for the purchase of property own it as:

    a. Joint tenants.
    b. Partners.
    c. Tenants in common.
    d. Tenants in severalty.

Ans.
c.

45. Which one of the following does not relate to lands and buildings?

    a. In rem.
    b. Hereditaments.
    c. Realtors.
    d. Subdivisions.

Ans.
c.

46. John Barr and Mary Miller take title to a residence as John Barr and Mary Barr, his wife, on September 29, 1991. Actually, they are not married. John died on March 3, 1992. Mary and John's mother, Anna, both claim title to the property. Under these circumstances:

    a. The property will go to Mary.
    b. The property will go to Anna.
    c. Mary and Anna will each own a one-half interest.
    d. The property will escheat to the state.

Ans.
a.

47. If you contract to sell the SW of the Sw of the NW of a section of land, how may acres would pass with the deed?

    a. 15 acres.
    b. 10 acres.
    c. 40 acres.
    d. 160 acres.

Ans.
b.

48. Restrictions in a deed are created by:

    a. Order of the court.
    b. Grantee.
    c. Grantor.
    d. The municipality.

Ans.
c.

49. The appropriation of land by an owner to some public use together with the acceptance for such use by or on behalf of the public, constitutes:

    a. Eminent domain.
    b. Dedication.
    c. Condemnation.
    d. Adverse conveyance.

Ans. b.

50. If title to real property remains in the seller's name after it is sold on a monthly payment plan, the buyer would have purchased it under:

    a. An FHA mortgage.
    b. A conventional mortgage.
    c. A real estate contract.
    d. A VA mortgage.

Ans. c.

51. Title to real property passes by voluntary alienation by:

    a. Quit claim deed.
    b. Grant deed.
    c. Court decree.
    d. Trustee in bankruptcy.

Ans. b.

52. The person who cannot take an acknowledgement is:

    a. An alderman.
    b. A justice of the peace.
    c. An interested party.
    d. A judge.

Ans. c.

53. The instrument which conveys title to a trustee is:

    a. A mortgage.
    b. Trustee's guarantee.
    c. An indenture.
    d. Trust deed.

Ans. d.

54. A cloud on a title would probably be discovered upon:

    a. Application for mortgage.
    b. Delivery of deed.
    c. Appraisal of the property.
    d. Title examination.

Ans. d.

55. An acknowledgement to a deed must be made before:

    a. An attesting witness to the deed.
    b. A court tipstaff.
    c. Recorder of deeds.
    d. Any qualified official.

Ans. d.

56. Rights to the use of, or access to, waterways are called:

    a. Water rights.
    b. Marine rights.
    c. Portage rights.
    d. Riparian rights.

Ans. d.

57. Property is identified in a conveyance instrument by the:

    a. Habendum.
    b. Consideration.
    c. Description.
    d. The warranty.

Ans. c.

58. A proper escrow, once established, should be:

    a. Held by a licensed broker.
    b. Voidable at the seller's option.
    c. Voidable at the option of one of the interested parties.
    d. Beyond the control of any one of the interested parties.

Ans. d.

59. Chain of title means:

    a. A measurement used by a surveyor.
    b. A listing of all recorded instruments affecting the subject title.
    c. Certificate of title.
    d. Heirs named in a will to inherit property after the death of the testator.

Ans. b.

60. The right of a water company to lay and maintain water mains along a designated line in the rear of a lot would be called:

    a. An encroachment.
    b. An easement.
    c. Adverse possession.
    d. An Appurtenance.

Ans. b.

61. A title insurance policy, standard form, insures:

    a. That there is no judgment against the property.
    b. That the property is free and clear of all encumbrances.
    c. The title only as it appears on record, subject to stated exceptions.
    d. None of these.

Ans. c.

62. A section of land is:

    a. 360 acres.
    b. 6 square miles.
    c. 6 miles square.
    d. 1 mile square.

Ans. d.

63. The party appointed by the court to settle a deceased person's estate is called:

    a. A trustor.
    b. A trustee.
    c. A guardian.
    d. An administrator.

Ans. d.

64. A valid declaration of homestead may be filed on a home by:

    a. The lessee.
    b. Trustee.
    c. Mortgagee.
    d. Head of family.

Ans. d.

65. The number of square feet in an acre of ground is:

    a. 5,280.
    b. 25,120.
    c. 43,560.
    d. 50,560.

Ans.
c.

66. In the West a township is:

    a. An incorporated city.
    b. A 640-acre plot of land.
    c. Five square miles.
    d. Six miles square.

Ans.
d.

67. A system of registration by which a state guarantees the title to land is called:

    a. Torrens system.
    b. Land registration.
    c. Land equalization system.
    d. Land protection system.

Ans.
a.

68. Title to real property passes to the grantee at the time the deed is:

    a. Written.
    b. Delivered.
    c. Notarized.
    d. Signed.

Ans.
b.

69. A quit claim deed conveys only the interest of the:

    a. Grantee.
    b. Property.
    c. Claimant.
    d. Grantor.

Ans.
d.

70. An authorization for a person to act for and on behalf of another in his absence is called:

    a. An option.
    b. An easement.
    c. A power of attorney.
    d. A release.

Ans.
c.

71. Unpaid taxes on real estate become:

    a. A lien.
    b. An easement.
    c. A judgment.
    d. None of these.

Ans.
a.

72. The taking of property for public use is:

    a. Zoning.
    b. Condemnation.
    c. Escheat.
    d. Reversion.

Ans.
b.

73. A charge levied against real estate for municipal functions is:

    a. A tax.
    b. A lien.
    c. An assessment.
    d. A judgment.

Ans.
a.

74. The grantor's guarantee that he is the owner of the property and has the power to convey title is called a covenant of:

    a. Seizin.
    b. Further assurance.
    c. Certificate of no defense.
    d. Warranty deed.

75. The rights to the water thereon of a person owning land containing or bordering upon a stream is called:

    a. Water rights.
    b. Riparian rights.
    c. Eminent domain.
    d. A reservation.

76. A policy of title insurance, "purchaser's form" insures the record title in the name of:

    a. The mortgagee.
    b. A broker.
    c. The grantor.
    d. The grantee.

77. Severalty ownership is ownership:

    a. By several persons.
    b. By title passing to the survivors upon the death of one.
    c. Of an undivided interest in property.
    d. By one person only.

78. Owner of an undivided interest in land with no right of survivorship owns it by:

    a. Joint tenancy.
    b. Severalty.
    c. Absolute ownership
    d. Tenancy in common.

79. Which one of the following is not an appurtenance?

    a. Right of way.
    b. Easement for egress and ingress.
    c. A garage.
    d. Driveway servicing two properties.

80. Which indicia of the following pertain to fee simple ownership?

    a. Can mortgage the property.
    b. Can alien the property.
    c. Can devise the property.
    d. All of these.

81. Horne sold a tract of land next to his residence to Bellows in 1987. The deed contained a covenant against the building of any structure by Bellows which would interfere with Horne's view of the lake, a half mile distant. Upon Horne's death in 1987, his heirs sold the residence to Greene in 1987, who filed plans with the city for a nine story apartment building which would obscure a view of the lake. Under these circumstances, the restriction:

   a. Is a covenant running with the land and the building will be
      enjoined.
   b. Is a personal covenant, which terminated with Horne's death.
   c. Will not be enforced, as a form of unjust enrichment.
   d. Is enforceable, as consonant with public policy.

82. The tax on a given piece of property is determined by multiplying the tax   Ans.
    rate (millage) by: d.

   a. The selling price.
   b. Appraised value of the property.
   c. Insured value.
   d. Assessed value.
   e. Market value less depreciation.

83. The legal rights which a wife has in her husband's property, at his death,   Ans.
    are known as: b.

   a. Curtsey.
   b. Dower.
   c. Share by entirety.
   d. Share by survivorship.

84. In order to accurately determine the boundaries of real property, one should   Ans.
    obtain: b.

   a. A title policy.
   b. A survey.
   c. An abstract.
   d. A decree of court.

85. The state of ownership in real property by which the husband and wife   Ans.
    hold title to real estate and in which the right of survivorship cannot be   b.
    destroyed by either party is known as:

   a. Estate in joint tenancy.
   b. Estate by entireties.
   c. Estate in common.
   d. Estate by dower right.

86. A roadway over Taylor's land existed for 25 years. Wagner sought a court   Ans.
    decree for a perpetual easement and an injunction against interference.   d.
    Heretofore, Taylor gave permission for its use to people asking permis-
    sion. Under these circumstances, the court should:

   I. Grant a decree for an easement.
   II. Grant a perpetual injunction, preventing Taylor from obstructing the
       roadway or interfering with Wagner's use.
   a. I only.
   b. II only.
   c. Both I and II.
   d. Neither I or II.

87. A policy of title insurance in favor of the mortgagee will also insure: Ans.
                                                                                     d.
   a. The owner.
   b. The buyer.
   c. The buyer's purchases.
   d. No other person.

88. Mrs. Elsie M. Sims, wife of Alfred D. Sims, should sign a deed to real estate in which manner?

   a. Elsie M. Sims.
   b. Mrs. Alfred D. Sims.
   c. Mrs. Alfred D. (Elsie) Sims.
   d. None of these.

Ans.
a.

89. In order for a would be buyer of real estate to be certain of the validity of the title, he should order:

   a. A survey.
   b. A title search.
   c. An estoppel certificate.
   d. None of these.

Ans.
b.

90. An encumbrance on real estate may be:

   a. Unpaid broker's commission.
   b. Live stock.
   c. Easement granting another a right of way over the land.
   d. A building.

Ans.
c.

Appendix E
PROBLEMS AND SOLUTIONS

1. How much would it cost to develop a parking lot allowing 300 ft^2 for each parking space on a plot 500 front feet and 300 feet deep, if paving costs $1.69 per ft^2, curbs and gutters cost $20 per front foot to be installed only on a front foot basis and lighting costs $10,000?

Ans.
500 ft. × 300 ft. = 150,000 ft^2
150,000 ft^2 × $1.69 = $253,500
500 ft. × $20 = $10,000
$253,500 + $10,000 + $10,000 = $273,500
Total Cost

2. How many parking spaces will be provided on the above lot?

Ans.
150,000 ÷ 300 = 500 Spaces

3. McDonald buys a storage building containing 8,000 ft^2 for $160,000. His gross rental is based at $5.00 per ft^2 of rental area. His total expenses are $15,000 per year. What is annual return on investment?

Ans.
8,000 ft^2 × $5.00 = $40,000
$40,000 − $15,000 = $25,000
$25,000 ÷ $160,000 = .156 or $15.6%

4. Jack Elder has a 2.0 acre plot of land which he is subdividing into lots. He plans to make each lot 60 ft × 190 ft in depth. If he provides a center street 28 ft × 210 ft, how many full lots can he market?

Ans.
2.0 Ac. × 43,560 = 87,120 ft^2
28 ft. × 210 ft. = 5,880 ft^2 (street)
87,120 − 5,880 = 81,240 ft^2 (lots)
60 ft. × 190 ft. = 11,400 ft^2 per lot
81,240 ft^2 ÷ 11,400 = 7 lots

5. On a plot prepared for a subdivision, 1/8 inch represents one foot of land. One lot is shown as 6 1/2 inches wide. What is the width of the lot, according to scale?

Ans.
6.5 in. × 8 ft per inch = 52 ft

6. Brown listed a commercial lot for $50,000. The lot has a 90 ft front and is 180 ft deep. He received an offer for $500 per front foot. He received another offer for $2.75 per ft^2. Which is the best offer?

Ans.
90 ft × $500 per front ft= $45,000
90 ft × 180 ft × $2.75 per ft^2 = $44,550.
The front-foot offer is best.

7. An apartment building has 3 floors containing 4 units each. First floor units rent for $350, second floor units rent for $300 and third floor units rent for $250. The owner receives a 11 percent return on his investment. What is the value of the property?

Ans.
Income = ($350 × 4) + ($300 × 4) + ($250 × 4) = $3,600 per mo. or $2,600 × 12 = $43,200 per year
Value = Income ÷ Rate
Value = $43,200 ÷ .11 = $392,727

8. A broker sells the NW1/4; NW1/4; SE1/4; Sec. 31,T4N R5 EMB for the owner @ $2,000 per acre. The commission was 6 percent. The broker must pay 10 percent of the commission to the salesperson, who listed the property. What is the net amount the broker receives in the sale?

Ans.
$1/4 \times 1/4 \times 1/4 = 1/64$th of a section
$1/64 \times 640 = 10$ Ac. sold
$10 \times \$2,000 \times 6\% = \$1,200$ Tot.Comm.
$(100\% - 10\%) \times \$1,200 = \$1,080$
   Broker's share

9. A tract of land contains 348,480 ft^2. It sold for $14,000 per acre. What was the total selling price?

Ans.
$348,480 \div 43,560 = 8.0$ ac.
$8.0 \times \$14,000 = \$112,000$ Sell Price

10. How many acres are in the S. 1/2 of the N.E. 1/4 of the S.W. 1/4 of the S.W. 1/4 of a section?

Ans.
$1/2 \times 1/4 \times 1/4 \times 1/4 = 1/128$ Acre
$1/128 \times 640 = 5.0$ acres

11. $20,000 is equal to 8 percent of the selling price of a dwelling. What was the selling price?

Ans.
$\$20,000 \div 8\% = \$250,000$

12. What is the annual interest rate on a $80,000 loan when the interest payments are $1,200 per quarter?

Ans.
$\$1,200 \times 4 = \$4,800$ per year
$\$4,800 \div \$80,000 = .06$ or 6%

13. If the interest rate is 8 percent per annum and your monthly interest payment is $500, what is the loan amount?

Ans.
$\$500 \times 12 = \$6,000$ per annum
$\$6,000 \div 8\% = \$75,000$ Loan Amt.

14. Which of the following tracts contains the most acres: (a) N 1/2 of the S. 1/2 of the N.W. 1/4 of Section 16 (b) W 1/2 of the E 1/2 of the S.E. 1/4 of Section 16?

Ans.
(a) $1/2 \times 1/2 \times 1/4 = 1/16$ acre
(b) $1/2 \times 1/2 \times 1/4 = 1/16$ acre
Equal

15. An apartment building is showing a profit of $850 per month and is earning 8 percent on the entire investment. What is the building worth?

Ans.
Value $= I \div r$ (rate)
$\$850 \times 12 = \$10,200$ Annual Income
$\$10,200 \div 8\% = \$127,500$

16. A real estate broker, at closing, deducted a commission of 6 percent. The owner then received $70,500. What was the selling price?

Ans.
$(100\% - 6\%) = 94\%$ or owner share
$\$70,500 \div 94\% = \$75,000$

17. A salesperson sells 2 1/2 sections of development land to a subdivider for $5,000 per acre. What is his commission if he receives 40 percent of the brokerage commission?

Ans.
$2 1/2 \times 640 = 1600$ acres in sale
$1600 \times \$5,000 = \$8,000,000$
$(40\% \times 6\%) \times \$8,000,000 = \$192,000$

18. A rectangular piece of property has a frontage 450 feet and a depth of 600 feet. At $10,000 per acre, what is the selling price?

Ans.
$450 \times 600 = 270,000$ ft^2
$270,000 \div 43,560 = 6.2$ acres
$6.2 \times \$10,000 = \$62,000$

19. Alberts and Briggs purchased an apartment house for $200,000. Alberts contributed $120,000 and Briggs invested $80,000. At the end of the year, the net profit is $120,000. How much will each partner receive based upon his investment?

Ans.
Albert's share = $120,000 ÷ $200,000 = 60%
60$ × $120,000 = $72,000
Brigg's share = 100% – 60% = 40%
40% × $120,000 = $48,000

20. Taxes of $924.60 are due and payable on January 1 of each year. If paid before January 31, a discount of 2 1/2 percent is allowed. Thompson pays his taxes on January 26, 1992. What amount does he pay?

Ans.
100% – 2 1/2% = 97 1/2%
97 1/2% × $924.60 = $901.49

21. Chandler bought a house for $67,000, paying $12,000 cash and a purchase money mortgage for the balance at 8 percent. In addition to the interest on the mortgage and an annual depreciation of 2 percent, his annual other expenses are $270. His rental income is $500 per month. What is the return on his cash investment?

Ans.
$67,000 – $12,000 = $55,000 loan
$55,000 × 8% = $4,400 Int. Exp.
$4,400 + $270 = $4,670 Total Exp.
$500 × 12 = $6,000 annual Inc.
$6,000 – $4,670 = $1,330 Net Inc.
$1,330 ÷ $12,000 = .111 or 11.1%

22. A rose bush grows in the middle of a circular plot that has a diameter of 3 yards. At $1.25 a linear foot, what will it cost to enclose the rose bush?

Ans.
Circumference = πD
D = 3 × 3 = 12 ft
12 × 3.1416 = 37.7 ft in diam.
37.7 × $1.25 = $47.12

23. Jones bought a 4-family apartment house for $100,000, paying $30,000 cash and giving a mortgage for the balance at 9 percent. The lot is valued at $20,000. Each apartment rents for $300 a month. Expenses on the mortgage interest at 9 percent; depreciation at 2 percent; taxes, insurance and repairs were $9,500. What is his rate of income?

Ans.
4 × $300 × 12 = $14,400 Gross Inc.
$14,400 – $9,500 = $4,900 Net Inc.
$4,900 ÷ $100,000 = .049 or 4.9%

24. A salesperson's half of a 6 percent commission on a $65,000 sale would be how much?

Ans.
$65,000 × 6% =$3,900
$3,900 × 50% = $1,950

25. If a woman's income is $1,950 per month and her home costs 2 1/2 times her annual income, what does her home cost?

Ans.
$1,950 × 12 × 2 1/2 = $58,500

26. On September 1, 1991, Jones purchased a 3-year HO-2 insurance policy for 90% of its $125,000 value. The insurance premium was $1.00 per $100 of the policy value. Jones sold the house on April 1, 1992. What was the prorata share of the premium owed by the buyer?

Ans.
$125,000 × 90% = $112,500 Ins.
($112,500 ÷ 100) × $1.00 = $1,125
   3-yr premium
Sept. 1 to Apr 1 = 7 months
$1,125 ÷ 36 × (36 − 7) = $906.25

27. Lane offers to sell an income property to Sloan. The income is $800 per month and the total expenses are $3,000. Sloan figures on a 9 percent return on investment. How much should he offer Lane?

Ans.
$800 × 12 = $9,600 Gross Income
$9,600 − $3,000 = $6,600 Net Inc.
$V = I ÷ i$
Value = $6,600 ÷ 9% = $106,667

28. What is the area of a circle with a radius of 6 feet?

Ans.
Area = πr^2
$3.1416 × 6^2 \approx 113.1 \text{ ft}^2$

29. Waldo owns a corner lot 250 feet wide and 350 feet deep. To keep people from trespassing, Waldo erects a fence around the lot. The fence costs him $1.27 per foot. What is the total cost?

Ans.
$(250 × 2) + (350 × 2) = 1200 \text{ ft}$
$1.25 × 1200 = $1,500

30. If an investor purchased an apartment building for $190,000 and received an annual net income of $18,000, what was the yield on his investment?

Ans.
$Y = I ÷ V$
$Y = $18,000 ÷ $190,000 = .095$ or 9.5%

31. Evans entered into a contract with Harper, a builder, to construct a house for him on a cost plus 15 percent basis. The contractor made the following expenditures: Foundation and Masonry $10,000; Lumber and Carpenter work $24,000; Plumbing $12,500; Heating & Air Conditioning $7,800; Electrical work and Equipment $7,000; Painting $4,000; Landscaping $3500; Roofing $2,500; Extras $1500. What was the total cost of the house?

Ans.
Contractor Cost = $10,000 + 24,000 + 12,500 + 7,800 + 7,000 + 4,000 + 3,500 + 2,500 + 1,500 = $72,800
$(100\% + 15\%) × $72,000 = $83,720

32. A mortgage company agreed to lend an owner 80 percent of its appraised value at 9 percent interest per annum. If the interest payment the first month was $600, what was the appraised value of the property?

Ans.
$600 ÷ (9% ÷ 12) = $80,000 Mtg.
$80,000 ÷ 80% = $100,000 Value

33. A broker sells a lot 50 ft × 100 ft for $4.25 per square foot. His commission is 8 percent. How much does the seller receive?

Ans.
$50 \times 100 = 5{,}000$ ft^2
$5{,}000 \times \$4.25 = \$21{,}250$
$(100\% - 8\%) \times \$21{,}250 = \$19{,}550$

34. What is the purchase price of a property, if a 20 percent earnest money deposit is $5,000?

Ans.
$\$5{,}000 \div 20\% = \$25{,}000$

35. A lot 150 feet wide and 200 feet deep sold for $90,000. What did the owner receive per square foot?

Ans.
$150 \times 200 = 30{,}000$ ft^2
$\$90{,}000 \div 30{,}000 = \$3.00$ per ft^2

36. The owner of a block of 14 building lots, each 75 feet front, desires to realize $45,000 from the tract, keeping two lots for himself. What would be the sales price per front foot?

Ans.
$(14 - 2) \times 75$ ft = 900 front ft
$\$45{,}000 \div 900 = \$50$

37. What is the cost of a tract of land 600 ft wide by 1000 ft deep at $20,000 per acre?

Ans.
$600 \times 1000 = 600{,}000$ ft^2
$600{,}000 \div 43{,}560 = 13.774$ Ac.
$13.774 \times \$20{,}000 = \$275{,}482$

38. A lot 100 feet × 200 feet deep costs $150 per front foot. What is the cost of the lot?

Ans.
$100 \times \$150 = \$15{,}000$

39. A man built a house which was rectangular in shape. The dimensions were 24 ft by 36 ft What is the total square feet of the house?

Ans.
$24 \times 36 = 864$ ft^2

40. A loan made April 17 is repaid June 26. How many days should the interest be calculated?

Ans.

April 30 days – 17 days	= 13
May	= 31
June	= 25
Total	69 Days

41. How many feet in 48 pieces of 2 × 4 lumber, each of which is 12 feet long?

Ans.
$(4 \div 12) \times 2 \times 12 \times 48 = 384$

42. 1/2 acre plus 5/8 acre plus 3/16 acre is equal to how many acres?

Ans.
1/2 = 8/16; 5/8 = 10/16
8/16 + 10/16 + 3/16 = 21/16 or 1 5/16

43. If a farmer sells 1/2 of 20 acres and plans to divide one fourth of the balance into lots, how many acres are left?

Ans.
$1/2 \times 20$ Ac. = 10 Ac.
$(1 - 1/4) \times 10$ Ac. = 7.5 Ac. left

44. What part of an acre is 5,445 square feet?

Ans.
$5{,}445 \div 43{,}560 = .125$ or 1/8 Acre

45. Add: 26 1/2 + 19 3/4 + 8 5/6 + 44 2/3

Ans.
26 1/2 = 318/12
19 3/4 = 237/12
8 5/6 = 106/12
44 2/3 = 536/12
318 + 237 + 106 + 536 = 1197/12 or 99 3/4

46. Divide: 18 1/2 by 4 1/6

Ans.
18 1/2 = 111/6
4 1/6 = 25/6
111/6 × 6/25 = 666/150 or 4 66/150 or 4 11/25

47. $223.65 is 5 1/4% of what amount?

Ans.
5 1/4% = .0525
$223.65 .0525 = $4,260

48. Multiply .75 × .83 1/3 and express the answer in lowest fraction form.

Ans.
.83 1/3 = 83 1/3 100 = 250/3
÷ 100 = 250/3 × 1/100 = 250/300
= 5/6
5/6 × 3/4 = 15/24 or 5/8

49. An owner lists property for sale with a broker to net him $90,000 after paying the broker a 6 percent commission. At what price would the broker have to sell the property?

Ans.
100% – 6% = 94%
$90,000 ÷ 94% = $95,745 say $95,800

50. A property was listed for sale with a broker for $30,000. The actual sale was made for 10 percent less than the listed price. The commission rate was 7 percent. What commission loss did the broker incur by not selling the property for the full listed price?

Ans.
Full Comm. = $30,000 × 7% = $2,100
Sale = $30,000 × 90% = $27,000
Sales Comm. = $27,000 × 7% = $1,890
Loss = $2,100 – $1,890 = $210

51. A room is 20 ft long by 17 ft wide by 9 1/2 ft high. What is the volume (cubic feet)?

Ans.
$20 \times 17 \times 9 \ 1/2 = 3,230 \ ft^3$

52. The legal description of a farm is NW 1/4 of the NW 1/4 and the N 1/2 of the NE 1/4 of the NW 1/4 of Section 17, Township 6 N, Range 3E of the Boise Meridian. How many acres in the farm?

Ans.
1/4 × 1/4 × 640 = 40 Ac.
1/2 × 1/4 × 1/4 × 640 = 20 Ac.
40 + 20 = 60 Acres

53. What would be the appraisal of a bungalow 30 ft by 40 ft at a replacement cost of $30 per ft^2, allowing 3 percent depreciation for 3 years?

Ans.
$30 \times 40 = 1,200 \ ft^2$
1,200 × $30 = $36,000
[100% – (3 × 3%)] × $36,000 = $32,760

54. Mary Crow receives a rental of $500 per month and her expenses are $2,000 per year. What is her net income per month?

Ans.
$500 × 12 = $6,000 Gross Inc.
$6,000 – $2,000 = $4,000 Net. Inc.
$4,000 ÷ 12 = $333.33 per month

55. A tract of land is bisected by a stream, leaving two triangular plots. One lot has a street frontage of 500 ft and a depth of 760 ft. How many acres does the one lot contain?

Ans.
Area = (Base × Altitude) ÷ 2
$(500 \times 760) ÷ 2 = 190,000 \ ft^2$
190,000 ÷ 43,560 = 4.36 Ac.

56. A farm earns $3,600 net after allowing $24 per month for expenses. A buyer wants to 6 percent return on his money. What would he have to pay for the farm so as to gross 6 percent?

Ans.
Net Income = $3,600
Expenses = 12 × $24 = $288
$3,600 + $288 = $3,888 Gross Inc.
$3,888 ÷ 6% = $64,800

57. A subdivider purchased a parcel of land 1320 ft by 1980 ft. How many 1/3 acre lots can he obtain allowing 16 2/3 percent of the total for streets and a school site?

Ans.
1320 × 1980 = 2,613,600 ft^2
(100% − 16 2/3%) × 2,613,600 = 2,177,991 ft^2 Available
2,177,991 ÷ (1/3 × 43,560) = 150 lots

58. A lot 75 ft by 115 ft is assessed at $24 per front foot. The house is assessed at 4.8 times the lot. The tax rate is 68 mills. What is the annual tax bill?

Ans.
75 × $24 = $1,800 lot assessment
$1,800 × 4.8 = $8,640 House Asst'mt.
$1,800 + $8,640 = $10,440 Total
$10,440 × .068 = $709.92

59. The owner of a farm said that was not usable, 3/5 was under cultivation, the remaining 60 acres was a grass meadow. How many acres in the entire farm?

Ans.
1/4 + 3/5 = 17/20 not useful
20/20 − 17/20 = 3/20 useful
60 ÷ 3/20 = 60 × 20/3 = 400 acres

60. What is the interest on $4,000 for 3 years, 5 months, and 20 days at 6.5 percent per annum?

Ans.
$4,000 × 6.5% = $260 per year
$260 ÷ 12 = $21.67 per month
(260 × 3) + ($21.67 × 5) + (20/30 × $21.67)
= $902.80

61. Cole is asked to appraise an open lot with no improvements on it. The neighborhood is 75 percent built up. Most lots in the area are from 55 to 65 feet wide. The lot under appraisal is 60 ft Comparable sales are found which indicates lots are selling for $60 − $75 per front foot. What is a good estimate of the lot's value?

Ans.
($60 + $75) 2 = $67.50 Average
60 × $67.50 = $4,050

62. What will the taxes be for six months on property valued at $8,000 if the tax rate is $2.27 per $100 valuation per year?

Ans.
($8,000 ÷ 100) × $2.27 = $181.60
6/12 × $181.60 = $90.80

63. An acre of land contains 43,560 ft^2 What is the cost of a lot 132 ft by 330 ft at $8,000 per acre?

Ans.
(132 × 330) ÷ 43,560 = 1.0 Ac.
1.0 × $8,000 = $8,000

64. How much additional cash must a buyer furnish in addition to his $1,000 deposit if the lending institution grants a 60 percent loan on a $80,000 home?

Ans.
(100% − 60%) × $80,000 = $32,000 loan
$80,000 − $32,000 − $1,000 = $47,000

65. If you bought two lots for $10,000 each, then made three lots out of the parcel and sold the three lots for $12,000 each, how much did you make? What was your return on investment?

Ans.
$2 \times \$10,000 = \$20,000$ Cost
$3 \times \$8,000 = \$24,000$ Sale
$\$24,000 - \$20,000 = \$4,000$ Profit
$\$4,000 \div \$20,000 = .20$ or 20%

66. Compute the cost of excavating a basement 25 ft wide, 30 ft long and 5 ft deep at $5.00 per cubic yard.

Ans.
$(25 \times 30 \times 5) \div 27 = 138.89$ yds^3
$138.89 \times \$5.00 = \$694.44$

67. Bell wishes to build a flat roof building 130 ft long, 30 ft wide and 24 ft high. Dusch offers to build for $22.00 per ft^2 and Sherwin bids $1.10 per ft^3. How much would Bell save by giving the job to Dusch?

Ans.
$130 \times 30 \times \$22.00 = \$85,800$ Dusch Bid
$130 \times 30 \times 24 \times \$1.10 = \$102,960$ Sherwin bid
$\$102,960 - \$85,960 = \$17,000$ Saving

68. In a contract for sale of real estate, the sales price is fixed at $60,000 and of this amount $12,000 is paid down at the time the sale is closed with the balance payable at $500 per month plus interest. The contract is dated January 1, 1992 and the first payment is due February 1, 1992. Assuming all payments are made on schedule, when will the contract be paid in full?

Ans.
$\$60,000 - \$12,000 = \$48,000$ Mtg.
$\$48,000 \div \$500 = 96$ months or 8 yr.
Last Payment Jan 1, 2000.

69. A certain two-story commercial building measures 46 ft by 80 ft. The height of the first floor is 16 ft and the second floor 14 ft. The estimated reproduction cost is $2.40 per ft^3 for the first floor and $1.90 per ft^3 for the second floor. What is the reproduction cost?

Ans.
$46 \times 80 \times 16 \times \$2.40 = \$141,312$ 1st Floor cost
$46 \times 80 \times 14 \times \$1.90 = \$97,888$ 2nd Floor
$\$141,312 + \$97,888 = \$239,200$ Total Cost

70. Lawrence leased a storeroom to Davis on a percentage rent basis. The lease called for a minimum monthly rental of $800 plus 5 percent of the gross yearly business over $100,000. How much rent would Lawrence receive yearly if Davis grosses $120,000?

Ans.
$\$800 \times 12 = \$9,600$ Regular Rent
$(\$120,000 - \$100,000) \times 5\% = \$1,000$
$\$9,600 + \$1,000 = \$10,600$ Total

71. There is a close relationship between the monthly rent obtainable for a property and the price the property will bring on the market (Gross Rent Multiple). In an area that was beginning to run down, properties were selling for 92 times monthly rental. In a newer district they were selling for 112 times monthly rental. If a property had a monthly rental of $300 per month, what would it be worth in each area?

Ans.
$92 \times \$300 = \$27,600$ Old Area Value
$112 \times \$300 = \$33,600$ New Area Value

72. An office building has a total income of $132,000 per year. The yearly expenses are: Taxes $20,000; Insurance $6,500; Heating and Air Conditioning $14,800; Miscellaneous Expense $9,600. If the owner of the building values the building at $1,000,000, what will be his net return?

Ans.
$20,000 + $6,500 + $14,800 + $9,600 = $50,900 Expenses
$132,000 – $50,900 = $81,100 net

73. Davis decides to construct a driveway. Concrete costs $33.00 per yd^3 and labor is $.80 per ft^2. What will be the cost of the driveway which is 36 ft long, 8 ft wide and 4 inches thick?

Ans.
$(36 \times 8 \times 4/12) \div 27 = 96$ yd^3
$96 \times \$33.00 = \$3,168$

74. A loan made April 17 is repaid June 26. How many day's interest should be charged?

Ans.
$30 – 17 = 13$ days left in April
31 days in May
25 days in June
$13 + 31 + 25 = 69$ days

75. Jim Underwood and John Davis traded properties. Underwood's property was valued at $142,500. Davis' property was appraised at $173,500. The difference in equities was $20,150.70. Underwood's equity was $49,012.50. His equity is greater than Davis' equity. What was the total mortgage against each property?

Ans.
$142,500 – $49,012.50 = $93,487.50 Underwood Mtg.
$49,012.50 – $20,150.70 = $28,861.80 Davis' Equity
$173,500 – $28,861.80 = $144,638.20 Davis' Mtg.

76. How many cubic yards of gravel would be needed to fill a trench 36 ft long, 9 ft wide and 18 in. deep?

Ans.
$(36 \times 9 \times 18/12) \times 27 = 18$ yd^3

77. If 8 1/2 percent is the annual interest rate and the monthly interest charge is $708.33, what is the amount of the debt?

Ans.
8 1/2% ÷ 12 = .0070833 Monthly rate
$708.33 ÷ .0070833 = $100,000 Debt

78. A grocery store building was leased to a national chain for 1 1/2 of gross sales, with a minimal rent of $20,000 annually. (a) If the first year's sales were $800,000, what was the rent? (b) If the second year's sales were $1,500,000, what was the rent?

Ans.
1 1/2% × $800,000 = $12,000 1st Year
1 1/2% × $1,500,000 = $22,500 2nd Year

79. An owner lists a property with a broker, under an agreement that the owner will receive $16,500 for the property. The owner agreed to pay the broker a 6 percent commission. What is the selling price?

Ans.
100% + 6% = 106% or 1.06
$16,500 × 1.06 = $17,490

80. If 24 acres of land cost $36,000. What would 87 1/2 acres cost?

Ans.
$36,000 ÷ 24 = $1,500 per acre
$1,500 × 85 1/2 = $128,250

81. What is the amount of the quarterly interest on a $12,000 loan at 8 percent per annum?

Ans.
$12,000 × .06/4 = $240

82. John Kane is a salesperson working on a 50/50 split commission with his broker. Kane sells a 280 acre farm for $1,050 per acre. The commission schedule calls for 6 percent on the first $100,000; 4 percent on the next $50,000 and 2 percent on the balance. What is Kane's commission?

Ans.
280 × $1,050 = $294,000
$100,000 × 6% = $6,000
$50,000 × 4% = $4,000
$294000 – $100,000 – $50,000 = $144,000 Balance
$144,000 × 2% = $2,880
($6,000 + $4,000 + $2,880) × 1/2 = $6,440 Kane's Comm.

83. The assessed value of all property in the city of Uranium is $12,000,000. The city budget is $600,000. Your property is assessed at $40,000. What tax would you be required to pay?

Ans.
$600,000 ÷ 12,000,000 = .050
.050 × $40,000 = $2,000.00

84. A broker receives half of the first month's rent of $450 for leasing an apartment and 5 percent of the monthly rent for collecting it. At the end of 18 months what commission would he have collected?

Ans.
$450 × 1/2 = $225
(17 × $450) × 5% = $337.50
$225 + $337.50 = $562.50

85. The schedule of commissions for negotiating a 20-year lease was 6 percent for the first year, 2 percent for the next 4 years, 1 1/2 percent for the next 10 years and 1 percent each year thereafter. What was the total commission earned if the annual rent was $16,500?

Ans.
6% × $16,500 = $ 990.00
2% × 4 × $16,500 = $1,320.00
1.5% × 10 × $16,500 = $2,475.00
1% × 5 × $16,500 = $825.00
990 + $1320 + $2475 + $825 = $5,610.00 Total Comm.

86. A man has an opportunity to buy a lot for $10,000 with a guaranteed resale value one year later of $12,000. He also has the opportunity to lend $10,000 at 10 percent interest. Which is the better deal? By how much?

Ans.
$12,000 – $10,000 = $2,000 Profit on purchase
$10,000 × 10% = $1,000 Interest
$2,000 – $1,000 = $1,000 better to buy the lot.

87. A woman borrows money for 6 months at 12 percent payable in advance. How much must she borrow to have $1,000 now?

Ans.
12% ÷ 2 = 6%
100% – 6% = 94% or .94
$1,000 ÷ .94 = $1,063.82

88. A lending institution advertises that it has no hidden charges or costs—that the charge for loans is simply 3 percent on the unpaid balance each month. If a man borrows $120 and pays $40 each month plus interest, what is the actual rate of interest paid per year?

Ans.
$3\% \times \$120 = \$3.60$
$3\% \times \$\ 80 =\ \ 2.40$
$3\% \times \$\ 40 =\ \ \underline{1.20}$
Total Int.　　$7.20
$(\$7.20 \times 4) \div \$120 = .24$ or 24% per annum

89. A man bought a farm for $88,000 and sold it for $100,000. His selling expenses were $6,000. His profit was what percent of the cost?

Ans.
$\$100,000 - \$88,000 - \$6,000 = \$6,000$
$\$6,000 \div \$88,000 = .068$ or 6.8%

90. If Mr. Jones had a furnished patio at the rear of his home, he could sell the property for $95,000. Without this addition, he can get only $85,000. If a 12 ft × 18 ft pavement 4 inches thick costs $38.00 per cubic yard and labor $1.90 per cubic yard, barbecue pit $135 and furniture $660, how much profit would Mr. Jones make by adding and furnishing a patio?

Ans.
$12 \times 18 \times 4/12 = 2.667$ yd^3
$(\$38 + 1.90) \times 2.667 = \$106.40$ Concrete cost
$\$106.40 + 135 + 660 = \$901.40$
$\$901.40 + \$85,000 = \$85,901.40$ Remodeled value
$\$95,000 - 85,901.40 = \$9,098.60$ Profit

91. How many acres are there in a right triangular property with 1,320 ft base and altitude?

Ans.
$(1320 \times 1320) \div 2 = 871,200$ ft^2
$871,200 \div 43,560 = 20.0$ Acres

92. Ray Upton inherited $65,000, which was 2 1/6 times as much as his sister Ann received. How much did Ann inherit?

Ans.
$\$65,000 \div 2\ 1/6 = \$65,000 \times 6/13 = \$30,000$

93. A building burned 16 bulbs of 25 watts each, 24 hours a day, and two 25 watt bulbs 12 hours a day. What is the June electric bill if it is based on a cost of 8 per kilowatt-hour?

Ans.
$(25 \times 24) + (25 \times 12) = 900$ watt-hrs per day.
$[(900 \times 30) \div 1000] \times \$.08 = \$2.16$

94. The perimeter of a rectangular lot is 108 yards. The length is 6 yards greater than twice the width. What are the length and width of the lot?

Ans.
108 yds. – 12 yds = 96 yds.
96 yds. ÷ 6 = 16 yds. width
(16 yds. × 2) + 6 yds.= 38 yds. long

95. A man can buy a house for $125,000 cash or $40,000 down and $90,000 at the end of the year. If his money is invested at 10 percent compounded semi-annually, which plan should he follow? Why?

Ans.
$(\$40,000 + \$90,000) - 125,000 = \$5,000$ extra cost by time payment
$\$90,000 \times 10\%/2 = \$4,500$ 6 mo. interest
$\$94,500 \times 10\%/2 = \$4,725$ 2nd 6 mo. interest
$\$4,500 + \$4,725 = \$9,225$ total interest earned in the year
$\$9,225 - \$5,000 = \$4,225$ Profit by time plan

96. A note is dated January 15, 1991, and the amount is $17,000; the interest rate is 10 percent per annum payable quarterly. None of the interest has been paid. How much interest is due on January 15, 1992?

Ans.
April 15th to January 15th = 9 mo. or 3 quarters
($17,000 × 10%/4) × 3 = $1,275
(Assumes no interest on interest)

97. The value of a 6-year-old frame house was estimated to be $76,500. What was the original value of the home if the yearly rate of depreciation was 2 1/2 percent?

Ans.
6 × 2 1/2% = 15% depreciation
Present value = 100% – 15% or 85%
$76,500 ÷ 85% = $90,000

98. The commission rate for selling an apartment house was 6 percent of the first $50,000 and 4 percent for all over that amount. The broker received a commission of $4,600. What did the apartment sell for?

Ans.
$50,000 × 6% = $3,000
$4,600 – $3,000 = $1,600 extra Com.
$1,600 ÷ 4% = $40,000 sale
$40,000 + $50,000 = $90,000 Total

99. How much would it cost, per parking space, to develop a parking area, with each space to contain 200 ft². The lot has a 250 ft frontage and is 200 ft deep. Asphalt cost is $2.80 per ft², curb and gutter across the front only will cost $30 per front foot and lighting costs will be $10,000. How many spaces will the lot contain?

Ans.
250 ft × 200 ft = 50,000 ft²
50,000 × $2.80 = $140,000 for Asphalt
250 × $30 = $7,500 curb and gutter
$140,000 + $7,500 + $10,000 = $157,500 Total cost
50,000 ft² ÷ 200 = 250 spaces

100. Change 7/8 to a decimal.

Ans.
7 ÷ 8 = .875

101. Taxes on a parcel of property are $1,325.28 for the current year. The first one half were paid by the seller. The deal will be closed as of December 15. In prorating the taxes, how much should be charged to the sell for his share?

Ans.
$1,325.28 ÷ 12 = $110.44 per month
$110.44 × 5.5 mo. = $607.42

102. The selling price of a certain property is $130,000. The sale can be financed if the buyer can pay 18 percent down plus a loan commission of 1.5 percent of the loan (points). How much money must the buyer have to pay the down payment and loan cost?

Ans.
$130,000 × 18% = $23,400 Down
($130,000 – $23,400) × 1.5% = $1,599 Loan cost
$23,400 + $1,599 = $24,999

103. A tract of land 65 ft wide and 150 ft deep sold for $5.25 per ft² plus $100 per front foot. What was the total selling price?

Ans.
(65 × 150) × $5.25 = $51,187.50
65 × $100 = $6,500
$6,500 + $51,187.50 = $57,678.50

104. The length of the south side of the NE 1/4 of the NE 1/4 of a section is how many feet?

Ans.
1 section = 1 mile or 5,280 ft
$5,280 \div (1/2 \times 1/2) = 1,320$ ft

105. John Ford is building two patios. One is a square of 30 ft per side and the other is a circle with a diameter of 27 ft. Which is the larger and by how much?

Ans.
$30 \times 30 = 900$ ft^2 for the square
Radius = $27 \div 2 = 13.5$ ft
Area of Circle = πr^2 where $\pi = 3.14$
$\pi(13.5)^2 = 572.56$ for the circle
$900 - 572.56 = 327.74$ larger

106. You have determined that there are 1,600 ft^2 in a house and the garage is 20 ft $\times$ 30 ft. The cost of building the house is \$30 per ft^2 and \$11 per ft^2 for the garage. If the 50 ft lot cost \$100 per front-foot, what is the total cost of the project?

Ans.
$1,600 \times \$30 = \$48,000$ house cost
$(20 \times 30) \times \$11 = \$6,600$ garage cost
$50 \times \$100 = \$5,000$ lot cost
$\$5,000 + \$6,600 + \$48,000 = \$59,600$ Total Cost

107. A room in an office building is 40 ft long, 24 ft wide and 15 ft high. How many workers should occupy the room if 200 cubic feet of air space is allocated to each person?

Ans.
$40 \times 24 \times 15 = 14,400$ ft^3
$14,400 \div 200 = 72$ people

108. A basement is 20 ft long, 15 ft wide and was dug to a depth of 9 ft. If it cost the owner \$10.20 per cubic yard of earth removed, what was the total cost?

Ans.
$20 \times 15 \times 9 = 2,700$ ft^3
$2,700 \div 27 = 100$ yd^3
$100 \times \$10.20 = \$1,020$ Total Cost

109. Smith employs a well digger, whose rate is \$9.00 for the first foot dug and \$1.25 increase for each additional foot dug. The well was dug to a depth of 60 ft. What was the cost?

Ans.
60 ft $\times \$.9.00 = \$540$
$59 + 58 + 57 ...+ 4 + 3 + 2 = 1770$
$1770 \times \$1.25 = \$2,212.50$
$\$2,212.50 + \$540 = \$2,752.50$

110. Stone has moved into a new office which is 15 ft by 24 ft. He purchases wall to wall carpet for \$14.95 per square yard. What did the carpet cost?

Ans.
$15 \times 24 = 360$ ft^2
$360 \div 9 = 40$ yd^2
$40 \times \$14.95 = \$598$

111. Mr. A is exchanging his house for a farm owned by Mr. B. A agrees to allow B, the owner of the 240 acre farm, \$600 per acre to apply on A's home, which is valued at \$150,000. How much more will B be required to pay A?

Ans.
$240 \times \$600 = \$144,000$
$\$150,000 - 144,000 = \$6,000$

112. Mr. Stone has a principal balance of \$60,000 on his mortgage. His interest rate is 12 percent per annum. His monthly payment of \$700 is applied first to interest and then to principal. What will be the mortgage balance after the first payment?

Ans.
$12\% \div 12 = 1\%$ per month Interest
$\$60,000 \times 1\% = \$600$
$\$700 - 600 = \$100$ for Mtg. Reduction
$\$60,000 - \$100 = \$59,900$ Balance

113. The sales price of a property is $100,000. The land is valued at $15,000. How much fire insurance should the owner carry?

Ans.
$100,000 – 15,000 = $85,000 Building Value

114. Assume that a $90,000 fire insurance policy is dated March 1, 1992. It was issued for three years at a premium of $1,584. What is the prorated value of the unused portion as of November 16, 1992?

Ans.
$1,584 ÷ 36 = $44 cost per month
March 1 to Nov 16 = 8.5 months
$1,584 – (8.5 × 44) = $1,210

115. The value of a house at the end of eight years was estimated to be $144,000. What was the value of the home when new if the home had depreciated at a 2 1/2 percent rate per year?

Ans.
2 1/2% × 8 = 20%
$144,000 ÷ (100% – 20%) = $180,000 When new.

116. A property is assessed for $50,000. The tax rate is $3.50 per hundred with a 5 percent discount for promptness and a 5 precent penalty for tardiness. What are the three possible payments?

Ans.
($50,000 ÷ 100) × $3.50 = $1,750 Full rate
$1,750 × (100% – 5%) = $1,662.50 Early Payment
$1,750 × (100% + 5%) = $1,837.50 Late Payment

117. A real estate broker is given a contract to manage an 8-unit apartment house with each unit renting for $500 per month. The contract calls for 5 percent of rents collected and 1/2 months rent for each apartment rented. What is the maximum first year commission if all apartments are rented before the building is completed?

Ans.
($500 × 8 × 12) × 5% = $2,400 Collection Commission
($500 × 8) × 1/2 = $2,000 Rental Comm.
$2,400 + $2,000 = $4,400

118. At settlement on June 15, 1992, a purchaser assumes the existing mortgage of $45,000 on which interest at the rate of 10 percent per annum has been paid up to December 15, 1991. Prorate the amount due at settlement and state whether this item is a debit or credit to the purchaser.

Ans.
($45,000 × 10%) ÷. 12 = $375 per month
Dec. 15 to Jun. 15 = 6 months
$375 × 6 = $2250 Credit to Purchaser

119. A house valued at $100,000 was insured on a home owner policy for 80 percent of value. The rate was $.75 per 100 dollar value. What was the three year insurance cost?

Ans.
$100,000 × 80% = $80,000 Ins. Value
($80,000 ÷ 100) × $.75 = $600 per Yr
$600 × 3 = $1,800

120. A property is assessed at $58,000. The school tax rate is $1.55 per 100 dollar of assessed value. What is the school tax on the property?

Ans.
($58,000 ÷ 100) × $1.55 = $899

121. A purchaser has decided to insulate his dwelling by covering the attic floor, measuring 24 ft by 32 ft, with rock wool. Each bag of rock wool will cover 36 ft². How many bags should he buy?

Ans.
$24 \times 32 = 768$ ft²
$768 \div 36 = 21.33$ (22 bags)

122. What investment in principal, must be invested at 8 percent per annum interest to receive $5,600 interest each year?

Ans.
$\$5,600 \div 8\% = \$70,000$

123. At the end of the calendar year, Hope Realty found that it had earned $300,000. Commissions paid and overhead amounted to 18 percent. What was the company's gross sales?

Ans.
$\$300,000 \div (100\% - 18\%) = \$365,853.66$

124. There are 20 fence posts, each 6.85 ft apart. How many yards from the beginning of the first post to the end of the last post, if each post is 4 3/4 inches wide?

Ans.
$20 \times 4\ 3/4 = 95$ in.
$95 \div 12 = 7.92$ ft
$(20 - 1) \times 6.85$ ft $= 130.15$ ft
$130.15 + 7.92 = 138.07$ ft
$138.07 \div 3 = 46.023$ yds

125. If a tract of land comprising 108,900 ft² was sold for $12,500 per acre, what was the total amount of the sale?

Ans.
$(108,900 \div 43,560) \times \$12,500 = \$31,250$

126. A rectangular piece of land containing an acre is 5 1/2 rods wide. What is the length?

Ans.
160 sq. rods = 1 acre
$160 \div 5\ 1/2 = 29.09$ rods long

127. From 160 acres of land, 42 1/4 acres were sold to one man and 1/3 of the remainder to another. How many acres remained unsold?

Ans.
$160 - 42 = 117\ 3/4$ acres left after the first sale.
$117\ 3/4 \times 1/3 = 39.21$ Acres in second sale.
$117\ 3/4 - 39.21 = 78.54$ acres left

128. A man paid $78,883 for a farm containing 89 acres and 90 rd² of land. What was the price per acre?

Ans.
160 rd² = 1 acre
$90 \div 160 = .563$ acre
$89 + .563 = 89.563$ acres in sale
$\$78,883 \div 89.563 = \$880.76$ per acre

129. The owner of a parcel of land 500 ft by 350 ft laid a sidewalk and curb around the entire parcel, placing the curb along the lot lines. Sidewalk cost $9,600 and curb $20.00 per lineal yard. What was the total cost?

Ans.
$2(500) + 2(350) = 1,700$ ft
$1,700 \div 3 = 566.67$ lin. yds.
$566.67 \times \$20 = \$11,333.40$
$\$11,333.40 + \$9,600 = \$20,933.40$

130. If you bought a house for 20 percent less than the listing price and sold it for the listing price, what percent profit would you make on the investment?

Ans.
$100\% - 20\% = 80\%$ Purchase price
$100\% - 80\% = 20\%$ profit
$20\% \div 80\% = 25\%$ on investment

131. McDevitt has a principal balance of $60,000 on his mortgage. The interest rate is 9 percent and taxes and insurance is $1,200 per annum. His monthly payment is $582.77 per month. What is the principal balance aft er the first payment?

Ans.
$1200 ÷ 12 = $100 per mo. for taxes & Ins.
$60,000 × (9%/12) = $450.00 interest
$582.77 – $100 – $450 = $32.77 left for Principal payment
$60,000 – 32.77 = $59,967.23 Balance

132. How many acres are there in a section?

Ans.
1 section = 1 mile square
$5,280 × 5,280 = 27,878,400$ ft^2
$27,878,400 ÷ 43,560 = 640$ acres

133. How many sections in a township?

Ans.
1 Township = 6 sections square
$6 × 6 = 36$ sections

134. What is the length of each side of a square acre?

Ans.
$\sqrt{43,560}$ – 208.7 ft

135. A man bought two lots for $30,000 each, divided them into three lots and sold these new lots for $24,000 each. What was his percent profit?

Ans.
$30,000 × 2 = $60,000 cost
$24,000 × 3 = $72,000 sales price
$72,000 – $60,000 = $12,000 profit
$12,000 ÷ $60,000 = .20 or 20%

136. If a seller wishes to trade his residence at a price of $157,000 subject to a mortgage of $62,400 for an apartment house costing $623,500 and subject to a mortgage of $366,750, what would be the amount of the cash difference?

Ans.
$157,000 – $62,400 = $94,600 Home equity
$623,500 – $366,750 = $256,750 apt. equity
$256,750 – $94,600 = $162,150 cash required

137. A property is worth $120,000, and the furniture and household goods are worth $40,000. The owner insures them for 80 percent of their value. The annual rate on the dwelling is $2.80 per $1,000 and $3.30 per $1,000 on household goods and furniture. If the premium for a three-year policy is 2 1/2 times the premium for one year, what savings would be effected by purchasing a three-year policy?

Ans.
$120,000 × 80% = $96,000 home policy
$40,000 × 80% = $32,000 hsld. policy
($96,000 ÷ 1000) × $2.80 = $268.80
($40,000 ÷ 1000) × $3.30 = $132.00
$268 + $132 = $400.00 cost per yr
$400 × 2 1/2 = $1000 for 3-yr policy
($400 × 3) – $1000 = $200 saving

138. If Dan McClure purchased an apartment building for $400,000 and the total amount of rents received was $60,00 annually, and the annual expense was $20,000, what percent will his investment pay?

Ans.
$60,000 – $20,000 = $40,000 Net Inc.
$40,000 ÷ $400,000 = .10 or 10%

139. Lawrence leased a storeroom to Davis on a percentage basis. The lease called for a minimum rental of $4,000 and 5% of the gross yearly business over $800,000. How much yearly rent would Davis receive from Lawrence if Lawrence did a gross business of $1,200,000 in 1992?

Ans.
$4,000 × 12 = $48,000 base rent
($1,200,000 – $800,000) × 5% = $20,000 overage rent
$48,000 + $20,000 = $68,000 Total

140. In appraising a one-story house 32 ft by 40 ft at a replacement cost of $39.50 per square foot, and allowing 5 percent depreciation for one year, what would your appraisal be?

Ans.
$(32 \times 40) \times \$39.50 = \$50,560$
$(100\% -5\%) \times \$50,560 = \$48,032$ appraised value

141. A broker has the problem of dividing a 10-acre tract into 50×100 foot lots; aft er allowing 85,000 ft^2 for streets. How many lots can he obtain?

Ans.
$10 \times 43,560 = 435,600$ ft^2 plot
$435,600 – 85,000 = 350,600$ ft^2 available for lots
$350,600 \div (50 \times 100) = 70.12$ lots or 70 lots

142. By how much does the sum of 2,583 and 4,905 exceed the difference of 9,421 and 2,892?

Ans.
$2,583 + 4,905 = 7,488$
$9,421 – 2,892 = 6,529$
$7,488 – 6529 = 959$ difference

143. Shields purchased the W 1/2 of NE 1/4 of section 10, T-16, R 18E for the sum of $2,500 per acre. He subdivided the land into 100 lots. The cost of the development was $65,000. Lots were sold for $7,500 each. What profit did Shields make?

Ans.
$(640 \times 1/2 + 1/4) \times \$2,500 = \$200,000$ cost
$\$200,000 + \$65,000 = \$265,000$ total cost
$\$7,500 \times 100 = \$750,000$ sales price
$\$750,000 – \$265,000 = \$485,000$

144. A tract of ground 30 rds by 16 rds contains how many acres?

Ans.
160 rd^2 $= 1$ acre
$(30 \times 16) \div 160 = 3.0$ acres

145. A developer purchased a parcel of land 2,640 ft × 9,900 ft . How many 1/2 acre lots can he obtain allowing 10 percent of the total for streets, 10 percent for play grounds and 20 percent for a factory?

Ans.
$2,640 \times 9,900 = 26,136,000$ ft^2
$10\% + 10\% + 20\% = 40\%$ loss
$(100\% – 40\%) \times 26,136,000 = 15,681,600$ for lots
$15,681,600 \div (43,560 \times 1/2) = 720$ lots

146. What is the cost of roofing a gable-type house (24 × 32) if the roof measures 15 ft from eaves to peak and 34 ft long; if shingles cost $40,000 per square (100 ft^2), and labor an additional $5.00 per square?

Ans.
$2(15 \times 34) \div 100 = 7.2$ squares
$7.2 \times (\$40.00 + \$5.00) = \$324$

147. A lot with a 50 ft lake frontage and 150 ft deep sold for $75,000. What was the price per square foot? per front foot?

Ans.
$\$75,000 \div 50 = \$1,500$ per front foot
$\$75,000 \div (50 \times 150) = \$10.00$ per ft^2

148. Of a certain farm, 1/6 is in pasture, 5/8 is under cultivation, and the remainder is in woodland. If the woodland is 50 acres, how many acres are there in the farm?

Ans.
1/6 + 5/8 = 38/48 acre other than woodlands
48/48 – 38/48 = 10/48 or 5/24 in woodland
50 ÷5/24 = 50 × 24/5 = 240 acres total

149. A perch or rod of land is how many feet?

Ans.
16 1/2 ft

150. How many feet in a chain? How many square chains in an acre?

Ans.
66 ft = 1 Chain
10 sq. chains = 1 acre

151. A percentage lease calls for a base rent of $6,000 per month plus 5 percent of the gross business over $1,150,000 per month. If the total rent paid by the end of the year was $93,000, what was the tenant's gross volume of business for the year?

Ans.
$93,000 – ($6,000 × 12) = $21,000 overage rent
$21,000 ÷ 5% = $420,000 overage gross
$420,000 + ($1,150,000 × 12) = $14,222,000

152. The assessed valuation of a residence is $100,000. If the tax rate is $19.00 per $1000 valuation, what is the tax bill?

Ans.
($100,000 ÷ 1000) × $19 = $1,900

153. A ranch contains 3 square miles. How many acres is the ranch?

Ans.
1 square mile = 1 section = 640 acres
3 × 640 = 1,920 acres

154. A lot is 300 ft wide and 450 ft long. A building was erected on the lot 27 ft from the front and 18 ft from the rear. The building contains 12,825 yd^2. How wide is the building?

Ans.
450 – 18 – 27 = 405 ft long
12,825 × 9 = 115,425 ft^2 in bldg.
115,425 ÷ 405 = 285 ft wide

155. Thompson and Tyler agreed to trade properties—each to assume the encumbrances on the property taken in trade and the difference in equities to be paid the party with the greater equity by paying 20 percent cash and the balance to be carried on a second mortgage. Thompson's property was valued at $200,000 with a first mortgage of $85,550 and a second mortgage of $16,551. Tyler's property was valued at $184,500 with a mortgage of $138,417.90. (a) What is Thompson's equity? (b) What is Tyler's equity? (c) Who is due the difference in equity? (d) How much of the difference will be paid in cash? (e) How much will be carried on a mortgage? (f) Against whose property (after transfer) will the mortgage be carried?

Ans.
(a) $200,000 – $85,550 – $16,551 = $97,899 Thompson's equity
(b) 184,500 – 138,417.90 = $46,082.10 Tyler's equity
(c) Thompson's equity is higher by $97,899 – $46,082.10 = $51,816.90
(d) 20% × $51,816.90 = $10,363.38 cash due to Thompson
(e) $51,816.90 – $10,363.38 = $41,453.52 carried on mortgage
(f) On Tyler's new property

156. The taxes on a certain house were $1,260 paid by the owner on January 1, 1992. What tax refund would the owner receive from the buyer who purchased the property on March 15, 1992?

Ans.
$1,260 ÷ 12 = $105 per month
105$ × (12 – 2) = $997.50

157. The assessment on a property is $133,000 on the building and $10,500 on the land. When re-assessed the land was increased $3,500. If the tax rate is raised 4.25 mills, what will the increase in taxes be?

Ans.
$133,000 + $10,500 + $3,500 = $147.000
new assessment total
4.25 mills = .00425
$147,000 × .00425 = $624.75

158. A broker leases a store measuring 30 ft by 100 ft for a period of five years at an annual rental of $10.00 per square foot. What would be the broker's total earnings if the rate of commission was 6 percent per year?

Ans.
30 × 100 × $10 = $30,000 annual rent
$30,000 × 6% = $1,800 comm. per year
$1,800 × 5 = $9,000 total comm.

159. An agent collects rents monthly as follows: $250 for each of four flats; $400 for each of six flats; $500 for each of 2 flats. He paid out $180 for water and $60 for repairs. He was to receive 3 percent of the gross rentals as a commission. What were the total collections per year and net to the owner?

Ans.
($250 × 4)+($400 × 6)+($500 × 2) = $4,400 per mo. collections
$4,400 × 12 = $52,800 total collections
$52,800 × 3% = $1,584 total comm.
$52,800 – $1,548 – $60 – $180 = $50,976 net to owner

160. J. James paid $484 property tax. If his property was assessed at $11,000, what was the tax rate in mills? Express this in dollars per $100 evaluation.

Ans.
$484 ÷ $11,000 = .044 or 44 mills
.044 × $100 = $4.40 per $100

161. The monthly rent for a high-rise office is $750. The size of the office is 12 ft by 20 ft What is the annual rate per square foot?

Ans.
$750 × 12 = $9,000 annual rent
$9,000 ÷ (12 × 20) = $37.50 per ft^2 annually

162. Mr. Brown built a house 33 ft × 45 ft which had an offset for the family room of an additional 5 ft × 15 ft. If construction costs were $40 per ft^2, how much did it cost to build the house?

Ans.
(33 × 44)+(5 × 15) = 1,527 ft^2
1,527 × $40 = $61,080 cost

163. Taxes on a parcel of property are $1,325.28, for the current year. The first 1/4 of the taxes were paid by the seller. You sell the property and will close the deal as of December 15. How much will you charge the seller for his share of the taxes?

Ans.
$1,325.28 ÷ 12 = $110.44 per mo.
11 1/2 × $110.44 = $1,270.06 seller's share
$1,270.06 – ($110.44 × 3) = $938.74 due from seller

164. You are to ascertain the value of a ranch home, which the owner will list with your office, based upon the following information: The lot is 75 ft front and 125 ft deep, cost $50,000, and has appreciated 4 percent in value each year. The swelling, built 4 years ago, is 28 ft × 38 ft in size; would cost $40 per square foot to reproduce today. Allowing 2 1/2 percent depreciation per year, what is the current Fair Market Value?

Ans.
$50,000 × (100% + 16%) = $58,000 present lot value
(28 × 38) × $40 = $42,560 dwelling reproduction cost
$42,560 × (100% – 10%) = $38,304 current dwelling value
$38,304 + $58,000 = $96,304 FMV

165. Crouch is employed as a salesperson for REALTOR® Evans. Crouch receives 40 percent of earned commissions on sales. A sub-division is listed for sale. Flynn, Sales Manager for Evans receives an override commission of 10 percent. Crouch sold lots with a total value of $150,000 during June 1992. The subdivision owner pays Evans 6 percent commission on sales. How much did Evans earn in commissions during the month on Crouch's sales?

Ans.
$150,000 × 6% = $9,000 total comm.
$9,000 × 40% = $3,600 Crouch's cut
$9,000 × 10% = $900 Flynn's cut
$9,000 – $3,600 – $900 = $4,500 left for Evans

166. A man bought a home for $141,600. Due to health conditions, he was forced to sell for 8 percent less than he paid. Find the selling price and the loss.

Ans.
$141,600 × (100% – 8%) = $130,272 selling price
$141,600 × 8% = $11,328 loss

167. How much additional cash must a buyer furnish in addition to his $1,000 earnest money deposit, if the lending agency makes a loan of 80 percent of the sales price of $120,000?

Ans.
(100% – 80%) × $120,000 = $24,000 down payment required
$24,000 – $1,000 = $23,000 Adn'l cash required

168. An insurance premium for three years is $1,800. The buyer is going to set up an insurance reserve with his loan to pay the premium when it comes due three years later. What will be the amount of his monthly reserve?

Ans.
$1,800 ÷ (12 × 3) = $50

169. The rental income from a duplex is $1,200 per month. Find the value of the property if the gross return on investment is 9 percent per annum.

Ans.
$1,200 × 12 = $14,400 Gross Inc.
$14,400 ÷ 9% = $160,000

170. Johnson bought his new home for $160,000. The assessed value is 60 percent of the market value. The tax rate is $4.00 per $100 assessed valuation. What is the assessed value and the annual tax bill?

Ans.
$160,000 × 60% = $96,000 assessed value
($96,000 ÷ 100) × $4 = $3,840 Tax

171. A lending institution requires that a buyer have a net income 4 1/2 times his monthly mortgage payment, and the use a 10 percent flat deduction of the gross income to compute net income. What would the minimum gross annual salary to qualify for a loan with a monthly payment of $900?

Ans.
$900 × 4 1/2 × 12 = $48,600 net Income
$48,600 ÷ (100% -10%) = $54,000 annual gross income required

172. A mortgage company agrees to lend a buyer 80 percent of the appraised value, at 8 percent per annum. The first month's interest was $960. What was the appraised valuation?

Ans.
$960 ÷ (8% ÷ 12) = $144,000 Mtg.
$144,000 ÷ 80% = $180,000 Value

173. An apartment had a gross income of $1,200 with annual expenses of $5,900 per annum, including depreciation. What price would a buyer pay for the property to show a net return of 9 percent on his investment?

Ans.
($1,200 × 12) – $5,900 = $8,500 net income
$8,500 ÷ 9% = $94,444 say $94,500

174. A vacant piece of land, of irregular terrain, has been appraised as follows: 3,250 ft^2 of slope at 40 per ft^2; 2,000 ft^2 of creek area, 24 per ft^2 and 7,250 ft^2 of lat land at $3.00 per ft^2 If the entire tract is sold, what would be the price per ft^2 to obtain the appraised value of the property?

Ans.
3,250 × $.40 = $1,300 slope value
2,000 × $.24 = $480 creek value
7,250 × $3.00= $21,750 flat land value
$1,300 + $480 + $21,750 = $23,530 total value
$23,530 ÷ (3,250 + 2,000 + 7,250) = $.57 per ft^2 average value

175. An appraiser, using the income approach is estimating the value of a single family residence. He finds comparable properties rent for $550 per month. Recent sales in the area of comparable properties averaged $79,000. Estimate the gross rent multiplier.

Ans.
$79,000 ÷ 550 = 143.6 Say 144

176. Edwards paid $84,000 for a home. He sold to Oliver for 4 percent profit. Oliver was forced to sell the property to Jordan and suffered a 11 percent loss. What was the sales price to Jordan?

Ans.
$84,000 × (100% + 4%) = $87,360 sales price to Oliver
$87,360 × (100% – 11%) = $77,750

177. On the scale of the plan of a lot. 1/8 inch equals one foot. If the plot plan measures 13 1/2 by 17 3/4 inches, what is the size of the lot?

Ans.
13 1/2 × 8 = 108 in.
17 3/4 × 8 = 142 in.
108 × 142 = 15,336 in.^{2}

178. If a concrete mix contains 105 parts of course gravel and 45 parts of fine gravel, what percent of the total does the course gravel represent?

Ans.
105 + 45 = 150 parts total
(105 ÷ 150) × 100 = 70%

179. A subdivision contains 5 blocks. Each block is divided into 4 sections, and each section contains 7 lots. How many lots in the subdivision?

Ans.
5 × 4 × 7 = 140 lots

180. Douglas purchased a lot 75 ft wide by 125 ft deep. Thirty-five percent of the total area was used to construct a building. The State Highway Department took 20 percent of the total area for road widening. How many square feet remained in the lot after the house was build and the condemnation was completed?

Ans.
75 × 125 = 9,375 ft^2 lot size
9,375 × (100% -20%) = 7,500 ft^2
Note:
Although the house occupied 35 percent of the lot, the lot size was not diminished by the construction.

181. A gross profit that is 25 percent of the selling price is what percent of the cost?

Ans.
100% – 25% = 75% cost
25% ÷ 75% = 33 1/3%

182. Mrs. Snyder owns a ten-unit apartment house. Each units rents for $500 if the owner pays the utilities, or $400 if the tenant pays the utilities. The utilities cost $800 per month for the 10 units. How much more income would Mrs. Snyder receive if she paid for the utilities?

Ans.
$800 ÷ 10 = $80 per mo. Util. cost
$500 – $400 = $100 additional rent where owner pays utilities.
$100 – $80 = $20 per unit profit
$20 × 10 = $200 additional income

183. A savings account has a $9,500 balance and a bi-monthly interest rate of $79.17. What is the annual interest rate paid?

Ans.
$79.17 × 6 = $475.02 annual interest
$475.02 ÷ $9,500 = 5% rate

184. John Hall has $50,000 invested in stocks that yield 8 percent per annum. He now pays $400 per month rent. He decides to take the $50,000 and buy a duplex, live in one side and rent the other for $450 per month. How much will he effectively realize from his investment, if maintenance and utilities cost $3,600 per year?

Ans.
$50,000 × 8% = $4,000 return
12 × $400 = $4,800 present rent
12 × $500 = $6,000 duplex rent
$6,000 – $3,600 = $2,400 net income
$2,400 + $4,800(rent) = $7,200 effective return on investment
$7,200 – $4,000 = $3,200 increase

185. If an owner pays 8 1/4 percent interest on a mortgage and the first month's interest is $275. What is the amount of the mortgage?

Ans.

8 1/4% ÷ 12 = .00688 interest per mo.
$275 ÷ .00688 = $40,000 Mtg.

186. A property owner is forced to sell his home so as to realize $75,000 aft er real estate sales commissions of 6 percent. At what price should he list the home?

Ans.
$75,000 × (100% + 6%) = $79,500

187. Jane is buying a bungalow that measures 52 ft by 48 ft on the outside. If the walls are 6 inches thick, what is the interior size?

Ans.
52 ft – (6 in. × 2) = 51 ft
48 ft – (6 in. × 2) = 47 ft
51 × 47 = 2,397 ft^2

Appendix F
A STUDY OF
SALES AGREEMENTS

QUESTIONS AND ANSWERS

1. What is an action for specific performance of an agreement of sale? It is a suit instituted by one party, to compel the other party to consummate the agreement of sale according to its terms.

Ans.
The suit is brought in a court of equity as an extraordinary remedy. If money damages only are sought, the suit would be brought in a civil court.

2. Can an aggrieved party to a contract of sale sue only for money damages?

Ans.
Yes. An action in assumpsit would lie for the breach in contract.

3. In a suit for specific performance of a sales agreement, the law requires special formality. What is meant by special formality?

Ans.
The agreement of sale must be in writing in order to bring an action for specific performance.

4. What is the distinction in law between communications of an acceptance of an offer and revocation (or withdrawal) of an offer.

Ans.
The communications of the acceptance of an offer takes effect from the time it is sent, if the medium of acceptance is the same as the method used in communicating the offer (for example, postal service used in both instances). A revocation takes effect when *received* by the offeree, if made before acceptance of the offer.

5. Chase listed his property for sale with Bender, under an exclusive right to sell contract. The listing stated that Bender was employed "for the sale" of premises, and so on. Bender obtained a buyer, Doland, upon the listed terms. He signed an agreement of sale with Doland—Herbert Chase, by Tom Bender, Agent. Chase, at the time, was on an extended cruse. Upon his return, Chase repudiated the agreement. Doland sues for specific performance. Will he succeed?

Ans.
No. Bender is a special agent, with limited powers. His employment "to sell" merely authorizes him to obtain a buyer, but did not include the right to sign an agreement of sale, binding on the owner.

6. Can a broker acquire rights to a commission under an agreement of sale, since he is not a party to it?

Ans.
Yes, if the agreement states that the broker negotiated the deal and the seller owes the broker a commission.

7. Is an oral agreement of sale invalid?

Ans.
It is invalid in so far as maintaining an action for specific performance is concerned, but it may give rise to an action for damages.

8. If the date is omitted in an agreement of sales, is it invalid?

Ans.
No. A date is merely evidence of the time when the agreement of sale was signed, but it is not essential for the validity of the instrument.

9. What information should an agreement of sale include?

Ans.
Name of the parties, consideration of price, description, and terms of sale.

10. In order for an agreement of sale to be enforceable, how many elements of the law of contracts must be represented?

Ans.
Six

11. What are they?

Ans.
Offer and acceptance, consideration (or seal in some states), capacity of the parties, reality of consent, legality of object, and special formality.

12. What is meant by reality of consent?

Ans.
The contract must be free of mistakes, misrepresented, fraud, duress, or undue influence.

13. Chappel, seller, and Stone, buyer, entered into an agreement of sale for a farm, located in Erie County. The farm is locate in the Harrison School District. Stone believes the farm is located in the Baldwin Township School District. It is located in Hayes Township, three miles from the school. Can Stone rescind the agreement on the grounds of a mistake?

Ans.
No, this is a unilateral mistake, not a mutual mistake, so that Stone is bound by his agreement to purchase the farm.

14. What is the purpose of the Statute of Frauds and when was it first enacted?

Ans.
It is an act for the prevention of fraud and perjury. It was first enacted in England, 29 Charles II, year 1676. It requires certain real estate contracts to be in writing.

15. What recourse would a seller have against a broker, if the buyer backed out of the transaction, before it was closed?

Ans.
None, the broker is not responsible for the buyer's default.

16. Wilson and Peters execute an agreement of sale for Wilson's property at $90,000, under and subject to a mortgage of $50,000 which Peters assumes and agrees to pay. Peters signs the agreement to Crane. Wilson refuses to recognize Crane. Can Crane compel Wilson to execute a deed to him?

Ans.
No. Ordinarily an agreement of sale is assignable. However, where the financial responsibility of the buyer is involved, as here, the seller has a right to select his debtor.

17. Beaty lists certain property with Coleman for sale at $40,000. He informs the broker that the property contains 3.5 acres. Coleman obtains a signed offer from Dixon at the listed price, which Beaty accepts. The agreement states, "3.5 acres more or less." The recorded deed description measures 2.5 acres. This is confirmed by a survey. Dixon demands a refund of his deposit money. Beaty refuses, relying on the "more or less" clause in the agreement. Decide who will win.

Ans.
Dixon will win. "more or less" is no defense where there is substantial difference in acreage. A one acre discrepancy in a 3 1/2 acre tract is substantial.

18. Does the term "valuable consideration" mean only money consideration?

Ans.
No. A valuable consideration may consist of services, chattels, or anything which could be measured in monetary terms.

19. Assume that after a sales contract has been written and executed, a slight change is made in the terms and conditions, and that the broker, in the presence of the interested parties, alters the writing to conform to the new agreement: what precaution should the broker take to protect himself against future controversy?

Ans.
He should have both parties to the agreement place their signatures or initials in the margin opposite or nearest the alterations.

20. An agreement of sale is made between Sims, vendor, and Cox, vendee. It is signed, however, by Sims and his wife, as well as by Cox. The wife refuses to execute the deed on the grounds that she is not a party in the agreement proper. Must she join in the deed?

Ans.
Yes, Her signature on the agreement indicates her intention to be bound by the agreement.

21. Abrams signs an agreement to purchase Bell's property at $50,000 and pays $5,000 as deposit money. Later, Abrams fails to complete the deal and bell keeps the deposit money. Three months later Bell sells the same property for $40,000 to Clark and now sues Abrams for an additional $5,000. Can he recover?

Ans.
No. When Abrams failed to perform, Bell elected to keep the deposit as liquidated damages. He has no other remedy.

22. A broker negotiated the sale of a property for $40,000, his commission to be 6 percent. The buyer deposited $4,000 as earnest money. Before the deal is closed, the buyer and seller mutually agree to call the deal off, with the owner to keep the $4,000 deposit. The owner offers the broker a commission of 6 percent of the $4,000 deposit. The broker claims $2,400. Decide who is right.

Ans.
The broker is entitled to $2,400 as he fully performed his contract with the owner in obtaining a buyer acceptable to the owner.

23. An agreement of sale calls for the closing to be on February 1. The buyer is unable to close on that date. Will he forfeit his earnest money if he fails to close on the stipulated date?

Ans.
No. The buyer has a *reasonable* time after the February 1 date to close the deal. What is considered a reasonable time depends upon the circumstances of each case. Thirty days is considered, in most instances, reasonable.

24. Suppose, in the preceding case, the seller has certain commitments on February 1 and wants to be certain that the deal is closed on time. How can he protect himself?

Ans.
By providing the time of closing is "of the essence" of the agreement.

25. When a buyer defaults, what steps should the seller take?

Ans.
Make a formal tender of the deed and *demand* of the *consideration* price.

26. When is a tender excused?

Ans.
When there is an anticipatory repudiation by the buyer or when the buyer has notified the seller of his intent to default.

27. Must an agreement of sale of real estate be in writing?

Ans.
Yes, unless the purchaser has gone into possession, paid part of the purchase price, and made improvements.

28. Why is it important that a broker have the seller sign an agreement of sale and deliver a signed copy to the buyer as soon as possible.

Ans.
Because the purchaser may revoke the offer up to the time the seller's acceptance is communicated to him.

29. Can a contract of sale be enforced if the description is not sufficient to identify the property?

Ans.
No.

30. An offer to purchase is signed by a purchaser on January 28, and he pays $1,000 as a deposit at that time. It contains a clause to the effect that the buyer agrees to keep the offer open without fail for 5 days, within which time the seller may accept the offer. On January 30, the buyer notifies the seller that he is withdrawing his offer and demands the return of his earnest money. Can he do so?

Ans.
Yes. He can withdraw his offer at any time up until it is accepted by the owner. The five-day simply means that the offer will automatically expire at that time unless accepted or previously withdrawn.

31. A broker holding a listing on a property secures from a prospect a deposit and a signed agreement to purchase. What steps should be take next?

Ans.
Four copies of the agreement should be signed by the buyer. The broker leaves one copy with the seller and takes three copies to the seller and has him sign all three copies. He leaves one copy with buyer and seller signatures with the seller and delivers one copy to the buyer. The broker keeps one copy for his file.

32. What is meant by the clause commonly found in contracts for the sale of real property reading, "rents, taxes, interest on mortgages, and all premiums on insurance policies in force at date hereof are apportioned?"

Ans.
The items mentioned are prorated between buyer and seller as of the date of closing.

33. A broker had a $5,000 bond filed when he obtained his real estate license. The broker is sued on a furniture claim and the creditor obtains a judgment for $1,750. Can the creditor recover on the broker's real estate bond?

Ans.
No. The claim did not result from a real estate transaction.

34. In relation to real property, in what instances are the following terms employed? (1) "Time is of the essence," and (2) "To apportion as of the date of deliver of the deed."

Ans.
(1) A provision in the contract that specifies the date of closing and makes that date mandatory for the parties to perform on that date. (2) Refers to the prorating of taxes, rents, interest, and insurance.

35. An agreement of sale includes the sale of rugs and draperies. After the deal is closed and the buyer takes possession, he finds that the seller has removed the kitchen linoleum, which was not cemented to the floor. Does the buyer have any remedy?

Ans.
No. The linoleum is personal property, which could be removed from the premises by the seller.

36. John Steel owns certain real estate clear of mortgages or unpaid taxes. Name three other types of encumbrances which might cloud the title.

Ans.
Judgments, a lease, a right of way.

37. In arranging for the closing of a real estate transaction, list several items that the broker should look after or check.

Ans.
1. Have a copy of the agreement of sale at the closing.
2. See that tax receipts, sewer, water, and rent receipts are available.
3. Leases are properly assigned to the buyer.
4. Endorsements for transfer of insurance policies prepared and signed.
5. Statement from mortgagee as to the exact balance due upon the mortgage; also eceipts for last payments of interest.
6. Prepare new deed to buyer.
7. Prepare a bill of sale for all personal property.
8. Prepare an estimate of closing expenses for both buyer and seller.
9. Transfer of keys.
10. Ascertain that the buyer has made his final inspection of the property if called for in the agreement.

38. Harris, owner of certain real estate, executed an exclusive listing contract of January 2, 1992, in favor of Stewart, a broker, for a period of three months, with power "for me and in my name to sell and execute contracts of sale" for the property in question. Stewart signed an agreement of sale with Snyder, the deal to close on March 1, 1992. Harris refused to convey the property, contending that where the principal-agent relationship is limited in time, the agent is without authority to enter into a contract to be performed subsequent to the expiration of the agency contract. Snyder brought suit for specific performance. Who will win?

Ans.
Snyder will win. Under the listing agreement, Stewart is authorized to execute a binding agreement for sale for the owner, Harris. It is of no consequence that the agreement of sale will be consummated subsequent to the expiration of the listing contract.

39. Name five items that are normally adjusted or prorated at the time of closing.

Ans.
Taxes, insurance, water and other utilities, insurance, rents, and interest on mortgages.

40. A and B sign a binder for the sale of a parcel of real property, with a provision that a formal contract would be signed the next day. The following day A refuses to complete the transaction. Can B force A to go through with the transaction since no formal contract was signed?

Ans.
No, since the terms of the contract have not been agreed upon. Courts do not make contracts for the parties.

41. You have obtained an offer for the purchase and have an earnest money signed by the prospective purchaser. The listing is signed by John and Mary Brown, his wife. You find that the property is owned by John Brown and Mary Brown, his wife, and Martha Brown, the mother of John Brown. The offer is acceptable to the Browns. Who would you have sign the agreement?

Ans.
John Brown, Mary Brown, and Martha Brown.

42. The following earnest money receipt was submitted as evidence:
May 10, 1992. Received from John Doe $8,000, Eight Thousand Dollars, earnest money on lot and house number 960 Union Street. Price $50,000, Five Thousand Dollars and balance of $45,000 to be paid when papers and title insurance are completed. It is understood this deal will be closed and house vacated on/before June 10, 1992. All furniture except personal belongings included in the transaction. Is this document binding?

Ans.
No. The agreement is too incomplete as it contemplates a subsequent instrument. In Oregon, omission of city is considered as fatal; in Pennsylvania, parol (oral) evidence permitted for purpose of giving a more precise description.

43. If a broker accepts a check from a buyer, who signs an agreement of sale which is accepted by the seller, and then the buyer stops payment on the check, is the agreement of sale void?

Ans.
No. The contract came into being when the agreement was signed by both parties. The check is incidental or collateral to the contract and has no effect on the validity.

44. A broker negotiates a real estate deal upon his oral promise that the will "find suitable or comparable quarters" for the seller. He fails to do so. Is he liable on his oral promise which is not contained in the agreement?

Ans.
Yes, the broker is personally responsible for damages to the seller for his failure to perform his promise.

45. In order to prevent the assignment of a real estate contract, what clause should be inserted?

Ans.
"It is agreed that the rights under the within agreement are not assignable."

46. A recorded agreement of sale constitutes a cloud on the title. How may it be removed?

Ans.
1. By a deed from the vendor.
2. By a quit claim deed from the vendee to vendor's purchaser.
3. By court decree.
4. By an instrument of extinguishment.

47. Identify the following whether realty or personalty: (1) growing corn, (2) cut logs, (3) growing wheat, (4) growing meadow grass, (5) nursery trees, (6) window shades, (7) electric chandeliers, (8) wall-to-wall carpet, (9) potted plants, and (10) gas grating setting in fireplace.

Ans.
1-2-3-5-6-9-10 are personalty.
4-7-8 are realty.

48. Where an offer has been mailed to the seller, is there a contract if the seller mails his acceptance, and due to some delay in the mail service, it does not reach the buyer in 15 days?

Ans.
Yes. The contract came into being when the letter of acceptance was mailed. The mail service is deemed the agent of the buyer since he used that medium in communicating the offer.

49. What is the difference between cancellation and recision of a contract of sale?

Ans.
Cancellation is by mutual consent. Recision is by court action.

50. To whose advantage is it to prorate taxes and rents from an income property as of the date of possession, rather than the closing date, which came earlier?

Ans.
Seller. He will continue to receive rents, which should exceed taxes and expenses.

51. A husband purchases a residence and take title, as such. Shortly thereafter the husband leaves and his whereabouts are unknown. The wife cannot afford to keep up the payments. Can she sell the house?

Ans.
No. Unless she has him declared legally dead after the years specified in the statute.

52. If a broker has good reason to suspect the competency of owner, due to his age and senility, and the owner wishes to sell, what protective steps can the broker take to avoid difficulty with some members of the owner's family?

Ans.
Have an interested party petition the court to appoint a guardian for the owner and have the guardian sign the agreement.

53. In selling a home, can the owner take with him the bedroom air conditioner, or does it belong to the buyer?

Ans.
This type of unit is considered as personal property.

54. John Davis, 21 years of age, signs an agreement to purchase a home. He is drafted by the Army before the deal is closed. He writes the owner to cancel the deal. Will he succeed?

Ans.
Yes, as a practical matter he is protected by law from any court proceedings on the contract during his military service. Rather than tie up the property indefinitely, the owner's interests would be best served by selling the property to another party.

55. Can a real estate salesperson be held responsible for earnest money that was turned over to his broker, who dies insolvent?

Ans.
No. The salesperson is required to turn over all deposits of earnest money to his broker.

56. Clayton lists his property with Moore Realty for $150,000. He obtains a prospect at $137,500. Clayton uses the offer of $137,500 to sell the property to his own prospect for $145,000. Is the broker entitled to a commission?

Ans.
No. This is one of the "risks of the trade." To protect himself, the broker should have communicated the terms of the offer to the owner but not left the written offer with him.

57. Under what circumstances can a broker represent a buyer?

Ans.
When employed by the buyer. The broker may not represent both buyer and seller, at the same time, unless both parties are informed and agree.

58. Is an agreement between broker and salesperson legal that states that if a salesperson leaves the broker's employ, he will never again engage in the real estate business?

Ans.
No. Contracts in restraint of trade must be reasonable as to area and time.

59. Should a broker quote any other price than the listing price to a prospect?

Ans.
No. He can entertain a lower price offered by the prospect and submit it to the owner and negotiate.

60. Alice Ritter agrees to sell her residence to James O'Donnel for $87,000 and agreements, dated June 17, 1991 are signed to this effect. The sale was to be closed on September 2, 1991. On August 14, 1991 O'Donnel agreed to sell the property to Steven Hill for $97,500 and assigned the agreement with Ritter to Hill. On September 14, 1991, Ritter is willing to deed to O'Donnel but she is unwilling to do business with Hill. Can Hill enforce O'Donnel's agreement?

Ans.
Yes. An agreement is assignable, unless it contains a clause to the contrary.

61. Saxman signs an agreement to sell vacant ground of 2 1/2 acres to Troop for $39,000, on June 23, 1991. Deal to be closed on September 11, 1991. The property is in a city zone which permits residential and commercial building use. Troop expects to erect retail store units, since none presently exist in the area. On August 9, 1991, the municipality adopts an ordnance restricting the subject area to residential only. Can troop rescind the deal because of the zoning change?

Ans.
No. When he signed the contract to purchase the land, he became the equitable owner of the property and as such is bound by the zoning change which affects the property.

62. How could have Troop protected himself in the above case?

Ans.
He should have included a clause in the agreement as to the proposed commercial use—that the seller knew that the property was being purchased for that intended use.

63. Henry Dunn and Margaret Dunn have signed an agreement for the sale of their home to Ben Eaton for $66,000. Eaton has paid $4,000 to them as a deposit. The date of the settlement was December 31, 1991, but the deal was not closed on that date. Eaton was very evasive as to when he would close. On February 15, 1992, the Dunns received a $65,000 offer from Hughes for the same property. Should the Dunns accepted the Hughes offer and keep Eaton's deposit?

Ans.
If the Dunns accept the Hughes offer and sign an agreement with him, it is quite possible that Eaton would sue for return of his deposit. The Dunns should tend the deed to Eaton and make demand for the purchase price, *before* they enter into an agreement with Hughes.

64. Allen Graham and Mary Stone, who plan to marry on Thanksgivings Day, 1991, sign an agreement on September 25, 19191, to purchase the residence of Margaret Wilson, a widow, for $70,000. Allen gives Mrs. Wilson his check for $7,000, as a deposit. The closing was to be on December 24, 1991. However, both Allen and Mary agree on October 1, 1991 to call off their engagement, and Mary elopes with a former suitor from Brazil a few days later, and moves to Brazil. Can Mrs. Wilson hold Allen Graham responsible on the agreement?

Ans.
Yes. Each named purchaser is responsible for the agreement of sale. Mrs. Wilson can keep the $7,000 deposit; or she can sue Graham for specific performance of the agreement.

65. An agreement of sale described the property as 3635 Buckner Street, Lots 1 & 2, excluding Triangle in southern part of Montana Industrial Park. The buyer sued for specific performance of the agreement. Will he succeed?

Ans.
No. The agreement is too indefinite. There is no way to know how large or how small the Triangle is; whether a major or a minor part of the land is to be conveyed.

66. A buyer and seller entered into a written agreement for sale which provided for Title Guarantee Co., to be escrow holder of the deposit money. Because it was representing an individual claiming title to the same property, it refused to accept the deposit. The seller's attorney told the buyers to deposit the earnest money in Providence Title Co. In a suit by the buyer for Specific Performance, the seller contends that the change in escrow holder had to be in writing under the Statute of Frauds. is his contention valid?

Ans.
No. The change was "an incidental condition" and did not change the character of substance of the agreement of sale, and it did not have to be in writing.

67. What are some attributes (or incidents) of a land contract?

Ans.
Vendee obtains possession of the property; pays annual taxes and assessments; discourages waste; must pay insurance premiums; any payments under the contract are applicable to the purchase price.

True and False

		Answer
1.	Agreements to exchange real estate of equal value need not be in writing.	False
2.	If there is a conflict between a printed clause and a written clause in an agreement, the written clause will prevail.	True
3.	Where a clause in a land contract provides for foreclosure upon default, advanced notice of intent to foreclose must be given.	False
4.	Misrepresentation in law is the same as fraud.	False
5.	An agreement for sale and a contract for sale are one and the same thing.	False
6.	Earnest money is paid to close the transaction.	False
7.	An agreement of sale must always be closed on the date specified in the agreement.	False
8.	An offer to purchase or an earnest money receipt can have the same effect as an agreement of sale.	True
9.	Once an offer to purchase is signed by the buyer, and is signed by the broker, there is an enforceable contract.	False
10.	Under the law every agreement of sale is assignable, even though a clause states it is nonassignable.	False
11.	The marital status of the parties to an agreement of sale should be stated.	True

12. The agreement of a minor to purchase a lot is voidable.   True
13. The buyer is entitled to a prompt return of his earnest money deposit if he   True
    withdraws his offer before the owner accepts it.
14. An offer to purchase is often called a preliminary contract.   True
15. Provided the broker and the buyer agree, it is permissible not to cash the   False
    earnest money check until the deal is closed.
16. If agreements of sale are signed between the buyer and seller, it is not necessary False
    for the broker to prove that the buyer is ready, able and willing to buy.
17. The broker is a third party creditor under the agreement of sale.   True
18. A purchaser under a land contract usually takes possession of the property.   True
19. A contract for the purchase of real estate for cash may be assignable to   True
    another.
20. Either the salesperson or the broker must witness the purchase contract to   False
    make it valid.
21. The term *option* and *listing* have the same meaning.   False
22. An option contract must be bound by a consideration.   True
23. Conditional land contracts of sale may be assignable.   True
24. The amount of the consideration determines the amount of the earnest   False
    money deposit.
25. Agreements of sale are subject to a government *freeze* on wages and prices.   False
26. A real estate broker is not required to give the buyer a copy of the closing   False
    statement until the deed is recorded.
27. The earnest money check should be made payable to the broker instead of   True
    the seller.
28. Where the sole owner is a married woman, the husband's signature is   True
    necessary on a contract of sale.
29. Land divided into six parcels is known as a subdivision.   True
30. Chattel is another name for the wife's interest in her husband's property.   False
31. In an option, the optionor has the right to collect rents on the property   False
    during the term of the option.
32. A broker should close the deals negotiated by his salesmen.   True
33. The full consideration in any real estate transaction must always be in legal   False
    tender.
34. Any broker can be given a valid power of attorney.   True
35. Contracts to exchange real property need not be in writing to be enforce-   True
    able.
36. The purchaser cannot rescind the deal and receive his earnest money after   False
    the seller has approved the deal.
37. Real estate sold on *conditional sales contracts* or *land contracts* can be   True
    subject to liens for indebtedness of the seller.
38. There is no difference between a voidable contract and a void contract.   False
39. It is important that the broker sign the contract of sale for real estate.   False
40. A sales agreement takes effect from the date it is signed by the seller.   True
41. When a prospect submits an offer to buy real estate to a broker, the prospect   False
    cannot withdraw his offer until the seller has had an opportunity to act
    upon it.

42. Both parties to an agreement for sale should receive signed copies of the agreement.   True

43. A contract of sale must be accompanied by a deposit to bind the transaction.   False

44. The real estate broker is not a principal party to an agreement of sale.   True

45. There must be at least three persons and a witness to form a binding agreement of sale.   False

46. An agreement of sale must be acknowledged by the vendor in order to be binding.   False

47. An option should always be signed by the optionee.   False

48. A *bill of sale* is the instrument by which title to real estate is conveyed.   False

49. Once an agreement of sale is signed, the broker may file a lien for his commission, if not paid.   False

50. An attorney-in-fact who signs an agreement of sale must be an attorney at law.   False

51. Restrictions as to the use of a property in an agreement are encumbrances but are not liens.   True

52. Fence posts are personal property.   False

53. An *abstract of title* guarantees a clear title.   False

54. An equity represents the actual amount of money a purchaser has paid on the property.   False

55. An option for which no consideration is given is not enforceable.   True

56. If a prospective purchaser revokes his offer in writing before he receives an accepted copy, of the offer to purchase, signed by the seller, he is entitled to the return of his deposit.   True

57. The sale of a property for cash automatically cancels a lease for less than one year.   False

58. An oral agreement for the sale of real estate, never reduced to writing, usually cannot be enforced.   True

59. Where money is actually paid as consideration for an option the option cannot be assigned by the holder thereof.   False

60. A purchaser cannot rescind the deal and get his earnest money back after the broker has told him that the seller accepted.   False

61. If the earnest money, received by a broker, is in the form of a note, it is essential that the agreement show that fact.   True

62. In a counter proposition the original offerer becomes the offeree.   True

63. If a seller is married, it is the duty of the broker to procure the signature of the seller's husband or wife, on the agreement of sale.   True

64. If a *slight* alteration is made on the earnest money receipt, after it is signed by the purchaser, this does not invalidate the earnest money receipt.   False

65. Once an owner accepts an offer to purchase even on different terms from those contained in the offer, there is a binding contract.   False

66. A purchaser buying real estate under a land contract does not usually have title to the property.   True

67. A valid written sales contract is binding even if the seller dies.   True

68. An agreement signed on Sunday is enforceable in most states.   False

69. If a person signs a joint and several note with other persons, it is possible that he may become liable for the entire sum of the note.   True

70. *Trade fixtures* means the brands, labels, names of products, and the good will of a business. — False

71. There must be an agreement of sale in order to bring action for specific performance. — True

72. When a property is sold, all insurance policies then in effect should immediately be canceled and new policies written. — True

73. An agreement of sale, which requires the purchaser to place his mortgage through the broker who negotiated the deed, is contrary to good ethics. — True

74. One who has taken an option on certain real estate may refuse to complete the transaction. — True

75. If the property is held by husband and wife as tenants in the entireties, neither may agree to sell to a third party his or her interest separately. — True

76. Unless expressly released in writing by the vendor, the vendee making an assignment of his interest in a land contract is not released from his liability for the unpaid balance of the contract. — True

77. Apportionment of taxes means prorating taxes between vendor and vendee as of the time of closing. — True

78. All rights under an agreement of sale are merged in the subsequent deed. — True

79. The seller is always entitled to keep the earnest money if the buyer defaults without cause. — True

80. A tender of deed and demand for payment of the consideration is necessary in order to place the buyer in default. — True

81. Any item of movable property is called a chattel. — True

82. A contract for deed and a land installment purchase contract are the same. — True

83. A broker, employed by an owner *to sell* his property, has authority to sign a binding agreement for the owner. — False

84. If the buyer notifies the seller that he will not complete the deal, the buyer is entitled to the return of his deposit. — False

85. Time in an option is of the essence. — True

86. Communication of the acceptance of an offer to purchase is essential to have an enforceable contract. — True

87. A counteroffer is the same as a rejection of the original offer. — True

88. When the title to real property is transferred, the insurance policies on the property are usually prorated at the closing. — True

89. An owner can refuse to sign a sales agreement for a store unless the buyer is sui juris. — True

90. Once the seller signs the sales agreement, he cannot later demand that the down payment be turned over to him. — True

91. A broker is not liable for an misstatements he makes because he is not a party of the sales agreement. — False

92. A broker is personally responsible, if he promises the buyer that he will procure a mortgage and is unable to do so. — True

93. If the sale is contingent upon the buyer selling his present home, the broker should include this fact in the sales contract. — True

94. A broker is within his rights in accepting a *postdated* check even if the sales agreement acknowledges cash. — False

95. It is acceptable practice for a broker to tell a salesperson to attend the closing in his sted, even if the salesperson did not negotiate the deal.   False

96. A broker should not compromise his commission claim in order to resolve a financial dispute between seller and buyer.   True

97. A broker cannot collect an earned commission if it is contingent upon a settlement that does not materialize.   True

98. An offer to buy may be withdrawn after the prospective purchaser and the seller have signed the writing, but before the seller's signed copy is delivered to the buyer.   True

99. An oral contract to sell real estate is not void but unenforceable.   True

100. If a buyer defaults on a sales contract, the broker should turn the entire earnest money deposit over to the seller.   False

101. A broker should not advise a buyer as to his legal rights where there is a dispute between buyer and seller.   True

102. Hand money, deposit money, and earnest money are one and the same thing.   True

103. Every state has a statute of frauds which requires real estate contracts to be in writing in order to be enforceable.   True

104. An acceptance of an offer to purchase after expiration of the time limit of the offer constitutes a *counter-proposition*.   True

105. Once an agreement of sale is signed, the broker may advance a salesperson part of the commission from the earnest money deposit.   False

106. Where a buyer withdraws his offer after he has signed the contract of sale, he is liable to the broker for his commission.   False

107. Where a single woman, who is engaged to be married, executes a sales contract for her own property, it is necessary to have her fiancé join.   False

108. An inmate of a home for the aged cannot execute a real estate contract without a court order.   False

109. A land purchase contract is generally used to purchase real estate by people of limited means.   False

110. A buyer may rescind an agreement of sale, where the broker, without authority of the seller, has misrepresented the property.   True

111. Where the broker knows that the property is infested with termites, and fails to disclose that hidden fact to the buyer, the latter can rescind the contract.   True

112. At the closing of a real estate deal, the seller can refuse to accept the buyer's personal check in payment of the consideration price.   True

113. The vendee pays the cost of preparing the mortgage or deed of trust papers.   True

114. A broker is entitled to a fee for preparing the mortgage papers.   False

115. Action by a buyer for specific performance of a contract of sale must be brought within two years from the specific date for performance.   False

116. Where the closing date in a sales agreement is more than three months in the future, the broker should insist upon a large than usual down payment.   True

117. One co-owner can bind another co-owner by signing an agreement of sale.   False

118. An article can change from personalty to real estate and then back to personalty.   True

119. Trade fixtures are usually so affixed to the property that they become part of the property and may not be removed. — False

120. Property classed as real property can become personalty. — True

121. A 30-day month is usually used in prorating real estate transactions. — True

122. Wall-to-wall carpeting in the bedroom can be removed by the vendor. — False

123. A buyer, under a land contract who erects improvements may remove those improvements, if he defaults on his contract. — False

124. An escrow holder is considered the agent for both the buyer and the seller. — True

125. Hand money paid upon signing a contract of sale is called an option. — False

126. An agreement of sale is usually more complex than an offer to purchase. — True

127. Under a land contract, the seller usually retains title until certain stipulated conditions are performed. — True

128. The consideration for a deed must always be shown in dollars and cents. — False

129. Where the money is placed in escrow, the buyer may reclaim it at any time prior to the closing date. — False

130. The court will not reform an ambiguous agreement for the parties. — True

131. A contract for sale involving financial responsibility is not assignable. — True

132. The unexpired premiums on an insurance policy are debits to the purchaser at time of settlement. — True

133. Unpaid city taxes at the time of settlement, are credited to the buyer. — True

134. In a purchase money mortgage, the buyer is the mortgagee. — False

135. The owner is the optionee in an option agreement. — False

136. The contractee is the same as purchaser. — True

137. A quit claim deed from a vendee to vendor may be used to extinguish an agreement of sale. — True

138. It is not necessary for all officers of a corporation to sign a deed. — True

139. A purchaser may rescind the transaction and recover his earnest money even after the seller orally approved the sale. — True

140. The optionor can enforce the terms of an option agreement by legal action. — False

141. $1 is sufficient consideration to support an option to purchase property worth $1,000,000. — True

142. Under an installment land purchase contract, the seller upon default can enter judgment for the balance. — True

143. An option is a bilateral contract binding both parties. — False

144. The agreement of sale controls the deed. — True

145. The first instrument a buyer signs is usually the offer to purchase. — True

146. An agreement of sale may be enforceable by the courts, even if no earnest money is received. — True

147. An aggrieved purchase can recover greater damages for fraud than for misrepresentation. — True

148. A licensed broker has the right to render an opinion on the validity of title to real estate. — False

149. If a buyer is to obtain a mortgage, the agreement should specify the amount, acceptable interest rate and terms. — True

150. A postdated check which is not paid, voids an executed agreement of sale. — False

151. Title insurance protects the buyer if the property is destroyed by fir before the deal is closed. — False

152. Gross inadequacy of consideration of price is always grounds for recision of an agreement of sale. — False

153. Laches and the statute of limitations are the same. — False

154. An oral agreement in the presence of two witnesses, accompanied by a handshake, will be enforceable. — False

155. A contract of sale of real estate differs from the sale of an automobile in that the real estate contract must be in writing. — True

156. If a deposit of earnest money is returned N.S.F. by the bank, the agreement is void. — False

157. The real estate broker is an important signatory to the agreement of sale which he negotiates. — False

158. An option may be extended by mutual consent, without an additional consideration. — False

159. Where property is under contract by the owner, a widow, and she remarries, a broker can recover a commission, if the husband refuses to sign the deed. — True

160. A recorded agreement of sale constitutes an encumbrance on the title. — True

161. Only a court of law can void a recorded agreement of sale. — False

162. A deed delivered by the vendor to the vendee will per se, extinguish a recorded agreement of sale between the same parties. — True

163. A seller can refuse to accept an assignee of the purchaser for any reason. — False

164. Courts abhor penalties in agreements of sale. — True

165. A broker, who is a Notary Public should not take the acknowledgement of the seller in a deal he negotiated. — True

166. A broker should recommend that the buyer consult an attorney before he signs an agreement of sale. — True

167. A builder *impliedly* warrants that a house he built is habitable. — True

168. A buyer can recover only deposit money and expenses where the seller fraudulently breaches a sales agreement. — False

169. A buyer assumes the risk for a change in zoning, after the agreement of sale is signed. — True

170. A *SOLD* sign is good advertisement for the broker. — True

171. The seller is charged with the marginal release of liens. — True

172. The pay-off figure on an existing deed of trust is a credit to the seller. — False

173. The buyer pays for the recording of the deed of trust. — True

174. A credit report fee is a credit to the buyer. — False

175. When rugs and draperies are included in a real estate sale, title to these items are usually transferred by a bill of sale. — True

176. The *time is of the essence* clause can be extended by verbal agreement of the parties. — True

177. The term of an option agreement can be extended if the optionee pays the optionor something of value. — True

178. A suit for specific performance is brought in a court of equity. — True

179. Permitting several consecutive defaults in payment on a land contract will stope the vendor from insisting on future timely payments. — False

180.	Under an installment contract, the vendee pays the property taxes.	True
181.	A land sales contract cannot be recorded.	False
182.	Where an agreement of sale is not closed on the date specified for closing, either party can sue for specific performance immediately.	False
183.	An agreement of sale must have a seal in order to be enforceable.	False
184.	A broker who participates in a duel mortgage contract is guilt of a criminal offense.	True
185.	In an equity action, the judge hears the case without a jury.	True
186.	Passive concealment of a defect by a vendor places duty upon the vendor to disclose.	True
187.	It is lawful to provide an agreement of sale that is not assignable.	True
188.	Life insurance on the life of the mortgagor is good protection in even the mortgagor dies.	True

Multiple Choice

1. An agreement of sale provided that it was "subject to the buyer's obtaining available financing." The only mortgage that the buyers were able to obtain was from a federal savings and loan association, at 9 1/2 percent interest for a term of 25 years. The offer of a loan also provided "that the stipulated rate of interest may be increased, but only after a 3-month written notice to the borrower." There was also a penalty on payment in excess of 20 percent of the original principal amount, but not on a bona fide sale of the property. The purchaser refused the loan because of these terms and conditions and they were unable to obtain a satisfactory loan elsewhere. Under these circumstances:

   Ans. d.

   I. The purchaser can recover his deposit.
   II. The purchaser should be reimbursed for all expenses incurred.
       a. I only.
       b. II only.
       c. Both I and II.
       d. Neither I or II.

2. Lester listed his home for sale at $95,000 with Walker, broker. Walker obtained a prospect, Wood, who made an offer of $88,000, which was refused. A month later he called Walker and told him he would pay $89,000. Walker told Wood, "If you want the house, you will have to act fast, because we just got an offer of $91,000." Wood offered $91,250, which was accepted by Lester. Deposit was $4,000, which Walker retained as his commission. Later Wood learned that Walker had no other offer and he seeks to rescind the agreement. Under these circumstances:

   Ans. c.

   I. Wood can rescind the agreement.
   II. Wood can recover the $4,000 retained by Walker.
       a. I only.
       b. II only.
       c. Both I and II.
       d. Neither I or II.

3. Margaret Doland agreed to purchase a dwelling through Henry Steel, broker, on Saturday, November 12, 1991. She signed an offer to purchase, and gave the broker a check for $1,000 as a deposit. The next day, another broker persuaded her to look at a house in another development. She looked at it and liked it much better. She called Steel the same day and told him that she had changed her mind and did not want the house. He told her that she was too late, as she had already signed a contract. She stopped payment on her check the next day. Under these circumstances:

Ans.
d.

I. Broker is entitled to a commission.
II. The agreement of sale is valid.
   a. I only.
   b. II only.
   c. Both I and II.
   d. Neither I or II.

4. Sawyer signed an agreement to purchase Wilson's property on March 21, 1992 for $96,000, subject to the contingency that he could get a variance of a prohibited use by June 16, 1992. He paid a deposit of $5,000. On June 1, 1992 the Zoning Board of Appeals denied the petition. The same day Sawyer took an appeal to Court and notified Wilson, in writing, that he would waive the variance and go through with the deal. Wilson thereupon notified Sawyer that the transaction was terminated and refunded the $5,000 deposit. Under these circumstances:

Ans.
a.

I. Sawyer can compel Wilson to deed the property to him.
II. Wilson can compel Sawyer to await the outcome of the appeal.
   a. I only.
   b. II only.
   c. Both I and II.
   d. Neither I or II.

5. An agreement of sale, to be enforceable against an owner, can be signed by:

Ans.
c.

   a. The broker, for the owner, in the owner's absence.
   b. The broker, upon the owner's verbal authorization.
   c. By the recorded owner.
   d. The broker for the owner, by telephone call from the owner, in the buyer's presence.

6. An agreement of sale is a contract between:

Ans.
c.

   a. Buyer and Broker.
   b. Between seller and broker.
   c. Between buyer and seller.
   d. Between buyer, seller, and mortgagee.

7. Adams sells his home, which is 22 years old, to Baker in June 1991. Baker does not check the furnace nor does Adams make any representations concerning it. In January 1992, the furnace "quits." Under these circumstances:

Ans.
a.

I. Baker must pay for the new furnace.
II. Baker can collect from Adams the "junk" value if the old furnace.
   a. I only.
   b. II only.
   c. Both I and II.
   d. Neither I or II.

8. Where a buyer causelessly defaults, the question whether to forfeit the earnest money deposit should be decided by the:

   I. The broker.
   II. The seller.
      a. I only.
      b. II only.
      c. Both I and II.
      d. Neither I or II.

Ans.
b.

9. Once an agreement of sale is signed, the purchaser has:

      a. Legal title.
      b. Equitable title.
      c. Ostensible title.
      d. Naked title.

Ans.
b.

10. Adams executes a contract for the sale of his dwelling to Berger. Thirty-one days before the closing, Adams dies. The result is:

      a. The deal is canceled.
      b. Berger can compel Adam's executor or heirs to complete the sale.
      c. The deal is in "limbo" for one year.
      d. The deal is voidable at the option of the deceased's heirs.

Ans.
b.

11. Broker A in cooperation with broker B made a sale, in which no earnest money was paid. The deal was closed and the buyer gave the broker the full amount due. The broker paid the net proceeds to the seller at the same time. The balance should be:

      a. Deposited in A's regular business account.
      b. Balance due B should be paid in cash.
      c. The balance should be run through A's trust account.
      d. B's share of the commission should be drawn by A to B's trust account.

Ans.
c.

12. When legal title is transferred as the result of the sale of real estate, which is encumbered by a trust deed (a mortgage), it is always necessary to:

      a. Obtain the consent of the mortgagee.
      b. Pay off the mortgage.
      c. Have the grantor deliver a deed.
      d. Completely refinance.

Ans.
c.

13. Gary, a Nebraska broker, represents to Hill, a former mill worker from Steelton, Pa., that the 200 acre farm he is selling him is in good condition. In fact, it has been cash cropped and the soil is in poor condition. Gary has been selling farms and ranches for 16 years and is a neighbor of the farm's owner. Upon hearing the true facts, Hill can:

      a. Rescind the deal.
      b. Can do nothing.
      c. Keep the farm but have the court reduce the price.
      d. File a complaint with the federal loan board.

Ans.
a.

14. Rushton enters into a contract for deed of a tract of land in Miami with the owner Alton. The consideration price is $400,000 and Rushton pays $50,000 on account. The balance is to be paid in installments of $2,800 per month with interest at 8 percent. This land contract is:

   I. In the nature of a purchase money mortgage.
   II. In the nature of a warranty in future.
     a. I only.
     b. II only.
     c. Both I and II.
     d. Neither I or II.

Ans.
a.

15. Broker Adams negotiated a transaction between Morgan, seller, and Zeigler, buyer. The agreement of sale provided for earnest Money of $1,500, and the date for performance, May 11, 1992 was "of the essence of the contract." At the oral request of the buyer, the broker agreed to an extension for performance to May 20, 1992. On May 12, 1992, the seller claimed that the agreement was breached and demanded the $1,500 deposit.

     a. The seller is entitled to the deposit.
     b. The seller is not entitled to the deposit.
     c. The buyer is entitled to a refund of the $1,500 deposit, less half of the broker's commission.
     d. The broker is entitled to his commission from the deposit money and any balance is due the buyer.

Ans.
a.

16. Bennett entered into an agreement of sale to sell his home to Randall. The deal was to be closed on June 21, 1991. Time was of the essence and the agreement was subject to the buyer obtaining a mortgage. Randall made a $3,000 deposit on the purchase price. Since Randall was unable to obtain a mortgage by June 21, 1991, Bennett verbally agreed to extend the time of closing until August 1, 1991. Randall still was unable to obtain a loan by that time. Randall demanded the return of his $3,000 deposit. Under these circumstances:

     a. Randall can recover his deposit.
     b. Bennett can keep the deposit.
     c. Randall can recover his deposit less Bennett's expenses.
     d. Randall must continue efforts for a reasonable time to obtain financing.

Ans.
a.

17. Whenever all parties to a real estate contract agree to terms, there has been:
     a. Legality of object.
     b. A meeting of the minds.
     c. Reality of consent.
     d. Bilateral consideration.

Ans.
b.

18. Unless there is a stipulation to the contrary, when real estate under a lease is sold, the lease:
     a. Must be renewed.
     b. Is immediately canceled.
     c. Remains binding on the new owner.
     d. Becomes a tenancy from month to month.

Ans.
c.

19. A broker receives a $5,000 deposit on January 1, 1992 on a property, the deal to be closed on July 3, 1992. He should deposit the money:

    a. In his checking account.
    b. In his trust account.
    c. In an interest bearing account.
    d. In G.M.A.C. notes.

    Ans. b.

20. Ames, a prospective purchaser writes a letter to Brown on January 7, 1992, offering to buy certain described real estate owned by brown for $20,000. Brown replies promptly by letter stating, "I accept your offer contained in your letter of January 7, 1992." Which of the following describes the situation?

    a. There is an offer but no acceptance.
    b. There is a valid contract between Ames and Brown.
    c. There is an acceptance but no offer.
    d. There is no contract between the parties.

    Ans. b.

21. Once the real estate transaction is closed, the closing statement, approved by the seller and buyer, should be:

    I. Recorded.
    II. Filed with the mortgage.
    a. I only.
    b. II only.
    c. Both I and II
    d. Neither I or II.

    Ans. d.

22. Tender of deed to the buyer is not necessary, where:

    I. Time is of the essence of the agreement.
    II. There has been an anticipatory repudiation.
    a. I only.
    b. II Only.
    c. Both I and II.
    d. Neither I or II.

    Ans. b.

23. In pro-rating $400 rent paid for June 1992, agreements were signed on June 15, 1992, and the deal was closed on July 1, 1992, you would:

    a. Credit the buyer with $400.
    b. Credit the buyer with nothing.
    c. Charge the seller with $200 (half).
    d. Charge the seller with $400.

    Ans. b.

24. A copy of the closing statements in a real estate transaction must be:

    a. Recorded.
    b. Kept by the broker for six years.
    c. Given to the seller and buyer.
    d. Given to the mortgagee.

    Ans. c.

25. An agreement of sale did not state when the deal was to be consummated. The agreement is:

    a. Void.
    b. Voidable at the option of the vendor.
    c. Voidable at the option of the vendee.
    d. Valid and enforceable, within a reasonable time.

    Ans. d.

26. One who has the right to sign the name of his principal to a contract of sale is:

    a. A special agent.
    b. An optionee.
    c. An attorney-in-fact.
    d. An attorney at law.

Ans.
c.

27. When real property is sold on an installment contract, and a warranty deed to be delivered at a future date, the warranty deed should be placed in the custody of:

    a. The real estate broker.
    b. The seller.
    c. The buyer.
    d. An escrow agent.

Ans.
d.

28. On January 1, 1991, Clay agreed to sell his residence to Dorrance for $122,500. Dorrance gave Clay a $5,000 deposit. The closing date was set for March 21, 1991. Dorrance failed to appear, and the broker, Hines, finds him very evasive as to when he will close. On June 16, 1991, Haines advises Clay "to forget" about Dorrance and he will try to get him another buyer. On July 3, 1991, Haines obtains another buyer, Joyce, to whom the property is sold, under an agreement of sale, with the deal to be closed on August 17, 1991. On July 17, 1991, Dorrance notifies Clay that he was ready to close immediately. Under these facts:

    I. Clay is bound to convey the property to Dorrance.
    II. Joyce can recover damages from Clay.
        a. I only.
        b. II only.
        c. Both I and II.
        d. Neither I or II.

Ans.
c.

29. Adams on March 21, 1991, obtains an option, for six months, to purchase Baker's property for $180,000. On September 15, 1991, Baker notified Adams that he will exercise his option on September 25, 1991, at the offices of the Tri-State Title Company. Baker appeared at those offices on that date and notified Adams that the option was canceled. Under these facts:

    a. The option is void.
    b. The option is valid, since Baker's appearance at the title company impliedly extended the option period.
    c. Adams can assert unjust enrichment to enforce the option.
    d. The doctrine of nunc pro tunc would apply to give Adams relief.

Ans.
a.

30. Which of the following instruments is not delivered to the buyer at the closing of the sale?

    a. Deed.
    b. Lease.
    c. Affidavit of title.
    d. Mortgage.

Ans.
d.

31. Under the usual form agreement of sale, the option to declare the deposit money forfeited belongs to:

    a. Seller.
    b. Buyer.
    c. Broker.
    d. Court of equity.

    Ans.
    a.

32. A purchaser's part ownership or interest in a parcel of real estate is called an/a:

    a. Equity.
    b. Equality
    c. Inheritance.
    d. Fee.

    Ans.
    a.

33. To each sales agreement there must be:

    a. An offer and acceptance.
    b. Earnest money payment.
    c. Notarial acknowledgement.
    d. A recordation.

    Ans.
    a.

34. When the contract of sale of real property includes the sale of certain removable fixtures, such as a refrigerator, radiator covers, etc., upon deliver of the deed the seller should also deliver:

    a. A bill of sale.
    b. A chattel mortgage.
    c. An estoppel certificate.
    d. A satisfaction piece.

    Ans.
    a.

35. A licensed broker promises a buyer of commercial property that a new post office will be built next door within six months. The post office is erected elsewhere.

    I. This is puffing the goods.
    II. This constitutes material misrepresentation.
    a. I only.
    b. II only.
    c. I and II.
    d. Neither I or II.

    Ans.
    b.

36. The statute of frauds was passed to prevent:

    a. Bribery.
    b. Forgery.
    c. Perjury.
    d. Embezzlement.

    Ans.
    c.

37. If the seller breaches an agreement of sale because he cannot deliver good title, the buyer can recover:

    a. Deposit money and expenses.
    b. Punitive damages.
    c. Exemplary damages.
    d. Full value of his bargain.

    Ans.
    a.

38. An option contract differs from a contract of sale in that:
    a. The option need not be consummated.
    b. The option needs no consideration.
    c. The contract of sale is enforceable by either party to it.
    d. The contract of sale requires money consideration.

Ans.
a.

39. A memorandum agreement of sale, dated March 21, 1992 is signed by Cook, seller, and Doran, buyer. No date is specified for performance, but in other respects the memorandum is adequate. Under these circumstances:
    a. The agreement is nudum pactum.
    b. The buyer has a reasonable time to close.
    c. Each party has one year to close.
    d. The agreement is ultra vires.

Ans.
b.

40. On October 3, 1991, Burns, a broker, negotiates a sale for Chapel at $98,000 and receives a $4,000 deposit from the buyer, Glean. The closing date is November 1, 1991. On October 28, 1991, Glean notified Burns that he will not be able to close on November 1st and desires an extension to December 15, 1991. Chapel refuses, unless Glean will put up an additional $3,000 deposit. Glen refuses to increase his earnest money deposit. Under these circumstances:

Ans.
d.

    I. The deal is cancelled.
    II. Glean is entitled to a return of his earnest money deposit.
    a. I only.
    b. I and II.
    c. II only.
    d. Neither I or II.

41. In most states, an action in court can be brought upon a formal (under seal) contract within:
    a. Five years.
    b. Six years.
    c. Ten years.
    d. Twenty years.

Ans.
d.

42. An owner delivers an option to purchase certain real estate to Smith upon Smith's payment of $10,000 within 30 days; the option recites that it is given in consideration for one dollar, the receipt of which the owner acknowledges; as a matter of fact, *nothing* is paid for the option. Under these circumstances the option is generally:
    a. Valid.
    b. Void.
    c. Voidable.
    d. Unenforceable.

Ans.
a.

43. The amount of deposit money is fixed:
    a. By the real estate licensing act.
    b. Agreement of the parties.
    c. A minimum of 5 percent of the consideration price.
    d. Determined by the broker.

Ans.
b.

44. A "binder," accompanied by a deposit, binds the:

    a. Buyer.
    b. Seller.
    c. Buyer and seller.
    d. Neither buyer or seller.

Ans. c.

45. The usual procedure is to deposit the earnest money payment:

    a. The next day after receipt.
    b. Within five days.
    c. Within one week.
    d. Anytime before closing.

Ans. a.

46. Where the seller defaults, the deposit money should be:

    a. Kept by the broker.
    b. Returned to the buyer.
    c. Placed in an escrow account.
    d. Paid in to the court.

Ans. b.

47. An oral agreement may be enforced where:

    a. The consideration price is less than $2,500.
    b. There is a down payment of 20 percent of the consideration.
    c. The purchaser has gone into possession, paid part of the purchase price, and made improvements.
    d. The broker guarantees performance.

Ans. c.

48. Breach of an oral agreement gives rise to:

    a. An action for specific performance.
    b. An action for damages, if there is fraud by the vendor.
    c. A suit by the broker against the buyer for commission.
    d. A suit for a written agreement of sale.

Ans. b.

49. An agreement of sale recites that the property is purchased "as is" and as a result of the buyer's inspection, that the "broker, and seller are not responsible for any oral representations made." After the closing, the buyer discovers that the basement walls have been recently painted to conceal water leaking into the basement. After a heavy rain, the buyer discovers he now has a wet basement. The buyer can recover damages:

  I. From the broker.
  II. From the owner.
    a. I only.
    b. II only.
    c. Both I and II.
    d. Neither I or II.

Ans. c.

50. A contract based on an illegal consideration is:

    a. Valid.
    b. Void.
    c. Legal.
    d. Enforceable.

Ans. b.

Appendix G
A GUIDE TO
TENANT/LANDLORD RELATIONS

QUESTIONS AND ANSWERS

1. What is a tenancy called where the lessee holds the land at the will of the lessor?

Ans.
Tenancy at sufferance or in some states, a tenancy at will.

2. Can a lease be enforced when the consideration is expressed in terms of farm products instead of money?

Ans.
Yes.

3. In computing the income from an apartment house, there are several major items taken from the gross income in order to arrive at the net. Name at least six.

Ans.
(1) Taxes, (2) insurance, (3) repairs, (4) depreciation on the building, (5) depreciation on the furnishings, (6) management expenses, and (7) license fees.

4. In a long-term lease, what provisions should be made in regarding to taxes?

Ans.
A clause that the tenant will pay any increases in taxes during the term of the lease.

5. In the management of property, name four duties which an agent owes to his owner.

Ans.
(1) Collect rents, (2) remit proceeds promptly, (3) keep good records, and (4) maintain and repair the property.

6. What is a sublease?

Ans.
A lease granted to another person by the lessee.

7. Name the essentials of a valid written lease.

Ans.
Parties, description, rental, term, and demising (leasing, signatures, and delivery).

8. In the investigation of a prospective tenant to determine his desirability, what information should be ascertained?

Ans.
Size of family, occupation, approximate income, previous address, former rental agent, and a credit report.

9. Where the tenant defaults in the payment of rent, can the landlord terminate the lease and evict a subtenant as well as the tenant?

Ans.
Yes. The subtenants rights rise no higher than those of the tenant.

10. Arthur verbally leased certain premises to James on February 1, 1991, for a one-year term from May 1, 1991 to April 30, 1992, with an option of two additional years at increased rental. On April 1, 1992, Arthur notifies James that the property has been leased to Black. Does James have any cause of action against Arthur?

Ans.
No. Under the Statute of Frauds, the lease from Arthur to James had to be in writing in order to be enforceable. In most states, the period is one year from the making of a lease, or from February 1, 1992. In Pennsylvania the period is three years.

11. A lease is made by the Rapid Realty Co. agent to John J. Flynn for a term of five years. The lease is approved by the owners. Prior to the expiration of the five-year term, the Realty Co. executed a new lease for an additional five-year period. Three months before the expiration of the original lease term, the owners notify Flynn to vacate the premises at the end of the term. The tenant insists that he has a lease for another five years. Is he correct?

Ans.
No. The agent's authority to execute a new lease beyond the period set by the statute of frauds must be in writing, and it does not appear that the agent had such written authority.

12. Rogers leases a premises to Pike for a one year term. The lease provides that if Pike lawfully holds over after the expiration of the term, he would be a tenant from "year to year" and so on from year to year. The original lease term ends on April 30, 1991. On April 20, 1991, Rogers notifies Pike to vacate the premises at the end of the current term, April 30, 1991. Pike refuses. Can Pike claim possession for another year?

Ans.
Yes. Rogers should have given Pike statutory notice (30-90 days, depending upon the state).

13. Jones leases a property to Brown for one year. The lease provides that if Brown remains over he shall be a tenant from "month to month". After 14 months' occupancy, Jones gives Brown 30 days notice to vacate. Brown claims he has a lease for an additional 10 months. Is Brown correct?

Ans.
No. The lease contract determines Brown's rights. It specifically provides that upon Brown's holding over, the tenancy shall be from month to month and this provision will be enforced.

14. A store lease provides that in the event of a sale, the lessee "agrees to vacate the said premises at any time after receiving -0- days notice in writing to do so. Archer sells the property to Connor, who notifies the tenant, Benson, to vacate the premises in 30 days. Benson claims that he has the right to remain in possession until the expiration of the lease term, a period of 20 more months. Who will win?

Ans.
Benson will win. It is a matter of intention of the parties, and it is inconceivable that the lease could be terminated in advance of the expiration date without any previous notice.

15. Lloyd leases certain property to Barns in February 1991, effective May 2, 1991. Before Barns took possession, Lloyd permitted Cox to dump earth on the premises so that Barns latter refused to take possession. Can Lloyd collect rent from Barns?

Ans.
No. Upon execution of a lease, there is an implied warranty that the conditions of the premises described in the lease shall remain the same during the time of the execution of the lease and the beginning of the term.

16. Adams leased certain property to Thomas and executed a release in favor of Clark, relinquishing his right to distrain upon certain articles owned by Clark and stored upon the premises. Later Adams sold the property to Dwight, who distrains for delinquent rent due him, upon Clark's property. Clark claims his property is exempt from levy because of Adams' release. Decide.

Ans.
Dwight can sell Clark's property, because Adams' release is personal in nature and not binding upon Dwight. A new release should have been obtained from Dwight.

17. A bank is a mortgagee in possession. It executes a lease to Casey for a two-year term. During the lease term the mortgage debt is paid by Boone, the mortgagor, who ousts Casey from possession. Does Casey have cause for action against the bank?

Ans.
Yes. The landlord guaranteed the tenant quite enjoyment of the premises which was broker by Boone, asserting a paramount title.

18. How could the bank have protected itself?

Ans.
By inserting a clause in the lease such as: "The lessee herein understands and agrees that the lessor is executing this lease under rights as a mortgagee in possession and does not in any way or manner covenant, agree, promise, or guarantee to the lessee, his heirs, or assigns, possession, quite enjoyment, or otherwise against any person having a paramount title or interest to the within leased premises, anything contained in the within lease to the contrary notwithstanding."

19. What are the interests of the lessor and the lessee in a lease called?

Ans.
Lessor's interest is called "Reversion" and the lessees interest is "an estate for years."

20. Ashley leases certain properties to Bridger for a motion-picture theater for 10 years, with the rights of assignment. Bridger expressly covenants to pay rent. Later Bridger forms a corporation and assigns the lease to the corporation. Upon subsequent insolvency of the corporation, Ashley seeks to hold Bridger personally liable. Will he succeed?

Ans.
Yes. By virtue of Bridger's covenant to pay rent, he continues liable during the term of the lease. He would be released from liability only if his lease was canceled an a new lease mad to the corporation.

21. A banking corporation leased certain premises to an oil company. Later the oil company refused to pay rent, claiming that the banking corporation's lease was *ultra vires* (beyond the powers of the corporation). Will it succeed?

Ans.
No. The contract is executed so that the *ultra vires* doctrine would not apply. In addition, it is a long-established rule in law that a lessee cannot impeach the title of his lessor for any cause except fraud.

22. Allen leased certain premises to Beck for a period of one year beginning on March 2, 1991. The lessee remained in possession through March 2, 1992. Is Beck liable for another year's rent?

Ans.
Yes. The lease expired at midnight March 1, 1992. Where the lessee holds over and continues to occupy the premises during all of the day of March 2 of the following year, he will be liable for the whole rent for the second year.

23. Ash leases certain premises to Blake for three years at $500 monthly. At the expiration of the three months, a flood damages the premises to such an extent that the premises are uninhabitable for five months. What, if any, is Blake's liability?

Ans.
He is liable for rent for the five month period. If the lease has no "Act of God" clause, Blake would also be liable for the cost of repairing the premises, exempted by statute.

24. Appel owns certain premises leased to Brent. There is a mortgage against the property, which is in default, and Cooper, the mortgagee, as well as Appel, demands rent from the tenant. To whom should Brent pay the rent?

Ans.
To Cooper. The mortgagee in possession, where the mortgage is in default, is entitled to collect rents.

25. A guest fell upon a landing in front of an apartment, due to a hole in the flooring. Is the lessor or tenant liable?

Ans.
The lessor. In an apartment the lessor is bound to make necessary repairs to stairways, landings, and the like.

26. What is the compensation or income received for the use of property called?

Ans.
Rent.

27. What type of property, as a general rule, may be distrained on the rented premises in order to collect delinquent rent?

Ans.

All property upon the premises irrespective of ownership unless specifically exempted by statute or previously released by the lessor.

28. Miller was a tenant of Stone in a small apartment house in Washington, D.C. 14 years. He planted flowers, plants, and shrubbery in the front yard. After the sale of the property to Wheeler, he moved and wanted to remove certain rose bushes. The owner took action to restrain him. Can the tenant remove the rose bushes.

Ans.

No. The bushes are *fructus naturales* and belong to the property. The tenant may not remove them.

29. What is meant by a percentage lease?

Ans.

A lease which provides that the rental shall be a percentage of the gross volume of business done upon the leased premises. The lease usually calls for a minimum rental.

30. Where Anders leases property to Brown, a person of dubious financial responsibility, for the term of five years, what steps can Anders take to protect his interests?

Ans.

(1) Require a surety on the lease.
(2) Require Brown to pay six month's rent in advance to be applied towards the last six months of the lease.

31. Axton leased the roof of a building to Barnes for three years for the purpose of erecting advertising signs. At the end of one year, Colfax, who owned an adjacent property, erected an addition that upon his property which obstructed the view of Barne's signs. Barnes refused to pay further rent. Can Axton collect?

Ans.

Yes. The lessor was in no way responsible for the interference. It is a "bad bargain" on Barnes's part.

32. If a number of the tenant's family is seriously ill or the premises are quarantined at the expiration date of the lease, what redress does the lessor have?

Ans.

None, until the condition abates.

33. In commercial leases what important clauses should be included for the lessor's protection?

Ans.

(1) Tenant to pay any increased insurance premiums due to the lessee's occupation of the property.
(2) Subordination clause so that lessor may place a first lien mortgage upon the premises.
(3) Tenant to pay an increased taxes during the term of the lease.
(4) Tenant to carry plate glass insurance.

34. A lease is drawn between P. Kelly and Kay Semel, beautician, for certain premises. Her father, Joseph Semel, has signed the lease as surety. Miss Semel, with the consent of her landlord, subleases the entire premises to Dorothy Adams. Is Miss Semel relieved from liability for the rent?

Ans.
No. As the original lessee, she continues liable for the rent during the term of the lease as she expressly covenanted to pay rent under the lease executed by her.

35. In what ways may a lease be terminated?

Ans.
(1) By performance; automatically terminates at the end of the period.
(2) By surrender; mutual cancellation of the lease prior to expiration of the term.
(3) By breach; act of the lessor is known as eviction; acts of the lessee is known as forfeiture.

36. Under the terms of a valid lease, must the landlord keep his tenant safe from trespassing of others upon the leased property?

Ans.
No. It is the duty of the tenant to enjoin such trespass.

37. Can a tenant after leasing a property for 25 years claim ownership by adverse possession against the heirs of the original lessor?

Ans.
No. Occupancy was permissive throughout and not hostile or adverse.

38. What articles belonging to others are usually exempt from a landlord's levy for delinquent rent?

Ans.
Leased articles, in most states, providing that notice of the leased articles is given to the lessor.

39. Albert leases certain property to Bold for a cigar store. In six months the place is raided five times as a "numbers joint." Court action is taken to padlock the premises. What is the status of rent for the unexpired period of the lease?

Ans.
The tenant would be liable for rent. If the landlord had guilty knowledge that the premises were to be used illegally, the courts would not enforce the lease.

40. Bates leased a warehouse to Chase on May 1, 1991 for a five-year term, with an option to purchase the property during the lease term for $900,000. The property was totally destroyed by fire on June 16, 1992. It was rebuilt within nine months. Is the lease terminated?

Ans.
Yes. The complete destruction of the building terminated the lease as of the date of the fire.

41. What do you understand by "distraint is a statutory procedure?"

Ans.

All steps must be strictly followed, such as notice, posting, appraisal, advertising and sale of tenant's goods. Where a distress for rent statute was applied so that corporate tenant did not receive service of process upon his person, when it could be found within the State of Florida, the statute was unconstitutionally applied and the distraint was invalid. *Phillips v. Gruin and Hunt, Inc. 344 So. 2d 568 (Fla. 1977)*

42. Where a member of a minority group has been refused a lease on that account, can he recover damages for mental anguish?

Ans.

Yes. (*Hinish v. meir & Frank Co., 115 P. 2d 438, Ore. 1941*)

43. A tenant, five months delinquent in rent, moves before expiration of the lease. He asks the owner to obtain a new tenant. The owner obtains a tenant at a higher rental. The first tenant then claims that the increased rent for the balance of the term should apply to his rent arrearages. Decide who will win.

Ans.

In favor of the first tenant, as decided in the case of *Wanderer v. Plainfield Carton Corp., 351 n.c. 2D 630 (Ill. 1976)*

True and False | Answer

1. A lease is a contract.	True
2. A lease given by a lessee is called a "release."	False
3. An estate for years and a tenancy for years means the same thing.	False
4. The terms "tenant" and "lessee" are generally used in the same context.	True
5. Where a tenant has been transferred to another city by his employer, he may terminate his lease.	False
6. "First right of refusal" is the same as an option to purchase the property under lease.	False
7. A tenant in a four-story apartment finds the elevator service is permanently discontinued. The tenant may move on that account.	True
8. Joint tenancy means ownership of real estate, not the leasing of it.	True
9. A lease stated that the rent was to be paid monthly, but did not specify that the rent should be paid in advance. In that case, the rent was due and payable on the last day of the month.	True
10. When a lease of a store does not provide who shall make necessary repairs to the premises, the cost of such repairs falls upon the lessor.	False
11. An oral lease for one year is valid.	True
12. An agent's authority to execute a lease for more than three years must be in writing.	True
13. A lease usually favors the tenant.	False

14. A married woman has the authority to execute a lease to property owned by herself and her husband. — False

15. The beneficiary of a trust estate must always join in the lease by the trustee. — False

16. A lease is assignable if there is no clause to the contrary. — True

17. A sky lease is one for space above the 25th floor. — False

18. A tenant can refuse to pay rent where the owner failed to make repairs agreed upon. — True

19. A lessor is not liable for damages where he voluntarily makes repairs and does so negligently. — False

20. The lease of a tenant on a store building expires if there is a change of ownership of the property. — False

21. On a percentage lease the monthly rental is always the same and does not vary. — False

22. A lease for less than one year need not be in writing to be enforceable. — True

23. City property may be leased from 1 to 99 years. — True

24. A 22 year lease on a farm is valid. — True

25. Where leased property is condemned by the municipality, the lessee has the right of action against the lessor for damages. — False

26. A tenant in an apartment building must pay rent if the building is destroyed by fire. — False

27. A tenant in possession of the entire building is liable for injuries suffered upon the leased premises. — True

28. A tenant is always entitled to the first right of refusal if the property is put up for sale. — False

29. Where the leased property is taken under eminent domain, the tenant can recover for the value of his lease from
    a. The lessor.
    b. The body or corporation condemning the property.
    — a. False
    — b. True

30. Where a lessor accepts delinquent rent for five months, he cannot refuse to accept the rent for the next month because it is after the due date. — True

31. A sale clause in the lease refers to the period of time a tenant must be given in order to terminate the lease. — True

32. A tenant for one year, who holds over after the term would be a tenant for an additional year. — True

33. A lessor may levy for back rent against a stranger's goods found upon the premises. — True

34. In case of ambiguity in a lease, it is construed most strongly against the lessor and his agent. — True

35. On levying for delinquent rent, the lessor, or his agent may break open an outer door in the tenant's absence. — False

36. A landlord is liable for injuries to a guest suffered in the collapse of a public building such as a grandstand. — True

37. Where a landlord distrains for rent, he cannot, at the same time, terminate the lease. — True

38. An estate for years is a leasehold. — True

39. A landlord may send mechanics into leased premises to make alterations even though the lease contains no specific authority to do so. — False

40. A mortgagee i. possession c!nnot lease the e/rtgaged property.   False

41. A tenant is required to repair frozen water pipes.   True

42. Where a lease contains a "first right of refus may file a lien for his   False
    commission, if not paid.

43. There is an implied warranty that the tenant will enjoy quiet and peaceful   True
    possession during the term of his lease.

44. A mortgagee in possession of leased premises must account to the owner   True
    for all rents received.

45. A broker's right to a commission for rents, containing a sales clause, ceases   True
    under the lease prepared by the broker if the property is sold.

46. Broker windows in a leased property are the tenants liability.   True

47. A writing which transfers possession of property but does not transfer   True
    ownership is a lease.

48. A tenant, who installs a fancy chandelier in a rented property and destroys   False
    the old one, is permitted to remove it at the expiration of his lease.

49. Failure of a tenant to pay his rent when due does not constitute a termina-   True
    tion of his lease automatically.

50. A tenant, who assigns a lease to a third party, is still liable for rent, even   True
    though the lease permits the assignment.

51. No lease is assignable unless the lease specifically grants this right to the   False
    lessee.

52. "Graduated" lease can provide for a change in the rent to be paid, either   True
    lowering or raising it.

53. An owner can compel a tenant to remove store shelving at the end of his   True
    lease term.

54. A lease given by an owner to his tenant is considered personal property.   True

55. Parol testimony can always be introduced to explain the terms of a written   False
    lease.

56. Under a net lease, the lessee is liable for increased property taxes.   True

57. Death of a lessor, during the term, terminates the lease.   False

Multiple Choice

1. A lease for 50 years is: Ans.
    a. Realty.   b.
    b. Personalty.
    c. Lis Pendens.
    d. A lease in perpetuity.

2. The manager of a multi-unit commercial building usually receives as   Ans.
   compensation: c.
    a. A straight salary.
    b. A percentage of net income.
    c. A percentage of gross income.
    d. A percentage fixed by the local apartment manager's association.

3. A property owned by Margaret and William Rushton, man and wife, was leased by William alone, to Commercial Sales Inc., for a five-year term. Rent was paid for the first two years to William. The following rent for two months was paid to Margaret. William brought a distraint action for breach of lease. Under these facts:

I. Payment to the wife was satisfaction of the rent claim.
II. The court would hold that William acted for himself and as agent for Margaret in executing the lease.
   a. I only.
   b. II only.
   c. Both I and II.
   d. Neither I or II.

Ans. c.

4. Clark leased a commercial property to Monroe for a tavern, for a term of five years. Within the second year, Monroe is convicted twice by the Liquor Control Board for permitting gambling and selling liquor to minors. Clark brings an action to terminate the lease. Under these circumstances:

I. Clark's action is void because the rent is not in default.
II. Monroe can recover damages for an illegal termination of the lease.
   a. I only.
   b. II only.
   c. Both I and II.
   d. Neither I or II.

Ans. d.

5. Which one of the following will not terminate a lease?
   a. Performance.
   b. Breach.
   c. Surrender.
   d. Vacancy.

Ans. d.

6. Which one of the following tenancies does not apply to a lessor-lessee relationship?
   a. Tenancy at will.
   b. Tenancy in common.
   c. Tenancy for years.
   d. Tenancy at sufferance.

Ans. b.

7. The legal compensation of income received from the use of real property is called.
   a. Ground rent.
   b. Interest.
   c. Rent.
   d. Owner's equity.

Ans. c.

8. Which one of the following is ordinarily not essential to the validity of a month-to-month lease?
   a. Offer and acceptance.
   b. Consideration.
   c. In writing.
   d. Reality of consent.

Ans. c.

9. A clause in a lease by which a lessor agrees with the lessee that the latter shall have the first right to purchase the property at the same price as offered by a prospective purchaser is called:

    a. An option clause.
    b. First right of refusal.
    c. An election clause.
    d. A prime clause.

Ans. b.

10. A landlord rents a store to a men's clothier on a "percentage basis." On which of the following is the percentage based?

    a. Market value.
    b. Assessed value.
    c. Tenant's gross sales.
    d. Tenant's net income.

Ans. c.

11. When a tenant is delinquent in his rent under a written lease, the owner may have him evicted by:

    a. Notifying the Real Estate Commission.
    b. Having the Office Housing Expeditor take legal action.
    c. Giving the tenant 30 days notice.
    d. Bringing court action.

Ans. d.

12. When a guest is injured on a leased dwelling, he may bring action (in most states) against:

    a. Lessor.
    b. Lessee.
    c. Broker, who collects the rent.
    d. Person, who has equitable title.

Ans. b.

13. Under a lease for three years, if the tenant remains in possession after the expiration of the term, the lease is:

    a. Canceled.
    b. Renewed for three years.
    c. Renewed for one year.
    d. None of these.

Ans. c.

14. Distraint is a proceeding to:

    a. Prevent a tenant from removing.
    b. Collect delinquent rent by lessor.
    c. Impeach the lessor's title.
    d. Prevent lessor from showing property to a sales prospect.

Ans. b.

15. A lease by an infant lessor is:

    a. Void.
    b. Voidable by lessee.
    c. Voidable by lessor.
    d. Not renewable.

Ans. c.

16. A pedestrian injured due to the negligent accumulation of snow and ice in from of an apartment building can recover damages from:

    a. The municipality.
    b. The real estate broker who negotiated the lease.
    c. The first-floor tenant.
    d. The lessor.

Ans. d.

17. Pedestrian traffic counts are usually taken to determine the:

    a. Urban population.
    b. Size of the shopping area.
    c. Rental value of the location.
    d. Average age group.

Ans.
c.

18. A lease gives the tenant an option to purchase the property for $40,000. The owner receives an offer from a third party for $55,000.

    a. The tenant can purchase the property for $40,000.
    b. The tenant can purchase the property for $55,000.
    c. Third party can buy it.
    d. Owner must pay the tenant $15,000.

Ans.
a.

19. Where a tenant's furniture is damaged by water due to the negligence of an upstairs tenant, he can:

    a. Refuse to pay rent until made whole.
    b. Move out if this happens again.
    c. Bring a civil suit against the upstairs tenant.
    d. None of these.

Ans.
c.

20. Where a four-room apartment is leased to a young couple and later the parents of the couple move in with them, the landlord can:

    a. Do nothing.
    b. Terminate the lease.
    c. Increase the rent proportionally.
    d. Require tenant to post bond against damages.

Ans.
a.

21. A lease which requires the tenant to pay all expenses of the property in addition to his rent is called:

    a. A gross lease.
    b. An assigned lease.
    c. A percentage lease.
    d. A net lease.

Ans.
d.

22. According to the Statute of Frauds, a verbal lease for five years is:

    a. Enforceable.
    b. Not enforceable.
    c. Assignable.
    d. Renewable.

Ans.
b.

23. Under a "net rental agreement," the tenant usually meets all but one of the following charges:

    a. Taxes.
    b. Mortgage interest.
    c. Plate glass insurance.
    d. Liability insurance.

Ans.
b.

24. A tenancy at will is:

    a. Tenancy for a specific time.
    b. Possession of property under a will.
    c. Life estate.
    d. None of the above.

Ans.
d.

25. Cancellation of a lease by mutual consent of lessor and lessee is called:

    a. Action of rescission.
    b. Action of revocation.
    c. Surrender and acceptance.
    d. Lis Pendens action.

Ans. c.

26. Ground rent is a fixed rental.

    a. Paid for vacant property.
    b. Rental paid on a parking garage.
    c. Rental paid by a grantee to a grantor.
    d. Paid by an upper tenant to a first-floor tenant.

Ans. c.

27. A lease which provides for a step-by-step increase in the ental at regular intervals is called:

    a. An installment lease.
    b. A percentage lease.
    c. An open lease.
    d. A graduated lease.

Ans. d.

28. Net return on investment property is computed by deducting all expenses from:

    a. Gross annual income.
    b. Gross annual income less depreciation.
    c. Appraised value.
    d. Market price.

Ans. a.

29. Accepting rebates on purchased materials for an office building is unlawful for which ones of the following:

    a. Owner.
    b. Tenants.
    c. Broker managing the property.
    d. Building manager.

Ans. c. & d.

30. The unlawful taking of possession of real estate from a person in possession is known as:

    a. An ejectment.
    b. An eviction.
    c. Ouster.
    d. Recapture.

Ans. b.

31. A life tenant may convey:

    a. A fee simple title.
    b. A perpetual easement.
    c. A tenancy per autre vie.
    d. None of these.

Ans. c.

32. A lessor has the right to show the premises to a prospective purchaser, because:

    a. An implied right under the law of landlord and tenant.
    b. Provision in the lease contract.
    c. He has a bona fide prospect.
    d. The showing is between 10 A.M. and 5 P.M.

Ans. b.

33. Under a ten-year commercial lease, the lease can provide that the tenant: Ans.

    I. Pay increased taxes.   c.

    II. Pay for repairs.

      a. I only.

      b. II only.

      c. Both I and II.

      d. Neither I or II.

34. Adams was a tenant in an industrial building. Due to the loud noises from   Ans.
printing presses in the space of an overhead tenant, he refused to pay rent,   a.
claiming a constructive eviction. The landlord sued for rent. Under these
circumstances:

    I. The landlord can recover the rent.

    II. The landlord must abate the nuisance.

      a. I only.

      b. II only.

      c. Both I and II.

      d. Neither I or II.

35. A lease for a bowling alley did not require the landlord to make repairs. A   Ans.
severe rain storm flooded the building three feet deep. The bowling alleys   a.
were damaged beyond repair. The building suffered only minimal damage
and could be repair within one week. Under these circumstances:

    I. The tenant continues to be liable for rent.

    II. The owner must restore the alleys.

      a. I only.

      b. II only.

      c. Both I and II.

      d. Neither I or II.

36. An apartment was rented for one year. The tenant remained over for the   Ans.
second year. Near the end of the second year, the owner notified the tenant   b.
and the other eleven tenants to vacate their units at the end of the month,
as the leases would not be renewed; and that eviction would be brought if
they remained for a third year. The tenants claimed that the owner was
retaliating against them, because they had filed complaints alleging city
housing building code violations. In a suit:

      a. Owner will win.

      b. Tenants will win and the lease renewed for one more year.

      c. The lessor can only recover the rent plus a penalty.

      d. The lease will become a month to month lease, and lessor can
collect the delinquent month.

37. A tenant was delinquent for four weeks in rent on a one-year lease with   Ans.
rent payable weekly. During the tenant's absence, the landlord entered the   d.
premises and changed the entrance lock. The tenant was unable to enter
her apartment. She sued for damages.

      a. The tenant cannot recover.

      b. The tenant can recover.

      c. The tenant will have free rent for the remainder of the term.

      d. The tenant can recover nominal damages, since she suffered no
physical harm.

38. In a lease to a mercantile establishment, it is preferable, from the standpoint of the lessor, to have:

    a. A straight lease with no assignment clause.
    b. A percentage lease, on volume of sales, with a minimum rent provision.
    c. A net lease.
    d. A first right of refusal.

Ans. b.

39. A commercial lease in a shopping center usually requires the lessee to:

    I. Pay the same monthly rental stated in the lease.
    II. Pay a percentage based upon the gross volume of sales over a certain minimum amount.
    a. I only.
    b. II only.
    c. Both I and II.
    d. Neither I or II.

Ans. b.

Appendix H
A GUIDE TO OTHER
REAL ESTATE KNOWLEDGE

QUESTIONS AND ANSWERS

1. How long has an owner of property sold for taxes the right of redemption?

   Ans.
   The period varies from state to state from one year in Oregon to five years in California.

2. What is the effect of a recorded judgment on the real property of the judgment debtor?

   Ans.
   It is a lien upon all of the property of the debtor in the County in which the judgment is recorded.

3. What is a deficiency judgment?

   Ans.
   A judgment for the difference between what the debtor owed and the amount realized from the debtor's property at the foreclosure sale.

4. Does compliance with the bulk sales law relieve the purchaser of liability for outstanding indebtedness of the seller?

   Ans.
   All except back sales taxes which constitute a lien against the assets of the business.

5. Define a judgment.

   Ans.
   It is an decree of a court of competent jurisdiction which determines that one individual is indebted to another and fixes the amount of the indebtedness.

6. What kind of judgments are there?

   Ans.
   In personam - which bind the person against whom they are rendered and all of his real estate.
   In rem - which bind a particular piece of real estate only and are against a particular person because he is the owner of the property.

7. Do judgments bind personal property?

   Ans.
   Not in the sense that it is a lien; however, personal property can be sold in satisfaction of a judgment.

8. Suppose Adams obtains a judgment for $10,000 against Brant, the owner of three tracts of property. Can Brant sell one of the tracts to Chalmers and give good title?

Ans.
No. Adam's judgment is against all of Brandt's property.

9. Is a judgment a lien on property acquired by the debtor after the judgment was recorded?

Ans.
No. The new property can be brought under the judgment only by reviving the judgment.

10. In what three ways may a judgment be entered?

Ans.
1. By confession.
2. By default, and
3. By Verdict of the court.

11. How long does a judgment remain a lien?

Ans.
Depending upon the state, from 5 to 10 years.

12. Is title acquired by a purchaser at a treasurer's sale for unpaid taxes good and marketable?

Ans.
No. Not until the owner's right of redemption has expired.

13. What is the best way for a purchaser of a new home to protect himself against the filing of contractor and subcontractor liens?

Ans.
The best way is title insurance.

14. A borough ordnance required that a person engaged in soliciting or canvassing required a license and payment of a fee. A real estate broker was prosecuted under the license law. Was the law valid?

Ans.
No. A broker licensed by the state would be exempt from the ordnance. The legislature, in delegating authority to the Real Estate Commission, to license and regulate brokers state-wide precludes a municipality form exercising local control (*City of Chicago v. Barnett, 88 N.E. 2d 477, Ill. 1949*).

15. Danton obtained a judgment against Fenton, a licensed real estate broker, in a civil suit arising out of a real estate transaction. The Real Estate Commission instituted an action against Fenton for revocation of license. Was the transcript of evidence, findings, and conclusions of the civil suit, admissible as evidence in the hearing under the license law?

Ans.
No. The court so held in the case of *Dittmeir v. Missouri Real Estate Commission, 237 S.W. 2d 201 (1951)*.

16. In regarding real estate licensing fees, what is the distinction between an occupational tax and a regulatory fee?

Ans.
An occupational tax is paid to the state treasurer and used by the state in any way. A regulatory fee, such as a real estate license fee, is one for the regulation and enforcement of real estate licensing. It must bear a reasonable relationship to such cost, and if excessive, will be held invalid (*C. Dan Blackshear et al. v. G.W. Hogan et al., File No. C-22561, Civil Action, Fulton County Superior Court, Ga., 1977*)

17. Can a person lawfully act as a broker or as a salesperson in a single isolated transaction without having a license?

Ans.
In almost all states the answer is no.

18. What must a builder do if he wishes to hire a salesperson to sell the houses built by himself?

Ans.
He must secure a broker's license. A salesperson can be employed only by a licensed broker.

19. Can a salesperson lawfully accept a commission from a purchaser or seller in addition to the compensation paid him by his broker, even with his broker's approval.

Ans.
No. A salesperson may only accept compensation from his employing broker.

20. A licensed broker tells his milk man to keep his eyes open in meeting his customers and says, "If you get me any leads that result in a sale, I'll pay you $50 for each sale I make." Two sales are made. Can the broker legally pay him $100?

Ans.
No. A broker may pay licensed salespeople in his employ or other licensed brokers. The milk man would also be subject to prosecution for operating as a broker without a license.

21. List four classes of persons who are not required to be licensed to sell real estate.

Ans.
1. Owners.
2. Persons operating under a power of attorney.
3. Attorney-at-law in the performance of their duties.
4. Executors, receivers, and trustees.

22. The Metropolitan Realty Corporation is duly licenses, with Mr. Smith, the secretary, holding the original broker's license, and Mr. Thomas, the treasurer, an additional broker's license. Mr. Price, the president, has inadequate experience to qualify for a broker's license. Can he be issued a salesperson's license?

Ans.
In some states, an *officer* of a corporation must be licensed as a broker, if he actively engages in the real estate business. In others only one officer must be licensed as a broker and other active officers may be licensed as associate brokers or salespeople.

23. In the event an officer of a real estate brokerage corporation, who is unlicensed to represent it, negotiates a sale of real estate which is listed with the corporation, is the corporation or the officer entitled to the usual commission for making the sale?

Ans.
The officer must be licensed in order to claim a commission by the corporation which he represents. The corporation, being an artificial person, can only operate through its officers and representatives.

24. John Adams, a small-town broker, is duly licensed and has built up a substantial business. He has one licensed salesperson. John dies, survived by his widow, Mary.
    1. Can Mary operate the business, as John's widow and sole heir?
    2. Can Mary operate the business through the salesperson?

Ans.
1. No. A broker's license is personal and not transferable.
2. No. A salesperson may only operate only if employed by a broker.
In actual practice, the local REALTOR® Board would probably appoint a broker to operate the business until Mary could obtain her own broker-employee or sell the business.

25. Higgins, a licensed broker in New York, but not in Florida, contacts Wiggins, a Florida licensed broker, and together they contacted Pickens at West Palm Beach, Florida, regarding the purchase of the Sea Breeze Hotel listed with Wiggins for sale. Higgins and Wiggins have agreed to split the commission 50-50 if Pickens buys. The sale is made and Wiggins pays Higgins one-half of the agreed commission. Has Wiggins violated the license law?

Ans.
Yes. Higgins is not a licensed broker in Florida and because he carried on active negotiations in Florida, he is required to have a Florida license. It was illegal for Wiggins to pay a commission to an unlicensed person.

26. What are the two basic requirements for a real estate license under the various state laws?

Ans.
Competency and trustworthiness.

27. Distinguish between the work of a broker and that of a salesperson.

Ans.
A broker represents the owner or purchaser. The salesperson operates under the supervision of his employing broker.

28. In a partnership one member has asked to be licensed as a broker and the other as a salesperson. Can licenses be issued in accordance with these applications?

Ans.
In a partnership every active partner must be licensed as a broker or an agent. In some states all active partners must be licensed as brokers with one being designated principal broker and the others as associate brokers.

29. How many real estate transactions must a salesperson complete in order to be eligible for a broker's license?

Ans.
The criteria is not number of transactions but the number of years licensed as a salesperson. Normally the requirement is two or more years experience as a licensed salesperson.

30. Adams files a complaint against Brown, a real estate broker, alleging serious fraudulent misrepresentations made by Brown to Adams in connection with a real estate transaction. At the hearing scheduled on the complaint, Brown offered to surrender his license voluntarily and requested that the hearing be called off. The Real Estate Commission refused to accept the surrender of license and proceeded with the hearing. Brown filed an appeal from the commission's revocation of license. Was Brown within his rights in offering to surrender his license in lieu of a hearing?

Ans.

No. Brown could not waive hearings on the charge. The hearing was proper. The Commission has the duty, as well as the right, to proceed upon the complaint, to determine if the broker was a fit person to hold a real estate license at a *later date*. There is a serious difference between surrender of license and revocation for cause.

31. Alden is president and sole stockholder of a real estate corporation. He employs a number of salesmen. A number of complaints are filed against the firm alleging misrepresentations by its salespeople. When a complaint is filed, the salesperson is fired and his license surrendered for cancellation. Is the corporation subject to any disciplinary action?

Ans.

Yes. License laws generally provide for that the broker's license be suspended or revoked where he is deemed guilty of "of a continued or flagrant pattern of misrepresentation or making of false promises through agents or salesmen." A broker cannot close his eyes to the actions of his agents and thus escape personal liability.

32. Where a real estate salesperson, employed by one broker, is assisted by another salesperson, employed by a second broker, under an agreement to share commissions, is it lawful for one salesperson to pay a commission directly to the assisting salesperson?

Ans.

No. Payment to the second salesperson must be through his employing broker.

33. What is the effect upon the licenses of salespeople, employed by a broker, whose license has been revoked or suspended?

Ans.

Immediate and automatic suspension. The salespeople may apply for a license with another licensed broker who agrees to hire them.

34. What is the difference between a REALTOR® and a real estate broker?

Ans.

A REALTOR® is a licensed broker and in addition is a member of the local, state, and THE NATIONAL ASSOCIATION OF REALTORS®.

35. Adams, a real estate broker, sells his real estate business to Brady, a licensed real estate broker, and agrees not to engage in the real estate business within a distance of two miles for a period of five years. Shortly after the sale, Adams opened a real estate office within two blocks of Brady. The latter files a complaint against Adams with the Real Estate Commission, claiming that Adams is guilty of untrustworthiness. May the commission revoke Adam's license?

Ans.
Yes. So held in *O'Hare v. Gilchrist, 210 N.Y. App. Div 518.*

36. Roberts sued Clark for a real estate commission. He failed to set forth in his statement of claim or to prove that he was a licensed broker. May he recover?

Ans.
No. Failure of a broker to prove he is licensed is fatal to his claim.

37. Ash sells Beale certain property for $35,000 and says that he thinks it will be worth $50,000 in two years. At the end of two years, Beal can sell the property for only $20,000. Is Ash guilty of misrepresentation?

Ans.
No. Ash has expressed his opinion. His statement constitutes "puffing of goods."

38. If you desire to use the word REALTOR® in your advertisements, what must you do to obtain that privilege?

Ans.
Become a member in good standing with the local, state, and NATIONAL ASSOCIATION OF REALTORS®.

39. Is it ethical for a broker to sell his own property to a client? Under what conditions?

Ans.
Yes. Providing the broker makes it known that he is, in fact, the owner of the property.

40. Does a Real Estate Commission have authority, on its own, to investigate any action of a broker or salesperson and call the matter to a hearing?

Ans.
It not only has the authority but has a duty to investigate any such problems which comes to its attention.

41. What constitutes misrepresentation?

Ans.
Misstatements of material fact which induce the contract. It may be innocent or wilful. If willful, it may constitute fraud.

42. The Ajax Realty Company advertises that it will give a 50-inch television to every purchaser of a dwelling through its office. Is this legal?

Ans.
No. It is illegal to pay a commission or anything in value to anyone other than a licensed broker.

43. What recourse does an applicant have in the case where the Commission arbitrarily refuses to license an applicant, found to be competent by State examination?

Ans.
The applicant can institute a mandamus action in court against the Commission.

44. The "Square Inch-Square Deal Co." advertises for a person to sell square-inch tracts of land, owned by the company, on Pikes Peak. The purchasers pays $1.00 and receives a deed, signed by the President, Chief Running Deer. The persons hired are to receive 50 for each sale made. Must these salespersons be licensed?

Ans.
Yes. The sale is of *real estate* and the sales persons must be licensed.

45. What legal papers may a licensed broker prepare?

Ans.
Only those State approved forms which are directly related to his employment—listing contracts, earnest money agreements, leases, and so on. In some states the broker is also empowered to close deals and prepare all papers, such as deeds, required to complete the sales transaction. In other states these closing actions are reserved to attorneys or specified agencies such as licensed escrow companies, or land title firms.

46. In endorsing the application of a prospective salesperson, what statements does the broker make?

Ans.
That he intends to hire the salesperson when licensed. In some states he may also be required to certify to the applicants character, determined by personal knowledge or proper investigation.

47. Does the Real Estate Commission have jurisdiction in commission disputes between (a) seller and broker, and (b) broker and salesperson?

Ans.
(a) No. (b) In most states, no. In New Jersey and Florida, yes. In other states disputes are usually handled by the arbitration committee of the local board of REALTORS®.

48. The real estate license law is said to be a valid exercise of the police power of the state. Why?

Ans.
As public protection in real estate dealings.

49. When and where was the first license law passed?

Ans.
A 1917 California law was declared unconstitutional. Oregon, Michigan and California passed valid licensing laws in 1919.

50. What is a *Real Estate Recovery Fund*?

Ans.
A state fund which provides financial relief for a defrauded buyer, or seller, against a financially irresponsible licensee. Over half of the states now have a Real Estate Recovery Fund, as a part of the licensing law. These funds are accumulated through an additional assessment, a part of the licensing fee.

51. Is it necessary for a real estate licensee to be a citizen of the United States?

Ans.

The United States Supreme Court held such requirements invalid in the case of *Indiana Real Estate Commission v. Satoskar, 417, U.S. 938 (1974).*

52. Is the broker responsible for the misconduct of his salespersons in their real estate transactions?

Ans.

Yes. If the broker knows or should have known of the act in question; or if it can be shown that the broker failed to give proper supervision and direction.

53. Define "Moral Turpitude."

Ans.

"An act of baseness, vileness, or depravity in the private and social duties which a man owes to his fellow man, to society in general and which is contrary to the accepted customary rule of right and duty between man and man." *Jennings v. Karpe, as Real Estate Commissioner, 111 Cal. Rptr. 776 (1974).*

True and False   Answer

THE FOLLOWING 27 QUESTIONS REFER TO FEDERAL FAIR HOUSING LAW PROHIBITIONS.

1. Statements by persons selling or renting dwellings which indicate a preference based on age.		False
2. A broker or sales associate who makes public speeches opposing equal housing opportunities.		False
3. A sales associate who attempts to induce a homeowner to list his property for sale by representing that minority groups are moving into the neighborhood, even when the statement is accurate.		True
4. Lending institutions which charge persons of certain races or religions higher mortgage interest rates.		True
5. Brokers or associates who mention the subject of race while dealing with a prospective purchaser, including the giving of accurate and complete answers to racial questions asked by the prospects.		False
6. Refusal by a broker to cooperate with another broker on the grounds of race are covered by the Federal Fair Housing Law.		True
7. Sellers may lawfully discourage black buyers by requiring larger down payments than required of white buyers, as long as the selling price is the same.		False
8. Brokers and salespersons may never mention the subject of race to sellers and prospective buyers.		False
9. The Federal Fair Housing Law only covers homes repossessed by the F.H.A and V.A.		False
10. The Fair Housing Law covers discrimination on the basis of sex.		True
11. The Fair Housing Law covers discrimination on the basis of national origin.		True

12. The Fair Housing Law covers discrimination in real estate board member-   True
    ship requirements.
13. White persons are protected by the Fair Housing Law and have a right to   True
    bring suit when they receive threatening phone calls for having sold their
    property to a minority family.
14. A broker interested in attracting black prospects can never use media   False
    directed primarily at black audiences.
15. The best way to deal with a minority prospect who makes inquiry about   False
    the availability of homes is to refer him to a minority broker.
16. When a minority prospect calls or visits the office to make an inquiry about   False
    a home located in an all-black residential area, the broker may assume that
    the prospect is interested only in homes located in black neighborhoods.
17. Discrimination in housing against American Indians is prohibited by the   True
    Fair Housing Law.
18. If a broker presents a contract for the listed price from a ready, willing, and True
    able black buyer, and the offer is refused by the seller, because of race, the
    broker may warn the seller that his refusal is a violation of the Fair Housing
    Law.
19. If a broker presents a contract for the listed price from a ready, willing, and True
    able black buyer, and the offer is refused by the seller, because of race, the
    broker may advise the black prospect of his right to complain to the United
    States Department of Housing and Urban Development.
20. All church-owned houses and apartment buildings are exempt from the   False
    Fair Housing Law.
21. If a black prospect does not ask to be shown homes located in a white   False
    neighborhood, the broker or sales person may legally assume that the
    prospect is not interested in such homes.
22. In 1968, at the federal level, the Congress enacted the Fair Housing Law   True
    (Title VIII of the Civil Rights Act of 1968) which contains broad fair
    housing provisions. The Law forbids discrimination and discriminatory
    practices in connection with the selling or renting of residential real estate
    not only by owners but also by lenders, investors, builders, brokers and
    real estate organizations and services.
23. Membership or participation in real estate organizations or multiple listing   True
    services cannot be denied on the basis of race, color, religion, sex or
    national origin.
24. The real estate licensee is obligated to provide equal professional services   True
    to all persons regardless of race, color, religion, sex or national origin.
25. The 1866 Civil Rights Act provides that "All citizens of the United States   True
    shall have the same right, in every state and territory, as is enjoyed by
    white citizens thereof to inherit, purchase, lease, sell, hold and convey real
    and personal property."
26. Violent interference with the right to acquire property of all kinds is   True
    prohibited by the Fair Housing Law.
27. Statements by persons selling or renting dwellings which indicate a   True
    preference based on religion are not allowed by the Fair Housing Law.
28. All full-time brokers are REALTORS®.   False

29. Local realty boards are affiliated with the Real Estate Commission. False
30. The real estate license law is a police measure. True
31. The "Code of Ethics" is a part of the real estate license law. False
32. A salesperson must renew his own license. False
33. Each real estate office must prominently display the licenses of its broker and salesperson. True
34. A salesperson who conceals the existence of termites in selling a home is guilty of fraud. True
35. A broker must notify the real estate commission if he changes his business address. True
36. A contractor who employs salesperson must be a licensed broker or hire a licensed broker to whom the salespeople will are licensed. True
37. A real estate broker can be disciplined for the misconduct of his salespeople, if he has knowledge or should have knowledge of their actions. True
38. A broker may not employ another broker in the capacity of a salesperson. False
39. A broker who collects rents for clients and co-mingles the money with his own so that he cannot make proper accounting may have his license revoked. True
40. REALTORS® are members of the NATIONAL ASSOCIATION OF REALTORS®. True
41. A real estate broker's or salesperson's license can, under no circumstances, be suspended without a formal hearing first being granted to the offender. True
42. A person may not engage in the real estate business until he has received his license. True
43. Placing a "For Sale Sign" on a vacant property, without the owner's permission may jeopardize the broker's license. True
44. A municipality has no part in regulation of real estate brokers under the licensing act. True
45. Brokers licensed in Michigan may act as a broker in any other state of the United States. False
46. A builder cannot employ salespeople to sell his properties unless the builder is a licensed broker or hires a broker to which the salespeople will be licensed. True
47. A licensed real estate salesperson must be prepared, at all times, to show his license upon request. True
48. The act of a real estate salesperson, within the scope of his authority, is considered to be the act of his employing broker. True
49. A salesperson may not sue anyone except his broker for the collection of real estate commissions. True
50. If a real estate salesperson works on a straight salary basis and does not participate in the commissions, he nevertheless requires a license. True
51. A salesperson may not leave the employ of one broker and go to work for another broker without having his license reissued to the new broker. True
52. Charging less than the going rate of commission is grounds for suspension of license. False

53. When an unlicensed officer of a real estate corporation negotiates a deal, neither the corporation nor the officer is entitled to a commission. — True

54. Every state of the United States and possessions now requires the successful passing of a written examination as a prerequisite for a broker's license. — True

55. A broker is bound to turn over his books of record to a Commission investigator. — True

56. The Island of Guam requires a broker to be licensed. — True

57. The license law of most states provides that every salesperson is an independent contractor. — False

58. A broker's license may be revoked for hiring a part-time salesperson. — False

59. A charge by a water company, if unpaid, is a lien on the real estate served. — False

60. A judgment must be recorded to become a lien against the real estate. — True

61. In a "joint and several" obligation, suit must be entered against all of the obligators. — False

62. The lien of a judgment binds real estate only. — True

63. Personal property may be sold upon a judgment. — True

64. A first mortgage is always a first lien. — False

65. A DSB judgment is one entered by confession. — True

66. Where one joint obligator dies, the note can be entered as a judgment against the survivor. — True

67. A leasehold is subject to the lien of a judgment. — False

68. A judgment against a husband will operate as a lien against property owned by husband and wife. — False

69. A judgment is void after the lien period has expired. — False

70. Any excess of funds realized at a foreclosure sale belongs to the owner. — True

71. A right or interest in real estate that diminishes its value is called an encumbrance. — True

72. Negotiability is the same as assignability. — False

73. A judgment entered against the seller of real estate, but before the deed is recorded, will be a lien against the real estate. — True

74. The effect of a mortgage is to create a lien. — True

75. The lien of a judgment is 20 years. — False

76. A suit in equity for real estate operates as a cloud on the title, when the suit is filed. — True

77. Where the judgment has been assigned of record, the debtor must pay the assignee and not the original creditor, even if he has not been notified of the assignment. — False

78. A property against which a judgment has been entered, must be sold within ten years or the judgment is void. — False

79. The lien of a trust deed is released by the recording of a properly executed deed of reconveyance. — True

80. Judgment entered against Catherine Lynn is a good lien against the property of Kathrine Lynn, who is the same person. — False

81. Lis pendens is a form of public notice filed against a named property that a suit is about to be filed. — True

82. A property can be sold even if there are judgments against it. — True

83. A defendant's automobile can be sold to satisfy a judgment.   True

84. When a deed of trust note is secured by a deed of trust, the latter but not   False
    the former should be recorded.

Multiple Choice

1. Judgments are entered by: Ans.
    a. An Alderman.   b.
    b. Court of competent jurisdiction.
    c. Real estate Commission.
    d. A justice of the peace.

2. When a firm furnishes materials for a house, and not paid, it may file: Ans.
    a. A mechanic's lien.   a.
    b. A deficiency judgment.
    c. A Lis pendens.
    d. An estoppel certificate.

3. A deal is closed on February 15, 1991 and the buyer, Jones, did not record   Ans.
    the deed until April 24, 1991. A judgment is filed against the grantor,   a.
    Adams, on April 19, 1991. The judgment is:
    a. A lien against the property.
    b. Is invalid against the property.
    c. Jones can rescind the deal.
    d. Constitutes a judgment inchoate.

4. A judgment is entered into record, is a lien on the debtor's: Ans
    a. Automobile.   b.
    b. Residence.
    c. Bank account.
    d. Wages.

5. If a debtor owns three pieces of real estate and a judgment is entered against Ans.
    him, it will be a lien on: c.
    a. The property first acquired by him.
    b. The property last acquired by him.
    c. All three properties.
    d. Homestead property only.

6. The type of property of a debtor which can be sold on execution of a   Ans.
    judgment is: b.
    a. Real Property only.
    b. Real or Personal property.
    c. Incorporeal property.
    d. Personal property only.

7. Judgment notes can be confessed by: Ans.
    a. An attorney in fact.   d.
    b. An agent.
    c. A Justice of the Peace.
    d. An attorney at law.

8. A judgment entered against a person, who owns property, would be good against which of the following?

    a. A Life estate.
    b. Tenancy in common.
    c. Leasehold.
    d. Estate by the entireties.

Ans. d.

9. Property which is acquired by a debtor after judgment has been entered against him will be liened by the issuance of:

    a. An action to quiet title.
    b. *Scire facias* proceedings.
    c. Filing a civil suit in assumpsit.
    d. Suit to annul a debtor's exemption.

Ans. b.

10. A judgment *in rem* binds only debtor's:

    a. Personal property.
    b. Real Property.
    c. Household effects.
    d. Automobile.

Ans. b.

11. A judgment is entered against the owner of a property on December 6, 1991, a first mortgage entered on January 21, 1992, a second mortgage entered on February 14, 1992, and a second judgment entered on March 3, 1992. In a foreclosure action brought by the second judgment creditor, the first judgment creditor would be paid:

    a. First.
    b. Second.
    c. Third.
    d. Fourth.

Ans. a.

12. A *scire facias* (sci fa) proceeding is brought:

    I. To revive a judgment after the statutory lien period has expired.
    II. In order to attach the lien of the judgment against property, acquired by the debtor, after the judgment was entered.
    a. I only.
    b. II only.
    c. Both I and II.
    d. Neither I or II.

Ans. c.

13. A debenture is a:

    I. Writ of attachment.
    II. Debt evidenced by a bond.
    a. I only.
    b. II only.
    c. Both I and II.
    d. Neither I or II.

Ans. b.

14. An agreement to waive the rights of a judgment creditor in favor of a mortgagee is:

    I. Subordination.
    II. Subjugation.
    a. I only.
    b. II only.
    c. Both I and II.
    d. Neither I or II.

Ans. a.

15. Willard Fry and Margaret Fry, his wife, own their home. A judgment is entered by Allen Crowe against Willard Fry on February 13, 1992 for $14,000. Margaret Fry died on April 4, 1992. Under these facts:

   I. Crowe can now sell the residence to satisfy his judgment.
   II. Mrs. Fry's two children, from a prior marriage, can claim her dower right in the property.
      a. I only.
      b. II only.
      c. Both I and II.
      d. Neither I or II.

Ans. a.

16. Which of the following provisions will be found in the Federal Fair Housing Law?

      a. A provision allowing for mortgage subsidies, insurance, and government lending procedures.
      b. A provision that real estate licensees shall not discriminate in the sale of any real estate.
      c. A code of ethics requiring brokers to follow the "Golden Rule."
      d. A provision requiring all prospective buyers to be given the same opportunity to select among available houses in their price range without restriction because of race, color, creed, or national origin.

Ans. d.

17. Which of the following is *not* covered by the Fair Housing Law, but *is* covered by the 1866 Fair Housing Law?

      a. Homes sold by a part-time real estate sales person.
      b. An owner of a 10-unit apartment house who lives in one of the units.
      c. An apartment building rented to the general public, but owned by a bona fide religious organization.
      d. A single family residence sold by an owner without a broker or salesperson and without discriminatory advertising.

Ans. d.

18. Punitive damages in a suit brought under the Federal Fair Housing Law are limited to which of the following amounts?

      a. $100.
      b. $250.
      c. $500.
      d. $1,000.

Ans. d.

19. Which of the following is the best response to sellers who have indicated that their homes are not to be shown to minority prospects?

      a. "Don't worry, they probably won't want to see it anyway."
      b. "I'm sorry, under these conditions, you'll have to sell without the services of a real estate broker."
      c. "I'll do my best, but Ill have to show it if anyone asks to see it."
      d. "All brokers must comply with the Federal Fair Housing Laws; I cannot accept the listing on your house under those conditions.

Ans. d.

20. Which of the following statements made by a real estate licensee soliciting a listing in a racially changing neighborhood violates the provisions of the Fair Housing Law?

    a. "You'd better sell while you can."
    b. "This area won't be the same a year from now."
    c. "List with me; I have many customers who are interested in this area."
    d. Not enough information given to the question.

Ans. d.

21. Under which of the following conditions may a real estate company lawfully place advertisements for homes in minority neighborhood in media specifically directed towards minorities?

    a. When advertising rates in such media are cheaper.
    b. When the same houses or homes in the same area are also advertised in media of general circulation.
    c. When the company also advertises representative homes from other than minority neighborhoods in the minority media.

Ans. c.

22. Under which of the following circumstances may a salesperson lawfully refuse to show a home to a black prospect who has specifically asked to see it?

    a. When the owner has exercised his exemption under the 1968 Fair Housing law and designated his home as not available to black persons.
    b. When the agent sincerely believes that such showing will cause panic in the neighborhood.
    c. When the owner is out of town and has instructed the agent that no showings may be made in his absence.

Ans. c.

23. When a white prospect inquires about a listing in a racially changing neighborhood, is it legally permissible to say, assuming all statements are true:

    a. "I don't think you would like that area."
    b. "You know where that is don't you?"
    c. "I'll show it to you if you want, but I wouldn't live in that area on a bet."
    d. "I don't think you can afford that house."

Ans. d.

24. Under which of the following circumstances may a broker exclude a home from showing to minority prospects?

    a. A covenant in the deed restricts the sale of the home to Caucasians.
    b. Approval of the sale is required by the homeowner's association.
    c. The broker knows that local lending institutions will not give a mortgage to minority buyers in the area in question.
    d. None of the above.

Ans. d.

25. A broker obtained a ready, willing, and able black buyer who signed an offer to buy a house at the listed price. Because of the buyer's race, the seller refused the offer. The broker may:

    a. Sue the seller for his commission.
    b. Advise the black prospect of his right to complain to the U.S. Department of Housing and Urban Development.
    c. Warn the seller that his refusal is a violation of the Fair Housing Law.
    d. Do any of the above.

Ans. d.

26. Real estate licensees who engage in racial steering may be:

    a. Sued in Federal court by the Attorney General of the United States.
    b. Subject to investigation by the U.S. Department of Housing and Urban Development.
    c. Subject to a private suit for money damages.
    d. Subject to all of the above.

Ans. d.

27. What is the best policy for a real estate licensee to follow concerning discussing the subject of race with sellers and prospective buyers?

    a. Race may be discussed when the facts are accurate.
    b. Licensees should never discuss race.
    c. Race may be discussed when the buyer is of the same race as the licensee.
    d. Race may be discussed at the time of accepting the listing.

Ans. a.

28. Discrimination based on the following considerations are prohibited by the Federal Fair Housing Act of 1968, except:

    a. National origin.
    b. Home repair financing.
    c. Age of a person.
    d. Sex of a person.

Ans. c.

29. The U.S. Supreme Court handed down one of the most famous decisions on fair housing in which of the following cases?

    a. Dred Scott v. Sanford.
    b. Jones v. Mayer Co.
    c. Corregan v. Buckley.
    d. Hurd v. Hodge.

Ans. b.

30. Which of the following U.S. Supreme Court Cases is most often cited as authority for prohibiting discrimination on the part of owners of property?

    a. Wilson v. Stearns.
    b. Shaffer v. Beinhorn.
    c. Jones v. Mayer.
    d. There is a conflict of authority.

Ans. c.

31. The fundamental basis for fair housing throughout the United States stems from the:

    a. National Association of License Law Officials.
    b. First amendment to the U.S. Constitution.
    c. Thirteenth amendment to the U. S. Constitution.
    d. Fifth amendment to the U.S. Constitution.

Ans. c.

32. In order to collect a commission, an executor or administrator of an estate must be licensed as:

    a. Real estate broker.
    b. Trustee.
    c. Cestui que trust.
    d. None of these.

Ans. d.

33. An unlicensed clerk or secretary may properly give information to a caller:

    a. From a property listing card.
    b. By driving a prospect to a sample house and acting as a guide in the house.
    c. By accepting a check for $25 "to hold" the house for a prospect.
    d. None of these.

Ans. d.

34. A person may be prosecuted in criminal court, under the license law, where said person is guilty of:

    a. Perjury.
    b. Operating an automobile without a driver's license, while driving a prospect to see a model home.
    c. Failure to file a Federal income tax return.
    d. Negotiating the sale of real estate, without a real estate license.

Ans.
d.

35. A salesperson may operate a branch real estate office when:

    a. The broker directs the person to do so.
    b. The salesperson is bonded.
    c. That person has passed all the required courses for a broker's license.
    d. None of these.

Ans.
d.

36. A real estate deal is made between seller and buyer, without the services of a broker. They arrange with a licensed broker for a fee to prepare the instruments. Indicate whether he may lawfully prepare:

    a. Contract of sale.
    b. Deed.
    c. Purchase money mortgage.
    d. None of these.

Ans.
d.

37. Operating without a license subjects the person to:

    a. Injunctions and proceedings.
    b. Fine and/or imprisonment.
    c. Commission reprimand.
    d. A fine by the Commission.

Ans.
b.

38. Ethical standards which must be observed by brokers in real estate deals are determined by:

    a. The Better Business Bureau.
    b. The local Real Estate Board.
    c. THE NATIONAL ASSOCIATION OF REALTORS®.
    d. Law.

Ans.
d.

39. Which group is exempt from the licensing law?

    a. Referee in bankruptcy.
    b. Person handling leases only.
    c. Salesperson employed by a builder.
    d. Person employed to sell sub-division lots.

Ans.
a.

40. A salesperson, upon receipt of his license, may operate from:

    a. The broker's principal office.
    b. An branch office in the county.
    c. Address on the license.
    d. Any office the broker designates.

Ans.
c.

41. A salesperson applicant for a license must be recommended by:

    a. Two property owners.
    b. Two citizens.
    c. His former employer.
    d. His prospective broker-employer.

Ans.
d.

42. A salesperson employed by another broker desires to join your firm: what ethical procedure should you follow?

    a. Employ him immediately.
    b. Write to the Real Estate Commission.
    c. Notify the other broker in writing.
    d. Call the other broker and have an understanding with him.

Ans.
d.

43. For a broker to act for more than one party in a real estate transaction without the knowledge and consent of all parties is:

    a. Ethical.
    b. Grounds for disciplinary action.
    c. Contrary to the Administrative Code.
    d. All right if no party suffers monetary damage.

Ans.
b.

44. When a real estate broker discharges a salesperson in his employ for dishonesty or any other reason, he must notify the Real Estate Commission.

    a. Within ten days.
    b. Immediately.
    c. Within 30 days.
    d. Any time during the licensing period.

Ans.
b.

45. The executor of an estate, in order to sell real estate, must be licensed by:

    a. The probate court.
    b. The real estate licensing agency.
    c. The county.
    d. No one.

Ans.
d.

46. What is the origin of the statement, "No sign should be placed on any property without the consent of the owner."

    a. State law.
    b. Regulations of the Real Estate Commission.
    c. Code of Ethics of THE NATIONAL ASSOCIATION OF REALTORS®.

Ans.
a.

47. The license law requires a broker to:

    a. Spend all of his time in the real estate business.
    b. Spend more than half of his time in the real estate business.
    c. Makes no provision as to time a broker must spend in the real estate business.
    d. Makes the real estate business his major activity.

Ans.
c.

48. For his acts in connection with business, a real estate salesperson is usually responsible to:

    a. The seller.
    b. The mortgagee.
    c. A buyer.
    d. His employing broker.

Ans.
d.

49. There are three elements necessary to constitute fraud in a misrepresenta-   Ans.
tion. Two of these are that the misrepresentation concerns material fact   d.
and that the party to whom the statement was made has a right to rely on
it. The third element is:

   a. The property will resell for a particular amount.
   b. The statement is funny.
   c. The broker knows the truth.
   d. The party to whom the statement is made acts on it to his
      detriment.
   e. The prospect did not employ the broker.

50. Deposit money, received by a salesperson, must be turned over to: Ans.
   a. The owner.   b.
   b. Broker for deposit in his trust account.
   c. Real Estate Commission.
   d. Seller's attorney.

51. Broker listed real estate should not be advertised except in the name of   Ans.
the: c.

   a. Seller.
   b. Salesperson who obtains the listing.
   c. Principal-licensed broker.
   d. Real estate salesperson on the premises.

52. Where broker A has an exclusive listing for 90 days from an owner, who,   Ans.
30 days later, desires to list the property with broker B, the latter broker   b.
should:

   I. Notify broker A and accept the listing after 30 days.
   II. Refuse to take the listing.
      a. I only.
      b. II only.
      c. Both I and II.
      d. Neither I or II.

53. A broker licensed in California who wishes to sell property in an adjoining   Ans.
state: b.

   a. Can also operate in the other state since he is licensed in California.
   b. Should immediately contact the appropriate agency in the adjoining
      state to obtain a license there.
   c. Must contact a broker in the adjoining state and work through him.

54. In the process of transferring from broker A to broker B, a salesperson   Ans.
should: c.

   a. Notify broker A that he is leaving.
   b. Start working immediately for broker B and notify A within 10
      days.
   c. First notify the Real Estate Commission of a desired change and
      request the transfer of his license to broker B.
   d. Post his license in broker B's office.

55. Adams does business as the Excelsior Realty Co. He has a broker's license, but has not registered his trade name.

    a. He can be fined by the Real Estate Commission.
    b. He will loose his commission on any sale.
    c. He can be fined by a court.
    d. He will receive a reprimand.

    Ans. c.

56. Which persons are specifically exempt from the Real Estate Licensing Act?

    a. War veterans.
    b. Executors and Administrators.
    c. Part-time salespersons.
    d. Listers of real estate.

    Ans. b.

57. A licensed broker selling property on which he holds an option must notify the buyer that he is:

    a. The Optionee.
    b. The Optionor.
    c. A tenant.
    d. An escrow holder.

    Ans. a.

58. James Stone passes the license law examination and can forthwith have the license issued in the name of:

    a. James Stone and Company
    b. James Stone d.b.a. Ajax Realty Co.
    c. James Stone
    d. James Stone, REALTOR®

    Ans. c.

59. A licensed broker may share a commission with:

    a. The person who introduced the buyer to the broker.
    b. The salesperson of another broker, who assisted in the sale.
    c. A licensed broker who assisted in the sale.
    d. An attorney at law, who is a friend of the seller.

    Ans. c.

60. The number of educational credits required before taking the real estate examination may be increased by:

    a. State Department of Education.
    b. Real Estate Commission.
    c. Legislature.
    d. Regional College Accreditation Board.

    Ans. c.

61. Bales, a buyer, filed a complaint with the Texas Real Estate Commission against Brown, a licensed broker, on February 21, 1992, claiming Brown had wrongfully withheld $8,000 due him on March 24, 1989. He also asked for payment of the $8,000 under the Recovery Fund Act. Upon the hearing held, Bales proved his case. Under these circumstances:

    I. The license of Brown should be suspended or revoked.
    II. Bales should be reimbursed from the recovery Fund.
    a. I only.
    b. II only.
    c. Both I and II.
    d. Neither I or II.

    Ans. a.

Appendix I
A GUIDE TO CONDOMINIUMS, COOPERATIVES, ETC.

Multiple Choice

1. Title to unit is both condominium and in cooperative housing developments are vested
   a. In a corporation owning the building.
   b. In an association owning the building.
   c. The owner of each unit.
   d. The unit owner of a condominium: the corporation owner of the
      cooperative.

   Ans.
   d.

2. Cooperative housing developments are usually organized:
   a. Under State business corporation laws.
   b. Under special State statutes governing creation of cooperatives.
   c. Under federal tax laws.

   Ans.
   a.

3. The proprietary interest of a cooperative tenant-stock holder is:
   a. Real estate for all purposes.
   b. Personal property for all purposes.
   c. Realty for some purposes, personalty for other purposes.

   Ans.
   c.

4. First mortgages are obtainable in most states:
   a. By the owners of condominium units.
   b. By the tenant-share holders of cooperatives.
   c. By either the condominium owner or the cooperative tenant-
      shareholder.

   Ans.
   a.

5. Upon default in payment of real estate taxes by a condominium owner:
   a. The taxing authority can levy on the entire condominium project.
   b. Title to the unit which he owns can be foreclosed.
   c. The taxing authority must first look first to his unit for satisfaction
      of the debt, then to the assets of the condominium project.

   Ans.
   b.

6. Under the federal income tax laws, mortgage interest and real estate taxes
   are deductible.
   a. By a condominium unit owner but not by a cooperative tenant-
      shareholder.
   b. By a cooperative tenant-shareholder but not by a condominium
      unit owner.
   c. By neither.
   d. By both.

   Ans.
   d.

643

7. Taxes levied on the individual units of a condominium are the responsibility of:

    I. The management association.
    II. The occupant under a lease.
      a. I only.
      b. II only.
      c. Both I and II.
      d. Neither I or II.

Ans. d.

8. Which one of the following does not apply to condominium ownership?

      a. Ownership of stock in a corporation.
      b. Common ownership in a swimming pool.
      c. Fee simple title to unit.
      d. Mortgage liability as to a single unit.

Ans. a.

9. A Florida developer attempted to create a separate unit of individual ownership designated as "recreation unit" or "recreation hall," claiming that each unit was a portion of the common elements, belonging to each unit owners in the condominium. Under these facts:

    I. The unit owner will win the suit, since the unit was a part of the common element.
    II. The developer will win, but must refund part of the purchase price to the unit plaintiff.
      a. I only.
      b. II only.
      c. Both I and II.
      d. Neither I or II.

Ans. a.

10. Jacobs, owner of a condominium unit, brought suit against Krig for a declaratory judgment, challenging the validity of a regulation prohibiting the keeping of animals in condominium units. Decide.

    I. The plaintiff will win.
    II. The prohibitions of animals must be by a by-law, and not by a rule or regulation.
      a. I only.
      b. II only.
      c. Both I and II.
      d. Neither I or II.

Ans. a.

11. Responsibility for taxes levied on the common elements is that of:

    I. The individual owner.
    II. The management association.
      a. I only.
      b. II only.
      c. Both I and II.
      d. Neither I or II.

Ans. b.

12. In a condominium, the unit owner has a:

      a. Fee simple title.
      b. Base fee title.
      c. Joint estate, with the other unit owners.
      d. Lease in perpetuity.

Ans. a.

QUESTIONS ON REAL ESTATE SYNDICATIONS

1. Real estate syndications are usually organized as:

   a. Business corporations.
   b. Limited partnerships.
   c. Nonprofit corporations.
   d. Lease in perpetuity.

   Ans. b.

2. A basic difference between a general partner and a limited partner(s) is:

   a. The different amount of capital each contributes.
   b. The general partner manages the enterprise and the limited partner(s) furnishes the capital and does not contribute to the management of the partnership.
   c. The general partner is liable for the debts of the partnership only if the limited partner(s) fail to discharge the partnership debt.

   Ans. b.

3. Under the federal income tax laws, limited partnerships:

   a. Are taxed like corporations.
   b. Are taxed like associations.
   c. Are not taxed as an entity.

   Ans. c.

4. Under the federal income tax laws, a limited partner:

   a. Cannot take advantage of losses for tax purposes.
   b. Includes his pro rata share of the partnership mortgage in his tax basis.
   c. Is not entitled to a tax deduction for mortgage interest payments and real estate taxes.

   Ans. b.

5. In order to qualify under the federal income tax laws, a limited partnership:

   a. Must have perpetual existence.
   b. Must have interests which are freely transferable.
   c. Must have centralized management.
   d. Must provide limited liability to investors.
   e. Must not have more than two of the above characteristics.

   Ans. e.

6. The Tax Reform Acts of 1976 and 1986:

   a. Eliminated all of the tax benefits of real estate limited partnerships.
   b. Changed the treatment with respect to the deductibility of construction period interest and taxes.
   c. Treats limited partnership losses and gains as passive income and losses for its investors.
   d. Greatly diminished the tax advantages for investors.

   Ans. b, c & d.

QUESTIONS ON REAL ESTATE TRUSTS

1. Mortgage trusts differ from equity trusts in that:

   a. A mortgage trust is a Massachusetts trust.
   b. An equity trust is a regulated investment company.
   c. Each invests in different types of real estate interests.

   Ans. c.

2. Under the federal tax laws, a real estate investment trust:

    a. Must engage actively in the real estate business.

    b. Is a passive investor in real estate interests.

    c. Must manage property in which it invests and render all services to tenants of property it manages.

Ans. b.

3. The Massachusetts trust is:

    a. A legal entity which is recognized in Massachusetts.

    b. The form of organization which is most often used to qualify for real estate investment status under the tax codes.

    c. Is recognized by all of the States as a common law form of legal organization which provides limited liability to investors and free transferability of shares.

Ans. c.

4. Under the federal tax laws, a real estate investment trust:

    a. Must be organized as a corporation.

    b. Must be organized as a limited partnership.

    c. Must be limited in size to 100 beneficial owners.

    d. Must have freely transferable shares of ownership.

Ans. d.

5. In a Massachusetts trust, legal title to all property belonging to the trust is vested:

    a. In the beneficial owners.

    b. In the trustees.

    c. In a limited partnership established by the trust.

Ans. b.

QUESTIONS ON REAL ESTATE SECURITIES

1. The federal securities laws regulate:

    a. The sales of stocks, bonds, and other corporate securities.

    b. Syndications and real estate sales only.

    c. The sale of U.S. Savings Bonds and other federal securities.

    d. Public offerings of securities.

Ans. d.

2. The sale of real estate is the sale of a security.

    a. If it is offered to the public in general.

    b. If it is an investment contract.

    c. If it is sold on the stock exchanges.

Ans. b.

3. When a public offering of a real estate security must be registered under federal law the registration statement is filed with:

    a. The S.E.C.

    b. H.U.D.

    c. F.H.A.

    d. The lands division of the Department of Justice.

Ans. a.

4. The "Blue Sky" laws are:

    a. Federal laws regulating the sale of securities.

    b. State laws regulating the sale of securities.

    c. Interstate land sales full disclosure regulations.

    d. None of the above.

Ans. d.

QUESTIONS ON INTERSTATE LAND SALES

1. The interstate land sales full disclosure act regulates:

   a. All interstate real estate transactions.
   b. The sale or lease of unimproved lots in subdivisions as a part of a promotional plan.
   c. Cooperative and condominium sales.
   d. The sale of real estate through the mail.

   Ans. b.

2. The act, where otherwise applicable, does not apply:

   a. If less than 50 improved lots are involved in the promotional plan.
   b. If the sale is registered with the S.E.C.
   c. If the sale is registered under the "Blue Sky Laws."
   d. If it falls within the "Limited offering-Intrastate Exemption."

   Ans. a.

3. A "Statement of Record," where required by the Act, is:

   a. Filed with the S.E.C.
   b. Filed with H.U.D.
   c. Furnished to the purchasers of lots sold in promotional plans subject to the Act.

   Ans. b.

4. A plaintiff, to recover against a developer, under the Act, for misrepresentation or omission of a material fact in the statement of record or in the property report, must establish that the defendant:

   a. Intended to deceive or defraud him and that he relied on such document(s).
   b. Was negligent.
   c. Actually made a material misrepresentation or omission of a fact required to be stated therein.
   d. Had *scienter* (knowledge) of the misrepresentation.

   Ans. c.

Appendix J
A GUIDE TO APPRAISALS
AND EVALUATION

QUESTIONS AND ANSWERS

1. What is an appraisal?

Ans.
An expression of opinion, by a licensed or certified appraiser, which gives an estimate of value as of a given date and under certain limiting conditions.

2. What is the relationship between cost, price, and value?

Ans.
Cost is the expenditure required to create something, price is the amount it sold for and value is (1) the power to command other commodities in exchange, or (2) the present worth of future benefits of ownership.

3. What is Fair Market Value?

Ans.
The most probable price a property will bring in a competitive open market under all conditions requisite to a fair sale. This would include the buyer and seller acting prudently, knowledgeably, and the assumption that the price is not affected by undue stimulus. Implicit in the definition is the consummation of a sale as of a specified date and the passing of title from seller to buyer under conditions whereby:

a. buyer and seller are similarly motivated;

b. both parties are well informed or well advised, and each acting in what he/she considers his/her best interest;

c. a reasonable time is allowed for exposure to the open market;

d. payment is made in terms of U.S. dollars or in terms of financial arrangements comparable thereto; and

e. the price represents the normal consideration for the property sold unaffected by special or creative financing or sales concessions granted by anyone associated with the sale.

4. In the appraisal of land, to estimate its value, what is the first consideration?

Ans.
Highest and best use.

5. Name the three generally accepted approaches to value determination.

Ans.
(1) Market data approach.
(2) Cost approach.
(3) Income capitalization approach.

6. What is the difference between *real estate* and *real property?*

Ans.
Real estate is the *land* and those things which are permanently fastened to it. Real property is all the rights and benefits to be derived from ownership of real estate.

7. Why is the appraisal of real estate considered more of an art than a science?

Ans.
It is people's actions in the market which determine price; therefore an appraiser must *estimate* the thinking of people to determine Fair Market Value.

8. What is meant by "Highest and Best Use?"

Ans.
Is the fundamental concept of value which implies maximum profitability by best utilization of an asset.

9. How has the passage of Title XI, of the Financial Institutions Reform, Recovery and Enforcement Act (FIRREA) effected the appraisal of real estate?

Ans.
The passage of FIRREA, in 1989, has set the standards for real estate appraisals and the mandatory state licensing of real estate appraisers.

10. How does the definition of value used by the F.H.A. and the V.A. differ?

Ans.
The F.H.A. stresses "what a buyer is warranted in paying" whereas the V.A. states that the Certificate of Reasonable Value (CRV) is a price that a certified appraiser would recommend, under prevailing conditions.

11. Name three kinds of depreciation which might affect the value of property.

Ans.
(1) Physical deterioration—wear and tear.
(2) Functional obsolescence—such as a poor floor plan or inadequate space.
(3) Economic depreciation—forces outside the property itself such as poor police protection and the type of neighborhood.

12. Must the appraiser be aware of the reason for the appraisal? Why?

Ans.
Yes. In order to stress certain types of information used in the formation of the opinion of value.

13. Names several different reasons or purposes for a real estate appraisal.

Ans.
Tax assessment, insurance, sale, mortgage loans, estate taxation, condemnation, liquidation, and partition of ownership.

14. Name four types of city data which affect value.

Ans.
(1) Economic conditions.
(2) Population trends.
(3) Cultural facilities.
(4) Public transportation.

15. What qualities, in an appraiser, is important for his selection?

Ans.
Whether he is a *Certified or a Licensed appraiser* under state licensing laws, his formal training, experience, local knowledge, and expertise in appraisal of your type of property.

16. What are the benefits of three approaches to value versus one?

Ans.
The three approaches to value help in setting the upper and lower limits of value to assist the appraiser in estimating the true Fair Market Value.

17. Is it possible that a property would be worth less than its cost? Why?

Ans.
The building can be an overimprovement on the land, a change in economic conditions or functional depreciation may limit its current value.

18. In estimating value by the income capitalization approach, what charges against gross income should be made?

Ans.
Allowances for vacancies and rent losses, fixed expenses (taxes etc.), operating expenses, and reserves for replacements.

19. What additional factors should be taken into account in the evaluation of a business other than goods, fixtures, equipment, and other tangible assets?

Ans.
"Goodwill" or that intangible asset which contributes to profitability of the business.

20. What is the difference in assessed valuation and fair market value?

Ans.
The assessed value is the value set for tax purposes—often a set percentage of fair market value.

21. What is meant by straight-line depreciation?

Ans.
An equal amount per year calculated by dividing the cost by the number of years over which it is depreciated.

22. Give a brief definition of accrued depreciation as it applies to real estate.

Ans.
Loss of value, due to all causes, deducted from the current reproduction cost.

23. What is the difference between accrued depreciation and deferred maintenance?

Ans.
Accrued depreciation is the total loss of value, from all causes whereas deferred maintenance is the value of physical deterioration which can be restored by repairs and proper maintenance.

24. Why is location so important in the evaluation of real property?

Ans.
The surroundings are the source of economic obsolescence, which destroys more value than any other cause.

25. On what type of property would the cost approach be most accurate?

Ans.
Newly improved property in a good neighborhood and in an active market.

26. On what kinds of property would the income capitalization approach be most valid?

Ans.
On income and investment properties.

27. When can it be said that the sales of other properties are comparable to a subject property?

Ans.
When they are of similar size, quality, age, lot size, the same or comparable neighborhood, and comparable architecture style.

28. What is the difference between replacement cost and reproduction cost?

Ans.
Reproduction cost means the cost of reproducing a building exactly as it was built with the same or comparable materials at present cost of materials and labor. Replacement cost means the cost of constructing a building which would serve the same purpose as the subject property.

29. Why is it sometimes difficult to determine the true net income from rental properties?

Ans.
Because of poor bookkeeping either deliberate or inadvertent.

30. To what extent is the judgment of the appraiser involved in the appraisal?

Ans.
Good judgment based on knowledge and experience are all important. The data gathered requires a careful weighing to determine value.

31. Do houses ever sell above their cost?

Ans.
Yes. When demand exceeds availability.

32. In what way does the income of people in an area affect market price?

Ans.
Income limits the price people can pay. The usual rule is 2 1/2 times annual income.

33. What portion of available sales data is useful as comparables in the market approach?

Ans.
Only a small percentage will meet the requirements for comparability.

34. What is the difference in market price and market value?

Ans.
Market value is what a prudent, informed person free of duress or compulsion would pay. Market price is what he must pay to obtain the property.

35. Does the fact that three methods of appraisal are used indicate three values will be obtained?

Ans.
No. The three-method approach is used to determine a range of values from which the estimate can be made. One or more of the three values obtained may be about the same.

36. How does the real estate market differ from other markets?

Ans.
There is no common meeting place where buyers and sellers gather. The chances are that a very small percentage of either will be aware of the other's intentions or needs.

37. Explain the essential steps in an appraisal by the cost approach.

Ans.
(1) Compute the cost of reproduction.
(2) Reduce the reproduction cost an appropriate amount to account for depreciation.
(3) Add the value of land obtained by comparable sales or the land residual method.

38. If a building has a life expectancy of 50 years and an effective age of 30 years, what is the remaining economic life.

Ans.
20 years.

39. What are the three residual techniques employed by appraisers?

Ans.
Land, building, and property residuals.

40. In the appraisal of leased real estate, is the total value always an asset of the lessor?

Ans.
No. If the contract rent is less than the economic rent, the lessee is said to have a leasehold interest in the total value of the property.

41. Name the three types of depreciation.

Ans.
Physical, functional, and economic.

42. What are the four categories of forces affecting real estate values?

Ans.
Social, governmental, economic, and physical.

43. Give the formula for the determination of value, where income and rate of return are known.

Ans.
Value = Income ÷ Rate of Return.

44. How can the going rate of return be determined from market data?

Ans.
By dividing the income produced by comparable properties by their market value...
r = Income ÷ Value

True and False   **Answer**

1. The term "MAI" means made as instructed.   False
2. Loss to a building from any cause is called deterioration.   False
3. Market value of real estate is usually the true value.   True
4. "Improved to the highest and best use" means that the improvements which   True
   produce the largest amount in money or amenities over a certain period
   of time.
5. A house is never worth less than its cost.   False
6. The economic life of a buildings is the time during which the income   True
   justifies its existence.
7. Zoning regulations limit the usefulness of real estate.   True

8. Two adjacent lots on a main business street, having the same area and the same topography but one having a frontage of 40 feet and the other a front of 35 feet, have the same value.	False
9. There are three kinds of depreciation which affect property.	True
10. Reproduction costs tend to set the upper limit of value.	True
11. Economic obsolescence is caused by undesirable neighbors.	True
12. The word "appraisal" means the process or method by which an opinion of value of a property is derived.	True
13. Depreciation is a loss in value from any cause.	True
14. In appraising residential property, the possible income is given the greatest consideration.	False
15. The rate of capitalization of the net income is that rate demanded by the public and which reflects the risk involved as compared with other investments.	True
16. The term "assessed valuation" always means market price.	False
17. The term "appraised value" means the present market price.	True
18. The valuation of residential property makes up about one-half of all appraisals in the United States.	False
19. An appraisal for a mortgage loan is usually very close to the selling price.	True
20. The valuation of a part of a lot taken by condemnation to widen a street would be very close to the market price for that part of the lot.	False
21. Economists tend to favor the idea that value of a material thing is its value in exchange.	True
22. Most people who buy homes could be said to be "well informed" as to the uses of the property.	False
23. The typical real estate sale fits quite closely the definition for determining value.	False
24. If a piece of property cannot be sold on the existing market then the appraiser would have to say that it has no exchange value at that time.	True
25. It would be correct to say that cost and value are approximately the same thing.	False
26. "Judgment" as far as appraising is concerned could be said to be made up largely of the ability to discriminate between the relevant and the irrelevant.	True
27. The general information gathered for an appraisal may be used over and over for different appraisals if the data is kept up-to-date.	True
28. There has been an increased use of the right of eminent domain by governmental bodies in recent years.	True
29. The population trend in the United States is probably of more importance to an appraiser than the trend within the city itself.	False
30. A city of many small factories would tend to have a more stable economy than one in which there are a few large factories.	True
31. The overflow movement of minority groups from one district to another is usually dictated by economic compulsion rather than a desire of the group to move.	True
32. Real estate carries a larger tax load proportionately than other types of wealth.	True
33. Values in a neighborhood will not be affected by rentals as long as the percentage of such rentals is less than 50% of the housing.	False

34. Local codes and ordinances have little effect on values for they apply to all buildings in the area. — False

35. The appraiser need not be concerned with the status of the title to the property because he is not expected to render a legal opinion. — False

36. Optimum values will be achieved when a property offers the most utility to the greatest number of people. — True

37. Only one bathroom in a five-bedroom home would be classified as functional obsolescence. — True

38. It is presumed that land does not depreciate. — True

39. As a general rule the quality of materials and labor in a building designed by an architect will be of satisfactory quality. — True

40. The shape of a lot is not important as long as there is sufficient room for the building. — False

41. The cubic foot is often used as the unit in computing reproduction costs. — True

42. An appraiser need not inquire into the motives of a buyer or seller of a property which is used as a benchmark, if it seems to be a normal transaction in other ways. — False

43. If two houses are in the same block, they can be assumed to be comparable for appraisal purposes. — False

44. In the final analysis the comparative approach is a comparison of prices rather than a comparison of properties. — False

45. The capitalization of income to arrive at a value was first used on commercial properties. — True

46. Value could be said to be present worth of all rights to future benefits arising from ownership of the property. — True

47. In appraising single family homes, one can often use a gross income multiplier instead of capitalizing the net income. — True

48. A residential lot with a frontage of 25 feet would be worth 1/2 as much as one with a 50-foot frontage. — False

49. The appraisal of residential real estate involves all of the techniques use in the evaluation of real estate. — True

50. If a building has excessive wear and tear which can be cured, the "cost to cure" would be deducted in arriving at an estimate of value by the cost method. — True

51. When using the unit in place method, it is assumed that all of the costs of building are included in the unit cost. — False

52. The economic obsolescence of homes in America is probably greater than in other countries. — True

53. When one is using the unit-in-place method any differences in such things as heating systems are added or subtracted from the other costs. — True

54. In arriving at the cubic feet in a house a person would take the measurements inside rather than outside. — False

55. A home built with a poor floor plan would have a loss of value due to functional depreciation as soon as it was built. — True

56. An over improvement of land would create economic obsolescence. — True

57. Accepting employment or compensation for appraisal of real property contingent upon reporting a predetermined value, is a ground for revocation of license and/or certification. — True

58. The gross money expectancy from any income property is the gross income less the operating expenses. False

59. In appraising income producing property, allowance would be made for vacancies even though the property is completely rented. True

60. Assessed valuation is generally considered to be market value. False

61. The tax on a given piece of property is the product of the tax rate and the assessed value. True

62. The gradual increase in the value of property over time is called appreciation. True

63. A competent appraiser develops the three approaches to value in every appraisal. False

64. An appraisal is merely an opinion of value. True

65. Accrued depreciation is all of the depreciation which has taken place up to the time of the appraisal. True

66. The ratio between the gross monthly income and the selling price of a dwelling is known as the gross multiplier. True

67. Replacement cost and reproduction cost are the same for appraisals. False

Multiple Choice

1. A "rule of thumb" method of determining the price range a wage earner can afford to pay for a home is to multiply his annual income by: Ans. b.
    a. One and one half.
    b. Two and a half.
    c. Four.
    d. Six.

2. No depreciation is allowed for tax purposes on: Ans. b.
    a. A 15 year-old improvement.
    b. Land.
    c. Auxiliary warehouses.
    d. Life tenant's interest as lessor in an estate.

3. A report setting forth the estimate and conclusion of value is: Ans. c.
    a. An abstract.
    b. A critique.
    c. An appraisal.
    d. Closing statement.

4. Amortization means: Ans. b.
    a. Appreciation.
    b. Liquidation.
    c. Depreciation.
    d. Adolescence.

5. Physical deterioration results from: Ans. b.
    a. Tax liens.
    b. Deferred maintenance.
    c. Poor basement drains.
    d. Overcrowded occupancy.

6. The three main approaches to residential appraising are replacement cost, capitalization approach and:

    a. Net income approach.
    b. Market data approach.
    c. Building-residual technique.
    d. Highest and best use determination.

Ans.
b.

7. Marginal real estate is:

    a. Border strip between two lots.
    b. Yielding farm land.
    c. Land which barely repays the cost of operation.
    d. Waste land due to erosion, swamps, and so on.

Ans.
c.

8. Which of the following creates greatest value in retail income property?

    a. Type of construction.
    b. Parking facilities.
    c. Pedestrian traffic.
    d. Vehicular traffic.

Ans.
c.

9. An appraiser in his work:

    a. Finds value.
    b. Determines value.
    c. Computes value.
    d. Estimates value.

Ans.
d.

10. By far the largest volume of work of real estate appraisers is the appraisal of:

    a. Single-family homes.
    b. Multiple-family residences.
    c. Commercial income property.
    d. Industrial acreage.

Ans.
a.

11. In computing the square footage of a home, the appraiser would use the:

    a. Inside measurements.
    b. Outside measurements.
    c. Both the inside and outside measurements.
    d. Neither the inside or outside measurements.

Ans.
b.

12. Highest and best use is defined as:

    a. Industrial property rezoned for single-family use.
    b. That use which will yield the highest return on investment.
    c. Exclusive hilltop "view" lots.
    d. Property purchased for owner use and occupancy.

Ans.
b.

13. The income approach for an appraisal would be most widely used:

    a. On newly open subdivisions.
    b. On commercial and investment property rented to tenants.
    c. On property heavily mortgaged.
    d. On property heavily insured.

Ans.
b.

14. Land suitable for citrus growth must be:

    a. Nearly level.
    b. Free from fog.
    c. Available to good drainage.
    d. Relatively free from frost.

Ans.
d.

15. Capitalization is a process used to: Ans.
    a. Convert income to value.   a.
    b. Determine cost.
    c. Establish depreciation.
    d. Determine potential future value.

16. An allowance in an income tax return for periodic decrease in value of   Ans.
    income property is called: b.
    a. Obsolescence.
    b. Depreciation.
    c. Deterioration.
    d. Fringe benefit.

17. Gross income and effective gross income, in appraisal terminology, are   Ans.
    not the same. In determining *effective* gross income, which one of the   d.
    following would be deducted?
    a. Insurance and taxes
    b. Repairs.
    c. Depreciation on appliances and furniture.
    d. Vacancy and credit loss.

18. The selling price of homes is usually determined by: Ans.
    a. A minute inspection.   c.
    b. Opinion of the builder.
    c. Comparison with similar properties.
    d. Cost to construct.

19. Estimating the value of real property is called: Ans.
    a. Assessment.   b.
    b. Appraising.
    c. Surveying.
    d. Tabulating.

20. The appraised value of a new structure that represents the highest and best   Ans.
    use of the land is likely to be similar to: b.
    a. Assessed value.
    b. Replacement value.
    c. Cost.
    d. None of these.

21. Loss of value due to a building being unsuitably located is: Ans.
    a. Functional obsolescence.   b.
    b. Economic obsolescence.
    c. Economic depreciation.

22. In order to estimate the market value of an improvement, it is important to: Ans.
    a. Obtain the amount of income.   d.
    b. Consider the tax millage.
    c. Ascertain amount of mortgage commitment.
    d. Estimate depreciation.

23. To obtain a gross rent multiplier, the appraiser must obtain from com-   Ans.
    parable properties: b.
    a. The cost and annual income.
    b. The monthly rent and selling price.
    c. The net income and selling price.
    d. The net income and rate of capitalization.

24. The average selling price of dwellings in a district can be ascertained by:

    a. Assessed value.

    b. Estimated unearned increment.

    c. Comparative analysis.

    d. Sidewalk judgment of an experienced broker.

Ans. c.

25. A single structure designed for two-family occupancy is called:

    a. A triplex.

    b. An apartment house.

    c. A duplex.

    d. None of these.

Ans. c.

26. A common unit, other than square foot, used to determine value in an urban center is:

    a. Cubage.

    b. Front foot.

    c. Square yard.

    d. The quotient.

Ans. b.

27. The average real estate appraiser is called upon most often to make appraisals for purposes of:

    a. Taxation.

    b. Condemnation.

    c. Insurance.

    d. Market value.

Ans. d.

28. The market approach to value is the method of appraisal in which the value of property is:

    a. Based on factual data related to the income yield of the property.

    b. Based on sales of comparable properties.

    c. Based on the cost of duplicating the improvements on today's market.

    d. Determined by capitalizing the annual income.

    e. None of these.

Ans. b.

29. Which two of the following should have no influence on an appraiser's compensation?

    a. The closeness of his value estimate to the owner's honest opinion of the property's value.

    b. The length of the report.

    c. The complexity of the appraisal.

    d. Time required to make the appraisal.

    e. The appraiser's knowledge and experience.

Ans. a. & b.

30. The function of an appraiser is to:

    I. Set value.

    II. Estimate value.

    a. I only.

    b. II only.

    c. Both I and II.

    d. Neither I or II.

Ans. b.

31. The income value approach for an appraisal would be most widely used:
    I. On dwellings in new subdivisions.
    II. On leased property in a shopping center.
    a. I only.
    b. II only.
    c. Both I and II.
    d. Neither I or II.

    Ans.
    b.

32. To obtain a gross rent multiplier, an appraiser must obtain from comparable properties the:
    I. Monthly rent and selling price.
    II. Net income and selling price.
    a. I only.
    b. II only.
    c. Both I and II.
    d. Neither I or II.

    Ans.
    a.

33. An appraiser, in determining depreciation, will consider:
    I. Wear and tear from use.
    II. Lack of modern facilities.
    a. I only.
    b. II only.
    c. Both I and II.
    d. Neither I or II.

    Ans.
    c.

34. "Value before and value after" taking is associated with:
    a. Eminent domain proceedings.
    b. Forcible retainer.
    c. A referendum.
    d. Adverse possession.

    Ans.
    a.

35. A M.A.I. is a certified appraiser of the:
    a. Society of Industrial REALTORS®
    b. Society of Residential Appraisers.
    c. The highest qualified member of the Appraisal Institute.
    d. Society of Independent Fee Appraisers.

    Ans.
    c.

36. What would you estimate the value of a lot 60 ft wide by 100 ft deep, considering that 60 ft is the average width for most lots in the neighborhood? A number of lots have recently sold for $60 to $70 per front foot.
    a. $3,000 to $4,000.
    b. $3,600 to $4,200.
    c. $4,500 to $5,500.
    d. $2,700 to $3,200.

    Ans.
    b.

37. A bank is considering a loan to a customer for the purposes of purchasing a commercial building. The loan will most likely be resold on the secondary market. The appraisal should be performed by:
    a. A State licensed appraiser.
    b. A State certified appraiser.
    c. A local appraiser who is familiar with properties in the area.
    d. An appraiser with a minimum of 5 years experience.

    Ans.
    b.

Appendix K
A STUDY OF
MORTGAGES AND FINANCE

QUESTIONS AND ANSWERS

1. Financial intermediaries are those institutions and businesses that accept money from savers and lend it to borrowers. Name five financial intermediaries that invest in mortgages.

Ans.
Commercial banks, insurance companies, mutual savings banks, pensions funds, and savings and loan associations.

2. Does the appraisal by the V.A. determine the purchase price the veteran can pay for a home?

Ans.
No. The Certificate of Reasonable Value (CRV) establishes the maximum that the V.A. will insure. The veteran may pay more but must pay cash for the difference in the selling price and the CRV.

3. Explain the terms "Secondary Mortgage Market" and "Secondary Financing."

Ans.
The Secondary Mortgage Market refers to the resale of existing mortgages. Secondary Financing means loans other than the first mortgage.

4. In its relation to real property, what is the meaning of "amortization?"

Ans.
The liquidation of a real estate loan on a regular payment or installment basis.

5. To what extent is the real estate business dependent upon the availability of loanable funds?

Ans.
The business is based on the assumption that qualified buyers will be able to obtain necessary funds at affordable rates.

6. What is a mortgage?

Ans.
A mortgage is an instrument pledged by the borrower as security for a loan.

7. How are interest rates determined for different kinds of loans?

Ans.
Interest rates are determined by free market forces based on availability of funds and demand plus the assumed risks involved in lending.

8. What do people mean when they say, "I am paying on a mortgage?"

Ans.
They are making periodic payments on a mortgage loan consisting of interest and principal.

9. Does a mortgage on a particular property prevent the owner from selling it?

Ans.
No. If the loan is assumable, the new buyer may assume the existing indebtedness. If not assumable, the mortgage must be paid in full from the proceeds of the sale in order for the Owner to be able to pass clear title.

10. How do savings and loan institutions differ from banks?

Ans.
Savings and loan institutions accept deposits from their customers and reloan the funds to others.

11. Why have large numbers of savings and loan associations gone broke recently?

Ans.
Changes in Federal laws during the middle 80s allowed savings and loan institutions to invest in commercial mortgages, where as the prior authority was limited to the less volatile home market.

12. Why are life insurance companies one of the leading sources of mortgage funds?

Ans.
Life insurance companies accumulate large amounts of cash from policy payments, which must be invested to reduce the cost of insurance to the policyholder.

13. Why is it said that insurance companies have a kind of "revolving" fund which can be made available for real estate loans?

Ans.
These companies have about 1/3rd their total assets invested in mortgages which are amortized on a periodic basis, thereby producing a constant flow of funds for additional loans.

14. Why are private individuals often willing to make real estate loans?

Ans.
Home loans provide a relatively high yield on investment with low risk.

15. Why responsibility does the lending institution have towards the borrower?

Ans.
They should assure that the loan is appropriate based on the borrower's ability to repay and that it meets the borrower's needs.

16. What is meant by the statement, "A VA loan is guaranteed?"

Ans.
The veterans administration guarantees the lending institution that the loan will be repaid.

17. Is a widow of a veteran eligible for a VA loan?

Ans.
Yes. If her husband is living, would have been eligible.

18. For how long a time period may a VA loan be made?

Ans.
For any period up to 30 years.

19. How widespread were loan defaults on home mortgages during the great depression of the early 30s?

Ans.
It has been estimated that as many as 80 percent were in trouble at one time or the other.

20. Does the government pay the cost of insurance on F.H.A. loans?

Ans.
No. The lender pays 1/2 percent per annum of the unpaid balance of the loan as an insurance premium.

21. What are points paid to obtain an F.H.A. or a V.A. loan?

Ans.
A cash payment up front which compensates the lender for the difference in the "real" rate of interest and the rate dictated by the government agency which insures the loan. A point is one percent of the loan amount.

22. Who must pay the points required for a buyer to obtain a V.A. or a F.H.A. loan?

Ans.
By law, the seller is required to pay any points required to obtain the loan.

23. Who *really* pays the points on a V.A. or F.H.A. loan?

Ans.
The buyer. The seller thinks in terms of "How much will I receive." He would probably sell for a lower price if he didn't have to pay the points. Thus, the buyer really foots the bill.

24. What is meant by the term variable interest rate as applied to a mortgage loan?

Ans.
The lender reserves the right to periodically adjust the interest rate up or down in accordance with some economic indicator.

25. How does the government participate in the secondary mortgage market?

Ans.
Several government and quasi-governmental organizations are authorized to buy mortgages from lenders. These purchases replenish the lenders available funds.

26. What is a conventional loan?

Ans.
A loan which is not insured by a governmental agency.

27. What is a land sales contract also known as a land contract?

Ans.
The seller becomes the lender and agrees to payment on a periodic basis. The seller usually retains title to the property until the debt is paid. The buyer obtains immediate possession after the deal is closed.

28. What rights does the seller have who agrees to a land sale contract in the event of default by the buyer?

Ans.
The seller has the right to dispossess the buyer in the event of default. Procedures for such actions vary from state to state as well as to what losses the buyer may or may not suffer as a result of the default.

29. Can a land contract be used to finance a purchase if a mortgage exists on the property too large for the buyer to clear at closing?

Ans.
Yes. The buyer's payments can be made to an escrow agent who makes the necessary mortgage payments on behalf of the seller and remits the balance of each payment to the seller. If the mortgage is assumable, the seller can assume that obligation as part payment of the selling price.

30. Can a purchaser of a veteran's property assume the existing V.A. loan? What is the veteran's obligation thereafter?

Ans.
Any purchaser can assume a V.A. loan; however, the veteran still remains liable for payment unless the buyer is qualified to assume and the veteran released from responsibility.

31. What are private mortgage insurance companies? What are their functions?

Ans.
Private mortgage insurance companies insure the lender against possible losses over and above that which the lender is allowed or willing to assume. PMI allows lenders to provide higher loans as a percentage of fair market value than otherwise. Conventional home mortgages of 90 to 95 percent are possible with PMI.

32. Why does a borrower execute a note when he executes a mortgage?

Ans.
The note of evidence of debt and expedites the entry of judgment (by confession) in case of default.

33. What two theories are there in regard to mortgages?

Ans.
In some states, a mortgage is a conveyance of real estate (via trust deed) while in others a mortgage is considered a lien, similar to a judgment.

34. What is the difference between a first and a second mortgage?

Ans.
A first mortgage is the first one recorded and has priority over the distribution of assets at a foreclosure sale. The second mortgage is subordinate to the first.

35. Who are the parties to a mortgage?

Ans.
The mortgagor (borrower), owner of the property and the mortgagee (lender). The mortgage is executed by the mortgagor in favor of the mortgagee.

36. What additional security does a borrower give in addition to the mortgage proper?

Ans.
A note for the debt and a warrant of authorizing an attorney at law to appear for and confess judgment against the debtor in the event of default.

37. What is a deed of trust?

Ans.
A written instrument, signed, sealed, and acknowledged wherein a property owner pledges his property as security for a debt by conveying title to one or more trustees for the purpose named in the deed of trust.

38. What are two functions of trustees named in the deed of trust?

Ans.
(1) To foreclose in the event of default under any of the terms of the deed of trust, and (2) To release the property upon payment or satisfaction of the debt.

39. Can a corporation execute a mortgage?

Ans.
Yes. If in the ordinary course of its business, but not for the purposes of increasing its indebtedness.

40. What is meant by the debtor's "equity of redemption?"

Ans.
A period of *grace*, after default, in which the debtor may redeem his property, providing it has not been foreclosed. Equity of redemption should not be confused with right of redemption, which is the right of the debtor to redeem his property after it has been sold for taxes.

41. Johnson has a mortgage on three contiguous tracts of equal value owned by Lee. The mortgage is for $90,000. Lee desires to sell one tract for $50,000 and asks Johnson to release the tract upon payment of $30,000. Johnson refuses. Can Lee compel Johnson to release the tract in question?

Ans.
No. Johnson has a "blanket mortgage" upon the three parcels and is entitled to the full security until the debt is paid.

42. What is meant by an acceleration clause in either an mortgage or contract?

Ans.
A clause giving the mortgagor the right to pay more than the regular payments at any time or to pay the contract in full. It also means that a mortgagee can accelerate the balance due under a mortgage immediately after default of terms, such as resale.

43. Does a purchaser assume personal liability for the mortgage debt?

Ans.
It depends upon the terms of the mortgage. If the purchaser buys the property "under and subject to a mortgage," he assumes no personal liability. If he buys "under and subject to mortgage, which he assumes and agrees to pay," he is personally liable.

44. Why is it important that a deed of release be promptly recorded after the debt is paid or satisfied?

Ans.
To guard against a careless accident which might result in loss of the canceled note.

45. Where a mortgagor makes extensive improvements to the property, can he off the cost against the mortgage debt in case of foreclosure?

Ans.
No. All improvements become part of the freehold and go to increase the mortgagee's security for the debt.

46. What is the purpose of the "mortgage clause" attached to a fire insurance policy?

Ans.
To protect the mortgagee against the destruction of the mortgaged premises, as the mortgagee's interests may appear. The insurance policy is kept by the mortgagee and a policy certificate furnished the property owner. The mortgagor pays the insurance premiums.

47. Can a mortgagee accept a voluntary deed from the mortgagor in lieu of foreclosure?

Ans.
Yes. The mortgagee should make certain that there are no liens or encumbrances entered subsequent to his mortgage as he will take the property subject to them.

48. What should be done when the mortgage is paid off?

Ans.
The mortgagee should acknowledge payment and satisfaction and execute a satisfaction piece. The mortgagor should require the return of all mortgage documents executed by him and the fire insurance policy.

49. What is the name of the clause inserted in a contract when it is desired by the purchaser of real property to place a mortgage at a later date on the property to take precedence over a purchase money mortgage given at the time of the purchase?

Ans.
A subordination clause.

50. Who executes the deed to real property when it is sold by the court in an action to foreclose a mortgage?

Ans.
The sheriff.

51. Ash obtained a mortgage from the Peerless Mortgage Company for $60,000. On the same day, Peerless assigns the mortgage to the Traders' Bank, and Ash executes an Estoppel Certificate. Later the Traders' Bank assigns the mortgage to Rex Tile Co. for value. At maturity, Ash refuses to pay more than $52,000, claiming that he has made payments of $8,000 to the Traders' Bank. If Ash can establish this fact, how much can Rex Title Co. collect?

Ans.
$52,000.

52. A mortgage with amortization provisions and in the original sum of $100,000 is offered for sale two years after its inception. Name two legal documents to be used in effecting a proper transfer of the mortgage to a purchaser.

Ans.
(1) An assignment of mortgage to the purchaser from the mortgagee.
(2) An Estoppel Certificate signed by the mortgagor.

53. What is the difference between a *purchase money mortgage* and a *blanket mortgage*?

Ans.
A purchase money mortgage is one given by the buyer to the seller in part payment of the consideration price. A blanket mortgage is one mortgage covering more than one property.

54. Does the death of a mortgagee have any effect upon the mortgage?

Ans.
No. It passes as personal property in the estate of the mortgagee.

55. What is the main reason for a lender to require a provision in the mortgage that failure to pay the taxes constitutes a default of the mortgage?

Ans.
The lien, created by the unpaid taxes, have priority over the mortgage on the property.

56. What are the essentials of a mortgage on real property?

Ans.
(1) Be in writing.
(2) Executed between competent parties.
(3) The purpose must be stated.
(4) Contain a mortgaging clause.
(5) Contain a description of the mortgaged property.
(6) Contain the Mortgagor's convenants.
(7) Must be signed by the mortgagor.
(8) The document must be acknowledged by the mortgagor.
(9) Mortgage delivered to the mortgagee.

57. What is the main difference between a mortgage and a deed of trust?

Ans.
A mortgage usually contains a one-year redemption period upon default. A deed of trust can be foreclosed in 120 days, unless reduced by agreement of statue.

True and False   Answer

1. The interest in or value of real estate in excess of the mortgage indebtedness is called an equity.   True

2. A private lender is prohibited from lending more than 80 percent of the market value of property.   False

3. The building and loan associations were the first to amortize mortgage loans.   True

4. The whole business structure of the country is based upon the assumption that responsible persons who have the ability and willingness to repay can borrow money.   True

5. At any time investors are competing with each other to obtain the best investments at the most favorable rate. — True

6. The interest rate which a lender charges is usually fixed by the Federal Government. — False

7. At any time the amount of money available in the banking system is controlled to a considerable extent by the Federal Reserve System. — True

8. Banks are allowed to make loans on real estate from the savings of individuals, which are deposited in savings accounts. — True

9. Investors tend to put their savings into the same types of investments regardless of business conditions. — False

10. One of the principals followed by investors is to diversify their investments regardless of business conditions. — True

11. The making of loans to individuals backed by mortgages on real estate as security has been in common use for only about 50 years. — False

12. A mortgage and a note might be incorporated into one instrument. — True

13. A mortgage could be called a dead pledge for it is inoperative as long as the owner of the property makes the payments and does not violate the convenants of the mortgage. — True

14. If a buyer purchases property "subject to" and existing mortgage, he would be liable for the debt as well as the original mortgagor. — False

15. When real estate is sold and the buyer assumes the mortgage, both the seller and the buyer are liable for the unpaid balance of the mortgage. — True

16. Modern savings and loan associations are much like banks in that they also offer their members checking privileges. — True

17. Most lending institutions feel that amortizing the loan is beneficial to the borrower and the lender. — True

18. Life insurance companies are an important factor in providing funds for investment in mortgages. — True

19. Real estate mortgages make up the largest type of investments held by life insurance companies. — False

20. A mortgage clause which provides that the unpaid principal balance shall become due upon the sale of the property, is illegal restraint upon the alienation of the property. — False

21. People that have funds to loan are often more willing to lend it on real estate because they feel it is a more secure type of investment. — True

22. Private lenders will seldom accept loans on real estate if institutional investors have turned down the loans. — False

23. Institutional lenders are supervised by government agencies because of the responsibilities they undertake with regard to investments of funds belonging to others. — True

24. G.I. loans are made direct to the individual by the Federal Government. — False

25. A lender cannot charge a veteran closing costs on a loan even though the costs appear reasonable. — False

26. Veteran's loans are the budget type where each monthly payment includes payments on such things as insurance and taxes. — True

27. The F.H.A. makes loans directly to home owners. — False

28. The government pays the cost of insuring F.H.A. loans. — False

29. The "Fannie Mae" organization was set up by the government to create a secondary mortgage market to which lending institutions could sell their mortgages when they needed funds for additional loans.   True

30. The purpose of the discounting of real estate mortgages is to increase the yield to the mortgagee.   True

31. Conventional loans usually carry a higher interest rate because they are not insured or guaranteed.   True

32. Title to property financed by a land sale contract remains in the hands of the seller's or an escrow agent until the final payment is made.   True

33. The seller of a piece of property under a land sales contract could not sell the contract because the buyer might object.   False.

34. A construction loan requires little supervision by the lender because the builder has agreed to build according to plans and specifications.   False

35. An F.H.A. mortgage gives the purchaser greater security as to construction than a conventional mortgage.   True

36. An F.H.A. insured loan may be repaid prior to maturity, but only with an added penalty fee.   False

37. Savings and loan associations cater mainly to investors of large sums of money.   False

38. In spite of longer mortgage terms, up to 30 years, mortgage loans have an average life of 12-13 years.   True

39. Some major insurance companies take equity positions in real estate.   True

40. Conscientious, careful lending benefits both the borrower and the lender. True

41. Veterans· may use his/her eligibility more than once.   True

42. The Veterans Administration does not guarantee loans beyond the "reasonable value" point.   True

43. Regulation "Z" implements the "Truth in Lending Act."   True

44. G.N.M.A. securities have revolutionized the approach of lenders to mortgage financing.   True

45. Investors in G.N.M.A. mortgage-backed securities secure yields comparable to those of high-grade corporate issues.   True

46. The recording fee for a mortgage is paid by the mortgagee.   False

47. A lending institution cannot refuse to give a veteran a loan if the veteran has a certified entitlement.   False

48. The date of recording determines the priority of a mortgage.   True

49. A minor cannot affirm his purchase of a property and disaffirm his purchase money mortgage.   True

50. A deed of trust is usually conveyed to a trustee.   True

51. Taxes have priorities over mortgages.   True

52. In a joint estate, either party can execute a valid mortgage.   False

53. In the sale of real estate, it is more advisable to sell the property with a clause that the buyer assumes the mortgage than merely "under and subject to a mortgage."   True

54. A veteran purchaser is not allowed to pay the appraisal fee.   False

55. It is lawful for a purchaser to give a second lien to the owner and assume the outstanding balance of an F.H.A. mortgage.   True

56. When a mortgage is overdue, and it is the desire of the owner to negotiate the continuance of the mortgage to a later date, he negotiates an extension agreement.   True

57. There is no difference between a purchase money mortgage and one given to secure a loan.   False

58. A mortgage is personal property.   True

59. A construction mortgage is one for a limited period of time.   True

60. It is lawful for the borrower on an F.H.A. mortgage to give a second mortgage on the same property covered by the F.H.A. mortgage.   False

61. There is a substantial difference between buying a property subject to a mortgage and buying the property and assuming the mortgage.   True

62. Where an applicant for a mortgage loan is an excellent moral risk, a higher appraisal of the property is permitted than if the applicant is a poor risk.   False

63. A mortgagee is bound to accept a voluntary deed from the mortgagor in lie of foreclosure.   False

64. A mortgage clause which permits the mortgagee to advance the maturity ate of the principal is called an acceleration clause.   True

65. Where a mortgagee takes possession and control of a property, he, and not the owner, is liable for injuries on the property.   True

66. Even though a mortgaged property is sold 3 or more times, the original mortgagor continues liable upon his note, until paid off.   True

67. Where a purchaser of mortgaged property "assumes and agrees to pay" the debt, he is liable to the mortgagee for full payment.   True

68. An agent appointed to collect interest on a mortgage debt has authority to also collect principal payments.   False

69. A mortgage clause is valid, which provides that in the event of a sale of the property, a higher named interest rate will be charged.   True

70. A minor is not permitted to own a mortgage.   False

71. It is to the seller's advantage to have a buyer obtain a new mortgage rather than assume and agree to pay the existing mortgage.   True

72. A blanket mortgage is a single mortgage on two or more parcels of real estate as security for a single loan.   True

73. Certain real estate was sold in a foreclosure sale bought by the mortgagee for $54,000. There is a first mortgage of $60,000 and a second mortgage of $24,000. The second mortgage will receive $18,000.   False

74. Where a mortgage has been assigned, the law requires a debtor to give the assignee a Declaration of No Setoff, or a Certificate of No Defense.   False

75. A Certificate of No Defense is obtained from the mortgagee by the purchaser of the mortgage.   True

76. The holder of a mortgage may transfer or sell the mortgage to a third party and the new holder obtains no greater interest than which the original holder had at the time of transfer.   True

77. An instrument which transfers possession of property by does not transfer ownership, is a mortgage.   False

78. A mortgage on an industrial plant covers the machinery and equipment necessary to operate the plant.   True

79. A purchase money mortgage is one taken by the seller in part payment of the purchase price.	True
80. The closing statement to the seller should reflect all of the mortgage costs to the buyer.	False
81. The "pay-off" figure on an amortized mortgage changes from month to month.	True
82. A mortgagee can enjoin the removal of a building from the mortgaged premises.	True
83. If a person "assumes" a mortgage, the most he can lose, in the event of foreclosure, is the amount of the equity in the property.	False
84. In order for a note to be legally enforceable it must be acknowledged.	False
85. The recording of a "Satisfaction Piece" is the only way a mortgage record can be released.	False
86. A property subject to a G.I. guaranteed mortgage cannot be sold except to another qualified veteran.	False
87. It is possible to exchange one mortgaged property for another mortgaged property even though the mortgage amounts are unequal.	True
88. The amount of a construction loan must be the same as the permanent mortgage amount.	False
89. The mortgagor pays the costs of title insurance.	True
90. A mortgagee is protected by the recording act.	True
91. A mortgagee is bound to accept payment of the mortgage at any time offered.	False
92. A mortgage must be recorded to become a lien.	True

Multiple Choice

1. The dollar value of a property over and above the total of the mortgage constitutes the owner's:

    Ans. c.

    a. Redemption value.
    b. Largess.
    c. Equity.
    d. Personality.

2. Alvin loaned Boyd, a carpenter, $5,000 on a mortgage on Boyd's home on January 12, 1991, for the term of three years at 7 1.2 percent interest. In May, 1991, Boyd built an additional den to Alvin's home, at an agreed price of $2,200. On September 6, 1991, Alvin assigns the mortgage to Citizen's Loan Co. Boyd tenders the Citizens Loan Co. $2,800 in full payment of the mortgage debt, which is refused. Under these circumstances:

    Ans. a.

    I. The full mortgage debt is discharged.
    II. Citizen's Loan Co. can now sue Boyd in assumpsit, alleging unjust enrichment.

    a. I only.
    b. II only.
    c. I and II.
    d. Neither I or II.

3. If a lender releases an original mortgagor from liability, the substitution must be evidences by an instrument called:

    a. A certificate of no defense.
    b. A novation.
    c. An estoppel certificate.
    d. Subordination.

Ans. b.

4. The right of a mortgagor to redeem the property by paying the debt after maturity is called:

    a. Reversion.
    b. Ademption.
    c. Redemption.
    d. Recapture.

Ans. c.

5. The Trustor in connection with a trust deed is a party who:

    a. Lends the money.
    b. Receives the payment on the note.
    c. Signs the note.
    d. Holds the property in trust.

Ans. c.

6. A deed of trust is usually conveyed to:

    a. The Grantor.
    b. Broker.
    c. Public trustee.
    d. Mortgagor.

Ans. c.

7. A mortgage is released by:

    a. Reversion.
    b. Reconveyance.
    c. Quit claim deed.
    d. Satisfaction.

Ans. d.

8. An agreement to waive prior rights in favor of another is called:

    a. Subordination.
    b. Subjugation.
    c. Subjacent.
    d. None of these.

Ans. a.

9. One mortgage theory is that a mortgage is a lien. The other is:

    a. An escrow.
    b. An estate in fee tail.
    c. A transfer of title.
    d. A reversionary estate.

Ans. c.

10. A chattel mortgage is given to secure:

    a. An eviction.
    b. Livestock.
    c. The seller.
    d. Money borrowed on real property.
    e. A loan on personalty.

Ans. e.

11. A mortgage is usually released by recording:

    a. Quit claim deed.
    b. Satisfaction piece.
    c. Reconveyance.
    d. Estoppel certificate.

Ans.
b.

12. In the sale of a mortgaged property, it is necessary:

    a. To obtain the consent of the mortgagee.
    b. To pay off the mortgage.
    c. For the grantor to deliver the deed.
    d. To obtain a court order.

Ans.
c.

13. The acceleration clause in a mortgage is for the benefit of:

    I. The mortgagor.
    II. The mortgagee.
    a. I only.
    b. II only.
    c. Both I and II.
    d. Neither I or II.

Ans.
b.

14. Where a lease antedates a mortgage, the mortgagee in possession has a right to:

    a. Evict the tenant.
    b. Collect the rent.
    c. Foreclose the property and terminate the lease.

Ans.
b.

15. An estoppel certificate is required when:

    a. The mortgage is sold by the mortgagee.
    b. The property is sold.
    c. A new mortgage is placed.
    d. The property is being foreclosed.

Ans.
a.

16. In the absence of an agreement to the contrary, the mortgagee normally having priority will be:

    a. The one for the highest amount.
    b. The one which is a first mortgage.
    c. The one that is recorded first.
    d. The one that is a construction loan mortgage.

Ans.
c.

17. A mortgage which has both realty and personalty as security is a:

    a. Chattel mortgage.
    b. Package mortgage.
    c. Blanket mortgage.
    d. An open end mortgage.

Ans.
b.

18. The owner of a property places a bank mortgage on it. He later sells the property with the buyer assuming and agreeing to pay the existing mortgage. In the event the bank later forecloses and sells the property at an amount less than the balance of the mortgage, which statement is correct?

    a. Only the original owner is liable for the deficiency.
    b. Only the buyer is liable for the deficiency.
    c. Neither is liable. The bank can only collect what is realized on the sale of the property.
    d. The bank can look to both the buyer and seller for payment of the deficiency.

Ans.
d.

19. The instrument which may conditionally convey title is:

    a. An option.
    b. A patent.
    c. A mortgage.
    d. A quit claim deed.

Ans.
c.

20. A "satisfaction piece" is a writing that:

    a. Record payments of a deed of trust indebtedness.
    b. Records and acknowledges a paid-off deed of trust.
    c. Pays a landlord for damages to his property.
    d. Renders satisfaction to a lessor for personal damages.

Ans.
b.

21. A mortgage which is past due and subject to foreclosure at any time is called:

    a. An open mortgage.
    b. A senior mortgage.
    c. A primary mortgage.
    d. A closed mortgage.

Ans.
a.

22. Money realized at a foreclosure sale on a mortgage in excess of the mortgage indebtedness belongs to:

    a. Purchaser at the sheriff's sale.
    b. Sheriff.
    c. Mortgagee.
    d. Mortgagor.

Ans.
d.

23. The borrower under a trust deed is the:

    a. Grantor.
    b. Grantee.
    c. Cestuique trust.
    d. None of these.

Ans.
a.

24. A clause releasing one lot in a mortgaged subdivision is:

    a. Release.
    b. An exoneration.
    c. Prepayment clause.
    d. An equity.

Ans.
a.

25. The Federal National Mortgage Association purchases:

    a. Chattel mortgages.
    b. F.H.A. mortgages.
    c. Government insured mortgages.
    d. Conventional mortgages.

Ans.
d.

26. The usual remedy on a defaulted mortgage is:

    a. Issue a court citation.
    b. Sequestration.
    c. Foreclosure sale.
    d. Eviction.

Ans.
c.

27. A clause in a mortgage whereby the mortgagee waives his rights in favor of another party is known as subordination. Under these circumstances:

   I. The first lien holder is called an assignee.
   II. The first lien holder has no further security.
      a. I only.
      b. II only.
      c. Both I and II.
      d. Neither I or II.

Ans. d.

28. Where a property is foreclosed upon a mortgage and the mortgagee buys the property at a foreclosure sale, he should receive a deed from:

   I. The owner.
   II. The sheriff.
      a. I only.
      b. II only.
      c. Both I and II.
      d. Neither I or II.

Ans. b.

29. A mortgage contained a clause, making the entire debt due, if the mortgagor conveys title to the property to a third party. The mortgagee brought an action to accelerate the date.

      a. The mortgagor will win.
      b. The mortgagee will win.
      c. The purchaser will be held liable.
      d. The acceleration clause is void as against public policy.

Ans. b.

30. The instrument which conditionally conveys title to real estate is a:

      a. Chattel mortgage.
      b. Conditional bailment lease.
      c. Escrow deed.
      d. Mortgage.

Ans. d.

When a purchaser of a property assumes and agrees to pay an existing mortgage, it is to the legal benefit of the:

   I. Purchaser.
   II. Seller.
      a. I only.
      b. II only.
      c. Both I and II.
      d. Neither I or II.

Ans. b.

31. When a mortgagor can secure additional amounts up to but not exceeding the original amount, it is known as:

      a. An escalating mortgage.
      b. Construction mortgage.
      c. An open end mortgage.
      d. An F.H.A. mortgage.

Ans. c.

32. A certificate of eligibility applies to:

      a. A former bankrupt.
      b. An applicant for a V.A. loan.
      c. An applicant for a second mortgage.
      d. An applicant for an F.H.A. mortgage.

Ans. b.

33. A borrower, who pays only the interest semi-annually until the debt matures, has:

    a. A closed mortgage.
    b. An open-end mortgage.
    c. A blanket mortgage.
    d. A straight mortgage.

Ans. d.

34. A broker negotiated a sale for $270,000. The buyer requires a mortgage of $260,000. The broker then prepares a second agreement, which are signed by the seller and the buyer, reciting a purchase price of $290,000. The latter are presented to a federal savings and loan association for a loan. Under these circumstances:

    I. The broker is liable for a criminal act.
    II. The seller and buyer are liable for criminal acts.
        a. I only.
        b. II only.
        c. Both I and II.
        d. Neither I or II.

Ans. c.

35. The Federal Truth in Lending Law was passed by:

    a. The United States Congress.
    b. The Federal Department of Housing and Urban Development.
    c. The office of equal opportunity.
    d. The Real Estate Commission.

Ans. a.

36. "Discount Points"

    a. Decrease the yield to the lender.
    b. Increase the yield to the lender.
    c. Increase the yield to the seller.
    d. Decrease the yield to the seller.

Ans. b.

37. The best way for a homeowner to liquidate a mortgage debt is to:

    I. Have his employer withhold payments from his salary.
    II. Amortize the loan on a monthly basis.
        a. I only.
        b. II only.
        c. Both I and II.
        d. Neither I or II.

Ans. b.

38. Construction loans for apartment buildings are paid off:

    I. Through amortization.
    II. By means of permanent financing at the end of construction.
        a. I only.
        b. II only.
        c. Both I and II.
        d. Neither I or II.

Ans. b.

39. In lending funds in the mortgage market, the mortgagee must guard particularly against:

    I. Obsolescence, whether functional or economic.
    II. The inability of the borrower to repay the debt.
        a. I only.
        b. II only.
        c. Both I and II.
        d. Neither I or II.

Ans. c.

40. The greater risk to a mortgage lender is found in:

    a. Construction loans.
    b. Permanent loans.
    c. Variable interest loans.
    d. Fixed interest loans.

Ans.
a.

41. Federal Savings and Loan Associations make a major contribution through their lending activities to:

  I. Standardized underwriting requirements.
  II. Housing for the population of the United States.
    a. I only.
    b. II only.
    c. Both I and II.
    d. Neither I or II.

Ans.
b.

42. Mortgage loans entailing more than standard risks are usually made by:

  I. Pension funds.
  II. Private lenders.
    a. I only.
    b. II only.
    c. Both I and II.
    d. Neither I or II.

Ans.
b.

43. Commercial banks are classified as either:

  I. Nationally chartered.
  II. State chartered.
    a. I only.
    b. II only.
    c. Both I and II.
    d. Neither I or II.

Ans.
c.

44. A land sale or installment purchase contract can sometimes be used as:

  I. Vendor's lien.
  II. A junior financing instrument.
    a. I only.
    b. II only.
    c. Both I and II.
    d. Neither I or II.

Ans.
b.

45. Pension funds as mortgage lenders are a force in the mortgage market. During recent years, their position with regards to this type of lending has:

  I. Increased.
  II. Decreased.
    a. I only.
    b. II only.
    c. Both I and II.
    d. Neither I or II.

Ans.
b.

46. The secondary mortgage market refers to:

  I. Sources of second mortgage loans.
  II. Investors who provide mortgage funds by purchasing them from the originators.
    a. I only.
    b. II only.
    c. Both I and II.
    d. Neither I or II.

Ans.
b.

47. Truth in Lending and Regulation "Z" have the effect of:

    a. Setting ceilings for interest rates and other loan charges.

    b. Requiring disclosure of interest and other loan charges.

    c. Both of the above.

    d. Neither of the above.

      Ans. b.

48. To what does the "annual percentage rate" referred to in the Truth in Lending and Regulation "Z" refer?

    a. The annual interest rate.

    b. All finance charges on the loan expressed as an annual percentage rate.

    c. The payment required for a default in the loan expressed as a percentage.

    d. The prepayment penalty expressed as a percentage.

      Ans. b.

49. The use of pledges is common to:

    I. Savings and Loan Associations.

    II. Commercial banks.

    a. I only.

    b. II only.

    c. Both I and II.

    d. Neither I or II.

      Ans. a.

50. Conventional mortgage loans:

    I. Are sometimes insured in part by private mortgage insurance companies.

    II. Are insured by the Federal Housing Administration or guaranteed by the Veterans Administration.

    a. I only.

    b. II only.

    c. Both I and II.

    d. Neither I or II.

      Ans. a.

51. In the case of a V.A. guaranteed or insured loan, the borrower may:

    I. Sell the property subject to the loan.

    II. Not repay the loan ahead of schedule.

    a. I only.

    b. II only.

    c. Both I and II.

    d. Neither I or II.

      Ans. a.

52. The following refers to those institutions which function to make credit available to borrowers:

    I. Financial intermediaries.

    II. F.H.A., V.A., G.N.M.A., and F.N.M.A.

    a. I only.

    b. II only.

    c. Both I and II.

    d. Neither I or II.

      Ans. a.

53. Banks are restricted from using the following sources of funds for investments in real estate mortgages.

   I. Checking accounts.
   II. Capital.
      a. I only.
      b. II only.
      c. Both I and II.
      d. Neither I or II.

54. Savings and loan associations were pioneers in:

   I. Use of amortized loans.
   II. Functioning as financial intermediaries to assist purchasers of single family homes.
      a. I only.
      b. II only.
      c. Both I and II.
      d. Neither I or II.

55. Institutional lenders, because they undertake the responsibility for lending the savings of others:

   I. Are carefully controlled by law.
   II. Evidence a high degree of responsibility.
      a. I only.
      b. II only.
      c. Both I and II.
      d. Neither I or II.

56. The buyer of a property subject to a mortgage loan:

   I. Assumes complete liability for repayment of the debt.
   II. Does not assume any liability unless he enters into a contract of assumption between himself and the seller-borrower.
      a. I only.
      b. II only.
      c. Both I and II.
      d. Neither I or II.

57. In order to simplify the calculations of mortgage payments, we have available a set of tables which express payments of interest and principal as a percentage. These tables are called:

   I. Constant payment tables.
   II. Interest percentage tables.
      a. I only.
      b. II only.
      c. Both I and II.
      d. Neither I or II.

58. Determining the needs and the abilities of the prospective purchasers with a suitable property is known as:

   I. Underwriting the risk.
   II. Qualifying the prospect.
      a. I only.
      b. II only.
      c. Both I and II.
      d. Neither I or II.

59. Who pays the service charge on an F.H.A. mortgage?

    a. The seller.
    b. The mortgagee.
    c. The mortgagor.
    d. The broker.

60. In making a loan covered by RESPA, the lender is required to:

    a. Make a disclosure of all charges not later than 12 days in advance of the date of the settlement.
    b. Provide only a statement of settlement charges and fees at the time of the settlement.
    c. Provide the borrower with the HUD-approved Special Information Booklet and a good faith estimate of settlement costs within three business days after the application is received for the loan.
    d. Advise the borrower that he has the right in all cases to rescind the loan for at least three days after the loan is made.

61. In a mortgage payable at the end of five years:

    a. The principal debt is usually reduced monthly plus interest for the month.
    b. The loan to value ratio does not exceed 66 2/3 percent.
    c. The principal is usually paid at the end of the term.
    d. The lender has greater options, upon default by the mortgagor.

Index